The zemstvo in Russia

An experiment in local self-government

Edited by

TERENCE EMMONS and WAYNE S. VUCINICH
Department of History
Stanford University

CAMBRIDGE UNIVERSITY PRESS

Cambridge

London   New York   New Rochelle

Melbourne   Sydney

Published by the Press Syndicate of the University of Cambridge
The Pitt Building, Trumpington Street, Cambridge CB2 1RP
32 East 57th Street, New York, NY 10022, USA
296 Beaconsfield Parade, Middle Park, Melbourne 3206, Australia

First published 1982

Printed in the United States of America

Library of Congress Cataloging in Publication Data
Main entry under title:
The Zemstvo in Russia.
Includes index.
Contents: Introduction/Wayne S. Vucinich – Local
initiative in Russia before the zemstvo/S. Frederick
Starr – Zemstvo organization and role within the
administrative structure/Kermit E. McKenzie – [etc.]
1. Zemstvo – Addresses, essays, lectures.   2. Local
government – Soviet Union – Addresses, essays, lectures.
I. Emmons, Terence.   II. Vucinich, Wayne S.
JS6058.Z46   352'.00722'0947   81–3897
ISBN 0 521 23416 6   AACR2

Contents

CONTENTS

Contributors

DOROTHY ATKINSON is an assistant professor of history at Stanford University, with research interests in Russian peasant society and the agrarian economy.

JEFFREY BROOKS is an assistant professor of history at the University of Chicago. He has published elsewhere on literacy and social change in prerevolutionary Russia.

TERENCE EMMONS is a professor of history at Stanford University and editor of the *Russian Review*. His new book, *The Formation of Political Parties and the First National Elections in Russia*, will appear soon.

THOMAS FALLOWS wrote his Ph.D. dissertation at Harvard University on the zemstvo movement in Saratov and Simbirsk provinces, 1890–1906. He works for Chase Manhattan Bank.

NANCY M. FRIEDEN is an adjunct assistant professor, Department of History, at Marymount Manhattan College. Her book *The Russian Physician, 1856–1905: Professional, Reformer, Radical* is being published by Princeton University Press.

WILLIAM GLEASON is Kenneth R. Rossman Professor of History at Doane College, where he teaches European and East Asian history. His current research includes a political biography of Alexander Guchkov.

ROBERT E. JOHNSON, an associate professor in Erindale College, University of Toronto, is the author of *Peasant and Proletarian: The Working Class of Moscow in the Late Nineteenth Century* (Rutgers University Press, 1979).

ROBERTA THOMPSON MANNING is an associate professor of history at Boston College. A managing editor of the journal *Russian History*, she is the author of *The Crisis of the Old Order in Russia: Gentry and Government, 1861–1914* (Princeton University Press, 1981).

KERMIT E. McKENZIE, a professor of history at Emory University, is the author of *Comintern and World Revolution, 1928–1943* (Columbia

University Press, 1963) and editor of a forthcoming edition of the memoirs of F. I. Rodichev.

SAMUEL C. RAMER is an assistant professor of history at Tulane University. He is currently preparing a study of public health in rural Russia during the late nineteenth and early twentieth centuries.

WILLIAM G. ROSENBERG, a professor of history at the University of Michigan, is author of *Liberals in the Russian Revolution* (Princeton University Press, 1974) and other work on twentieth-century Russia.

S. FREDERICK STARR is vice-president for academic affairs at Tulane University and former secretary of the Kennan Institute for Advanced Russian Studies, The Wilson Center. He is the author of *Decentralization and Self Government in Russia, 1830–1870* (Princeton University Press, 1972).

WAYNE S. VUCINICH, Robert and Florence McDonnell Professor of East European History at Stanford University, is the author of many works on Slavic history. He is the president of the American Association for the Advancement of Slavic Studies.

Editorial preface

The studies presented here issue from a conference, "The Zemstvo: An Experiment in Local Self-Government," held at Stanford University on April 14–15, 1978. The idea of holding a conference to assess the present state of knowledge about this important institution in the political and cultural life of prerevolutionary Russia and to suggest new directions for research on it belongs to Wayne Vucinich: he was able to convince his somewhat skeptical colleague that the time was ripe for such an undertaking, in view of the absence of any comprehensive work on the zemstvo in the postrevolutionary literature, either Soviet or Western, on the one hand, and the existence of a wealth of accessible documentation on the history of the zemstvo, both published and unpublished, on the other.

That the time was indeed ripe for a conference on the zemstvo became clear to us once we began to make a preliminary inventory of scholars in North America with relevant research interests: it turned out that many more scholars than we had thought, especially younger colleagues, were currently engaged in major research projects involving substantial use of zemstvo-related materials. The number of them who expressed interest in presenting papers to the conference was unusually high.

The intensity of current interest in the structure and workings of local self-government in prerevolutionary Russia that we discovered is clearly reflected in the following pages. It will also be apparent from what follows that research work on the zemstvo is not merely a response to a "fresh topic" but has arisen from an understanding that the zemstvo provides a firm institutional framework for inquiries into many complicated problems concerning state and society in late Imperial Russia, problems all linked in one way or another to the major historical problem of the origins of the Russian Revolution.

At the same time, this book does not pretend to reflect fully the dimensions of current work on the zemstvo. We were able to accommodate, either as rapporteurs at the conference or as contributors to this volume, only a few of the qualified scholars we knew to be interested in our subject. We were guided in our search for participants by our sense of the major topical issues that needed to be covered and by what we knew of the work that had been done on them. Errors of oversight undoubtedly were made. We claim only that this book presents some of the best work currently being done on the history of modern Russian institutions and social relations.

We said at the beginning of this Preface that these studies issue from a conference. They are not papers read at the conference, however. Although a few of the essays that were circulated preliminarily to conference participants found their way into this volume almost unchanged, most of these studies existed only as working papers at conference time and were substantially altered – partly because of ongoing research and partly because of constructive criticism, from coparticipants at a remarkably stimulating conference or from the editors in subsequent months. We are pleased to recognize the willing cooperation of all our authors throughout the long process of preparing this volume.

We wish to express our thanks to all the conference participants (for various reasons, not all of them could be represented in this volume). We are especially grateful to the American Association for the Advancement of Slavic Studies for a grant that made the conference, and ultimately this book, possible, and to the Center for Russian and East European Studies of Stanford University for its sponsorship and support. Special recognition is due Mrs. Betty Herring for her skillful handling of the logistics of the conference and for keeping the lines of communication open with a particularly peripatetic group of authors during the editing process. Several young colleagues and graduate students also did much to make the conference a success; among them, we particularly wish to thank Dr. Constantin Galskoy and Mr. Nicholas Pappas.

T.E.
W.S.V.

Note on terms, abbreviations, transliteration, and dating

The terms and abbreviations listed below appear throughout the volume. Translated terms are followed by the original Russian; abbreviations and Latinized terms are followed by the original Russian and a translation.

A simplified version of the Library of Congress transliteration system has been used throughout the book – omitting diacritical marks and, in the main text, hard (") and soft (') signs in proper and geographical names.

Unless specifically noted otherwise, all dates in this book are given according to the Julian calendar in use in Russia until 1917. It was 12 days behind the Gregorian calendar in the nineteenth century and 13 days behind in the twentieth century.

Text term/abbreviation	Russian original/translation
delegate	*upolnomochennyi*
deputy	*glasnyi*
desiatina	*desiatina* (a land measure equivalent to 1.1 hectares)
district	*uezd*
district (zemstvo) assembly	*uezdnoe (zemskoe) sobranie*
district (zemstvo) governing board	*uezdnaia (zemskaia) uprava*
elector	*vyborshchik*
feldsher	*fel'dsher* (medical assistant, paramedic; from German *Feldscher*)
governing board	*uprava*
Kulak	*kulak* (a rich peasant; literally, *fist*)

mir	*mir* (peasant commune)
muzhik	*muzhik* (in colloquial usage, a male peasant)
obshchina	*obshchina* (peasant land commune, or commune)
province	*guberniia*
provincial (zemstvo) assembly	*gubernskoe (zemskoe) sobranie*
provincial (zemstvo) governing board	*gubernskaia (zemskaia) uprava*
TsGAOR	*Tsentral'nyi gosudarstvennyi arkhiv Oktiabr'skoi revoliutsii* (Central State Archive of the October Revolution, Moscow)
TsGIA	*Tsentral'nyi gosudarstvennyi istoricheskii arkhiv* (Central State Historical Archive, Leningrad)
ukaz	*ukaz* (an imperial edict)
village community	*sel'skoe obshchestvo*
volost	*volost'* (a peasant administrative unit usually comprising several village communities)
zemets (pl. zemtsy)	*zemets, zemtsy* (an elected zemstvo member)
zemstvo	*zemstvo* (the general name for the system of rural self-government introduced in 1864)

1

Introduction

WAYNE S. VUCINICH

This book represents the first serious attempt since the Revolution of 1917 to assess the overall character and significance of Russian experience with the principle and practice of rural local self-government embodied in the elective institutions called zemstvos (*zemstva*) over the half-century of their existence (1864–1918).

Postrevolutionary Western writing on Russian history has, by and large, presented the zemstvo as "a school preparing Russia for parliamentary government" and in so doing has tended to dwell primarily on "the obstacles continually placed in the zemstvo's way by an autocratic regime jealous of its own political monopoly."[1] Studies devoted specifically to the history of the zemstvos have been rare.[2] Soviet historiography, albeit more inclined to remark the shortcomings and "limited class character" of the zemstvos, has also, following Lenin, paid attention primarily to their role in the history of the political opposition movement.[3] In terms of substantive research, it would be more precise to say that until quite recently Soviet historiography has not paid much attention at all to the zemstvos: Only a few monographs devoted to them specifically have appeared in the Soviet Union, all within the last few years.[4]

The studies in this volume attempt to look beyond the rather well-known story of the liberal reform movement to the substantial elements of tension and conflict that existed within and especially between the principal groups associated with the zemstvo: the landed gentry, whose deputies generally dominated the zemstvo institutions; the peasants, who constituted the overwhelming mass of the population and were the social group toward whose improvement the bulk of the cultural and economic programs of the zemstvo were ostensibly directed, yet in the formulation of which they took very little part; and the "third element," the teachers, doctors, statisticians, agronomists,

1

and other technical and clerical personnel employed by the zemstvos for carrying out their programs. Relations between the zemstvos and the central goverment, in particular the conflicting interests represented in the zemstvo constituency and in the government, are also examined here, with results that call into serious question widely accepted ideas about the nature of those relations. At the same time, the chapters in this book give a general assessment of the major aspects of the zemstvo's contribution to Russian cultural and political development. All the chapters are based on extensive knowledge of their respective subjects; many provide relevant new information from unpublished materials in Soviet and U.S. archives.[5]

Since the zemstvos were intimately involved in the history of the constitutional reform movement in prerevolutionary Russia, this book also provides new evidence on the character of that movement, its strengths and weaknesses, and should consequently encourage new reflection by the reader about the perennially debated question of the peculiarities of Russian political development.

Notes

1 I take the liberty of quoting here the just words of the Cambridge University Press's anonymous reviewer of the manuscript version of this work.

2 Although there are several recent and as yet unpublished doctoral dissertations, there is to my knowledge only one Western book devoted primarily to the history of the zemstvos: S. F. Starr, *Decentralization and Self-Government in Russia, 1830–1870* (Princeton, 1972), which deals with the origins and promulgation of the zemstvo legislation. Those studies that devote considerable attention to the zemstvo do so within the framework of the history of Russian liberalism and the political reform movement: V. Leontovitsch, *Geschichte des Liberalismus in Russland* (Frankfurt/Main, 1957); G. Fischer, *Russian Liberalism: From Gentry to Intelligentsia* (Cambridge, Mass., 1958); J. Walkin, *The Rise of Democracy in Prerevolutionary Russia* (New York, 1962).

3 V. V. Garmiza, "Zemskaia reforma i zemstvo v istoricheskoi literature," *Istoriia SSSR*, 1960, no. 5, pp. 82–107; V. G. Chernukha, "V. I. Lenin o zemstve," in *V. I. Lenin i problemy istorii* (Leningrad, 1970), pp. 283–310.

4 Principally the following: V. V. Garmiza, *Podgotovka zemskoi reformy 1864 goda* (Moscow, 1957); L. G. Zakharova, *Zemskaia kontrreforma 1890 g.* (Moscow, 1968); and N. M. Pirumova, *Zemskoe liberal'noe dvizhenie: Sotsial'nye korni i evoliutsiia do nachala XX veka* (Moscow, 1977).

2

5   In this latter respect, the present work may be compared to the recent volume edited by Leopold H. Haimson, *The Politics of Rural Russia, 1905–1914* (Bloomington, Ind., 1979).

2

Local initiative in Russia before the zemstvo

S. FREDERICK STARR

Were the zemstvos an anomaly in the political and social history of Russia? On the one hand, they brought about a dramatic expansion and improvement of local services as diverse as medicine and fire insurance, in the process attracting a dedicated band of talented men and women. During the last half-century of the tsarist state's existence, they constituted the most vital public presence at the district and provincial levels. On the other hand, in the extent of purely local initiative they fostered, the elective zemstvos would appear to have had little relation to anything that preceded or followed them. Contemporary partisans of the zemstvos took pains to disassociate them from the local institutions that had existed down to the abolition of serfdom in 1861. After 1917, the Communist government made similar efforts to show that the local institutions it introduced owed nothing to zemstvo voluntarism.

Both had a case. Numerous zemstvo specialists did continue in responsible positions after the Bolshevik coup, but the institutional environment in which they functioned had been fundamentally altered. Likewise, the notion of discontinuity between the prereform local institutions and the zemstvos is tenable however one looks at the zemstvos themselves. If their introduction is seen as a government concession to the gentry, they can be contrasted to the virtually moribund gentry assemblies under serfdom.[1] If they are viewed as an attempt to embody a new principle of local self-government, one can point to the contrary ideal of centralization, which was defended in theory as well as practice prior to the Great Reforms.[2] Finally, if the introduction of zemstvos was intended to be a practical solution to a long-standing problem of undergovernment in the Russian countryside, then one can cite convincing evidence of the extent of the change wrought by these innovative organs.[3]

However strong the case for discontinuity between the prereform local government and the zemstvos, it cannot be pressed so far as to

5

ignore various types of continuity that in fact existed. On one level it is obvious that, since the zemstvos were not introduced onto a tabula rasa, they were heir to various attitudes and patterns of behavior formed under serfdom. A 60-year-old provincial governor in 1880, for example, would have spent approximately two-thirds of his civil service career working under the old system – ample time to form habits that were bound to influence his behavior under the new.

On another level, though, no matter how revolutionary the purely theoretical differences between the principle of self-government and the state's virtually limitless right before 1864 to intervene in local affairs, the actual practice of local government before and after Alexander II's reforms shows greater continuity than has generally been acknowledged. Stated differently, the zemstvos were far from being the radically new form of organizing human endeavor in Russia that their partisans have sometimes claimed, and the continuities account in part for both the strengths of the zemstvos and their weaknesses.

It is this proposition that the present chapter seeks to examine. To this end it will be necessary, first, to identify the zemstvos' relevant antecedents in prereform Russian local government. With these before us, it will then be possible to consider the relationship between the zemstvos and Russian political culture as a whole and to place the question of continuity and discontinuity in a broader context embracing not only legal theory but day-to-day practice as well. By this process one can demonstrate that certain tendencies in the life of the zemstvo – the style of participation they encouraged; their internal management; and especially the relation of the zemstvos to one another, to their constituents, and to the local and central agencies of government – all derive from characteristics of Russian political life that antedated and also outlived the zemstvos.

Three characteristics of the zemstvos are most pertinent to this inquiry: (1) they were elective agencies composed of representatives drawn from the three groups or estates (sosloviia) into which Russian society was divided by law; (2) they were charged with executing a variety of purely local functions, which they did by employing professional executive staffs; and (3) in carrying out their assigned tasks, the zemstvos were placed in a state of constant interaction with the Petersburg ministries and their representatives, an interaction which often led to conflict due to both the mutual dependencies that existed between them and the inadequate integration of zemstvos with all the other institutions operating in or near their jurisdictions.

6

Prior to 1864, many of the essential functions later assigned to the zemstvos were executed not by "societal" organizations but by the central ministries and their field staffs. Indeed, in several instances, notably medicine,[4] the zemstvos were to build more upon this governmental heritage than upon activities under the jurisdiction of the estates. But the prereform system called for a greater sphere of action for the estates and their representatives than advocates of the zemstvo and their scholarly legatees have acknowledged. True, the old system failed signally at eliciting the activity that it mandated in law and did much to hamper it when it did exist. But the estate organizations were assigned broad responsibilities, which they executed through elected representatives who worked alone and with representatives of the other estates and also with governmental officials, whom they treated with the same mixture of dependence and hostility that prevailed after 1864.

Let us, then, turn to the manner in which Russian "society" participated in the work of local government prior to the Great Reforms. In Russia this participation was compartmentalized into the structures of the three estates, or *sosloviia*, which derived, at least outwardly, from the model of the German *Stände*.[5] It is more than a convenience, therefore, to base our examination upon the estate organizations of the peasantry, the gentry, and the townsmen.

The peasant estate

Down to the mid-nineteenth century, most subjects of the tsar had more contact with the organs of peasant self-government than with any other institutions serving the public good. Whether one speaks of the communal institutions of mir and volost on landlord's estates or of the same institutions as they were extended first to appanage peasants and then to state peasants through the Kiselev reforms of the 1840s, one confronts institutions that enjoyed extensive authority to address local needs. Far from being merely objects of ethnographic curiosity, peasant institutions of prereform Russia should rightly be considered the primary political experience of the overwhelming majority of the population and, as such, an inevitable influence on the later zemstvos.

At least since 1765, when the Free Economic Society attacked it as harmful to economic growth, the practice of periodic repartition of the peasants' common land had come under harsh criticism in Russia.[6] The policy of retaining and even expanding periodic repartition, which the imperial government pursued for nearly a century before 1861, was defended not so much on economic grounds as for political and

7

especially administrative reasons. Wherever it was practiced, repartitional tenure strengthened the collective institutions of the peasantry rather than the individual, causing the historian S. G. Pushkarev to compare its effects to those of Stalin's collectivization.[7] The fact that it was promoted by state action indicates the extent to which the tsarist autocracy intervened in the administrative as well as economic affairs of the peasantry. Hence, it is quite appropriate to view the Russian peasant commune by the nineteenth century as a quasi-governmental institution, whatever its ancient origins in patriarchal and clan life may have been.[8]

Officials (starosty) elected by each commune were charged with upholding state laws, with catching and returning fugitive soldiers, serfs, and criminals, and even with provisioning state agencies locally.[9] Communes on lords' lands managed everything from child welfare to the construction of roads in the eighteenth century. Later, the Ministry of the State Domains called upon the communes of state peasants to collaborate in providing fire prevention measures and insurance, stockpiling food and seed reserves, and executing numerous other public functions.[10] Beyond this, of course, the commune was responsible for apportioning and collecting state levies and for supplying recruits. Its responsibilities in these important areas were in no way diminished by the presence of overlords on gentry lands. As a recent Soviet student of the subject has written, "To a greater or lesser degree all personal aspects of the life of the peasant were controlled by the commune."[11] To be sure, this would have been true of village communities all over Europe in an earlier age.[12] But the inability of the tsarist state to erect any more solid presence than the gentry at the local level perpetuated the communes' local political and administrative role longer than would otherwise have been the case.

What were the political practices encouraged by the commune that might have been carried over to the zemstvos as peasants came to participate in those institutions? Three images dominate the literature on the subject: first, the Slavophile notion of a benign and simple village anarchism, which has gained acceptance even among students who are otherwise unsympathetic to Slavophile ideology;[13] second, a tendency to view peasant self-government as little more than a debased and brutish gathering of village oligarchs whose knowledge of the elective process was limited to an awareness of the need to provide vodka for recalcitrant voters;[14] and third, an image spread by Baron Haxthausen in the 1840s, when he laid stress on the "despotic powers" of the commune, citing such peasant proverbs as "Whatever the mir decides will come to pass."[15]

Each of these images has some basis in the often contradictory life of the Russian peasant village. Their common shortcoming – and for our purposes a serious one – is that they all underestimate the extent to which the obshchina (the land commune) and volost had acquired fairly sophisticated institutional lives by the nineteenth century, and hence the degree to which their various structures and practices would be pertinent to the later zemstvos experience. Thus, the image of peasant elections as irregular, primitive, and, by implication, irrelevant to the electoral processes introduced with the zemstvos,[16] must be revised in light of important evidence brought forward by the Soviet scholar Aleksandrov. In the late eighteenth century, at least, the skhod or assembly, at which elections were held and other public business conducted, would normally congregate monthly, if not more frequently. Such meetings took place not simply on the village square, as certainly occurred in summer months, but also in specially designated cabins (izba), which were, in effect, the village administrative offices.[17]

Who ruled in the commune? Although strong men certainly emerged at various times in specific communes, they were not at bottom autocratic institutions. Rather, they tended to be oligarchies, in which groups of leading village figures played the dominant role in local life for years at a time. In those villages which have been studied in depth, not uncommonly a small coterie filled most of the public jobs of the locality.[18] However, with a substantial number of diverse responsibilities to be executed, ranging from burmistr (Burgermeister) to church elder, it would have been hard for a very small group, let alone a single village autocrat, to dominate affairs completely.

The infrastructure of communal and volost life further supports this conclusion. Pay for village functionaries was rare, but most received compensation in the form of additional land.[19] In contrast to the Slavophile or Tolstoyan image of the peasant as noble savage, most communes had at least one scribe (pisar'), whose written records, presumably known to the members, would have constituted a kind of institutional memory to supplement the collective memory of the group. Accountants (shchetchiki) also existed. Even if such skills were so rare as to make the post of shchetchik virtually hereditary in many communes, a district zemstvo would later be able to call on almost as many such skilled peasants as there were volosts or even obshchinas.

By the late eighteenth century many communes in central Russia had adopted the practice of designating or electing commissions from within the commune to handle special tasks as they arose. The idea for such bodies probably reached the peasantry from the local gentry, who would have had contact with such commissions through government

9

service. Although far from common, these commissions were charged with such diverse assignments as settling land disputes, reviewing complaints against a *burmistr*, or even checking the commune's books. Aleksandrov reports on one eighteenth-century peasant commission that drew from the 38 villages of a volost and included 50 members![20]

Such evidence suggests that peasantry entering the zemstvos could have enjoyed a far more sophisticated political schooling than many of the reformers themselves suspected. At the least, such practices as we have outlined here must be squared with the notion of peasant corporate institutions being ground under the heel of gentry caprice and governmental condescension. The lords' powers over the communes were indeed extensive.[21] Some exercised them tyrannically; others exerted their despotism in the manner of the Enlightenment, issuing erudite instructions and *ulozheniia* (codices) like village tsars. Still other lords retired from the countryside and handed their authority over to vicious overseers (*prikazshchiki*), who wielded it in their absence. If state peasants were relatively freer of such interventionism, the onerous taxes and particularly the levy of recruits poised a constant sword of Damocles above their communal autonomy.

Yet this is by no means the whole picture. The notorious written instructions from lords to their peasant communes almost all date to the eighteenth century, suggesting that gentry zeal for manipulating peasant life faded rapidly upon direct exposure to it. Consultation and negotiation rather than order and confrontation were the norm in communal–gentry relations. Payments to the lords were generally worked out through discussions culminating in an agreement (*mirskii prigovor*). There existed many other possibilities for political compromise between a lord's command and outright rebellion by the peasantry. Collectively sponsored petitions were common, and more parliamentary forms of pressure also existed. When a Penza lord called for a speedup, his peasants rejected the *burmistr* whom the landlord named to accomplish it and elected their own man. Upon their failure to resolve the issue, the peasants continued to meet without gentry approval, thus anticipating forms of zemstvo defiance in the post-1864 era.[22]

Conscious of the peasants' corporate unity and sense of propriety, most lords adopted a hands-off policy toward the commune, a policy which in turn contributed to its autonomy. Government agents followed the same course out of necessity. Despite the state's century-long attempt to intensify its local presence, the peasants' own countercampaign was on the whole effective. Communal account books frequently exhibit regular entries to cover the cost of bribes to local officials, payments which obviously had their intended effect in that they recur year after year.[23] In a similar spirit, peasants accurately assessed the very limited ability of the government and lords to extract state taxes from them. Realizing that money payments were far easier to avoid than was the duty to provide recruits, they built up huge arrears that went uncollected for generations. Historians who have accepted the increase in arrears as proof that the peasantry was being impoverished might do well to consider the possibility that the same figures attest to the decreasing ability of the state and gentry to oppose the organized peasantry at the communal level. Such a hypothesis accords well with the skill that many peasant delegates to the zemstvos showed in keeping "alien" forces, including the government, at bay.

It goes without saying that no brief overview can do justice to all the regional variations to which peasant communal institutions were subject. Nonetheless, the evidence presented above suggests that the corporate institutions of the central Russian peasantry fostered a wide range of political skills involving both the internal and external relations of community life and that these skills involved a high degree of local initiative and the defense of local interests against external claims. Despite the physical isolation of most peasants, the more active members of their communes gained considerable experience at dealing with representatives of other estates and of the central government. Furthermore, these same corporate institutions gave peasants experience with both elections and representation.

The zemstvos certainly differed from peasant institutions in important respects, notably their all-class character and the extent to which they were subject to external and juridical norms. Nonetheless, peasant leaders who were elected to zemstvos arrived at the first meeting with a considerable fund of relevant experience.

The gentry's estate

In Russia neither the peasantry nor the townspeople rivaled the gentry in the amount of governmental attention showered on their group prior to the Great Reforms, and neither could boast of so elaborate a body of legislation defining and protecting its character as an estate. Thanks to Catherine's Provincial Reform of 1775 and her Charter to the Nobility of 1785, the gentry was given an extensive role in local life, both indirectly through the active participation of its elected representatives on governmental boards and directly through its corporate assemblies.[24] Even someone as skeptical of the gentry as the reformer Mikhail Speranskii turned naturally to gentry leadership

11

when he sought to strengthen the public presence at the district level. As Speranskii knew perfectly well, the gentry already controlled district and local courts[25] and dominated practically every other local agency.[26] Hence, the solicitude that Alexander II's government showed towards the gentry by assuring its role within the new zemstvos did not, in itself, constitute a new departure.

That gentry privileges could form the basis for a functioning system of local government was assumed by gentry activists over the century prior to the debates leading to the establishment of the zemstvos. Yet no clear notion of the gentry's corporate rights had existed in Russia before the gentry's emancipation from compulsory state service in 1762.[27] Even when polled by Catherine II in connection with her Legislative Commission of 1767, all but 14 percent of local gentry groups submitting responses preferred to involve themselves in local government by having their assemblies elect representatives to state agencies rather than exercise authority independently.[28]

Compared with Western Europe, the "rights" of the Russian gentry that were to figure so large in the zemstvo debates were far closer to duties. More than one of Catherine's advisors recoiled at the possibility that the emancipated nobility might sink into idleness and sought means of preventing this.[29] The bloody Pugachev Revolt of 1773–5 convinced many other officials of the need to invite the gentry into local government in order to deter anarchy, which gentry were eager to do anyway, since it was they who suffered most from brigandage.[30] Hence, at this crucial juncture the gentry very much wanted a share in rule but was little inclined to press for full autonomy for its assemblies, as opposed to participation with the state.

This peculiar genesis of the gentry's estate institutions accounts in good measure for their failure to assume a strong and independently corporative character. Thanks to the state's effort to expand its own presence in the provinces – an effort which bore fruit precisely during the so-called Age of the Nobility – this initial tendency was never reversed over the decades prior to the establishment of the zemstvos. Between 1775 and 1795, the staffs of provincial agencies more than doubled,[31] whereas the growth of the provincial civil service during the reign of Nicholas was even more dramatic.[32] Although gentry assemblies remained fairly constant in terms of both membership and staffs,[33] they actually diminished in importance relative to the provincial state agencies.

This relative decline in authority and capacity to act caused the gentry's exclusive institutions to fall into a moribund state by the time of the Crimean War. In spite of all Nicholas I's efforts to the contrary, the gentry assemblies atrophied. A special term, the *Naysayers* (*net-chiki*), was used to describe those many gentry, especially the wealthier, who avoided elections or service as a fruitless and time-consuming bore.[34] Unlike the peasantry's, then, the gentry's locus of political life prior to 1864 was not their purely corporative institutions.

If the gentry's independent organizations failed to become a major component of provincial rule in prereform Russia, what about the public agencies in which gentry participated as elected representatives of their estate? Thanks to the reforms of 1775, these collegial bodies were responsible for the dispatch of nearly all public affairs at the provincial and district levels, including many pertaining largely to the interests of the central government rather than of the locality. In them, the elective principle prevailed and embraced all but the governor, who sat as chairman of most such boards, and the ministerial representatives. Even the police, to whom fell the actual execution of governmental decisions at every level, were elected from the local gentry rather than appointed from Saint Petersburg.

The involvement of the elected representatives of the gentry in government committees, boards, and councils at the district and provincial levels was thus a major factor in the gentry's political education prior to 1864. What lessons did this "school" impart? One need not look far to discover evidence that gentry participation in such bodies was as often as not a source of frustration to all involved. The tendency, increasingly widespread over time, for only the poorer gentry to stand for election has been noted. The low social prestige of *ispravniki* (police officials) and other elected officials is also well known to readers of novels and plays of the period. The reasons for it are clear. None of the matters dealt with by the elected representatives of "society" in the provinces was under their sole jurisdiction but were instead subject to review and approval by ministerial agents and the governors at every step.[35] Added to this, issues of the most divergent nature were lumped together under single jurisdictions.

It is scarcely surprising that gentry came to look cynically at the public institutions to which they were elected by their assemblies and sought at every turn to exploit them to their own advantage. In this context the case of the Social Welfare Boards (*Prikazy obshchestvennogo prizreniia*) is particularly instructive and directly pertinent to the later zemstvos. Catherine II had instituted the Social Welfare Boards in her 1775 legislation as a means of reversing the deepening atrophy of provincial life that had set in after the death of Peter I.[36] Down to their replacement by the zemstvos in 1864, these boards were to be the chief institutional patrons of local social development in Russia.

13

No institution of the prereform era bears a closer resemblance, in theory at least, to the later zemstvos. The responsibilities of these protozemstvos covered hospitals, orphanages, insane asylums, reformatories, workhouses, schools, and numerous other vital public functions.[37] According to Catherine's legislation, they were to be composed of two elected representatives each from the gentry, the towns, and the peasantry and presided over by the provincial governors. The representatives were to be drawn from the estate courts of each constituent group.

When the plans for the zemstvos were being drawn up, one of the keenest subjects of debate was the tax powers of the new bodies. The prereform Social Welfare Boards had been able to skirt this problem because the government had provided them with 15,000 rubles each at the time of their establishment in 1775. These funds were to form the basis of a mortgage loan operation that was intended to provide all the needed revenue. It is revealing of the gentry's attitude toward these agencies that they were promptly turned into mortgage banks for the exclusive benefit of the gentry themselves.[38]

Why had the gentry done this? Realizing correctly that the central government was milking the provinces for the sake of the army and court, the gentry, in an exceptional show of corporate solidarity, diverted whatever funds they could get their hands on to their own needs. Like state peasants who built up tax arrears with the confidence that the government could never collect them, the gentry pocketed the government's modest welfare contribution knowing that they would never be held to account. In a similar vein, the gentry proved quite effective at extracting the money and labor duties that the peasantry owed them as lords but were wondrously inept at turning over the duties that they collected for the government.

The contrast between the gentry's universal show of independence and resolve in the case of the social welfare boards and its avoidance of both its own corporate institutions and elective service with governmental bodies is instructive. It indicates that the prereform gentry was quite capable of identifying and acting on its real corporate interests. It indicates, further, that the gentry had judged rightly that both their own corporate assemblies and the elective positions open to them in the provincial administrations were at best forms of cooptation and at worst mere busy work. Against this background, one cannot explain the degree of gentry activism in the zemstvos merely in terms of the greater sphere of competence that the zemstvos enjoyed. After all, many gentry continued to avoid zemstvo service. The difference is not so much in the institutions as in the circumstances of the

14

gentry, which made service in elective bodies a chore prior to 1861 and, for many, a useful means of advancing their own interests thereafter.

If gentry self-government and elective service with the provincial bureaucracy were both failures before 1861, the two experiences did bring certain benefits relevant to the zemstvos. They placed gentry in close touch with government at the provincial level and schooled them in the means needed to manipulate ministerial agents to their advantage. These skills, analogous to those acquired at the same time by the peasantry through their institutions, were later to prove thoroughly applicable to the zemstvo experience.

One might think that the natural consequence of this state of affairs would have been for government officials to call for the elimination of elective offices in the provinces and their replacement with bureaucratic appointees. Baron Haxthausen acknowledged the existence of such sentiment when he noted that in 1843 there were those who felt it desirable simply to abolish the corporate state institutions of the gentry and reduce the gentry's role in local administrative agencies.[39]

The sixfold increase in the number of provincial officials during the reign of Nicholas I may reflect the implementation of such a policy, but it is by no means conclusive evidence. Rather, what is surprising is the number of leading tsarist statemen of the first half of the nineteenth century who, even in the face of these circumstances, called for the expansion of the number and authority of elected offices in provincial Russia. Thus, in the Committee of December 26 (1825), it was proposed to establish an elective council at the district level, to be made up of representatives of the various estates and with broad responsibilities over those matters not explicitly singled out for the jurisdiction of the police.[40] Mikhail Speranskii also proposed the creation of assemblies of deputies at the provincial and district levels, to be made up of six elected representatives each from the gentry, the peasantry, and the towns.[41] Even General Muravev, who consistently championed a strong governmental presence wherever possible, favored the expansion of public involvement in the government at the provincial level for the simple reason that he saw no other means of keeping the burgeoning bureaucracy in hand.[42] Each of these proposals represents a reworking of the social welfare boards, which is the more surprising since ministerial officials could only have judged them a failure. This indicates that, for all their limitations and shortcomings, the gentry were acknowledged to constitute a force in the provinces that could not forever be permitted to go untapped by the government.

The urban population

The third group or estate that was to be represented in the zemstvos was the townsmen. To be sure, they were to be severely underrepresented under the 1864 statutes, but they were there nonetheless, carrying the entire baggage of their prior political experience. For at least two reasons this experience is in many respects quite distinct from that of both the peasantry and the gentry. First, in terms of sheer numbers the urban population was small, and that part of the urban population that enjoyed the formal rights and duties of citizenship was smaller still. Notwithstanding recent claims that the agglomeration of townsmen in Russia was greater,[43] the total urban population at the time of Peter I was scarcely 3 percent of the peasant population, and even by the 1840s only 23 towns in the entire empire, including the more settled Baltic region, could claim populations of more than 25,000.[44] Thanks to the highly restrictive legal definition of membership in the urban political community, only a fraction of these played any direct role in local public life. Even after the extremely restrictive Charter to the Cities of 1785 was broadened for Saint Petersburg in 1846, only 2 percent of the population of the capital was empowered to vote in the local elections.[45] The General Municipal Statute of 1870, which brought about the first real reform of urban government since 1785, opened up the political process within Moscow to fewer than 20,000 people on the basis of their ownership of real property or capital, although by that time the ancient capital had a population of a third of a million.[46] The underrepresentation of the urban population within the zemstvo thus represents a continuation of a century-old policy rather than a new concession to the rural classes.

Urban representatives tended to play a less vigorously independent role in the zemstvos than did their rural colleagues, whether gentry or peasants. This is not surprising given the relatively weak development of corporate autonomy in the prereform Russian city. It has been said that the secret of commercial and political development of such Western European cities as Venice was due to the ease with which townsmen there could form corporations in order to coordinate behavior beyond familial and other traditional limits.[47] No real analog to these bodies existed in the Russian city before the late eighteenth century. The church brotherhoods of Belorussia and the Ukraine are perhaps closest in that they successfully organized schools, printing houses, almshouses, and other such institutions, but they were unknown within Great Russia.[48] The absence of a concept of limited liability in Russian law before 1805 effectively denied Russians down

16

to that date what might have been another major school of autonomous administrative activity in the cities.[49]

Urban life at the larger communal level was scarcely more developed than at the level of firms, societies, and corporations. Muscovite tsars issued few charters of immunity to the urban communities (*posady*)[50] but readily coopted individual commercial "guests" (*gosti*) to do what was in effect the state's own work.[51] Only with the *Ulozhenie* of 1649 did the state endow the *posady* with a firm legal existence by confirming their communal monopoly over trade.[52] Even this degree of autonomy was qualified by the townsmen's heavy dependence upon the state to limit the activity of foreign traders in their midst.[53] Thanks to this dependence and to the increasingly heavy burden of taxes and military recruiting that the state imposed on the urban communes, the several measures to establish elective *ratushi, burmistry,* and *magistry* (*Rathaus, Bürgermeisters, magistrates*) under Peter I came to naught, although the legislation establishing them assigned these officials responsibility over welfare, medicine, and other functions that were later to fall to the zemstvos.[54]

The very constraint placed upon their free activity by the government at times provoked the urban communes into impressive shows of defiance, if not real independence. Thus, in 1740 the town of Pskov was ordered to pay for the maintenance of a doctor there. Already impoverished by the demands of the central government, the commune of Pskov flatly refused to obey, proposing instead that the doctor's salary be covered by the patients themselves.[55] The government had no choice but to back off.

Such actions by the urban communes have led some observers to doubt the interest of Russia's urban community in the kind of public programs that the zemstvos were later to foster. According to this line of argument, the merchantry was so traditional in outlook that they virtually abdicated the developmental function, forcing the central government and its agents to take it up. The proposals by various communities to Catherine II's Legislative Commission belie this view. In its response, the merchantry of Moscow asked for a school for teaching "various languages, bookkeeping, and other sciences and studies essential for merchants"; the merchants of Astrakhan sought a navigation school; and the Tver merchants asked for schools to teach "grammar, arithmetic, history, geography, rhetoric, philosophy, jurisprudence, and dogmatic theology."[56] Clearly, the urge to develop urban life was present among these groups, but, as each declared, the existing structure of central levies prevented the urban populace from acting in this area on its own initiative, just as it prevented the gentry from taking the lead to develop rural society.

Superficially, Catherine's provincial and urban reforms might seem to have improved the basis for corporate initiative in the cities. They expanded and codified the elective principle in urban affairs, exempted urban dwellers from the capitation tax, formalized the system of urban merchant guilds and raised the amount of capital necessary to gain admission, exempted guild merchants from corporal punishment, and called upon the urban corporations to establish school, orphanages, lunatic asylums, workhouses, and homes for the aged.[57] Simultaneously, the empress and her collaborator, Jacob Sievers, set out to replan the cities of European Russia and to elevate many settlements to urban status as a means of strengthening the overall urban network.[58] Indeed, had Sievers had his way, provincial Russia would have been dotted with little Petersburgs, from which programs for the betterment of civil welfare would radiate outward to the villages, just as they were to have radiated into the provincial capitals from Saint Petersburg itself.[59]

In the end, Catherine's urban reforms failed, as did all subsequent efforts in this direction until 1870. As one student of the problem has observed, "Catherine had little faith in the civic responsibility of her subjects."[60] Provincial cities were denied most of the essentials of self-administration, even as they were expected to manage many affairs locally. Urban communes were granted no substantial power to tax themselves even for local needs; they were excluded from the process of urban planning yet expected to pay for the state's projects; and they were denied effective control of their own police, which became instead the "agents and guardians of Catherine's urban programs."[61]

Worse, the reforms that defined the life of Russia's urban estate down to 1870 succeeded in pitting town against countryside. For example, the state based medical services in urban centers and made those same centers bear the costs, even though rural folk were to have benefited equally from them; naturally, this caused the urban communes to resent what might otherwise have been sympathetic forces among the gentry.[62] Other policies fanned the same hostilities. The government's decision to permit gentry to own manufacturing and trading enterprises nullified the privilege that had defined the urban estate as a group since 1649. Its related decision in 1807 to grant to urban gentry the right to join the urban guilds and, through them, to play a role in elective government in the towns further diluted the political coherence of the so-called third estate.[63]

18

It is scarcely surprising that Russia's urban estate – like the gentry – avoided service in its own elective organs and that control over the election of magistrates and other officials became increasingly oligarchic.[64] By the time Paul I temporarily abolished urban elections, Catherine's 1785 reforms were already inoperative, even in the capital. The desperate attempt of the government in 1825 to force urban residents to serve in elective offices indicates the extent to which elective office holding had been bureaucratized and hence demoralized.[65]

Can one conclude, then, that the urban leaders who were called upon to play a role in the self-governing zemstvo institutions had lost all sense of the kind of independent corporate activity to which Catherine seemed to have summoned their forebears? Certain evidence from the early nineteenth century suggests otherwise. Just as peasants lied to the state about the resources of their villages and gentry lied to the state over their holdings and those of their serfs as well, so the urban electors systematically underreported the capital of their towns in order to avoid state taxes. According to one authoritative modern analyst, this practice caused the part of urban wealth upon which the government could levy taxes to shrink to a tenth and even a twentieth of its actual value.[66] Such brazen falsification, like the gentry's subversion of the Social Welfare Board, was a corporate action and hence must be weighed against claims of the passivity of the urban estate. Beyond this, the urban communes gauged carefully the ability of the state to extract taxes from them and, like the peasantry and gentry, avoided payment whenever they could get away with doing so. Suffice it to say that in the capital city of Saint Petersburg absolutely no personal property taxes were collected by the urban commune between the urban reform of 1785 and the establishment of a State Council committee to investigate urban governance in 1815![67] The organization of such systematic corruption and its maintenance over two generations testifies to a stronger corporate sense and coordination than any of the cities positive activities might suggest.

The system of corporative government

On the basis of this cursory review, it is possible to suggest a number of conclusions about the character of corporative rule by estates in the prereform Russian provinces. In doing so it is important to identify both similarities and differences among the experience of the three estates; both were to be pertinent to their participation in the zemstvos after 1864.

That significant differences existed among the political cultures of the three constituent estates is itself an important conclusion, one that contradicts the intent of the cameralists who constructed the system under Catherine II and of the reformers who perpetuated it in 1864. Such differences are to be discerned in at least three areas. With respect to the extent of organizational activity among the three corporative groups, the peasantry must take first place. Notwithstanding the comparatively recent origins of the repartitional commune in Russia, the peasant communes met more frequently than either the gentry assemblies or the urban communes and exercised control over a far broader spectrum of their members' lives than did either of the others. Furthermore, they wielded that control with a greater degree of autonomy from governmental interference, especially in the case of crown and state peasants. This was not because the various ministries were disinterested in the communal affairs of the peasantry but because the latter were conducted in the villages themselves, remote from the provincial and district capitals in which the corporate lives of the gentry and urban communes were centered and where the central ministerial agents were also domiciled.

Although available data do not suffice to compare the budgets of the corporate institutions of the gentry and townspeople, it is clear that both were accustomed to deal with larger sums of money than was the peasantry. The gentry in particular, thanks to its elective role in the local ministerial agencies, had experience with handling relatively substantial amounts of capital. The peasantry, on the other hand, had extensive experience with the execution of public works projects, thanks to its labor obligations. This latter, however, was to prove of less significance under the zemstvos, when so many labor duties were transformed into taxes in money in 1864 and subsequently.

These differences in the range of activity and resources of the three estates account for the differing corporate sense that existed among them. The urban communes, demoralized and with their prerogatives undercut by tsarist legislation, exhibited a weak corporate sense, except in the negative area of resisting ministerial pressure through corrupt means. The gentry's identity as an autonomous corporation was also vitiated by the state's refusal to entrust it with major functions and its preference instead to co-opt gentry into its own bureaucratic system. Although the corporative sense of the peasantry was diluted by the process of economic differentiation that was steadily occurring among members of the village communes – a process that was paralleled among both gentry and urban communes – the expansion of duties in cash (obrok) at the expense of corvée (barshchina) tended to

20

strengthen the mir.[68] Similarly, the policies of the Ministry of State Domains under Count Kiselev strengthened corporatism among state peasants just as it was waning in the towns and among the gentry.

A further and significant difference between the political cu'tures of the three estates that were called upon to join in the zemstvos was the extent to which their affairs were governed by norms derived from state law as opposed to custom. In this respect, the peasantry and even the urban communes lagged behind the gentry. Thanks to its status as a service class, a status that continued de facto long after it had been eliminated de juris in 1762,[69] the gentry could boast thousands of members with a good knowledge both of state law and bureaucratic procedure, skills that they were to apply to their advantage in the zemstvos.

Having acknowledged the significant differences among the political environment of the three estates before 1864, it must also be noted that they demonstrated numerous common characteristics. All three estates were of recent origin and owed their prerogatives as much to the state having acted in its own interests as from any concessions that the peasantry, gentry, or townspeople had extorted from the crown. None could cite a body of corporate law confirming its special position, although both the gentry assemblies and urban communes liked to pretend that their claims against the state were analogous to the privileges enjoyed by the Germanic noble and urban corporations in the Baltic. By the mid-nineteenth century, the norms of the central ministries had penetrated all three to the extent that their elected officials were viewed as being virtually indistinguishable from civil servants.[70] Baron Haxthausen saw this clearly and piled up evidence to show that the "estates" of Russia were no estates at all either juridically or in their ability to control their own actions or even to define their own membership.[71]

Oligarchic tendencies were universal among the three groups that later made up the zemstvos, and these tendencies were becoming more pronounced in the nineteenth century. This, combined with the provincial administrators' extensive power to influence their internal life by refusing to confirm elected officials in their offices[72] and the various legal and financial restrictions on their ability to raise taxes for local needs, did much to dilute the meaning of the elective principle. Yet, through the district and town level, most offices among all three groups were elective. Though Count Kiselev restricted somewhat the elective principle among state peasants in the 1840s, all three estates had considerable experience with elective office holding well before the zemstvos systematized it up to the provincial level.[73]

21

Whatever the restrictions on their ability to take positive measures in their own behalf, all three estates proved that they could at least show great cunning and resourcefulness in resisting the government's claims against their resources. As we have seen, the single best evidence for the existence in Russia of strong and independent estates managed by elected officials was their ability to cheat the government out of the taxes that it sought to collect. On the other side, there exists no better evidence of the limited desire among the three estates for a greater degree of autonomy than their failure, both individually and together, to translate their willingness to cheat the government into a broader theory of pluralism, self-government, or voluntarism.

Hence, it is no wonder that even the more cautious tsarist officials could support the zemstvo without abandoning their commitment to bureaucratic ideals, even as they were later to oppose the more ambitious claims of zemstvo activists. Though informed by a new theory of self-government, the zemstvo was built upon practices and relationships that had been worked out without danger to the state during the century since Catherine's reforms.

Nor was there any ready alternative to the zemstvo, given the demonstrated inability of the tsarist state to force leaders of "society" and its elected officials to pay the taxes that were so desperately needed to sustain the army and court. Like the earlier decentralizing reforms of Catherine II, zemstvo self-government was instituted at a moment when the state's finances were in a state of chaos. Unable itself to pay for the local services that the populace demanded and dependent upon that same populace for its own support, the tsarist state turned to the estates.

It might well be asked whether many of the same functions that the zemstvo was to perform could not have been turned over to the local communities to be handled through voluntary associations, for example, philanthropic societies, clubs, membership associations, and private foundations. In Western Europe and North America, after all, such self-organized bodies constituted a major component of the system providing local services, and even in Russia they were to assume great importance by the end of the nineteenth century.[74] It is true that voluntarism was on the rise in the very years when the zemstvo reform was being drafted.[75] Yet the reformers scarcely considered the possibility of truly autonomous bodies playing a central role in the provision of local services, probably for the simple reason that local leaders themselves could scarcely conceive of such a notion. With limited liability introduced only in the nineteenth century, the first private insurance company founded only in 1827, and the first

22

detailed law on joint stock companies issued only in 1836, this was hardly unrealistic of them.[76] True, Freemasons had advocated private philanthropy in the eighteenth century, and Catherine herself had taken the lead in establishing various schools and homes. But up till the Crimean War it was the court itself that stood behind most private philanthropy and indeed dominated the field through the Imperial Philanthropic Society (founded 1802), whose officers, quite incongruously, were awarded civil service ranks![77] During the entire reign of Nicholas I, only some 25 voluntary associations were awarded charters by the government, and most of these were either organized by foreigners or founded in the Baltic provinces, where the social and historical basis for public action did exist.[78] Without liquid capital and a strong system of private credit, voluntarism had even less strong a financial base than did the system of estates, with their nominal powers of taxation.[79]

The isolation of local initiative

In our review of the organizational life of three estates into which the Russian population was divided from the late eighteenth century to the founding of the zemstvos we have assumed that, for better or worse, these institutions were the schools in which were formed many of the political attitudes and habits that were later to appear in the zemstvos. This assertion must be qualified to the extent that numerous gentry and smaller numbers of men from the urban estate and peasantry gained administrative experience through service on the staffs of ministerial agencies at the provincial or district level, whether in career appointments or through elective posts. Such service was certainly of significance on a functional level. Along with the penetration of governmental practices into the organizations of the estates, this experience must have gone far to foster communications, if not actual coordination, between governmental and estate institutions that were, at bottom, starkly different from one another.

Let us now turn to the differences between the organization of the three estates, on the one hand, and that of the government, on the other, for these differences may reveal the roots of many of the anomalies that characterize the relationship of the zemstvos to Russian political culture as a whole. Viewed from the perspective of any of three estates, the differences were great in theory but insignificant in practice. Gentry marshalls, urban magistrates, and peasant elders inevitably felt somehow beholden to the members of the estate that had elected them to office. Even if estate officials or representatives gained office through bribery or the machinations of an oligarchy, as often occurred, they nonetheless were linked to the group from which they were drawn and subject in varying degrees to its influence or control. Given this, the cooptation of the elected official by local administrators would not so much reverse his loyalties as complicate them. From his perspective, the elective estate official's constant fate was to be subjected to interference from the side of the central ministries and their agents – an interference that was rarely, if ever, offset by financial benefit to the local constituency.

The local governor or appointed official was bound to see things differently. Subject to rapid turnover[80] and rarely able to sink deep roots at the provincial, let alone the district, level, the appointed official could not but envy the degree of attachment to the locality that the estate representatives could claim. The appointed official and, still more, his minister in Saint Petersburg, was inclined to view the estate institutions as a kind of state within a state, a *status in statu*, in the expression made popular during the debates of the late 1850s.

This difference of perceptions accurately reflected a basic condition of the tsarist state in the eighteenth and nineteenth centuries. Notwithstanding its aspirations as an absolutist monarchy, tsardom was composed of various poorly integrated institutions founded on basically different principles. This lack of integration among themselves was formalized when Catherine II established the system of three estates and at the same time expanded the central bureaucracies at the provincial and district levels. Retained intact until the end of serfdom, the clash of state and estate (or "society") was then perpetuated down to the end of the old regime.

The conflict between "state" and "society" as represented by the zemstvo has frequently been noted in descriptions of the period 1864–1917. As we have seen, in matters of local government its emergence dates not to the establishment of the new self-governing bodies under Alexander II but to the era of Catherine II, when the system of estates was formally constituted. Now, given the fact that nearly a century passed between Catherine's reforms and those of her great-grandson, it is worth asking why the conflict was not meliorated under the impact of daily contact between the three estates and the central ministries. The answer lies in both the nature of the tsarist administration and the character of the estates themselves.

As an autocratic state, tsarist Russia was committed to the ideal of a single, integrated system linking ruler to ruled. Provincial governors were to be the bosses (*khoziaeva*) of their districts – virtual despots – and gentry were to play the same grandiose role at the most local level.

24

This simple ideal proved impossible to attain. For the governors to have fulfilled the role of provincial autocrats, they would have needed local agencies corresponding to each of the central agencies in the capital. Yet neither before nor after 1864 did such agencies exist. The central ministries simply lacked the authority to replicate themselves locally, although, as Herbert J. Spiro has observed, such replication is a fundamental drive of most political systems: "In all modern governments, each ministry tends to replicate the overall structure of the government, and each bureau tends to replicate the overall structure of the ministry of which it is a part."[81] Far from being replications of patterns in Saint Petersburg, provincial agencies were organized on collegial, rather than ministerial, lines both before and after 1864. Ministries had been introduced in 1802, but vocal advocates of the older system continued to be heard not only in the 1840s but even amidst the reforms of the 1860s![82] This failure of replication meant that even within the purely bureaucratic agencies of the tsarist state a lack of integration reigned, giving rise to a sense of utter powerlessness among the nominally all-powerful provincial officials. It need scarcely be said that the lack of integration was felt even more keenly at the more local levels.

Merely to state that the government in Saint Petersburg was unable to provide effective rule at the provincial level before 1864 is actually to minimize the gravity of its problem. It was unable even to set up local agencies corresponding to the major ministries and bureaus in the capital. This basic organizational failure and the sense of insecurity it engendered underlay the local bureaucrats' inherent suspicion of all "societal" initiatives arising from the three estates and their elective organs. After 1864 the same sense of insecurity on the part of provincial officialdom was directed toward the zemstvos, and for the same reasons. What did they fear? Quite simply, that the estate-based elective system would seek to replicate itself upward, culminating in a national zemstvo.

Given the frequency with which ministerial officials and their local agents registered this fear after 1864, it is worth asking whether such a fear had existed earlier as well and, if so, with what justification. It did, of course, and was reinforced every time a group of townsmen, gentry, or peasants sought to petition the crown directly or to send their elected representatives to the capital. But it did not ripen into open conflict before the establishment of the zemstvos because the possibility that the estates would actually seek to replicate themselves upward seemed so slight. On the one hand, the Catherinian reforms left such scant resources to the organized gentry, townspeople, and peasants that, with the exception of the Decembrists, few subjects dared entertain any ambitions reaching beyond their immediate problems. On the other hand, the existence of serfdom placed the gentry in such a state of dependence upon the central government, and the peasantry in such a position of subordination to it, as to discourage any independent organizational initiatives.

Against this background the zemstvos can be seen as exacerbating a tension between state and "society" that was fully present under the prereform system but in latent form, held in check by the poverty of rural life and the institution of serfdom. The abolition of serfdom dramatically reduced the gentry's dependence upon Saint Petersburg and thereby opened the way for its elected representatives to strike out vigorously in behalf of local needs and the interests of their estate. The abolition of serfdom and the ensuing urbanization destroyed the rationale for the subordinate position in which the urban communes had been placed vis-à-vis the gentry estate, thus expanding the political aspirations of urban leaders. The peasantry, too, could engage more actively in local affairs once its servile status was reduced. Each estate thus had ample grounds for asserting its needs and interests more vigorously than before.

We have seen that the new zemstvo institutions owed much to the organizational forms of the preexistent system of local rule based on the three estates. Moreover, in their day-to-day practice the zemstvos called upon techniques and attitudes that had been built up over nearly a century of interaction between the elective estate organs and local agents of the central government. In these respects the establishment of the zemstvo culminated a phase of Russian history that began with Catherine's provincial reform of 1775.

Were it not for the changed social environment brought about by the end of serfdom, the zemstvo reforms might have been little more than what Minister of Internal Affairs Valuev expected them to be: a carefully devised and eminently conservative step to increase the public presence at the most local level. But the altered social climate gave meaning to the calls for self-government that were fashionable in the 1850s and forced to the surface the fundamental contradiction between the ideal of an administered society and a self-governing community that had been present in Russian political culture since the 1770s. Down to 1917 the activism of zemstvo leaders caused this unstable situation to be resolved in a manner that left a broad sphere of activity for communal self-government. After 1917 a reverse tendency set in. The replication of ministerial agencies to the most local level that had eluded tsarist administrators for a century and a half was finally achieved.

26

Notes

1 This argument underlies the study of V. V. Garmiza, *Podgotovka zemskoi reformy 1864 goda* (Moscow, 1957).
2 See, for example, the remarkable statement of Senator Muravev in 1843, cited in E. Anuchin, *Istoricheskii obzor razvitiia administrativnykh politseiskikh uchrezhdenii v Rossii* (St. Petersburg, 1862), p. 62. See also S. Frederick Starr, *Decentralization and Self-Government in Russia, 1830–1870* (Princeton, 1972), ch. 2.
3 Starr, ch. 1.
4 See Nancy M. Frieden, "The Roots of Russian Zemstvo Medicine," *Actes du Congrès, I: Colloque* (Proceedings of the 25th Congress of the History of Medicine, Quebec, 1976).
5 See N. Lazarevskii, "Sosloviia," *Entsiklopedicheskii slovar'*, (Brokgauz – Efron) vol. 60, pp. 911–13.
6 Steven A. Grant, "The Peasant Commune in Russian Thought, 1861–1905" (Ph.D. dissertation, Harvard University, 1973), p. 73; see also Michael Confino, *Systèmes agraires et progrès agricole: l'assolement triennal en Russie aux xviiie–xixe siècles* (Paris, 1969).
7 S. G. Pushkarev, *Krest'ianskaia pozemel'no–peredel'naia obshchina v Rossii* (Newtonville, Mass., 1976), p. 113.
8 Pushkarev, in making this point, traces the roots of "governmentalization" to the seventeenth century; ibid., pp. 99 ff.
9 V. A. Aleksandrov, *Sel'skaia obshchina v Rossii s xvii–nachalo xix v.* (Moscow, 1976), p. 130.
10 Olga Crisp, *Studies in the Russian Economy Before 1914* (New York, 1976), p. 94.
11 Aleksandrov, p. 294.
12 This is not to deny, of course, the equally extensive and universally prevalent powers of lords over their serfs throughout Europe; see Jerome Blum, *The End of the Old Order in Rural Europe* (Princeton, 1978), chs. 2–3.
13 Andrzej Walicki, *The Slavophile Controversy: History of a Conservative Utopia in Nineteenth-Century Russian Thought* (Oxford, 1975), pp. 230 ff; also, Grant, pp. 7 ff.
14 This image received support in the 1840s from the findings of Count Kiselev's inspectors, from whose reports it has entered the scholarly literature. See Jerome Blum, *Lord and Peasant in Russia from the Ninth to the Nineteenth Century* (Princeton, 1961), p. 525; Crisp, p. 82.
15 August von Haxthausen, *Studies on the Interior of Russia*, ed., S. Frederick Starr, (Chicago, 1972), pp. 277 ff.
16 Richard Pipes, *Russia Under the Old Regime* (New York, 1974), p. 150.
17 Aleksandrov, p. 157

18 Haxthausen, p. 63; Aleksandrov, p. 138.

19 Aleksandrov, pp. 130 ff.

20 Ibid., pp. 140 ff.

21 See Blum, *Lord and Peasant*, ch. 21.

22 Aleksandrov, pp. 126 ff.

23 Ibid., p. 142.

24 See Robert E. Jones, *The Emancipation of the Russian Nobility* (Princeton, 1973), pp. 191 ff. 264–5; also A. Romanovich-Slavatinskii, *Dvorianstvo v Rossii ot nachala xviii veka do otmeny krepostnogo prava* (St. Petersburg, 1870).

25 M. P. Pavlova-Sil'vanskaia, "Sotsial'naia sushchnost' oblastnoi reformy Ekateriny II," in N. M. Druzhinin, ed., *Absoliutizm v Rossii XVII–XVIII vv.* (Moscow, 1964), pp. 467–9.

26 P. A. Zaionchkovskii, "Gubernskaia administratsiia nakanune Krymskoi voiny," *Voprosy istorii*, 1975, no. 9, pp. 38–9.

27 Romanovich-Slavatinskii, pp. 402–10.

28 Paul Dukes, *Catherine the Great and the Russian Nobility* (Cambridge, 1967), pp. 168 ff.

29 Ibid., p. 162.

30 Jones, p. 196; Dukes, p. 172.

31 Jones, p. 127.

32 Starr, *Decentralization*, pp. 9–26.

33 Jones, pp. 264–5.

34 Romanovich-Slavatinskii, p. 491. Curiously, this occurred precisely in the decades when the corporate bodies of the nobility in Austria and Hungary underwent a kind of revival; Blum, *End of the Old Order*, p. 27.

35 Iv. Blinov, *Gubernatory: istoriko-iuridicheskii ocherk* (St. Petersburg, 1905), pp. 186–299.

36 On the decline of provincial institutions after the death of Peter I see Iu. Got'e, *Istoriia oblastnogo upravleniia v Rossii ot Petra I do Ekateriny II*, Vol. 1 (Moscow, 1913), pp. 354 ff.

37 *Polnoe sobranie zakonov Rossiiskoi imperii (PSZRI)*, 4th series, vol. 20, no. 14392, Statute on the Provinces, November 7, 1775, p. 1, art. 38–9; see Jones, p. 329.

38 Adele Lindenmeyr, "The Origins of Collective Charity in Russia" (Ph.D. dissertation, Princeton University, 1979).

39 Haxthausen, p. 253.

40 Anuchin, pp. 117 ff.

41 Ibid., p. 121.

42 Ibid., pp. 132–3.

43 See Gilbert Rozman, *Urban Networks in Russia, 1750–1800, and Pre-Modern Periodization* (Princeton, 1976), ch. 4.

44 L. Tengoborskii, *Commentaries on the Productive Forces of Russia*, 2 vols. (London, 1855–56), 1:89 ff; for the seventeenth century see Pavel Smirnov, *Goroda moskovskogo gosudarstva v pervoi polovine xvii veka*, vol. 1. (Kiev, 1917).

45 Walter Hanchett, "Tsarist Statutory Regulation of Municipal Govern-ment in the Nineteenth Century," in Michael Hamm, ed., *The City in Russian History* (Lexington, Ky., 1976), pp. 91 ff.
46 Ibid., p. 101.
47 William H. McNeill, *Venice, the Hinge of Europe, 1051–1797* (Chicago, 1974), p. 14.
48 Λ. Λ. Papkov, *Tserkovnye bratstva: kratkii slulislicheskii ocherk o polozhenii tserkovnykh bratstv k nachalu 1893* (St. Petersburg, 1893).
49 These circumstances are reviewed by N. N. Firsov, *Russkaia torgovo-promyshlennye kompanii v l-oi polovine xviii stoletiia* (Kazan, 1896); William C. Blackwell, *The Beginnings of Russian Industrialization, 1800–1860*, vol. 1 (Princeton, 1968), pp. 92–3.
50 Marc Zlotnik, "Muscovite Immunity Charters," unpublished paper, 1978, p. 107.
51 V. I. Sergeevich, *Russkiia iuridicheskie drevnosti*, vol. 1 (St. Petersburg, 1890); also, Pipes, p. 197.
52 A. Kizevetter, *Istoricheskie ocherki* (Moscow, 1912), p. 1; also Iu. P. Klokman, "Gorod v zakonodatel'stve russkogo absoliutizma vo vtoroi polovine xvii–xviii vv.," in Druzhinin, ed., *Absoliutizm v Rossii*, p. 322.
53 David H. Miller, "State and City in Seventeenth Century Muscovy," in Hamm, ed., *The City in Russian History*, p. 46.
54 Klokman, p. 332.
55 PSZRI, 1st series, vol. 6, no. 3708 (1740), p. 1721.
56 Kizevetter, pp. 504 ff.
57 Ibid., pp. 553–4; Iu. P. Klokman, *Sotsial'no-ekonomicheskaia istoriia russkogo goroda vtoroi poloviny xviii veka* (Moscow, 1967), pp. 77–88.
58 Klokman, "Gorod v zakonodatel'stve," p. 330; Robert E. Jones, "Urban Planning and the Development of Provincial Towns in Russia, 1762 –1796," in John Garrard, ed., *The Eighteenth Century in Russia*, (Oxford, 1973), pp. 327 ff.
59 Pavlova-Sil'vanskaia, pp. 476–7; Robert E. Jones, "Jacob Sievers, En-lightened Reform and the Development of a 'Third Estate' in Russia," *Russian Review*, (October 1977), pp. 424–37; Klokman, "Gorod v zako-nodatel'stve," p. 330.
60 Jones, "Urban Planning," p. 341.
61 Ibid., p. 332. For a detailed review of this situation, see I. Ditiatin, *Gorodskoe samoupravlenie v Rossii* (Iaroslavl, 1877), pp. 115 ff.
62 Compare with the pre-1775 situation, in which provincial towns were pitted against district centers; Kizevetter, p. 539.
63 Romanovich-Slavatinskii, pp. 164–5; see also W. Bruce Lincoln's excel-lent review of urban legislation, "The Russian State and Its Critics: A Search for Effective Municipal Government, 1786–1842," *Jahrbücher für Geschichte Osteuropas*, December 1969, pp. 531 ff.
64 This had always been the case to some degree; Kizevetter, p. 659.
65 Hanchett, p. 91.
66 Lincoln, p. 534.

67 M. V. Varadinov, *Istoriia Ministerstva vnutrennykh del*, 2 vols. (St. Petersburg, 1858–63), 2:69 ff.

68 Aleksandrov, pp. 177 ff.

69 That this was in keeping with Catherine's intentions is affirmed by Robert E. Jones, "Catherine II and the Provincial Reform of 1755: A Question of Motivation," *Canadian Slavic Studies*, 1970, no. 3, pp. 503 ff.

70 Lincoln, p. 535; and Romanovich-Slavatinskii, p. 491 ff.

71 Haxthausen, pp. 214, 247–53.

72 John P. LeDonne, "The Judicial Reform of 1775 in Central Russia," *Jahrbücher für Geschichte Osteuropas*, 1973, no. 1, pp. 42 ff.

73 See Boris Chicherin's counterargument to this, *Oblastnye uchrezhdeniia Rossii v xvii-om veke* (Moscow, 1856), pp. 453 ff.

74 For a full development of this thesis see Lindenmeyr's dissertation, cited above.

75 Starr, p. 187 ff.

76 Blackwell, pp. 88–90

77 Lindenmeyr, p. 36.

78 Nikolai Anufr'ev, "Pravitel'stvennaia reglamentatsiia obrazovaniia chastnykh obshchestv v Rossii," *Voprosy administrativnogo prava*, vol. 1 (Moscow, 1916), p. 24.

79 S. Ia. Borovoi, *Kredit i banki Rossii, seredina xvii v.–1861 g.* (Moscow, 1958), pp. 235 ff.

80 Zaionchkovskii, p. 39.

81 Herbert J. Spiro, "Interdependence and Replication: America's Unique Role in the World," (Paper delivered at The Wilson Center, 1978), p. 28.

82 Count Vorontsov's defense in the 1840s is to be found in Anuchin, p. 59; for A. D. Gradovskii's defense see *Sobranie sochinenii*, 9 vols. (St. Petersburg, 1899), 1:292.

3

Zemstvo organization and role within the administrative structure

KERMIT E. McKENZIE

Basic pattern of the zemstvo

The zemstvo was introduced in the Russian Empire on January 1, 1864, with the confirmation by Alexander II of the Statute on Zemstvo Institutions. This statute authorized the establishment of zemstvo institutions in the local territorial–administrative units of the empire: the province (*guberniia*) and the district (*uezd*). Entrusted with the management of affairs relating to "the local economic welfare and needs of each province and each district" (article 1), these institutions were to consist of an assembly (*sobranie*) and an executive board (*uprava*) at each level. The assembly was to hold decision-making power (*rasporiaditel'naia vlast'*), and the board, executive power (*ispolnitel'naia vlast'*). The assemblies were to be composed (almost entirely) of elected representatives of the local population, called deputies (*glasnye*). At the lower or district level, these deputies were to be chosen by three electoral groups formed by distinct categories of the local citizenry and meeting separately to cast their votes. The deputies to the provincial assembly were to be elected by the district assemblies from their own memberships. The presiding officer of the district assembly was to be the district marshal of nobility, and, of the provincial assembly, the provincial marshal of nobility. The executive boards at the provincial and district levels were to be chosen by their respective assemblies. No enforcement or police power was assigned to the zemstvo.

These basic features of the zemstvo institutions were to be preserved throughout the following years down to the Revolution of 1917. Subsequent legislation, including the second Zemstvo Statute of 1890, interpretations by the Senate, and the very practice of the zemstvos were to modify and refine, add to and subtract from, the competence and powers of zemstvo institutions. The mode and degree of supervision exercised by the government over the zemstvo was also to change. The specific terms of suffrage were to undergo substantial modification. But the basic features outlined above were to remain constant during the more than half-century of zemstvo history.

The new zemstvo institutions, popularly known as organs of self-government (*samoupravlenie*; the word is not used in the Statute of 1864), joined a host of existing institutions, governmental and societal, in the provincial and district arenas of Russian life. The appearance on the local scene of the zemstvo did not cause the displacement, save in small part, of the existing structure of administration. True, certain matters formerly dealt with by the provincial bureaucracy were now transferred to the zemstvo, but provincial government remained in the hands of the governor, who was endowed with broad powers of supervision and control over local affairs, including those now to be managed by the zemstvo.[1] Subordinate to the Ministry of Interior, the governor was aided by a provincial board (*gubernskoe pravlenie*), which was composed of a general bureau (*obshchee prisutstvie*) and a chancellery divided into departments and staffed with a growing bureaucracy.[2] The governor was also chairman of numerous specialized bodies of a collegial nature, variously called committees, commissions, and bureaus.[3] These bodies usually included, besides bureaucrats of the Interior Ministry, certain local representatives of other ministries and agencies and also the provincial marshal of nobility and in some cases had subordinate counterparts at the district level. With the creation of the zemstvo, it too was to gain representation on several of these committees and bureaus. The governor's chief subordinate at the district level was the police captain (*ispravnik*), who headed the local police and was himself a member of several district committees and bureaus. Besides these institutions of the Ministry of Interior, a host of lower branches of other central civil and military ministries and agencies – justice, finance, education, war, and so forth – cluttered the local scene.[4]

If one adds to the local picture the several existing class or estate (*soslovie*) organizations – provincial and district corporations of the nobility, village communities, and the societies of the various urban classes – as well as the ecclesiastical institutions, it is obvious that an elaborate array of veteran governmental and societal entities was to coexist with the new zemstvo institutions. And the activist in zemstvo matters, the *zemskii deiatel'*, was to be confronted by a wide variety of personages and dignitaries in the provinces, each with his own pursuits, interests, and loyalties.[5]

32

Establishment, extension, and duration
of zemstvo institutions

The zemstvo was introduced by no means simultaneously and universally throughout the provinces and regions of the Russian Empire. During the first decade of the existence of the Statute of 1864, zemstvo institutions were opened in 34 provinces, compactly clustered in the heartland of European Russia. Thereafter, with the exception of the short-lived zemstvo of the Don region, it was not until 1911 and 1912 that nine additional provinces obtained zemstvos, and only in 1917 were zemstvos authorized throughout the realm, on the very eve of their displacement by revolutionary soviets. Thus the history of the Russian zemstvo is, by and large, the history of the original 34 zemstvos.

The imperial ukaz (edict) that presented the Zemstvo Statute of 1864 provided for zemstvos in 33 provinces: Chernigov, Ekaterinoslav, Iaroslavl, Kazan, Kaluga, Kharkov, Kherson, Kostroma, Kursk, Moscow, Nizhnii Novgorod, Novgorod, Olonets, Orenburg, Orel, Penza, Perm, Poltava, Pskov, Riazan, Saint Petersburg, Samara, Saratov, Simbirsk, Smolensk, Tambov, Tauride, Tula, Tver, Viatka, Vladimir, Vologda, and Voronezh.[6] In each of these provinces, except Orenburg, zemstvo institutions were in fact opened in the years between 1865 and 1870.[7] In addition, zemstvos also appeared in two provinces not mentioned in the Statute of 1864 – in Bessarabia in 1869,[8] and in Ufa in 1875.[9] The process was irregular: in 1865, 19 zemstvos were opened; in 1866, 9; in 1867, 2; in 1869, 1; in 1870, 2; in 1875, 1.[10] The total number of district zemstvos within these 34 provinces was 359. These provinces thereafter retained their zemstvo institutions uninterruptedly, with two exceptions, until the establishment of Bolshevik power in Russia. In Saint Petersburg province the action of the statute was suspended for six months in 1867, and in the Cherepovets district of Novgorod province the zemstvo was replaced during 1881–91 by a temporary commission appointed by the minister of interior.[11] There was, it may be noted, no provision in either the 1864 or the later 1890 zemstvo statute for dissolution of zemstvo institutions.

The original intention of the government to extend zemstvo institutions to other parts of the empire is clear. On the very day the Statute of 1864 was promulgated, another measure instructed the minister of interior to prepare proposals to be introduced in the State Council for the establishment of zemstvos elsewhere: specifically, Archangelsk, Astrakhan, Bessarabia, the nine western provinces, and, more generally, those parts of the empire "governed by special insitutions."[12] But, until 1911, no additional zemstvos were created except in the Don region, where zemstvo institutions existed only from 1876 to 1882.[13] The introduction of zemstvos in the Baltic provinces was discussed in the State Council in 1887, but this body concluded that such would be impossible, "for, in its opinion, no matter how skillfully self-government would be organized, it would be entirely in the hands of the German nobility."[14]

By the Imperial Ukaz of March 11, 1911, zemstvo institutions were granted to the six western provinces of Kiev, Minsk, Mogilev, Podolia, Vitebsk, and Volynia.[15] Originally designed by Stolypin to include also the northwestern provinces of Grodno, Kovno, and Vilna, the bill as presented to the Duma in March 1910 omitted the latter three. The reason for the omission was that in these three provinces even Stolypin's electoral tinkering could not ensure the Great Russian predominance that he was able to achieve in the six western provinces.[16]

Three more provinces – Astrakhan, Orenburg, and Stavropol – obtained zemstvo institutions prior to World War I by virtue of three separate laws receiving imperial confirmation on June 9, 1912, after having passed both houses of the Russian parliament.[17] Thus, on the eve of war, zemstvo institutions were functioning in 43 of the 84 provinces and regions of the empire (not including the 8 provinces of Finland and the 9 of Poland), comprising 441 districts. Virtually two-thirds of the country's population lived in these areas.[18]

Following the overthrow of the monarchy and the establishment of the Provisional Government in 1917, the zemstvo was universalized, democratized, and given the foundation long denied by zemstvo activists – a volost, or subdistrict, zemstvo. The law of June 9, 1917, extended to all parts of the country the right to establish zemstvo institutions.[19] Prior to this and pending the elaboration of a new overall zemstvo statute, temporary rules democratizing the election process had been issued on May 21.[20] The voting age was lowered from 25 to 20, females were enfranchised, and property or tax-paying qualifications were abolished. Also on May 21, volost zemstvos were authorized by a temporary statute, as a result of which a three-tiered structure came into being.[21] According to a Soviet study, in 1917 there were 9,305 volosts in the 43 provinces having zemstvo institutions; volost zemstvo elections were carried out in August (in 9 provinces), September (31 provinces), and October (3 provinces).[22]

The establishment of Bolshevik power and the beginning of the Russian Civil War brought an end to the existence of the zemstvo. A Soviet decree of December 24, 1917, declared that "the organs of local power are soviets" and ordered that former organs of local government everywhere be replaced.[23] Forced closings, self-liquidation, or simple renaming were the means.[24] Sustained for a time in areas under anti-Bolshevik control, the zemstvos lingered longest in the Russian Far East, vanishing there only in 1922.[25]

The Statutes of 1864 and 1890

Twice in its history the zemstvo received comprehensive definitions of its fundamental attributes – jurisdiction, competence, obligations, electoral basis, composition of its assembly and executive board, and relationship to the government. Dissimilar circumstances and political attitudes surrounded each definition.

The original Statute (*Polozhenie*) of January 1, 1864, was a product of the classic, early phase of the era of Great Reforms.[26] An initial draft of the new institutions was elaborated in a special Commission on Provincial and District Institutions, established within the Ministry of Interior in March 1859, and headed first by N. A. Miliutin and later by P. A. Valuev. Confirmed by Alexander II in June 1862, and subsequently published, this draft became the subject of much debate and revision before emerging in final form and receiving the approval of the emperor.[27]

A quarter-century later, a new reformed statute emerged during the illiberal reign of Alexander III.[28] This second statute was the result of virtually a decade of study, first by the abortive commission (1881–5) headed by M. S. Kakhanov and then by Minister of Interior D. A. Tolstoi and his head of chancellery, A. D. Pazukhin. Rejecting the more liberal recommendations of the Kakhanov commission, Tolstoi and Pazukhin desired a reform of the zemstvo that would place it directly under bureaucratic control, virtually destroy its independence, further enhance the already dominant role of the gentry, and reshape the electoral colleges upon an estate (*soslovie*) basis. Modified further by I. N. Durnovo, Tolstoi's successor, these reactionary aims met considerable resistance and change during the State Council's deliberations in the spring of 1890. The resulting measure received imperial approval on June 12, 1890.[29]

These lengthy documents (120 articles in 1864, and 138 in 1890) sought, in quite different political climates, to provide the country with a workable institution at the local level. To what extent do they reflect a change in attitude respecting the very nature of the zemstvo? Do the two statutes demarcate two distinct phases in zemstvo history? Do they provide for qualitatively different sets of zemstvo institutions? Some general remarks may serve to place a detailed examination of zemstvo organization in better perspective.

What has been termed the public or societal theory (obshchestven-naia teoriia) of self-government appears to have been held more or less consciously by the framers of the Zemstvo Statute of 1864 and by educated opinion at that time. According to this theory, there is a juxtaposition of society's local interests and affairs to the interests and affairs of the state. Each are distinct and legitimate categories. Local self-government has to do with society's interests alone, which stand apart from the interests of the state. The management of society's interests, which are essentially economic in nature as distinguished from the essentially political interests of the state, should be entrusted to special societal institutions standing outside the governmental hierarchy and acting independently. The organ of self-government is similar in status to a private person and, like a private person, has itself no function of police power but rather must turn to the police for cooperation and aid.

This societal theory gave way in subsequent years to the state theory (gosudarstvennaia teoriia) of self-government, according to which local society takes on the realization of certain tasks of state administration; that is, local society serves state interests and goals. Here there is no juxtaposition and isolation of self-government and the state. A division of interests into separate and distinct categories (societal vs. state) is considered false. There are only state interests, and local self-government organs are brought into existence because they are believed to be best able to carry out certain of these state interests.[30]

Thus, at first, zemstvo institutions were considered to be special extragovernmental bodies, coexisting alongside the latter and creating with them a kind of dualism in the management of local affairs. In 1870, responding to protests of zemstvos against the loss of their franking privileges the previous year, the Committee of Ministers emphasized that zemstvo institutions possessed a character similar to that of private persons and societies and "were not, either in composition or in basic principle, governmental authorities."[31] But Tolstoi and Pazukhin were to come to the conclusion in the 1880s that the basic problem of local government lay in the isolation of the zemstvo from governmental institutions and in an artificial distinction between societal and state interests. Insisting that zemstvo matters be recognized as state matters, they argued however not for greater powers for the zemstvo but rather for greater subordination of these bodies to the bureaucracy.[32] The Imperial Ukaz of June 12, 1980, announcing the introduction of the new statute, explained that necessary improvements had been introduced into the 1864 statute so that the zemstvos

"in proper unity with *other governmental institutions* could carry
out with greater success the important *state business* entrusted to
them."[33] These acknowledgments illustrate well that the zemstvo
was now being interpreted in terms of the state theory of self-
government. It may be added that the restricting adjective *economic*, used in article 1 of the 1864 statute to characterize the
concerns of the zemstvo and much beloved by proponents of the
societal theory, was omitted in the corresponding article 1 of the
1890 statute.[34] With the introduction of the new statute, many
undoubtedly shared the optimistic belief of the governor of Voronezh province that the old dualism of societal interests and state
interests had been abolished. "Now," he declared, "it will not be
possible to say: this is our affair, and that – yours."[35]

Do the two statutes, each effective for somewhat more than a
quarter-century, divide zemstvo history into distinct phases? The
great historian of the zemstvo, B. B. Veselovskii, answered in the
negative: "Having carefully analyzed zemstvo activity in various
fields, we can say that the *reform of 12 June did not produce a
demarcation line in zemstvo life*, and in any case it did not by and
large alter the current of this life."[36] Similarly, N. N. Avinov, in his
review of 50 years of legislation respecting the zemstvo, cautioned
that it would be inappropriate to divide either this legislation or
zemstvo history into periods corresponding to the periods of existence of the two statutes.[37]

Avinov also concluded that the 1890 statute did not establish a
completely new set of zemstvo institutions, "but only supplemented, modified, pared, and preserved" what had been created by
the 1864 statutes.[38] N. M. Korkunov perceived the 1890 statute as
not at all producing a total transformation of the zemstvo. In his
view, the essence of zemstvo self-government was preserved, and
only corrections and partial changes had been introduced.[39] The
leading Soviet authority on the 1890 "counterreform," L. G. Zakharova, concurs: "The Law of 12 June 1890 is much closer to the
Statute of 1 January 1864 than to the original draft of Pazukhin-
Tolstoi."[40] All emphasize, however, that the power of the imperial
government to control the zemstvo was much increased.[41]

These opinions suggest, then, that the second of the two fundamental statutes, while reflecting acceptance of the state theory at
the expense of the societal theory of self-government, neither
served to periodize zemstvo history into markedly different eras nor
produced a wholesale reconstruction of the zemstvo structure.

Elections according to the Statute of 1864

The Statutes of 1864 and 1890, although differing greatly in their respective electoral arrangements, did have certain common basic features. First, deputies to the assemblies were to be elected, at the district level, by the local population and, at the provincial level, by the district assemblies. Second, the elective principle was preserved intact, despite repeated proposals that large landowners be granted, without undergoing election, the status of deputy by virtue of their ownership of considerable property. Third, a property qualification prevailed under both statutes, and other possible standards, such as those of education or service, were never employed. As Korkunov says, "Our legislation establishes for zemstvo representation a property qualification alone."[42]

The electoral system as established by the 1864 statute separated voters into three groups, defined not by their class (*soslovie*) (as later in the 1890 statute) but by the kinds of property they held: (1) rural property held in private ownership, (2) urban property held in private ownership, or (3) communal property held by village communities. Differentiated by their relationship to these kinds of property, voters were grouped into three electoral curiae: (1) a congress (*s"ezd*) of district landowners, (2) a congress of town voters, and (3) congresses of electors from the village communities. Excluded from participation in these congresses were the following categories: persons younger than 25 years of age, persons under criminal investigation or on trial, persons sentenced by a court or by the estate to which they belonged, and foreigners (article 17).[43]

Participating in the congress of district landowners were: (1) persons owning a certain minimum expanse of land (specified for each district in an appendix to the statute),[44] (2) persons owning in the district other immovable property valued at not less than 15,000 rubles or industrial or economic establishments of the same value or having an annual turnover of not less than 6,000 rubles, (3) authorized persons representing private owners as well as institutions, societies, companies, and associations that owned similar property, (4) representatives of small landowners and institutions owning at least one-twentieth of the land qualification, and (5) representatives from the clergy owning a certain amount of land (article 23).[45] Persons of all classes, including peasants who owned nonallotment land, participated in this curia provided only that they met the property qualification (*tsenz*). In calculating whether he met the *tsenz*, the landowner included land he leased to others and land allotted in continuous usage to the peasantry. Once peasants began buying this land, however, it could no longer be included as part of the former owner's property (article 26). It will be recognized that this curia, although designated in the statute as the congress of district landowners (*s"ezd uezdnykh zemlevladel'tsev*), included owners of certain other kinds of property situated outside city limits.

This curia was unique in its provision for a special preliminary congress or congresses of small landowners (categories 4 and 5 above). These bodies elected representatives to the congress of district landowners equal in number to that number of full *tsenzy* to which their total landholdings amounted (article 25).

In the urban electoral congress participated: (1) persons possessing merchant certificates (*svidetel'stva*), (2) owners of factories and other industrial and commercial establishments within the town with an annual turnover of not less than 6,000 rubles, (3) owners of immovable property valued at least at 3,000 rubles (in towns over 10,000 in population) or 1,000 rubles (towns of 2,000 to 10,000) or 500 rubles (other towns), and (4) authorized persons representing private owners as well as various institutions, companies, and so on, meeting the above *tsenz* (article 28).

In these two curiae, it should be noted, authorized persons (*poverennye*) acted on behalf of those private owners who were males under 25 or females (or absentees). Only males over 25 could actually participate in the electoral congresses. Persons younger than 25 and females, if they satisfied the *tsenz*, retained the suffrage but could not personally exercise it. Their proxies had themslves to meet the property qualification, except in the case of proxies who were relatives of the females they represented (article 18).[46] Leaseholders could be proxies for owners under certain conditions (article 21).[47]

Congresses for the election of deputies from village societies were composed of electors chosen by volost assemblies from their memberships, which included one representative for every 10 households in the several constituent villages. These electors could not exceed one-third of the total number of persons having the right to participate in the volost assembly, but each village community (*sel'skoe obshchestvo*) was to have at least one representative among the electors (article 30). Such congresses were to be arranged either in each peace arbiter's circuit (*uchastok*) or police ward (*stan*) within the district. The total number of zemstvo deputies to be elected from this curia was divided among these several congresses of electors (article 31).

The presiding chairman at the landowners' congress (and at the special preliminary congresses) was the district marshal of nobility (articles 24 and 27). His counterpart at the urban electoral congress was the mayor of the district seat (article 29). The peasant curia was handled somewhat differently. These congresses were opened by the peace arbiters, who invited the electors to choose from themselves a chairman. Having confirmed in office the newly elected chairman, the peace arbiter remained on the scene to settle any "misunderstandings" that might arise during the voting. Once the office of justice of the peace had been established in the district, this personage replaced the peace arbiter at meetings of the peasant curia (article 32).

The electoral congresses chose deputies only from their own memberships, with the important exception that peasant congresses might also elect as deputies members of the congress of landowners as well as parish priests and other clerics (article 35). Certain officials could not be elected as deputies even if they qualified as voters: the governor, vice-governor, members of the governor's provincial board, provincial and district procurators, and police officials (article 36). If the number of voters at a congress was less than the number of deputies to be elected, then no elections took place and all the voters present were simply recognized as deputies (article 34). No one could have more than two votes, one by personal right and one as proxy (article 22).

Such were the electoral provisions as stated in the Statute of 1864. Voting was carried out in three separate curiae, and these curiae did not each elect the same number of deputies. There was variation within each district and among the districts of each province. One of the supplementary documents to the 1864 statute[48] gave for each of the 354 districts (within 33 provinces) the allocation of district zemstvo assembly deputies among the three electoral curiae (and also specified the number of deputies each district assembly was to elect to its provincial assembly). No curia was allotted more district deputies than were allotted to the other two curiae combined. My calculations show that the first curia had a plurality in 267 districts; the town curia, in 4 districts; and the peasant curia, in 72.[49] The number of deputies to be elected by first curiae ranged from as many as 40 to as few as 2; by second curiae, from 22 to 2; by third curiae, from 40 to 4.[50] Bobrinets in Kherson province had the largest district assembly, with 96 deputies; the smallest district assemblies had only 12 deputies.

How were elections actually carried out? On May 25, 1864, the government issued a set of rules on the method of bringing the 1864 statute into operation.[51] Chapter 1 of these rules dealt with the first zemstvo elections, and this portion of the rules was reaffirmed in directives issued for the second round of zemstvo elections in 1867.[52] From these documents the following picture emerges. The district zemstvo executive board was charged with the preparation and confirmation of lists of eligible voters, which were published at the end of the third (and last) annual meeting of the outgoing assembly. During a one-month period following publication, the board could receive complaints from those omitted from these lists and consider and rule on such complaints. Its corrected lists were then sent to the provincial executive board, along with proposals about the time and place of meeting of the several electoral congresses. The provincial board then made, within a month's time, final confirmation of the voting lists and election dates and places and forwarded this information to the governor, who in turn sent it to the minister of interior.

Barring objection, the process went into motion, and the several congresses opened under their respective chairmen on the appointed days. By law sessions could last only three days. Each congress verified its own membership after a warning that unlawful participants would be brought to court. Any member could nominate himself or others having by law the right to become a deputy. Evidently to prompt peasant electors to choose nobles as their deputies, article 45 of these rules required that peasant electors be notified "in good time" of the names of members of the landowners' congress. Candidates were voted on individually and, to be elected, had to receive a majority of the votes from those present. Witnessing an election in the first curia, the French observer Anatole Leroy-Beaulieu noticed that the practice was to vote on all members in alphabetical order. As the voting progressed, this procedure caused those with names low in the alphabet more and more frequently to vote down those preceding them, in order to save some of the diminishing number of seats for themselves.[53]

Each curia was to elect not only its allotted number of deputies but several more, for replacement of those elected deputies who declined office or who had been elected by another curia or, later, those who moved from the district or had died. Once the elections were complete, the list of deputies was compiled and then signed by all voters present. Especially noteworthy is article 49 of these rules; it declared that the electoral congresses did not have the right to give any instructions to the elected deputies. The list of victorious deputies then went to the district executive board for verification and transmission to the governor for publication. Article 37 of the 1864 statute placed final verification of the deputies and the legality of the elections in the hands of the district assembly, but the governor even at this stage could raise objections and suspend the assembly's decision.[54]

Elections according to the Statute of 1890

The new electoral arrangements of 1890, while retaining the property qualification, grouped voters according to estate (*soslovie*). If formerly voters were grouped according to kind of property, now what mattered was the estate to which a voter belonged. The new categories became: (1) noble, both hereditary and personal, owners of private property (and *where* this property was located, in town or countryside, was of no consequence); (2) nonnoble owners of private property, wherever located (but with two restrictions, namely, peasants and Christian clergy were excluded); and (3) members of village communities. As for those who acted as representatives of various institutions, societies, companies, and associations that met the property *tsenz*, these were simply placed in the second category.[55]

A new structure was erected whereby noble and nonnoble property owners each had an electoral assembly (*sobranie*) for those meeting the full property qualification and a preliminary electoral congress (*s"ezd*) for petty property owners (article 15). But for the peasantry no similar institutions were created, and they lost (until 1906) the electoral congress created under the Statute of 1864.

The regulations governing the two electoral assemblies were quite the same, as were those pertaining to electoral congresses; the only distinction that must be kept in mind is that one set of assembly-plus-congress was for nobles and the other set for commoners. In the assemblies participated (1) persons who owned in the district for at least a year as private property either a minimum expanse of land (specified for each district in an appendix to the statute)[56] or other immovable property valued, for purposes of local taxation, at not less than 15,000 rubles; (2) authorized persons representing either private owners or philanthropic, educational, and economic institutions, societies, and companies that owned property described above; and (3) representatives elected from the congress of petty property owners possessing at least one-tenth the property described above (article 16).

Authorized representatives of males under 25 years of age and of females were regulated by much the same conditions as in the 1864 statute, except that now females could have as their proxies only close relatives (article 18). Individuals who were petty property owners participated in the preliminary electoral congresses; no longer were institutions or companies represented here. These petty owners could not be represented by a proxy (article 24).

The impact of these and other changes in the 1890 statute was to deprive numerous categories of the vote: Christian clergy (article 26),[57] Jews,[58] peasants and peasant associations owning nonallotment land[59] (by virtue of article 26), merchants, the "six thousanders" (owners of commercial and industrial establishments with an annual turnover of at least 6,000 rubles), and those under public surveillance (*glasnyi*

42

nadzor) of the police (article 27). The land *tsenz* was lowered in many districts, as noble landholdings now had declined since 1864. As noted above, petty property owners now had to own one-tenth rather than the previous one-twentieth of a full *tsenz*.

As for the peasants, they henceforth participated in the electoral process only as members of village communities and no longer as owners of private land. Their volost assemblies each elected one person, and from this group of candidates the provincial governor confirmed the required number of deputies. If the number of volosts in a district was less than the required number of deputies, the more populous volosts were allowed to elect two each.[60] From the unconfirmed candidates the governor designated future replacements of peasant deputies who, for whatever reason, did not complete their terms. Under these rules the peasantry clearly lost their independent choice of deputies (article 51).[61]

The statute defined electoral procedures for the other social classes more elaborately. The district marshal of nobility chaired the first or nobles' electoral assembly and congress; the town mayor, the second or nonnobles' assembly and congress. These bodies, except for the nobles' assembly, could be divided into sections meeting in different towns, in which case the governor appointed additional chairmen.[62] Lists of voters, maintained by the district zemstvo executive board, were published four months before each election, and during one month the board received and decided upon declarations by those excluded. Those still dissatisfied had a seven-day period in which to protest to the governor, who transmitted these along with his recommendations to the Provincial Bureau of Zemstvo Affairs (*Gubernskoe po zemskim delam prisutstvie*) (see below for further discussion). Following the provincial bureau's final decisions in respect to the lists, these were published one month before the election and could no longer be changed. Election meetings were to last only two days, and voting was secret. At the preliminary electoral congresses only those present could be elected, whereas at the electoral assemblies absentees could be elected. No electoral body, however, could elect anyone not having the right to vote in that body. Those chosen by the electoral assembly in excess of the number of allocated deputies were regarded as candidates (to replace deputies when and if necessary). A special provision provided that, if by 3:00 p.m. on opening day the number of voters present was less than two-thirds the number of delegates to be chosen, then all present would be declared deputies. Lists of those elected were sent to the district zemstvo executive board, then to the governor, and finally to the provincial bureau, which also reviewed complaints of illegality and could make decisions to replace incorrectly elected deputies with candidates or to cancel the entire election and call a new meeting of the electoral bodies. Once elections were approved, the governor ordered publication of the results.[63]

The new arrangements under the 1890 statute had a number of consequences. A new schedule reduced the overall number of zemstvo deputies at both levels: district deputies dropped from a total of 13,196 to 10,236, a loss of 22.4 percent, and provincial deputies were decreased from 2,284 to 1,618, a loss of 29.1 percent.[64] The percentage of nobles in the district assemblies increased from 42.4 percent in the period 1883–86 to 55.2 percent in 1890; in provincial assemblies, from 81.9 percent to 89.5 percent in 1897.[65] The amount of land represented by a landowner-deputy in 1877 was on the average 9,200 desiatinas and, by a peasant-deputy, 16,200 desiatinas. In 1905 these figures had changed to 4,700 and 30,400 desiatinas.[66] But the persistent decline of noble land ownership led to the steady reduction of the number of nobles having a full tsenz and, consequently, to problems in filling the nobles' quota of deputies. For instance, by 1912 in Kaliazin district of Tver province there were 20 noble voters who had to elect 12 deputies.[67]

To complete the story of the electoral arrangements for the 34 zemstvo provinces[68] one must take notice of the important Imperial Ukaz of October 6, 1906, which redefined the status of the peasantry.[69] In respect to participation in zemstvo elections, this document altered the 1890 rules to benefit the peasant in two ways. First, those peasants owning private (nonallotment) land in sufficient amount to meet the tsenz were granted the right to participate in the nonnoble electoral assemblies and congresses, and this regardless of their other participation in zemstvo elections through volost electoral assemblies (article 9). Second, the governor's power of confirmation of zemstvo candidates elected by the volost assemblies was abolished, and these candidates henceforth constituted themselves as a special congress (osobyi s"ezd) and chose from themselves the designated number of zemstvo deputies (article 10).

Jurisdiction, competence, and obligations of the zemstvo institutions

Here these subjects will be treated with respect to the zemstvo as a whole, standing alongside but apart from the local echelons of the government. Discussion of the specific powers and obligations of the assembly and of the executive board will be, for the most part, deferred.

The Statutes of 1864 and 1890 included statements about the overall jurisdiction and competence of the zemstvos that are on the whole similar. However, whereas the 1864 statute defined the jurisdiction of the zemstvo as the management of "local economic welfare and needs," the 1890 statute omitted the word *economic*, possibly reflecting recognition of a broader scope for zemstvo activities. The 1864 statute listed 14 objects of zemstvo jurisdiction: (1) management of properties, funds, and revenues of the zemstvo; (2) arrangement and maintenance of zemstvo buildings and other structures; (3) measures for securing public food supplies; (4) management of philanthropic and other forms of public welfare, including looking after the building of churches; (5) administration of mutual zemstvo property insurance; (6) looking after the development of trade and industry; (7) participation, chiefly in economic terms, in looking after public education, public health, and prisons; (8) cooperation in preventing cattle disease and preserving crops from destruction by insects and animals; (9) fulfillment of the demands put on the zemstvo by civil and military administration and participation in postal duty; (10) apportionment of those state taxes that were assigned to the zemstvo for distribution; (11) fixing, allocating, collecting, and spending of local taxes to satisfy local needs; (12) presentation of information respecting local welfare and needs to the government and the right to petition about these subjects; (13) holding elections; and (14) matters that were to be entrusted to the zemstvos on the basis of special charters, statutes, or enactments (article 2). In overall content the Statute of 1890 was much the same on these subjects,[70] with the important exception that it restricted the right of petition to the provincial zemstvo (article 64).[71] Obviously points 9 and 14 were especially vague; point 14 did leave room for future growth of zemstvo jurisdiction, but at the government's discretion.

Korkunov and others have noted the specific language used in these clauses and have suggested that basically a twofold categorization should be made. That is, certain local matters were transferred wholly to the management (*zavedyvanie*) of the zemstvo, and other matters remained under the direct management of the state with the zemstvo being granted rights of "cooperation" (*sodeistvie*), "participation" (*uchastie*), or "looking after" (*popechenie*).[72] The latter category was bound to produce friction between administration and zemstvo, especially with respect to public education. What were to be the proper limits of zemstvo "participation" or "cooperation" in affairs remaining essentially under state management?

Matters within zemstvo jurisdiction may be viewed also as either obligatory or nonobligatory. In the budgets that the zemstvos were to establish, certain needs or expenses had to be met; beyond these, the zemstvo acted at its own discretion, depending on its inclination and resources. Obligatory expenses had to do with the nonstate local taxes levied in the past to fulfill the so-called local obligations (zemskie povinnosti). As governed by the Charter of 1851, local obligations were either monetary, that is, fulfilled by payment of local taxes, or natural, that is, fulfilled by labor and materials. Such obligations were, at least in theory, directed toward local (provincial, district, and estate) needs, as distinguished from state needs, and were handled separately in each province. What happened in 1864 was the transfer to zemstvo management of all natural and a good part of the monetary obligations. Temporary rules, issued on January 1, 1864, specifically allocated certain of the monetary obligations to the zemstvo, others to the state budget, and still others to societal groups.[73] The major obligations that befell the zemstvo included: certain expenses for support of local civil administration; support of the institutions of local justice; road maintenance and repair; cartage; military quartering; operations and expenses of the Bureau of Public Social Welfare Boards (now to be dissolved); and expenses of local institutions supervising peasant affairs.[74]

The taxing power of the zemstvo was restricted to taxes on land, industrial and commercial establishments, and other immovable property in general and to levies on guild certificates and commercial and industrial licenses.[75] Further restrictions came in 1866. Zemstvos were allowed to tax only the immovable properties of business establishments but not the manufactured articles and products, and strict ceilings were put upon the levies on guild certificates and business licenses.[76] In 1900 zemstvos were limited to an annual 3 percent increase in taxes on immovable property.[77] To be sure, there were favorable developments to counter these restrictions. One was the considerable scope of state grants to the zemstvos, which developed mainly in the twentieth century. Polner's estimate is that by 1914 governmental subsidies to the zemstvos amounted to 20 percent of their total revenue.[78] In his study of the Tver zemstvo, Veselovskii reported that in 1912 24.72 percent of its income came from state grants.[79] Despite restrictions on zemstvo taxing power, zemstvo budgets grew. The example of the Tver budget shows a doubling between 1868 and 1890, when it reached 1,298,800 rubles; by 1913 it had reached 7,958,000 rubles.[80] Another favorable development over the years was the state's assumption of several of the obligatory expenses laid upon the zemstvos in 1864: the military quartering obligation was largely ended by the law of June 8, 1874; the law of June 1, 1895, released zemstvos from expenses in support of the office of land captain, local peasant affairs institutions, and provincial statistical committees; the laws of June 12, 1900, and of December 15, 1912, relieved them of a variety of petty obligations in regard to housing, travel expenses, and transportation of local officials, convicts, and exiles.[81] Obligatory expenses declined from 50.6 percent of the total zemstvo budget in 1874 to 15.1 percent in 1901.[82]

The zemstvo was endowed with decision-making power (*rasporiadi-tel'naia vlast'*). The Russian word that was consistently employed in the two statutes to denote a zemstvo decision or enactment is *postanovlenie* (and not, for example, *zakon*). Korkunov and Malinovskii, as well as others, emphasize that in the 1864 statute the zemstvo's decision-making power was limited and could be expressed only in the form of a particular directive affecting an object of zemstvo jurisdiction, such as a decision to establish a local economic exhibition, and that the zemstvo did not as yet have the power to issue general rules that would be obligatory for all local citizens.[83] (For such an obligatory general rule Korkunov employs the term *ukaz*). The Urban Statute of 1870 did, however, grant to town governments the power to issue obligatory decisions binding upon all urban inhabitants.[84] Only in 1873 was the zemstvo allowed a similar privilege, granted to its provincial assembly and limited initially to the making of obligatory rules on methods of preventing fires.[85] In 1879 two more measures followed, granting to the district assemblies the right to issue obligatory decrees concerning means of preventing epidemic and epizootic diseases[86] and to the provincial zemstvos the same right with respect to the removal and destruction of diseased livestock.[87] No additional similar measures seem to have been issued by the government until, with the Statute of 1890, the power to issue obligatory decisions binding upon all the local population (but outside town limits) was considerably enlarged and extended to the provincial zemstvo assembly (chapter 4). Here 13 subjects are listed (fire prevention, sanitation, means of communication, food supply, fairs and markets, and so on). All such enactments were to be drafted in close cooperation with local officials (article 110), confirmed by the governor (article 111), enforced by the police and zemstvo-appointed overseers (*popechiteli*) (article 113), all of whom were empowered to bring violators before the court (article 114).

This enlargement of zemstvo competence is one of the few aspects of the 1890 statute of which Veselovskii approves. And, in general, other authorities agree that zemstvo competence was not constricted but extended by the 1890 statute.

Apart from the stipulations in the two statutes, zemstvo jurisdiction and competence could be expanded or contracted by other legislation. For example, the matter of food supply was taken out of zemstvo jurisdiction by the law of June 12, 1900, and transferred to the administration.[88] On the other hand, the district zemstvo was empowered to elect justices of the peace from 1864 to 1889, and again in 1912. And, of course, in 1906 the provincial zemstvo assemblies were granted the right to elect deputies, one each, to the State Council.[89] Over the years still other legislation established numerous committees and bureaus on which the zemstvos were entitled to have representation (to be discussed later).

Serious limits were placed upon the zemstvo's capacity to act freely and effectively, even within its assigned range of jurisdiction. No police powers were ever given to the zemstvo. Its capacity to tax was restricted. Moreover, article 3 of each statute specified that the sphere of activity of zemstvo institutions was limited by the boundaries of the province or district, and for decades thereafter governmental officials pursued a policy of prohibiting interzemstvo contacts. As early as 1866, a Senate ruling forbade such contacts on the basis of this article.[90] To be sure, during the period of General Loris-Melikov's "dictatorship," as Veselovskii notes, permission was granted for two regional zemstvo congresses in February 1881, but these were exceptional concessions.[91] A major breakthrough was the measure of December 16, 1902, which permitted zemstvos to establish amongst themselves, with confirmation by the minister of interior, arrangements with respect to mutual reinsurance of property against fire.[92] Another measure of January 31, 1906, offered zemstvos the right to create joint associations for the acquisition and sale of agricultural machinery.[93] During both the Russo-Japanese War and World War I the government allowed the formation of all-Russian unions of zemstvos to aid in the relief of sick and wounded soldiers.[94] In general, following the Revolution of 1905, interzemstvo contact became more and more accepted. Polner goes as far as to assert that, after 1905, "the zemstvos won the unconditional and definite recognition of the Government."[95]

An even more serious restraint upon the zemstvos' freedom to act was the administrative control (nadzor) exercised over them by governmental institutions, a subject which will receive special attention in a later section herein.

The zemstvo assemblies

Composed of elected deputies and a few other individuals by virtue of office or appointment, the zemstvo assemblies underwent changes from their original size and composition as a result of the reformed Statute of 1890 and other legislation. The reduction in 1890 of the total number of deputies led, in the great majority of cases but not everywhere, to smaller assemblies than under the 1864 statute. For example, the average number of deputies in the 11 district assemblies of Novgorod province fell from 33 to 28, yet 4 of these district assemblies were actually enlarged. At the provincial level the only assembly not reduced in number of deputies was that of Olonets, which kept its 15 deputies and remained, as before, the smallest provincial assembly. Whereas the largest provincial assemblies had formerly been those of Poltava and Tambov, with 100 deputies each, after 1890 the largest was that of Poltava, with 62 deputies. Apart from the overall changes in size brought about in 1890, specific legislation could alter the size of assemblies in particular provinces and districts, as was the case in 1902 when assemblies were increased in size in five provinces.[96]

The composition of assemblies also underwent change. Under the Statute of 1864 the district assembly was composed of elected deputies (only these members of the assembly bore the title *glasnyi*) and of one to three representatives appointed by the local offices of state properties and of appanages, depending upon the amount of land held within the district by these agencies (articles 41 and 42). The Statute of 1890 stipulated one representative each from state properties and appanages and added a representative of the clergy (at the discretion of the church authorities), the mayor of the district town (article 57), and also all members of the district executive board (article 121). The chairman of the assembly was the district marshal of nobility.

The provincial zemstvo assembly was composed, under the 1864 statute, of deputies elected from the district assemblies[97] and of representatives appointed by the local offices of state properties and appanages.[98] The 1890 statute added to the provincial assembly all district marshals of nobility, a representative of the clergy (if desired by the church authorities), and all members of the provincial zemstvo executive board (articles 56 and 121). And in 1899 chairmen of the district executive boards were added.[99] The chairman of the provincial assembly was the provincial marshal of nobility, unless the emperor wished to name another person.[100]

Deputies to both assemblies were governed in general by the same rules. They had to take an oath, served for three years, but could resign at any time, whereupon previously chosen candidates replaced them. The Statute of 1890 made attendance at assembly sessions obligatory, a specification absent in the earlier statute; if the reasons for absence were deemed insufficient the deputy was liable to punishment (articles 59 and 60).[101] Veselovskii calculates that the right to punish absentees

49

was used in only 38 cases between 1891 and 1909.[102] Absenteeism was a persistent problem, especially before 1890, and assembly sessions were often shortened because the drifting away of deputies reduced the attendance below the legal quorum.[103] Partly the problem derived from the fact that the deputies were not paid a salary, nor could they receive an expense allowance.[104] An 1866 ruling of the State Council stated that the zemstvo budgets could not include any expenditure to the benefit of deputies.[105] Peasant deputies were especially hurt by the prohibition against salaries. Tardiness was also a problem that moved some assemblies to impose penalties.[106]

Meetings of the assemblies were either regular, once a year, or extraordinary. Regular meetings of the district assembly had to begin not later than October 1, and, of the provincial assembly, not later than December 1.[107] Both statutes limited the duration of annual sessions to 10 days for the district assembly and to 20 days for the provincial assembly.[108] As time passed and zemstvo work increased, these periods became too limited for some assemblies. The Tver provincial assembly petitioned for a one-month session in 1900.[109] On the other hand, as late as 1915, the Voronezh district assembly still needed only six days for its annual session.[110]

Extraordinary sessions of assemblies were allowed by permission of the minister of interior; the 1890 statute extended authorization to the governor in emergency situations (national calamity, war). Such assemblies could consider only the specific question for which they were called (article 68).[111] For these assemblies no quorum was set (article 74).

Provincial sessions were opened and closed by the governor; district sessions, by the marshal of nobility. On opening, the assembly selected a secretary from its membership. A quorum for conducting business was fixed, in 1864, at not less than one-third of the total number of deputies and in any case not less than 10 deputies (article 42); in 1890 the minimum was raised to one-half and in any case not less than 10 (article 74).[112] Business was brought before the assembly by (1) proposals from the governor; (2) presentations by the executive board, (3) proposals of the chairmen and members, and (4) requests and complaints of private individuals. Experts or "informed persons" not belonging to the assembly could be invited to the sessions of the assembly (article 73). Decisions were made by a majority vote, with ties broken by the chairman. No member had more than one vote, and this vote was not transferable to another member (article 75). Voting was secret in elections, in deciding whether to bring officials to court, and in matters of salaries and other financial aid to employees; on all other matters voting could be open (article 76).

The powers of the assembly chairman deserve attention. The Statute of 1864 confined itself to one brief article endowing the chairman with keeping order and directing the course of business (article 84). But soon the chairman's role was to be given detailed attention by the State Council in its measure of June 13, 1867, and this law was reaffirmed in article 77 of the 1890 statute.[113] Considerable powers and responsibilities were thereby assigned to the chairman. He determined the order of business and could change that order. He was to maintain orderly procedures and prevent interruptions of speakers. He could stop debate if digressions persisted, deprive a member of the right to speak, and even close a sitting. He could expel disorderly spectators or all nonmembers present. He was charged with seeing that the assembly did not exceed its jurisdiction; if he allowed violations he was responsible and liable to punishment.[114]

All enactments of the assemblies were to be entered into a journal, to be signed by the chairman, secretary, and members. Some assemblies kept more elaborate records that included summaries of debates, but most journals were probably quite laconic.[115] The journal for 1915 of the Voronezh district assembly is a terse listing of its decisions, in three to six pages for each day. On the other hand, the reportage of provincial assembly proceedings in Tver was rather extensive.[116]

The chief work during assembly sessions was always concentrated in commissions formed of its membership. The Statute of 1864 had specified only one commission – a revision commission – to review financial reports of the executive board (article 71). Veselovskii reports that the number of commissions remained small until the 1890s but increased thereafter, so that few provincial assemblies came to have less than four or five (budget, judicial, road, school, medical, and so forth). Often the practice was to have each district represented on each of the provincial assembly's commissions. These commissions studied materials presented to the assembly by its executive board and made recommendations when the matter came before the assembly.[117]

If the 1915 session of the Voronezh district zemstvo assembly is typical, the dominant figure in assembly proceedings must have been the chairman of the executive board, who gave one report after another at the six sittings of the assembly.[118] Each report was followed by the assembly's decision (the exact vote not recorded, save in the case of elections). Reports were also heard from the assembly's commissions. Besides hearing reports and voting on measures, budgetary and other, the Voronezh assembly's business included the adoption of petitions to be sent to governmental ministries and agencies, sometimes with a request directed to the provincial assembly that it also give support.

Veselovskii provides much interesting information on the relation-ship between the district and provincial assemblies. For a long time, he reports, the provincial assembly was looked upon by the district zemstvo people as a mechanical aggregate of deputies from the dis-tricts, and "an assembly of delegations," without acceptance of its claim to represent the interests of the province as a whole. Veselovs-kii explains that, up to the mid-1890s, the district bodies in general had been the more active, that the sphere of competence of the provincial bodies was in practice restricted by the "method of exclu-sion," that is, only what could not be done directly by the district zemstvo devolved upon the provincial body. A change began in the 1890s, and the center of zemstvo gravity moved to the provincial level. A more aggressive leadership came forward and sought to make the provincial zemstvo a true regulator of all zemstvo activity within the province.[119]

As a general provision both statutes assigned jurisdiction in matters having provincial scope or affecting several districts to the provincial assembly and jurisdiction within the district to the district assembly. Beyond this, the statutes provided lists of subjects of jurisdiction for each level of zemstvo institutions.[120] These lists defy summary, but in general it can be said that the more important matters were allocated to the provincial assembly and that its jurisdiction was increased by the 1890 statute as compared with that of 1864. Under both statutes the provincial assembly was given such an important power as the allocation, between provincial and district zemstvos, of zemstvo buildings, other structures, ways of communication, local obligations, and institutions of societal welfare, and it could make subsequent changes in this distribution. As noted previously, only the provincial assembly could issue general obligatory decrees. The provincial zem-stvo assembly could also issue directives and instructions to the district institutions on provincial matters requiring support from the district. But practice often deviated from the formal arrangements. Such a specific matter as fire insurance was assigned to the provincial assembly, but, as Veselovskii points out, in practice this activity was long dominated by the districts.[121]

The zemstvo executive boards

The *uprava* or executive board was the workhorse of the zemstvo. If the assemblies convened for only a brief period once a year, the executive boards labored all year long, in constant super-vision and management of zemstvo activities and operations. And it

52

was the board that hired and dealt with the growing mass of zemstvo employees known popularly as the "third element."

The executive board was subjected to much greater transformation by the Statute of 1890 than was the assembly, although under each statute it remained elective.

Under the 1864 statute the district zemstvo board was to be composed of a chairman and two members, elected for three years by the district assembly from its membership. The assembly could increase the number of members to six if it deemed such action necessary (article 46).[122] The provincial board was to consist of a chairman and six members elected for three years by the provincial assembly from its midst (article 56).[123] The governor's confirmation was required for the district board chairman; in case of his absence his replacement (one of the members) likewise required confirmation (article 48). The chairman of the provincial board was confirmed in office by the minister of interior, who also confirmed his substitute (article 56). As Korkunov notes, the statute did not state the consequences of nonconfirmation, and apparently the only outcome was the election of a new chairman.[124]

Under the Statute of 1890 these matters change a good deal. Both district and provincial boards were to be composed of a chairman and two members; the number of members could be increased up to four by decision of the relevant assembly, and, with permission of the minister of internal affairs, up to six in the case of the provincial board (article 96). More important, now chairmen and members of the boards could be elected not only from among the deputies of the assemblies, but from nondeputies who had the right to vote in the two electoral assemblies (article 116).[125] This interesting extension of eligibility is viewed favorably by Veselovskii, who asserts that it permitted peasants and townspeople in certain zemstvo assemblies to elect able persons who had earlier been defeated in deputy elections by the nobles.[126]

But an added stipulation in 1890 was that the chairman of the board had to be a person eligible by law for state service (article 117). For years this proviso hurt those boards on which the chairman had usually been a peasant or townsman.[127] However, with the law of October 6, 1906, peasants together with all other unprivileged classes received the same rights in respect to state service as applied to the gentry estate.[128] The Statute of 1890 had another innovation: the chairman and members of the executive boards were to be considered as being in state service. Those members who did not have the right to enter state service were not promoted into the Table of Ranks but were to enjoy during their tenure on the board the rights and privileges of those ranks (*chiny*) in state service that corresponded to the class of their offices on the board (article 124).[129]

Confirmation was now required of *all* members of the boards, both district and provincial. Chairmen of provincial boards were confirmed by the minister of interior; chairmen of district boards and all members of both boards, by the governor (article 118). In case of nonconfirmation, new elections were held, in which the rejected person could not be voted on a second time. If a second nonconfirmation occurred, then eligible persons were appointed to these offices by the minister of interior (article 119). Substitutes for the chairman, in case of illness or temporary absence, were appointed from the board membership by the governor for the district board, and by the minister of interior for the provincial (article 120). In 1899 the right of choosing these substitutes was restored to the assembly, but confirmation was still required.[130]

The right of confirmation, exercised by the bureaucracy and now applied to all members of the elected executive organ, did not remain a dead letter. If, before 1890, only five persons had not been confirmed as chairman, after 1890 the number of nonconfirmed chairmen and members of the board significantly increased, and Veselovskii's evidence shows about 80 such persons for the years 1891 to 1909.[131]

Under both statutes, chairmen and members of the executive boards received salaries, in an amount determined by the assemblies.[132]

The impact of the 1890 statute upon the class composition of the boards was to strengthen the already dominant role of the nobles. If in 1886 nobles and officials comprised 55.5 percent of the membership on district boards and peasants 30.9 percent, in 1903 the figures were 71.9 percent and 18.3 percent, respectively. On provincial boards nobles and officials comprised 89.48 percent in 1886, and rose to 94.12 percent in 1903. Of the 153 members and chairmen of provincial boards in 1903, 144 were nobles or officials, 3 were peasants, and 6 were from other classes.[133]

Some board chairmen and members served for an impressive number of years. Up to 1905 15 persons had held the position of provincial zemstvo board chairman for at least 15 years each. One of these had served for 37 years, another for 32. Others had equally long records as members. At the district level 83 chairmen had held office for at least 20 years each. A peasant of Ves"egonsk served on its board from its inception in 1865 until 1894.[134]

An even more extraordinary aspect of board service occurred when the same individual, as marshal of nobility, not only presided over the zemstvo assembly but also was elected chairman of the executive board. Veselovskii cites 8 instances of this occurrence at the provincial level (none for more than 8 years) and lists about 200 instances at the district level (up to 1910), where the individual record appears to have been 25 years.[135]

The responsibilities of the zemstvo boards were manifold. They directly managed the affairs and administration of the zemstvo, governed by the statutes and other charters and state legislation and by the decisions of the assemblies. More specifically, the boards managed the properties of the zemstvo, compiled budgets and financial reports, supplied the assemblies with needed information, watched over zemstvo revenues, disbursed payments for expenses, represented the zemstvo in court suits, reported to the assembly concerning its work, and, in general, sought ways to improve zemstvo economy (1864: article 69; 1890: article 97). The district board was, moreover, obligated under both statutes to carry out locally, within the district but under the provincial board's directives, certain responsibilities with respect to means of communication, obligations to civil and military administration, and insurance; to report on these matters to the provincial board; and to supply that board with information needed for the provincial budget (1864: article 72; 1890: article 97). In regard to the execution of these functions, the Statute of 1890 contained an innovation, namely, that certain functions should be assigned each member of the board, while other functions should be treated collegially. Such allocation was to be worked out with assembly confirmation (article 101).

With the passing of time the board developed into a rather elaborate organization. For example, by the early twentieth century the Tver provincial board possessed an impressive apparatus divided into several departments: (1) a chancellery, headed by a secretary, with five section heads, three clerks, two typists (*remingtonisty*), and two registrars; (2) a staff library; (3) a bookkeeping office with about nine persons; (4) a statistical department; (5) a road department, with a dozen engineers plus others; (6) a chaussée department; (7) a pedagogical bureau; (8) a sanitation department; (9) an economic department; (10) an insurance department; (11) an assessment department; (12) a drugstore; (13) a bookstore; (14) a printing press; and (15) two special hospital colonies.[136] This central office comprised about 60 or more hired persons. For each district board there were similar structures and hired personnel.

In addition to those who worked in the central offices of the executive boards there were, of course, growing numbers of zemstvo employees scattered throughout the districts and working as teachers, doctors, feldshers, agronomists, and so forth. Constituting the "third element" in the countryside, these people increased especially rapidly after the early 1890s. By 1908 the total number of zemstvo employees throughout the 34 zemstvo provinces ranged, in Veselovskii's estimate, from 65,000 to 70,000.[137] In seeking to attract into its service specialists of various kinds, zemstvos did not have the resources to offer competitive salaries and tried other inducements such as bonuses for so many years of service, regular if modest salary increases, leaves with pay, and grants for children's education. The main expression of concern for zemstvo employees in Tver province was the early establishment of a pension fund, the first such in zemstvo history.[138] A contract between the Voronezh district board and an agronomist in 1915 stipulated an annual vacation of one month, full salary for up to four months if seriously ill, and a four-month leave for schooling after two years of service.[139]

Both statutes had granted the assemblies the right to elect from their memberships persons to assist the executive board in the management of specific branches of its work.[140] These persons might be paid or unpaid in practice, and they performed a variety of tasks including such simple chores as watching over the condition of roads. One district zemstvo in Tver province paid each of its peasant deputies 10 rubles a year to watch over roads in their localities.[141] One suspects that this money was in actuality a disguised form of the prohibited expense money that some zemstvos desired to give their peasant deputies. Other persons might become trustees for particular schools or hospitals, or be sanitation trustees, or concern themselves with zemstvo postal stations in their neighborhoods. Eventually zemstvos developed the practice of forming specialized commissions or councils of these people, and such a right was given official recognition in an 1899 State Council ruling despite governors' protests.[142] These commissions, known as commissions *pri upravakh*, were an important source of support for the executive boards, helping them to oversee zemstvo activities and furnishing information and advice. Sometimes a commission or council established a substructure of its own. In Voronezh district a trustee sanitation council directed 17 sectional sanitation trusteeships, each of which had a chairman, deputy chairmen, and members. The council consisted of the zemstvo board, all 17 chairmen, 2 deputies from the zemstvo assembly, zemstvo doctors, and 1 member elected by each trusteeship.[143] This apparatus was one means of combatting the problem of the large territorial units in which the zemstvo boards were compelled to operate.[144] By 1914 there came to be many such substructures.

Administrative control over the zemstvo

In the matter of administrative supervision or control (*nadzor*) over the zemstvo institutions the two statutes present major differences. In brief, the Statute of 1864 established a very limited measure of administrative control over the personnel of the assembly and executive board and, with respect to enactments of the zemstvo, arranged a relatively simple procedure in which the Senate was the final arbiter. The 1890 Statute greatly increased administrative control over personnel and constructed a much more complex structure for settling disputes between zemstvo and administration.

The Statute of 1864 required confirmation only of the chairmen of the executive boards – the provincial chairman by the minister of interior, and the district chairman by the governor (articles 48 and 56). No confirmation was required of board members or assembly deputies. The verification of the deputies and of the legality and validity of elections was placed on the assembly itself (article 37). The executive boards were responsible to their assemblies, and the governor could not demand an accounting from them of their activity. To the provincial assembly alone was given the authority to bring actions of the chairmen and board members, both district and provincial, to the attention of the courts (article 116). Removal from office of board members was by decision of the Senate; they could be temporarily removed, however, by a decision of the provincial assembly confirmed by the governor (article 117).

In respect to its enactments, the assembly was required to communicate these without delay to the governor (article 93). Enactments fell into two categories: those on matters requiring confirmation, either by the governor (listed in article 90) or by the minister of interior (listed in article 92); and those not requiring confirmation. These latter went into effect immediately but could be suspended. There were two grounds for nonconfirmation or suspension: violation of the law and violation of "general state interests" (article 9).

For those assembly decisions which required confirmation, the governor had seven days in which to act, and the minister, two months. If no reply was received by the zemstvo by the end of these periods, the decision was considered confirmed and went into effect. Notification of refusal to confirm had to be accompanied by an explanation to the assembly. If in its review of the matter the assembly was not convinced by the explanation and reissued its decision in a form unsatisfactory to the governor or to the minister, he could suspend its execution and refer the matter to the Senate.[145]

The right to suspend an enactment not requiring confirmation could be exercised by the governor during a seven-day period following receipt of the measure from the assembly. The same right could be exercised by the minister of interior in the interval between two sessions of the assembly. In suspending an enactment, the governor or minister was required to notify the assembly and give reasons for suspension. The assembly then reviewed its decision and returned it, modified or not. If the governor or minister still disagreed with the assembly the matter was presented to the Senate for solution.

This procedure seems fair and reasonable. It allowed, as Blinov points out, both sides opportunity to reconsider, weigh the arguments, and make concessions.[146] Korkunov notes that the organ of state power was, in this procedure, in the role of a plaintiff, on whom lay the obligation of proving that a zemstvo decision was illegal or contrary to state interests.[147]

In the interval between the two statutes, other measures were introduced that increased administrative control. On June 13, 1867, the State Council decreed that all assembly decisions and reports of sessions, including debates and speeches, were to be printed only with the permission of the governor's office.[148] Another important measure was that of August 19, 1879, which empowered the governor to deny confirmation of or to dismiss from zemstvo service any employee he considered to be unreliable.[149]

Chapter 2 of the Statute of 1890 set up an entirely new organ of control over the zemstvo, the provincial bureau of zemstvo affairs.[150] Established "to consider, in appropriate cases, the correctness and legality of the enactments and orders of zemstvo institutions and for the solution of other matters" designated in the statute, the provincial bureau was to include, under the governor's chairmanship, the provincial marshal of nobility, the vice governor, the manager of the treasury chamber, the procurator of the regional court, the chairman of the provincial zemstvo executive board, and one member of the provincial zemstvo assembly, elected by the latter from the board members or from the assembly deputies. There was also a secretary, appointed by the governor (article 8).[151] Decisions of this new body were to be by majority vote, with the chairman deciding a tie (article 11). However, if the governor disagreed with the majority, he could suspend its decision and refer the matter to the minister of interior, who could either endorse the decision or refer it to the Senate with a proposal for its abolition (article 12). Such are the contents of chapter 2. How did it affect the zemstvo?

In respect to the assembly, the provincial bureau, as already noted, was the verifier of the correctness and legality of elections to the district assemblies. In addition, the provincial bureau had jurisdiction over

58

illegal actions of those chosen by the assembly to perform certain special tasks; that is, those who had been elected to help the executive board in managing individual branches of zemstvo economy and administration, those who were members of the assembly's revision commission and other financial commissions, and those who were elected trustees to enforce the assembly's obligatory decrees (article 137). In this way the provincial bureau could reach into assembly affairs and affect a good many deputies.[152]

Control by the provincial bureau over the zemstvo executive boards was extensive but not exclusive. It will be remembered that the chairmen of these boards had to possess eligibility for state service and that all members on these boards were considered to be in state service. If the governor or zemstvo assembly brought charges that a crime or misdemeanor had been committed by the chairman or by members of the board, the matter was turned over to the bureau, on which now the procurator was replaced by the chairman of the regional court (article 133). Possible punishments ranged from a simple rebuke to a reprimand (without entry into the individual's service record), to removal from office (article 134). The provincial bureau was empowered to levy only the first two punishments, and only upon members of the district executive boards. Chairmen of both boards and members of the provincial board were punished by the council[153] of the minister of interior, with the minister's confirmation. This council alone had the power, again with the minister's confirmation, to remove from office the chairmen and members of the zemstvo executive boards (article 135). In this important process the Senate lost its former role. If the matter in question warranted court action, the provincial bureau brought members of the district boards to court; chairmen of both boards and members of the provincial board were brought to court by decision of the council of the minister of interior, with the minister's confirmation (article 136).

Under the 1890 statute the governor was granted the right to conduct an inspection (*reviziia*) of the zemstvo executive boards, of other executive organs of zemstvo administration, and of all institutions subordinate to the zemstvo. No such privilege had existed under the Statute of 1864. If the governor's inspection uncovered incorrect activities and if the executive board refused to make changes, then the matter went to the provincial bureau, whose decision was binding. But the zemstvo assembly could then appeal to the Senate (article 103).[154]

With respect to the zemstvo assemblies' enactments, a new basis for nonconfirmation of suspension was authorized in the 1890 statute. To the existing grounds of (1) illegality and (2) violation of state interests was added (3) clear violation of the interests of local inhabitants. The right to suspend an enactment was now exercised by the governor only (and no longer by the minister of interior) during a two-week period after receiving the enactment. Suspended enactments were not returned to the assembly for reconsideration (as under the 1864 statute). If a suspension had to do with the *legality* of the enactment, it was brought before the provincial bureau, against whose decision the assembly could appeal to the Senate (articles 88–9). If the suspension was based on other grounds, a district assembly's enactment was turned over to the provincial assembly for decision,[155] and a provincial assembly's enactment was brought to the ministry of interior, with a recommendation from the provincial bureau. The minister could then either approve the enactment or recommend its abolition or modification to the Committee of Ministers, which decided the matter (articles 90–94).[156] A quite complicated procedure indeed, and one which must have involved much time and paperwork! The Senate, it will be noted, is excluded from cases involving grounds other than legality.

Those assembly enactments requiring confirmation by the governor (listed in article 82) or by the minister of interior (listed in article 83) did not go into execution unless confirmation was explicitly given, and no time limit for confirmation was fixed (article 81). Thus a measure could be delayed indefinitely, a situation not possible under the Statute of 1864. If the enactment was given explicit rejection by the governor, it was not returned to the assembly for a second consideration. Instead it went to the provincial bureau, which decided the matter unless the governor disagreed with the bureau, in which case the minister of interior decided. Enactments requiring ministerial confirmation were forwarded to the minister together with a recommendation by the bureau. The minister again made the final judgment. In both cases, the Senate was not involved (articles 84–5).

But the Senate's relationship with the zemstvo institutions was not exhausted by the roles described above. For instance, the Senate possessed its own right of *nadzor* over provincial institutions, and its inspections of local bodies included scrutiny of the zemstvo. A senatorial inspection of Samara province in 1888 by I. I. Shamshin resulted in recommendations entirely favorable to zemstvo autonomy (for example, election of assembly chairman and publication without censorship). Unfortunately, these recommendations were ignored in the drafting of the 1890 statute.[157]

The Senate could also entertain appeals (*zhaloby*) against enactments of the zemstvo assemblies. Under the 1864 statute, such appeals could be made by governmental and societal institutions (article 118) but not by private individuals. The latter did win the right of appeal to the Senate under the 1890 Statute (article 128). As a matter of fact, even before 1890 the governor had begun the practice of forwarding complaints of private citizens to the Senate, and the Senate had come, somewhat hesitantly, to consider such appeals.[158] Appeals against zemstvo enactments already in operation went directly to the Senate; if the enactment was not yet in operation, then the appeal went to the provincial bureau, except in the case of bills requiring ministerial confirmation (article 128).[159] If there was dissatisfaction with a decision of the bureau, appeal could then be made to the Senate (article 131). It may be added that, under both statutes, private persons as well as societies and institutions could bring suit against the zemstvo in instances of violation of their civil rights, that is, if legal grounds existed for a court trial.[160]

Outside the zemstvo structure

This chapter concludes with, first, a brief look at the zemstvo's representation on other local bodies and, then, a schematic consideration of certain modes of its relationship to the central government.

Over the years the zemstvo was accorded the right to participate in a variety of bureaus and councils of governmental and other institutions at the provincial and district levels of Russian administration. The zemstvo did not lead an isolated existence, and its officials, especially the executive board chairman, assumed a multitude of roles on the local scene. The following brief list indicates something of the extent to which the zemstvo participated on nonzemstvo bodies.

1. In 1864, by the Statute on Primary Schools, district and provincial zemstvo assemblies each elected two members to the school councils established at the district and provincial levels.[161]
2. In 1870 the Town Statute establishing urban self-government also created a supervising agency in the form of a provincial bureau (*prisutstvie*) on town affairs, chaired by the governor and including as member the chairman of the provincial zemstvo executive board.[162] The zemstvos were obligated to cooperate with the new organs of town government, which could appeal to the governor against zemstvo measures (articles 6 and 8).
3. In 1874 a new primary school statute, placing district and provincial school councils under the chairmanship of marshals of the nobility, maintained the previous zemstvo representation on these councils.[163]
4. In 1874 the Charter on Military Duty created provincial and district bureaus to handle recruitment, under the chairmanship respectively of the governor and the district marshals of nobility. The provincial

61

bureau included the chairman and one other member of the provincial zemstvo executive board. On the district bureau was to serve one member of the district zemstvo board.[164]

5. In 1874 the Statute on Changes in the Arrangement of Local Institutions of Peasant Affairs abolished the office of peace arbiter and created district bureaus of peasant affairs chaired by the marshals of nobility and including as a member the chairman of the zemstvo executive board. A similar bureau at the provincial level had existed since 1861, and its membership included the chairman of the zemstvo executive board.[165]

6. Following the establishment of the Peasant Land Bank in 1883, local branches were opened in several provinces, and on their governing bodies, headed by an official of the Ministry of Finance, were two members elected by the provincial zemstvo assembly.[166]

7. In 1885, Rules on the Retail Sale of Spirits set up provincial and district bureaus, under the chairmanship of the governor and the district marshals of nobility, to authorize the opening of taverns and inns, and so on, and to supervise the sale of liquor in general. Each bureau included a member of the zemstvo executive board.[167]

8. In 1888 the Statute on Forest Preservation, designed to protect forests from exhaustion and to encourage development of new forests, created in each province a forest protection committee, under the supervision of the Ministry of State Properties. Under the governor's chairmanship, each committee included, from the zemstvo, the provincial board chairman or one of the board members and, in addition, two local forest owners, elected by the zemstvo assembly. Decisions of the committee were considered operative only if certain members, including a representative from the zemstvo board, were present.[168]

9. In 1889 the bureaus of peasant affairs were replaced by the new institution of land captain, around which was constructed a new apparatus of surveillance over the peasantry. At the district level was set up a congress of land captains, subdivided into two bureaus, administrative and judicial, with each chaired by the district marshal of nobility. Zemstvo participation was limited to the administrative bureau, on which the chairman of the zemstvo board had membership. At the provincial level was established a body simply called the provincial bureau, chaired by the governor, and on which the chairman of the zemstvo board participated when administrative, but not judicial, matters were being considered.[169]

10. In 1892 the new Town Statute affected the zemstvo in certain ways: The provincial bureau of zemstvo affairs was renamed the provincial bureau of zemstvo and town affairs, to which were added the mayor and one deputy from the city government of the provincial capital. That member previously elected to the bureau by the provincial zemstvo assembly now had to be confirmed by the minister of

interior. And the board chairman of the local district zemstvo became a member of the city council (*duma*).[170]

This list is not meant to be exhaustive, but it does include some of the more important local institutions in which the zemstvo was granted representation and participation. And it cannot fail to communicate some sense of the busy life led by the chairmen and members of the zemstvo board.

Finally, in schematic fashion the modes and forms of interaction between zemstvo and central government (other than that expressed by state legislation and administrative control) might be identified by the following list.

1. Submission by the zemstvo of petitions (*khodataistva*) to higher governmental bodies. This right was granted in the Statute of 1864, but restricted to matters concerning local interests and needs, and exercise of this right was not direct but through the governor's office.[171]
2. Submission by the zemstvo of an address to the throne. The Tver Address of 1894, provoking the famous "senseless dreams" retort of Nicholas II, is undoubtedly the most famous case.
3. Presentation by the central government of a specific issue to the zemstvos for discussion and recommendation. This practice began in 1866, and Veselovskii calculates that 34 questions were sent to the zemstvo in the 1870s.[172]
4. Establishment by the central government of special temporary commissions to which are appointed experts or "informed persons," selected from various organizations including the zemstvos. Some few zemstvo people were appointed. Participation was limited and was a distinct privilege granted at the government's discretion. An early case – perhaps the first to include zemstvo participation – was the Valuev commission of 1872, on the condition of rural agriculture.[173]
5. Creation of a countrywide network of committees with zemstvo participation. A major example was the Special Conference on the Needs of Agricultural Industry, which existed from 1902 to 1905 and involved the creation of local committees throughout the empire.[174] Here a massive participatory role was assigned to zemstvo men, although not to the zemstvos formally.
6. Creation of a special advisory council, more or less permanent in nature, to be attached to an organ of the central administration and to include designated individuals from local self-government. An example would be the council attached to the Chief Administration for Affairs of Local Economy within the Ministry of Interior (1907). The central government appointed representatives from the zemstvos to this body (ignoring protests that these representatives be elected).[175]

7. Representation in the organs of the central government through election, not appointment. This was achieved in very limited form after the Revolution of 1905, when each provincial zemstvo assembly gained the right to elect one member of the State Council. But, indirectly, zemstvos and zemstvo interests could now also be represented in the State Duma by those numerous Duma deputies with long experience in zemstvo work.

There is suggested here a gradation, perhaps not too forced, by which the zemstvo moved from the relatively helpless position of suppliant to a more respected and acknowledged role as advisor and consultant and finally to virtually complete acceptance.

Concluding remarks

Designed originally to perform a limited number of tasks, and intentionally laden with restrictions, the zemstvo institutions, partly through their own efforts, however "small-deedish" in character, and partly through developments and circumstances quite beyond their control, came to occupy a stable place in Russian life. The ultimate, albeit grudging, acceptance of the zemstvo has been frequently noted, but the reverse point can also be made: The zemstvo, once established, was never destroyed. Even Tolstoi perceived its usefulness. Under just what kind of arrangement would this usefulness be best preserved was the debated issue. Fortunately the State Council saw that Tolstoi's plan of emasculation would discourage local support and interest in the zemstvo. In his great work, perhaps never to be rivaled, Veselovskii has shown the uneven evolution of relations between the state administration and the zemstvo, and Witte has also provided the story of governmental harassment and distrust.[176] Not with the 1890 statute but with the 1905 revolution, one may argue, is to be found the demarcation point to be used in periodizing state–zemstvo relations. A qualitatively new situation arose after 1905. The Duma displaced the zemstvo as the major object of bureaucratic distrust; and there were to be found, with the passing of time, more and more bureaucrats with zemstvo backgrounds. Zemstvo activists, now in the role of Duma deputies, were a numerous group requiring and receiving recognition. Hosking has recently illustrated the importance of the veteran zemstvo contingent in the Octobrist party and Stolypin's appreciation thereof.[177]

The zemstvo was a flawed structure in many respects. It did present a contradiction, an institution dominated by a very small minority of the population, but a minority whose labors were directed mainly toward promoting the welfare not of itself but of the broad masses in the countryside. Set against the array of other governmental institutions of the last 50-odd years of the old regime, the zemstvo exhibited many tendencies that would incline one to agree with Walkin that this institution did contribute to the "rise of democracy" in pre-Soviet Russia.[178] Without doubt, the zemstvo would have made an even greater contribution if certain reforms in its structure and in its relationship to the administration had been carried out in good time, and at the very latest in the years immediately following the Revolution of 1905.

Among these desirable reforms three, at least, seem preeminent: (1) initiation of a process leading toward equalization of the franchise, even if only by gradual stages; (2) creation of a small zemstvo unit, perhaps based on an all-class *volost*, with the goal of bringing the zemstvo and its personnel closer to the people; and (3) recasting the system of *nadzor* to exclude the administrative bureaucracy and to base supervision over the zemstvo squarely upon the judicial branch and upon the sole criterion of legality, rather than appropriateness, of zemstvo activities. There were other desirable reforms, to be sure, but of lesser urgency: election of the assembly chairman, establishment of a zemstvo police, accountability of the executive board exclusively to the assembly, and, as Tverdokhlebov suggested, the separation of sizable towns and cities from district and provincial zemstvo jurisdiction.[179] These brief lists could easily be expanded.[180]

In hindsight, too much should not be asked of the zemstvo, given the difficult and peculiar conditions under which it existed. Yet, if one considers the active participation of elected citizens in the business of governing themselves to be the best expression of political life, then the zemstvo has considerable claim to a valuable place among the governmental organs of Old Russia. Perhaps the judgment of Leroy-Beaulieu remains valid: With all their limitations, the zemstvos did for the country "about all that sober-minded people could expect of them."[181]

Notes

1 For a discussion of the governor's role in provincial administration see N. L. Lazarevskii, *Lektsii po russkomu gosudarstvennomu pravu*, 2d ed. vol. 2 (St. Petersburg, 1910), pp. 223–34. By the law of May 3, 1829, never abolished, the governor was to be appointed by the emperor on the recommendation of the Committee of Ministers. In practice, however, the recommendation of the minister of interior became decisive. Lazarevskii, 2:224.

2 Ibid., pp. 235–40. the term *prisutstvie*, a much used title for a variety of governmental bodies, has been translated herein consistently as "bureau."

65

3 Lazarevskii lists 14 such bodies at the provincial level, of which no less than 10 were chaired by the governor (p. 252, n. 1). Evidently not all of these bodies existed in each and every province.

4 A convenient chart of local government from 1861 to 1914 is presented as *skhema* 5 in the packet of charts included in N. P. Eroshkin, *Istoriia gosudarstvennykh uchrezhdenii dorevoliutsionnoi Rossii*, 2d ed. (Moscow, 1968).

5 The Russian provincial milieu with its variety of officials, local dignitaries, and classes is charmingly presented in W. H. Bruford, *Chekhov and His Russia* (New York, 1947). For a valuable account of Russian local institutions by an intelligent foreign observer, see Anatole Leroy-Beaulieu, *The Empire of the Tsars and the Russians*, vol. 2 (New York, 1903), passim.

6 *Polnoe Sobranie Zakonov Rossiiskoi Imperii (PSZRI)*, 2d series, vol. 39, no. 40457 (January 1, 1864), pp. 1–2.

7 Samara province was the first to open zemstvo institutions. For a study of this process, see N. L. Khaikina, "Organizatsiia zemskikh uchrezhdenii v Samarskoi gubernii," *Nauchnye doklady vysshei shkoly: istoricheskie nauki*, 1959, no. 2, pp. 47–60.

8 *PSZRI*, 2d series, vol. 43, no. 46404 (October 28, 1868). All seven districts of Bessarabia received zemstvos at that time. An eighth district, Izmail, created from annexed territory after the Russo-Turkish War of 1877–8, did not receive a zemstvo.

9 Ibid. vol. 49, no. 53461 (May 2, 1874).

10 For specific dates see the lists in K. A. Pazhitnov, *Gorodskoe i zemskoe samoupravlenie* (St. Petersburg, 1913), p. 76; and in N. N. Avinov, "Glavnye cherty v istorii zakonodatel'stva o zemskikh uchrezhdeniiakh (1864–1913 gg.)," in B. B. Veselovskii and Z. G. Frenkel', eds., *Iubileinyi zemskii sbornik, 1864–1914* (St. Petersburg, 1914), p. 31.

11 V. Skalon, "Zemskie uchrezhdeniia," *Entsiklopedicheskii slovar'* (Brokgauz-Efron), vol. 1 (St. Petersburg, 1894), p. 540. The law of January 16, 1867 (*PSZRI*, 2d series, vol. 42, no. 44114) stopped the operation of the 1864 statute in Saint Petersburg province "until further notice"; the statute became operative again on July 7, 1867 (*PSZRI*, 2d series, vol. 42, no. 44813). For Cherepovets, see *PSZRI*, 3d series, vol. 8, no. 5303 (June 7, 1888).

12 *PSZRI*, 2d series, vol. 39, no. 40459 (January 1, 1864).

13 The 1882 law provided for the "temporary cessation" of the zemstvo in the Don region (*PSZRI*, 3d series, vol. 2, no. 759 [March 23, 1882]). Rostov district of Ekaterinoslav province lost its zemstvo in 1887, when this district was joined to the Don region. But Ekaterinoslav had gained another district zemstvo in 1869 in its newly formed Mariupol' district. *PSZRI*, 2d series, vol. 44, no. 46748 (Feruary 10, 1869).

14 P. A. Zaionchkovskii, ed., *Dnevnik gosudarstvennogo sekretaria A. A. Polovtsova*, vol. 2 (Moscow, 1966), p. 502, n. 52.

15 *PSZRI*, 3d series, vol. 31, no. 34903 (March 14, 1911).

16 Detailed discussions of the "western zemstvo crisis" are in Geoffey A. Hosking, *The Russian Constitutional Experiment: Government and Duma, 1907–1914* (Cambridge, 1973), pp. 116–49; and in A. Ia. Avrekh, "Vopros o zapadnom zemstve i bankrotstvo Stolypina," *Istoricheskie zapiski*, 1961, vol. 70, pp. 61–112; and in Ben-Cion Pinchuk, *The Octobrists in the Third Duma, 1907–1912* (Seattle, 1974), pp. 111–18 and 137–52.

Not to be confused with zemstvo institutions are the provincial and district committees and boards set up in the nine western provinces by the Statute of April 2, 1903. Although resembling zemstvos in terms of jurisdiction, these bodies were composed of governmental officials and of deputies appointed by the minister of interior. See *PSZRI*, 3rd series, vol. 23, no. 22757. Popularly known as "margarine" zemstvos, these bodies were replaced after 1911, save in Grodno, Kovno, and Vilna.

17 *PSZRI*, 3d series, vol. 32, nos. 37238, 37239, 37240 (June 9, 1912).

18 Estimate based on figures in Tikhon J. Polner, *Russian Local Government During the War and the Union of Zemstvos* (New Haven, 1930), p. 36.

19 Charles E. Timberlake and James A. Malloy, Jr., "Introduction," in B. B. Veselovskii, *Istoriia zemstva za sorok let*, 4 vols. (St. Petersburg, 1909–11), 1:vi. Special acts authorizing zemstvos in various regions are in R. P. Browder and A. F. Kerensky, eds., *The Russian Provisional Government, 1917: Documents*, 3 vols. (Stanford, 1961), 1: 300–6.

20 Browder and Kerensky, 1: 272–6.

21 Ibid., pp. 284–90. On the average, it appears that a district included about 20 or 21 volosts.

22 P. N. Abramov, "Volostnye zemstva," *Istoricheskie zapiski*, 69, 1961: p. 28. The author notes that the volost soviets were weakly developed at that time; by the end of October, of a group of 1,926 volosts, only 25 had soviets.

23 S. S. Studenikin, ed., *Istoriia sovetskoi konstitutsii v dokumentakh, 1917–1956*, comp. A. A. Lipatov and N. T. Savenkov (Moscow, 1957), pp. 93–6.

24 Several volost zemstvos continued to function after merely changing their name to soviet. Abramov, p. 39.

25 Polner, p. 291n. On the zemstvo in 1917 see Chapter 12 in the present volume.

26 For the text of the statute, see *PSZRI*, 2d series, vol. 39, no. 40457 (January 1, 1864).

27 For the preparation of the 1864 zemstvo statute, see S. Ia. Tseitlin, "Zemskaia reforma," in *Istoriia Rossii v XIX veke*, 9 vols. (St. Petersburg, 1907–11), 3: 179–231; S. Frederick Starr, *Decentralization and Self-Government in Russia, 1830–1870* (Princeton, 1972), pp. 185–291; V. V. Garmiza, *Podgotovka zemskoi reformy 1864 goda*

(Moscow, 1957); and James A. Malloy, Jr., "The Zemstvo Reform of 1864: Its Historical Background and Significance in Russia" (Ph.D. dissertation, Ohio State University, 1965).

28 On the background to the 1890 statute, see L. G. Zakharova, *Zemskaia kontrreforma 1890 g.* (Moscow, 1968); and S. Ia. Tseitlin, "Zemskoe samoupravlenie i reforma 1890 g.," in *Istoriia Rossii v XIX veke*, 5: 79–138.

29 *PSZRI*, 3d series, vol. 10, no. 6927 (June 12, 1890).

30 For discussions of theories of self-government, see N. M. Korkunov, *Russkoe gosudarstvennoe pravo*, 6th ed., vol. 2 (St. Petersburg, 1909), pp. 488–501 and 533–7; and P. P. Gronskii, "Teorii samoupravleniia v russkoi nauki," in *Iubileinyi zemskii sbornik*, pp. 76–85.

31 *PSZRI*, 2d series, vol. 45, no. 48309 (May 1, 1870). The committee decided to permit free mailing of zemstvo correspondence with officials and institutions of government. It pointed out that several zemstvos had, in protest, simply refused to answer their mail unless it was accompanied by the necessary payment for a reply.

32 Korkunov, 2:535; Zakharova, pp. 97–100.

33 *PSZRI*, 3d series, vol. 10, no. 6922 (June 12, 1890). My emphasis.

34 This shift toward state theory did not mean that zemstvo institutions became state institutions. It is true, however, that under the new Statute of 1890 members of the executive boards were considered to be in state service (article 124).

35 Quoted in Veselovskii, 3:368.

36 Ibid. Original emphasis.

37 Avinov, p. 1.

38 Ibid.

39 Korkunov, 2:536–7. Korkunov did concede that the balance between the zemstvo and the bureaucracy had shifted in favor of the latter.

40 Zakharova, p. 162.

41 Tseitlin called the 1890 statute a "second, much worsened edition" of the 1864 statute. "Zemskoe samoupravlenie," p. 138. The historian A. A. Kizevetter saw the new statute as "a great step backwards." *Na rubezhe dvukh stoletii (vospominaniia, 1881–1914)* (Prague, 1929), p. 147.

42 Korkunov, 2:554.

43 Subsequent legislation added persons who had been dismissed from office (for the three years following dismissal) and persons in bankruptcy. *PSZRI*, 2d series, vol. 44, no. 46945 (April 7, 1869).

44 A specific amount of land was set for each district, and these figures often varied within a province. There were initially six categories: 200, 250, 350, 475, 650, and 800 desiatinas. For a complete listing for all districts, see the *prilozhenie* to article 23 of the 1864 statute, located under the heading "Shtaty i tabeli" on pp. 3–4, in part 3 of *PSZRI*, 2d series, vol. 39.

45 Land requirements for the clergy were based on articles 462–5 of the Code of Laws, vol. 10, part 3, book 2.

46 According to Russian law, age 21 gave a person "civil majority" (*grazhdanskoe sovershennoletie*). Those between ages 17 and 21 were *nesovershennoletnye* and were legally able to manage their affairs but only through a trustee (*popechitel'*). Those under 17 years of age were termed *maloletnye*, and a guardian (*opekun*) managed their affairs for them. See V. N., "Popechitel'stvo," *Entsiklopedicheskii slovar'*, (Brokgauz–Efron), vol. 24. These trustees and guardians served as proxies in zemstvo electoral bodies.

47 Article 20 allowed *neotdelennye synov'ia*, which I take to mean adult sons still living with their parents, to represent their fathers. By a law of December 12, 1865, these sons could also represent their mothers and be elected to the zemstvo assembly. *PSZRI*, 2d series, vol. 40, no. 42771.

48 The *prilozhenie* to articles 33 and 52 of the 1864 statute, located under the heading "Shtaty i tabeli" on pp. 5–9, in part 3 of *PSZRI*, 2d series, vol. 39.

49 In each of the remaining 11 districts two curiae had an equal number of deputies. The strong town curiae were in Shadrinsk district of Perm province, in Simferopol, Yalta, and in Berdiansk district of Tauride province. Peasant strongholds were concentrated in Viatka, Olonets, and Vologda provinces and, to a lesser extent, in Perm, Kazan, and Samara.

50 The number of deputies set by the *prilozhenie* to the 1864 statute for each curia appears to have undergone little change during the period 1864–90. I have found only one law making such changes, namely, for town curiae in Perm province. *PSZRI*, 2d series, vol. 41, no. 43012 (February 14, 1866).

51 *PSZRI*, 2d series, vol. 39, no. 40934 (May 25, 1864).

52 Ibid., vol. 42, no. 44622 (May 26, 1867). But with the exception that now the *uprava* performed the role assigned in the first elections to the Temporary District Commission, a body created in each district to set up the zemstvo institutions.

53 Leroy-Beaulieu, 2:161–2.

54 Articles 9 and 94–6 of the 1864 statute. In Tver province the governor protested the correctness of elections in eight cases between 1865 and 1890; in six of these the zemstvo yielded, in one the governor, and the eighth case went to the Senate for decision. B. B. Veselovskii, *Istoricheskii ocherk deiatel'nosti zemskikh uchrezhdenii Tverskoi gubernii* (Tver, 1914), p. 30.

55 Section 1 of chapter 3 in the 1890 statute, which describes the electoral system, is indeed a rather peculiar piece of legislation. Of its 39 articles, only 1 deals with peasant voting. All the other articles have to do with the first two curiae – who was and was not eligible, exact procedures to follow in voting, and so on – and none of this was

made applicable to the peasant communities. In his commentary Korkunov makes much of this and more than once points to the carelessness shown by the drafters of the statute. See Korkunov, 2:537–62 and passim.

56 Instead of the existing seven categories (to the original 6 there had been added a seventh, of 300 desiatinas, in 2 districts of Bessarabia), there were now to be no less than 16: 125, 150, 175, 200, 225, 250, 275, 300, 325, 350, 400, 425, 475, 550, 700, and 800 desiatinas. Korkunov, 2:549. For a complete list of the land tsenz for each district in all 34 provinces, see the prilozhenie to article 16 of the 1890 statute, located under "Shtaty i tabeli" on pp. 384–99, in part 2 of PSZRI, 3d series, vol. 10.

57 Korkunov notes that the law, unintentionally, did not exclude non-Christian clergy (2:557).

58 Jews were not excluded in the statute proper but in article 12 of the mnenie of the State Council preceding the statute text.

59 These peasant owners had constituted 4.8 percent of all full-tsenz voters in the 1883–4 elections. Zakharova, p. 145.

60 Such decisions were to be made by the Provincial Bureau of Zemstvo Affairs. This was an important new supervisory body created by the Statute of 1890.

61 Korkunov points out that the statute stipulated no conditions of electability as far as the peasants were concerned (as it did in the case of the other two curiae), and volost voters could elect even persons not belonging to the volost. "This," he remarks, "is no doubt the consequence of the hasty editing of the statute" (2: 561).

62 The statute provided for only one electoral assembly and one electoral congress in all districts of Viatka, Olonets, and Perm provinces, and also in seven of the ten districts of Vologda province, with their chairmen appointed by the governor (article 32). In these districts the few nonpeasants participated together in voting, noble and commoner alike. But again, carelessness is revealed in the drafting of the 1890 statute, for the acompanying prilozhenie to article 14 gives no electoral assembly and no electoral congress for two districts of Vologda, and here the peasants apparently had a clean monopoly in the election of deputies. PSZRI, 3d series, vol. 10, part 2, "Shtaty i tabeli," p. 370.

63 Based on articles 34–50 and 52 of the 1890 statute. It will be noted that, unlike the 1864 statute's arrangement, the zemstvo assembly has no role in confirmation and is in fact bypassed.

64 Veselovskii, Istoriia zemstva, 3; 677. Veselovskii points out that only in Olonets and Saint Petersburg provinces did the total number of district deputies increase. He is, however, in error in saying that the number of provincial deputies increased in Viatka province; in fact, they fell from 35 to 29 and decreased in every provincial zemstvo except that of Olonets.

65 Zakharova, p. 153; Veselovskii, *Istoriia zemstva*, 3:680–81.

66 Veselovskii, *Istoriia zemstva*, 3:673.

67 Zakharova, p. 156.

68 The electoral system in those nine provinces in which zemstvos were established in 1911 and 1912 may be briefly noted. In the six western provinces (Vitebsk, Volynia, Kiev, Minsk, Mogilev, and Podolia) the arrangement was dictated by the nationality question. In each province there were three curiae: an electoral assembly and congress for non-Polish property owners; the same for Poles; and village communities. The only exceptions to this scheme were the western, Lettish districts of Dvinsk, Liutsin, and Rezhitsa in Vitebsk province, where the first curia was for Russians and the second curia for non-Russians. In Astrakhan, Stavropol, and Orenburg provinces the special feature was the existence in each district of only one electoral assembly and one congress, plus of course the curia of village communities. In Astrakhan a new form of property qualification permitted owners of fisheries with annual net income of 600 rubles to vote in the electoral assembly.

69 *PSZRI*, 3d series, vol. 26, no. 28392 (October 6, 1906).

70 It did add a clause about "solicitude" for preventing and extinguishing fires and for the better arrangement of villages (article 2, point 9).

71 This right was restored to the district zemstvo by the law of February 2, 1904 (*PSZRI*, 3d series, vol. 24, no. 23980) but exclusively in matters concerning the "local interests and needs of the district." The Statute of 1890 had not stipulated a territorial limitation in petitions from the provincial zemstvo assembly.

72 Korkunov, 2:578–9, and I. A. Malinovskii, *Lektsii po istorii russkogo prava* (Rostov, 1918), p. 25.

73 *PSZRI*, 2d series, vol. 39, no. 40458 (January 1, 1864). See especially the *prilozhenie* to article 3.

74 Veselovskii, *Istoriia zemstva*, 1:241.

75 Article 9 of the temporary rules. It may be noted that the zemstvo also drew income from such sources as sales of various articles, equipment, and books and from fees paid by travelers using zemstvo conveyance services.

76 Veselovskii, *Istoriia zemstva*, 1: 106–7. See also the discussion in Starr, pp. 306–11.

77 *PSZRI*, 3d series, vol. 10, no. 18862 (June 12, 1900), article 7. Witte assured D. N. Shipov that the state would fill the gap if zemstvos found themselves short of money as a result of the 1900 law. V. I. Gurko, *Features and Figures of the Past* (Stanford, 1939), p. 699.

78 Polner, p. 34. In 1910, subsidies had amounted to only about 7 percent of the zemstvo budget.

79 Veselovskii, *Istoricheskii ocherk*, p. 115.

80 Ibid.

81 Veselovskii, *Istoriia zemstva*, 1:241–2.

82 Ibid., p. 243.

83 Korkunov, 2:580–3; Malinovskii, p. 251.

84 *PSZRI*, 2d series, vol. 44, no. 48498 (June 16, 1870), article 103.

85 Ibid., vol. 48, no. 52396 (June 16, 1873). The local police were obligated to cooperate (point 7), and, of course, the governor's confirmation was required (point 3).

86 Ibid., vol. 54, no. 59399 (March 9, 1879). The measure also allowed the zemstvos to divide the district into sectors, each with its own overseer (*popechitel'*) appointed by the zemstvo.

87 Ibid., vol. 54, no. 59739 (June 3, 1879).

88 Kizevetter reports that, when serious crop failures occurred in the fall of 1901, Minister of Interior Sipiagin ordered the convening of extraordinary sessions of the zemstvo assemblies to help cope with the problem. In his circular, Sipiagin asserted that the law of June 12, 1900, was applicable only in good years, "but not in years of serious hardship." Kizevetter, p. 322. Kizevetter sees this statement as a remarkable admission of the inadequacy of the government.

89 In 1864 the district assembly was granted the right to elect local justices of the peace, usually four or five for each district, and also honorary justices. *PSZRI*, 2d series, vol. 39, no. 41475, (November 22, 1864), article 24. This privilege, terminated in 1889 with the replacement of the peace justices by the land captains, was again extended in 1912 with the restoration of the institution of peace justice. *PSZRI*, 3d series, vol. 32, no. 37328, (June 15, 1912). The provincial assembly received the right to elect one member each to the revamped State Council by the law of February 20, 1906. *PSZRI*, 3d series, vol. 26, no. 27425, article 1, point 5. It is interesting that this law explicitly stated that elected members of the State Council were not obliged to make reports to their constituencies (article 1, point 18).

90 Veselovskii, *Istoriia zemstva*, 3:126–7. See also the similar interpretation of the Committee of Ministers in 1879 (p. 230).

91 Ibid., p. 248. These congresses, held in Kharkov and Odessa, were concerned, respectively, with combatting diphtheria and crop-damaging insects.

92 *PSZRI*, 3d series, vol. 22, no. 22284 (December 16, 1902).

93 Ibid., vol. 26, no. 27300 (January 31, 1906).

94 In his *Russian Local Government*, Polner discusses the first of these unions briefly but then devotes the bulk of the volume to a full-scale portrayal of the zemstvo union during World War I. For a more analytical study, see chapter 11 in the present volume.

95 Ibid., p. 33.

96 In Kherson, Tauride, Viatka, Novgorod, and Saint Petersburg provinces. *PSZRI*, 3d series, vol. 22, no. 22286 (December 16, 1902).

97 A schedule stipulated the number to be elected from each district assembly. See the *prilozhenie* to articles 33 and 52 of the 1864 statute in *PSZRI*, 2d series, vol. 39, part 3, "Shtaty i tabeli," p. 5–9.

98 Deputies were also elected by the city councils of Saint Petersburg, Moscow, and Odessa to the provincial zemstvo assemblies of Saint Petersburg, Moscow, and Kherson provinces (article 52). A similar arrangement obtained after 1911–12 in respect to the cities of Kiev, Minsk, Astrakhan, Orenburg, Troitsk, Cheliabinsk, and Stavropol. Unlike other cities and towns in those provinces having zemstvo institutions, these 10 cities lay outside the jurisdiction of local district zemstvos.

99 *PSZRI*, 3d series, vol. 19, no. 17837 (December 6, 1899).

100 Article 53 of the 1864 statute and article 54 of the 1890 statute.

101 Reasons stipulated as adequate excuse for absence included personal illness, serious illness or death of a close relative, breakdown in communications, and call to state service (article 59). The punishments were: for a first offense, a reprimand; second offense, a fine of 75 rubles; third, a fine plus exclusion from the assembly for a time not longer than until the next zemstvo elections. See the *mnenie*, article 6, in *PSZRI*, 3d series, vol 10, no. 6927 (June 12, 1890), p. 494.

102 Reprimands accounted for 36; fines for 2. The Senate ruled that levying of such punishment was a right, not an obligation, of the assembly and that the assembly need not punish absentees (even on the governor's demand). Veselovskii, *Istoriia zemstva*, 3:353–4.

103 Ibid., pp. 143–6.

104 Article 39 of the 1864 statute stipulated that deputies were to receive no remuneration or service privileges.

105 *PSZRI*, 2d series, vol. 40, no. 45353 (May 30, 1866). It did, however, permit support of deputies by societal groups. In 1890, the *mnenie* prefacing the text of the zemstvo statute specifically allowed volost assemblies to support peasant deputies from volost levies (article 4, in *PSZRI*, 3d series, vol. 10, no. 6927 [June 12, 1890], p. 493).

106 The Voronezh assembly in 1866 fined tardy deputies three rubles, to be deposited in a school fund. Veselovskii, *Istoriia zemstva*, 3:71.

107 *PSZRI*, 3d series, vol. 20, no. 18790 (June 10, 1900). Prior to this legislation, the Statute of 1890 simply stated that these meetings were to convene not later than October and December; the Statute of 1864 not later than September and December.

108 Sessions could be postponed by permission of the minister of interior and could be prolonged by permission of the governor (articles 66 and 67 of the 1908 statute).

109 *Sbornik materialov dlia istorii Tverskogo gubernskogo zemstva*, vol. 6 (Tver, 1911), pp. 46–7.

110 *Zhurnal Voronezhskogo uezdnogo zemskogo sobraniia ocherednoi sessii, 1–6 oktiabria 1915 g.*, vol. 1 (Voronezh, 1916), pp. 1–32.

111 Extraordinary sessions were not uncommon; between 1886 and 1908 there were 16 such of the Tver provincial assembly. *Sbornik materialov*, 6:10–14.

112 Insufficiency of deputies could not be compensated for by including the *appointed* members of the assembly in a quorum count; the quorum was to be determined exclusively by the number of deputies (*glasnye*) present.

113 *PSZRI*, 2d series, vol. 42, no. 44690 (June 13, 1867).

114 The chairman could be punished even for failure to carry out a governor's demand that spectators be removed from the assembly room (article 19 of the 1867 law). The Senate ruled, however, that the governor could not remove a subject from the agenda (only the chairman could), but he could send the chairman his opinion on the matter. *Istoriia Pravitel'stvuiushchego Senata za dvesti let, 1711–1911 gg.*, vol. 4 (St. Petersburg, 1911), p. 165.

115 The number of assemblies that kept stenographic reports was not great, according to Veselovskii, *Istoriia zemstva*, 3:68–9.

116 See Veselovskii, *Istoricheskii ocherk*, pp. 51–2. The abolition of preliminary censorship in 1906 also applied to zemstvo publications.

117 Veselovskii, *Istoriia zemstva* 3: 460–4. A. I. Koshelev was the chairman in 1866 of a hard-working "general commission" that kept its sessions going until midnight. He reports that two kinds of deputies were chosen to the commission, those who appeared to be especially useful to its work and those who loved to talk (with the idea that the latter would talk themselves out in the commission and be less inclined to delay matters in the assembly sittings). A. I. Koshelev, *Zapiski, 1806–1883* (Berlin, 1884), pp. 185–6.

118 *Zhurnal Voronezhskogo uezdnogo zemskogo sobraniia*, 1: 1–31.

119 Veselovskii, *Istoriia zemstva*, 3:412–21. His figures show that the provincial zemstvo budget, as a percentage of the whole zemstvo budget, increased from 24.2 percent in 1890 to 36.3 percent by 1906 (p. 412).

120 In the 1864 statute, articles 61–64 and 68; in the 1890 statute, articles 63–4.

121 Veselovskii, *Istoriia zemstva*, 3:414.

122 But it could not elect those deputies who had participated in the electoral congresses as representatives of females and underage males or as leaseholders representing landowners, nor members of the judiciary (except peace justices), local treasury officials, and clergy (article 47). Aside from treasury officials, other persons in state service could be elected but could not take office without permission of their superiors.

123 Altered in 1867 to read, instead of six members, from two to six members. *PSZRI*, 2d series, vol. 42, no. 45163 (November 15, 1867). Article 47 of the 1864 statute also applied to the provincial zemstvo board (see preceding note).

124 Korkunov, 2: 574.

125 This rule did not exclude all peasants, despite the fact that they had no electoral assembly. A peasant who had been elected as deputy to

74

the zemstvo assembly would be eligible for election to its board as a member (but not, until 1906, as chairman).

126 Veselovskii, *Istoriia zemstva*, 3:358.

127 Thereupon the merchant–chairman of the Totma district board in Vologda province lost his post after having held it since 1873. Veselovskii, *Istoriia zemstva*, 3:355.

128 *PSZRI*, 3d series, vol. 24, no. 28392 (October 6, 1906), article 1. The only remaining exception were the *inorodtsy*.

129 The *prilozhenie* to this article placed the provincial board chairman in the fifth class (*klass*) of the Table of Ranks; the district chairman and members of the provincial board, in the sixth; the members of the district board, in the seventh. See *PSZRI*, 3d series, vol. 10, part 2, "Shtaty i tabeli," p. 399. Those members not having the right to enter state service could, however, be promoted into the Table of Ranks after having served three terms on the zemstvo board (article 124 of the 1890 statute).

130 *PSZRI*, 3d series, vol. 19, no. 17899 (December 20, 1899).

131 Veselovskii, *Istoriia zemstva*, 3:357–8. Nonconfirmations occurred most often in Viatka, Ufa, and Tver provinces. The most famous case was that of the widely respected D. N. Shipov, chairman of the Moscow provincial board from 1893 to 1904.

132 Articles 49 (1864) and 126 (1890). But, after 1890, if board personnel were appointed rather than elected, their salaries were fixed by the Provincial Bureau of Zemstvo Affairs.

133 Veselovskii, *Istoriia zemstva*, 3:433–4. For a detailed study of the peasants' relationship to the zemstvo, see Chapter 4 in the present volume.

134 Ibid., pp. 437–41.

135 Ibid., pp. 218–23.

136 See the chart in *Sbornik materialov*, 6:292–3, and also 289–90.

137 Veselovskii, *Istoriia zemstva*, 3:465. By 1914, in an especially active zemstvo such as that of Tver province, there were approximately 3,500 zemstvo employees. Veselovskii, *Istoricheskii ocherk*, p. 68. For zemstvo activities in the fields of medicine, public health, and education, see Chapters 9, 8, and 7, respectively, in the present volume.

138 Veselovskii, *Istoricheskii ocherk*, p. 74. The fund provided pensions, special grants, and annual salary supplements. By 1914 it was able to offer a pension of 50 percent of salary after 15 years of service and 100 percent of salary after 25 years.

139 *Zhurnal Voronezhskogo uezdnogo zemskogo sobraniia*, 1: 146–9.

140 Articles 59 of the 1864 statute and 105 of the 1890 statute. The 1890 statute also allowed the election of nondeputies who met the property qualification (article 105).

141 Veselovskii, *Istoricheskii ocherk*, p. 65.

142 *PSZRI*, 3d series, vol. 19, no. 17145 (June 7, 1899). See also Veselovskii, *Istoriia zemstva*, 3: 446–7.

143 *Zhurnal Voronezhskogo uezdnogo zemskogo sobraniia*, 1: 579–89. The richness, scope, and detail of the material contained in the annual reports of zemstvos at this mature stage (1915) in their history is remarkable. The two-volume *Zhurnal* of the Voronezh district zemstvo for this one year includes over 2,800 pages of *doklady*, *otchety*, and other documents. Unfortunately, however, the terse reportage of the annual assembly session in October amounts to only 34 pages.

144 If Voronezh district were of average size (for districts within Voronezh province), its area would have been 5,491 square kilometers, much larger than the territory of the average county in Virginia today (1,080 square kilometers), New York (2,007 square kilometers), or Georgia (958 square kilometers).

145 Based on articles 9, 11, and 94–7 of the 1864 statute.

146 *Istoriia Pravitel'stvuiushchego Senata*, 4: 152. I. A. Blinov wrote that part of the volume dealing with senatorial supervision of local institutions (pp. 108–214).

147 Korkunov, 2:588.

148 *PSZRI*, 2d series, vol. 42, no. 44691 (June 13, 1867).

149 Ibid., vol. 54, no. 59947.

150 In 1892 combined with the provincial bureau of town affairs and renamed the provincial bureau of zemstvo and town affairs.

151 If desired, experts could be invited to advise the bureau (article 10). The member of the bureau elected by the assembly had to be a deputy who had the right to enter state service (article 117). A "permanent member" was added to the bureau by the law of May 29, 1900. He became its workhorse. See Veselovskii, *Istoriia zemstva*, 3:362.

152 The bureau's procedure against such persons was the same as against board members (article 137).

153 This council (*sovet*) was composed of the minister, the deputy minister, directors of departments, and other high-ranking bureaucrats of the ministry. Such councils existed in several of the ministries. See Eroshkin, p. 164.

154 On governors' inspections, see Veselovskii, *Istoriia zemstva*, 3: 548–51. Here Veselovskii also discusses revisions initiated by Pleve in 1903–4. The ministerial revision of Tver is especially interesting. It was conducted by B. V. Shtiurmer, the future prime minister and himself a landowner in Tver province. This *reviziia* violated lawful procedures in that a provincial board as well as a board for Novotorzhok district were appointed following the inspection without observance of article 119 of the statute, which stipulated that a board could be appointed only after *two* elections by the assembly had not been confirmed. In this case the second elections were not allowed, and the minister was explicitly directed to ignore this lawful procedure. See article 1 of *PSZRI*, 3d series, vol. 24, no. 23861 (January 8, 1904). Nicholas II evidently cherished a distaste for the Tver zemstvo

ever since the Address of 1894. Gurko reports that Pleve showed him a note in the tsar's handwriting and signed "Nicholas," which said: "I have been thinking a great deal about our conversation concerning the Tver zemstvo; they must be dealt a severe blow." Gurko, pp. 240–1.

155 If the governor disagreed with the provincial assembly's decision, the matter went to the provincial bureau for its recommendation and then to the minister (articles 90–1).

156 There was an additional finesse: if the enactment involved an increase in zemstvo taxes, the State Council and not the Committee of Ministers made the final judgment (article 94).

157 *Istoriia Pravitel'stvuiushchego Senata*, 4:209–10.

158 Ibid., p. 153. Appeals to the Senate, both by the zemstvo and by other parties, are analyzed in Chapter 6 in the present volume.

159 An enactment not in operation would be one either not yet confirmed or still in the two-week waiting period mandatory for other enactments.

160 Article 119 of the 1864 statute; article 127 of the 1890 statute.

161 *PSZRI*, 2d series, vol. 39, no. 41068 (July 14, 1864), article 19. The zemstvo representatives were obligated to make annual reports to their assemblies on the condition of schools that the zemstvo supported (article 21).

162 Ibid., vol. 45, no. 48498 (June 16, 1870), article 11.

163 Ibid., vol. 49, no. 53574 (May 25, 1874), article 27.

164 Ibid., no. 52983 (June 8, 1874), articles 81, 84.

165 Ibid., no. 55678 (June 27, 1874), articles 2 and 26. On these bureaus there was to be a "permanent member," from the local landowners, who received his salary from the zemstvo (articles 9 and 27).

166 Gurko, p. 592.

167 *PSZRI*, 3d series, vol. 5, no. 2946 (May 11, 1885), articles 5, 7.

168 Ibid., vol. 8, no. 5120 (April 4, 1888), articles 23–6.

169 Ibid., vol. 9, no. 6196 (July 12, 1889), articles 69–73, 105.

170 Ibid., vol. 12, no. 8708 (June 11, 1892), articles 7 and 8 of the *mnenie* of the State Council and articles 12, 13, and 57 of the statute.

171 Article 2, point 12 of the 1864 statute; article 63, point 14 of the 1890 statute. The Senate ruled that the governor had no power to suspend a zemstvo enactment that was a petition but must forward it to the governmental agency to which it was addressed. *Istoriia Pravitel' stvuiushchego Senata*, 4: 162.

172 Veselovskii, *Istoriia zemstva*, 3:152–3 and note 2.

173 Ibid., pp. 158–9.

174 Gurko, pp. 222–5, 615.

175 Ibid., pp. 124–6, 532.

176 S. Iu. Witte, *Samoderzhavie i zemstvo* (Stuttgart, 1903), pp. 107 ff.

177 Hosking, ch. 2.

178 Jacob Walkin, *The Rise of Democracy in Pre-Revolutionary Russia* (New York, 1962), ch. 7, esp. pp. 178–80.

179 V. N. Tverdokhlebov, "Vydelenie gorodov v samostoiatel'nye zemstva," in *Iubileinyi zemskii sbornik*, pp. 206–18.

180 A very detailed program of reforms is presented in the editors' preface to *Iubileinyi zemskii sbornik*, pp. vii–xviii.

181 Leroy-Beaulieu, 2:196.

4

The zemstvo and the peasantry

DOROTHY ATKINSON

Throughout the half-century of zemstvo self-government, the governed – for the most part – were peasants. Few aspects of zemstvo life failed to affect the peasantry in some way, yet the general relationship between the zemstvo and the peasants has drawn suprisingly little attention. The investigator confronts a number of basic questions: To what extent did the peasants actually take part in the zemstvo system? What benefits did they derive from it? What did it cost them? And what was their attitude toward the institution?

A full discussion of the zemstvo and the peasantry would encompass all of these issues. But since major zemstvo contributions to peasant welfare are dealt with in other chapters, this inquiry will bypass the question of benefits received and focus on the three remaining problems: participation, the price of zemstvo progress, and peasant perspectives.

Peasant participation in the zemstvo

Background of the legislation

The Statute of January 1, 1864, establishing the zemstvo system decreed that participation in the zemstvo was to be based on property holding. The property that mattered most in agrarian Russia was land, and the very name of the zemstvo derived from the word for land (*zemlia*). The amount of land that entitled a private proprietor to a vote in zemstvo elections depended on the average size of a peasant allotment in the district. Oddly enough, though, the amount of allotment land actually held by a peasant had nothing to do with his electoral rights. This curious situation, like the zemstvo legislation itself, was the product of the differing viewpoints and different objectives that emerged in the elaboration of the reform.

From the outset there was general agreement that the peasants should take part in the new system of local government – along with general disagreement as to precisely *what* part.[1] The zemstvo was not only a logical extension of the emancipation, it was a necessity occasioned by that reform. The serf-owning landlord had carried out a number of local administrative functions that had to be handled differently once serfdom was ended. To some extent the formal institutionalization of the old commune and of the new (restructured and extended) volost transferred administrative responsibilities to the peasants themselves; but the competency of these peasant organs of self-government was strictly limited. The zemstvo, however ambiguous its official status, stood above the volost in the administrative hierarchy and was to serve as a critical link between state and society.

It was the intermediate nature of its role that made possible the debate over whether the zemstvo should be locally autonomous or integral (and subordinate) to the centralized bureaucratic system of government.[2] Whatever the stand taken by contenders on this point, the necessity of peasant participation in the new zemstvo institutions was universally conceded. Once the hand of the landlord had been lifted from the village, it became more important to gain peasant support for local programs. With the loss of traditional mechanisms of social control the need for social cooperation appeared more urgent. The peasants had been accustomed in their communes to accept collective decisions as well as mutual responsibility for the payment of taxes. The presence of their representatives in the zemstvos, it was reasoned, would legitimate zemstvo policies and zemstvo taxation in their eyes. The only question to be decided was how to arrange for peasant participation.

It had been suggested in the commission formulating the legislation that participation be based on social estates. But objections were raised. Members representing different estates might view themselves as defenders of special interests; such particularism would undermine the responsibility of the zemstvo to concern itself with the interests of the local economy as a whole. Furthermore, separation of the estates would deprive peasant deputies of the beneficial tutelage of the educated classes.[3] But if the representation of social sectors did not have to be separate, it did not have to be equal either. Members of the nobility expected to be compensated for their loss of seigneurial authority by receiving a leading role in the new regime of local government. The expectation was well founded. Even before the terms of the emancipation had been settled, the minister of internal affairs had insisted on the need to "reward the nobles with primacy in economic administration."[4] Yet to flaunt that primacy before the newly liberated peasantry would be decidedly impolitic.

The problem facing the legislators, then, was to find a formula that, without making reference to social estates, would bring the peasants into the zemstvo but guarantee the predominance of the nobility. The ready solution was to establish a property qualification for participation, bringing the two groups together through the most vital economic interest of each: land. The general idea of a property-based franchise had wide-ranging appeal in Russia. Commending itself to conservatives, who saw it as a means of reinforcing the existing power structure, and to liberals, who hoped to use it to modify that structure, it held out promise to radicals also. The prevalence of communal land tenure among the Russian peasantry made it uniquely possible here to reconcile arguments for a propertied franchise with a call for broad popular participation in government.

Whatever its promise in theory, the property qualification in fact best served the socially conservative objectives of the legislators. As Kermit McKenzie has described in Chapter 3, three categories of property were recognized: privately owned land, urban immovable property, and the allotment land of peasant communities. Each category gave rise to a curia of proprietors which had the right to elect locally a stipulated number of deputies for the district zemstvo. Since nobles constituted the largest group of private proprietors by far, claiming title to at least 80 percent of all private holdings of 100 or more desiatinas and to much urban property, it was a relatively simple matter to assure their control of the zemstvo. Peasants were not likely to own urban property; they held relatively little land as private property, and very little of this was in large parcels.[5] So the property qualification – along with the curial system and the distinction drawn between privately owned and peasant allotment land – secured the preponderance of the nobles in the zemstvo. Yet because the extent of noble landholding and the average size of noble properties varied sharply in different localities, the establishment of a uniform qualification norm for the first curia proved impossible. It was necessary to work out a series of local norms and to determine the quota of zemstvo deputies to be chosen by each of the three curias in different localities. The State Council rejected the first electoral scheme submitted by the legislative commission. The proposed procedures, it was feared, would give the nobles such overwhelming numbers in the zemstvo as to create misgivings about the institution among the peasantry.[6]

Concern about popular reaction surfaced again in the discussion of the property norm for the peasant curia. Baron Korf questioned the advisability of any property qualification for peasants. The need to qualify for participation in the zemstvo, he suggested, would only call peasants' attention to the distribution of land and make disturbingly evident the disparity between the average amounts of land held by members of the different social estates. As an alternative he proposed that one peasant deputy be elected for every 4,000 male peasants.[7] Although the figure was ultimately revised, the proposal to avoid any specific land require- ments for the peasantry was incorporated into the final legislation. The commission itself had suggested that peasant elections for the zemstvo might be circumvented. Instead of holding special elections for peasant deputies, the zemstvo could simply co-opt the peasant officials – the *starosty* and the *starshiny* – chosen by the peasants to run their communes and volosts, respectively. But the State Council rejected this on a number of counts. First, the peasants were likely to consider these officials as under administrative control. Further, since the numbers of peasants in each commune and volost differed significantly, this pro- cedure would result in highly uneven representation. Finally, many of the "wealthiest and best" householders were reluctant to serve in the peasant organizations but might willingly enter the zemstvo.[8] Armed with such arguments, the proponents of peasant elections won their case. The result was that peasants not only could participate in the elections for the zemstvo but, due to the absence of property restrictions, could participate more fully than any other social category.

The zemstvo legislation established virtually universal suffrage for the male peasantry. This was a monumental step in Russian political institutional development, and all the more dramatic for the fact that the peasantry was only just emerging from centuries of enserfment. The social conservatism of some of the framers of the legislation had been tempered by anxiety about the mood of the peasantry whose disappoint- ment with the terms of the emancipation was manifest. If the nobility was to be compensated in the zemstvo for the emancipation, compensa- tion to the peasantry was no less advisable. But the zemstvo presented to Russian society was more than a bill of exchange. The emancipation of 1861 had sundered the old degrading bond of serfdom joining lord and peasant in Russia. Enthusiastic reformers viewed the zemstvo of 1864 as the new bond that could reunite them and all of Russian society in a form of local self-government that joined noble enterprise to common cause.

The Statute of 1864 and the Third Estate

Although the general features of the zemstvo legislation have been described in Chapter 3, several specific points of law with respect to landed property are of particular interest here. Article 33 of the general Statute on District and Provincial Zemstvo Institutions stipulated that, in determining the number of deputies to be elected by each curia, the following criteria were to be "taken into consideration": the number of landowners and the amount of usable land they owned; the number of urbanites along with the value of urban immovable property; and the number of volosts, the size of the rural population, and the amount of productive allotment land held by rural societies (communes).

For the landowners' curia the number of deputies to be elected to the district zemstvo was based on the total amount of usable land held by all private proprietors within the district. There were 30 electors qualified to vote for each deputy.[9] The formula used to determine the amount of land needed to qualify (the *tsenz*) was supposed to yield one deputy for every section of privately owned land equivalent in area to 3,000 average peasant allotments in that district. No landowner was permitted more than one vote in the zemstvo regardless of the extent of a holding, but a second vote was permitted to each elector in the electoral session as a proxy or delegate of a group of partial *tsenz* holders. Private owners with at least 5 percent of the amount of land necessary for full qualification could select – in a special preliminary assembly – a number of electoral delgates equal to the number of full *tsenzy* represented by their aggregate holdings.

For the peasant curia, however, the number of deputies was set simply at one for every 3,000 male peasants, without reference to the amount of land actually held by particular peasant societies.[10] That amount, in any case, was somewhat ambiguous since article 26 of the zemstvo statute stipulated that, in calculating the extent of an owner's land for purposes of electoral qualification, the land transferred to the peasantry for "permanent use" at the time of the emancipation was to be treated as still part of the original owner's property. Only after final confirmation of a redemption agreement was the redeemed land deducted from the noble's account.[11]

The provisions of the law dealing with the representation of rural societies made no mention of voting rights for peasant women, although other sections of the statute established that women who owned sufficient private property to meet the *tsenz* could vote in zemstvo electoral sessions through male proxies. Under communal tenure peasant allotment land was usually distributed to households according to the number of males in each, and generally only the male heads of households participated in the commune or volost meetings where peasant electors were to be chosen.

Despite the fact that the peasants' allotment land was indirectly linked to their participation in the zemstvo, the connection was by no means as apparent as it was in the case of private landowners (or urban proprietors), who had to meet specific property requirements. In effect, the peasants, despite the legislators' abjuration of the "class principle" of social segregation, were treated as a distinct social estate, and this inconsistency in the law was a significant modification of the "property principle" that had been nominally adopted. Nobles with landholdings below 5 percent of the local qualifying norm were denied representation in the zemstvo; other citizens were excluded for lack of adequate property; but no peasant in a rural society was similarly disqualified. Private property gave rise to individual political rights, whereas collective property gave group representation to all peasants in the zemstvo. But just as private property limited the political rights of some individuals, so collective property limited the political rights of all peasants. The zemstvo system did not give representation to peasants as citizens so much as it gave recognition to the peasantry as a social estate.

Representation of the peasantry in the zemstvo

The 1864 regulations provided for the election of some 13,000 district deputies in the 33 provinces in which zemstvos were initially to be introduced. According to the schedules appended to the law, 40 percent of the total number of deputies were to be elected by rural societies, and 48 percent by the landowners.[12] Unlike the landowners and the urban proprietors, who could elect only members of their own electoral colleges, the peasants could also elect members of the landowners' electoral college and members of the clergy as their representatives.

The option to elect nonpeasant deputies could have considerably limited their own direct participation in the zemstvos had the peasants made extensive use of it. And there were arguments favoring such use. In many cases public-spirited members of the local gentry were committed to improvement of the peasants' lot. Well-qualified by education, experience, and social status to work effectively for the peasants in the zemstvo, these men were often seen as invaluable spokesmen by the peasants themselves. Yet the elections for the first zemstvos in 1865–6 indicated that the peasantry as a whole strongly preferred peasant representatives. Of the deputies chosen by the peasant curia 90 percent were peasants, only 8 percent were landowners, and 2 percent were from the clergy.[13]

In the elections of 1865–7, which established zemstvos in 29 provinces, 42 percent of all district deputies elected were members of the nobility and 38 percent were from the peasantry.[14] Most of the peasant deputies were from rural societies, and this group accounted for 36 percent of all district zemstvo deputies. Peasant owners of private land who were elected by the landowners' curia accounted for the remaining 2 to 3 percent. In a few cases independent peasant landowners – colonists – were elected by the peasant curia, but apparently such instances were rare.[15]

The number of peasants elected to the district zemstvos, then, was largely a function of the quotas established by the zemstvo legislation. But the number elected to the provincial zemstvos had been left to the members of the district zemstvos. Peasants held over a third of the votes in the district zemstvos, yet they won only a tenth of the seats in the provincial zemstvos. Since each candidate needed the vote of a majority of those present for election, the support of all peasant district deputies was ordinarily insufficient in itself to secure the election of a peasant to the provincial zemstvo. Moreover, there were factors that discouraged peasants from voting for other peasants or advancing their own candidacy: social deference, less interest in provincial affairs, travel expenses, and loss of working time associated with membership in a provincial zemstvo.

With such limited representation in the provincial zemstvos, peasants were all but excluded from the executive boards of those zemstvos. At the district level they fared somewhat better. In the elections of 1865–7 peasants and Cossacks held 19 percent of all the seats on zemstvo boards.[16] The Statute of 1864 had provided for compensation of zemstvo board members, or rather, made it possible for the zemstvos to provide it. In the case of the provincial boards, the provincial assembly was authorized to determine the appropriate amount of compensation for board members; at the district level, however, the assemblies were to decide whether or not financial support was necessary before determining the amount.[17] Board membership was an important, time-consuming responsibility which the peasants in some cases were content to turn over entirely to the gentry. But on occasion they fought to place their own representatives on zemstvo boards. In one instance when the nobles in a district zemstvo insisted that only private landowners could serve on the zemstvo board, the peasants refused to take part in the elections. The governor of the province thereupon dispatched a telegram, deciding the dispute in favor of the peasants. In response, the irate nobles elected an entire board of peasants. The affair ended when the outmaneuvered peasants capitulated and issued a written statement, declining to serve on grounds of their "unfamiliarity with paperwork."[18]

The most impressive showing made by the peasantry in the zemstvo system was in the district assemblies where the general level of peasant delegates – although hardly supporting any claim of equal representation based on landholding – was secured by the law. Over the quarter of a century following the appearance of the zemstvo, the ratio of peasant district deputies remained almost unchanged. In the elections of 1883–5, peasants still accounted for 38 percent of the total number of district deputies. They had gained on the district zemstvo boards, where they now accounted for 31 percent of all members, but had dropped to below 7 percent of all provincial deputies.[19] By this time, however, the disparity between land rights and voting rights had widened considerably due to the substantial loss of land by the nobility. A zemstvo seat held by a landowner in 1877 represented an average of 9,200 desiatinas, whereas that occupied by a delegate from a rural society represented 16,200 desiatinas.[20]

By the mid-1880s peasant owners of private land accounted for half of all smallholders with fractional electoral rights in the landowners' curia and for one-tenth of the fully qualified electors. They constituted 7 percent of all deputies elected by the landowners' curia and 3.4 percent of all district zemstvo deputies.[21] Although their number was still relatively quite small, it was clearly growing. Yet this interesting development was offset by a slight decline in the number of zemstvo representatives from the communal peasantry. Despite a growth in the population of 34 percent between 1863 and 1885,[22] the number of peasant deputies from rural societies had diminished slightly two decades after the introduction of zemstvos. The peasant curia now chose only 85 percent of its deputies from the peasantry and 12 percent from the nobility, as compared with the earlier rates of 90 and 8 percent.[23] The overall share of peasant deputies in the zemstvos remained constant only because of the growing role of the peasant proprietors.

The contradictory tendencies of the two groups of peasant deputies were not apparent to earlier investigators because they relied on aggregate data that combined the two. Statistics on the social composition of the zemstvo have generally grouped the peasant private holders with the peasants in rural societies, but although the independent proprietors shared the burden of social, fiscal, and legal disabilities that continued to differentiate the peasantry from other sectors of Russian society, they were likely to be in circumstances quite different from those of the communal peasantry. Zakharova's recent study of zemstvo electoral statistics, although concerned with other problems, provides data that make it possible to distinguish the two groups of peasants in the zemstvo. It also brings to light some conflicting regional tendencies that had similarly cancelled one another out of the earlier statistical picture.

The increase in the number of peasant proprietors in the zemstvos – an increase that appears rather modest overall – was more impressive in parts of the central industrial region, the southern steppe, and the southeast. In the extreme case of Tauride province peasant owners of private land rose from 1 to 14 percent of all district zemstvo delegates. Yet in other localities the pattern was reversed. In Poltava, for example, this group dropped from 13 to 1 percent.[24] Regional differentiation may account, if only in part, for the larger number of peasants on district zemstvo boards in the 1880s. Local concentration of peasant landowners in some district zemstvos improved the prospects of peasant candidates for board membership more significantly than the slightly increased number of peasant proprietors would have done if evenly distributed. In this connection it is especially interesting to note that the peasant proprietors were the most active group among the smallholders with electoral rights in the landowners' curia. Not only did the qualified peasant smallholders outnumber their noble counterparts by a ratio of three to one, but the peasants' rate of participation in elections for the zemstvo was twice as high as that of the noble smallholders.[25]

Opportunities for participation increased as the peasants acquired more private land. In Moscow province only 13 peasants had qualified for a full vote in 1865. By 1885 there were 151. Between the same years the number of nobles in the province who owned enough land to meet the full electoral qualification dropped from 1,887 to 709.[26] The land lost by the nobility was not going to the peasantry alone, but the peasants, often through collective purchases by associations formed for that purpose, were taking over a considerable part of it. In 1877 the nobles held 78 percent of all private land; the peasants, 7 percent. A decade later the nobles were down to 68 percent, and the peasants had climbed to 12 percent.[27] In the first three decades after the emancipation the nobility lost about a third of its landholdings.[28] Under these conditions a land-based franchise was clearly a questionable means of assuring continued control of local government. The zemstvo counterreform of 1890 was an attempt to deal with that problem.

The counterreform of 1890 and the peasantry

The revised zemstvo statute of June 12, 1890, is often viewed as basically a replacement of the property franchise with a class (or estate) franchise. The landowners' curia disappeared, and membership in the first electoral assembly was now open only to members of the nobility. But the old "property principle" did not really disappear, and, as Veselovskii and others have pointed out, the system of 1864 too had been constructed essentially on the "estate principle."[29] The estate nature of the earlier legislation was evident not only in the predominance assigned to the nobility, the feature emphasized in most of the literature on the zemstvo, but also in the special treatment of the peasantry. Yet, despite the important continuities between the statutes of 1864 and 1890, it is difficult to accept the assertion of some writers that there was little real difference between them. Anyone approaching the counterreform from the perspective of the peasantry is more likely to agree with the historian Kornilov, who described the 1890 law as a "complete perversion of the statute of 1864, especially with respect to the peasantry."[30]

Already in 1889 the relative autonomy of the peasants in their own rural societies and volosts had been seriously undermined by the establishment of a new order of appointed rural officials: the land captains (zemskie nachal'niki). These officers, selected ordinarily from the local nobility, were given broad administrative and judicial powers within district boroughs and were charged with responsibility for the "economic welfare" of the peasants in their territory insofar as this was related to matters within the competency of the peasant institutions.

Just a year later the legislative revision of 1890 deprived the peasantry of the right to elect deputies to the zemstvo. Thereafter the volost assemblies were permitted only to nominate candidates, and peasant deputies were appointed by the provincial governor from the lists submitted. All peasant candidates had to be members of rural societies now; the peasants could no longer choose representatives of other social estates or even peasants who were not members of rural societies. The latter, the independent peasant proprietors, who accounted for a substantial share of the deputies in some zemstvos, were now completely disfranchised. Just as the "non-estate" legislation of 1864 had actually treated the peasants in rural societies as an estate, so the "estate" legislation of 1890 – consistent in its inconsistency –ignored the social estate of the peasant proprietors. Ownership of private property no longer qualified peasants for participation in the zemstvo, but neither did membership in the peasant estate for the minority of peasants who did not belong to a rural society. This meant the exclusion from the zemstvo of all of the independent peasant landowners as well as of peasant private landholding associations. In view of the active part taken by this group of peasants in zemstvo life earlier, this was an unfortunate amputation. Despite the differences between the peasant landowners and the rest of the peasantry, they shared certain common interests, and through the participation of the peasant proprietors the entire peasantry had been more closely linked to the zemstvo system of self-government.

Refusal to accept the peasants' private property as a basis for zemstvo electoral rights was in flagrant contradiction to the retention of the property franchise for the first and second electoral assemblies. By 1905 peasants owned one-fourth of all private land in European Russia. Not only were the peasants set back politically, but all smallholders had lost out when the minimum amount of land qualifying an owner for a fractional electoral vote was raised in 1890 from 5 to 10 percent of a full qualification. D. A. Tolstoi, as minister of internal affairs, had argued for the upward revision on the grounds that the 5 percent minimum "gave entry into the electoral sessions to a multitude of persons belonging to the most unreliable elements of the rural population – small businessmen, tavern keepers, money lenders, kulaks and such."[31] The higher qualification meant that about one-third of all smallholders lost their voting rights, and the loss was all the more serious because, as the electorate was narrowed, the scope of zemstvo activities was broadened. The 1890 statute dropped the terminology limiting zemstvo concerns to "economic" matters and recognized the rights of zemstvos to deal with questions of local welfare and needs.

Due to the ongoing loss of land by the nobility and to land acquistions by the peasantry, each zemstvo seat held by a noble in 1905 represented an average of 4,700 desiatinas, whereas each peasant deputy now represented 30,400 desiatinas.[32] Comparing the situation of 1905 with that of 1877, Veselovskii noted that the land base of the nobles in the zemstvo had been halved, while that of the peasants had doubled. The new law reduced the total number of deputies to the district and provincial zemstvos (by 22 and 29 percent) but strengthened the representation of the nobility. The amount of land necessary to qualify a noble for a full vote in the elections was lowered in most provinces, and the nobility now had a deputy for every 20 (rather than 30) qualified electors.[33]

As for the peasants, not only were their numbers and relative weight in the zemstvos cut down, but they were cut off from any opportunity for leadership. When it became necessary after 1890 for presidents of zemstvo boards to meet qualifications for state service in order to be confirmed in office, peasants were effectively excluded from that role.[34]

As a result of the changes introduced in 1890, the number of peasants declined in the district zemstvos to 31 percent of all deputies, and in the provincial zemstvos to less than 2 percent. Peasant membership on zemstvo boards also dropped sharply.[35] The law had fixed the number of noble deputies at the level of those who met the land qualification in 1890. In the course of time the number of those who met the qualification norm shrank steadily as noble landholding continued to decline, but the number of zemstvo seats allotted to the nobility remained constant. Eventually, in many localities there were few nobles qualified to take part in zemstvo elections, but elections were not always necessary. According to the law, when there were fewer electors present at an election than the number of delegates to be chosen, those present were automatically elected. Where it was impossible to find qualified candidates, or where the delegates elected were unacceptable to the government, individuals were sometimes simply appointed to the zemstvo by the authorities.[36]

Discontent with the system of zemstvo representation led to a call for change, articulated most clearly from the side of liberal elements in society (including those within the zemstvo), and voiced also by the peasantry.[37] From the 1890s there was a growing demand for a "small zemstvo unit," below the district level and encompassing all social estates. The importance of involving the peasants more closely with zemstvo activities was widely acknowledged. In the opinion of one contemporary observer, the legislation of 1890 was based on the notion of noble guardianship over the peasantry and its representatives, but "in the true sense of the word, the peasants have no representatives in the district zemstvo."[38]

Although the nobility retained its predominance in the zemstvo to the end, some of the retrograde provisions of the counterreform were repealed or relaxed after the Revolution of 1905. When the provincial zemstvos were permitted to send representatives to the State Council in connection with the institution of the Duma in 1906, there were no peasants among the group elected. However, seven peasants who were zemstvo deputies were elected to the Duma itself.[39] The decree on peasants' rights promulgated by Stolypin on October 6, 1906, curtailed the authority of the land captains and restored the right of peasants in rural societies to elect deputies to the zemstvo rather than just nominate candidates for gubernatorial appointment. Peasants (along with all others) were now given rights held previously only by the nobility with respect to state service, making it possible once more for a peasant to be elected president of a zemstvo board. Needless to say, such instances remained rare.

A more immediately important change granted rural residents with sufficient private land the right to participate in the second (urban and smallholder) electoral assembly independently of any participation in the elections for the delegates of rural societies. Subsequent interpretations by the Senate, however, established that peasant societies or associations that had acquired land with the help of the Peasant Land Bank could participate in the second electoral assemblies only if the property share of *each member* met the regular qualifying norms. Similarly, it was ruled that peasants who had left their communes and established independent farmsteads under the Stolypin reform legislation of November 1906 were not entitled to participate in zemstvo elections along with other small landowners.[40]

Although these peasants could continue to take part in elections held by rural societies, this policy ran counter to the official agrarian program of the time, which encouraged individualization of land tenure. The contradiction, like the collision of the "estate principle" with the "property principle" in the zemstvo, is evidence of a pervasive confusion about the proper bases of the social and political order – in the face of a steady and dramatic shift in the foundations of the economic order. That shift, painfully impressing itself on a declining nobility still – and more urgently – seeking "compensation" in the zemstvo, is recorded in the property statistics of the zemstvo era (Table 4.1).

By 1911 the nobility had lost over half of the land it owned at the time of emancipation. Nobles in the 34 zemstvo provinces now held 30 million desiatinas of land, only 12 percent of the total for these provinces, however they still occupied over half of the seats in the zemstvo.[41] Deputies elected by peasant societies continued, in accordance with the legislative schedule, to hold less than a third of the zemstvo seats. These ratios of representation persisted even after the entry of additional provinces into the zemstvo system after 1911, and right up to the end in 1917.[42] By this time, however, the amount of private land owned by peasants was approaching parity with that owned by the nobility (see Table 4.1).

The social composition of the zemstvo is more difficult to reconstruct for the institution's final years than for earlier periods. Archival materials reveal that the government was less interested at the end in collecting data on this question. This in itself is striking evidence of the social flux occurring at the time, of the dissolution and increasing irrelevancy of the old social order shaping the zemstvo. The absolute predominance of the nobility within the zemstvo had been secured, but after 1905 it was not the social status of zemstvo members as much as their political orientation that concerned the central administration. This is clearly reflected in the type of information gathered from local authorities in the last few years.

91

Table 4.1. *Ownership of private property in 47 provinces of European Russia 1862–1915*

Year	Land (in millions of desiatinas) owned by	
	Nobles	Peasants (individuals and associations)
1862	87.2	5.7
1872	80.7	7.3
1882	71.2	10.7
1892	62.9	16.2
1902	53.2	22.8
1905	51.3 (49.8)	24.7 (24.6)
1911	43.2	30.4
1915	39.0	34.4

Source: N. P. Oganovskii, ed., *Sel'skoe khoziaistvo Rossii v XX veke. Statis-ticheskii sbornik* (Moscow, 1923), pp. 60–61 (1862–1911); A. M. Anfimov and I. F. Makarov, "Novye dannye o zemlevladenii Evropeiskoi Rossii," *Istoriia SSSR*, 1974, no. 1, p. 85 (1915 and parenthetical data for 1905).

Nonetheless, it can be established from the records of the Ministry of Internal Affairs that despite the unchanging general statistical picture, the position of the peasants in the zemstvo did not remain static. On the contrary, some extremely interesting developments took place. Thanks to the legislative changes effected by the Revolution of 1905, the peasantry made a decided comeback in the provincial zemstvos and on zemstvo boards, where they resumed or approached their pre-1890 levels (Table 4.2). Their stronger showing in these bodies appears to be directly related to another change that emerges from the data: the growing role of the peasant proprietors in the second electoral assembly.

It was the shifting pattern of land ownership that was responsible for this development. Of the total amount of land held by all three electoral assemblies in the 34 zemstvo provinces, the share of the second rose over the two decades following 1890 from about 12 to over 26 percent.[43] As a result, the number of full land-based electoral votes (including the sum of all partial votes to which smaller proprietors were entitled) dropped between 1893 and 1912 in the first (noble) electoral assembly by about one-fourth (roughly, 22,000 to 17,000), whereas it rose in the second electoral assembly by about one-half (17,000 to 25,000).[44] The change in the total number of those qualified to participate in zemstvo elections was even more dramatic since large numbers of smallholders

Table 4.2. *Peasant participation in zemstvos, 1865–1915*

Type of zemstvo	1865–7 Number	1865–7 Percent of total membership	1883–6 Number	1883–6 Percent of total membership	1897 Number	1897 Percent of total membership	1903 Number	1903 Percent of total membership	1913–15[a] Number	1913–15[a] Percent of total membership
District zemstvos	4,581	38	5,073	38	3,174	31			2,647	31
Provincial zemstvos	317	11	157	7	29	2			76	7
Zemstvo boards										
District			389	31			226	18	326	26
Provincial			2	1			3	2	4	2
Combined	304	19		28				17		23

[a]District zemstvos in 30 provinces, provincial zemstvos in 23 provinces, district boards in 23 provinces, provincial boards in 33 provinces, district boards in 32 provinces.

Sources: B. B. Veselovskii, Istoriia zemstva za sorok let, 4 vols. (St. Petersburg, 1909–11), 3:49, 433–4, 680–1; Entsiklopedicheskii slovar' (Brokgauz–Efron) vol. 12, p. 538; TsGIA, F. 1288, Ministerstvo vnutrennykh del, Glavnoe upravlenie po delam mestnogo khoziaistva, op. 3 (47 dela).

were replacing the small group of noble landowners who had held full votes. In Penza province, for example, the group of zemstvo electors more than doubled in these two decades, while nobles dropped from 57 to 14 percent of the electorate.[45]

Peasants were not the only gainers here, of course, but after 1905, just as in the period before 1890, the peasant proprietors were clearly beginning to play a more important role in the zemstvo. In 1913–15 they accounted for over half of the qualified electorate in the second electoral assembly in Kostroma province, about half in Iaroslav and Tula provinces, almost a third in Vladimir province, and over a quarter in Kharkov province.[46] Although increasing peasant ownership of private property in land was the major factor here, local records show that peasants sometimes qualified through ownership of other forms of immovable property, usually related to an industrial or commercial enterprise.

Since the entire second electoral assembly supplied less than a sixth of all zemstvo deputies, peasant gains here had limited impact on the general situation in the zemstvo. Yet the addition of these peasant deputies to the zemstvo after 1905 was no longer offset by the election of nonpeasant representatives by rural societies. The institutionalization of the estate principle in 1890 had precluded this. Therefore, although the share of deputies elected by rural societies remained virtually constant after 1905, the ratio of deputies who were peasants was actually improving somewhat. The improvement directly involved only the most prosperous sector of the peasantry, but, as previously, this sector appears to have taken a relatively active role in zemstvo affairs.[47] That role invites further study, but it is noteworthy that deputies chosen by the second electoral assembly were less likely than those from the noble or peasant electoral assemblies to belong to the political right. In the 1909–10 elections only 40 percent of all deputies returned by the second assembly were officially identified as rightists, as compared with 57 percent from the noble assembly and 52 percent from the rural societies.[48]

Another noteworthy feature of the zemstvo electoral scene, and one that seems to have been quite overlooked in the literature on the zemstvo, is the surprisingly high number of women qualified by property ownership to participate (through male proxies) in the electoral assemblies. In Tula province in 1913, for example, 4 out of every 10 persons who qualified for the first electoral assembly and almost 2 in 10 eligible for the second electoral assembly were women.[49] In the lists for the second assembly these women are described most often as someone's wife, widow, or daughter, but some are listed as shopkeepers or owners of businesses. Far less common but appearing from time to time in the lists are the names of women peasants. Occasionally they amounted to a significant group: in Soligalich district of Kostroma province, for example, women accounted in 1913 for a full quarter of all the peasant electors and for a sixth of all electors in the second assembly.[50] Yet the electoral rights of the women could be exercised only through their male relatives, and to the end they were denied the right to participate directly in the zemstvo as deputies. When liberals raised the question of women's right to serve in the zemstvo during the Moscow district zemstvo of 1903, all of the peasant deputies (among others) were adamantly opposed.[51]

The attitude of the peasant men was quite different when it came to their own service in the zemstvo, or at least to service on zemstvo boards. The compensation of board members, accepted everywhere as a necessity, became an important factor attracting peasants into the zemstvo. Contemporary reporters repeatedly noted that peasants sought election to the zemstvo in hopes of being appointed to the salaried board.[52] Compensation varied substantially among and within provinces: service as a district board member in 1915 could yield from 600 rubles (Kargopol district, Olonets) to 3,600 rubles (Elizavetgrad district, Kherson), and the president of a provincial board could earn from 3,600 rubles (Riazan) to 8,400 rubles (Kiev).[53] Despite their interest, though, and despite some improvement of the situation after 1905, peasants in most areas were poorly represented on zemstvo boards; they were absent from almost all provincial boards and were rarely to be found as board presidents.

The question of peasant participation in the zemstvo can be addressed in the most general terms by calculating the number of peasant deputies in district zemstvos over the life of the institution. Peasants accounted for approximately a third of the total membership, not an especially impressive figure considering that they constituted over four-fifths of the population. Yet it is quite substantial in comparison with popular representation in some other parts of the contemporary Western world, particularly at the beginning of the zemstvo period. (In 1864, after all, the second English reform bill was still in the wings.) There were, in round numbers, some 65,000 three-year terms in the zemstvo that were filled by peasants and, allowing for instances when a peasant served more than one term, there may have been roughly 50,000 peasants who served as deputies and gained some political experience in the new system of local self-government. But numbers tell only part of the story. It is clear that popular participation in the zemstvo system not only failed to increase over time but actually declined significantly after 1890. And before concluding this survey of the quantitative aspects of peasant participation, it should be noted that the number of deputies provided for by law, as well as the number elected, indicate only the upper limits on peasant participation. Although they are revealing, the numbers are not necessarily reliable evidence of actual involvement because the number of deputies elected was often below the allotted quotas, and in any case election was no guarantee of attendance at zemstvo meetings.[54] Absenteeism was a problem that extended beyond the peasantry, but to see that problem from the peasant point of view and to understand that viewpoint in general one must turn to the question of the cost of the zemstvo to the peasantry.

The price of peasant progress

Pre-zemstvo local taxation

In prereform Russia the question of local economic needs and of taxation to cover such needs was left largely to local estate owners or to local agents of the state treasury. The collection of local taxes was disorganized and highly arbitrary. Only from the beginning of the nineteenth century was there an attempt on the part of the government to deal systematically with problems of local economic administration. In 1805 local taxes were organized on a provincial basis, but not until 1851 was a general regulation issued on "local obligations" (zemskie povinnosti).[55] These included both monetary and "natural" obligations. Monetary taxes fell into three categories: state (general), provincial (local), and "particular" (falling on specific social estates or groups). Natural obligations included payments in kind or in labor and could apply to residents of a village or of an entire province, but by law these were divided among the revision souls in rural societies and thus the nobility was exempt from them.[56]

The provincial institutions charged with supervision of local taxes were loose bodies which met rarely and exerted little control. Since taxes fell almost entirely on the peasantry and merchants, most nobles had little interest in this area, and in general the nobles demonstrated little interest in the local economy beyond the borders of their own estates. Local economic affairs were left to the provincial governor and a sparse handful of bureaucrats; at the district level the police was virtually the only agency of local economic administration.[57] At the time of the emancipation an array of pressing needs demanded attention, but it was beyond the government's competence to cope effectively with such problems as local roads, food supply, medical and veterinary care, fire protection, or insurance. Administrative mechanisms were lacking, and financial resources were inadequate. Yet by 1864 the average annual loss from fire damage alone amounted to 10 million rubles, almost half of the total tax revenues.[58]

Zemstvo finances

The decree of January 1, 1864, announcing the creation of the zemstvo made it clear that the new institution had been brought into being specifically to deal with affairs "relating to the economic interests and needs of each province and district." In the era of Great Reforms as in the days of Muscovite reforms, it was fiscal considerations that led to the introduction of institutions of local self-government in Russia.[59] Upon the establishment of the first zemstvos, most of the provincial zemskie taxes and certain other revenues (in all, over 5 million rubles or about 20 percent of the total annual state revenue) were transferred to the zemstvo budgets.[60]

A set of "temporary rules" covering zemstvo taxation was issued simultaneously with the zemstvo statute in 1864.[61] These rules, regulating zemstvo monetary and natural taxation, were to become a permanent part of the system. State taxes remained, as before, essentially under the contol of the provincial governor and, along with the particular taxes, were beyond the purview of the zemstvo. However, the former provincial taxes and all others in the hands of the zemstvo (known together now as the zemskie taxes) were henceforth to be applied to district needs as well as to provincial needs. Those provinces where zemstvo institutions were not introduced remained without administrative agencies for local economic affairs below the provincial level.[62] The zemstvos were to take care of the specific local needs described above (Chapter 3), which included, but extended beyond, those covered by zemskie taxes in the regulation of 1851. Beyond the stipulated responsibilities, the zemstvos were permitted to attend to other local economic concerns at their own discretion. The old revenues turned over to the zemstvos were to be applied to the "obligatory" expenditures, but since these revenues were already inadequate to their expanded purpose, and in order to meet "nonobligatory" expenses, the zemstvos were given the right to levy new supplementary taxes. All zemstvo taxes, as well as the annual zemstvo budgets themselves were subject to the approval of the provincial governors. Property taxes were to be levied in accordance with the value and income of the property; and all taxable land – private or public, individually or collectively held – was to be taxed on the same basis.

A special rule was devoted to clarification of the status of the lands transferred to the "permanent use" of the peasantry under the terms of the emancipation. As mentioned earlier, these lands had been credited to their former owners for purposes of electoral qualification. But when it came to tax payments, the same land was debited to the peasants' account. The logic of the latter procedure was apparent: the peasants now received the income from the land. But the pointed inconsistency of the former was no less apparent.

Natural obligations captured an even greater amount of attention in the legislation than did monetary taxes. This was hardly surprising since natural obligations had been considerably heavier under serfdom than those paid in money and at the time of emancipation may have been approximately equal to monetary taxes.[63] Natural obligations included such services as road work, quartering soldiers (until 1874), and transporting officials. The zemstvos were permitted to convert natural obligations into monetary form or to extend existing forms of natural taxation, but they could not convert an existing monetary tax into a natural tax or impose new forms of natural taxation. The 1864 regulations stated that only those specifically excused by law were exempt from the payment of natural taxes, but they also directed the zemstvos to be guided by the rules laid down in 1851. Certain natural obligations were due only from the peasantry, but in some cases the nobility contributed materials, for example, wood for road construction. Although some peasants preferred natural imposts to additional demands for money, these obligations were generally viewed as discriminatory and were unpopular with the peasantry. Over the course of time they were increasingly converted into monetary taxes, and by the mid-1880s they had been completely replaced by monetary taxes in two-thirds of all zemstvo districts.[64] By the beginning of the twentieth century the obligation to perform road work, once the most important of the natural duties, had been converted to a money tax in three out of four zemstvo districts.[65]

The zemstvo, however, was not the only local institution calling on the peasant for taxes. The emancipation legislation had made it clear that the peasants would continue to be subject to state, provincial, and particular taxes.[66] The distribution of taxes (monetary and natural) within the rural society was left to the peasant assembly (the mir) itself. Both the rural society and the volost had the right of self-taxation to provide at will for churches, schools, and "other social and economic needs of the peasants," but these institutions were also required to meet a number of stipulated "mir obligations," including responsibilities later assigned to or assumed by the new zemstvos as well; road maintenance, public welfare, public health, pest control, fire control, and so forth.

The delineation of functions, therefore, remained somewhat unclear within the districts. The overlapping competencies of the zemstvos and the peasant societies created a certain amount of administrative confusion and potential for fiscal competition. In some cases a mutual accommodation was arranged by the withdrawal of one of the competitors. Thus in the early years of the zemstvo over half of the district zemstvos had no budget provision at all for roads, whereas other zemstvos turned their road funds over to rural societies.[67] The emancipation statute had promised a later reexamination of the question of zemskie taxes, and the promise was repeated in the title of the "temporary rules" of 1864; but provisional arrangements became permanent regulations, and the situation remained unchanged in the years ahead.[68] Given their own limited participation rights and the dominance of the nobility in the zemstvos, it was clearly preferable from the peasants' point of view to deal with local economic problems on the level of their own peasant institutions. Taxes adopted by their own assemblies were likely to seem more urgent and be more acceptable. The result was that "mir taxes" (the sum of rural society and volost taxes) in many places significantly exceeded zemstvo taxes in the earlier period.[69] But the situation was to change in time.

Despite the competition for peasant kopeks, the zemstvo budgets grew with remarkable vitality and by the end of the century were gaining slightly even on the rapidly expanding state budget.[70] From a modest beginning of 5.6 million rubles in 1865, zemstvo income had increased to 220 million in 34 provinces by 1912, and to 291 million rubles the following year with the addition of the 6 western provinces. Following an initial spurt as the zemstvos were introduced, the budget growth rate slowed in the 1870s and especially in the depressed 1880s, but picked up momentum in the 1890s and raced ahead after the turn of the century. Between 1893 and 1903 alone the total zemstvo budget almost doubled as zemstvos extended and intensified their activities. This abrupt escalation alarmed the government and led to the law of June 12, 1900, which limited zemstvo increases on already taxed immovable property to a maximum of 3 percent annually. Increases above this level required the approval of the provincial governor. Yet in

Table 4.3. *Zemstvo budgets, 1865–1914*

Year	Number of provinces	Amount (millions of rubles)	Percent average annual growth
1865	18	5.6	
1873	34	23.5	
1883	34	41.3	7
1893	34	54.2	3
1903	34	105.0	9
1913	34	253.8	14
1913	40	290.6	
1914	40	336.4	16

Sources: B. B. Veselovskii, *Istoriia zemstva za sorok let*, 4 vols. (St. Petersburg, 1909–11), 1:15; V. F. Karavaev, "Zemskie smety i raskladki (istoricheskii ocherk razvitiia zemskikh biudzhetov)," in B. B. Veselovskii, ed., *Iubileinyi zemskii sbornik* (St. Petersburg, 1914), p. 174; *Zemskoe delo*, 1915, no. 9, p. 579.

the decade between 1903 and 1913 the aggregate zemstvo budget rose by 141 percent (Table 4.3).

There was obviously a negative correlation between peasant participation rates in the zemstvo and the level of zemstvo budgets. Budgets were highest after 1890, when peasant representation was lowest. Some sources of zemstvo income had little to do with the peasantry; however, before turning to the question of the peasants' relationship to zemstvo income, it should be noted that a small part of the zemstvo budget increase was only apparent and not real growth. To the extent that the natural taxes were converted into monetary taxes and introduced into the financial accounts, income appeared higher without a genuine increase in zemstvo resources. Part of the real increase in tax income resulted simply from the rapid growth of population in this period, but the budget inflation far outpaced the population boom. Between 1863 and 1914 the population of European Russia slightly more than doubled;[71] in just about the same period, between 1868 and 1914, zemstvo budgets ballooned from 15 million to 336 million rubles.

Although the regulations of 1864 had given the zemstvos the right to tax industrial and commercial establishments, official concern arose at once over the possible constraining effects of such taxation on industrial development. As a result, a law of November 21, 1866 limited zemstvo taxation of such enterprises to their immovable property: the buildings themselves and the land under them. Inventories and business turnover were excluded from taxation.[72] This and other restrictions made the zemstvos dependent for income on three major categories of fixed taxation (land, other immovable property, and commercial and industrial licenses) and on a group of fees, fines, and payments that they were also entitled to collect. The latter group made up an increasingly important component of the zemstvo budget as time went on, accounting for about a fourth of all income in 1912.[73] Peasants provided the greatest part of this nonfixed income, which included such items as payments for medical care and for other services provided by zemstvos.

Under the category of immovable property, peasants along with others were subject to a house tax, but this was a significant source of zemstvo income only in urban localities. The house tax was used increasingly by district zemstvos in the latter part of the century but accounted for less than 2 percent of zemstvo income in 1900.[74]

Zemstvo taxation of land

The form of immovable property most important to the peasant, and the income category most important to the zemstvo, was land. A tax on land had been added to the soul tax (the most important source of state revenue at the time) in 1853. In 1862 the land tax yielded less than 2 million rubles, a scant 8 percent of state revenues. The Temporary Rules of 1864 established the right of the zemstvo to tax all land defined as "suitable" (*udobnyi*) under the regulations of 1851, that is, all land that was usable, including all land listed in previous tax registers, all arable land, meadowland, steppe, and forest land, whether held by private owners, societies, the state, or appanage proprietors. Land was taxable whether it was populated or not and regardless of whether it was producing income. The level of land taxation was up to the individual zemstvo, and there was considerable local variation in both the rate of taxation and the share of the resultant income in the zemstvo budgets. Among the district zemstvos the tax on land (or "land and forests" as it was usually recorded) supplied anywhere from 3 to 95 percent of income. Almost everywhere the tax was important, and in the majority of provinces the largest part of all zemstvo income was derived from land. Over the course of time the relative weight of income from land in the aggregate budget of the zemstvo dropped, although only very slowly in the first three decades. From the 1890s, however, as other sources of income expanded the share of income from land diminished more rapidly. Yet despite this relative decline, the amount of land tax collected by zemstvos doubled in the first decade of the twentieth century.[75]

If the land tax was the most important single source of zemstvo income, then the peasant was the most important provider of land tax revenues. In the period immediately following the establishment of the

101

zemstvo system the amount of allotment land held by peasants in the zemstvo provinces (70 million desiatinas) was close to the total amount of taxed land (73 million desiatinas) held by private owners or the state in those provinces; and the sum of zemstvo taxes from the peasants' land (4.8 million rubles) was equal to that collected from all the nonallotment land.[76] In 1914 allotment and nonallotment land were again contributing approximately equal shares of the zemstvo land tax.[77] Yet any appearance of equity or stability is misleading. Kornilov, who pointed with pride to the zemstvo's initial "equalization" of payments on allotment land, was inclined to overlook later developments and, for that matter, the explanation behind the earlier distribution of taxes.[78] As Vasilchikov noted, according to the land statistics collected by the editorial commissions at the time of emancipation, the land in the use of the peasantry in 49 provinces amounted to only 20 percent of that classified as "usable." Upon the introduction of the zemstvo and higher land taxes, however, a good deal of forested and unproductive land held by private proprietors and the state was withdrawn from the tax rolls, leaving the peasantry with a full half of the zemstvo tax burden. Later, as land values climbed and as the new zemstvo statisticians sharpened their skills, some of the withdrawn land found its way back onto the tax registers. By the end of the century the amount of state and private land was one and a half times the amount of allotment land in the zemstvo provinces, but allotment land was now providing 60 percent of all zemstvo land taxes.[79] It was only as an increasing share of nonallotment land came into the hands of the peasantry and urbanites that the relative burden on allotment land began to drop, but only back to the initial level. Admittedly, a higher percentage of allotment land than that of state or private land was likely to be "usable" and therefore taxable, but the share of zemstvo land taxes paid by allotment land appears to have been consistently high.

The data on the tax levied on each desiatina of allotment and nonallotment land support this conclusion. Peasant land was consistently taxed at higher rates than other land – in some localities at rates as much as ten times higher.[80] Part of the reason for the differential was the fact that "other land," and especially state land, included more forested and unpopulated lands producing little or no income. Such lands, by law, were subject to a lower rate of taxation. Yet privately owned lands subject to discretionary taxation by local zemstvos were also taxed at rates below those imposed on the peasants' allotment lands. In 1870, for example, when peasant land was taxed an average of 11 kopeks per desiatina, other land was taxed at an average rate of 7

Table 4.4. *Zemstvo income from land, 1868–1914*

Year	Number of provinces	Total income (millions of rubles)	Income from land (millions of rubles)	% of total income from land
1868	18	14.6	9.6	66
1871	34	20.1	13.5	67
1880	34	35.1	22.4	64
1890	34	47.0	29.4	62
1901	34	88.9	47.2	53
1906	34	124.2	64.5	52
1912	34	220.2	102.1	46
1913	34	253.8	112.3	44
1913	40	290.6	130.4	45
1914	40	336.4	142.5	42

Sources: V. F. Karavaev, "Zemskie smety i raskladki (istoricheskii ocherk razvitiia zemskikh biudzhetov)," in B. B. Veselovskii, ed., *Iubileinyi zemskii sbornik* (St. Petersburg, 1914), pp. 168, 172, 176; B. B. Veselovskii, *Istoriia zemstva za sorok let*, 4 vols. (St. Petersburg, 1909–11), 1:35; *Zemskoe delo*, 1915, no. 9, p. 579.

kopeks; in 1885 when peasants were paying 18 kopeks, private owners paid 13 kopeks. In 1903 the ratio was 26:20; in 1906, 37:23; in 1913, 52:47.[81]

The obligation of the zemstvos to take into account the "value and income" of land in setting tax rates left room for local interpretation – and appraisal. Zemstvo taxes ranged from 0.2 to 1.7 percent of the value of land, and from 2 to 29 percent of land income.[82] In 1879 allotment land was appraised higher than private land in almost two-thirds of the 233 districts for which data were published, and private land was higher in only about one-tenth of these districts. Yet private land was more productive in each of 17 grain-producing provinces studied in 1885. In only three of these provinces, however, was private land taxed at a higher rate than allotment land. Data for all 359 district zemstvos in 1890 still showed a higher evaluation of allotment land in two-thirds of all districts, but the market price of private land then, as earlier, contradicted the zemstvo appraisals.[83] Records of the Peasant Land Bank reveal that the average price paid for nobles' land between 1907 and 1910 was 121 rubles per desiatina, whereas peasant land sold for an average of 64 rubles per desiatina; yet peasant land was described at the time as almost universally appraised higher (for zemstvo tax purposes) than private land of comparable income.[84] There was marked regional variation in the differential between zemstvo tax assessments on allotment land and on private land. In the central industrial region, where the nobility had been most noticeably losing zemstvo delegates prior to the 1890 counterreform, the differential was larger than average, and a desiatina of peasant land was assessed at 55 percent above a desiatina of privately owned land. In agricultural regions the tax was higher, but the differential was less.[85]

Not only was there a disparity in the taxation of allotment and nonallotment land, but the allotment land itself was taxed quite differently and often arbitrarily by different zemstvos. Even a uniform rate might prove inequitable, as the work of zemstvo statisticians revealed. In Chernigov province, for example, zemstvo statistics showed that the productivity of a desiatina of land in the northern part of the province was less than that of a quarter of a desiatina in the southern part, and yields could vary by a ratio of five to one within the same district.[86] Land reappraisals carried out in the 1890s by provincial zemstvos helped to iron out some of the most troublesome disparities, but the unevenness of the land tax burden remained a serious problem.

Despite the elimination of the soul tax in the 1880s, the per capita tax on the peasantry was clearly rising in the late nineteenth and early twentieth century, and in the opinion of many contemporaries it was rising far faster than peasant income.[87] Increased indirect taxation, borne mainly by the peasantry, kept the much larger state budget growing at rates comparable to those of the zemstvo budgets, and local tax expenditures rose in the nonzemstvo as well as the zemstvo provinces.[88] Yet taxes were higher where there were zemstvos. In 1885, when taxes on the peasants' allotment land in 14 nonzemstvo provinces averaged 7 kopeks per desiatina, the allotment land tax in the zemstvo provinces averaged 18 kopeks per desiatina.[89]

The zemstvo land tax was especially onerous because it was a highly visible, direct tax and because it was generally considered inequitable.[90] Resistance to zemstvo taxation was highest where the amount of land held per capita was lowest,[91] and throughout the life of the zemstvo the average size of allotment holdings was shrinking due to rapid population growth. Although declining both as a component of zemstvo income and in the share it took of the income produced by land, the zemstvo land tax was still rising at the end both in absolute and per capita terms, with the greatest acceleration occurring in the twentieth century (Table 4.5).

The zemstvo legislation of 1890 had excluded the clergy from participation in the system on the widely accepted grounds that participation in the zemstvo should be limited to those who contributed to zemstvo income. Taxation and representation had been officially joined here, but again proportional equation of the two was no part of the zemstvo scheme. In fact, a suggestion that the two should be

104

Table 4.5. *Zemstvo land tax per capita,*
1868–1914

Year	Number of provinces	Tax per capita (kopeks)
1868	18	24
1885	34	46
1901	34	66
1914	34	125

Sources: Calculated from data in Table 4.4, and in A.
G. Rashin, *Naselenie Rossii za 100 let (1811–1913*
gg.) (Moscow, 1956), pp. 44–5.

more closely joined contributed to the widespread noble opposition to
Stolypin's zemstvo reform proposals. In the final decades of zemstvo
history the urban and industrial sector represented in the second
electoral assembly was contributing an increasingly larger share of
zemstvo income. This group, too, remained relatively underrepresented and, in terms of its zemstvo tax bill, even more so than the
peasantry. But the peasants were clearly less well equipped to support
the burden of taxation with or without representation.

Tax collection and arrears

To the Russian peasant as to most of mankind, one of two sure
harvests was taxation. The grim reaper in this case was the district
policeman. The zemstvo faced some difficulty in tax collection since
the agents on whom it was obliged to rely were entirely beyond its
control. Zemstvo efforts to change the system or to acquire authority
over the police were to no avail. The Senate, in fact, prohibited zemstvo
awards to the police for active cooperation and even forbade expression of thanks to them.[92]

The police collected all fixed taxes for both the state and the
zemstvo, gathering as much as possible of the total tax due and then
allocating it to the state or zemstvo. Under the regulation of 1851 the
zemskie taxes were to be discharged first unless the taxpayer stipulated
otherwise. In 1867 the law was revised, and the sums turned over to the
zemstvo were limited to 12 percent of each collection if the taxpayer
had not specified a different allocation; the rate was equivalent to the
zemstvo share of the total fixed tax bill at that time. Whether from
indifference or ignorance of the law, few taxpayers indicated a different
preference, and in practice the taxes were sent out to the state or the

zemstvo at the discretion of the police. This discretionary authority was employed most often in the allocation of the taxes paid by the peasants' rural societies. Because the zemstvo had no authority with respect to the police, and because arrears in state taxes were punished more severely by higher authorities, the natural tendency of the police was to meet the state tax bill first.[93] Levying taxes was one thing, but collecting them, as the zemstvos discovered, was another.

From the time of the international agricultural troubles of the 1870s the Russian rural economy had experienced mounting problems. The agrarian crisis made it all the more difficult for the peasants (and nobles) to meet the rising tax bills. Reviewing zemstvo taxes in 1871 shortly after the introduction of the new institution, Vasilchikov had concluded that the peasants were not being unreasonably taxed.[94] Yet within a few years observers of the rural scene were pointing to signs of economic stress in the countryside and blaming high taxation as one of the prime causes.[95] By the mid-1880s the tax obligations of the peasantry had grown considerably. Mir taxes alone increased by one-half within the decade.[96] In 1881 redemption payments to the state yielded only 7.6 million rubles, and the alarming number of peasants who were unable to meet their payments prompted the government to grant a substantial reduction in the annual amount due. But from 1883 all peasants who had not yet concluded redemption agreements were obliged to do so and thereby were saddled with redemption payments. By 1891 these amounted to almost 71 million rubles.[97]

As early as 1884 the accumulated arrears on zemstvo ledgers reached half of the budgeted annual fixed tax. Although the total income realized by all zemstvos in the mid-1880s fell only slightly short of their combined actual expenditures, a number of provinces experienced considerable deficits. Collections fell short of assessments for all categories of zemstvo taxpayers; however, the peasants followed next after the state with the best record of payments. The state paid some 85 percent of its zemstvo land tax bill in these years of agrarian crisis; the peasants, about 60 percent.[98]

By the end of the 1880s, due to the state's increasing reliance on indirect rather than fixed taxes, the zemstvo budget claimed a full third of the total fixed tax bill. Since fixed taxes accounted for the major part (75 percent) of the zemstvo budget, many zemstvos began to petition for a revision of the law limiting them to 12 percent of the tax receipts until the full state tax bill had been met. In 1899 zemstvo arrears amounted to 65 percent of the entire sum of fixed taxes budgeted for collection by the zemstvos that year. Arrears on peasant allotment land alone had climbed to 20 million rubles; those on privately owned land came to 10 million. According to Veselovskii's calculations these figures meant an average of 21 kopeks in arrears per desiatina of allotment land and 15 kopeks per desiatina of private land. Because allotment land was assessed about 30 percent higher than private land at this time, he concluded that the peasants' rate of tax payment was approximately the same as that of private landowners. In fact, however, the peasants' rate of payment was far better if their additional tax burdens are taken into consideration. Along with zemstvo land taxes the peasant faced heavy redemption payments and mir taxes for which nonpeasants bore no responsibility. The total tax bill on the 128 million desiatinas of allotment land in the 50 provinces of European Russia in 1899 came to over 173 million rubles, whereas taxes on the 102 million desiatinas of privately owned land amounted to only 20 million rubles (17.6 million to zemstvos and 2.5 million to the state).[99] Under the circumstances, it took special effort to maintain the critical flow of income from peasant land into zemstvo budgets.

The zestvo assemblies could impose fines for late payment (or nonpayment) of taxes, but, again, collecting them was another matter. Their only recourse was the police. Since the peasant commune was collectively responsible for the taxes of each of its members, households that had managed to pay their own share of taxes could be subject to additional exactions or penalties for the nonpayment of others. And as a last resort the police could requisition and sell the movable property of delinquents, including the livestock that was vitally important to the peasant's economy.[100] Such measures obviously did little to increase the tax-paying capacity of a defaulting household but were undertaken partly "*pour encourager les autres.*"

It was the communal peasant rather than the private landowner who was apt to be the target of such exercises, yet it was the private smallholders who defaulted most often. Within the zemstvo there was considerable discussion of possible alternative sanctions against tax delinquents and particularly of the desirability of depriving them of electoral rights. However, objections were raised that such a step would have no effect on private smallholders or on the independent peasant proprietors already disfranchised by the legislation of 1890. Ultimately the matter was dropped, the zemstvos concluding that they had no basis for such a move.[101]

Faced with growing discontent and unmistakable evidence of agrarian economic stress, the government passed a law on March 12, 1903, ending the mutual tax responsibility of the peasants in rural societies; at the same time it rescinded the "12 percent rule." All fixed tax payments and a part of all payments on arrears were to be assigned preferentially now to the zemstvos.[102] A year later, in May 1904, the state treasury assumed fiscal responsibility for all zemstvo arrears on allotment land and agreed to pay the zemstvos the entire sum over the course of the next five years. By this time the arrears had dropped somewhat (to 15 to 16 million rubles), thanks in part to the recent legislation.[103] But redemption payments to the government also had begun to fall off after reaching a high of 101 million rubles in 1895. By 1905 they were down to 76 million.[104]

Continued government financial assistance and the increasing flow of income from other sources helped the zemstvos to maintain a vigorous program of constructive activities but gave little tax relief to the peasantry. When the Revolution of 1905 broke out the peasants were quite prepared to move to their own direct solution to the agrarian problem. In some 66 districts in 1905–6 the peasants refused to pay taxes.[105] The government reacted by canceling the redemption payments (but not the outstanding arrears). Most peasant protests were against taxation in general rather than the zemstvo specifically, but in at least 17 districts the zemstvo was the specific target.

Discontent was concentrated in the non–black soil region (51 of the 66 districts; 15 of the 17), where the greatest difference prevailed between the zemstvo assessments on allotment and private land. There was another interesting feature of the tax situation in this region. Although this was not the area of highest land taxation (that distinction being reserved for the central agricultural region), the troubled central industrial and southern regions had a land tax that was higher per *working male peasant* than anywhere else due to the exodus of part of the male population for outside employment.[106] The rebellious anti-zemstvo peasants protested the estate nature of the institution, the inequity of zemstvo tax, and the excessive rate of zemstvo taxation. Because of their inadequate representation, they complained, they were unable to keep informed about, or even keep an eye on, zemstvo expenditures.[107]

Similar protests against zemstvo taxation were raised on the eve of and during World War I. In Volynia, where zemstvos were new, the governor informed central authorities in May 1914 of widespread and rising peasant discontent, and in reviewing the situation he conceded a certain legitimacy to their complaints.[108] A few months later cases of refusal to pay taxes were reported in Stavropol province, where the zemstvo had just been introduced; 27 rural societies "categorically refused" to distribute zemstvo taxes among their members. According to the governor,

> The dissatisfaction of the rural population with the introduction of the zemstvo was evident almost everywhere in the province shortly after the distribution of the tax lists. The peasants, being insufficiently informed about the tasks and sphere of activity of zemstvo institutions which were only in their first year of existence, noticed the exceptional increase in local taxation.[109]

Having noticed, the peasants promptly declined to send their children to zemstvo schools. They refused to take advantage of zemstvo medical assistance, rejected zemstvo aid to families of soldiers, and in short would have nothing to do with zemstvos. After several clashes with the villagers of Aleksandriia the local land captain ordered a public sale of the movable property of eight peasants who had been particularly active in the opposition to the zemstvo and to the payment of zemstvo taxes. A notice was posted: The sale was to be held in the district seat, the neighboring town of Blagodarnoe, on November 25, 1914. To prevent any disturbance, on November 23, the antizemstvo activists were arrested and dispatched under guard of a policeman to the Blagodarnoe prison. But a short way out of Aleksandriia the group met up with a band of 25 to 30 local peasants who beat off the policeman and returned to the village with the arrested men. There they ran into the volost *starshina* on the street and beat him as well. Part of the growing crowd then went off to threaten a local member of the Blagodarnoe zemstvo bureau, while a smaller group proceeded to incinerate the zemstvo school. That evening a constable, two policemen, and a dozen guards arrived at the village. At dawn small groups of peasants began to assemble, and by noon there was a gathering of 2,000. An attempt by the constable to talk to the crowd proved fruitless. Rocks and sticks were sent flying. After repeated warnings and after a shot from the crowd had wounded one of the policemen in the shoulder (according to the official report), the order was given to open fire on the villagers. The immediate result was three dead and seven wounded peasants.[110] The zemstvo survived.

Ironically, the repeal of mutual responsibility and the post-1905 attack on the commune with the Stolypin agrarian reform made such confrontations between peasant and official Russia more likely and more bitter. Reform policies designed to discourage collective resistance (among other objectives) brought individuals and authorities into conflicts sharpened by the attenuation of mediating institutions.

The events of November 24 at Aleksandriia had strong repercussions throughout the province, and antizemstvo feeling continued to erupt in Stavropol throughout the war. But it could be argued that the case, the wartime circumstances, and local conditions here were exceptional.[111] It is all the more interesting, then, to explore the question of peasant attitudes toward the zemstvo under more normal or, at any rate, different circumstances.

Peasant perspectives on the zemstvo

The "I" of the beholder

It would be as pointless to look for the peasant viewpoint on the zemstvo as to search for the typical peasant. There were potentially as many different opinions as there were peasants, and the variety of local conditions promoted diversity. Nonetheless, certain attitudes appear to have been widely shared among the peasantry. There were, after all, a number of factors – social, economic, cultural, and political – that bound the peasants together, separated them from other social sectors, and contributed to the shaping of uniquely peasant perspectives.

After the emancipation the peasants remained differentiated from the rest of the populace by a number of legal and institutional constraints limiting their rights and encumbering them with special responsibilities. Among these were the "soul tax," the need to fulfill "natural obligations," mutual tax responsibility, restricted property rights and lack of personal mobility in the communal system, subjection to corporal punishment, a separate system of peasant courts based on customary law and standing largely outside the formal legal structure, separate institutions of peasant self-government (the commune and volost), and, of course, representation as an estate within the zemstvo.

Within the relatively brief span of zemstvo history a striking number of these "class barriers" were removed or greatly diminished. The soul tax disappeared from European Russia in the 1880s; natural taxation was clearly on the wane; mutual tax responsibility was cancelled in 1903; and in the following year corporal punishment was ended. The Revolution of 1905 prompted the elimination of many of the remaining restrictions on peasant rights, and agrarian reform made it possible subsequently for peasants to appropriate communal land and/or leave the commune. In 1912 a judicial reform, though retaining the volost court system for peasants, reinstituted the office of the zemstvo-elected justice of the peace, replacing the judicial authority of the land captain.

The one area in which class/estate distinctions not only remained in full force but were actually reinforced was local self-government. The peasants retained their own institutions, and after 1890 their rights of participation in the zemstvo were more sharply limited, while their

fiscal responsibilities steadily increased. It was the dawning perception of the social, economic, and political implications of this situation
that inspired the growing liberal demand for a lower level, "all-class"
zemstvo unit in the final decades of Imperial Russia. But well before
the implications of the situation became apparent to others, the
situation had impressed itself upon the peasants. Their reaction can be
traced through contemporary reports.

Peasant attitudes

The opening of zemstvo institutions appears to have elicited a
certain amount of interest among the peasantry. Enthusiasm ran high in
some areas and in some social quarters; mothers, it is said, took their
children to the early zemstvo assemblies to develop their civic consciousness.[112] Although some rural societies proved reluctant to choose
electors,[113] the general attitude seems to have been one of curiosity and
guarded optimism. Initially, the peasants were not sure what to expect,
and even after the introduction of the local zemstvo they often
remained unsure of its nature and functions. In the early stages of
zemstvo activity such measures as the conversion of natural obligations
into monetary taxes enlisted lively peasant support. The first years also
witnessed charitable work that won popular approval. With emancipation many former house serfs found themselves abruptly deprived of
employment. These unfortunates had no claim to allotment land, and,
lacking economic resources, they became a serious problem in some
localities. The new zemstvos helped to organize public welfare assistance on their behalf and gained good will as a result.[114] But as time went
by peasant interest waned; and, as the populist ardor of the 1870s
abated, disappointed reformers began to complain of the "apathy" and
"indifference" of the peasants toward the zemstvo. In the opinion of
contemporaries, the rural masses viewed it as an alien intrusion into
the countryside. Although the government – at least initially – saw the
zemstvo as standing apart from the regular bureaucratic administrative
system, the peasants came to see it as just another arm of officialdom.[115]

Critics faulted the peasantry for lack of understanding of the institution. Yet if the peasants failed to appreciate the ultimate purpose of the
zemstvo, they understood well enough some of its immediate effects.
Observers agreed on the peasants' reaction: "All they understand about
the zemstvo is that it imposes additional taxes."[116] "Local [tax] rates
have been rising with alarming rapidity, and many people draw from
all this the conclusion that the zemstvo is a worthless institution which
has increased the taxation without conferring any corresponding

benefit on the country...The most commonplace complaint made against it is that it has enormously increased the [tax] rate." [117] "The zemstvo, which takes heavy taxes, gives back too little of benefit to the local population."[118] "In the election of delegates the muzhik sees only a new natural obligation...If the zemstvo were completely annihilated tomorrow the peasantry, en masse, would most definitely make no complaint about a loss of rights, but rather would feel a certain relief."[119]

Obviously, the zemstvo provided important local services in return for its exactions, and these services became more obvious, even to the peasants, as time went on and the scope of zemstvo activity expanded. But the peasants often complained that the zemstvos were out of touch with rural realities. In effect, they hurled the charge of "lack of understanding" right back at their educated critics. Writing to *Moskovskie vedomosti* in 1889, a zemstvo delegate complained that the peasants had no comprehension of such principles as representative government, equality before the law, or free trade.[120] But in 1905 a peasant correspondent complained to the same paper of zemstvo inattentiveness to peasant needs and charged that the zemstvo failed even to comprehend rural problems. True enough, conceded this literate rustic, some important gains had been achieved in such areas as education and medicine. "But is this a contribution of the zemstvo workers? I don't see it that way. Both here and elsewhere, the engine lever was the *means* – the pocket of the taxpayer."[121]

A certain failure in communication seems evident, and that impression is deepened by the arguments of activists justifying zemstvo taxation. In a committee reporting to Witte's Special Conference on the Needs of Agriculture in the early years of the century the point was made (with reference to the "3 percent" law of 1900) that it was ridiculous to impose limits on zemstvo taxation since the zemstvo was composed of local residents who were taxing themselves and obviously would not raise taxes beyond local capacity.[122] Zemstvo taxes were said to be the least burdensome of all direct taxes, both in extent and because they went to satisfy local needs.[123] The argument had merit but fell short of persuading most peasants. True, the zemstvo members were taxing themselves, but the effective majority of members consisted of nobles whose lands were not already encumbered with the additional taxes imposed on peasants. Peasants viewed the commune and the volost as "their own." The commune in particular also served the peasants' local needs, competing in the process for the peasants' tax rubles. In the decade between 1881 and 1891, when the zemstvo budget rose by 26 percent, the total budget of volosts in the 34 zemstvo

Table 4.6. *Mir expenditures in zemstvo and nonzemstvo provinces, 1881 and 1891, in millions of rubles*

Year	34 zemstvo provinces			12 nonzemstvo provinces		
	Volosts	Communes	Total	Volosts	Communes	Total
1881	10.8	15.4	26.2	4.3	1.9	6.2
1891	12.8	21.7	34.5	5.1	3.6	8.7
Percent growth	19	40	32	21	85	41

Source: Calculated from data in A. N. Diadchenko, ed., *Statisticheskii sbornik. Finansy*, 2d ed. (St. Petersburg, 1906), pp. 88–91.

provinces rose about 20 percent, while that of communes climbed by 40 percent. Between 1891 and 1905 communal taxes almost doubled (Table 4.6).[124]

The peasants' tax problem was not only – or even primarily – the fault of the zemstvo, but they could easily fail to appreciate that fact. When things went wrong, it was easy to blame the zemstvo. One of the sorest points in the village was the matter of property seizures for tax arrears. The impact of such confiscations is portrayed in Chekhov's 1897 tale, "Peasants." For inability to pay their taxes, the impoverished villagers described here are deprived of their last comfort, the household samovar. Later, they sit about ruminating on local affairs. Some hens and sheep, seized similarly from other families, had died for subsequent lack of care on the part of local officials.

And now the question was being settled: who was to blame?
"The zemstvo!" said Osip. "Who else?"
"It's well known, the zemstvo."
The zemstvo was blamed for everything – for the arrears, and for the oppressions, and for the crop failures, although not a one of them knew just what was meant by the zemstvo. And this came about from the time when rich muzhiks with factories, shops, and inns served as zemstvo deputies, became dissatisfied, and then began to inveigh against the zemstvo in their factories and taverns...
Earlier, fifteen or twenty or more years ago, conversations in Zhukhovo were a lot more interesting. In those days every old man looked as if he were guarding some sort of secret, knew something, and was waiting for something. They used to talk about a charter with a golden seal, about a redistribution of land, about new lands, about hidden treasures; they hinted at something. Nowadays, though, the villagers had no secrets whatsoever, their whole life was an open book, and they could talk only of need and food, and of the fact that there was no snow...

They grew silent. And once again they remembered the hens and sheep, and began to decide who was to blame.

"The zemstvo!" said Osip dejectedly. "Who else!"[125]

Zemstvo land taxes amounted to less than a quarter of all the direct taxes levied on the agricultural population of European Russia, but the peasants' allotment land paid 90 percent of all direct taxes, and due to the system of tax collection the peasant was not likely to draw much distinction between zemstvo and state direct taxes.[126]

Indirect taxes were another question, and one that was raised by the Kostroma district zemstvo board in the local conference committee. Board members were concerned about government motives in shifting to indirect taxation and with the implications of the shift for the zemstvo. At the very time the state had limited the zemstvo's right to raise taxes, they pointed out, it had itself raised the price of vodka in connection with the introduction of the state monopoly. This created an additional 96 million rubles in indirect taxes, and the increase alone was 8 million rubles higher than the entire zemstvo budget for all 34 provinces in 1900.[127] The Kostroma representatives feared that state fiscal policy was aimed at curtailing zemstvo activity rather than helping the taxpayer. But whatever other policy objectives were served, indirect taxes were less obvious to taxpayers and therefore promised to be less troublesome politically. To the peasant, however, zemstvo taxes remained a burden of conspicuous and growing magnitude.

While some nonzemstvo areas petitioned for the introduction of zemstvos, the Don Cossacks, who had received them in 1875, petitioned Alexander III for their removal (successfully). Noting that the populace of the Don region was predominantly peasant, Leroy-Beaulieu attributed its hostility to the zemstvo to the discovery that "the new-fangled institutions did not really pay." And, he added, "The people in many provinces would be of the same opinion if asked."[128]

The opinion of the peasantry was not frequently consulted, but it could become important at election time to would-be zemstvo deputies. There were reports of peasant votes being "bought" with vodka and of peasants pressured by local bureaucrats to elect acceptable deputies.[129] Peasants who actually took part in the zemstvo as deputies were in the best position to understand how the institution could serve peasant interests and to interpret it to the rest of the peasant population. Despite the negative impression conveyed by so many contemporary observers, it seems clear that there was some active support for the zemstvos among the peasant third of the district zemstvo membership. Individual cases of zemstvo activism among the peasantry were not unknown and, as observed above, both before 1890 and after 1905 the peasant proprietors appear to have participated with some interest.

Yet the peasant landowners were a special, small group, and on the whole the role of peasants in the zemstvos appears to have been quite limited. Some contemporaries considered this appropriate and contended that the low cultural level of the peasantry would make any broader participation harmful. But others disagreed. In 1902 a member of the Krasnoiarsk conference committee insisted that more peasants be brought into the zemstvo. The villagers, he argued, were used to working together on public affairs in their communes and were therefore actually better prepared for zemstvo activity than members of the intelligentsia or the commercial class. Far more experienced in matters of local self-government, the peasant was more of a "zemstvo person."[130]

Peasant delegates within the zemstvos

A vivid description of zemstvo sessions was penned by that venturesome Scot, Donald MacKenzie Wallace, who studied and actually worked in Russian zemstvos for some time. Arriving in Novgorod in 1870, Wallace soon had the opportunity to attend the annual meeting of the local district zemstvo. His observations are of interest:

> I found thirty or forty men seated around a long table covered with green cloth. Before each member lay sheets of paper for the purpose of taking notes...When any decided difference of opinion appeared, a vote was taken by handing around a sheet of paper, or by the simpler method of requesting the Ayes to stand up and the Noes to sit still.
>
> What surprised me most in this assembly was that it was composed partly of nobles and partly of peasants – the latter being decidedly in the majority – and that no trace of antagonism seemed to exist between the two classes. Landed proprietors and their ci-devant serfs, emancipated only ten years before, evidently met for the moment on a footing of equality. The discussions were carried on chiefly by the nobles, but on more than one occasion peasant members rose to speak, and their remarks, always clear, practical, and to the point, were invariably listened to with respectful attention. Instead of that violent antagonism which might have been expected...there was too much unanimity – a fact indicating plainly that the majority of the members did not take a very deep interest in the matters presented to them.[131]

A few months later Wallace was present at the assembly of the provincial zemstvo and found its general character and procedures quite similar. He was surprised, however, to find that the number of peasant deputies here was very small, especially since he knew that the provincial deputies were elected by and from the members of the district zemstvo. The explanation he was offered was that the district assemblies simply chose their most active members to represent them. The peasants were content with this arrangement, he was told, because attendance at provincial sessions was costly for them.

The Novgorod zemstvo was generally regarded as one of the best (and rightly so, as Wallace was later to confirm through personal experience). Prince Vasilchikov was one of the members here, and his colleagues included other public-spirited zemstvo enthusiasts. Elsewhere, the zemstvo functioned less ideally, although generally without the overt conflict between peasant deputies and their recent masters that some had initially anticipated.[132] Many of the peasant deputies were among the elected peasant "elders" originally earmarked for co-optation into zemstvos by the Valuev Comission; and many appear to have been among the wealthier peasants of the villages. In the later years especially, some were peasants by legal status only, having moved into trade or industry.[133] Given the expense of participation, this was only to be expected. As Wallace had learned, service in the zemstvo was apt to be costly for the average peasant even at the district level and far more so at the provincial capital. The possibility of reimbursement for per diem and travel expenses was one of the questions raised frequently by peasant members. In some cases this was arranged, but it required special authorization. The better-off villagers and the peasant officials who were already receiving some payment for their public service were clearly in the best position to participate in the zemstvos without (or with tolerable) personal loss. Another factor promoting the candidacy of these categories of peasants (and of the rural clergy also before 1890) was their generally higher rate of literacy. The illiterate peasant confronted with those sheets of paper for notes or votes was clearly at a disadvantage in the zemstvo among his educated peers.

However, despite their lack of formal education and the complaints of their critics, many peasants, as Wallace and others indicate, followed zemstvo discussions intelligently and showed a clear grasp of the issues raised. Zemstvo journals record a pattern of peasant interest in practical improvements coupled with a strong insistence on cost control. Peasants supported lower schools but opposed expenditures for higher schools as less essential to their immediate needs. They called for greater agronomic assistance and more medical aid. They discussed means of easing migration and spoke of the need to reform volost courts and improve volost administration.

On the other hand, peasants were often allied with the more conservative elements within the zemstvo and not only when it came to guarding the purse-strings. Interestingly enough, the peasants do not appear to have taken a prominent role in zemstvo discussions on the repeal of corporal punishment and in fact often called for sanctions of exceptional severity, for example, the banishment of discredited zemstvo members to Siberia or the introduction of harsher punishment for horse thieves.[134] And, as noted above, peasant delegates on the whole were opposed to the extension of political rights to women.

By all accounts the peasants' greatest single concern within the zemstvo was the general level of expenditures, and particularly the peasant share of the tax burden. Although some enthusiasts welcomed the expansion of zemstvo activities, an overriding preoccupation with costs made most peasant deputies cautious about innovations or extensions of programs. Their persistent attempts to limit and equalize taxation led observers to the conclusion that "to the extent that they were active in the zemstvo, the peasants were a constraining element."[135]

But there was also a widespread impression that the peasants themselves were under considerable constraint in the zemstvo. Some of this was internal, the result of social and cultural conditioning. According to some observers, peasant deputies were inarticulate and incapable of defending their interests by reasoned argument. They were unused to asserting their rights and seldom spoke up. They were at a loss to understand the foreign phrases and technical terms with which the speeches of some of their colleagues were embellished. As a result, they hung back in debate, uneasy in the presence of their "betters," and hung together in general, apart from the rest of the members. Such descriptions recall Miasoedov's 1872 painting of peasant deputies segregated at lunch. The interpretation accompanying the reproduction of that work in a standard Soviet history of Russian art is tendentious in claiming that it exposes "all the hypocrisy of the zemstvo reform," but a social message is suggested by the painting itself.[136] Despite Wallace's charming word portrait of former serfs and their masters rubbing comradely elbows on the green baize in Novgorod, the situation was rather different in other localities where peasant deputies were described as just "furniture" in zemstvo halls.[137]

Yet the passivity of the peasants was by no means their fault alone. Some constraints were external. There were cases when official pressure was brought to bear on them quite openly, when elections were "arranged" by local authorities, and even when the peasant deputies were simply appointed by the authorities in violation of the law. Peasant deputies were known to have been harassed in and out of zemstvo meetings: in one case a volost *starshina* on his way to take part in a Smolensk provincial zemstvo was arrested by the local police for inadequate collection of taxes from the peasants. In Riazan province, a peasant deputy was flogged by the police on his return from the provincial zemstvo.[138] Others were sent directly from the meeting hall to jail. Such instances appear to have been uncommon, but they point to the existence of pervasive, if less evident, forms of intimidation.

The situation of peasant deputies deteriorated with the introduction of the land captain in 1889, and the subjection of the peasantry to his authority. The Statute of 1864 had excluded local police from zemstvo membership – for good reason. But the land captain was often a member, and after 1889 the peasant "elders" under his administrative control almost completely lost their independence in the zemstvo. Reports to the special conference committees in 1902 reveal the widespread nature of the problem. Samara: "The peasant dignitary in the presence of his immediate superior is hardly going to be able to summon the heroism to stand in direct contradiction to the latter's interests." Tula: "The peasant deputies feel constrained in the presence of their immediate superior, the land captain." Riazan: "The peasant deputies are afraid of falling into a difference of opinion with their superior. A case is known when a peasant *starshina* who wanted to speak got a disapproving sign from his captain and sat down." "The deputies from the rural societies are rarely independent and usually vote in unison with their land captains." Kharkov: Deputies from the peasantry have "lost all independence and become playthings in the hands of the land captains seated in the zemstvo."[139] "At the present time," wrote one commentator, "frequently all business in the district zemstvo is dispatched by the magical pencil of the land captain: the pencil stands – and the peasant deputies stand; the pencil lies still – and the peasants sit still."[140] At the Congress of the All-Russian Peasant Union held in Moscow in the late spring of 1905, as popular disaffection mounted, the peasants themselves vigorously voiced their complaints about this state of affairs. "The only peasants permitted to be deputies are the down-trodden or stupid extortionists, the volost *starshiny* beloved of the land captains."[141]

Peasants who showed signs of independence or refused to cooperate with the authorities could easily be replaced with others from the candidate lists. After 1906 the lists disappeared, but the land captains remained and the zemstvos were swept by a conservative reaction that

118

harbored an atmosphere of open hostility to the recently rebellious peasantry.[142] Under such conditions it is hardly surprising that the peasants displayed scant interest in the zemstvo. Absenteeism was a common and persistent problem, although not confined to the peasantry alone. Wallace spoke of "thirty or forty men" at the Novgorod district meeting, when there were 50 members in that zemstvo. But that turnout represented excellent attendance, as zemstvos went. Poor attendance had been something of a problem from the start, but the problem grew worse with time. At the first meeting of the Chernigov provincial assembly in 1865, only 5 peasants put in an appearance, although 12 had been elected.[143] In the final years of the zemstvo's history it was often difficult to obtain an attendance of half of the deputies at zemstvo sessions even in Novgorod, and in some localities so little interest was shown in the zemstvos that concerned officials took to jailing peasants for nonparticipation in elections.[144] Yet if indifference was the rule among the peasants in some areas, it was by no means a universal rule. There were a few provinces where the peasants themselves ran the zemstvos, and these "peasant zemstvos" were characterized by a number of unique features.

The "peasant zemstvos"

Under the legislation of 1864 there were almost 50 districts where peasants were allotted at least 50 percent of the district zemstvo deputies because of the low number of private landholders in the area. Following the changes of 1890 the number of such "peasant" districts dropped to 32; but in these the peasants predominated even more highly, and in 5 of them *all* deputies were peasants. Most of the zemstvos with a predominance of peasant deputies were located in four provinces in the north and northeast: Olonets, Vologda, Viatka, and Perm. The zemstvos in this region became known as "peasant zemstvos." Due in part to their social composition, and even more to another peculiarity that soon became apparent, they attracted a great deal of attention. The peasant zemstvos, it turned out, had remarkably high levels of expenditure.[145]

The situation here seemed to refute the opinion gaining ground elsewhere that the peasants opposed zemstvo spending. Consequently, those who wanted to expand zemstvo services took to buttressing their arguments with references to the record of the peasant zemstvos. It was the per capita outlay of the peasant zemstvos that was relatively high, and especially so in education. Viatka took the lead here, devoting a substantial part of its zemstvo income to this purpose, and the other peasant zemstvos followed close behind. Leroy-Beaulieu advertised the situation in words sure to warm the heart of a Russian liberal or a modern educator: "The greater the number of peasant representatives in a provincial assembly, the greater the sacrifices made in favor of rural schools...These peasants themselves, generally so entirely unlettered, uninformed, give their poor substance freely in order that their children may be taught."[146]

Where other zemstvos typically spent more for medicine than education, the peasant zemstvos reversed the order of priorities and placed schooling – particularly elementary education – in first place. This was hardly because medical needs were less urgent in the northern provinces. At a time when the Russian infant mortality rate was a dismal 55 percent, the rate in Viatka was 64 percent.[147] Wallace opined that the zeal of the zemstvo liberals for popular education, though well intended, was a bit misplaced. Such problems as roads and agricultural aid required more immediate attention in his judgment. But it is hard to believe that the practical peasants and businessmen in the peasant zemstvos were seduced by liberal theories of the good society when they invested their limited resources in education. In these sprawling, lightly populated provinces where the land was often of low agricultural value, an investment in human capital promised the greatest return, and the commercial and industrial pursuits of many deputies enhanced their appreciation of the importance of literacy. Here, even more than elsewhere, the peasants were likely to be "kulaks" involved in local trade.[148]

The peasant zemstvos kept the cost of zemstvo administration relatively low, thanks to concentration in relatively few but large zemstvo centers and because of the low wages they paid their employees. But these zemstvos also profited from the labors of large numbers of the "third element" among their membership and staff. In many of the peasant zemstvos, especially Perm and Viatka, local community residents employed in various occupations (engineers, industrialists, pharmacists, doctors, foresters, agronomists, and peasant-agriculturalists) contributed their efforts to zemstvo projects as public service.

One important factor promoting the growth of civic spirit in the peasant zemstvos was their freedom from the blight of land captains. The 1889 reform introduced the office in the peasant provinces as elsewhere but because of the shortage of local nobles, bureaucrats had been sent out to fill the posts. These envoys were not ordinarily elected to the local zemstvo and therefore had less opportunity to influence its activities. The history of the peasant zemstvos, then, suggests that the peasants in general would have responded more positively to the zemstvo had they been permitted to play a larger role in the institution – larger in terms of participation and freedom from administrative pressure. However, the experience of these zemstvos does not necessarily prove that the peasants were prepared – or able – to pay for these privileges.

Although the expenditure rate of the peasant zemstvos was high, there were three good reasons for this, reasons which had little to do with any readiness on the part of the peasants to accept higher taxes. In the first place, the fact that the population was more dispersed made it more expensive to provide services here. Higher per capita expenditure did not necessarily buy more or better education. This does not alter the fact that these zemstvos were willing to meet their special needs or the fact that they gave high priority to education in their budgets. But the source of budget income was another and an important peculiarity of the peasant zemstvos. In the provinces where they were located there was an unusually large amount of state land. This land was taxed steeply by the local zemstvos and brought in considerable revenue, so much, in fact, that some peasant zemstvos were known as "zemstvos on the treasury account."[149] In Olonets the land tax alone brought in 85 percent of all zemstvo income.[150] Thus taxation in the peasant zemstvos involved more than self-taxation: there was a unique opportunity here to take advantage of "matching funds," and it was intelligently exploited. Finally, because these peasants were able to retain effective control over zemstvo expenditures, they were more willing to transfer functions and tax accounts from their communes and volosts to the zemstvos. Part of the expansion of the peasant zemstvo's role and the growth of its budget simply reflected this transfer operation. This meant that the competition of local institutions for tax rubles and the confusion of overlapping spheres of activity could be, if not eliminated, at least reduced. Local self-government was less at odds with itself here: stresses that impaired the rest of the zemstvo system were absent or relieved in the peasant zemstvos. Possibly the all-class volost zemstvo finally created in 1917 would have similarly relieved some of the stresses in the institutional structure of local self-government had it survived. But the history of the relationship between the peasantry and the zemstvo suggests that the structure itself was propped on weakening foundations.

The consent of the governed

The possibility that the volost zemstvo would lead to more active popular support for the zemstvo system hinged on the representation and role offered the peasantry. Most advocates of the "small all-class zemstvo unit" took it for granted that the volost zemstvo would provide a broader popular base for the zemstvo system. But there was also a possibility that it would open a path to even greater gentry control over the countryside.[151] Despite administrative surveillance and pressure, the all-peasant institutions of self-government had enjoyed a degree of autonomy in some spheres of activity. And, paradoxically enough, the "class principle" had from the start guaranteed the peasants a measure of zemstvo representation which, however limited, might not otherwise have been achieved under prevailing circumstances.[152] Yet democratization imposed by autocratic fiat has its limitations.

The thesis that government rests on the consent of the governed is among the many debatable propositions advanced in theories of political science. Yet it is difficult to imagine a viable system of *self*-government that does not rest on the consent of the governed. As noted at the beginning of this discussion, the governed in the case of zemstvo Russia were, for the most part, peasants.

In 1861, when it became necessary to replace the serf order with a system of local administration more appropriate to a modern state, the central authorities faced a set of contradictory imperatives. On the one hand, they were determined to compensate the nobility and enable it to maintain local authority. On the other, however, the reformers were persuaded of the necessity for popular participation in local self-government. The zemstvo system was an attempt to reconcile these objectives; in many ways it was an imaginative and far-reaching attempt, and to some extent it was successful. Through manipulation of the property qualification, the nobility was guaranteed control of the system while the peasants could be reassured that they had received "equal" representation. Yet, the limited resources available to the zemstvo, the way it assessed taxes, and the system of tax collection in general left the peasants feeling that the zemstvo was a luxury they could ill afford.

Retention of exclusively peasant institutions at the lower levels made the zemstvo appear superfluous, alien, and a competitor for local tax funds. The commune and the volost had a prior claim on the peasants' loyalties and resources. It is significant that the mir taxes, although considerably higher than zemstvo fixed taxes near the end of the nineteenth century, had far lower arrears.[153] The growth of mir expenditures, and especially of commune budgets, in the 1880s revealed that the peasantry was taking a more active role in local economic administration; but the counterreform of 1890 guaranteed that the role would remain outside of the zemstvo. At the time of the Great Reforms, publicists had written glowingly of an historic tie between the zemstvo and the mir. The two terms, it was said, were once synonymous. Both were used to describe associations based on the land and on the common need for it that made all men equal, and drew them together. The word zemstvo, like the word mir, wrote the populist historian Shchapov in 1862, meant a union of men, brotherhood.[154] A half-century later the promise of the rhetoric and of the name remained unfulfilled. Despite the disappearance of many of the legal barriers dividing Russian society, the peasants remained segregated in their "mir" institutions, and separated within the zemstvo.

There were three sets of tensions at play in rural Russia, all deriving from unresolved inconsistencies, and all operating within the system of local self-government. The first was the social tension between the two major rural estates: the peasantry and the nobility. Closely allied to this was the economic tension highlighted by the establishment of a zemstvo to deal with common local economic interests, but a zemstvo whose electorate was nonetheless divided into three separate economic categories. Finally, there was the institutional tension resulting from the incongruity in the administrative hierarchy between the lower-level all-peasant organizations and the "all-class" zemstvo above them.

The more democratic objectives of the reformers were jettisoned in the counterreform. The peasants did not graduate into a larger role in self-government as the result of their apprenticeship in the zemstvo but were demoted to stricter tutelage in 1889/90. In this at least, there was a measure of consistency and a line of continuity in policy that extended back even beyond 1762: rural self-government in Russia had tradition-ally meant noble self-government. When the Duma accepted a proposal to introduce zemstvos in Arkhangelsk province, the State Council rejected the project on the ground that there was no governing estate there, no nobility.[155] The government clearly did not look on the zemstvo as a peasant institution (peasant zemstvos notwithstanding), and the peasants were inclined to agree. The result was that the peasants identified their interests with neither the zemstvos nor the central government. This was surely one of the factors that made it easier for the governed to part company with the government in 1917.

If the imperial government remained unchanged to the end in some of its attitudes, the same can be said of the peasants. A report on the introduction of the zemstvo in Orenburg in late 1914 recalls another time of troubles at the opposite end of the Romanovs' reign. The recalcitrant rustics were refusing to pay taxes, reported the governor, and insisting that they had no need of zemstvos. In fact, they fell back on a tried and true–enough formula, announcing that the tsar himself did not want zemstvos either: it was only the bureaucrats who were forcing them on the peasants.[156] Rebels "in the name of the tsar" are a familiar phenomenon in Russian history, and even the tsar's bureaucrats understood that invocation of the name was only a device to legitimate resistance. But resistance, however legitimate, is far from consent. Considering the limited extent of their participation and the seemingly unlimited price they were being charged for zemstvo progress, the peasants' attitude is hardly surprising. Lenin stated that the Russian peasant was poorest of all in consciousness of his own poverty.[157] Yet, when it came to the zemstvo, the peasants showed themselves quite aware of their poverty. It was others who were apt to be unconscious of peasant financial problems. When the draft law on the volost zemstvo came up for discussion in the Duma in December 1916, K. A. Gorodilov, a "right" peasant deputy, argued against the project, stating that it was impossible to establish a volost zemstvo without the consent of the volost and communal assemblies. "The volost zemstvo will give rise to many expenses. Are we going to give those who come back from the war only a volost zemstvo in return for their service? A lot they need a volost zemstvo!"[158]

When the volost zemstvo finally was introduced in 1917, some of its supporters appeared totally oblivious to peasant concerns. A popular pamphlet that extolled the advantages of the new organ and contrasted it favorably with the "unruly" commune concluded with a casual – almost incidental – remark that the "monetary–tax side" of volost zemstvo affairs had not yet been resolved.[159] After the October Revolution, as the commune experienced a spontaneous and dramatic revival, the zemstvo was eliminated with the consent – and to the relief – of most of the governed.[160]

The picture of the zemstvo and the peasantry that has emerged here was shaped by the questions chosen for investigation. A study focused on the benefits secured for peasants with zemstvo tax rubles would doubtless convey a more positive picture. The historical balance sheet on the zemstvo must include the sum of benefits as well as costs, but the debit side of the record appears to have had less attention than it merits. This neglect is due to the fact that most of the literature on the zemstvo is the product of liberal historiography. The liberals projected their aspirations for a more democratic order onto the zemstvo, viewed it as the institutional embodiment of their hopes, and presented it as such in their writings. Their enthusiasm led them to overlook some awkward realities. As the historian Kliuchevskii had observed of his

124

contemporaries in the 1870s, the enthusiasts were so eagerly watching the reforms change the past that they failed to notice how the past was changing the reforms.[161]

The zemstvo experiment was a bold venture and, in more than one sense, a noble enterprise.[162] But new enterprises were appearing on the Russian scene, and the zemstvo itself contributed to their emergence by promoting education and providing employment for the new professionals. Not only the peasantry but the burgeoning middle class was inadequately represented in the zemstvo, and a growing industrial labor force of former peasants had no voice at all in the institution. The zemstvo presented an unparalleled opportunity to integrate Russian society and to integrate state and society, but the principles on which integration might have been possible were contradictory to those on which the social and political systems rested. The symbiotic bond between the autocracy and the nobility was maintained to the end, with a tenacity that imposed serious constraints on the development of local self-government in Russia.

Notes

1 See V. V. Garmiza, *Podgotovka zemskoi reformy, 1864 goda* (Moscow, 1957), esp. chs. 2, 3.

2 S. Frederick Starr, *Decentralization and Self-Government in Russia, 1830–1870* (Princeton, 1972), pp. 241–88.

3 Garmiza, p. 235.

4 S. Ia. Tseitlin, "Zemskaia reforma," in *Istoriia Rossii v XIX veke*, 9 vols. (St. Petersburg, n.d.), 3:197.

5 Garmiza, p. 213. Data from A. F. Fortunatov, *Raspredelenie pozemel'noi sobstvennosti v evropeiskoi Rossii* (Moscow, 1886).

6 Garmiza, p. 237.

7 Ibid., p. 219.

8 Tseitlin, pp. 227–28; Garmiza, 218, 236–7.

9 L. G. Zakharova, *Zemskaia kontrreforma 1890 g.* (Moscow, 1968), p. 102.

10 L. Demis, comp., *Zemstvo. Politiko-ekonomicheskii sbornik* (St. Petersburg, 1864), p. 117. This is a useful collection of legislative materials. The general statute is in the *Polnoe Sobranie Zakonov Rossiiskoi Imperii (PSZRI)*, 2d series, vol. 39, pt. 1, no. 40457 (1864).

11 According to Tseitlin, p. 229, the State Council viewed this as a temporary provision, but it continued in force up to the repeal of the Statute of 1864.

12 Tseitlin, p. 229. The schedule detailed the local quota for each curia and gave the total number of delegates for each province but omitted the totals for the separate curias in an apparent attempt to avoid publicization of the noble plurality.

13 Zakharova, p. 22.
14 B. B. Veselovskii, *Istoriia zemstva za sorok let* 4 vols. (St. Petersburg, 1909–11), 3:49.
15 Zakharova, p. 171n.
16 Veselovskii, 3: 49.
17 *PSZRI*, 2d series, vol. 39, pt. 1, no. 40934 (1864), articles 63, 76.
18 Veselovskii, 3: 57.
19 V. Skalon, "Zemskie uchrezhdeniia" *Entsiklopedicheskii slovar'* (Brokgauz-Efron), vol. 12, pp. 536, 538; Veselovskii, 3:434, 681.
20 Veselovskii, 3:673.
21 Ibid., 4:181; L. G. Mamulova [Zakharova], "Sotsial'nyi sostav uezdnykh zemskikh sobranii v 1865–1886 godakh," *Vestnik Moskovskogo universiteta*, 1962, no. 6, p. 38, table 2. Data for 24 provinces; comparable data are not available for 1865–7; Zakharova, pp. 170–71.
22 A. G. Rashin, *Naselenie Rossii za 100 let (1811–1913 gg.)* (Moscow, 1956), p. 45.
23 Zakharova, p. 22, table 3.
24 Ibid., pp. 18–19, 170–1.
25 Veselovskii, 4:181.
26 Mamulova, p. 39.
27 A. A. Kornilov, *Kurs istorii Rossii XIX veka*, 2d ed., 3 vols. (Moscow, 1918), 3:154. According to N. P. Oganovskii, ed., *Sel'skoe khoziaistvo Rossii v XX veke. Statisticheskii sbornik* (Moscow, 1923), p. 58, peasants held 8 percent of private land in 1877 and 14 percent in 1887.
28 Veselovskii, 3:50.
29 Ibid., 3:670–1.
30 Kornilov, 3:302.
31 Zakharova, p. 101.
32 Veselovskii, 3:673.
33 Zakharova, p. 102.
34 Veselovskii, 3:355.
35 Veselovskii, 3:434, 680–1.
36 TsGIA, f. 1288, Ministerstvo vnutrennikh del, Glavnoe upravlenie po delam mestnogo khoziaistva, op. 3, d. 77, *Lichnyi sostav zemskikh uprav Saratovskoi gubernii*, pp. 19–34, 91.
37 TsGIA, f. 1288, op. 3, d. 3 (1912) *Ob izmenenii chisla zemskikh glasnykh*, p. 3; d. 29 (1912) *O sozyvakh gubernskikh i uezdnykh zemskikh sobranii Viatskoi gubernii*, p. 21.
38 V. D. Kuzmin-Karavaev, *Zemstvo i derevnia: 1898–1903* (St. Petersburg, 1904), p. 348.
39 Veselovskii, 4:35.
40 *PSZRI*, 3d ser., vol. 26, pt. 1, no. 28392 (1906); Veselovskii, 4:177–8.
41 N. I. Lazarevskii, "Zemskoe izbiratel'noe pravo," in B. B. Veselovskii, ed., *Iubileinyi zemskii sbornik* (St. Petersburg, 1914), p. 66.

42 The last set of regular zemstvo elections took place in 1914. Elections scheduled for 1915 and 1916 were successively postponed, and the government was contemplating a further postponement when overtaken by revolution in 1917. The terms of previously elected delegates were extended to keep the zemstvo functioning; in some cases partial elections were held to fill vacancies that occurred, especially due to the military drain, and at times the government simply appointed individuals to vacancies. TsGIA, f. 1288, op. 3, d. 19, p. 2, and d. 8, p. 92 (postponement of zemstvo elections in 1915); d. 14, pp. 129, 132 (postponement in 1916).

43 B. B. Veselovskii, "Ocherednye zemskie zadachi," *Sovremennik*, May, 1913, p. 302.

44 B. B. Veselovskii, comp., *Kalendar'-spravochnik zemskogo deiatelia na 1914* (St. Petersburg, 1914), pp. 53–4.

45 *Zemskoe delo*, 1915, no. 8, p. 516.

46 TsGIA, f. 1288, op. 3, d. 9a (information on zemstvo elections for the term 1913–16), pp. 91–4, 134–45, 192–9 (Kostroma, Tula, Iaroslavl); d. 9, ch. 2, pp. 346–7 (Kharkov); d. 90, pp. 19–33 (Vladimir).

47 Ruth D. MacNaughton and Roberta Thompson Manning, "The Crisis of the Third of June System and Political Trends in the Zemstvo, 1907–1914," in Leopold H. Haimson, *The Politics of Rural Russia, 1905–1914* (Bloomington, 1979), p. 202.

48 Ibid., p. 199. Data for 33 provinces. Data for Perm not available.

49 TsGIA, f. 1288, op. 3, d. 9a, pp. 200–26.

50 TsGIA, f. 1288, op. 3, d. 9a, pp. 142–3.

51 "Zemskie shalosti," *Moskovskie vedomosti*, October 7, 1903, p. 1.

52 TsGIA, f. 1288, op. 3, d. 9 ch. 2, pp. 2–3, 74.

53 *Kalendar'-spravochnik*...no. 1916, pp. 386–404.

54 TsGIA, f. 1288, op. 3, d. 8 (1915). *Kalendar' spravochnik*...*na 1915*, pp. 34–5.

55 *PSZRI*, 2d series, vol. 26, pt. 1, no. 25398, (1851); V. F. Karavaev, "Zemskie smety i raskladki (istoricheskii ocherk razvitiia zemskikh biudzhetov)," in *Iubileinyi sbornik*, p. 156.

56 Tseitlin, pp. 189–90.

57 Tseitlin, p. 189.

58 Garmiza, p. 27.

59 The point has been made by Veselovskii, among others, 1: 8.

60 V. Skalon, "Zemskie finansy," *Entsiklopedicheskii slovar'* (B-E), 12: 520.

61 *PSZRI*, 2d series, vol. 39, pt. 1, no. 40458 (1864).

62 Skalon, "Zemskie finansy," p. 516.

63 Veselovskii, 1:176; Skalon, "Zemskie finansy," p. 515.

64 Kornilov, 3:109.

65 Veselovskii, 1:182.

66 *PSZRI*, 2d series, vol. 36, pt. 1, no. 36657 (1861), article 164.

67 Veselovskii, 1: 184.

68 Karavaev, p. 161.
69 A. Vasil'chikov, *Zemlevladenie i zemledelie v Rossii i drugikh evropeiskikh gosudarstvakh*, 2 vols. (St. Petersburg, 1876), 1:546; S. I. Shidlovskii, comp., *Zemel'noe oblozhenie* (St. Petersburg, 1904), p. 4; A. I. Shingarev, "Vopros ob uluchshenii zemskikh finansov," in *Iubileinyi sbornik*, pp. 134, 137n; Veselovskii, 1:105, 172n; P. Kh. Shvanebakh, *Nashe podatnoe delo* (St. Petersburg, 1903), pp. 88–90.
70 Veselovskii, 1:32.
71 Rashin, p. 45.
72 In response to zemstvo petitions, a subsequent decision (1867) permitted plant machinery and equipment to be taken into account for zemstvo tax appraisals. However, further limitations were imposed in 1868. Railroad land and immovable property were exempted from taxation; taxation of church and monastery property, state factories, and state immovable property in towns was limited. Shingarev, p. 109.
73 Shingarev, p. 127.
74 Veselovskii, 1:99–102.
75 Karavaev, p. 176.
76 Vasil'chikov, 1:496.
77 Veselovskii, 1:89; Shingarev, pp. 134–5, *Zemskoe delo*, 1915, no. 9, p. 578–9.
78 Kornilov, 3:110.
79 Vasil'chikov, 1:498–9; Shvanebakh, pp. 139–40.
80 Shvanebakh, p. 144.
81 Veselovskii, 1:65–6, 150, 656–7; 4: 27.
82 A. N. Diadchenko, *Statisticheskii spravochnik*, 2d ed. (St. Petersburg, 1906), pp. 74–7.
83 Veselovskii, 1:48, 72, 644–7.
84 Lazarevskii, p. 71n.; V. Lind, "Zemskie sobraniia tekushchego goda," *Russkaia mysl'*, 1909, no. 6, p. 143.
85 Zakharova, p. 170; Shvanebakh, p. 142; Veselovskii, 1:66.
86 Charles E. Timberlake, "The Birth of Zemstvo Liberalism in Russia: Ivan Il'ich Petrunkevich in Chernigov" (Ph.D. dissertation, University of Washington, 1968), p. 131.
87 S. N. Prokopovich, *Mestnye liudi o nuzhdakh Rossii* (St. Petersburg, 1904), p. 168.
88 Karavaev, p. 168; Diadchenko, p. 90.
89 Veselovskii, 1:66.
90 I. Ivaniukov, "Ocherki provintsial'noi zhizni," *Russkaia mysl'*, 1894, no. 12, p. 208.
91 P. Chizhevskii, "Vliianie sostava zemskikh sobranii na resul'taty zemskoi deiatel'nosti," *Vestnik Evropy*, August, 1909, pp. 580–6.
92 Veselovskii, 1:193.
93 Ibid., p. 190.
94 A. Vasil'chikov, "Zemskaia povinnost' v Rossii," *Vestnik Evropy* February, 1871, p. 658.

95   For example, I. Davydov, "Smolenskoe zemstvo," *Vestnik Evropy* November, 1875, pp. 341, 361. Yet as perceptions of the extent of the agrarian problem heightened, there were calls for *increased* zemstvo activity to aid agriculture. See, for example, E. Maksimov, "Ekonomicheskii krizis i otnoshenie k nemy zemstva i sel'skokhoziaistvennykh obshchestv," *Russkaia mysl'* July, 1887, pp. 120–50.

96   Shvanebakh, p. 9; Diadchenko, pp. 88–90.

97   Diadchenko, pp. 94–5.

98   Skalon, "Zemskie finansy," p. 529.

99   Veselovskii, 1: 200–2; Shvanebakh, pp. 125, 139–40.

100 *Krest'ianskoe dvizhenie v Rossii v 1881–1889 gg. Sbornik dokumentov*, (Moscow, 1960), doc. 340, pp. 705–8; see also doc. 276, and *Krest'ianskoe dvizhenie v Rossii v 1890–1900 gg.* (Moscow, 1959), docs. 1–3.

101 Veselovskii, 1:198.

102 *PSZRI*, 3d series, vol. 23, pt. 1, no. 22629. Mutual tax responsibility for state, zemstvo, and mir taxes had already been limited by the law of June 23, 1899. In 1903 it was completely repealed, and tax payment became the responsibility of the individual heads of households.

103 Veselovskii, 1:191–2, 200. By 1914 regular government "subsidies" to zemstvos amounted to 58 million rubles, almost 20 percent of the entire zemstvo budget. See Tikhon J. Polner, *Russian Local Government During the War and the Union of Zemstvos* (New Haven, 1930), p. 34.

104 Diadchenko, pp. 94–5.

105 Veselovskii, 4:26–34.

106 Shvanebakh, pp. 142-3.

107 Veselovskii, 4:30.

108 TsGIA, f. 1288, op. 3, d. 88 (1914), p. 104.

109 *Krest'ianskoe dvizhenie v Rossii v gody pervoi mirovoi voiny – iiul' 1914 g.–fevral' 1917. Sbornik dokumentov* (Moscow, 1965), doc. 62, pp. 131–6. See also doc. 60–4, 142, 144–5.

110 Of the 63 peasants brought to trial in this affair, 4 were sentenced to death, 17 were released, and the remainder received varying prison terms. A petition was moved by the provincial zemstvo requesting clemency for those sentenced to capital punishment. *Zemskoe delo*, 1916, no. 3, pp. 151–2.

111 In fact, though, a very similar report on peasant attitudes toward the zemstvo had been sent in by the governor of Orenburg province in June 1913. TsGIA, f. 1288, op. 3, d. 76b (1912), pp. 3–4.

112 D. M. Wallace, *Russia on the Eve of War and Revolution* (New York, 1961), p. 35.

113 TsGIA, f. 1288, op. 3, d. 76b (1913), p. 3; *Krest'ianskoe dvizhenie v Rossii v 1861–69 gg.* Moscow, 1964), doc. 131, p. 346.

114 Kornilov, 3: 103.

115 N. Shishkov, "Nashe zemstvo, ego trudy i nedochety; 1864–1900," *Vestnik Evropy* September, 1901, p. 322.

116 A. Leroy-Beaulieu, *The Empire of the Tsars and Russians*, 3 vols. (New York, 1893–6), 2 (1894); 170.

117 Wallace, pp. 37, 39.

118 TsGIA, f. 1288, op. 3, d. 38 (1914), p. 104.

119 Veselovskii, 4; 189.

120 "Nuzhna li reforma mestnogo upravleniia: Pis'ma iz derevnii," *Moskovskie vedomosti*, January 14, 1889, p. 2.

121 "Zemtsy pred sudom krest'ian," *Moskovskie vedomosti*, June 24, 1905, p. 2.

122 Prokopovich, p. 123.

123 T. I. Tikhonov, *Zemstvo v Rossii i na okrainakh* (St. Petersburg, 1905), p. 21.

124 *Kalendar'-spravochnik...na 1916*, p. 48.

125 A. P. Chekhov, "Muzhiki," *Sobranie sochinenii*, 12 vols. (Moscow, 1960–4), 8 (1962); 222–3.

126 Direct taxes on the agricultural population of the 50 provinces of European Russia amounted to 193.5 million rubles, of which 173.4 million was paid by lands of rural societies. Shvanebakh, pp. 139–40.

127 Prokopovich, p. 123. State revenue from the liquor monopoly amounted to 270 million rubles in 1900, when the total zemstvo budget was 88 million. By 1913 the monopoly brought in 899 million rubles – one-fourth of all state income and still over three times the entire zemstvo budget.

128 Leroy-Beaulieu, 2:170.

129 Veselovskii, 1:190n.; 3: 210.

130 Prokopovich, p. 115. Others shared the opinion, insisting that the peasant was better equipped for practical self-government than either the intelligentsia or the zemtsy. See N. M. Pirumova, *Zemskoe liberal'noe dvizhenie* (Moscow 1977), p. 156.

131 Wallace, pp. 29–30. The "peasant majority" described here is questionable since the law provided for a district zemstvo in Novgorod of 50 members, including only 17 peasants.

132 Veselovskii, 4:183, 188.

133 *Zemskoe delo*, 1913, no. 8, p. 1138.

134 Veselovskii, 3:696–700; 4: 193–4.

135 Veselovskii, 4:31–3, 192.

136 Miasoedov's painting is reproduced, with commentary, in *Istoriia russkogo iskusstva*, vol. 2 (Moscow, 1960), p. 141. Peasant social malaise at the zemstvo is noted by Shishkov, p. 326; Veselovskii, 4:180n.

137 Prokopovich, p. 119.

138 Veselovskii, 4:191.

139 Prokopovich, pp. 119–20.

140 Veselovskii, 4:195n.

141 Vestnik sel'skogo khoziaistvo, 1905, no. 24, p. 18.

142 According to D. N. Shipov, the real significance of the 1890 zemstvo legislation emerged only after 1905. Previously, he contends, the increase in noble representation was not harmful because only progressive nobles took active part in the zemstvo; after 1905, reactionaries made use of their electoral prerogatives to gain control. Vospominaniia i dumy o perezhitom (Moscow, 1918), p. 529. I. V. Chernyshev, writing in the Trudy vol'nogo ekonomicheskogo obshchestva, 1907, no. 1–3, p. 37, reflected a similar view and charged that the zemstvo had become the representative of the Black Hundreds.

143 Timberlake, p. 19.

144 TsGIA, f. 1288, op. 3, d. 33 (1912), pp. 318, 436–8; A. M. Anfimov, "Krest'ianstvo Rossii v 1907–1914 gg." (Paper presented at the annual meeting of the American Historical Association, 1971), p. 50.

145 Veselovskii, 4:196. Veselovskii states that only 17 of the 40 zemstvos in these provinces were properly "peasant" because raznochintsy, merchants, and landowners accounted for a majority in the remainder.

146 Leroy-Beaulieu, 2:183.

147 "Viatskoe zemstvo," Vestnik Evropy, October 1880, p. 873.

148 "Krest'ianskie zemstva," Moskovskie vedomosti, October 10, 1900, pp. 1–2.

149 Veselovskii, 4:198–200.

150 Diadchenko, pp. 74–5.

151 V.V. Garmiza, "Zemskaia reforma i zemstvo v istoricheskoi literature," Istoriia SSSR, 1960, no. 5.

152 The point had been noted earlier by Leroy-Beaulieu, 2:162.

153 Vremennik Tsentral'nogo statisticheskogo komiteta ministerstva vnutrennikh del, 1894, no. 32, p. xxvii; Shvanebakh, p. 125.

154 A. P. Shchapov, "Zemstvo," Sochineniia, 3 vols. (St. Petersburg, 1906), 1:753.

155 Because the government owned 95 percent of the land in Arkhangelsk, it was feared that zemstvos here too would be "at the treasury's expense." However, the treasury was already paying the bulk of land taxes in the province, and the essential concern appears to have been the "one-sidedly democratic" structure of the province. TsGIA, f. 1288. op. 3, d. 78 (1913) (on the legislative proposal of 54 members of the State Duma to introduce zemstvos in Arkhangelsk province), pp. 38–9, 68–70; Zemskoe delo, 1915, no. 18, pp. 1010–11.

156 Krest'ianskoe dvizhenie, 1914–1917, doc. 41, p. 104. In a similar case, reported in Zemskoe delo, 1916, no. 3, p. 151, peasants protested, "The Tsar knows nothing about the zemstvo."

157 V. I. Lenin, Sochineniia, 4th ed. 45 vols. (Moscow, 1941–67), 5:23.

158 Zemskoe delo, 1917, no. 1, pp. 27–8.

159 I. M. Vladislavlev, O volostnom zemstve (Petrograd, 1917), p. 11. Similarly, A. I. Shingarev, a former zemstvo doctor and minister of agriculture and of finances in the 1917 Provisional Government, wrote

glowingly in 1913 of how opposition to expenditures had faded in zemstvo assemblies. "Where sharp arguments could be heard five to eight years ago against a modest allotment for a new school or a new hospital, or for agronomy... where an increase in land tax of one-half or one kopek was considered an impossible burden, now tens of thousands are allotted [and] a tax hike of 10 to 12 kopeks per desiatina is greeted with good will." *Russkie vedomosti*, October 9, 1913.

160　K. V. Gusev, "Iz istorii soglasheniia Bol'shevikov s levymi eserami," *Istoriia SSSR*, 1959, no. 2, pp. 87–9 Gusev reports widespread peasant opposition to zemstvos but also cites documents indicating some peasant support.

161　V. O. Kliuchevskii, *Ocherki i rechi* (Petrograd, 1918), p. 50.

162　Compare Pirumova, p. 229: "Zemstvo liberalism was noble liberalism, gentry liberalism."

5

The zemstvo and politics, 1864–1914

ROBERTA THOMPSON MANNING

Very early in the history of the zemstvo, this local institution of self-government began to concern itself with the direction of state affairs, engaging in deliberate attempts to shape and influence national policies and political structures. Indeed, one is hard pressed to name another single Imperial Russian institution that played as great or sustained a role in Russian politics or one that contributed more substantially and in a more varied fashion to the constitutional development of the country in the last half-century of the old regime as did the Russian zemstvo. The political history of the zemstvo, however, does not form a continuous whole but can easily be divided into three distinct periods. The first and longest of these periods, 1864–1905, was marked by the growth of political opposition to bureaucratic rule within the zemstvos, culminating in zemstvo participation in the Liberation Movement of 1902–5, when zemstvos throughout the country used their influence to press for the establishment of representative government in Russia. The era of the Liberation Movement was immediately followed by a period of political reaction, 1905–7, which continued to influence the outlook and attitudes of zemstvo activists beyond the fall of the old regime, shaping their conduct during the 1917 Revolution and the Civil War that followed. Beginning at the end of 1905 and continuing through the middle of 1907, the zemstvos gradually turned against the broadly based representative institutions, which they had helped to create, while still maintaining their commitment to a less democratic form of representative government dominated by the upper strata of Russian society. To these ends, they worked for the dissolution of the radical Second Duma and the promulgation of a new, more restrictive election law by participating in a well-organized campaign to discredit the Duma in the eyes of the government and tsar.

These goals were attained by the start of the third and last period in the zemstvos' political history, which was launched by the Stolypin coup d'état of June 3, 1907, and continued until the fall of the old order in February 1917. During this period, the central government, contrary to much of its previous practice, sought to work closely with the zemstvos and to augment zemstvo authority, jurisdiction and responsibilities substantially. At the same time zemstvo men came to play a major role in the legislative branch of government through the Duma election law of June 3, 1907, which unduly favored the larger landowning elements that constituted the prime political constituency of the zemstvos, and through the existence of a large bloc of elected zemstvo representatives in the upper house of the new Russian legislature, the reformed State Council. World War I merely introduced a new factor into these political arrangements, prompting the zemstvos to use their authority within the political system to attempt to augment the power of the legislative institutions in the face of the demonstrated inability of the monarch and administration to deal with the war. For the local zemstvos (as opposed to the zemstvo union) entered the political opposition of 1915–16 in order to save the existing political system of which they were an integral part from itself, not – as in 1905 – to work for a fundamental restructuring of the Russian political order.[1]

The era of liberal opposition, 1864–1905

The initial period in the political history of the zemstvo, that of growing zemstvo involvement in the liberal opposition to the Old Regime, is by far the best-known epoch in zemstvo history, firmly enshrined in zemstvo mythology and Western historiography. In fact, the zemstvos' role in the Liberation Movement, coupled with the growing importance of the public services with which they provided the countryside in the form of schools, hospitals, aid to agriculture, and so forth, has greatly colored Western views of the zemstvo, giving rise to the widespread conception of the zemstvo as an institution that represented and served all classes of the Russian population while promoting Russian political development along Western constitutional lines.[2] To be sure, this view of the zemstvos, although it overlooks the complex motivations of ordinary zemstvo men, does possess some validity for the *first* period of zemstvo history in that the zemstvos at this time did make a substantial contribution to the first phases of the struggle for political liberty in Russia.

The involvement of the zemstvo in this struggle can be gauged from Table 5.1, which charts the growth of the zemstvo opposition by showing the ever increasing numbers of provincial zemstvo assemblies presenting the government with demands for the establishment of a central representative organ (or with petitions interpreted as such by the government). Advocates and adversaries of the zemstvo alike have often regarded the growth of the zemstvo opposition as the logical outgrowth of the foundation of zemstvo institutions in Russia. According to this fairly common line of reasoning, the zemstvo, as an elected body, could not avoid engaging ultimately in a head-on assault on the bureaucratic government, being bound – regardless of any conscious intentions on the part of the zemstvo activists themselves – to strive inexorably toward the expansion of the representative principle in the Russian government in the form of an augmentation of zemstvo authority and the foundation of a central zemstvo organ. At the same time, the bureaucratic government, motivated by a sense of self-preservation, could not help but seek to curb zemstvo autonomy and to resist zemstvo political demands, thus exacerbating the inherent antagonism between the zemstvos and government and prompting the zemstvos to engage ever more earnestly in oppositional activities. Therefore, it is not at all surprising that by the end of the nineteenth century half of all the provincial zemstvos in the land had openly expressed themselves at one time or another in favor of the establishment of representative government in Russia[3] and that in the course of the year 1904–5 they were joined by the remainder of their fellows as well as most of the traditionally sluggish and apolitical district assemblies.

Zemstvo involvement in the Liberation Movement, however, was not as unavoidable or continuous a development as this rather Whiggish – or, more properly speaking, Kadet – view of zemstvo history implies. Nor did the antagonism between the government and the zemstvo stem solely – or even mainly – from the differing natures of their respective political stuctures. In the first place, as Table 5.1 indicates, there were long periods, particularly in the initial decades of the zemstvos' existence, in which the zemstvos did not engage in oppositional activities of any kind but worked peacefully and harmoniously with the government. Indeed, the zemstvos went out of their way to avoid the conflict with the government that was supposedly inherent in their elective natures. They rarely if ever issued protests against government curbs on zemstvo authority until the mid-1890s, even failing to complain about the introduction of the Zemstvo Statute of 1890, which greatly enhanced the government's ability to control the zemstvos.[4] Those relatively few times when the zemstvos did engage in overt oppositional activities coincided with major political crises: the unsettled condition of the country after emancipation; the dislocations of the

Table 5.1. *Growth of the zemstvo opposition, 1867–1905*

Year	Number of provincial zemstvo assemblies adopting oppositional resolutions	Most typical political demands of the period
1865–7	1[a]	Central zemstvo institution to administer state land taxes
1878–81	9[b]	"A constitution like that given the Bulgarians" (consultative assembly, elected by a limited franchise; freedom of speech, press, and opinion)
1894–5	12[c]	"Allow the voice of the zemstvo to reach the heights of the throne"[d]
1903	25[e]	Zemstvos participation in the composition of legislation affecting them through elected zemstvo representatives
1904–5	34[f]	A fully constitutional regime, based on guarantees of the "rights of man" (freedoms of speech, press, assembly, etc., right of habeus corpus) and a national assembly with legislative powers elected by universal, equal, and secret suffrage

[a] The zemstvo concerned was the Saint Petersburg provincial zemstvo, which upon learning of the government's negative reaction to such a petition decided not to transmit this resolution to the tsar.

[b] The zemstvos concerned were the Chernigov, Tver, Kharkov, Poltava, Samara, Novgorod, Riazan, Tauride, and Kazan provincial zemstvos.

[c] The zemstvos concerned were the Tver, Ufa, Poltava, Tambov, Saratov, Kursk, Orel, Chernigov, Pskov, Smolensk, and Novgorod provincial zemstvos. Of these, the latter three failed to transmit their addresses to the tsar upon learning of his extremely negative reaction to the previous addresses.

[d] These petitions were interpreted by Nicholas II as evidence of latent constitutionalism within the zemstvos.

[e]The assemblies concerned were the Bessarabia, Vladimir, Vologda, Voronezh, Viatka, Ekaterinoslav, Kaluga, Kursk, Moscow, Olonets, Orel, Penza, Perm, Pskov, Riazan, Samara, Saint Petersburg, Saratov, Simbirsk, Smolensk, Tauride, Tula, Kherson, Chernigov, and Iaroslavl provincial zemstvos. Of the remainder seven assemblies (the Kazan, Nizhnii Novgorod, Poltava, Tula, Ufa, and Kharkov provincial zemstvos) were not allowed to consider this issue by the local administration, prompting strong protests from Nizhnii Novgorod and Ufa. Of the assemblies considering this issue, only the Tambov and Kostroma provincial zemstvo assemblies refused to make such demands upon the government, calling instead for freedom of speech for zemstvo representatives invited to serve on government commissions.
[f]This accounts for all the provincial zemstvo assemblies then existing in Russia, all of which called for the foundation of representative institutions in the course of the year. Three-quarters of these assemblies went further and supported legislative powers for the national assembly (which entailed placing limitations on the autocratic powers of the tsar), whereas two-thirds of them endorsed a "three-tail" franchise – universal, equal, and secret suffrage.
Sources: B. B. Veselovskii, Istoriia zemstva za sorok let 4 vols. (St. Petersburg, 1909–11), 3:98–101, 231–63, 498–504, 590–7; I. P. Belokonskii, Zemskoe dvizhenie, 2d expanded edition of Zemstvo i revoliutsiia (Moscow, 1914); S. Mirnyi, Adresy zemstv 1894–1895 i ikh politicheskaia programma, 2d ed. (Geneva, 1896); S. Iu. Witte, Samoderzhavie i zemstvo: konfidentsial'naia zapiska Ministra finansov Stats-Sekretaria S. Iu. Vitte (1899) (Stuttgart, 1901), pp. 92–169; D. N. Shipov, Vospominaniia i dumy o perezhitom (Moscow, 1918), pp. 225–6; and Roberta T. Manning, "Zemstvo and Revolution, the Onset of the Gentry Reaction, 1905–07," in Leopold H. Haimson, ed., The Politics of Rural Russia, 1905–1914 (Bloomington, 1979), pp. 37–8.

Russo-Turkish War and the height of the terrorist activities of the People's Will; the aftermath of the Great Famine of 1891; the 1902 peasant rebellions; and major Russian defeats in the Russo-Japanese War and the onset of the 1905 Revolution. These crises revealed serious weaknesses in the existing political structures, which the zemstvo men tended to overlook in periods of normalcy, and prompted the zemstvos to seek to remedy these deficiencies by calling them to the attention of the government, scarcely a subversive activity.

Likewise the government's attitude toward the zemstvos was far more ambiguous than the prevailing liberal interpretation of the rise of the zemstvo opposition suggests. Throughout this period there were influential forces in the government seeking to work with the zemstvo, soliciting zemstvo opinion on a wide variety of issues affecting the countryside, and going so far as to appoint zemstvo activists to various government commissions entrusted with the preliminary phases of the preparation of legislative projects, such as the Valuev Commission of 1872, the Kakhanov Commission of 1881–3, and the local committees on the needs of agriculture of 1902.[5] Indeed, several times in the course of the 1861–1905 period the government came close to institutionaliz-ing the ad hoc involvement of zemstvo men in the legislative process by including zemstvo representatives on the State Council or some other such assembly of high officials and exofficials entrusted with the drafting of legislative proposals.[6]

Meanwhile, the numbers of zemstvo and other local gentry activists invited to assume important posts in the administration – usually as provincial governors and vice governors – steadily grew from 1 such appointment in the 1860s to 15 in the 1898–1904 period, reaching its pre-1905 peak during Pleve's tenure as minister of internal affairs. It appears that Pleve, who has gone down in history as the arch foe of the zemstvo, nevertheless considered zemstvo service excellent prepara-tion for an administrative career.[7] The growing reliance of the govern-ment on zemstvo men to staff the upper levels of the provincial administration appears to have been a conscious attempt on the part of officialdom (including Pleve) to temper the escalating conflict between the administration and the zemstvos by appointing men to local administrative positions who would be more likely to be able to work harmoniously with the zemstvos. In pointing out some of the complex-ities in the government's relationship with the zemstvo, I do not mean to absolve the government of any responsibility for the rise of the zemstvo opposition. It is clear that the 1890 statute's substantial augmentation of government powers over the zemstvos, coupled with the often inept and ill-advised usages to which ministers of internal

138

affairs, such as Sipiagin and Pleve, put these powers, did contribute greatly to the mounting tensions between the zemstvos and the government.

Nevertheless, accommodation between these two main forces in Russian political life was not out of the question before 1905, despite the different principles – elective versus bureaucratic – upon which their respective political structures rested, as the post-1907 experiences of these two branches of government indicate. Until the summer of 1905, when a majority of the provincial zemstvos came to endorse a national representative assembly with *legislative* powers, elected by a three-tail franchise (universal, equal, and secret suffrage), zemstvo political demands were quite modest and could be accommodated without upsetting the basic political or social order of the country. The pre-1905 zemstvo program as outlined in zemstvo addresses and resolutions neither threatened the autocratic powers of the tsar and bureaucracy, as the 1905 calls for a *legislative* rather than a consultative assembly were to do, nor challenged the foundations of the social order of the old regime, which was based on the inequality of the various estates (*sosloviia*) of the Russian Empire as the zemstvos' subsequent endorsement of universal and equal suffrage did imply.

To be sure, as Table 5.1 demonstrates, the Saint Petersburg zemstvo in 1867 and nine other assemblies in the period 1879–81 espoused the foundation of a central representative chamber. But the body demanded by the Saint Petersburg zemstvo was to be elected by the gentry-dominated zemstvos and limited in scope to the establishment and appropriation of government land taxes,[8] whereas the nine oppositional zemstvos of the 1878–81 address campaign endorsed a constitution like that recently given the Bulgarians by force of Russian arms in the Russo-Turkish War. This constitution established a consultative chamber composed of both elective and appointed deputies. The elective deputies were to be selected by Bulgaria's counterpart of zemstvos and city dumas, bodies themselves chosen by a similarly limited franchise. Under this arrangement, the king was allowed to appoint a sizable bloc of deputies – one-third of the chamber – and retained a veto over the legislative projects passed by the representative body.[9] The limited representation allowed by this system far more closely resembled the 1881 "constitutional" project of Loris-Melikov than the political structures that actually emerged from the Revolution of 1905.[10]

Even then, in 1894–5, the zemstvo opposition retreated considerably from this limited political program. The addresses of this period went no further than to hint vaguely that the zemstvos should be regarded as the representatives and spokesmen of the local population and to express the modest hope that in the future "the voice of the zemstvo would be allowed to reach the heights of the throne." It is difficult to understand in retrospect how Nicholas II could have interpreted these pitiful petitions as a threat to the autocracy, characterizing them as "senseless dreams." When the zemstvos resumed making more clear-cut political demands upon the government in 1903, they merely attempted to institutionalize their own growing ad hoc involvement in the legislative process by calling for the election, rather than the appointment, of zemstvo representatives on government commissions. Yet these elected representatives were not to deal with legislation in general but were to be confined in their deliberations to matters directly concerning the zemstvos.[11]

Despite the zemstvo opposition's reluctance to challenge the political and social structures of the Russian Empire, their influence within zemstvo circles was rather limited before 1905. At any given time before the Revolution of 1905 (except for 1903), the number of politically "loyal" zemstvos always greatly outweighed those in the camp of the opposition. In 1867 not a single other zemstvo moved to support Saint Petersburg, whereas 19 provincial zemstvos in 1878–81 and 22 provincial assemblies in 1894–5 pointedly presented the sovereign with loyal addresses, resplendent with declarations of their "limitless" devotion and support for his policies.[12] Not a few of these resolutions were intended as a response to the concomitant upsurge in the activities of the zemstvo opposition. In addition, conservative elements satisfied with the political status quo quite often made significant gains in the zemstvo elections immediately following each major address campaign. This was particularly true of the 1878–9 and 1883 elections.[13]

In general the form in which zemstvo political protests were couched was no more resolute or rebellious than their contents. The zemstvo opposition inevitably limited their activity to petitioning the government for political change, expressing their opinions most frequently in the form of a loyal address to the tsar. In drafting these petitions, all the ritualized, deferential conventions of the loyal address were rigorously observed before 1905, save in the case of the Tver resolution of 1894, which deliberately omitted the title "autocrat" to the horror not only of Nicholas II and his advisors but of many zemstvo men as well, including members of the opposition.[14] Not until 1905 did it become the standard practice of the zemstvo opposition to drop the autocratic title (and all references to the autocracy) from their communications with the monarch.[15]

140

Moreover, the zemstvos never did proceed beyond humbly soliciting government support for political reforms to more active forms of oppostion. Not even at the height of political excitement in zemstvo circles in 1905 did any zemstvo so much as discuss the possibility of refusing to carry out some of the vital functions that they performed for the government in an attempt to place more effective pressure upon the administration. Although some zemstvos engaged in so-called political strikes in the course of the 1905 revolution, terminating their meetings without completing all their regular business in order to register their objections to government-placed limitations on zemstvo debates, these actions constituted merely a token gesture. In all such cases, zemstvo enterprises and services continued to function, despite the fact that the budget had not been officially approved by the assembly – not exactly most people's idea of a strike![16] And when the third-element employees of the zemstvo actually did join the nationwide general strike in the autumn of 1905, thus interrupting zemstvo services to the population, the elected deputies, outraged and scandalized, retaliated with widespread dismissals of those employees who had "shirked" their duties.[17]

It was not until the summer of 1905 – and then only briefly – that the zemstvos ever sought to go outside their chambers and mobilize popular support for their political demands. This they attempted to do by involving the local population in public discussions of the country's future constitutional order. These activities, however, were terminated fairly soon after their initiation, since the local peasants found the political forums provided by the zemstvos splendid occasions to express their land hunger and press their claims to the estates of the local landowning gentry.[18] Even then, the main concern of zemstvo opposition leaders at this time was to direct the rapidly developing peasant movement into peaceful channels.[19]

In light of the zemstvo opposition's moderation before 1905, the harsh reaction of the government appears quite unwarranted. Before the outbreak of the first revolution, when zemstvo protests escalated beyond the government's ability to control and chastise, the administration tended to deal with the leaders of zemstvo protests in a draconian fashion, subjecting them to administrative exile from their home province and/or deprivation of their political rights, including the right to participate in the zemstvo. As time passed, particularly after the turn of the century, the government tended to resort to these measures ever more frequently, imposing such penalties on anyone it deemed to be persistently trying to politicize the zemstvos, regardless of whether his activities elicited much of a response from the local zemstvos. At the same time, the government increasingly attempted to ward off future political protests by using its augmented authority under the Statute of 1890 to refuse to confirm in office increasing numbers of elected zemstvo officials of a known oppositional bent.[20] Such harassment of the zemstvo opposition on the part of the government, however, merely estranged more and more zemstvo men from the administration, greatly augmenting the oppositional forces in the zemstvos. The growth of the zemstvo opposition, in turn, provoked more government intervention in zemstvo affairs, thus giving rise to a vicious circle in zemstvo–government relations in the form of an ever escalating conflict between the zemstvos and the central authorities from the mid-1890s on.

To understand fully how zemstvo–government relations came to this impasse despite the better intentions of both parties involved, we will have to turn our attention away from political structures and programs to the underlying social structure of the zemstvos. For the conflict between the zemstvos and government was prompted by the social evolution of the dominant element in the zemstvos' constituency – the landed gentry – whose way of life had undergone substantial changes since the emancipation of the serfs. The involvement of the zemstvos in the Liberation Movement is directly rooted in these social changes, being not so much the product of the inevitable response of elective institutions to bureaucratic government but, rather, the result of the interaction between this recently altered element of the nobility and a unique set of liberal and progressive leaders capable of articulating the zemstvo nobility's aspirations and grievances and translating these as yet often scarcely perceived feelings into political demands.

While it is widely recognized that noble landowners played a predominant role in zemstvo affairs, the scope, extent, and implications of noble influence in these bodies both before and after the introduction of the Statute of 1890 was never fully explored until quite recently. As a consequence, Western historians have tended to regard the zemstvo above all else as an "all-class," if not democratic, institution which embraced all elements of the population of the zemstvo provinces: the landed nobility, the peasantry, urban inhabitants, and the intelligentsia in the form of zemstvo employees, the so-called third element. In part, this view of the zemstvo was perpetuated by the fact that the oft-cited statistics on zemstvo membership, which reveal that nobles occupied 55.2 percent of the seats in the district zemstvos and 89.5 percent of the seats on the provincial level under the 1890 law, tended to obscure the real extent of noble domination of the zemstvos in most provinces, especially in the more "political" (that is, oppositional), provincial zemstvo assemblies. For these well-known figures

142

include membership statistics for the four so-called peasant provinces of Viatka, Vologda, Olonets, and Perm, areas in which relatively few noble landowners resided.[21] Memoir literature, the Soviet historian N. M. Pirumova's thorough analysis of the election returns for 25 provinces in the 1890–3 period, and my own probings into the incomplete files of the Ministry of the Interior on the social composition of the zemstvos after the 1906–7 elections indicate that outside the peasant provinces (and a handful of highly urbanized and industrialized areas) gentry political influence in the zemstvo was even more crushing, accounting for at least two-thirds of all zemstvo deputies at the district level and virtually all the provincial deputies.[22] A good case in point was the Poltava provincial zemstvo assembly elected in 1907. Not only were all zemstvo members elected at this time hereditary noblemen save for two nonnoble landed proprietors (one Cossack and one "honorary citizen") and two personal nobles, but almost all the deputies were quite substantial landowners, possessing on the average 640 desiatinas of land, with a median holding of a little more than 500 desiatinas in a province where the average noble estate amounted to 111.1 desiatinas, considerably below the national average of 470 desiatinas.[23]

Since social elements other than the landed gentry were at best only weakly represented in the zemstvos, these institutions should not be regarded as all-class political institutions so much as the almost exclusive political preserve of the local gentry landowners, whose grievances, aspirations, and dilemmas were reflected in the opposition movements that these institutions spawned. It may seem somewhat incongruous that gentry-dominated institutions like the zemstvos provided fertile soil for a growing liberal opposition to the old political order. But by the time the Liberation Movement swept over the zemstvos, the hereditary landed nobility that controlled these bodies had ceased to be a highly privileged social order, having been transformed in the course of the previous century into a social group engulfed in crisis – a crisis that was both economic and political. In the second half of the nineteenth century, landed noblemen in Russia were simultaneously confronted with the well-known precipitous decline of noble landownership, launched by the emancipation of the serfs, *and* a concomitant, equally swift erosion of their once influential political position, as landless men of diverse social origins, in the main hereditary career bureaucrats, increasingly supplanted the old hereditary landed nobility as the dominant element at *all* levels of the Russian civil service and military officers corps.[24]

Under these conditions, ever larger numbers of noble proprietors, especially the members of the younger generation of landed noblemen who came of age from the end of the 1880s on, responded to the landed

143

nobility's growing crisis by eschewing traditional careers in government service in order to resettle in the provinces and to occupy themselves with agriculture and local affairs. Indeed, in the words of Nicholas II's future foreign minister, Alexander Izvolskii, who was reared in a family of provincial nobles in the second half of the nineteenth century, "It became the fashion for young nobles to shun the bureaucratic institutions of Saint Petersburg and to serve in the provinces as marshals of the nobility, members of the zemstvos, judges, and arbitrators of the peace."[25] In this way, the crisis of the Russian nobility led not to its disappearance but to its disintegration and transformation, giving rise in the process to a new social stratum that hitherto had not existed in Russia – a provincial gentry in the true sense of the term, that is, a group of locally based, politically active, and involved agrarians.

The social disintegration of the noble estate and the rather sudden, belated appearance of a provincial gentry on the Russian political scene was directly responsible for the growing political tensions between the zemstvos and government and the rise of the liberation movement among the landed gentry. As the zemstvo gentry and the state bureaucracy became ever more differentiated socially from one another, these two key elements in the Russian political order began to harbor quite different, even divergent, views of the zemstvos' political role. The state bureaucracy, which still tended by and large to consider the zemstvo gentry as an integral component of the service class, looked upon the zemstvo as a convenient means to extend government control into the rural localities, which hitherto remained ungoverned save for the peasant village assemblies and gentry-elected institutions. To these ends, the government at the end of the nineteenth century moved to incorporate the zemstvos ever more firmly into the administrative apparatus of the country. The zemstvo gentry, on the other hand, as a result of their life experiences had come to value their new, more autonomous role in the Russian socio-political order, viewing themselves primarily as independent country gentlemen and public activists in their own right rather than the state servants of yesteryear.[26] Indeed, not a few such local activists were oriented toward provincial life in the first place due to a deep-seated antipathy toward the higher standards, new norms, customs, attitudes, and practices injected into government service by the professionalization of the civil service and military officers corps, which entailed the gradual substitution of talent, education, expertise, and hard work for birth and social status as the main criteria for career success in government service. Thus finding the newly modernized and upgraded "bureaucratic" norms of official

144

life inimical to their own traditional values, mores, outlook, and lifestyle, increasingly numbers of noble proprietors left government service in the second half of the nineteenth century and sought refuge on their estates and in local elective institutions. Increasingly such men included significant numbers of the descendants of some of the country's ancient, and formerly more distinguished, influential, highly cultured, and wealthy families (although not necessarily the very wealthiest), a stratum of the Russian nobility which hitherto had maintained little contact with local life.

The conflict between this new provincial gentry (or Russia's old power elite transformed) and the increasingly "bourgeois" professional bureaucracy, which owed its status ever more to talent, education, and work,[27] assumed an overtly political form from the mid-1890s on, when the bureaucracy and its policies began to impinge upon and even threaten the new way of life that the gentry had managed to create for itself in the provinces. By imposing ever more stringent controls on the zemstvos in an attempt to integrate these institutions more thoroughly into the government apparatus and by stimulating the industrial development of the country through the adoption of tariff, taxation, and monetary policies detrimental to agriculture at the very time when Russian landowners were confronted with a worldwide depression in the price of grain, their chief marketable commodity, the bureaucracy appeared to be launching a direct, even deliberate attack on the last bastion of gentry influence in the Russian socio-political order – their new-found sanctuaries in the countryside. The end result was the provincial gentry's counterassault in the form of its growing involvement in the opposition to the existing political order. In this way, a significant portion of the country's old power elite came to look upon the zemstvos as a political base from which they could strike out to regain their recently lost influence in state affairs.

That such an essentially reactionary movement took on the highly unlikely veneer of liberalism and modern constitutionalism was the result of the presence within the zemstvos and among the provincial gentry of a highly unique group of liberal and progressive political activists, who subsequently were to adhere to the liberal Constitutional Democratic (Kadet) party or to one of the minuscule progressive political entities located somewhere between the Kadets and Octobrists on the post-1905 Russian political spectrum. Among them could be found the leading lights of the zemstvo movement, men whose names are still virtually synonymous with the zemstvos in the historical writings on these institutions, such as the Petrunkevich brothers, the Princes Dolgorukov, F. I. Rodichev, Prince D. I. Shakhovskoi, Count

145

P. A. Geiden, and the grand old man of the pre-1905 zemstvos—the long-time Moscow provincial board chairman, D. N. Shipov.[28] These men, who provided the bulk of the nationally recognized leadership of the zemstvo movement before and during the Revolution of 1905, tended to espouse quite liberal, sometimes even democratic views and quite often concluded *before* beginning their zemstvo service or fairly soon thereafter that the greatest service they could render the nation was the politicization of the zemstvos and the involvement of these institutions in the struggle for representative government in Russia.

To these ends, the zemstvo liberals and progressives devoted considerable time and effort to the organization of the zemstvo movement on the national level through the convocation of periodic national zemstvo congresses of the leading local activists and the establishment of permanent organizations of the more active and politicized elements among the local zemstvo men, ranging from the theoretically "apolitical" Beseda, which included zemstvo activists of quite diverse political views, to the militantly constitutionalist Union of Liberation and its fraternal organization of zemstvo constitutionalists.[29] At the same time the left-wing leadership of the pre-1905 zemstvos did not neglect their political base in the local assemblies but emerged the dominant element within the local zemstvos as well as the recognized national spokesmen of the zemstvo movement by virture of their demonstrated managerial skills, hard work, and intensity of commitment to the mundane tasks of daily zemstvo life.[30] They were also responsible for the growing politicization of the zemstvos, the increasing coordination of zemstvo oppositional activities, and the organization of the well-known zemstvo address campaigns, which entailed the adoption of similar resolutions by as many local zemstvos as possible on a wide variety of issues, ranging from the abolition of corporal punishment to the dispensation of famine relief funds. As a result, once the Russian defeats in the abortive war with Japan and the initial popular outbursts of the Revolution of 1905 convinced the zemstvo rank and file that immediate changes in the Russian political order were mandatory, the liberal and progressive leaders of the zemstvos were able to utilize their past organizational experiences to rally the local zemstvos to the Liberation Movement. In the course of 1904–5, a series of national zemstvo congresses, immediately seconded by unanimous votes or overwhelming majorities in most local assemblies, committed the zemstvo movement to clearly constitutionalist demands, calling for the establishment of a modern parliamentary regime based upon a national assembly with legislative powers elected by universal, equal, and secret suffrage and guaranteed by a broad range of civil liberties and human rights.[31]

146

The achievement of these goals in the form of the October Manifesto and the relatively democratically elected first two State Dumas ironically resulted in the immediate demise of liberalism as an important political force in the zemstvos and the onset of a period of reaction, beginning in November 1905 and continuing unabated for over two years. In this period, the local zemstvos gradually turned against their former liberal and progressive leaders, subjecting these elements to increasing and ever more bitter and hostile criticism and finally eliminating them altogether from the zemstvos in the elections of 1906–7 and 1909–10.[32] By then ongoing events had revealed to many provincial noblemen that the political goals of the old left-wing leadership of the zemstvo movement and the tactics utilized to achieve these goals were incompatible with the basic interests of the zemstvo gentry. Not only did the liberal-sponsored zemstvo movement to the people in the summer of 1905, coupled with the unsettled conditions of the time, help contribute to the outbreak of widespread peasant disorders in the autumn of 1905, rivaling in scope and intensity the Great Pugachev Rebellion of the eighteenth century.[33] The zemstvo liberals and progressives, especially those among them who joined the newly formed Kadet party at this time, failed completely to respond to these developments, as did other provincial noblemen. Instead of organizing armed guards to protect their estates and issuing frantic appeals for the institution of "law and order" in the Russian countryside,[34] the left wing leaders of the pre-1905 zemstvo movement calmly prepared to appeal for the votes of the rebellious peasants in the coming Duma elections on the basis of a platform calling for far-reaching expropriation of gentry lands.[35] In this they were motivated by their own unique position in Russian society as an element that shared much in common in terms of education and professional orientation with the professional intelligentsia, possessed far more varied interests and career options than the average provincial nobleman, and hence related far differently to their landed estates. Such elements readily decided, as one Kadet zemstvo man put it, that the sacrifice of gentry landholdings was "a small price to pay for political liberty"[36] (and their own political hegemony in the new representative chamber). However, this move clearly entailed a sacrifice that the liberals' gentry constituency in the local zemstvos were not at all prepared to pay, prompting the zemstvo rank and file to turn against its former liberal leaders and cast them out of the zemstvo movement as an alien element among the provincial gentry willing to sacrifice the gentry's vital economic interests to their own political ambitions and concerns.

147

The era of reaction, 1905–7

The rank-and-file revolt against the former left-wing leadership of the zemstvo movement marked the start of the second period in the political history of the zemstvos: the era of reaction. This period until quite recently has been overlooked in the Western writings on the zemstvo, which tend to skip directly from the involvement of the zemstvos in the Liberation Movement to the period of World War I and the activities of the zemstvo union and progressive bloc, with scarcely a glance at the intervening decade. In this way, the political history of the zemstvo generally has been portrayed quite inaccurately as one of constant "liberal" opposition to the old political order, directed toward the revamping of Russian political structures along Western constitutional lines. The Revolution of 1905, however, represented a major watershed in zemstvo history, prompting these institutions to renounce their former liberal and progressive leaders and to work at crosspurposes to the alleged political goals of the zemstvo movement.

To be sure, the zemstvo gentry did not rush to replace their former liberal leaders with outright reactionaries committed to the restoration of the pre-1905 political order. Such elements apparently did not exist in significant numbers among the gentry landowners of the provinces, who collectively did not waver in their commitment to the foundation of representative institutions as a necessary, long-awaited check upon the authority of the alien bureaucracy.[37] The Kadets and progressives were supplanted as the dominant element within the zemstvo leadership, therefore, by political moderates, in the main veterans of the Liberation Movement, who had provided the zemstvo movement with its "second-string" leadership before 1905, including many of the assistants and protégés of their more liberal predecessors. Most of these new zemstvo leaders, who had been converted to a moderate constitutionalism in the course of 1905, adhered (as did so much of the zemstvo gentry at this time) to the Octobrist party, a political formation which accepted the October Manifesto as a sufficient basis for a constitutional order by virtue of the broad legislative powers that it conferred on the national assembly and its guarantees of civil liberties.[38] In this, they were opposed by the Kadets, who wished to press on for the establishment of a more democratic, fully parliamentary regime, complete with a ministry responsible to the legislative chamber (although the Kadets were by no means opposed to reaching a political accommodation with the old order).

The actual functioning of the political order established by the October Manifesto and the political situation of the times, however, severely strained the fledgling constitutionalism of the new Octobrist leadership of the zemstvo movement and their gentry constituency, inducing many, if not most, of them to act quite contrary to their professed political principles. For example, confronted with widespread agrarian disorders and sporadic peasant attacks on their estates, the Octobrist gentry and their zemstvo following soon found themselves condoning the repressive measures used by the government to curb the spreading revolution. As Table 5.2 demonstrates, instead of calling for the immediate observation of the civil liberties granted by the October Manifesto and criticizing the government for violations of the rights of citizens, especially zemstvo personnel, as the zemstvos have done repeatedly in the past, local zemstvo assemblies now ignored large-scale government violations of human rights, even when such actions affected zemstvo members and employees, while venting their spleen against acts of revolutionary terrorism against government personnel, which the government often cited to justify its own repressive actions. At the same time, incidences of right-wing terrorism were generally overlooked, and a significant proportion of the provincial zemstvos – at least a third – went as far as to petition the government to postpone the introduction of the "freedoms" promised by the October Manifesto until "law and order" were restored in Russia.

Such initiatives were strongly opposed by the few remaining Kadets in the local zemstvos, who pointed out that the zemstvos' talk of "law and order" and frequent condemnations of acts of revolutionary violence were tantamount in the absence of resolutions to the contrary to zemstvo sanctioning of the ever mounting government repression (as, indeed, high state officials, from the minister of internal affairs to the provincial governors, tended to interpret such resolutions on the part of the zemstvos).[39] But these arguments carried little weight with most zemstvo men, like the Octobrist A. D. Protopopov of Simbirsk, who maintained at the end of 1906: "It is necessary to say not enough to courtmartials but enough to revolution."[40] The courtmartials to which Protopopov referred were, of course, Stolypin's notorious roving military tribunals, which were sent to areas of revolutionary unrest with the power to try, sentence, and even execute persons charged with revolutionary "crimes" within the course of a single day, without allowing those condemned any opportunity to appeal their sentences.

Similarly, the zemstvo gentry's nominal commitment to modern parliamentarism was deeply eroded by the actual experiences of the first two State Dumas. The social and political composition of these

Table 5.2. *Provincial zemstvo assemblies and the civil liberties of citizens, 1904–7*

Political demands	Number of assemblies espousing such demands
November 1904 to November 1905	
Immediate guarantees of civil liberties; i.e., freedom of speech, press, assembly, and the right of habeas corpus	34
November 1905 to June 1907	
Immediate introduction of the civil liberties promised by the October Manifesto	2[a]
Postponement of the introduction of civil liberties promised by October Manifesto until "law and order" had been restored in Russia	12[b]
Protests against government violations of civil liberties	2[c]
Refusals to protest against government violations of civil liberties	5[d]
Support for Stolypin's repressive measures (including the use of field courtmartials)	10[e]
Condemnations of left-wing terrorism	56[f]
Attack on Stolypin's life	18[g]
Plot against the tsar's life	23[h]
Assassination of Admiral Dubasov[i]	3[j]
Assassination of Ignatev[k]	12[l]
Condemnations of right-wing terrorism (assassination of the Moscow zemstvo member and First Duma Deputy M. Ia. Gertsenshtein)[m]	0[n]

[a]The assemblies concerned were the Ufa and Kazan provincial zemstvos.

[b]The assemblies concerned were the Ekaterinoslav, Kaluga, Moscow, Olonets, Orel, Perm, Poltava, Pskov, Smolensk, Saint Petersburg, Vologda, and Voronezh provincial zemstvos.

[c]The assemblies concerned were the Vladimir and Kharkov zemstvos, which protested the arrest of zemstvo deputies. No zemstvos issued a protest against the use of field courtmaritals.

[d]The assemblies concerned were the Ekaterinoslav, Moscow, Penza, Smolensk, and Tauride provincial zemstvos.

[e]The assemblies concerned were the Bessarabia, Iaroslavl, Kherson, Olonets, Poltava, Tambov, Tula, Tver, Saint Petersburg, and Vologda provincial zemstvo assemblies.

[f]Many provincial zemstvos protested more than once against various acts of left-wing terrorism.

[g]The assemblies concerned were the Bessarabia, Chernigov, Iaroslavl, Kazan, Kaluga, Kherson, Kursk, Olonets, Penza, Poltava, Pskov, Simbirsk, Saint Petersburg, Tambov, Tula, Tver, Viatka, and Vologda provinical zemstvos. In addition, 157

of the 359 county zemstvos expressed their horror at the attack on Stolypin's life.
ʰThe assemblies concerned were the Chernigov, Ekaterinoslav, Iaroslavl, Kaluga, Kostroma, Kursk, Moscow, Nizhnii Novgorod, Olonets, Orel, Penza, Perm, Poltava, Pskov, Riazan, Simbirsk, Smolensk, Saint Petersburg, Tver, Tula, Ufa, and Vladimir provincial zemstvos. All the assemblies plot was revealed save the peasant-dominated Viatka zemstvo accepted such resolutions.
ⁱAdmiral Dubasov was responsible for the bloody suppression of the Moscow uprising in December 1905.
ʲThe assemblies concerned were the Orel, Saratov, and Simbirsk provincial zemstvos.
ᵏIgnatev was a former "liberal" minister of education of the early 1880s who was currently serving as a member of the Tver zemstvo.
ˡThe assemblies concerned were the Bessarabia, Kazan, Kaluga, Kursk, Moscow, Penza, Pskov, Saint Petersburg, Saratov, Simbirsk, Tver, and Tula provincial zemstvos.
ᵐGertsenshtein was the author of the Kadet land project in the First Duma and a current member of the Moscow zemstvo.
ⁿAlthough resolutions to express indignation upon Gertsenshtein's assassination were introduced into the Tambov assembly and Gertsenshtein's own Moscow zemstvo, such proposals were soundly defeated.
Source: TsGIA, f. 1288, op. 2, ed. khr., pp. 76–1906; B. B. Veselovskii, Istoriia zemstva za sorok let, 4 vols. (St. Petersburg, 1909–11), 4:50; and the printed proceedings of the provincial zemstvos concerned for 1905–7.

legislative chambers came as an enormous shock to the zemstvo members, who fully expected to play a prominent, if not dominant role in the new political order. Now, notwithstanding a multi-staged electoral system deliberately weighted to favor the propertied elements of Russian society, the near universal manhood suffrage allowed by the October Manifesto, combined with the numerical preponderance of the peasantry and the prevailing high levels of class antagonisms in the countryside, resulted in the election of peasant-dominated chambers in which virtually all the delegates of gentry origins – in the main the outcast Kadets and progressives – were committed to the far-reaching and possibly unlimited expropriation of gentry lands.[41] As a result, the mainstream of zemstvo political opinion was not only effectively deprived of a voice in the reconstructed Russian government, which had been the goal of the zemstvo gentry's political activity in 1905, but the new State Dumas, which were preoccupied with the land question, threatened the propertied interests of the gentry far more severely than the old bureaucratic regime had ever done.[42]

Under these conditions, the zemstvo gentry failed to defend the prerogatives of the First Duma in its prolonged struggle with the government, although the zemstvo movement had overwhelmingly insisted on legislative powers for the national assembly throughout 1905. Instead the zemstvos concealed their growing disapproval of the Duma behind a wall of silence on the subject, which was maintained even after the escalating conflict between the national assembly and government had terminated in the dissolution of the Duma on July 8, 1906.[43] The zemstvos' failure to rally to the cause of the First Duma greatly weakened the legislative chamber in its confrontation with the forces of the old political order, for liberal political strategy had always counted heavily on substantial zemstvo support for any representative assembly on the grounds that no Russian government would dare dismiss any chamber that enjoyed the backing of the chief organs of local self-government, the zemstvos.[44] The zemstvos' indifference to the fate of the Duma was all the more striking (and carried all the more weight) in face of the active opposition shown the legislative chamber by the new national association of provincial noble corporations, the United Nobility, whose membership, a significant proportion of whom were zemstvo men, strongly criticized the Duma at its constituent congress in May and whose leadership immediately began to place behind-the-scenes pressures on the government for the dissolution of the Duma.[45]

The zemstvos' official neutrality with respect to the national assembly was rapidly abandoned when the elections to the Second Duma produced results quite similar to the first elections, despite minor government tampering with the electoral system. Indeed, the zemstvo movement soon became actively involved in a campaign to exacerbate relations between the Second Duma and government in hopes of inducing the government to dismiss the legislative chamber once again *and* to revise Duma electoral procedures to enhance substantially the political role of the more prosperous elements of the Russian population, especially the zemstvo gentry. To these ends, the zemstvos launched an attack on the government's most far-reaching attempt to cooperate with the Duma in the enactment of long-needed social and political reforms – the plans of the new prime minister, P. A. Stolypin, to reorganize and somewhat democratize local government, including the zemstvos, by basing electoral rights not on estates (*sosloviia*) as did the 1890 zemstvo law, but on the amount of zemstvo taxes paid.

Explicitly denying the prerogatives of *both* the Duma and the government to legislate on matters concerning local government without prior consultation with the zemstvos, the new Octobrist leadership of the zemstvos hastily convened a series of conferences of zemstvo leaders between January and April 1907. These relatively unknown meetings, the last of which attracted more participants than any of the zemstvo congresses before 1904–5, called upon the local zemstvos to hold special sessions in the spring of 1907 to discuss the issue of local reforms and to elect delegates to a national zemstvo congress scheduled to meet on June 5, 1907, to deal with this and "other current issues."[46]

To be sure, the ostensible – and one very real – purpose of these endeavors was to block a series of reforms that probably would have had the effect of excluding much of the zemstvo gentry from their cherished role in local government. Yet a majority of the zemstvo men who organized the 1907 congress currently favored an electoral system for the zemstvo quite similar to the government reform proposals (that is, a zemstvo franchise based on the amount of zemstvo taxes paid),[47] so it appears that the State Duma even more than the government was the main target of these initiatives. The unofficial yet frequently quoted motto of the 1907 zemstvo congress – Is not the opinion of five hundred zemstvos worth more than five hundred Duma deputies?[48] – was not only a direct attack on the power of the Duma to legislate but also counterposed the zemstvos to the Duma as an alternate, possibly even more authoritative source of public opinion. At any rate, the zemstvo men clearly hoped that their activities would place additional strain on the already tenuous relations between the government and Duma. With these goals in mind, the special sessions of the provincial zemstvos, meeting in April and May, insisted in no uncertain terms on the zemstvos' right of preliminary consideration of all legislation affecting them. Many assemblies went as far as to demand that the government immediately withdraw all its local reform projects from legislative consideration, including those bills which the cabinet had *already* submitted to the Duma.[49] Yet the few remaining Kadets and progressives in the local zemstvos, including D. N. Shipov, once the most authoritative zemstvo leader in the country, tended to regard such demands as a deliberate attempt to provoke a political confrontation between the Duma and government.[50] When confronted with such charges, A. A. Naryshkin, an influential member of the Orel zemstvo and of the Permanent Council of the United Nobility, simply confirmed them, maintaining that if the gentry's political activities terminated in a clash between the Duma and government "then this will serve as a pretext for the dissolution [of the Duma] and in such case we will actually aid the cause, if only indirectly."[51]

The local zemstvos also "aided the cause" by joining in the right wing's campaign against political terrorism with hopes of further discrediting the Duma, since the current majority of the legislative chamber was most reluctant to express itself on this issue, being far more concerned about the government's large-scale violations of human rights in its attempts to suppress the revolution. The Duma's reluctance in this matter, however, was viewed most negatively in government – and court – circles, especially after the Duma was able to endorse unanimously a right-sponsored resolution expressing the chamber's indignation at the revelation of a year-old abortive plot against the life of the tsar on May 8 only after more than a third of the Duma deputies abstained from voting. In order to keep this sensitive issue continually before the government, all the local zemstvo assemblies meeting after the Duma vote (with the sole exception of the "peasant" Viatka zemstvo) unanimously proclaimed their concern for the personal safety of the monarch; and the organizers of the 1907 zemstvo congress pointedly planned to place the issue of left-wing terrorism first on the agenda of their coming congress, removing this issue from their agenda only after the dissolution of the Duma.[52]

Precisely what role all this agitation played in the coming of the June 3, 1907 coup d'état – Stolypin's dismissal of the Second Duma and his simultaneous promulgation of a new, highly restrictive electoral law – cannot be determined due to the fact that, at Stolypin's instigation, few government records pertaining to the coup were kept.[53] What is known, however, is that much of the left and liberal press at the time as well as highly respected progressives like M. A. Stakhovich, the Orel marshal of the nobility, firmly believed that the 1907 congress and the coup d'état were somehow linked.[54] The remarks of various important figures on the organizational bureau of the zemstvo congress, such as Count D. A. Olsufev and M. D. Ershov, also indicate that some congress organizers clearly intended for the congress to play more than an "indirect" role in the revision of Duma electoral procedures. As early as November 1906, before the election results to the Second Duma were in, Olsufev, who was a close personal friend of Stolypin's and took the lead in calling for the convocation of a zemstvo congress in 1907, advocated the convocation of an assembly of public activists (the usual euphemism for zemstvo men) which was to meet "publicly" to work out a new electoral system for the Duma "not with the goal of promoting a coup d'état but with the goal of keeping the law in its briefcase as a restraining influence on the activity of the Duma." On April 12, 1907, in a private session of the Permanent Council of the United Nobility of which he was a member, Olsufev went further, hinting broadly that the zemstvo congress would indeed perform such a function by composing a new electoral law for the Duma if Duma electoral procedures had not been revised by the time the congress convened in June.[55]

154

Moreover, the timing of the coup d'état, which occurred two days before the 1907 zemstvo congress was originally scheduled to meet, indicates that the zemstvo conclave must have played some role in the government's political calculations, as does the rather cryptic remark made to the Extraordinary Investigatory Commission of the Provisional Government of 1917 by Stolypin's Deputy Minister of Internal Affairs, S. E. Kryzhanovskii, the actual author of the June 3 electoral law, to the effect that the June 3, 1907 coup d'état represented "the reconciliation of Stolypin with the zemstvo men."[56] At the very least, it is likely that an open political confrontation between the zemstvos and the Duma would have ensued had not the June 3 coup d'état intervened.

In this way, the zemstvo movement in the First and Second Duma periods did not promote Russian constitutional development along Western lines as much as it did constitutional deformation, contributing to the establishment of the truncated, semi-demi-constitutional order of the Third of June, with its questionable guarantees of civil liberties and human rights, unclear division of authority between government and Duma, uncertain rights of the national assembly, and highly restrictive electoral system which unduly favored the propertied elements of Russian society, especially the landowning gentry.

The Stolypin era, 1907–14

The June 3 coup d'état did represent, however, as Kryzhanovskii pointed out, the reconciliation of the Russian government in the person of its new prime minister, P. A. Stolypin, with the zemstvo men. Henceforth throughout the prewar years, the government would seek to work closely and harmoniously with the zemstvos and to involve these institutions in the formulation and implementation of government policy. Stolypin, who began his political career not in the bureaucratic chancelleries of Saint Petersburg but as a local gentry activist and improving landowner in Kovno province,[57] tended quite naturally to identify closely with the zemstvo gentry and to allow the zemstvos a key role in the administration of many of his pet legislative projects in the localities, from the so-called Stolypin land reform to the introduction of compulsory primary education in the countryside. To these ends, the government, which only recently had attempted to curb zemstvo spending severely, now poured ever increasing sums into zemstvo coffers, thus financing the rapid expansion of zemstvo services characteristic of these years. By 1904 almost 40 percent of the funds spent by the local zemstvos came directly from the state treasury, with the government accounting for a very significant proportion of zemstvo budgetary allocations in the key fields of education and agriculture.[58] At the same time, zemstvo institutions were introduced into 9 additional provinces, thereby increasing the number of zemstvo provinces from 34 to 43,[59] while plans were frequently discussed in government circles in the Stolypin years to establish zemstvos in other areas of the country, to replace the current separate peasant volost administration with zemstvo institutions elected by all classes of the Russian population, and to enhance zemstvo authority and responsibilities substantially.

Even more importantly, as a result of the Stolypin-sponsored coup d'état of June 3, 1907, the zemstvo gentry emerged as the single most significant socio-political force in the legislative branch of government. The new Duma electoral law essentially limited the representation of the outlying, nonzemstvo areas of the country and, to use the words of the law's author, Kryzhanovskii, "filtered" the electoral process through the conservative medium of the larger private landowners[60] by granting this element, close to two-thirds of whom were nobles,[61] the lion's share of the seats in the provincial electoral assemblies, which selected the Duma deputies. In 27 provinces, including most zemstvo provinces, landowners accounted for an actual majority of provincial electors. Elsewhere, it was assumed that the landowners could form electoral alliances with what was presumed to be the equally conservative larger urban property owners, many of whom were also members of the noble estate (soslovie).[62] In this way the landowning gentry replaced the land-hungry peasantry as the dominant element among the electorate to the lower house of the new Russian parliament.

Given these conditions it is not surprising that an actual majority of the deputies to the Third and Fourth State Dumas were indeed landed noblemen.[63] The zemstvo gentry alone, as Table 5.3 demonstrates, occupied half the seats allocated to the zemstvo provinces in these chambers, thus providing almost a third of all Third and Fourth Duma deputies, including almost all of the more prominent and influential legislators, such as S. I. Shidlovskii, M. V. Rodzianko, N. A. Khomiakov, Count V. A. Bobrinskii, F. I. Rodichev, and P. N. Krupenskii, as well as the gadflies of the Duma right, the notorious and highly vocal V. M. Purishkevich and N. E. Markov.

The influence of the zemstvo gentry in the legislative branch of government was by no means restricted to the Duma. As Table 5.4 demonstrates, zemstvo men originally contributed at least half of the elected delegates (and a quarter of the total membership) of the upper house of the Russian legislature, the reformed State Council, accounting for all 34 of the representatives of the provincial zemstvo assemb-

Table 5.3. Zemstvo men in the legislative branch of government: the State Dumas, 1906–17

Duma	Deputies with zemstvo backgrounds	Number of representatives allotted the zemstvo provinces	Percent representatives of zemstvo provinces with zemstvo service	Total duma deputies	Percent zemstvo men in Duma
First	95	288	33.0	524	18.1
Second	53	288	18.4	524	10.1
Third	141	281	50.2	442	31.9
Fourth	136[a]	281	48.4	442	30.8

[a] Actually, there were at least 152 zemstvo men in the Fourth State Duma if one includes 16 additional members of the new western zemstvos, which were just in the process of being introduced at the time of the Duma elections.

Source: B. B. Veselovskii, Istoriia zemstva za sorok let, 4 vols. (St. Petersburg, 1909–11), 4:80–3; and Chetvertyi sozyv gosudarstvennoi dumy, khudozhestvennyi fototipicheskii al'bom s portretami i biografiiami (St. Petersburg, 1913).

Table 5.4. *Zemstvo men in the legislative branch of government: the State Council, 1906–9*

Categories of members	Total number	Zemstvo men
Appointed members	98	no data
Elected members	98	no data
From the provincial zemstvo assemblies	34	34
From the Russian nobility	18	15
From the western landowners	22	0[a]
Others (from the universities, trade, and industry)	24	no data
Total	196	49

[a] No zemstvos existed in the western provinces at this time.
Sources: B. B. Veselovskii, *Istoriia zemstva za sorok let*, 4 vols. (St. Petersburg, 1909–11), 4:36; and Alexandra Deborah Shecket, "The Russian Imperial State Council and the Policies of P. A. Stolypin, 1906–1911: Bureaucratic and *Soslovie* Interests versus Reform" (Ph.D. dissertation, Columbia University, 1974), pp. 62–81.

lies as well as almost all the 18 members allocated to the Russian nobility.[64] Subsequently the share of zemstvo men in this chamber was further enhanced by the introduction of zemstvo institutions into the seven western provinces in 1911, thus enabling gentry zemstvo representatives of Russian ethnic origins to replace most of the Polish nobles who had previously represented this area in the upper house.[65] To these figures should also be added the undeterminable number of appointed members and members of other categories (especially the representatives of the Russian universities) who possessed zemstvo backgrounds. Moreover, one must remember that the weight of the elected members in the State Council was all the greater than their actual numbers because the appointed members (primarily high government officials and former officials) appear to have been almost evenly divided – as indeed was the higher bureaucracy as a whole in the early twentieth century – between reformist and antireformist elements, and this chamber passed or rejected most key legislative projects by rather narrow margins.[66] Indeed, as we shall see, the addition of zemstvo men to the State Council actually increased the weight of conservative elements in this key legislative chamber.

Finally, the zemstvo gentry provided a majority of members of a highly important but relatively unstudied quasi-legislative institution, the Council on the Affairs of the Local Economy (*Sovet po delam*

Table 5.5. *Zemstvo men in the legislative branch of government: the Council on the Affairs of the Local Economy, 1907–11*

Categories of members	Total number	Zemstvo men
Appointed members[a]	24	—[b]
Elected members		
Representatives of the provincial zemstvo assemblies	36[c]	36
Representatives from the city dumas of major urban centers	12	—[b]
Representatives of the nobility	8	8
Total	70	44

[a]Appointed members consisted of Minister of Internal Affairs (and Prime Minister) Stolypin, his Deputy Minister Kryzhanovskii, and 22 selected provincial governors. In view of the zemstvo backgrounds of increasing numbers of provincial governors, it is quite likely that some of these men were also former zemstvo activists.
[b]Because a number of high officials in the Ministry of the Interior, from which most government appointees on this body came, possessed backgrounds as former local gentry activists, some no doubt served on the zemstvo at one time or another. Biographical information on government appointees was not available to me; however, such information does exist in Soviet archives.
[c]Two zemstvos, Kursk and Pskov, were represented by two delegates.
Source: P. P. Koropachinskii, *Reforma mestnogo samoupravleniia po rabotam Soveta po delam mestnogo khoziaistva* (Ufa, 1908), p. 2.

mestnogo khoziaistva), which contemporaries often considered a "pre-parliament," if not a third legislative chamber in the post-1907 political order due to the fact that this assembly was empowered to review all government legislation pertaining to local government before such bills could be submitted to the Duma (see Table 5.5).[67] Pleve had originally conceived the Council on the Affairs of the Local Economy in 1904 as an advisory council consisting of both appointed members and members elected by the local zemstvo assemblies, which was to be established under the auspices of his ministry in hopes of tempering the growing conflict between the zemstvos and government.[68] The council, which was not founded at this time due to Pleve's assassination and the outbreak of the Revolution of 1905, was revived by Stolypin in the autumn of 1907, as a concession to persisting gentry agitation against his local reform projects in the form of the two zemstvo congresses of June and August 1907, and the petitions of many local zemstvos and noble corporations.[69]

The presence of such a large contingent of zemstvo men among the legislators of the Third of June system is sometimes viewed as a positive development that supposedly rendered the Third and Fourth State Dumas much more capable and effective legislative chambers than either of their predecessors.[70] Thus it is assumed that the zemstvos served as valuable schools of self-government, providing their members with political experience which had not been otherwise available under the pre-1905 political order and which later stood many zemstvo men in good stead in their subsequent legislative careers. In actual practice, however, the zemstvos were permeated with an ethos and spirit that was quite inimical to modern parliamentarianism and rendered many of those who passed through this particular political school unprepared for and ill-adapted to the demands, stresses, and strains of parliamentary life. The zemstvos were not the mini-parliaments that their myth would often have them be, but rather, highly peculiar, premodern institutions whose practices and traditions reflected the values and experiences of their dominant gentry element and the unique, ingrown provincial society over which the gentry held sway. As a result of the narrow social basis of the zemstvo electoral system and the closely knit, almost incestuous social relationships that prevailed among the relatively small provincial gentry, the zemstvos actually operated less as modern representative bodies than as a network of rather exclusive private gentlemen's clubs in which most participants were related if not by actual ties of blood and matrimony (as was quite often the case) then by bonds of friendship sometimes stretching back for generations.

The Tula zemstvo activist Sergei S. Podolinskii, a member of the Octobrist party and a nephew of Prime Minister Stolypin, described the zemstvo in his memoirs as "a compact family," pointing out that, in the zemstvo,

> Everyone was acquainted with one another from childhood on. Here one could not act a part; everyone had to behave naturally. Pathos, any remarks not to the point would be considered ridiculous. Expressions of approval or misrepresentation in general were inadmissible. It was not always easy to speak in the zemstvo.[71]

In the atmosphere of a family reunion, which permeated zemstvo life, partisanship was frowned upon, and consensus, if not political unanimity, was sought even amidst the heady political turbulence of 1905.[72] Indeed, factionalism based on political principles or ideology rather than what was deemed to be the more "natural" ties of friendship and kinship was not generally tolerated for long in zemstvo circles; much of the zemstvo gentry appear to have regarded the very

160

terms *politics, political,* and even *parliamentarism* as outright pejora-
tives. If gentry memoirs are any indication, one of the major and
enduring grievances harbored by the zemstvo gentry against the
zemstvo left wing, especially the Kadets, was the Left's injection of
partisanship and political conflict into what had previously been
peaceful, "businesslike" zemstvo life.[73] Generally shunning partisanship, the zemstvo gentry consequently tended to regard themselves in
or out of the legislative chambers as they were in the zemstvo – as
unattached, independently minded representatives of their localities –
whether or not they affiliated themselves with a political faction.
Hence they were most reluctant to accept party discipline or to form
firm partisan attachments based on anything other than personal
considerations, thereby contributing to the constant fragmentation of
Duma political parties and the weakly developed political factions and
partisan ties in the other legislative chambers and in the country at
large.[74]

At the same time, the extremely limited nature of the zemstvo
electoral system and the close personal relationships that generally
prevailed among zemstvo deputies precluded the development of
many vital parliamentary skills without which no representative
system can properly function. Thus, zemstvo men regarded oratorical
abilities, which were irrelevant if not ridiculous within the family
circle of the zemstvos, as evidence of demagoguery, insincerity, and the
conscious desire to dissimulate and deceive rather than an important
political skill to be cultivated by all those involved in public life.[75]
Likewise, all other means to move and mobilize people, such as
journalism and electioneering, were largely neglected by gentry activists, who had long felt no need to appeal to people outside the closed
world of the provincial gentry; the zemstvo gentry were accustomed to
representing their localities without much effort and without appealing
to anyone but their friends and relations among their peers.[76] The
zemstvo gentry's lack of experience in this regard accounts in part –
along with the class consciousness of the peasants and workers – for
the gentry's disastrous political defeats in the relatively democratic
elections to the first two State Dumas as well as the gentry's continuing
need for an extemely circumscribed political system like that provided
by the Third of June electoral law and the Zemstvo Statute of 1890.

In addition, being largely unaccustomed to any prolonged or deep-
seated political strife within their own ranks save for the relatively
short and highly uncharacteristic period of the first Russian revolution
(1905–7), many zemstvo men were quite unprepared for the constant
political infighting and conflicts among Duma parties and factions.

161

Indeed, at least two zemstvo representatives to the Third State Duma (N. A. Melnikov of Kazan and K. N. Grimm of Saratov), both Octobrists, were so repelled by the atmosphere of strife that they encountered in the lower house that they resigned their Duma seats in order to return to the more familiar, less conflict-ridden, "businesslike" world of the zemstvo; and they did so with the blessing and sympathy of Duma President N. A. Khomiakov, a fellow party member and a long-time activist in the Smolensk zemstvo who apparently shared many of Grimm's and Melnikov's misgivings about the nature of parliamentary life.[77] Finally, because the zemstvo movement throughout most of its history had been largely locally rather than nationally oriented and the zemstvos in most periods before and after 1905 sought actively to avoid outright conflict with the government, the zemstvo activists in the legislative chambers, especially those elected to the State Council, tended to neglect national issues for purely local concerns.[78] Virtually all of them (with the possible exception of some of the Kadets) preferred, as descendants of the old service estate, to cooperate and collaborate with the government rather than engage in open conflict with it (except, of course, when the gentry's vital interests – land or local government – were at stake).[79] In this way, the zemstvo experiences of much of the dominant gentry element within the Third of June system may very well account at least in part for many negative attributes and fatal weaknesses of the parliamentarianism of the post-1907 period, such as the virtual nonexistence of political parties outside the representative chambers, the persistent disintegration of Duma party structures, the lack of clearly delineated political factions in either legislative chamber, the reluctance of the legislative branch of government to expand the very narrow social basis of the political system either locally or nationally, and the inability of the legislative chambers in the prewar years to stand up for their political prerogatives with respect to the government.[80]

These deficiencies were greatly compounded by the fact that the zemstvo gentry did not hesitate to utilize their inflated position in the new, post-1907 political order to ward off all attacks on what they deemed to be the gentry's vital interests, which were most narrowly interpreted after 1907. To be sure, the Octobrists, who originally replaced the Kadets and progressives as the dominant political element among the gentry leaders of the zemstvo provinces, proved themselves – once law and order had been restored in Russia and the Duma franchise curtailed – to be sincere constitutionalists of a uniquely Russian variety, committed to a broad program of social and political reforms.[81] To these ends the Octobrists, especially their "left"-leaning

Table 5.6. *Political eclipse of the Octobrists: the political affiliation of zemstvo men in the State Dumas, 1906–17*

	Percent of members affiliated with			
	---	---	---	---
Duma	Revolutionary parties	Kadets and progressives	Octobrists	Right of Octobrists
First	5.2	78	16.8	0
Second	7.5	54.7	11.3	26.4
Third	0	21.2	49.6	29.2
Fourth	0	13.2	36.2	50.7

Source: B. B. Veselovskii, *Istoriia zemstva za sorok let*, 4 vols. (St. Petersburg, 1909–11), 4:80–3; and *Chetvertyi sozyv gosudarstvennoi dumy*, khudozhestvennyi fototipicheskii al'bom s portretami i biografiiami (St. Petersburg, 1913).

national leadership,[82] were willing to defend the prerogatives of the legislative chambers against the administration, and they were most insistent on the observation of legality and due process of law. At the same time, they sought in cooperation with the Stolypin government the restructuring of the sociopolitical order of the old regime into a modern secular society favoring men of property but based on the equality of all before the law. The implementation of such a program entailed the toleration of non-Orthodox religions, the expansion and secularization of education, and the restructuring of local self-government to enhance the role of men of property other than the landed nobility.

As such, the Octobrist program required the eventual curtailment – or even elimination – of many of the exclusive privileges of such influential pillars of the old political order as the landed gentry and the Orthodox Church. Consequently, the Octobrists were gradually replaced after the Stolypin coup d'état as the dominant political element among the gentry of the zemstvo provinces (as the 1906–7 zemstvo elections and the elections to the Third State Duma in the landowners' curia showed them to be) by a group of far more rigid and less enlightened political activists of a clearly rightist bent. These new gentry leaders, many of whom were closely associated with the highly conservative United Nobility, supplanted the Octobrists not only in the local zemstvo assemblies[83] but in the legislative chambers as well, as Tables 5.6 and 5.7 demonstrate. This third and final major political tendency within the early twentieth-century zemstvo leadership is exceedingly difficult to categorize and classify. The rightist label generally attached to these men is at best a political approximation.

Table 5.7. *Political eclipse of the Octobrists among the elected members from the zemstovs and nobility to the State Council, 1906–14*

Year	Number of members affiliated with				
	Kadets	Progressives	Octobrists/ Center	Right of Octobrists	Total
Zemstvo Representatives					
1906	6	3	13	10	34
1909	3	2	10	19	34
1913–14	2	2	9	21	34
Representatives from the nobility					
1906	1	0	7	10	18
1909	1	0	7	10	18
1913–14	0	0	2	14	17[a]

[a] One seat alloted the nobility was vacant in 1913–14.

Sources: B. B. Veselovskii, *Istoriia zemstva za sorok let*, 4 vols. (St. Petersburg, 1909–11), 4:36; A. D. Stepanovskii, "Politicheskie gruppirovki v gosudarstvennom sovete v 1906–1907 gg.," *Istoriia SSSR*, 1965, no. 4, pp. 49–64; *Novoe vremia*, 1906, no. 10808, p. 2; A. N. Naumov, *Iz utselevshikh vospominanii, 1868–1917*, 2 vols. (New York, 1954), 2:86; TsGIA, f. 699 (the diary of the Octobrist deputy I. S. Kliuzhev); *Adres-kalerdar' na 1913 g.* (St. Petersburg, 1913), pp. 138–40.

Although those among them who entered the legislative chambers adhered to political factions and groupings sitting definitely to the right of the Octobrists, their political commitment invariably fell far short of actual enlistment in a national political party that existed outside the legislative chambers. The Octobrists' successors tended to regard political parties in the light of their zemstvo experience as an outright obstacle to the proper "businesslike" functioning of representative bodies as well as an unnecessary encumbrance on their own freedom of political maneuver as independent country gentlemen and, hence, ipso facto the rightful representatives of their localities. Moreover, these rightist activists, although most conservative, were not outright reactionaries. None of them longed to return to the pre-1905 political order, tending rather to regard themselves no less than the zemstvo left and center as the heirs of the zemstvos' "liberal," that is to say, antibureaucratic, traditions.[84]

To these men, Stolypin's reform program, especially his plans to restructure local government, which generally received the support of the Octobrist leadership after 1907, appeared, as it did to the majority of the participants in the 1907 zemstvo congresses, as a devious bureaucratic plot to undermine gentry influence in the countryside. Consequently they were most unwilling to expand the zemstvo electorate to enhance the role of the wealthier urbanites and kulaks favored by Stolypin and the Octobrist leaders, going no further in their plans to "reform" the zemstvo than the inclusion of the larger nonnoble landowners in the first (nobles') curia and the lowering of the property qualification to vote in zemstvo elections (while being most careful in light of the experiences of the first two State Dumas to limit the political role of the peasantry).[85] At the same time, the gentry right viewed the Octobrist gentry's interest in the secularization of Russian society and the expansion of public education as an outright attack on the Orthodox faith that might ultimately entail the undermining of the rather precarious social stability of the countryside by vastly increasing the numbers of potentially subversive zemstvo employees in the localities. For the introduction of compulsory primary education and its concomitant secularization required the transfer of the parish schools of the Orthodox Church to the control of the zemstvos and Ministry of Education (and hence the replacement of the loyal parish priests by third-element teachers) as well as an enormous increase in the numbers of schools and teachers in the localities.[86] Finally, the Octobrist leaders' interest in the observation of due process and rule by law appeared to many rank-and-file noblemen who had not received legal educations – and to some zemstvo men with such educations as well – as an unwarranted obsession with senseless "formalism" alien to the healthy common sense of the Russian people. In short, it was a concern more congenial to the "alien," "plodding," "pedantic," "German" bureaucracy than to practical, pragmatic gentry proprietors of the central Russian provinces.[87]

In keeping with zemstvo traditions, the gentry right supplanted the Octobrists as the dominant element in the zemstvo leadership not through outright political conflict and struggle (as was done with the Kadets in 1906–7) but rather through the gradual estrangement of local gentry activists from the Octobrist party as a consequence of the alien concerns and interests of the national party leadership. Although some left-wing Octobrists were voted out of high zemstvo positions or lost their seats in the legislative chambers after 1907, the rightward shift in the political alignment of the local zemstvo assemblies and of gentry cadres in the legislative institutions was due as much to the growing conservatism and disillusionment with political parties on the part of existing officeholders as to the influx of new elements into these representative bodies.[88] Ironically, the advent of the right to the leadership of the provincial gentry of the zemstvo provinces was

165

marked by the depoliticization of gentry political life. Although the Kadets and many progressives were still excluded from the zemstvos as traitors to their estate throughout the prewar years and left-wing Octobrists and the more moderate progressives were admitted only after they had eschewed all extraneous political goals, distinct political factions based on considerations other than personal (or family) rivalries and preferences disappeared from zemstvo life to the extent that the government in reporting the 1912–13 zemstvo elections listed only the names of the zemstvo chairmen and board members elected without appending any political labels or descriptions to them or to the assemblies that elected them.[89] At the same time, the number of officially nonpartisan (usually rightist) gentry deputies in the legislative assemblies increased significantly as well as the number of zemstvo men in these chambers adhering to political splinter groupings and to factions that existed only within the walls of the legislative institutions.[90]

The increasingly conservative propensities of the zemstvo gentry – especially its representatives in the upper house of the Russian parliament, the State Council – in the final analysis played a large role in the frustration of all efforts at the peaceful transformation of the post-1907 political order on the part of the Stolypin government and reformist elements in the State Dumas. Although Stolypin's well-known agrarian reforms were enthusiastically embraced by the zemstvo gentry as a much-welcome alternative to compulsory expropriation,[91] all other major components of his reform program ultimately went down to defeat – or were amended beyond recognition – by rightist elements in the State Council or in the Council on the Affairs of the Local Economy, in whose ranks stood increasing numbers of zemstvo men. In this way, Stolypin's local reforms were defeated outright, leaving the country to enter the trials of World War I and the Revolution of 1917 with the limited local institutions of the counter-reform era preserved intact.[92] Likewise, the prime minister's plans to introduce universal primary education in the largely illiterate country-side were never formally endorsed by the legislative chambers but were implemented by executive decree (under the provisions of the well-known article 87 of the Fundamental Laws) proclaimed in the interim between the first two State Dumas.[93]

The involvement of the zemstvos by the government in the implementation of legislation in the localities gave the zemstvo gentry yet another lever to shape government policies to its liking after 1907. As the political control of the zemstvos slipped from the hands of the reformist-minded Octobrists into those of more selfish and self-centered conservative activists, the propensities of the zemstvos to utilize their administrative role to hinder various government programs deemed incompatible with the interests of the local gentry increased accordingly. In this way, a number of local zemstvos actively hindered the implementation of the Stolypin land reforms (which the gentry generally favored) by insisting that any government aid to agriculture administered by the zemstvo be made available to *all* agriculturists (including gentry proprietors) instead of being reserved – as the government originally intended – for those peasants who had consolidated their landholdings.[94] Likewise, some zemstvo assemblies interfered with the progress of the government's educational reforms by expanding the local school network at rates far lower than those envisioned by the government or by insisting on diverting funds from secular schools to the educational establishments of the Orthodox Church.[95] Elsewhere persistent quarrels and deadlocks within some zemstvo assemblies over these thorny issues greatly hindered the zemstvo activity in these important areas.

Consequently, the enormous role allotted the zemstvo gentry in the legislative process and in the implementation of legislation under the Third of June system accounts largely for the ultimate political defeat of Stolypin's reform program long before the prime minister's untimely assassination removed him from the Russian political scene. It also accounts for the do-nothing administrations that succeeded Stolypin, which were unwilling (and unable) to take any political action contrary to the interests of entrenched elite groups in Russian society, including the gentry landowners of the zemstvo provinces.

Conclusion

Thus, the zemstvo played a most ambiguous role in Russian constitutional development. Contributing both to the establishment of central representative institutions in Russia and to the eventual limitation and frustration of the new political order that emerged from the Revolution of 1905, the zemstvos acted in both cases not as liberal institutions inherently opposed by virture of their elective natures to bureaucratic rule but, rather, as they were in reality – the political power base of an as yet insufficiently studied but nonetheless highly important gentry fronde. As such, the zemstvos were utilized by the provincial gentry, which effectively dominated these institutions under the 1890 zemstvo law, to regain – and then to defend – the gentry's recently lost political influence in state affairs. In the process the zemstvos proved themselves to be staunch opponents of bureaucratic (and legislative) reformers no less than adroit adversaries of reactionary officialdom once reformist programs proved (as any meaningful reforms would ultimately have to) detrimental to the vital interests of the gentry landowners of the provinces. The zemstvos therefore did not, as many works on these institutions tend to imply, offer a solution to the political dilemmas of the old regime. For the gentry's zemstvos, especially after 1905, were an integral – and important – part of Russia's political problems, reflecting as they did the social tensions and contradictions of the old order. As such, the zemstvos contributed as much as – if not more than – any other Imperial Russian institution to the fundamental weaknesses of the Third of June system and, hence, to tsardom's eventual political demise.

Notes

1 The period of World War I is covered in Chapter 11. For the role of the local zemstvos – as opposed to the Zemstvo Union – in the fall of the old regime, see also Lonka Fogelman, "The Gentry Opposition at the End of the Old Regime" (M.A. thesis, Columbia University, 1974).

2 This view of the zemstvos' political role permeates much of the existing literature on the zemstvo movement. See also, for example, I. I. Petrunkevich, "Blizhaishchii zadachi zemstva," in B. B. Veselovskii and Z. G. Frenkel', eds., *Iubileinyi zemskii sbornik* (St. Petersburg, 1914), p. 429–36; I. P. Belokonskii, *Zemskoe dvizhenie* (Moscow, 1914); I. P. Belokonskii, *Zemstvo i revoliutsiia* (St. Petersburg, 1906); Prince Dmitrii Shakhovskoi, "Soiuz Osvobozhdeniia," *Zarnitsy*, 1909, no. 2; B. B. Veselovskii, *Zemstvo i zemskaia reforma* (Petrograd, 1918); George Fischer, *Russian Liberalism: From Gentry to Intelligentsia* (Cambridge, Mass., 1958); Alexander Vucinich, "The State and the Local Community," in Cyril E. Black, ed., *The Transformation of Russian Society* (Cambridge, Mass., 1960), pp. 209–25 Victor Leontowitsch, *Geschichte des Liberalismus in Russland* (Frankfurt/Main, 1957); and S. Iu. Vitte, *Samoderzhavie i zemstvo: konfidentsial'naia zapiska Ministra finansov Stats–Sekretaria S. Iu. Vitte (1899)* (Stuttgart, 1903).

3 Vitte, p. 168.

4 See B. B. Veselovskii, *Istoriia zemstva za sorok let*, 4 vols. (St. Petersburg, 1909–11), 3:117–38, 172–87, 558–577; and chapter 3 of this book.

5 Veselovskii, *Istoriia*, 3:153–9, 242–50, 315–62.

6 For these attempts, see Marc Raeff, *Plans for Political Reform in Imperial Russa, 1730–1905* (Engelwood Cliffs, N.J., 1966), esp. pp. 121–40.

7 Veselovskii, *Istoriia*, 3:583–9.

8   Ibid., pp. 3–5, 100–1.
9   For a more complete description of this constitution, compare C. E. Black, *The Establishment of Constitutional Government in Bulgaria* (Princeton, 1943), esp. pp. 65–9.
10 For the details of the constitutions of 1881 and 1905, compare Raeff, pp. 132–52.
11 When the question of the participation of zemstvo representatives in general legislation was raised at a national zemstvo congress at this time, congress participants, who were among the more politicized and liberal of zemstvo men, defeated it soundly. For this development, see D. N. Shipov, *Vospominaniia i dumy o perezhitom* (Moscow, 1918), pp. 219–26.
12 Veselovskii, *Istoriia*, 3:98–101, 251–63, 498–504.
13 Shipov, pp. 240–2, 285–8. This did not mean that these conservative assemblies would not defend oppositional deputies whose rights were violated by the administration in retaliation for their political activity. For a good example of such a case, see Charles E. Timberlake, "Ivan Ilich Petrunkevich: Russian Liberalism in Microcosm," in Charles E. Timberlake, ed., *Essays on Russian Liberalism* (Columbia, Mo., 1972), pp. 31–32.
14 I. I. Petrunkevich, "Iz zapisok obshchestvennogo deiatelia," *Arkhiv russkoi revoliutsii*, 1934, no. 21, p. 290.
15 Roberta Thompson Manning, "Zemstvo and Revolution: The Onset of the Gentry Reaction, 1905–1907," in Leopold H. Haimson, ed., *The Politics of Rural Russia, 1905–1914* (Bloomington, 1979), p. 37.
16 Roberta Thompson Manning, *The Crisis of the Old Order in Russia: Gentry and Government* (Princeton, forthcoming, 1982) ch. 9.
17 Manning, "Zemstvo and Revolution," pp. 45–6.
18 Manning, *Crisis of the Old Order*, ch. 6.
19 See the discussion that accompanied the adoption of this strategy at the July 1905 zemstvo congress, "Iiul'skii zemskii s"ezd," *Osvobozdenie*, 1905, no. 76, pp. 427–55; ibid., no. 75; and TsGAOR, f. 102 (Department of the Police), op. 5, ed. khr. 1000 (materials pertaining to the 1905 zemstvo congresses) ch. 2, t. 4, pp. 71–8.
20 As many as 22 elected zemstvo officials were denied such confirmation in the 1900–5 period alone. See Veselovskii, *Istoriia*, 3:347, 357–8.
21 Ibid., pp. 8–9, 14, 49, 600–2, 647.
22 N. M. Pirumova, *Zemskoe liberal'noe dvizhenie: sotsial'nye korni i evoliutsiia do nachala XX veka* (Moscow, 1977), pp. 75–87; (TsGIA), f. 1288 (Chancellery of the Ministry of Internal Affairs on the Affairs of the Local Economy, the department that oversaw the operation of the local zemstvos and collected data on zemstvo elections) op. 2 (for 1906 and 1907); Count Constantine Benckendorff, *Half a Life: the Reminiscences of a Russian Gentleman* (London, 1954) p. 123; A. N. Naumov, *Iz utselevshikh vospominanii, 1868–1917*, 2 vols. (New

York, 1954), 1:249; Petrunkevich in *Arkhiv russkoi revoliutsii*, 1934, no. 21, p. 17; A. P. Korelin, "Rossiiskoe dvorianstvo i ego soslovnaia organizatsiia (1861–1904 gg.)," *Istoriia SSSR*, 1971, no. 5, p. 71; and B. B. Veselovskii, "Ocherednye zemskie zadachi," *Sovremennik*, May 1913, p. 312.

23 TsGIA, f. 1288, op. 2, ed. khr. 15-1907 (zemstvo election returns for 1907), pp. 84–100. Even the Cossack and honorary citizen sent to the provincial zemstvo were quite well off, owning 100 and 318 desiatinas, respectively.

24 For the best published accounts of the nobility's political crisis, compare Walter M. Pintner, "The Russian Higher Civil Service on the Eve of the 'Great Reforms,' " *Journal of Social History*, Spring 1975, pp. 55–68; Waltner M. Pintner, "The Social Characteristics of the Early Nineteenth–Century Bureaucracy," *Slavic Review* 1970, no. 3, pp. 435–8; A. P. Korelin, "Dvorianstvo v poreformennoi Rossii (1861 –1904 gg.)," *Istoricheskii zapiski*, 87, pp. 91–173; Korelin; P. A. Zaionchkovskii, *Pravitel'stvennyi apparat samoderzhavnoi Rossii v XIX v.* (Moscow, 1978). For the nobility's economic crisis, see Geroid T. Robinson, *Rural Russia Under the Old Regime* (New York, 1932), pp. 129–37; Theodore H. von Laue, *Sergei Witte and the Industrialization of Russia* (New York, 1956), pp. 28, 109–10, 168–9; and Terence Emmons, "The Russian Landed Gentry and Politics," *Russian Review*, 1974, no. 3, p. 276.

25 Alexander Izwolsky, *The Memoires of Alexander Izwolsky* (London, 1921), p. 149.

26 Such views were widespread among both conservative and liberal zemstvo men at the turn of the twentieth century. For this, see Manning, *Crisis of the Old Order*, ch. 2.

27 Walter W. Pintner in a recent article has called the professional bureaucracy "a concealed third estate." See Walter W. Pintner, "The Evolution of Russian Civil Officialdom, 1755–1855," in Walter W. Pintner and Donald K. Rowney, eds, *Russian Officialdom from the Seventeenth to the Twentieth Centuries: The Bureaucratization of Russian Society* (Durham, N.C., 1979).

28 Manning, "Zemstvo and Revolution," 33–6.

29 See Shakhovskoi, pp. 86–168.

30 K. F. Golovin, *Vospominaniia*, 2 vols. (St. Petersburg, 1909–10), 1: 267–8.

31 For these developments, see Manning, "Zemstvo and Revolution," pp. 30–1, 37–9.

32 For zemstvo elections after 1905, see Ruth Delia MacNaughton and Roberta Thompson Manning, "The Crisis of the Third of June System and Political Trends in the Zemstvos, 1907–1914," in Haimson, *The Politics of Rural Russia*, pp. 184–218; and Manning, "Zemstvo and Revolution," p. 50.

33 For this, see *Krasnyi arkhiv*, 1930, no. 39, pp. 88–91, and *Krest'ian-skoe dvizhenie v simbirskoi gubernii v pervoi revoliutsii 1905–1907 gg.: dokumenty i materialy* (Ul'ianovsk, 1955), p. 83.

34 For the impact of the 1905–7 peasant movement on gentry political attitudes, see Manning, "Zemstvo and Revolution," pp. 43–6.

35 For the Kadet land program, see Judith Zimmerman, "The Kadets and the Duma, 1905–1907," in Timberlake, *Essays in Russian Liberalism*, pp. 110–38.

36 *Russkiie vedomosti*, December 2, 1905, p. 3.

37 Neither the highly conservative United Nobility nor such right-wing gentry diehards as V. M. Purishkevich and N. E. Markov opposed the existence of representative institutions. Indeed, Purishkevich and Markov actually resigned from the Union of the Russian People over this organization's continued opposition to the existence of the Duma after Stolypin's June 3, 1907 coup d'état. A. Chernopol'skii, *Soiuz russkogo naroda po materialam chrezvychainoi sledstvennoi kommissii vremennogo pravitel'stva 1917 g.* (Moscow, 1929); and *Obedinennoe dvorianskoe obshchestvo ob usloviiakh vozniknoveniia i o deiatel'nosti obedinennogo dvorianstva* (St. Petersburg, 1907), p. 13.

38 For the original program of the Octobrist party, see Ben-Cion Pinchuk, *The Octobrists in the Third Duma, 1907–1912* (Seattle, 1974), pp. 13–19.

39 TsGIA, f. 1288, op. 2, ed. khr. 76-1906 (governors' reports on the mood of the local zemstvos in the opening months of 1906), esp. pp. 197, 252.

40 *Zhurnaly Simbirskogo gubernskogo zemskogo sobraniia, ochered-naia sessiia 1906 g.* (Simbirsk, 1907), p. xxi. The left-leaning Octoberist leadership, however, reacted far differently to these developments. For this, see Shipov, pp. 411–22.

41 For the elections to the first two Dumas, see Warren B. Walsh, "The Composition of the Dumas," *Russian Review*, 1949, no. 2, pp. 111–16; S. N. Sidel'nikov, *Obrazovanie i deiatel'nost' pervoi gosudarstvennoi dumy* (Moscow, 1962); and Aleksei Smirnov, *Kak proshli vybory vo 2-iiu gosudarstvennuiu dumu* (St. Petersburg, 1907).

42 The main concern of both Dumas – and the reason for their dissolutions – was the agrarian question. See Zimmerman, "Kadets and the Duma," pp. 119–38.

43 Only the two nongentry zemstvos of Viatka and Olonets followed the practice of many city dumas and sent the First Duma their official greetings. Not one provincial zemstvos and only 6 of the 359 district zemstvos objected to the dissolution of the legislative chamber. When the First Duma deputies protested against their dissolution by issuing the Vyborg Appeal, the government retaliated by depriving the Vyborg signatories of their political rights, including the right to participate in the zemstvos. Although this move affected 42 of the

best-known zemstvo activists in the country, it encountered very little opposition in the zemstvos, unlike similar moves against zemstvo activists in the past. See Veselovskii, *Istoriia*, 4: 37–9; and Russia. Gosudarstvennaia duma, *Stenograficheskie otchety 1906 god, sessiia pervaia*, vol. 1 (St. Petersburg, 1906), pp. 6–7, 33, 37–8, 353, and 587.

44 See, for example, I. P. Belokonskii, *Ot derevni do parlamenta: rol' zemstva v budushchem stroe Rossii* (Berlin, n.d.) esp. p. 50.

45 See Geoffrey A. Hosking and Roberta Thompson Manning, "What Was the United Nobility?" in Haimson, *The Politics of Rural Russia*, pp. 152–61.

46 *Doklad Kostromskoi gubernskoi zemskoi upravy chrezvychainomu zemskomu sobraniiu 2-go maia 1907 g.* (Kostroma, 1907), pp. 15–18; and *Stenograficheskie otchety 1-go vserossiiskogo s"ezda zemskikh deiatelei v Moskve zasedanii 10–15 iiunia 1907 g.* (Moscow, 1907), pp. 1–3.

47 A majority of the members of the organizing bureau of the 1907 zemstvo congress favored a zemstvo electoral system virtually identical to that espoused by the Stolypin government, with the one exception that the zemstvo congress organizers wished to establish a special curia of small landowners separate from the larger property owners in order to prevent the zemstvo gentry from being overwhelmed by the numerically superior peasantry as they had been during the recent elections to the first two State Dumas. The congress itself – as opposed to its organizers – completely rejected a property qualification based on taxes, such as the government desired, in favor of a system similar to the Zemstvo Statute of 1864, based on landholdings rather than estates (sosloviia). *Stenograficheskie otchety 1-go vserossiiskogo s"ezda zemskikh deiatelei v Moskve*, pp. 111-15; and *Zhurnaly i postanovleniia vserossiiskogo s"ezda zemskikh deiatelei v Moskve s 10 po 15 iiunia 1907 goda* (Moscow, 1907), pp. 113–27.

48 Count D. A. Olsuf'ev, *Ob uchastii zemstv v obsuzhdenii zemskoi reformy* (St. Petersburg, 1907); TsGAOR, f. 434, op. 1, ed. khr. 76-1906 (stenographic proceedings of the Permanent Council of the United Nobility), p. 120; Saratovskoe gubernskoe zemstvo, *Doklad i protokoly zasedanii komissii po reforme zemskogo polozheniia* (Saratov, 1907); *Zhurnaly chrezvychainykh zasedanii moskovskogo gubernskogo zemskogo sobraniia sostoiavshikhsia v 1907 g. 15, 16, i 19 fevralia,) 10, 11 i 12 aprelia, 1 i 2 iiunia*, vol. 3 (Moscow, 1907), p. 4.

49 Manning, *Crisis of the Old Order*, ch. 4.

50 TsGAOR, f. 102, op. 265, ed. khr. 49 (police monitoring of private correspondence), p. 203.

51 TsGAOR, f. 434, op. 1, ed. khr. 76-1906–7, p. 93.

52 TsGAOR, f. 102, op. 265, ed. khr. 211 (police monitoring of private correspondence) p. 20.

53 P. Kh. Shvanebakh, "Zapiska sanovnika (politika P. A. Stolypina i vtoraia gosudarstvennaia duma)," *Golos minuvshego*, January–March 1918, pp. 132–3.

54 *Stenograficheskie otchety 1-go vserossiiskogo s"ezda zemskikh deiatelei v Moskve*, p. 142. See also the accounts of the congress in *Samoupravlenie*, May 22–June 30, 1907, nos. 22–6; *Golos Moskvy*, June 10–15, 1907, nos. 134–8; *Russkiie vedomosti*, June 12–15, 1907, nos. 132–5; *Russkaia mysl'*, July 1907; and *Obrazovanie*, July– November 1907.

55 *Trudy vtorogo s"ezda upolnomochennykh dvorianskikh obshchestv 31 gubernii 14–18 noiabria 1906 g.* (St. Petersburg, 1906), p. 74; TsGAOR, f. 434, op. 1, ed. khr. 76-1906–7, pp. 91–2; M. D. Ershov, *Zemskaia reforma v sviazi s gosudarstvennym izbiriatel'nym zakonom* (St. Petersburg, 1907).

56 *Padenie tsarskogo rezhima: stenograficheskie otchety doprosov i pokazanii dannykh v 1917 g. v chrezvychainoi sledstvennoi kommissii vremennogo pravitel'stva*, vol. 5 (Leningrad, 1925), p. 389.

57 Mary Schaeffer Conroy, *Peter Arkadevich Stolypin: Practical Politics in Late Tsarist Russia* (Boulder, 1976), pp. 1–11.

58 This figure has been derived from the data in B. B. Veselovskii, *Zemstvo i zemskaia reforma*, pp. 17–23; and G. L'vov and T. Polner, *Nashe zemstvo i 50 let ego raboty* (Moscow, 1914), p. 30.

59 The provinces concerned were the six western provinces of Vitebsk, Mogilev, Minsk, Volynia, Kiev, and Podolia, and the three southeastern provinces of Orenburg, Astrakhan, and Stavropol. L'vov and Polner, p. 16.

60 See Samuel Harper, *The New Electoral Law for the Russian Duma* (Chicago, 1908).

61 Of the private landholdings over 300 desiatinas, 62.4 percent were in noble hands in 1905. *Statistika zemlevlandeniia 1905 g. Svod dannykh po 50-ti gubernii Evropeiskoi Rossii* (St. Petersburg, 1906).

62 Once the revolution was crushed, however, urban proprietors of all estates and degrees of wealth proved themselves to be far less conservative than originally expected. See Haimson, *The Politics of Rural Russia*, pp. 6, 23.

63 See Walsh in *Russian Review* 1949, no. 2, pp. 111–18.

64 In 1906, 15 of the 18 representatives of the nobility in the upper house had zemstvo backgrounds.

65 Geoffrey A. Hosking, *The Russian Constitutional Experiment: Government and Duma, 1907–1914* (Cambridge, 1973), pp. 106–49.

66 For example, the Naval General Staff Bill passed the State Council by only an eight-vote margin. Ibid., p. 85.

67 Ibid., pp. 122, 150, 160; V. S. Diakin, "Stolypin i dvorianstvo (proval mestnoi reformy)," in *Problemy krest'ianskogo zemlevladeniia i vnutrennoi politiki Rossii: Dooktiabr'skii period* (Leningrad, 1972), pp. 231–74; and N. A. Mel'nikov, "19 let na zemskoi sluzhbe" (Ms. in the Columbia University Russian Archive), pp. 334–48.

68 V. I. Gurko, *Features and Figures of the Past: Government and Opinion in the Reign of Nicholas II* (Stanford, 1939), pp. 124–5.

69 TsGIA, f. 1276 (Chancellery of the Council of Ministers), op. 3, ed. khr. 22-1907–8 (meetings of the Council of Ministers), pp. 149–50.

70 See, for example, Vladimir Mikhailovich Andreevskii, "Vospominaniia i dr. material Vladimira Mikhailovicha Andreevskogo b. chlena Gos. Soveta" (Ms. in the Columbia University Russian Archive), p. 72.

71 Sergej S. von Podolinsky, *Russland vor der Revolution: Die agrarsoziale Lage und Reformen* (Berlin, 1971), pp. 29–33.

72 In 1905, most zemstvo political petitions were passed by unanimous votes or overwhelming majorities of at least two to one and hence represent a consensus of the opinions of the zemstvo members involved. For this, see Manning, "Zemstvo and Revolution," p. 43.

73 V. A. Aveskii, "Zemstvo i zhizn' (zapiska predsedatelia zemskoi upravy)," *Istoricheskii vestnik* 1912, no. 127, esp. pp. 180–2; Andreevskii, esp. pp. 29–50; Mel'nikov, 119–22.

74 By the time of the Fourth Duma elections (1912), political parties scarcely existed outside the walls of the legislative chambers, a consequence of government repression of parties that sought to appeal to groups outside the gentry and the gentry's reluctance to adhere to political parties.

75 This attitude estranged the gentry all the more from the Kadet party, which contributed a disporportionate number of the more articulate Duma deputies.

76 Zemstvo elections were not only rarely contested but delegates were chosen largely on the basis of their family or personal connections. For this, see Benckendorff, p. 84; and Mendeleev, p. 165.

77 Mel'nikov, pp. 129–63.

78 Andreevskii, pp. 71–7.

79 Even the Kadets, as the most perceptive commentators on the party have pointed out, were torn between conflicting desires to cooperate with the Imperial Russian government and to launch a head-on assault on it. See William G. Rosenberg, "The Kadets and the Politics of Ambivalence, 1905–1917," in Timberlake, *Essays on Russian Liberalism*, pp. 139–63.

80 The future premier of the Provisional Government of 1917, Prince G. E. Lvov, a Kadet deputy to the First State Duma, provides an excellent example of a zemstvo activist who harbored all these attitudes. See T. I. Polner, *Zhiznennyi put' Kniazia Georgiia Evgenievicha L'vova* (Paris, 1932), esp. pp. 110–12.

81 For the details of the reformist program of the Octobrist party, see Hosking, pp. 50–2, and Pinchuk, pp. 28–9, 35–9.

82 For the political differences within the Octobrist party, see Hosking, 50–2; Pinchuk, 28–39; and Michael C. Brainerd, "The Octobrists and the

Gentry, 1905–1907: Leaders and Followers?" In Haimson, *The Politics of Rural Russia*, 67–93.

83 For a discussion of these elections, see MacNaughton and Manning, pp. 184–218.

84 For a good example of such attitudes, see F. V. Shlippe, untitled memoirs (Ms. in the Columbia University Russian Archive), esp. p. 93.

85 *Stenograficheskie otchety 1-go vserossiiskogo s"ezda zemskikh deiatelei v Moskve zasedaniia 10–15 iiunia 1907 g. Stenograficheskii otchety 2-go vserossiskogo s"ezda zemskikh deiatelei v Moskve za zasedaniia 25–28 avgusta 1907 g.* (Moscow, 1908); and *Zhurnal i postanovlennia vserossiiskogo s"ezda zemskikh deiatelei v Moskve s 10 po 15 iiunia 1907 goda.*

86 MacNaughton and Manning, p. 193; and Hosking and Manning, pp. 167–9.

87 Prince A. V. Obolenskii, *Moi vospominaniia i razmyshleniia* (Stockholm, 1961), pp. 244–5.

88 Prince A. D. Golitsyn, "Vospominaniia" (Ms. in the Columbia University Russian Archive), p. 294; and MacNaughton and Manning, pp. 189–204.

89 MacNaughton and Manning, p. 207.

90 Hosking, pp. 182–8.

91 Manning, *Crisis of the Old Order in Russia*, chs. 8–10.

92 Diakin, pp. 231–72.

93 Hosking, pp. 178–9. Although the Duma and the State Council both passed bills to introduce universal education in Russia, the two legislative chambers were unable to agree on a common version of this project. The State Council insisted on providing aid to church schools, whereas the education bill adopted by the Third State Duma through Kadet–Octobrist collaboration sought to secularize the new primary school network. Octobrist support for school secularization, which was much more enthusiastically embraced by the party's left-leaning national leadership than by many rank-and-file Octobrists, cost the party gentry votes in the 1912–13 zemstvo elections and in the elections to the Fourth State Duma. For this, see MacNaughton and Manning, p. 198.

94 A. Petrishchev, "Khronika vnutrennei zhizni," *Russkoe bogatstvo*, November 1910, pp. 104–7; Vas. Golubev, "Zemstvo i zemleustroistvo," *Moskovskii ezhenedel'nik*, July 31, 1910, pp. 1–7; I. Zhilkin, "Provintsial'noe obozrenie," *Vestnik Evropy* December 1909, pp. 776–87; and November 1910, p. 333.

95 MacNaughton and Manning, pp. 191–3.

6

The zemstvo and the bureaucracy, 1890–1904

THOMAS FALLOWS

The Russian regime has never proved capable of satisfying in a peaceful and planned manner the growing needs of the people. In its relationship to the liberation movement the Russian government has always applied, if one may use this term, a sluice system. The instant it recognized the appearance of a "free spirit" within the population, it set up a floodgate. When the sluice began to fill up with discontent, and the latter began to flow over the first lock, the government placed a second, third and still more gates in its path, totally forgetting the fact that, facing this kind of resistance, the very source of discontent not only cannot be destroyed but in fact grows incredibly; and that, in the end, no sluice will ever be capable of holding back the pressure of discontent, which gradually becomes transformed into indignation, malice and despair.[1]

These words, written by the zemstvo publicist Ivan Belokonskii shortly after the Revolution of 1905, aptly capture the traditional image of the imperial bureaucracy in its relations with the zemstvo. Modern historians often succumb to the temptation of envisioning an unbreachable chasm separating the zemstvo from the bureaucracy. While the zemstvo stands as the liberal incarnation of virtue, the *zemskie nachal'niki*, the provincial governors and central ministers, are condemned as a monolithic bastion of reaction. Ever since one liberal émigré coined the phrase *"vlast' i obshchestvennost'"* (the state and the liberal public),[2] historians have been inclined to accept a "black–white" image of state–zemstvo relations. Liberals used words *proizvol* (capriciousness, arbitrary rule) and *biurokratiia* (bureaucracy) so synonymously in 1905 that historians have rarely

The author would like to express his gratitude to his many colleagues who commented on the first draft of this chapter, especially Roberta Manning, Terence Emmons, Richard Robbins, Daniel Field, Daniel Orlovsky, Reginald Zelnik, and William Rosenberg.

177

stopped to question whether things were in fact that bad for the zemstvo.

The more closely one looks into zemstvo–state relations, however, the clearer it becomes that the conventional idea of a virtuous zemstvo pursued by an evil bureaucracy is a distorted impression of a complicated reality. To be sure, zemstvo leaders did come into bitter conflict with the bureaucracy in 1905, and in a few celebrated provinces like Tver the zemstvo seemed endlessly at odds with local officials. Nevertheless, we should not allow these moments of discord to lead us to the conclusion that zemstvo–state relations were fundamentally antagonistic. An impartial investigation into the zemstvo's dealings with the bureaucracy would indicate that the zemstvo was much less innocent and the bureaucracy much less reactionary than the conventional image would allow. Considering the flaws in the zemstvo's services to the population, one can understand some of the suspicion felt by the bureaucracy toward the zemstvo. This chapter will attempt to demonstrate that the two sides of *vlast'* and *obshchestvennost'* had more in common than liberal publicists would have admitted.

One of the basic problems in studying the zemstvo is determining the status of the zemstvo within the structure of the imperial governmental system. After the creation of the zemstvo in 1864, legal scholars and journalists debated whether the zemstvo was a part of the government or belonged to the sphere of private organizations. The two theories put forward – the so-called public (*obshchestvennaia*) theory and state theory – reveal the ambiguity of the issue. The public theory, most prevalent in the 1860s and 1870s, stressed the separate status of the zemstvo from the state, whereas the state theory, dominant at the end of the century, saw the zemstvo essentially as one link in the chain of bureaucratic command from Saint Petersburg to the village.[3] Underlying these two theories on the nature of self-government lie two basic tendencies in the way historians study the zemstvo. One approach is to define the zemstvo politically, as a forum for Russian liberals. The other is to define this institution administratively, essentially as a welfare agency serving the educational, health, and economic needs of the population.

This traditional division between political and administrative approaches to the zemstvo can only distort our understanding of the zemstvo in its relations with the bureaucracy. From the standpoint of the tsarist administration, both aspects of the zemstvo – its danger of becoming the source for a constitutionalist movement and its usefulness as a welfare agency – carried weight in the thinking of high officials on the zemstvo. While one minister could warn the tsar of the threat posed by this liberal institution independent of bureaucratic control, another minister could rush to the zemstvo's defense, reminding His Majesty of the vital contribution it made to the development of Russian schools and hospitals. Accordingly, when we encounter complaints by zemstvo liberals of the bureaucracy's political conspiracy against it, we must also remember the basic administrative harmony uniting the zemstvo and the bureaucracy.

High government officials in the 1880s recognized the confusion created by the zemstvo's ambiguous status of 1864,[4] and drew up the counterreform of 1890 to make the zemstvo more clearly integrated into – or swallowed up by – the state bureaucracy. All elected officials of the zemstvo, once considered private citizens, now held the same legal status as officials in the administration. As we shall see below, the provincial governor gained new powers of supervision over the zemstvo, and liberal activists became alarmed at this growing threat to the autonomy of Russian self-government. In many ways the two decades preceding the Revolution of 1905 appear as an era of unrelenting attack by the state on the zemstvo's prerogatives, as the government issued a steady stream of laws limiting the zemstvo's role in the administration of hospitals, schools, veterinary care, and relief from famine and epidemics. These actions by the state undeniably struck zemstvo leaders as part of a political conspiracy against *obshchestvennost'*. Yet in retrospect modern historians must see through this political controversy to perceive the zemstvo and bureaucracy as two parts of one broader whole, the administrative apparatus of tsarist Russia. Even though in the minds of zemstvo liberals the bureaucracy may have been motivated by a vengeful desire to destroy self-government, a closer analysis of relations between the zemstvo and bureaucracy will reveal more generous motivations in the minds of state officials.

Another problem in studying zemstvo–bureaucratic relations is that we cannot generalize about "the state," since the government itself was deeply divided in terms of both territory and function. Unless one appreciates the distinction between the provincial and central bureaucracies, one will be forever doomed to use stereotypes, such as the one quoted on the first page of this essay, of a grand effort by "the regime" to restrain the growth of the zemstvo. The zemstvo came into contact with the bureaucracy on two levels; its relations with the provincial governors differed significantly from its relations with the central ministries. This chapter will accordingly be divided into two parts.

The first section, on the zemstvo's relations with the governor and provincial society, seeks to show the essential harmony of zemstvo –state relations on the local level. The central source in this section, a study of legal disputes among the zemstvo, the governor, and private plaintiffs, will demonstrate how poorly the conventional labels of *vlast'* and *obshchestvennost'* fit the reality of the zemstvo's relations with surrounding society. Where conflict did exist on the provincial level, the governor's opposition to zemstvo programs was motivated largely by his concern for protecting the local population from abuses by the zemstvo. Political divisions between a "liberal" zemstvo and a "conservative" provincial bureaucracy thus appear largely irrelevant for the majority of cases.

By contrast, the second section, on the zemstvo's relations with Saint Petersburg, will demonstrate where the *vlast'–obshchestvennost'* division is valid. Based on archival sources, this section attempts to explain the reasons for the growing hostility among state officials toward zemstvo leaders. Here another division within the bureaucracy will become apparent, the important functional split between the interior and finance ministries. This section will show how, by the eve of the Revolution of 1905, the pressure felt in Saint Petersburg by the government's effort to industrialize the country while simultaneously fighting the growth of revolutionary agitation led the central ministries to provoke the rise of a unified zemstvo opposition.

Zemstvo, society, and provincial administration: proizvol and taxes

Any effort to study relations between the zemstvo and bureaucracy stumbles immediately upon the problem of sources. The sources most commonly used by historians of the zemstvo, the memoirs and histories written by zemstvo activists themselves,[5] are useful in documenting the rise of a feeling of opposition among men of the zemstvo. They are of limited value, however, for an objective view of how the zemstvo fared within the imperial system.

One alternative to the problem of sources is to study the legal disputes between the zemstvo and the bureaucracy. Both the zemstvo and the governor enjoyed the right to appeal each other's actions to Russia's Supreme Court, the Senate. An analysis of these appeals would show us some of the most important concerns of the zemstvo and the bureaucracy, and it would offer a more systematic and impartial view of state–zemstvo relations than is normally available.

A source exists for studying these Senate appeals. Beginning in 1902, Nikolai Kuznetsov of the Voronezh provincial zemstvo board compiled a collection of all Senate rulings on local governmental disputes and started publishing them for reference use by other zemstvos. Demand for the collection led to the publication of subsequent volumes, so that by 1914 several thousand rulings had been printed.[6] The Voronezh compilations cannot be considered a complete index of all Senate rulings, but they do represent an adequate sample.[7] The Kuznetsov collection is a remarkable set of documents deserving further attention, but, as far as I know, it has been studied only once before.[8]

Previous studies of the Senate's relationship to local government have been concerned primarily with the Senate itself and the legal principles it upheld rather than with the contesting parties who brought their cases before it.[9] The approach here is the reverse: instead of concentrating on the Senate's reasoning in its decision, this chapter examines the types of disputes raised in local government, when they arose, which parties were involved, and who tended to win the Senate's favor. To study the bureaucratic origins of the rise of zemstvo liberalism before 1905, I have selected all Senate rulings in the Kuznetsov collection between June 12, 1890, when the new counterreform law was issued, and November 6, 1904, when the first zemstvo congress of the Revolution of 1905 took place. I entered each Senate ruling on a computer card and used the SPSS computer program to analyze the disputes according to the date, location, nature, and outcome of their conflict; the results are tabulated below.

Not only will this survey of Senate rulings reveal the types of conflicts engaging the "average" zemstvo men and local state officials, it will also display the significant strife that existed between the zemstvo and the population of the provinces. Nearly everyone who came in contact with the zemstvo brought suit against it, not just governors but also peasants, industrialists, town mayors, and women of rural Russia. Thus these cases provide a systematic picture of the zemstvo in its dealings with the surrounding society.

Some of the other chapters in the present volume demonstrate the contributions of the zemstvo to the local population – the valuable schools, hospitals, and economic facilities providing relief to the population. Here the Senate disputes will reveal the debit side of the ledger, the protests of the population to the high cost of those zemstvo services. Even zemstvo leaders themselves sometimes recognized that the gulf between *vlast'* and *obshchestvennost'* meant little to the provincial poor. Facing his associates at a Beseda meeting in August 1904, Count Geiden asked, "Could you imagine the peasant being ready for universal suffrage when he can't even distinguish between the zemstvo board and the police administration?"[10]

In his play *The Barbarians* (1906), Maxim Gorky satirized Russian society's readiness to take its adversaries to court. A hard-nosed, businesslike peasant named Cherkun threatens a peasant employee, "You

Table 6.1. *Number of appeals involving zemstvos, and plaintiffs lodging appeals, 1890–1904*

Plaintiff	Number of appeals
Zemstvo appeals vs. bureaucracy	422
Bureaucracy appeals vs. zemstvo	67
Provincial bureaucracy	40
Central bureaucracy	27
Appeals by local society vs. zemstvo	249
Trade and industry	68
Peasants	56
Municipal government	23
Meshchane (petty burghers)	21
Gentry	21
Women	20
Others	40
Total	738

Source: N. I. Kuznetsov, *Sistematicheskii svod ukazov Pravitel'stvuiushchego Senata, posledovavshikh po zemskim delam*, 12 vols. (St. Petersburg, 1902–15), vols. 1–3.

will work and I'll pay you for it. But if you try anything fishy, I'll throw you out and take you to court – understand?" The town mayor in turn used this same threat against Cherkun: "You came here to build the railway, mister...Build it! I don't interfere with you, and you'd better not interfere with other people's business! And don't stick your green eyes out at me...I'll complain...I'll go to the governor."[11]

Russia is not renowned as a stronghold of legalism, but the rise of a legal consciousness at the time of the Great Reforms helped make it possible for the appeal to become a regular feature of administrative life in provincial Russia.[12] Kuznetsov's Senate cases reveal the frequency of appeal: between 1890 and 1904 a total of 738 cases involving the zemstvo were submitted to the Senate, an average of about 50 cases a year.[13] Not surprisingly, the zemstvo exercised this right more than anyone else, initiating the appeal in over half the number of cases. However, appeals were also initiated against the zemstvo, as the governor, business representatives, and peasants each lodged another one-tenth of the complaints before the Senate (see Table 6.1).

To understand the history of these appeals, we must begin with Interior Minister Dmitrii Tolstoi's counterreform proposal of 1888. From the perspective of the state, one of the major defects in the original Zemstvo Statute of 1864 was that the governor had only the passive right of vetoing zemstvo bills he considered illegal and could not actively interfere in zemstvo legislation to change its content. In presentations to the tsar and in his final proposal, Tolstoi argued that the governor should be entitled both to veto a zemstvo bill if he considered it contrary to state or local interests and also to reword the bill himself, whereas the zemstvo should be stripped of its right to protest such vetoes to the Senate. Fortunately for the zemstvo, Tolstoi died before his proposal reached the State Council for approval, and under his successor, Ivan Durnovo, the project's harshness was softened. In the final legislation of 1890, the governor gained the right to veto a zemstvo bill on the basis of its "usefulness" (*tselesoobraznost'*) but would not be able to change its content, and the zemstvo retained its right to appeal to the Senate.[14]

The consequences of this reform were significant for it heightened the tensions between the state and zemstvo and foreshadowed an increased meddling by the central ministries in the affairs of local government. Prior to 1890, a harmonious system had allowed the zemstvo and governor to resolve their differences without the involvement of Saint Petersburg. Within a seven-day period the governor could register his protest to a zemstvo bill; the zemstvo then met a second time and reconsidered the bill; and if it insisted on its original provisions the governor then had his chance to reassess the bill. Only after both sides had given the issue a second hearing was the dispute sent to the Senate. As a result, compromises were often reached before the higher appeal became necessary.[15]

Tolstoi's counterreform eliminated the second hearing in this appeal process and created a new provincial office to enforce the governor's veto. The provincial office on zemstvo affairs (renamed the provincial office on zemstvo and town affairs after the municipal counterreform of 1892) was a collegial body chaired by the governor and attended by local finance and judicial officials and by two representatives of the zemstvo.[16] The 1890 law lengthened the period within which the governor could veto zemstvo bills to two weeks for budgetary questions and one month for other matters. Usually a rubber stamp for the governors, the provincial offices managed to overrule the governors' veto only on 18 occasions between 1890 and 1904.[17] As we shall see at the end of this chapter, frustrations with this collegial board led a later minister of internal affairs, Viacheslav Pleve, to propose major reforms in the provincial administration.

To be sure, Tolstoi's counterreform created other, more significant changes in the zemstvo, most notably the shifting of representation in the zemstvo assembly from a property basis to an estate (*soslovie*) principle, extending undeniable advantages to gentry members. From the standpoint of the zemstvo's relations with the governor, however, the law's extension of the governor's veto powers represented the most serious threat to zemstvo autonomy. Article 87 entitled the governor to halt a zemstvo bill not only it if violated law but also if it "did not correspond to general state needs and uses, or manifestly (*iavno*) violated the interests of the local population."[18] What constituted state needs or local interests depended on the governor's personal interpretation, and zemstvo writers complained that this law gave free rein to "individual *proizvol*" whereby one governor could outlaw zemstvo programs that had been approved by governors elsewhere.[19] Throughout the next decade, such zemstvo leaders as Konstantin Arsenev and Ivan Petrunkevich called for a campaign against article 87 at gatherings of early zemstvo constitutionalist associations.[20]

The counterreform introduced another innovation by allowing private citizens to bring suit against the zemstvo. Before 1890 individuals had managed to do this informally, persuading the governors to submit complaints to the Senate for them against the zemstvo,[21] but now a channel was cleared for direct appeal to the Senate. And it was used. In 15 years, a total of 226 private complaints against the zemstvo reached the Senate (30 percent of all appeals), most of them protesting zemstvo taxes.

Even before we glance at the specific disputes in the Senate rulings, we can discern a basic theme emerging. Partisans of the zemstvo movement claimed that the bureaucracy, in its efforts to harness the zemstvo, was motivated by its obscurantist hostility to liberalism and social progress. The Senate cases suggest, however, that this accusation served more as a political polemic than as a description of reality. Although by convention historians look unfavorably on the bureaucracy's "protectionism" (*popechitel'stvo*) of the population, regarding it as a cynical effort to hold the masses at bay, one cannot deny the sincerity of local officials in their concern for the welfare of provincial society.[22] The counterreform, so notorious for "strangling" the zemstvo, actually inaugurated a period of unprecedented growth in zemstvo welfare activities that swelled to twin peaks of spending around 1900 and 1905, and doubled the size of the zemstvo purse. As the taxes multiplied so too rose the protests, and the waves of citizens' complaints in the Senate rather closely followed the growth of zemstvo taxes (see Tables 6.2 and 6.3). Indeed, zemstvo taxation dominated the Senate cases. Of all categories of disputes, taxation was the most frequently encountered, accounting for 258 cases (35 percent) and also helping to provoke conflict in other categories of disputes. Above all, the steady rise of private complaints against zemstvo taxes strengthened the resolve of the local bureaucracy to watch the zemstvo with a suspicious eye.[23]

Table 6.2. Number of protests lodged by private plaintiffs, 1892–1904

Plaintiff	1892	1893	1894	1895	1896	1897	1898	1899	1900	1901	1902	1903	1904
Industry and trade	1	0	0	4	3	2	9	9	1	13	12	11	3
Peasants	0	3	4	1	6	4	8	7	3	10	6	3	1
Municipal government	0	0	2	6	0	2	3	2	1	2	2	3	0
Petty burghers	0	0	1	0	1	1	1	3	0	7	5	0	2
Gentry	0	0	0	0	0	3	1	2	4	4	5	1	1
Women	0	0	2	2	2	0	1	0	2	4	5	0	2
Church	0	0	0	1	1	0	1	2	2	0	0	3	0
Citizens	0	0	0	0	0	1	0	0	2	2	0	1	1
Total	1	3	9	14	13	13	24	25	15	42	45	22	10

Sources: Iubileinyi zemskii sbornik (St. Petersburg, 1914), pp. 101, 127–8, 166–7; Sergei Witte, Samoderzhavie i zemstvo, 2d ed. (Stuttgart, 1903), p. 159.

Table 6.3. *Growth of the zemstvo budget, 1885–1906, in millions of rubles*

	1885	1890	1895	1900	1901	1906
Zemstvo and government	49.3	53.8	75.2	93.4	NA	NA
Zemstvo alone	38.9	41.9	56.4	81.9	71.1	90

Sources; For zemstvo and government figures, *Iubileinyi zemskii sbornik* (St. Petersburg, 1914), pp. 101, 127–8, 166–7; for zemstvo figures alone, Sergei Witte, *Samoderzhavie i zemstvo*, 2d ed. (Stuttgart, 1903), p. 159.

Evidence for this contention that governors responded to public pressure against the zemstvo can be found by looking more closely into the timing of the private protests. Adding up the yearly totals of private tax complaints, we find that their peak years do not coincide with the crests of *all* tax disputes heard in the Senate. In other words, someone else must be bringing suit against zemstvo taxes in the years in which private tax complaints decline. The only person who could be making up for the private complaints, of course, is the governor. Taking the percentage of private tax complaints to the total tax disputes in a given year, we find that the ratio rises and falls fairly rhythmically. In 1896, all tax protests were initiated by private citizens; the following year, over half the protests were begun by the governor. Then private complaints stirred up again until they reached their peak in 1901, when they were responsible for 94 percent of the tax disputes heard before the Senate. Thereafter the governor increased his vigilance, vetoing zemstvo taxes more and more frequently (see Table 6.4).

One should not infer from this evidence that governors were solely motivated by their altruistic love for local society. Despotic governors certainly existed in Imperial Russia, one so bad that in the mid-1890s the Interior Ministry had to remove him from his post because of his illegal beating of peasants.[24] Another governor had such a notorious reputation that his appointment to a new province had to be rescinded after nearly a thousand citizens in that province signed petitions protesting his nomination.[25]

On the whole, however, it is difficult to say that the governors were more guilty of ruling capriciously than was the zemstvo or that the zemstvo objectively cared more for the province than did the governor. The zemstvo and the provincial bureaucracy were divided over important issues, such as whether the need for increased educational and

Table 6.4. Fluctuation in number of private and gubernatorial protest about zemstvo taxes, 1890–1904

Type of protest	1890	1891	1892	1893	1894	1895	1896	1897	1898	1899	1900	1901	1902	1903	1904
Private	0	0	1	3	7	8	13	7	20	21	8	32	28	16	8
Gubernatorial	1	4	1	2	7	1	0	9	12	8	6	2	18	10	10
Total	1	4	2	5	14	9	13	16	32	29	14	34	46	26	18
Percent disputes initiated by governor	100	100	50	40	50	11	0	56	30	28	43	5	30	38	55

Source: N. I. Kuznetsov, Sistematicheskii svod ukazov Pravitel'stvuiushchego Senata, posledovavshikh po zemskim delam, 12 vols. (St. Petersburg, 1902–15), vols. 1–3.

health services could justify the addition of new taxes to the peasants' fiscal burdens. Yet in retrospect the similarities between the zemstvo and the governor seem more striking than their differences.

One way to examine the issue of whether the zemstvo suffered from bureaucratic abuse is to consider the findings of the Senate on the issue of *proizvol*. The zemstvo was the winningest party of all the groups involved in Senate cases, receiving a favorable ruling in 365 out of 738 instances (49 percent). Local government officials came in second, winning 142 cases (19 percent); if we add all cases involving the central ministries as well, the total of government victories reaches 177 (24 percent). Hence the zemstvo was defeating the government in the Senate by a ratio of two to one (see Table 6.5).

The zemstvo's success in the Senate can also be measured by calculating the likelihood for an appealing party to win its case. The zemstvo initiated appeal in 418 cases and won over two-thirds of those appeals (267 cases). By contrast, local government officials could not even break even when they brought suit in the Senate. Of 40 cases appealed by provincial officials without the involvement of the central ministries, they won only 17 victories. However, once the central bureaucracy came into the picture, the balance heavily shifted in favor of the state: the senate yielded to pressure from the ministries, ruling in favor of the state in 20 out of 27 cases initiated by the central ministries. Not surprisingly, the Interior Ministry triumphed over all the rest, winning every single one of its 16 appeals (see Table 6.6).

One must be cautious in assessing the significance of these victories for the zemstvo. One way to understand the high success rate of zemstvo appeals is to see it as a vindication of the liberal claim that the bureaucracy governed capriciously: a third party, the Senate, had objectively weighed the evidence and ruled the zemstvo to be justified in its protests.

This impression that the bureaucracy really did rule capriciously becomes even stronger when we consider how corrupt the Justice Ministry was at the turn of the century. If the Russian Supreme Court, under heavy influence from the administration, could still rule in favor of the zemstvo, then we have a strong indictment against the governor. And this was certainly the case, particularly during the administration of Justice Minister Nikolai Muravev, who took over the ministry in 1894.

Muravev held a reputation throughout Saint Petersburg as an unscrupulous careerist, bribing officials in the Senate in order to influence their rulings and actually instructing magistrates to interpret decisions "according to the views of the government."[26] To make things worse,

Table 6.5. *Number and percent of a total of 738 cases won by various parties, 1890–1904*

Parties involved[a]	Cases won Number	Percent of total	Cases won Number	Percent of total
Zemstvo versus bureaucracy	365	49		
Provincial zemstvo			150	20
District zemstvo			215	29
Zemstvo and bureaucracy versus third party	36	5		
Bureaucracy versus zemstvo	177	24		
Provincial bureaucracy			142	19
Central Bureaucracy			35	5
Bureaucracy and third party versus zemstvo	6	1		
Private plaintiff versus zemstvo	154	21		

[a]In each case, winning party is listed first.
Source: N. I. Kuznetsov, *Sistematicheskii svod ukazov Pravitel'stvuiushchego Senata, posledovavshikh po zemskim delam*, 12 vols. (St. Petersburg, 1902–15), vols. 1–3.

Table 6.6. *Success ratio for appeals initiated by zemstvo, local government, and central government, 1890–1904*

Plaintiff	Winner Zemstvo	Bureaucracy	Other
Zemstvo			
Number of initiated appeals	418	—	—
Number of cases won	267	133	18
Percent of victories	64	35	1
Local government			
Number of initiated appeals		40	—
Number of cases won	20	17	3
Percent of victories	50	43	7
Central government			
Number of initiated appeals	—	27	—
Number of cases won	2	25	0
Percent of victories	7	93	0

Source: N. I. Kuznetsov, *Sistematicheskii svod ukazov Pravitel'stvuiushchego Senata, posledovavshikh po zemskim delam*, 12 vols. (St. Petersburg, 1902–15), vols. 1–3.

observers noted an increasing tendency for former governors, generals, and career bureaucrats, devoid of any legal background or any dedication to the principles of the Judicial Reform of 1864, to take positions in the Senate. The Senate's Cassation Departments (where appeals on civil crimes were heard) managed to escape this decay, but its First Department (in charge of zemstvo appeals), Second Department (on peasant affairs), and other divisions responsible for administrative appeals fell victim to this influx of retiring bureaucrats. No judicial or educational background was required to become a senator; officials were appointed directly by the tsar (who also personally fixed their salaries), and they enjoyed no permanent tenure.[27]

The high turnover rate of senators in the First Department certainly reflects this dependence of the judiciary on the whims of the executive branch of government. Over the 15-year period of review, an average of only 29 percent of the First Department senators remained in their position from one sample year to the next, and in 1894, 1897, and 1903, the turnover rate ranged over 85 percent (see Table 6.7). Moreover, the lack of legal training was manifest in the inconsistency of some Senate rulings. A prerevolutionary scholar on the Senate noted that it did not feel the need to follow precedent in its decisions and sometimes rejected appeals in which earlier Senate rulings were cited on the grounds that "the particular ukaz of the past cannot have any bearing on the present case."[28]

Despite this corruption, the Senate still managed to rule consistently in favor of the zemstvo. As stated above, one way to regard these zemstvo victories is to see them as proof of the governor's proizvol. Another way to look at the issue, however, is to recognize that the zemstvo was not as persecuted in fact as it perceived itself to be. Even though unqualified officials dominated the top of the Senate, the Russian Supreme Court employed enough young, highly trained jurists inspired by the Judicial Reform of 1864 to allow it to live up to its goal of protecting citizens from bureaucratic abuse.[29] One example of the moral power of the Senate appeared when Interior Minister Durnovo decided to yield to zemstvo resistance to the 1893 hospital statute, realizing that in the final court of appeals the Senate would only rule in favor of the zemstvo.[30]

Zemstvo leaders could reply, of course, that their victories in the Senate meant little since it took so long for the Senate to rule on an appeal. However, this argument is not altogether convincing. It took an average of little more than two years for a local dispute to be heard in the Senate: for cases originating between 1890 and 1900, the required

190

Table 6.7. Turnover of senators, First Department, 1891–1906

	1891	1894	1897	1899	1901	1903	1904	1906
Total number of senators	10	11[a]	12[a]	11	14[a]	13	11	18
New senators	2	8	6	3	5	5	2	11
Senators dismissed	2	7	6	4	2	6	4	5
Turnover rate (%)[b]	40	136	100	64	50	85	54	88
Average turnover rate (%)[b]	71							

[a]Year in which a new chief justice (prokurator) was appointed.
[b]New and dismissed senators as percent of total senators.
Source: Spisok vysshim chinam gosudarstvennogo, gubernskogo i eparkhial'nogo upravlenii (St. Petersburg, years cited).

duration was two years, one month, whereas between 1900 and 1905 that figure rose to two years, four months. To be sure, a two-year hiatus could damage zemstvo operations if the governor's office had vetoed a zemstvo budget because the veto would remain in effect until the Senate presented its ruling. Nevertheless, this two-year delay did not cripple zemstvo activity; the previous year's budget was renewed while the vetoed budget awaited a decision. For that matter, the two-year delay worked to the zemstvo's advantage when private citizens were the plaintiffs, for in these cases the zemstvo's own tax remained in effect until the Senate could overrule it.

In short, the imperial bureaucracy at the end of the century appears much less the unified bastion of reaction than liberal publicists would have us believe it was. The very frequency of zemstvo appeals to the Senate demonstrates the faith zemstvo members held in that body as an effective means of redressing grievances. Zemstvo activists cleverly used Senate rulings as precedents to challenge gubernatorial decrees, employing the Senate as a defense against bureaucratic abuse.[31] Still more, the frequency with which private citizens complained to the Senate about *zemstvo* capriciousness indicates that society, too, enjoyed in the Senate an institutional means of redressing grievances. Coupling this with the tendency of the governors to sympathize with citizens' complaints against the zemstvo, we find our image of a dichotomy between *vlast'* and *obshchestvennost'* eroded still further.

The 738 Senate cases can be broken down into 10 basic categories of disputes (Table 6.8). The most numerous category, as we have already mentioned, was zemstvo taxation. Appeals concerning zemstvo public programs (education, health, economic development, and road building) came in second, and the budget represented the third most numerous category.

These 10 types of appeals arose at different moments throughout the 15-year period before 1905, and by plotting the peak years for each category it is possible to show the chronological development of zemstvo–government conflict. The earliest category of dispute to peak was the "mandatory" obligations to local officials, followed by province–district relations, the zemstvo public programs, zemstvo–town relations, and budgetary disputes. (A description of these categories will follow below.) These categories flared up before 1900, and were directly related to the expansion of zemstvo services for the local population. After 1900, the disputes became more overtly political, now that the governor, particularly because of the pressure of complaints against zemstvo taxes, began to attempt to change the actual

192

Table 6.8. *Number and percent of appeals to Senate, 1890–1904, by category of dispute*

Dispute category	Number of cases	Percent of total
Zemstvo taxation	258	35
Public programs	107	14
Budget	81	11
Internal zemstvo operations	75	10
Obligations to local officials	56	11
Zemstvo–town relations	40	5
Province–district relations	37	5
Petitions and politics	30	4
Third element	28	4
Zemstvo elections	26	3

Source: Kuznetsov, *Sistematicheskii svod ukazov Pravitel'stvuiushchego Senata, posledevavshikh po zemskim delam*, 12 vols. (St. Petersburg, 1902–15), vols. 1–3.

composition of individual zemstvos, overruling elections, firing specialized personnel, and vetoing precedures within the zemstvo. The chronological development of zemstvo-governor disputes is shown in Table 6.9.[32]

Obligations to local officials

According to both the 1864 and 1890 zemstvo reforms, the zemstvo was required to pay the expenses necessary to maintain the offices of certain provincial officials and to provide transportation for local judicial and police officers. These "mandatory" payments symbolized the zemstvo's ambiguous status as fully neither a state nor a private institution but an awkward combination of both. What zemstvo leaders wanted was to free themselves from the stigma of being an auxiliary state body and leave more of their revenues for the "nonmandatory" programs, the schools and hospitals run by the zemstvo. The first way they set out to do this was by limiting funding to the *zemskii nachal'nik*, the gentry-staffed policeman of the village created in 1889.[33] When this new position was established, the zemstvo was required to support it, as it had previously assisted the local constable, by relinquishing all its funds formerly allocated to the justice of the peace (*mirovoi sud'ia*). Six times in the early 1890s, the zemstvo was brought before the Senate for reducing its contributions to the *zemskii nachal'nik*.

Table 6.9. Number of zemstvo–governor disputes, 1890–1904, by category of dispute

Dispute category	1890	1891	1892	1893	1894	1895	1896	1897	1898	1899	1900	1901	1902	1903	1904	Peak years
Obligations	1	7	1	3	1	7	4	3	1	6	4	6	5	2	2	1891, 1895
Province–district relations	0	0	2	0	2	4	4	2	8	6	3	1	2	3	0	1895-1899
Public programs	1	0	1	3	6	11	10	15	11	11	8	14	5	6	5	1895-1901
Zemstvo–town relations	0	0	0	0	5	7	1	3	4	4	3	4	5	3	1	1894-1895
Budget	0	1	0	5	6	4	11	4	16	7	12	6	2	5	1	1896-1900
Elections	0	0	0	0	1	0	0	6	1	2	3	3	6	3	1	1897, 1902
Third element	0	0	0	0	1	0	3	3	3	4	3	2	3	2	4	1899, 1904
Petitions and politics	0	1	0	1	1	1	4	1	4	1	1	7	2	7	0	1901, 1903
Taxation	1	4	2	5	14	9	13	16	32	29	14	32	40	26	18	1902
Internal operations	0	1	0	4	5	4	2	7	6	6	8	5	7	11	9	1903

Italicized figures indicate peak years.

Source: Kuznetsov, Sistematicheskii svod ukazov Pravitel'stvuiushchego Senata, posledovavshikh po zemskim delam, 12 vols. (St. Petersburg, 1902–15), vols. 1–3.

The second major issue in this category concerned the obligation to provide free transportation, in cash or in kind, to judicial and police officials. By the 1890s most zemstvos had already shifted or were in the process of shifting from a "natural" to a cash system of transportation. This reform caused some misunderstandings, as officials feared that their coupons would not entitle them to as many horses as they had formerly used and as zemstvo officials worked to prevent state officials from abusing this privilege of free horses.

On the whole, this problem became less and less an issue in zemstvo–bureaucratic relations. In 1868, nearly two-thirds of the zemstvo budget (61 percent) was channeled into "mandatory" expenses, but this proportion so declined that by 1890 only 39 percent of the budget went to police support. Then the road law of 1895 (to be discussed below) freed nearly 6 million rubles for the zemstvo, after which the notorious June 12, 1900 tax law actually relieved the zemstvo of most other obligations, amounting to another 1.5 million rubles.[34] Thus, paradoxically, despite the designs embodied in the counter-reform to integrate the zemstvo into the state, the actual practice of payments shows that the zemstvo was losing its ambiguous status and becoming more clearly a separate institution.

Relations between the provincial and district zemstvo

In the mid-1890s, the centralization of all zemstvo operations within the province became a main issue in zemstvo circles. Zemstvo services could vary drastically from one district to another, depending on the staff of the particular zemstvo and the economy of the district. Once liberal activists in the provincial zemstvo had embarked on their welfare programs, they noticed this disunity among the districts and tried to coordinate the districts through the intervention of the provincial zemstvo. This in turn provoked a campaign against the provincial zemstvo waged by the conservative journal, *Moskovskie vedomosti*, beginning in 1894; in reply the liberal *Vestnik Evropy* and *Russkie vedomosti* rushed to the province's defense.[35] At the Nizhnii Novgorod zemstvo congress of 1896, provincial centralization formed the main focus of debate between Dmitrii Shipov, leader of the provincial centralists, and Boris Chicherin, voicing the objections of the district separatists. This issue totally dominated zemstvo politics in Moscow from 1897 to 1899, so that in 1899 the provincial chairman Shipov had to resign temporarily in order to impress upon his colleagues the need for greater district unity.[36]

Most commonly the centralists and separatists debated this issue in the arena of education. Disciples of Shipov found a useful tactic to spur sluggish district zemstvos into increases in their welfare programs: the provincial zemstvo would pledge funds to the districts as long as the districts followed provincial procedures. In reply the separatists would cover their opposition to the province's goal of universal education by complaining that their districts were required to bear a disproportionate burden for other, less-developed districts.[37]

This part of the story is already common knowledge to historians of the zemstvo, but from the Kuznetsov collection we can see another, more surprising method used by provincial centralists. Often historians forget to ask how the provincial zemstvo acquired its funds to pay for the new programs it urged upon the districts. A rather crafty method was for the provincial zemstvo to claim district revenues as its own or to transfer to the district less vital responsibilities for which the province did not wish to pay. Of the 34 appeals in this category, 16 can be considered within this subcategory, in which the province seized district funds.[38]

Although the district separatists eventually lost this battle, the district did not fare badly in the Senate. It nearly broke even, winning 16 of 34 cases, against 18 victories for the province.

Public programs

In the minds of zemstvo men, the purpose of this institution was not to provide horses for police officers but to set up schools, hospitals, agricultural warehouses, and fire insurance programs. These "nonmandatory" programs represent the best of the zemstvo's legacy, and a glance into the disputes in this category will give us special insight into zemstvo–governor conflicts. The governors did attempt to resist the expansion of zemstvo services, but their actions cannot be dismissed casually as part of a blind attack on liberalism and progress.

Up until the twentieth century the zemstvo devoted more of its energies to education than to anything else; accordingly, most of the Senate disputes concerned education. Of the 107 appeals over public programs, 44 fell to education, 25 involved zemstvo medicine, 13 belonged to zemstvo road work and trade regulations, and the remaining 12 concerned fire prevention.

Not only was education the central issue of these disputes, it also provoked actions by the governor that most sharply tested zemstvo independence. In nearly two-thirds of the cases (25, or 61 percent), the

196

zemstvo was forced to challenge the Ministry of Education or state school council of the province for the right to establish a new school, determine its instruction, or open a library without state approval. In another six cases, the zemstvo challenged the church for the right to determine the type of education in the area, and in four instances the zemstvo found itself in litigation with peasants protesting the payments for education. Kursk province witnessed the greatest number of these appeals, with seven cases (all of which concerned "political" types of educational disputes, such as freedom of instruction and public libraries). Saratov came in second with five appeals; and Voronezh, Kazan, Poltava, and Kherson each brought in another three cases. Altogether the zemstvo was winning 67 percent of these appeals but did even better in the "political" cases, succeeding in 72 percent of its protests.

Zemstvo medicine must be seen as a less political issue. Whereas 33 percent of these disputes concerned such items as zemstvo resistance to the Hospital Statute of 1893 or a refusal to follow bureaucratic orders on public health, another 48 percent of the cases involved zemstvo attempts actually to *reduce* its hospital services or to compel peasants or *meshchane* (petty burghers) to pay for zemstvo medicine. Saratov and Tver are the provinces where the political disputes arose, and Kursk province was the scene of the greatest number of conflicts with peasants or townsmen over the cost of zemstvo medicine.

A few individual cases will show us that the zemstvo, despite its dedication to the welfare of the region, was not always appreciated by the surrounding society as a progressive institution. In Poltava province one village submitted a complaint to the Senate against a district zemstvo that had refused to subsidize a church school; zemstvo schools were no different from church schools, argued the peasants, and thus the zemstvo should continue to pay for the village school even though its authority had recently passed to the church.[39] In Saratov, peasants challenged both a district zemstvo and the governor's own provincial office, demanding the right to have a zemstvo school replaced by a church school; the church school would cost *no* money, reasoned the peasants, and its spiritual education would be more appropriate to the needs of the village.[40] The governor's rationale in vetoing some zemstvo programs emerges clearly. Recommending that his provincial office veto zemstvo funds to construct a new school, the governor of Kursk wrote that "under the presently troubled economic circumstances of zemstvo taxpayers, as well as the indebtedness of the provincial zemstvo, more severe here than elsewhere, and also considering the extensive funds already paid by the provincial and district zemstvos to education, the zemstvo should postpone its present construction of new school buildings."[41] Similarly, the Kherson governor vetoed a district school project to subsidize higher education, calling such an action an avoidance of the real need of the population for elementary popular education.[42] In these vetoes the governors' actions seem entirely reasonable, a display of dedication to the welfare of the population no less sincere than that of the zemstvo. In the long run, of course, the zemstvo's public programs were bound to raise the cultural level of the Russian countryside. But the governors also deserve credit for their defense of the peasants' more immediate fiscal interests.

Zemstvo–town relations

To pay for its projects of the 1890s, the zemstvo had to find new sources of revenue. One way it solved this problem was by squeezing the town. Of the 38 appeals of this type, 20 cases (52 percent) involve municipal protests to zemstvo taxation of urban property and industry. In two of these disputes, the Senate explicitly reprimanded the zemstvo for "capriciously" (proizvol'no) assessing urban property.[43] Town mayors and city councils became most outraged when the zemstvo fixed a fee for the town to pay to the zemstvo as an urban tax, demanding that the town government itself work out the distribution of this tax burden among city taxpayers. Perhaps in retaliation, after 1901 the town government began to tax zemstvo property located within city limits; this action produced 6 zemstvo protests to the Senate. Saratov stands as the hotbed of zemstvo–town disputes, with 6 cases; Smolensk and Voronezh followed with 5 and 3 cases, respectively. The zemstvo broke even in these appeals, winning 19 of the 38 cases, whereas the town triumphed in only 15 disputes.

The zemstvo budget

Although the subject of the budget would seem to hold little of interest to historians, the 81 disputes under this rubric actually offer some fascinating examples of zemstvo–governor conflict in this period. Here the budget experts on the zemstvo board emerge as crafty operators, capable of manipulating the budget in order to hide zemstvo activities from the watchful eye of the governor. To understand how this worked, we must consider the sources of revenue for the zemstvo. From 1890 to 1900, income from zemstvo taxes on land and industry,

198

although steadily rising, represented a declining percentage of total zemstvo revenues. In other words, revenues other than property taxes provided an increasingly significant share of zemstvo income (see Table 6.10).

The governor in these budgetary disputes appears to have distrusted the zemstvo in its competence to balance its budget and keep itself solvent. The zemstvo, in turn, showed little faith that the governor would approve its program if he knew how it was to be financed. Thus began a game of cat and mouse in which the zemstvo attempted to evade the governor's grasp by creating ambiguously defined budgetary articles, "slush funds" to draw from in the course of the year.

A few examples will illustrate how this game was played. In six districts of Vologda province in 1895, the assemblies voted to allow the executive board to transfer money from one paragraph of the budget to another; the governor protested with a veto, challenging the assembly to spell out the exact conditions under which the transfers would be made.[44] That same year in Moscow, the provincial assembly voted to build new offices for the executive board, drawing from the voluntary insurance fund and arranging to pay it back over a 10-year period; the governor vetoed this on the grounds that deductions from the insurance fund could be made only for short-term, emergency expenses.[45] The Kursk provincial zemstvo displayed a remarkable ability to sidestep the governor's obstruction in 1899. After the governor vetoed an allocation of 36,000 rubles for new schools, the zemstvo simply went ahead with its intentions, paying for the schools now through a mysteriously entitled *"zhdanovskii kapital"* (Zhdanov fund), which had already been established. The Senate overruled the governor's veto two years later.[46] The Riazan and Poltava provincial zemstvos both attempted to set up large reserve funds for emergency purposes, but the governor rejected this transfer since the zemstvos had not specified the destination of every kopeck from this fund.[47]

Although much of the governor's suspiciousness can be ascribed to his politically unsympathetic attitude toward the zemstvo, there is also reason to believe that he scrutinzed the budget to keep it from falling helplessly into debt. Many outside observers quite removed from the bureaucracy also saw a potential for the zemstvo to become an expensive agency wasting thousands of rubles.[48] The governor tried to prevent zemstvo waste by ensuring that the zemstvo eliminated all possible arrears from its estimates of income. Tax arrears became a central problem in the budgets of the government and zemstvo alike in the 1890s. The best available source on zemstvo arrears reports that in

Table 6.10. Source of zemstvo income, 1890 and 1900

Income source	1890		1900		Net gain or loss in percent of total	Percent increase over decade
	Thousands of rubles	Percent of total	Thousands of rubles	Percent of total		
Land tax	36,964	78.7	62,238	70.2	−8.5	68
Income from industrial certificates	3,673	7.8	4,159	4.7	−3.1	13
Customs duties			925	1.1		
Income from zemstvo property			419	0.5		
Credit operations (zachety)			10,284	11.6		
Subsidies and refunds			9,494	10.7		
Other			1,018	1.1		
All revenues except land and industrial tax	6,410	13.5	22,140	25	+12.5	245
Total	47,047		88,563			188

Source: Iubileinyi zemskii sbornik (St. Petersburg, 1914), p. 174.

the central black-earth provinces in that decade, only 41 percent of zemstvo taxes had actually been collected.[49] The governor of Voronezh vetoed a budget of a district zemstvo after he found that it had failed to account for arrears and was already running a major deficit in 1897; the governor of Orel encountered this same problem in 1903.[50] A dispute in Tauride province reveals the governor's fears even more clearly. Falling into debt, the provincial zemstvo had been forced to take out a loan from the treasury, and then proved incapable of repaying it; the governor attempted to fine the zemstvo for its arrears, but the zemstvo appealed and won its case in the Senate.[51]

Most protests in this category (45 out of 81 cases, or 55 percent) involved an effort by the zemstvo to transfer funds from one paragraph to another or to create reserve funds. The peak years for these disputes ranged between 1898 and 1900, precisely when zemstvo publicists were complaining of gubernatorial interference in the zemstvo budget. (This, by the way, was also the time when Witte and Sipiagin were preparing their notorious law of 1900 to limit zemstvo tax increases, to be discussed below.) A smaller subcategory of disputes (17 cases) represents zemstvo efforts openly to defy tax and budgetary laws: the 1895 road law requiring that zemstvo funds be deposited in treasury banks provoked five conflicts, and the 1900 tax law produced another four appeals. The zemstvo fared poorly on disputes involving fund transfers, losing 24 out of 45 cases (53 percent), but it enjoyed greater success when openly refusing to observe budgetary laws, winning 12 out of 17 appeals (70 percent).

Zemstvo elections

The Senate cases provide a convenient method for showing how zemstvo–governor disputes became increasingly politicized after 1900. Throughout the 1890s the central issues concerned the more mundane questions of zemstvo education, zemstvo payments to local policemen, and so on. Now we shall see how explicitly political issues rose to the fore. Of the 26 disputes involving zemstvo elections, only 10 occurred in the entire decade before 1900, whereas most appeals arose in the following five-year period.

Despite the common absenteeism which so many observers noticed in the zemstvo assembly, electoral disputes demonstrate that zemstvo elections could still be hotly contested. The most vexing issue of electoral disputes was the right of an individual to serve as a proxy for another individual in the zemstvo. Landowners (including women) could authorize proxies to serve in their stead as zemstvo members, and factories and industrial enterprises could also empower deputies. Confusion arose, naturally, once zemstvo voters tried to explore the unforeseen implications of this right to elect proxies. One nobleman had himself elected to the first (gentry) electoral curia and then ran for election again, now as a proxy in the second (urban–industrial) electoral curia.[52] One landowner authorized the steward of his estate to serve as his proxy in the first curia, even though the steward was a peasant.[53] Another nobleman appealed to the Senate when the governor invalidated his election: he had been serving as a proxy for a woman landowner, but the governor claimed that the woman had already sold her land.[54] The possibilities of proxy qualifications seem to go on indefinitely.

The gravity of the proxy issue becomes more apparent when we consider its effects on electoral corruption in the zemstvo. One nobleman sent a petition to the governor in 1903, requesting that another nobleman be denied his right to serve as a proxy for a mining company because one of its directors was a foreigner; upon appeal to the Senate it became clear that the first nobleman had no legal basis for complaint but was using this challenge to the man's proxy qualifications as a pretext for removing his enemy from the zemstvo.[55] The same year in Novgorod, the governor's provincial office overruled an election in which five noblemen had attended the electoral caucus but had refused to specify the curia which their proxies entitled them to attend; the Senate nullified the entire election, ruling that these five voters had a decisive influence on the outcome of the election.[56]

Even without the proxy issue, zemstvo elections could fall victim to corrupt influences, as was the case in three elections in 1903. The most outlandish incident occurred in Krestetsk district of Novgorod province. The local gentry marshal had failed to arrive in town to open the first curia electoral caucus but had sent a telegram to his deputy instructing him to preside over the session. Before the telegram had arrived, 12 landowners became impatient and returned to their hotel rooms, expecting to meet again the next day. In the meantime, the deputy marshal assembled a group of 17 landowners at 11:30 that evening, and under the cloak of night the gathering selected its 12 zemstvo deputies. When the other group of 12 landowners heard of this midnight caucus the following day, they challenged the election first before the provincial office and then successfully before the Senate. In their appeal they complained that "the deputy marshal had only invited those landowners who stood close to him." This action, they charged, "clearly indicates an effort by one part of the electors to eliminate another group from elections and from zemstvo matters in general."[57]

It is not altogether clear why the electoral disputes become more frequent as we approach 1905. One possibility is that the rise of a zemstvo oppositionist movement made the stakes of electoral politics so high that zemstvo members cared more about their elections and became increasingly willing to protest whenever the governor's office invalidated an election. Considered within the context of the entire body of Senate appeals, however, these electoral disputes seem to have been initiated more by the governor than by the zemstvo. Having vetoed a growing number of zemstvo budgets and public programs, the governor probably became more vigilant in his surveillance of zemstvo affairs in general; with this heightened watchfulness, the governor noticed many abuses in zemstvo elections that had previously been ignored.

The third element

A historian asked to envision the "typical" dispute between the zemstvo and the governor over hired zemstvo specialists would probably reply that the case occurred in Moscow province (because of its leadership in innovating new zemstvo programs) and involved the governor's veto of the zemstvo's appointment of new specialists. In some ways this image would be true, but not entirely.

True to our expectations, the dominant subcategory here proved to be instances in which the zemstvo had offered benefits to its specialists – salaries, pensions, transportation privileges, and housing – but encountered objections from the governor (11 cases out of 28, or 39 percent). However, the second leading subcategory were disputes of a contrary type, in which the zemstvo had attempted to fire a specialist and was challenged either by that specialist himself or by the governor (5 cases, or 18 percent). The situation becomes even more complicated when we consider the third subcategory, the 4 cases in which the zemstvo punished an employee for some improper action. Additionally, there were 3 cases in which the zemstvo conflicted with other employees or taxpayers after it hired a specialist: one zemstvo forced a doctor to sever his contract with a town on the grounds that he could not work for two employers; another zemstvo refused to pay the state after hiring a government doctor; and a third zemstvo sought to compel a village to provide free housing for a feldsher. Considering the additional two cases in which Zemstvo members themselves disagreed over their employees – one assembly rehired a feldsher after the board had fired him, and a provincial zemstvo liquidated a pension fund set up for employees by one district zemstvo – we begin to realize that the governor was not the only one to distrust the third element.

Moscow certainly enjoyed fame for the great number and high quality of its specialists, but this province is not represented in the disputes at all. Perhaps, then, Moscow could attribute its success to a certain acceptance of its specialists by the governor. In any case, Tver stands as the leading province, with three disputes (one case involving zemstvo benefits for its employees, and another two caused by the zemstvo's efforts to *punish* its employees!).

Petitions and politics

Up until this point the Kuznetsov appeals have told us little about zemstvo liberals, the people who led the zemstvo movement in the years leading up to 1905. The category of petitions allows us to trace the activity of this energetic and very vocal minority. Of the 28 petition disputes, over two-thirds (20, or 71 percent) clearly involved national political issues (peasant reform or state policies), whereas the remaining eight cases limited their focus to local zemstvo business. The cases also demonstrate once again that zemstvo–governor disputes became more political around the turn of the century and attracted the involvement of the central ministries in local zemstvo affairs.

Most studies of the liberal zemstvo movement in the 1890s maintain that the initial questions raised in liberal circles were issues of peasant reform, which gradually became transformed into political issues. The petition disputes before the Senate plot a similar course of evolution. The earliest petitions appealed for reform of the legal and economic status of the peasant. They represent a dominant subcategory, with eight cases. In two instances zemstvo men petitioned for the abolition of corporal punishment (a code phrase for protest against the *zemskii nachal'nik*, who was responsible for disciplining peasants).[58] A petition vetoed in 1892 advocated the reduction of peasants' redemption payments, and another called for a reform of volost taxes so that all classes, not just the peasants, would bear the burden. In another appeal, a district zemstvo of Poltava had unsuccessfully petitioned the government for the right to establish a legal consultant for peasants in order to counteract underground radical lawyers. These petitions on peasant problems appear to have been distributed somewhat randomly in both time and location: they began in 1893, continued throughout the 1890s, and then reached their peak in 1901–2. None of the celebrated liberal provinces are represented here: Novgorod, Samara, Riazan, Tambov, Chernigov, and Smolensk were the only provinces to produce disputes over petitions on peasant reform.

Whereas the petitions on peasant reform fall randomly throughout the period, the disputed petitions on state policies conform more closely to the broad lines of development of the liberal movement. The earliest few cases arose around the turn of the century, and four petitions were submitted in the crucial years 1902–3. The most politicized provinces produced the greatest number of disputes: Kursk province was the scene of three disputed petitions (two from Sudzha district alone, home of the prominent activist in Beseda and the liberation movement, Petr Dolgorukov), and Tver provided the setting for another two cases (one of which occurred in Ivan Petrunkevich's home seat of Novotorzhok, the district in which the entire zemstvo board was replaced by administrative appointees in 1904). One dispute involved an attempt by the zemstvo to subsidize zemstvo publications by the Free Economic Society; another was a protest against the hated veterinary law of June 12, 1902; and two disputes were related to Witte's Special Conference on the Needs of Rural Industry (see below).

A third subcategory of petitions (four cases) concerned zemstvo conferences. The government unequivocally prohibited national zemstvo conferences, but zemstvo leaders attempted to circumvent this restriction by arranging meetings on specialized topics – agriculture, statistical work, education, and so on – at which zemstvo activists could assemble to discuss common interests. A petition from Tver province, for example, protested the Interior Ministry's circular of August 23, 1901, forbidding that zemstvo from communicating with other provinces on national politics.

The zemstvo fared rather well in the court of appeal, gaining the Senate's recognition that it did indeed have the right to submit petitions on matters vetoed by the governor. Of the 16 political disputes, the zemstvo won 11; for the remaining petitions on local business, the zemstvo won 8 of 11 cases.

Zemstvo taxation

Now we finally come to the most important (certainly the largest) group of disputes before the Senate. Tax disputes were the dominant category of Senate cases in every year except 1893 and 1897, and significantly overshadowed the other disputes from 1898 onward. By no means does this contradict our thesis that disputes were becoming increasingly political after 1900. Rather, it shows how the governor changed from fighting the *symptoms* of the burgeoning zemstvo activity – overruling allocations for schools, resisting reductions in zemstvo payments to local policemen, and so on – to attacking the *causes* of this growth. This he did by scrutinizing the personnel who promoted the expansion and the taxes through which the public programs were financed.

The zemstvo received its revenues through two types of taxes: immovable property (land, homes, and urban property) and industrial property (the building and equipment of the enterprise but not its goods). Shortly after 1864 the question arose of whether the zemstvo also enjoyed the right to tax the actual turnover of industry. Rejecting what it considered a double tax on industry, the state issued a clarification of November 21, 1866, eliminating the possibility of a genuine industrial tax.[59] From that moment on, the burden of zemstvo taxation fell on the land, primarily on peasant property.

Despite the elimitation of the 1866 law, zemstvo men could not fail to see the wealth lying in the cities and factories, especially with the upsurge of industrial growth in the 1890s. In the two decades before 1905, the zemstvo sought to shift at least a portion of its tax burden to the shoulders of Russia's merchants and townsmen. This subtle alteration in the proportion of zemstvo taxation supported by the land, the town, and the factory is shown in Table 6.11. In a previous section we have already seen the protests this tax shift provoked among town residents. Even more vociferously did industry oppose the new zemstvo taxes.

One way to appreciate the strength of this opposition is to examine the type of plaintiffs who brought suit against the zemstvo and the years in which they protested. Of the 226 private appeals to the Senate, business representatives were the largest group, submitting 68 protests; peasants came in second with 56 complaints. Members of town councils, *meshchane*, noblemen, and women each lodged about 20 appeals. The population did not stand united in what it opposed about the zemstvo. For business representatives, women, and members of the clergy, zemstvo taxes were the primary matter of concern. Peasants and *meshchane*, however, divided their opposition more equally between taxes and zemstvo welfare programs (some of which, we should recall, actually went against the interests of the lower classes). Not surprisingly, gentry plaintiffs were hardly upset by zemstvo taxes and directed their opposition against zemstvo elections. (In fact, only three Senate cases involved a landowner actually bringing suit against a land tax.)

206

Table 6.11. Source of zemstvo income from taxation, 1890–1906

Income source	1890		1895		1901		1906	
	Thousands of rubles	Percent of all taxes	Thousands of rubles	Percent of all taxes	Thousands of rubles	Percent of all taxes	Thousands of rubles	Percent of all taxes
Land	29,961	81	37,803	80	47,177	75	64,533	72
Town property	2,624	7	3,665	8	5,588	9	8,777	10
Industry	3,721	10	5,345	11	9,338	15	14,632	16
Rural homes	658	2	615	1	986	2	1,406	2

Source: Iubileinyi zemskii sbornik (St. Petersburg, 1914), p. 176.

The tax issue provides a good litmus test of who was within the zemstvo and who stood outside it. All of the groups challenging zemstvo taxes were outsiders, people under- or disenfranchised from zemstvo elections. The clergy had no representation in the zemstvo at all after 1890. Women could empower direct relatives to serve as their proxies in the zemstvo, but they themselves were denied suffrage. Merchants comprised only 14 percent of district zemstvo deputies and 9 percent of provincial deputies; peasants supplied 31 percent of district deputies, but only 2 percent of provincial members.[60]

Thus we see a fundamental flaw in the political appeal of zemstvo liberalism. The social class enjoying the greatest chance of representation in the zemstvo, the landed gentry, also benefited from an understood tax advantage. By contrast, the strongest potential allies of the zemstvo movement, the social groups most needed by zemstvo liberalism – the industrialist, the merchant, the enterprising and well-to-do peasant – were precisely the people most aggrieved by zemstvo taxes.

The tax issue also helps us further examine the question of *proizvol* in local government. The Senate disputes have already shown us two basic points about bureaucratic abuse: first, considering the zemstvo's high success rate in its appeals, the governors truly were guilty of abusing their powers to veto zemstvo legislation; second, the governors had legitimate justification for scrutinizing zemstvo activity. On the specific issue of tax disputes, the Senate rulings again show how ambiguous the issue of *proizvol* can be. In 17 rulings the Senate explicitly reprimanded the zemstvo for "capriciously" (*proizvol'no*) assessing taxes. In most of these cases the zemstvo was found guilty of using rule-of-thumb estimates to calculate the profitability and value (*dokhodnost' i stoimost'*) on which the final tax on immovable property was based. Instead of using precise data on the factory's initial cost and operating expenses over a fixed period of time, zemstvo tax assessors used rough estimates or simply guessed. This problem arose most frequently in Perm province, with five counts of *proizvol* against the zemstvo, and Poltava province, with two counts.[61]

Internal zemstvo operations

To understand the bureaucratic origins of the rise of an opposition mentality among zemstvo members, we must appreciate the effect the governor's veto powers had on the personal careers of zemstvo activists. Historians often describe the end of the nineteenth century as an era of professionalization. Lawyers, teachers, doctors, engineers, and other trained specialists began to see themselves as a separate caste and organize themselves into professional bodies. Even governors are seen to have been forming into a professional corps.[62] Although no technical training was required to become a zemstvo activist other than experience in zemstvo affairs, one could argue that the zemstvo, too, was experiencing this tendency toward professionalization by the turn of the century.[63] The issue is too complicated to be treated in detail here, but we should recognize that a growing number of politicians in the provinces began to think of themselves not as landlords or members of the gentry but as "zemstvo activists," devoting the bulk of their time and thought to "the business of the zemstvo" (*zemskoe delo*). It was one thing for the governor to veto a proposed zemstvo school or hospital. However, when the governor began to question the way zemstvo members ran their own business or to question their very right to belong to the zemstvo, the matter became much more personal. It is not hard to imagine the fatal political consequences of the central government's decision to dispatch investigators into the provinces to harass the zemstvo and refuse confirmation of elected zemstvo leaders.

As was true for the other catgories of "political" disputes heard before the Senate, the protests over internal zemstvo affairs tended to occur in the five years after 1900. Whereas only 35 out of a total of 73 disputes of this nature occurred in the decade preceding 1900, over half the disputes (40, or 55 percent) fell in the remaining five-year period, above all in the critical years 1902–3.

A glance at the leading subcategories will indicate the ways in which the governor meddled in internal zemstvo affairs. One grouping holds first place with 15 cases: zemstvo efforts to extend benefits to the executive board or to deputies that were vetoed by the governor. The type of gubernatorial vetoes explains how zemstvo men could feel threatened by the governor's interference. On one occasion, zemstvo deputies voted for themselves the privilege of free transportation to assembly sessions; the governor overruled this. On another occasion the assembly voted, without official approval, a raise in the pension for former chairmen of the executive board; this the governor also overruled. Often the governor vetoed salary increases for board members with the excuse that the vote for this action had been an open ballot, which allowed influential members of the assembly, such as the board chairman, an opportunity to exert moral suasion over their colleagues. In addition to these disputes, there was also a smaller subcategory of appeals, 5 disputes in which the governor had vetoed zemstvo votes to hang portraits of former leaders in the chambers of the zemstvo assembly. Altogether, the governor was preventing the zemstvo from rendering honor to itself, either through higher salaries or through symbolic praise to its leaders.

Another subcategory of 12 cases (16 percent) involved disputes arising from the governor's effort to remove "outsiders" from the zemstvo, specialists and expert witnesses who had not been elected to the zemstvo. Another 10 cases concerned the governor's direct meddling in the business of the zemstvo board, questioning the right of the chairman to do things without the approval of the board itself or protesting the way a substitute chairman took over the duties of the permanent chairman. Still another 7 disputes involved gubernatorial resistance to arrangements made between the executive board and its statistical, sanitary, and medical commissions. Adding these three subcategories together, we reach a total of 29 disputes (40 percent of the total) in which the governor frustrated the zemstvo in the administration of its own business.

However, one should not think that the governor was the only one to begin to look hard at the way the zemstvo ran its own affairs. Deputies of the assembly themselves began to protest the actions of the executive board. Seven disputes arose over conflicts between the assembly and the board. The Tver provincial assembly, surprisingly enough, challenged its board for submitting a petition without the assembly's authorization.[64] In that same province another dispute arose over the right of the chairman to exclude minority opinions from the protocol.[65] In one district of Voronezh, a deputy brought a member of the board to trial for allegedly embezzling funds from the zemstvo agricultural warehouse.[66] Altogether, the total breakdown of these disputes is shown in Table 6.12.

Being probably the most politicized province of zemstvo Russia, Tver quite naturally produced the greatest number of disputes over internal zemstvo operations, with 10 cases. The major issue in this province was the participation by outsiders in zemstvo affairs (four cases). Saratov took second place with six disputes, two of which concerned outsiders, while another two cases involved absenteeism at zemstvo sessions. Kursk province came in third, with five cases (three of which resulted from the extension of benefits to the executive board). Vologda, Voronezh, Nizhnii Novgorod, Riazan, and Ufa provinces followed behind with four cases apiece. The outcome of these disputes is irrelevant; the events of 1905 were already in full swing before the Senate had ruled on most of them.

The Senate rulings provide a convenient source for exploring the relationship between the governor's persecution of the zemstvo and the rise of the zemstvo liberal movement before 1905. Several impressions

Table 6.12. Instances of gubernatorial meddling in internal zemstvo affairs, 1896–1904, by type of case

	1896	1897	1898	1899	1900	1901	1902	1903	1904	Total
Benefits to zemstvo	0	2	0	3	3	0	3	3	0	15
Honors for zemstvo leaders	1	1	0	1	1	0	1	1	0	5
"Outsiders"	0	1	4	0	1	0	0	1	2	12
Governor vs. zemstvo board	1	1	0	0	1	0	0	3	2	10
Commissions	0	2	1	0	1	0	0	1	1	7
Assembly vs. zemstvo board	0	0	1	2	1	0	1	1	0	7
Other	0	0	0	0	0	5	2	0	3	17
Total	2	7	6	6	8	5	7	10	8	73

Source: N. I. Kuznetsov, Sistematicheskii svod ukazov Pravitel'stvuiushchego Senata, posledovavshikh po zemskim delam, 12 vols. (St. Petersburg, 1902–15), vols. 1–3.

emerge from this study of the Kuznetsov collection. The Senate disputes reveal the ambiguity of relations between the zemstvo and the local bureaucracy: definite conflict existed between the governor and the zemstvo, but from the standpoint of an outsider neither party in these disputes appears either more virtuous or more capricious than the other.

Indeed, the celebrated gulf between *vlast'* and *obshchestvennost'* should not obscure our appreciation of the ties linking the two forces. It is becoming common for historians to point to the modest social background of tsarist bureaucrats as a reason for the tension between the state and the liberal gentry in late nineteenth-century Russia. This is certainly true for the upper bureaucracy in Saint Petersburg, primarily composed of commoners or landless gentry.[67] We should hesitate, however, before making this claim for relations between the zemstvo and the governor. Unlike the *chinovniki* in Saint Petersburg, both governors and vice governors tended to have a very high percentage of landed noblemen in their ranks.[68] Not only were zemstvo members and governors linked by common social origin, they also tended to share common patterns of service. Increasingly after 1900, a large number of governors tended to have served in the zemstvo before entering the bureaucracy.[69]

Once in the bureaucracy, however, these former zemstvo members began to view the problems of the province from a new perspective. The governor served as the "chief" (*nachal'nik*) of the province, the man who, officially at least, stood second only to the tsar in the administration of the region. Thus he saw himself as the tsar's personal agent, standing above all social classes, even above all public institutions, and defending the interests of the province as a whole.[70] Even if he were a landed nobleman experienced with a background of service in the zemstvo or as a gentry marshal, the governor could still come into conflict with the zemstvo. Such political labels as *left* and *right*, relevant in describing one's feelings on national politics, meant little in determining one's stand on most zemstvo issues, which more often than not turned on local, pragmatic considerations.[71] The English liberal Bernard Pares observed the change occurring in a man's thinking when he entered the bureaucracy: "In Russia, then, the difference is not so much between the official class and the rest of the nation, as the difference between a man in his official capacity and the same man as a private person."[72] In short, the demands of the office, not the social background, shaped the governor's mentality.

A local dispute appealed to the Senate illustrates how distorted our impression of reality becomes when we attempt to use labels based on class or national politics to describe zemstvo–governor relations. On

212

December 1, 1902, the governor of Kharkov, Prince Ivan Obolenskii, rose to address the provincial zemstvo for the opening of the regular session. Although a former zemstvo man himself, he managed to insult the audience and turn the occasion into one of the most embittering disputes of all cases heard before the Senate. Obolenskii began by discussing the problems of the zemstvo hospital, then turned to the question of the budget. The annual estimates and accounts serve as a prism for assessing the work of the zemstvo, claimed the prince, and they help one judge whether the population was getting a suitable return for its taxes. In nearly all district zemstvos of the province there were no funds for operating expenses; chaos reigned in the budget. Of course, Obolenskii went on, you men of the zemstvo might reply that you had not set up such a fund because governors of the past had not insisted on it. "I, however, as an old zemstvo man, have become accustomed to thinking that the orderly flow of zemstvo work depends not on the provincial chancellery and on the watchfulness of the governor, but depends solely on the zemstvos themselves and zemstvo assembly deputies...I invite you to find a way to correct your accounts." Obolenskii then closed with a phrase that touched off the fireworks: "In short, I will tell you only this, that I have known many zemstvos, but such zemstvo institutions as you have, I have never seen before."[73]

The Kharkov deputies were outraged. Once Obolenskii left the chambers, they launched into a debate over how to censure the governor for his offensive speech. What incensed them most was the governor's indiscretion of criticizing them for the failings of the district zemstvos, even though the law prevented them from intervening excessively in district business. After complaining to Saint Petersburg, the Kharkov zemstvo received a ruling from the Senate on November 15, 1905; the governor was to be admonished for improper behavior.

All the sources of misunderstanding were present in this case. The governor, once a zemstvo man himself, thought the present zemstvo careless and regarded himself as the sole guardian of the population. Moreover, eight months prior to Obolenskii's inflammatory speech, this same governor had attracted national attention for his brutal suppression of peasant unrest in Kharkov province.[74] Whatever harmony had united the governor and zemstvo prior to 1900, this bond was weakening under the weight of the growing revolutionary movement. Offended by Obolenskii's flogging of rebellious peasants in the spring of 1902, some Kharkov zemstvo members were ready to confront the governor at the first opportunity. Thus, reacting to Obolenskii's speech, the zemstvo leaders complained that state law had prevented them from correcting their own defects. Obolenskii to them personified the rude and capricious bureaucrat. The Senate, in turn, came to what it thought to be the rescue with its ruling of reprimand against the governor. By the time the decision arrived, however, the deputies had already forgotten the specific reason for their bitterness – 1905 was already underway. The governor had persecuted the zemstvo in style, not in substance, but symbolic pinpricks such as these could move the assembly to revolt.

The zemstvo and Saint Petersburg: Pleve and the third element

In order to complete our discussion of zemstvo–state relations, we must close with some comment on the attitude of the central ministries toward the zemstvo. To be sure, provincial governors were increasing their scrutiny of zemstvo business, particularly after 1900. However, the real basis for the zemstvo's hostility toward *vlast'* lay in its disagreements with the central bureaucracy, not with the provincial apparatus. The lasting impression one gains from the Kuznetsov collection is that the zemstvo and governor could get along harmoniously, conflicting at times over particular matters (much as a budget-minded school board director in America today would clash with his teachers over salary raises) but usually able to work a compromise. The situation changed totally, however, once the central ministries became involved. Then positions became rigid, issues took on a political overtone, and the zemstvo and the state retreated to their opposing poles in the *vlast'–oshchestvennost'* dichotomy. What we must understand, therefore, is the cause of the ministries' decision to involve themselves increasingly in local zemstvo affairs. (This, by the way, is the reverse argument of the claim, usually made by tsarist officials to explain the zemstvo–state polarization of 1905, that zemstvo leaders decided to involve themselves increasingly in *state* affairs.)

The essential question becomes, then, what did the imperial government do to provoke the rise of a unified zemstvo opposition in 1905? Although many theories have been advanced to solve this riddle, most historians emphasize one of two not incompatible arguments. The first theory, initially articulated by Russian liberals themselves, blames the counterreforms and the failure of the regime to follow through on the reforms of the 1860s. Characterized by Belokonskii's passage cited at the beginning of this chapter, this "sluice" theory sees the rise of the zemstvo movement as virtually an inevitable consequence of the government's inability to "crown the edifice" by accepting the "senseless dream" of a national representative body.[75] The second theory, first

214

argued by the Menshevik historian of the zemstvo, Boris Veselovskii, and now accepted by most modern specialists, sees the zemstvo opposition as a "fronde", an upper-class movement shaped by economic conflict with the state. According to this second theory, zemstvo activists, reflecting their gentry background, arose in opposition to the regime's economic policies which favored the interests of industry over those of the landed nobility.[76]

Although these two theories are useful in describing the background to the rise of liberal zemstvo opposition in 1905, they cannot explain clearly why the government began to meddle in zemstvo affairs after 1900. The counterreform theory may accurately convey the sense felt by liberal publicists that the government had abandoned the goals of the 1860s and was intent on liquidating the zemstvo. But it does not take into account the institutional and ideological diversity within the imperial bureaucracy, the absence of a reactionary consensus within the government capable of destroying local self-government.[77]

Similarly, although the agriculture-versus-industry theory does help us understand how Russian noblemen as a class could come to feel themselves estranged from the regime, it neither describes sufficiently the thinking of zemstvo leaders nor explains the motivation behind government policy on the zemstvo. One flaw in this "fronde" theory lies in the timing of the rise of the zemstvo movement. The most threatening period for Russian agriculture had been earlier, in the late 1880s and early 1890s, whereas the zemstvo movement began to organize into a coherent opposition only in the early 1900s. If we look at the personnel involved in the gentry campaign to challenge the state's economic policies, we find that these gentry leaders tended not to have been active in the leadership of the later zemstvo movement, and vice-versa.[78] A second flaw in this class-based theory is its unconvincing depiction of the regime as antigentry. Although landlords may have perceived the policies of the Ministry of Finance to be directed against them, this by no means proves that Finance Minister Sergei Witte abandoned the interests of gentry agriculture.[79]

To find the more specific cause of the government's provocation of the zemstvo, therefore, we must look elsewhere. Two trends in state policy at the turn of the century will help us understand the new turn against the zemstvo. The first theme, the government's response to the tax crisis of the mid-1890s, is already apparent from our discussion of the Kuznetsov collection of Senate disputes. As the zemstvo's explosive growth in expenditures in the 1890s began to compete with state expenditures for the diminishing supply of revenues from the peasantry, the central ministers began to see the need to restrict the zemstvo's welfare activities.

To understand the second theme in state policy on the zemstvo, however, we must reach beyond the material in the Kuznetsov collection to borrow a concept popular among modern Soviet historians on the zemstvo, the "fear of revolution" theory.[80] Soviet historians usually employ this theory to explain the motivation behind the zemstvo leaders' decision to revolt: state policies were leading the country into anarchy, zemstvo liberals argued, and so to preserve order the zemstvo activists must push for reform. This line of reasoning does accurately depict the thinking of zemstvo leaders at the turn of the century, particularly after the agrarian unrest of 1902. Space does not permit a full discussion of how zemstvo leaders came around to this way of thinking, especially since this process involved a very complicated attitude on the part of the gentry toward the peasant problem. For our purposes here, however, we should also consider the "fear of revolution" argument from the standpoint of the bureaucracy. Combatting the swelling wave of revolutionary unrest, the bureaucracy began to see the zemstvo as a sanctuary for radicals. Blurring the distinctions between zemstvo leaders and revolutionary agitators, state officials began to persecute the zemstvo with a vigilance exceeded only by its attack against Marxist and populist radicals.

The background to the tax crisis of the 1890s and the Finance Ministry's attack on the zemstvo lies in the expansion of that ministry's control over the affairs of the provinces. In his broad study of the imperial bureaucracy, George Yaney argues that the extension into the provinces of local agencies of the Interior and Finance Ministries created a situation in which local tensions sent shock waves to the capital, magnifying conflicts within the upper bureaucracy.[81] We should add to this that a tendency in the reverse direction was also occurring, such that conflicts between the Interior and Finance ministries in Saint Petersburg were being felt increasingly in the provinces. Much of the disagreement between the two ministries resulted from the difference in their functions. The Ministry of Internal Affairs served as the empire's police agency and thus sought to preserve the status quo, whereas the Finance Ministry was charged with the responsibility of increasing state revenues and public wealth, which led it to promote industrialization and other disruptive changes. Before 1890 only the Interior Ministry concerned itself with the zemstvo, but in the following decade the zemstvo became a central point of controversy between the two ministries.

216

The trouble began with the Finance Ministry's efforts to strengthen its authority in the provinces, thereby placing itself in competition with the Interior Ministry. Finance Minister Vyshnegradskii managed to establish tax inspectors in the districts (1885) and gained the right of provincial treasury directors to submit their remarks on the zemstvo budget to the governor's provincial office (1890).[82] Then Sergei Witte succeeded Vyshnegradskii in 1893, and began his industrialization program, which coincided precisely with the zemtsy's decision to expand their own spending dramatically. The poverty of the village, displayed so evidently in the famine of 1891–2, could only limit the resources available for public works, and the Finance Ministry was not about to let the zemstvo steal away scarce revenues. For the next 11 years in which he held office, Witte sought to channel as many funds as possible into state coffers and to limit expenditure on items not contributing to industry.[83]

Naturally this brought Witte into conflict with the zemstvo, especially since the zemstvo had fallen into debt after its spending during the famine of the early 1890s and needed loans from the treasury to pay for its *new* programs. While under Vyshnegradskii's stewardship, the Finance Ministry issued the law of June 8, 1893, establishing the supervision of zemstvo tax assessment work by provincial finance officials.[84] Then Witte produced the law of June 1, 1895, requiring zemstvos to deposit in the Treasury most funds not used for operating expenses.[85] To prevent the zemstvo from burdening the village with its taxes, his advisers drew up one of Russia's earliest progressive tax reforms, the state industrial tax of June 8, 1898. This law freed from industrial taxes "all rural dwellers, not only peasants of any description but also any other individuals registered in the village," thereby depriving the zemstvo of its claims on the handicraft taxes of peasants hiring no outside labor.[86]

The 1898 law also set off a major dispute with the Interior Ministry by its attempt to transfer authority for tax collection from the *zemskii nachal'nik* to the provincial tax inspectors of the Finance Ministry.[87] The following year, to sabotage Interior Minister Goremykin's proposal to introduce the zemstvo into the western, non-Russian provinces, Witte issued his polemical tract, *Autocracy and the Zemstvo*. To buttress his central argument that the principle of the zemstvo contradicted the principle of the monarch, Witte vigorously denounced the zemstvo for its costliness and fiscal irresponsibility.[88] Once Witte's influence prevailed upon the tsar to replace Goremykin with a friend of the finance minister, Dmitrii Sipiagin, the two ministries settled in an alliance that seemed to zemstvo leaders to mark the beginning of a conspiracy against them. On June 12, 1900, Witte and Sipiagin produced the twin laws placing a 3 percent per annum limit on the increase of the zemstvo budget and removing the zemstvo from the organization of food relief.[89] This cooperation between the Finance and Interior Ministries in regulating rural affairs continued in the law of March 12, 1902, outlawing the use of "collective responsibility" (krugovaia poruka) when collecting taxes in the village.[90]

The personal amity between the two ministries ended violently with the assassination of Sipiagin on April 2, 1902. The new interior minister, Viacheslav Pleve, unleashed a stubborn campaign to dislodge Witte from his position of primus inter pares among the tsar's ministers. Under Pleve, the government's efforts to combat the revolutionary movement began to affect relations between the zemstvo and the state. Thus we now can see the influence of the second factor embittering zemstvo–state relations, the threat of revolution. Whereas the tax crisis of the 1890s gave birth to the state's provocation of the zemstvo in the 1900 legislation, the efforts by police to remove radical influences from the zemstvo motivated the state's attack on the zemstvo after 1902.

Although most historians recognize that the problem of the third element formed a basis of the government's distrust of the zemstvo, the specific way this issue led to the worsening of zemstvo–state relations is not commonly known. Throughout the history of the zemstvo, radical professionals had managed to find employment in the zemstvo's health, educational, and economic programs, but the issue of radical zemstvo employees became a matter of state concern in the early 1900s when tsarist police uncovered a surprisingly large group of radicals working in the offices of the Samara provincial zemstvo.

The issue of radical employees in the zemstvo came to the attention of the tsarist police when the chief of the Samara provincial gendarmes filed his annual report to Saint Petersburg in January of 1900, summarizing problems in the province for the previous year. The gendarme labelled the zemstvo "the most dangerous institution in the province" because of the radical employees working in the provincial executive board. In the Statistical Department alone 38 employees were under police surveillance, he pointed out with alarm.[91] This report by the gendarme led to the coining of the phrase third element, as the vice governor of the province, Vladimir Kondoidi, warned of the threat posed by rootless radical professionals who had seized actual control of zemstvo affairs. In his speech opening the first session of the Samara provincial zemstvo assembly on January 11, 1900, Vice Governor Kondoidi directed attention to the steady growth recently of "a new, third element in the life of the zemstvo":

> Some will be pleased by this news and others will be dismayed, but all will agree with me that in the life of the zemstvo one can now see the participation of a new factor belonging neither to the administration nor to the ranks of representatives of local estates [*sosloviia*].

By using their authority as trained specialists, Kondoidi went on, these *intelligenly*, operating under the guise of freely hired employees of the provincial board, managed to convince the elected deputies in the assembly to approve projects undertaken by the *intelligenty* themselves. Kondoidi ended by warning of the "dangerous side" of these "people belonging neither to the administration or to representatives of *soslovie* in the zemstvo."[92]

We should not scoff at Kondoidi's remarks and think his argument a mere excuse for attacking the zemstvo. Even the leader of the zemstvo opposition at this time, Dmitrii Shipov, had exactly the same impression of third element control of zemstvo operations. In a letter to his close friend Mikhail Chelnokov of October 19, 1902, Shipov confessed his melancholy thoughts on the crisis of the Russian zemstvo:

> The difficult thing in zemstvo business is not only (and even not so much) the uselessness of debate aroused by policies of the government, so much as it is the apathy among deputies. After all, in essence *the zemstvo board has no choice but to rely exclusively on the third element*, since there is no participation by the assembly at all. In this regard, the upcoming session terrifies me.[93]

A month after Kondoidi's speech, the governor of Samara, Aleksandr Brianchaninov, launched his campaign to rid the zemstvo of the influence of the third element. In February 1900 he asked the provincial zemstvo board to present him with a list of all zemstvo employees so that he could check which had slipped into the zemstvo without his approval. Impatient with the sluggishness of the zemstvo's reply, which did not arrive on the governor's desk until a year later, Brianchaninov formed his own revision commission to investigate the zemstvo. A check on the total number of zemstvo employees showed that for 1899, 1900, and part of 1901, the provincial zemstvo board had failed to request the governor's confirmation of its appointments of over half its employees.[94] By October of 1901 the Department of Police in Saint Petersburg had become alarmed by the situation in Samara and began requesting information from Brianchaninov as to why so many zemstvo employees had been hired without his approval.[95]

As zemstvo members prepared for the forthcoming session of the provincial zemstvo that winter, the Samara governor challenged the zemstvo for its violation of required procedure. In a letter of December 14, 1901, Brianchaninov accused the provincial board of allowing the

219

director of each department of the zemstvo board to run its own affairs without consulting with the chairman and members of the board, as a result of which the unelected professionals in the board's departments were able to run zemstvo business de facto, skirting around the supervision of the nominal directors of the zemstvo, the elected (usually gentry) members of the zemstvo board. Although the director of the statistical department, Pavel Pegeev, was under police surveillance as a radical, he managed to hire like-minded statisticians and spend zemstvo money without any opposition from the provincial board.[96]

Now tensions broke out between the Department of Police in Saint Petersburg and the governor in Samara. On February 19, 1902, the director of the Department of Police sarcastically wrote to Brianchaninov of the illegality of the zemstvo board's practice of not requesting confirmation of its appointments and reminded the governor of his duty to prosecute the responsible (elected) officials of the provincial board.[97] Challenging this directive from the police, the Samara governor appealed for leniency to Interior Minister Sipiagin. Seeing the problem of the zemstvo more sympathetically because of his closeness to the zemstvo, Brianchaninov pleaded that he not be forced to bring the zemstvo leaders to court.[98] In the end, the governor held the upper hand: although Pegeev and other radical statisticians were finally dismissed at the end of 1902,[99] the elected members of the provincial board emerged unscathed.

Although the only concrete consequence of the Pegeev incident was the firing of the statisticians, the Samara experience strongly affected the thinking of police officials in Saint Petersburg on the problem of the zemstvo. In a landmark policy statement written by Aleksandr Voitov, director of the Department of Police's Special Division, the police equated the zemstvo with the revolutionary movement. Entitled "On the Legal Opposition," Voitov's memorandum of May 18, 1902, argued that the state should no longer draw a sharp distinction between the revolutionary movement and the legal opposition because they often had very close ties and supported each other. Indeed, he argued the strength of the liberals often determined the success of the revolutionaries: "The pressure of the revolutionary movement in a given moment and in a given region directly depends on whether or not an organized legal oppositional movement exists in that region.[100]

Then Voitov echoed Kondoidi in arguing that the third element, not the elected zemstvo gentry, actually ran the zemstvo: "Behind the backs of the zemtsy who get carried away and make protests, there always stands the prompter [whispering ideas in the zemtsy's ears] —

the zemstvo statistician, the zemstvo stenographer, the zemstvo doctor and so on."[101]

Voitov actually reprinted the text of Kondoidi's 1900 speech in his memorandum to prove his point, then carried the vice governor's thoughts to their extreme by arguing that the activity of this "third factor" was not accidental but a "systematic implementation of the revolutionary program" contained in a variety of Social Revolutionary and Social Democratic pamphlets.[102] Remarking that the "embryonic elements of constitutional life in contemporary Russia contain an absolutely stronger revolutionary spirit than developed constitutional forms in the West," Voitov concluded that the liberal, respectable, and wealthy elements in Russian society were working hand in hand with the revolutionaries. "Given these circumstances, such institutions as our organs of public self-government and our press, however innocent they may be on their own, must become instruments of the revolutionization [*revoliutsionizirovanie*] of the popular masses.[103]

The spring of 1902 marks a watershed in Russian politics, when the potential turmoil raging within the revolutionary movement finally broke to the surface. A month before Voitov wrote his memorandum "On the Legal Opposition," fierce agrarian disturbances erupted in Poltava, Kharkov, Saratov, and other provinces. In January of that year, Finance Minister Witte had founded his Special Conference on the Needs of Rural Industry to study peasant reform. Elected zemstvo representatives would not be invited to participate in the provincial and district committee of Witte's special conference. To protest this exclusion of the zemstvo from national politics and to discuss the agrarian crisis, Shipov gathered together a conference of zemstvo leaders in Moscow in May 1902. Although generally composed of moderate, uncertain zemtsy, the "Shipov Conference" also brought together some Beseda members who went on that summer to announce on the pages of *Osvobozhdenie* their entrance into the constitutionalist liberation movement.[104]

In the middle of this revolutionary crisis, the Interior Ministry fell into the hands of an official well suited to enforcing the new police mentality that now began to dominate government thinking on the zemstvo. That man was Viacheslav Pleve, former director of the Department of Police. Pleve's predecessor, Dmitrii Sipiagin, represented the traditional, yet now outmoded, approach to administering the Ministry of Internal Affairs. Like the two interior ministers before him, Sipiagin began his career in service as a representative of the landed nobility and then took a job as a provincial governor.[105] Sipiagin certainly bears responsibility for some pieces of antizemstvo legislation, such as the famine law of 1900,[106] but he never singled out the zemstvo as a scapegoat for the rise of revolutionary unrest. He did play the decisive role in the decision by Witte's special conference to exclude zemstvo representatives from its local committees.[107] Nevertheless, he was sensitive to the need not to alienate moderate members of the zemstvo and avoided the policeman's equation of the zemstvo with radical agitation.

The possibility of a nuanced appreciation of the zemstvo ended with Sipiagin's assassination, coming only days after word first reached Saint Petersburg of the village unrest in Poltava and Kharkov. With the inauguration of his successor, Viacheslav Pleve, a tougher, more uncompromising attitude toward the zemstvo took hold. Pleve's early months in office are famous for his half-hearted effort to woo Shipov away from the cause of Osvobozhdenie. Temporarily, at least, Pleve's overtures won Shipov's sympathy,[108] but by early October of 1902, the Slavophile zemstvo leader was already denouncing Pleve as an opportunist.[109]

A speech delivered by Pleve on the zemstvo reflects how deeply the new, post-Samara police mentality had penetrated state policy on the zemstvo. Addressing the February 28, 1904, session of Witte's special conference, Pleve made explicit his agreement with the Department of Police over the connection between the legal zemstvo opposition and the revolutionary movement. Pleve wholeheartedly endorsed the idea of consulting with "local people," especially the landed gentry, in order to clarify the needs of rural Russia. For this reason, he wrote, the local Witte committees had done the right thing by inviting gentry representatives, such as the provincial and district gentry marshals and the chairmen – almost universally gentry – of the zemstvo boards. But to call upon the zemstvo *as an institution* to participate in state affairs meant to open the floodgates to the influence of the third element:

> Petersburg assumes that by submitting a given issue to the zemstvo institutions for their comments, it is turning to local people who will explain everything that is needed; in reality what happens is the following: in the zemstvo the work force joining the ranks of zemstvo *chinovniki* have for a long time now been of a calibre much lower than that of Petersburg *chinovniki*, but unfortunately they arouse much alarm politically from the point of view of the Minister of Internal Affairs. Work done by these zemstvo *chinovniki* is essentially inspired by the doctrine demanding centrifugal aspirations in the name of the most detached principles. I am convinced that even road work provides an excuse in the zemstvo for the claim that under the present state structure the issue of roads not only cannot be resolved correctly but cannot even be discussed correctly. Such resolutions I have also heard expressed on the peasant matter.[110]

Because the third element held the zemstvo in a tight grip, Pleve continued, this institution of self-government could not be trusted:

> Until any change is made, until the organization of zemstvo activities is arranged so that local interests are represented not by statisticians under police surveillance, but are represented by people connected with the land, until then one should be very careful about organizing any survey of opinion by local people; and we should not be pleased to submit legislative projects to zemstvo institutions and receive their comments. We will receive a mass of comments from zemstvo institutions which will be sheer mush [*i budet deistvitel'naia kasha*] and the most talented presentations by people of the land (who write poorly, if at all) will have little influence on us, while people who have mastered an intelligent style by reading texts in their leisure time in prison will command our attention. And so, desiring to hear the thoughts of local people, we will receive doctrinaire replies from people having nothing in common with the local zemstvo.[111]

Armed with this new, post-Samara attitude to the zemstvo, Pleve set out to challenge the revolutionary threat in Russia. The contours of Pleve's program are too intricate to be detailed here, for they involved activity on a wide variety of fronts – against his arch rival, Finance Minister Witte, against the rise of an independently organized workers' movement, against the spread of revolutionary propaganda in the village, against Finnish separatists, and so on. But for our purposes of understanding state–zemstvo relations, Pleve's plans to reform the provincial administration merit comment here. Now we are finally able to see specifically how the heightened vigilance on the part of the central government soured the once stable relations between the governor and the zemstvo.

Once again, the Senate cases can help us see the background to changes in government policy on the zemstvo. Contrary to what we might expect, the peak years for zemstvo–governor disputes were not 1903 or 1904 but a few years earlier, between 1898 and 1902 (Table 6.13).

The years 1898–9 in fact seem to mark the period of the greatest turmoil. In Tver province alone, the governor vetoed over 160 bills on the zemstvo budget during the 1899 session.[112] These disputes clearly affected zemstvo liberals, for at the end of that same year the Beseda group was founded.[113] But they also left their mark on the Interior Ministry. Shortly before his assassination, Sipiagin was rumored to have been toying with the idea of proposing an elimination of the zemstvo's right of appeal. Pleve, a man of action, thought up a more fundamental solution to the problem, namely the elimination of all

223

Table 6.13.   *Frequency of all disputes, 1890–1904*

Year	Number of disputes
1890	3
1891	13
1892	7
1893	20
1894	42
1895	47
1896	52
1897	60
1898	86
1899	76
1900	59
1901	80
1902	77
1903	68
1904	42

Source: N. I. Kuznetsov, *Sistematicheskii svod ukazov Pravitel'stvuiushchego Senata, posledovavshikh po zemskim delam*, 12 vols. (St. Petersburg, 1902–15), vols. 1–3.

collegial bodies in the province and the consolidation of the governor's powers.

The initial sketch of his proposal appeared in a memorandum he drafted for the tsar on May 20, 1901 (even before he was minister of the interior). The govenor's authority was well-nigh nonexistent, Pleve wrote the tsar, and the collegial provincial offices attended by finance officials and zemstvo representatives had loosened the governor's grip on the province.[114] Once in the Interior Ministry, Pleve returned to the subject in two memoranda of October 23, 1902, and February 27, 1903. Echoing the thoughts of the minister responsible for the counter-reforms, Dmitrii Tolstoi, Pleve complained of the governor's inability to order the zemstvo to take an action or to alter the content of a zemstvo bill. If the governor recommended such a change, zemstvo leaders could claim they lacked sufficient funds and refuse to budge. The only way to avoid this "passive resistance" by the zemstvo, Pleve concluded, was to empower the governor to fix a time limit within which the zemstvo would be required to perform its mandatory duties. If the zemstvo dragged its feet, the Interior and Finance ministries could jointly authorize a forced transfer of funds from the zemstvo to the governor, who could then spend the money as he wished. Pleve also proposed the creation of a provincial council under the governor which would essentially remove local finance officials from any influence in the province.[115]

Pleve publically unveiled his plans at a banquet honoring the one-hundredth anniversary of the founding of the Interior Ministry on December 29, 1902.[116] Throughout the next month Pleve worked busily in Saint Petersburg with his "expert on the issue of strengthening gubernatorial power,"[117] Prince Ivan Obolenskii, governor of Kharkov (and, we should recall, the former zemstvo man involved in the bitter dispute with his provincial zemstvo described above).

To proclaim his support for Pleve's reform, Tsar Nicholas II issued his Manifesto of February 26, 1903, announcing the need to centralize the provincial administration in order to put an end to the "chaos" (*smuta*) in the realm.[118] The next day, Pleve chaired the opening session of his newly created the Imperial "special commission" for a Review of Provincial Administration, the first government effort to reexamine the provincial administration since the Kakhanov Commission of the early 1880s. Dominated by Pleve's leading assistants in the Interior Ministry,[119] the commission drafted a wide program of reforms corresponding closely to Pleve's principles of October 23, 1902, and February 27, 1903.

Nothing ever came of this reform effort due to the intervention of Pleve's own assassination in 1904 and the revolution of the following year. Nevertheless, the work of Pleve's commission reflects the drift in thinking among central officials on governor–zemstvo relations. For our purposes, the most significant aspect of this reform was Pleve's decision to submit copies of the proceedings of his commission to the governors for their comments. Although too lengthy to be summarized here, these remarks by the governors reveal the strong diversity of opinion between Saint Petersburg and the provinces. Some governors, most notably Governor Shlippe of Tula, wholeheartedly supported Pleve's plans and called for the transformation of the zemstvo into essentially a governor-appointed economic agency.[120]

However, other governors, such as those from Ekaterinoslav, Simbirsk, and Saint Petersburg provinces, consistently disagreed with the commission's proposals, mixing their arguments with objections on pragmatic grounds and disagreements in principle.[121] The most remarkable comment came from the pen of Count Keller, governor of Ekaterinoslav. Responding to the commission's proposal to create a provincial council (*gubernskii sovet*) to unify the activities of all local state agencies under the governor's control, Keller argued that such unity of administration was impossible "as long as there continues to exist a *disagreement in the views and directions of the central institutions themselves,* which among other things have the tendency to exert their influence on the course of affairs of local life."[122]

Faced with the disagreement among the governors themselves over the need to strengthen their authority over the zemstvo, Pleve took matters into his own hands to enforce his will on the provinces. Angered by the zemstvo campaign aganst the Witte committees, Pleve prevailed upon the tsar to issue formal rebukes to Shipov, Mikhail Stakhovich, Petr Dolgorukov, and others. Strengthening his surveillance of the provinces, Pleve dispatched two of his top advisers on zemstvo affairs, Nikolai Zinovev and Boris Shtiurmer, to inspect the zemstvos of Voronezh, Kursk, Tver, Moscow, and Viatka provinces.[123] Shortly after two members of the Voronezh committee had been arrested for liberal statements, Zinovev arrived in Voronezh to interrogate zemstvo members and gentry marshals. Rudely warning them of the consequences of their actions, Zinovev closed by saying, "You haven't seen the end of this."[124] Zinovev's inspection of the Moscow zemstvo totally outraged zemstvo leaders there.[125]

Despite a dissension within his own ministry,[126] Pleve used these reports by Zinovev and Shtiurmer as the basis for still more purges of zemstvo men in the followng year: on January 8, 1904, he prevailed upon the tsar to order the dismissal of the entire elected staff of the Tver provincial and Novotorzhok district zemstvo boards; and then in April he announced his decision not to confirm the election of Dmitrii Shipov as chairman of the Moscow provincial zemstvo board.

Pleve's handling of the governors at this time reveals how fundamentally his campaign against zemstvo leaders had disrupted traditional relations in the provinces. If we recall the events of the Samara incident at the turn of the century, we find that in March 1902, Governor Brianchaninov successfully defied the will of the Department of Police and convinced Interior Minister Sipiagin not to bring to trial the elected, gentry officials of the Samara zemstvo. However, after Pleve took over the reins of the ministry and clashed with the zemstvos over the Witte committees, leniency toward the governors' sympathies could no longer be tolerated in Saint Petersburg. After the incident in Voronezh, Pleve forced the governor there, Sleptsov, to resign.[127] A few months later, in early 1904, Pleve summoned several governors to Saint Petersburg to instruct them on how to steer their Witte committees away from political issues. An eyewitness recorded that he and his fellow governors behaved like docile, intimidated schoolchildren, lowering their glances to avoid the eyes of the schoolmaster.[128]

226

Conclusion

The famous zemstvo congress of November 6, 1904, the beginning date of the period of a unified zemstvo opposition, did not solely
result from Pleve's sacking of the Tver, Moscow, Kursk, and Voronezh
zemstvos. The tensions aroused by the Russo-Japanese War and the
new administration of Interior Minister Sviatopolk-Mirskii certainly
played their own role in the building of the banquet campaign of the
fall of 1904.[129] Nevertheless, Pleve's tactless provocations certainly
contributed to the decision of zemstvo leaders to gather and openly
challenge the regime. The governor's conflicts with the zemstvo over
budgetary matters help us understand the first underlying cause of the
central government's growing distrust of the zemstvo – the Finance
Ministry's competition with the zemstvo for increasingly scarce tax
revenues. In turn, the Samara incident of 1900–2 helps explain the
second cause of the state's provocation of the zemstvo, the police-
minded effort to root out radical, third-element influences within the
zemstvo.

As a consequence of their conflicts with the bureaucracy in the five
years before the Revolution of 1905, zemstvo leaders managed to
convince the quiet deputies in their assemblies of the impossibility of
getting along with the present regime. In the 1890s, the governor
questioned the usefulness of a new school or overruled a zemstvo tax
increase, but the bonds uniting the zemstvo and local officialdom
remained intact. After 1900, however, the bureaucracy's distrust of the
zemstvo became a personal affront to zemstvo men, a direct challenge
to their right to participate in an institution to which they had devoted
their careers.

By the middle of 1902, a group of zemstvo constitutionalists had
already become a visible part of the Liberation Movement. In December
of that year, a group of "old *zemtsy*" wrote an "open letter" in
Osvobozhdenie to their comrades, entitled "What Is There for Us to
Do?" Pointing to the rise of peasant and worker unrest, the "old
zemtsy" bitterly blamed the bureaucracy for the growing threat of
anarchy. Exhorting their comrades to join the movement, they cried out
aganst the rude treatment they had suffered from the bureaucracy:

> The attitude held by the Autocratic bureaucracy to you [fellow
> *zemtsy*] has now become totally clear. You are treated either like
> poorly educated kids on the street whom anyone passing by can smack
> or slap on the face without the slightest fear of being punished; or you
> are treated like dimwits and ninnies [*fofany i protofili*] in front of

whom anyone can play out any kind of comedy with the fullest
assurance of your simple-minded gullibility. Does it please you, dear
sirs, to remain in this position even into the future?[130]

Although only a few zemstvo members were ready to commit
themselves fully to the Liberation Movement in 1902, the government's
personal attack on zemtsy convinced most zemstvo members by the fall
of 1904 that they must link their fate with the opposition. The fatal
mistake on the part of Pleve, his willingness to blur the distinctions
between the legal zemstvo members and the radical agitators, now bore
its fruit.

Notes

1 Ivan Belokonskii, Zemskoe dvizhenie, 2d ed. (Moscow, 1914), p. 1.
2 Vasilii Maklakov, Vlast' i obshchestvennost' na zakate staroi Rossii, 3
vols. (Paris, 1936).
3 The best summary of these theories can be found in P. P. Gronskii,
"Teorii samoupravleniia v russkoi nauke," in Iubileinyi zemskii
sbornik, 1864–1914 (St. Petersburg, 1914), pp. 76–85. See also N. M.
Korkunov, Russkoe gosudarstvennoe pravo, 2 vols. (St. Petersburg,
1909), 2: 498–501.
4 One example poignantly illustrates the confusion reigning since
1864. Boris Chicherin, the liberal historian and zemstvo activist,
recalled that in 1871 he had been elected director of the Tambov–
Saratov railroad by a district zemstvo of Tambov province. Shortly
following this election, he heard that he had been appointed a
member of the jury in his district town. Knowing that his duties in the
railroad administration would require him to spend a great deal of
time in Saint Petersburg, Chicherin appealed to the local court
requesting exemption from jury duty. The court rejected his request
and threatened him with a fine of 100 rubles if he failed to serve on
the jury. Chicherin then complained to the judicial chambers of
Saratov for a repeal of this ruling – but was overruled on the grounds
that his job for the zemstvo was a matter of "private business" which
could not take precedence over his responsibility to the state to serve
on the jury. Chicherin chose to pay the 100-ruble fine. Boris
Chicherin, Voprosy politiki (Moscow, 1904), p. 90.
5 Among the many zemstvo memoirs are Ivan Petrunkevich, "Iz zapisok obshchestvennogo deiatelia," Arkhiv russkoi revoliutsii 31 (Berlin, 1934); Dmitrii Shipov, Vospominaniia i dumy o perezhitom
(Moscow, 1918); Tikhon Polner, Zhiznennyi put' Kniazia Georgiia
Evgen'evicha L'vova (Paris, 1932); V. M. Khizhniakov, Vospominaniia zemskogo deiatelia (Petrograd, 1916); and A. N. Naumov, Iz
utselevshikh vospominanii, 1868–1917, 2 vols. (New York, 1955).
The standard histories written by zemstvo men include Boris Vese-

lovskii, *Istoriia zemstva za sorok let*, 4 vols. (St. Petersburg, 1909–11); and Belokonskii, *Zemskoe dvizhenie*.

6   N. I. Kuznetsov, *Sistematicheskii svod ukazov Pravitel'stvuiush-chego Senata, posledovavshikh po zemskim delam*, 12 vols. (St. Petersburg, 1902–15).

7   A much more complete set of Senate rulings for the decade of the 1890s can be found in Ia. A. Kantorovich, *Sbornik opredelenii Pervogo Departamenta Pravitel'stvuiushchego Senata po gorodskim i zemskim delam za 10 let (1891–1900 gg.)* (St. Petersburg, 1903). I am grateful to Professor Richard Robbins for bringing this book to my attention. I saw this book after my computer analysis of the Kuznetsov collection had already been completed and decided that an additional study of Kantorovich's rulings would not be worth the extra month's work that this book would require. First, there would be the problem of what to do with the years after 1900, since Kantorovich's book cuts off then. Second, there is the question of whether an analysis of *all* disputes is necessary in order to comment on zemstvo–governor relations. Social historians use sampling techniques in studying census reports of populations, and there is no reason why the 738 disputes listed in Kuznetsov do not represent an adequate sample. If any bias exists in this sample, it would undoubtedly be in favor of the zemstvo, against the government. (The Voronezh provincial zemstvo board, which produced the Kuznetsov collection, had a reputation in the eyes of the police as a hotbed of radical agitation.) As we shall see below, a close reading of the Kuznetsov collection reveals the zemstvo to be just as blemished as the governor, so there is every reason to feel confident in the reliability of this source.

8   A. A. Bogolepov, "Resheniia Senata po administrativnym delam," *Zapiski russkogo nauchnogo instituta v Bel'grade*, 1928, no. 15, pp. 1–35.

9   Ibid.; S. A. Korf, *Administrativnaia iustitsiia v Rossii*, 2 vols. (St. Petersburg, 1910); I. A. Blinov, *Otnosheniia Senata k mestnym uchrezhdeniiam v XIX veke* (St. Petersburg, 1911); S. F. Platonov, ed., *Istoriia Pravitel'stvuiushchego Senata za dvesti let* (St. Petersburg, 1902); G. B. Sliozberg, *Dorevoliutsionnyi stroi Rossii* (Paris, 1933).

10 Gosudarstvennyi Istoricheskii Muzei (hereafter GIM), f. 31 ed. khr. 142 (Maklakov papers on *Beseda*), p. 155. The Samara *zemets* Shishkov also admitted this in an article written at the turn of the century: "For the overwhelming majority of the *narod*, the zemstvo is only one part of a towering structure known as *nachal'stvo* [the bosses] – less important, surely, than the *ispravnik*, and not as stubborn as the *stanovoi* [two police ranks], but that is all." N. A. Shishkov, "Nashe zemstvo, ego trudy i nedochety," *Vestnik Evropy*, 1901, no. 9, p. 322.

11 M. Gor'kii, *Sobranie sochinenii*, 30 vols. (Moscow, 1949–55), 16: 330, 334.

12 For more on the spread of legalistic thought within the judiciary, see Richard Wortman, *The Development of a Russian Legal Consciousness* (Chicago, 1976). This consciousness took root among private citizens as well and was reflected in the steady increase of private appeals to the Senate. Blinov, pp. 164–6.

13 Kuznetsov, vols. 1–3.

14 A. A. Polovtsov, *Dnevnik gosudarstvennogo sekretaria A. A. Polovtsova v dvukh tomakh*, 2 vols. (Moscow, 1966), 2:263–71, 500; Theodore Taranovski, "The Politics of Counter-Reform: Autocracy and Bureaucracy in the Reign of Alexander III, 1881–1894," (Ph.D. dissertation, Harvard University, 1976), pp. 413–15, 527, 541–64.

15 Blinov, p. 209. The zemstvo tended to respect the governor's objections, as one senator found in an 1880–1 revision of Samara and Saratov provinces. According to Veselovskii, there were only 11 instances of governor–zemstvo conflict that had to be reported to the Committee of Ministers in the 1880s. Veselovskii, 3:325–6.

16 *Polnoe sobranie zakonov Rossiiskoi imperii (PSZRI)*, 3d series, vol. 10, no. 6927 (June 12, 1890), p. 495.

17 The highwater mark for mutiny by the provincial offices was between 1893 and 1896, when they refused to confirm governors' vetoes on eight occasions.

18 *PSZRI*, 3d series, vol. 10, no. 6927 (June 12, 1890), article 87, p. 506. Ironically, the same appellation is used for the notorious article 87 of the 1906 Fundamental State Laws allowing the tsar to pass laws in defiance of the Duma.

19 Veselovskii claims that this paralyzed zemstvo life in Tver in the 1890s, and in Ufa and Kharkov in the early 1900s. *Istoriia zemstva*, 3: 362. See also I. A. Blinov, *Gubernatory* (St. Petersburg, 1905), pp. 295–8. The most interesting discussion of this problem can be found in V. D. Kuz'min-Karavaev, "Predely prava gubernatorov ostanavlivat' postanovleniia zemskikh sobranii," *Pravo*, 1900, no. 15, pp. 756–62.

20 P. I. Shlemin, "Zemsko-liberal'noe dvizhenie na rubezhe XIX–XX vekov " (*Kandidat* dissertation, Moscow State University, 1972), pp. 63–4, 90; N. M. Pirumova, *Zemskoe liberal'noe dvizhenie* (Moscow, 1977), p. 188.

21 Blinov, *Otnosheniia Senata*, p. 210.

22 For interesting remarks on the origins of the bureaucracy's attitude of protection for the population, see the work by David Anthony Macey, "The Russian Bureaucracy and the 'Peasant Problem': The Pre-History of the Stolypin Reforms, 1861–1907" (Ph.D. dissertation, Columbia University, 1976), pp. 20–6.

23 The governor's tradition of distrusting the zemstvo because of its fiscal irresponsibility extended back to the 1880s and late 1870s, and played an important role in persuading Count Tolstoi to embark on his plan

for a zemstvo counterreform. See Thomas Pearson, "Ministerial Conflict and Local Self-Government Reform in Russia, 1877–1890" (Ph.D. dissertation, University of North Carolina at Chapel Hill, 1977), pp. 270–6.

24 The governor in question was P. V. Nekliudov, governor of Orel. For details on this case and a stimulating discussion of the problem of central ministerial discipline of disobedient governors, see the unpublished manuscript by Richard G. Robbins, Jr., "Guarding the Guardians: Law and the Problem of Central Control over the Russian Provincial Governors in the Last Years of the Empire," pp. 1–14. See also P. A. Zaionchkovskii, *Pravitel'stvennyi apparat samoderzhavnoi Rossii v XIX v.* (Moscow, 1978), p. 213.

25 The appointed governor was Dmitrii S. Neidgardt, despised for his involvement in the Odessa pogroms of 1905, while serving as *gradonachal'nik* there. The public protest to Neidgardt occurred in Nizhnii Novgorod when he was appointed to the governor's post there in 1906. Gosudarstvennyi arkhiv Gor'kovskoi oblasti, f. 2, op. 3, ed. khr. 54, (Podpisnye listy gr-n N. Novgoroda, protestuiush-chikh protiv naznacheniia gubernatorom Neigarda), pp. 1–21.

26 A. F. Koni, "Triumviry," *Sobranie sochinenii*, 8 vols. (Moscow, 1966–9), 2:269; S. Iu. Witte, *Vospominaniia*, 3 vols. (Moscow, 1960), 1:320–8; V. I. Gurko, *Features and Figures of the Past: Government and Opinion in the Reign of Nicholas II* (Stanford, 1939), pp. 90, 292; Blinov, *Gubernatory*, p. 307; P. A. Zaionchkov-skii, *Rossiiskoe samoderzhavie v kontse XIX stoletiia* (Moscow, 1970), pp. 247–53.

27 Korf, 2:315–16; Sliozberg, pp. 147–8; Marc Szeftel, "The Form of Government of the Russian Empire Prior to the Constitutional Reforms of 1905–6," in John Curtiss, ed., *Essays in Russian History in Honor of Geroid Tanquary Robinson* (New York, 1963), pp. 112–13; Zaionchkovskii, pp. 104–7; Taranovski, pp. 322–3.

28 Blinov, *Otnosheniia Senata*, p. 194.

29 In the words of Sliozberg, "[The Senate's] main significance lies in the fact that, in the face of the tendency of executive organs of the state to display *proizvol*, it stood as the bastion of legality." *Dorevoliutsionnyi stroi*, p. 145. See also Blinov, *Otnosheniia Senata*, p. 183; Szeftel, p. 112; Taranovski, pp. 83–90.

30 Shipov, pp. 115–18.

31 The liberals' faith in the Senate as a safeguard against abuse is clearly articulated by Kostantin B. Veselovskii, a zemstvo activist from Saratov province and brother of zemstvo historian Boris B. Veselovskii: "I don't doubt for a minute that the ministry [of education] will honor our complaint; and if the ministry won't be there, there's always the Senate." Balashovskoe uezdnoe zemskoe sobranie, *Zhurnaly Balashovskogo uezdnogo zemskogo sobraniia ... za 1902 god* (Balashov, 1903), p. 20.

One can easily confirm the legalistic talent of the zemstvo by checking almost any appeal submitted to the Senate. Contrary to the popular image of gentry politicians at the turn of the century as amateurs poorly trained for bureaucratic and legal paperwork, zemstvo board members writing Senate appeals displayed a great ability to cite precedent and present legal evidence to argue their case. (This, by the way, is one of the main reasons why the zemstvo managed to beat the governor so frequently in appeals to the Senate: zemstvo writers were more skilled in writing legal arguments.) Even in the files of the Beseda circle there is mention of the Senate as a defense against the bureaucracy. In 1901, members of Beseda discussed the use of Senate appeal in order to challenge a proposed government order on education. Then in the late summer of 1904 each member of Beseda carried a copy of a ten-year-old Senate ruling back to the provinces, to prove that the zemstvo indeed had the right to elect people to advisory commissions. The fact that zemstvo leaders could recall a ruling of 1894 to buttress their strategy against the bureaucracy in the middle of the Russo–Japanese War truly indicates the significance of the Senate. GIM, f. 31, ed. khr. 142, pp. 10, 158.

32 A word must be said about the method employed here to determine the year in which these disputes arose. In nearly every instance Kuznetsov provides the date of the Senate ruling but fails to mention the date when the dispute arose in almost a third of the cases (235, or 32 percent). To obtain the initial date of the conflict, therefore, I have had to use the second date, the year of the Senate ruling, and assume that the dispute began two and a half years earlier.

33 For more on the close ties uniting land captains and zemstvo deputies, especially in the early 1890s, see Thomas Fallows, "Forging the Zemstvo Movement: Liberalism and Radicalism on the Volga, 1890–1905" (Ph.D. dissertation, Harvard University, 1981), ch. 7.

34 *Iubileinyi zemskii sbornik*, pp. 106–7, 166–8.

35 Veselovskii, 3:424–6.

36 A. A. Kizevetter, *Na rubezhe dvukh stoletii* (Prague,1929), p. 224; Shipov, pp. 31–54.

37 Chicherin, pp. 94–138; Veselovskii, 1:196, 244–5, 257–8; A. Novikov, *Zapiski zemskogo nachal'nika* (St. Petersburg, 1899), pp. 160–3.

38 For some examples of this tactic, see the appeals from Viatka, Saratov, and Samara provinces. Kuznetsov, 2: nos. 185, 195, and 276.

39 Ibid., 1: no 284.

40 Ibid., no. 534.

41 Ibid., no. 327.

42 Ibid., no. 305.

43 Ibid., 3: nos. 43, 217.

44 Ibid., 1: no. 340.

45 Ibid., no. 356.

46 Ibid., no. 358.

47 Ibid., nos. 308, 309.

48 It is remarkable how frequently outside observers found fault with the zemstvo. Even in Russian literature one can find criticism of zemstvo corruption. In Saltykov-Shchedrin's *The Gentlemen Golovlev*, Indushka's daughter, Anninka, receives a letter from Liubinka writing of a zemstvo activist making his living by stealing money from the zemstvo. Levin, in Tolstoi's *Anna Karenina*, refuses his brother's pleas that he participate in the zemstvo, exclaiming that "to me the zemstvo means nothing more than a tax of three kopeks a desiatina." Chekhov's "The Peasants" closes with a scene in which peasants foolishly blame "zemstvo!" for their travails. And in Chekhov's "Chamber No. 6," the doctor Andrei Efimych appears before the city council and asks that they transfer his hospital to the zemstvo. "Sure," replies another doctor with a knowing smile. "Turn over money to the zemstvo, and it will steal it."

Foreigners also saw reason to distrust the zemstvo. The reporter for the London Times, Donald MacKenzie Wallace, would hardly be considered an ally of the bureaucracy against the zemstvo. Yet he wondered why Russians had not questioned whether the zemstvo was "too expensive for the work to be performed" and noted that "many people draw from all this the conclusion that the Zemstvo is a worthless institution which has increased the taxation without conferring any corresponding benefit on the country." Donald Mackenzie Wallace, *Russia on the Eve of War and Revolution* (New York, 1961), p. 34, 37. The Frenchman Anatole Leroy-Beaulieu echoed Wallace's sentiments, scorning the zemstvo for its unfair tax policy. Anatole Leroy-Beaulieu, *L'Empire des tsars et les Russes*, 3 vols. (Paris, 1897–8), 2:198–200. See also Richard G. Robbins, Jr., *Famine in Russia, 1891–1892* (New York, 1975).

49 M. S. Simonova, "Otmena krugovoi poruki," *Istoricheskie zapiski* 1969, no. 83, p. 166. Although this is not the place for a full discussion of the issue, we should note here that the arrears problem seems to have resulted largely from the peasants' tax resistance. Once the government realized that collective responsibility for tax collection actually enabled the village to refuse to pay taxes, the Ministry of Finance became dedicated to its abolition. Ibid., pp. 170–6; and Novikov, p. 125. For an extreme statement of this view, see James Simms, "The Crisis in Russian Agriculture at the End of the Nineteenth Century: A Different View," *Slavic Review*, September 1977, pp. 377–98.

50 Kuznetsov, 1: no. 313; 2: no. 149.

51 Ibid., 3: no. 200.

52 Ibid., 2: no. 25.

53 Ibid., 3: no. 46.

54 Ibid., no. 53.
55 Ibid., no. 52.
56 Ibid., no. 55.
57 Ibid., no. 299.
58 An interesting discussion of zemstvo petitions against the use of corporal punishment and of the governor's abuse of article 87 to thwart these petitions can be found in E. Varb, "Neskol'ko slov o zemskikh khodataistvakh i otnosiashchikhsia k nim zakonopolozheniiakh," *Russkaia mysl'*, 1896, no. 11, pp. 178–87. I am grateful to Mr. Timothy Mixter for this reference.
59 For more on this see John Gantvoort, "Relations Between Government and Zemstvos under Valuev and Timashev, 1864–1876" (Ph.D. dissertation, University of Illinois at Urbana–Champaign, 1971), pp. 29–43. Gantvoort's thesis serves as a useful antidote to the liberal tradition seeing an antizemstvo conspiracy behind every piece of legislation restricting zemstvo activity. He shows how administrative necessity, rather than political conspiracy, led the state to curtail some of the rights zemstvo leaders felt they deserved after 1864.
60 L. G. Zakharova, *Zemskaia kontrreforma 1890 g.* (Moscow, 1968), p. 153.
61 This same problem came to the attention of state officials when Senator Ivan Shamshin inspected the Saratov and Samara zemstvos in 1880. Instead of carefully documenting the amount of money needed in famine relief funds, the Volga zemstvos were found guilty of submitting greatly inflated requests for loans from Saint Petersburg. Pearson, pp. 90–3.
62 For more on the governor's career patterns, see Richard G. Robbins, Jr., "Choosing the Russian Governors: the Professionalization of the Gubernatorial Corps," *Slavonic and East European Review*, October 1980, pp. 541–60.
63 *Professionalization* is used here in the broad sense, to describe a state of mind, rather than the more specific sense of professionalization as the result of technical training. For more on the corporate mentality among zemstvo leaders see Fallows, ch. 4.
64 Kuznetsov, 3: no. 17.
65 Ibid., 1: no.7.
66 Ibid., 3: no. 23.
67 A. P. Korelin, "Dvorianstvo v poreformennoi Rossii (1861–1904 gg.)," *Istoricheskie zapiski*, 1971, no. 87, pp. 158–64; Helju Aulik Bennett, "The *Chin* System and the *Raznochintsy* in the Government of Alexander III, 1881–1894" (Ph.D. dissertation, University of California, 1971), ch. 8; Don Karl Rowney, "Higher Civil Servants in the Russian Ministry of Internal Affairs: Some Demographic Characteristics," *Slavic Review*, March 1972, p. 102; Taranovski, p. 136–7; Daniel Orlovsky, "Recent Studies on the Russian Bureaucracy," *Russian Review*, October 1976, pp. 457–63; Jerome Blum, "Russia,"

in David Spring, ed., *European Landed Elites in the Nineteenth Century* (Baltimore, 1977), pp. 68–95; Daniel Field, "Three New Books on the Imperial Bureaucracy," *Kritika,* Spring 1979, p. 119–47; and Roberta Manning, *The Crisis of the Old Order in Russia: Gentry and Government, 1861–1914* (forthcoming), ch. 2.

68 Zaionchkovskii, pp. 211–17.

69 The evidence collected by Richard Robbins shows a very strong tendency for governors to have begun their service by working in the provincial bureaucracy, not the central bureaucracy, usually starting as gentry marshals or in the zemstvo. Robbins, "Choosing the Governors," pp. 549–55. See also Gurko, pp. 127–8, 143.

70 For more on this attitude, see the dissertation by Theodore Taranovski, especially chapter 3. See also Stephen Sternheimer, "Administering Development and Developing Administration: Organizational Conflict in Tsarist Bureaucracy, 1906–1914," *Canadian-American Slavic Studies,* Fall 1975, pp. 277–301.

71 K. F. Golovin, *Vospominaniia,* 2 vols. (St. Petersburg, 1899), 1: 260–8. One governor, Prince Urusov, reported that the provincial zemstvo of his province could promote liberal programs while refraining from any confrontation with him or with earlier governors. S. D. Urusov, *Zapiski gubernatora* (Moscow, n.d.), p. 146. Consider also the example of Tver province. After Fedor Rodichev had been removed from the provincial board in 1891 for criticizing the counterreforms, the governor appointed a zemstvo member of the extreme right, Boris Shtiurmer, to run the zemstvo. (This same zemstvo man was to assist Pleve in his persecution of the zemstvo in 1903–4, and then to head the Russian government in 1916 in opposition to the zemstvo Union of World War I.) Once in charge of the Tver zemstvo, however, Shtiurmer avoided conflicts with the zemstvo left by working out a compromise with Ivan Petrunkevich: Shtiurmer agreed to let the provincial board do its work without his interference in exchange for a pledge from Petrunkevich that the left deputies would not denounce him as the government's lackey. Gurko, pp. 186–7.

72 Bernard Pares, *Russia and Reform* (London, 1907), pp. 164–5.

73 Kuznetsov, 3: no. 30.

74 Edward H. Judge, "The Russia of Plehve: Programs and Policies of the Ministry of Internal Affairs, 1902–1904" (Ph.D. dissertation, University of Michigan, 1975), pp. 110–12. In retaliation for Obolenskii's brutal floggings, the SR Battle Organization pronounced a death sentence on the governor in the summer of 1902. *Revoliutsionnaia Rossiia,* August 1902, p. 25.

75 Besides Ivan Belokonskii's *Zemskoe dvizhenie,* other adherents to this theory include Aleksandr Kornilov, *Kurs istorii Rossii XIX veka,* 3 vols. (Moscow, 1912–14), 3; George Fischer, *Russian Liberalism* (Cambridge, Mass., 1958); Jacob Walkin, *The Rise of Democracy in Pre-Revolutionary Russia* (London, 1963). Boris Chicherin explains

the rise of zemstvo opposition similarly as an inevitable consequence of the nature of bureaucracies everywhere: "Bureaucracies hate independent forces which set limits to their love of power and their *proizvol*. From this arises their hatred for the zemstvo, which constitutes a permanent feature of a bureaucracy resting on its greatness and not knowing any limits to its power. The belittling of the zemstvo and its subordination to bureaucratic control are the goals of any true *chinovnik* in any country on the globe." Chicherin, p. 77.

76　Boris Veselovskii, "Dvizhenie zemlevladel'tsev," in L. Martov et al., eds., *Obshchestvennoe dvizhenie v Rossii v nachale XX-go veka*, 4 vols. (St. Petersburg, 1909–14) 1:291–312; Korelin; Iu. B. Solov'ev, *Samoderzhavie i dvorianstvo v kontse XIX veka* (Leningrad, 1973); M. S. Simonova, "Zemsko-liberal'naia fronda (1902–1903 gg.)," *Istoricheskie zapiski*, 1973, no. 91, pp. 150–216; Terence Emmons, "The Russian Landed Gentry and Politics," *Russian Review*, July 1974, pp. 269–83; Gary Hamburg, "The Russian Nobility on the Eve of the 1905 Revolution," *Russian Review*, July 1979, pp. 323–38; Manning, chs. 1, 2, 3.

77　The best recent disscusion of this problem can be found in the dissertation by Taranovski, "The Politics of Counter-Reform." See also George Yaney's remarks on the vitality and creativity within the pre-war bureaucracy: "Some Aspects of the Imperial Russian Government on the Eve of the First World War," *Slavonic and East European Review*, December 1964, pp. 69–90; and "Social Stability in Pre-Revolutionary Russia: A Critical Note," *Slavic Review*, September 1965, pp. 521–7. Consider also the dissertations by Pearson, passim; and Macey, p. 280.

78　Exceptions to this general rule did exist, of course, as in the cases of M. A. Stakhovich and, to a lesser extent, the Bobrinskii brothers and D. S. Sheremetev.

79　For more on this problem, see my review of T. M. Kitanina's book on tsarist grain policy in *Kritika*, Winter 1980.

80　Examples include E. D. Chermenskii, "Zemsko-liberal'noe dvizhenie nakanune revoliutsii 1905–07 g.," *Istoriia SSSR*, 1965, no. 5, pp. 41–60; Shlemin; K. F. Shatsillo, "Formirovanie programmy zemskogo liberalizma i ee bankrotstvo nakanune pervoi russkoi revoliutsii (1901–1904 gg.)," *Istoricheskie zapiski*, 1976, no. 97, pp. 59–98; Pirumova; K.F. Shatsillo, "Taktika i organizatsiia zemskogo liberalizma nakanune pervoi russkoi revoliutsii," *Istoricheskie zapiski*, 1978, no. 101, pp. 217–70.

81　George Yaney, *The Systematization of Russian Government* (Urbana, Ill., 1973), chs. 6, 8, 9.

82　Polovtsov, 2:264–7. After one round of negotiations in the State Council, Polovtsov told Grand Duke Mikhail Nikolaevich of his plan to speak with the tsar. "I wanted to dispel the idea in the mind of the tsar that the issue here involved a conflict over the rights of the zemstvo vis-à-vis the authority of the ministers, and to explain as clearly as possible that every zemstvo bill involved the use of money, and that therefore this issue should be resolved in the same manner as other financial issues, i.e., with the involvement of other ministers, not just the minister of internal affairs." Ibid., pp. 269–70.

83   As a result of the famine, Witte found that his treasury could not even pay the salaries for his officials. Witte, 1:363. Agriculture Minister Aleksei Ermolov complained that Witte refused to allocate sufficient funds to him for fear of draining funds from the treasury. Gurko, p. 71. For the effects of Witte's tight-fisted budgetary policy on the War Ministry, see William C. Fuller, Jr., "Civil–Military Conflict in Imperial Russia, 1881–1914" (Ph.D. dissertation, Harvard University, 1980), ch. 3.

84   *Sobranie uzakonenii i rasporiazhenii pravitel'stva izdavaemoe pri Pravitel'stvuiushchem Senate,* 2d series, no. 856 (St. Petersburg, 1893), pp. 2350–9.

85   Ibid., 2d series, no. 899 (1895).

86   Gurko, p. 97; *Sobranie uzakonenii* (1898), p. 1553; and article 27 of statute 6. The Kuznetsov collection contains numerous accounts of peasant protests to zemstvo taxes on village handicrafts.

87   *Sobranie uzakonenii* (1898), p. 1553, section 5.

88   Sergei Witte, *Samoderzhavie i zemstvo,* 2d ed. (Stuttgart, 1903), pp. 158–60. The previous year Witte had written a memorandum to the tsar criticizing the zemstvo for its tax *proizvol* which it inflicted on the peasant: "It can tax the ploughman over his ability to pay, and there is nothing to stop this. Such a right is not granted to local governments in the most liberal countries." Witte, *Vospominaniia,* 2:526. For more on Witte's commitment to minimizing the cost of local government, see the article by Richard G. Robbins, Jr., "Russia's Famine Relief Law of June 12, 1900: A Reform Aborted," *Canadian-American Slavic Studies,* Spring 1976, p. 32.

89   In a gloomy letter of May 1900 to his son, Ivan Petrunkevich wrote of his fears that the Witte–Sipiagin coalition would destroy the zemstvo: "Our public affairs are going from bad to worse and our zemstvo institutions are, apparently, nearing the end of their existence." Shmuel Galai, "A Note on the Establishment of the Liberation Movement," *Russian Review,* July 1978, p. 310. In July of that year, Dmitrii Shipov wrote a letter of a similar spirit to Mikhail Chelnokov: "I tell you this *completely secretly...* about my opinion. I have come to the conclusion that we zemstvo people, in view of the recent legislation, will not be passing on to our heirs an independent zemstvo institution; the only thing we should avoid is silence, what we need to do is come forward with the most resounding and specific word, not in the form of struggle but by passing declarations at the

forthcoming sessions and by presenting addresses to the throne in which we explain to the tsar that the idea of the zemstvo presents no contradiction to the idea of autocracy and in which we beseech him to return to the public institutions the trust they need" (emphasis in original). TsGAOR, f. 810 (M. V. Chelnokov fond), op. 1, ed. khr. 491, p. 5. For more on the zemstvo reaction to the perceived conspiracy of 1900, see Shlemin, pp. 133–42.

90 Simonova, "Otmena krugovoi poruki," p. 530; Witte, *Vospominaniia*, 2:530.

91 TsGAOR, f. 102 (Department of Police), 00 DP., 1900, no. 1, ch. 44, L. A. (Politicheskii obzor: Samarskoi gub.), pp. 3–4.

92 TsGAOR, f. 102, 00 DP., 1902, no. 835, p. 5.

93 TsGAOR, f. 810, op. 1, ed. khr. 492, p. 39. Emphasis added.

94 TsGAOR, f. 102, III DP., 1901, no. 1743 (O Samarskoi gubernskoi zemskoi uprave), p. 39.

95 TsGAOR, f. 102, 00 DP., 1900, no. 1, ch. 44, L. A., p. 1. The interesting question underlying the Samara incident is why the government finally chose this province as the center for its campaign against the third element. As I will show in my dissertation, a very lax policy toward the hiring of zemstvo employees prevailed throughout *all* of zemstvo Russia, and the Department of Police itself was responsible for radicals slipping into zemstvo service.

96 TsGAOR, f. 102, III DP., 1901, no. 1743, pp. 58–60.

97 Ibid., p. 42.

98 Brianchaninov used the excuse that circumstances would make such a trial impractical: "I would be forced to bring to trial an extremely large number of people from previous staffs of the zemstvo board, and for that matter I would have no assurance that a court would find them guilty." Letter of March 12, 1902. Ibid., p. 57.

99 This action sparked an angry protest by ten statisticians. Ibid., pp. 66–7.

100 TsGAOR, f. 102, 00 DP., 1902, no. 835, p. 1.

101 Ibid., p. 5.

102 Ibid.

103 Ibid., p. 9.

104 "Otkrytoe pis'mo ot gruppy zemskikh deiatelei," *Osvobozhdenie*, June 18, 1902, p. 2.

105 Sipiagin served as governor of Courland after holding the post of marshal of the nobility. Ivan Durnovo also served as a gentry marshal, while Ivan Goremykin gained his experience as a zemstvo man. Pleve, by contrast, spent the formative years of his youth in Warsaw as the son of a schoolteacher. From the 1880s on, Pleve concerned himself with criminal law and police matters, tracking down the plotters in the Winter Palace explosion of 1880. The only way he came to know Russian *obshchestvennost'* was through the eyes of the tsarist police. Judge, pp. 32–71.

106 Robbins, "Russia's Famine Law of 1900," pp. 35–6. Robbins' description of the preparation behind this law shows us one other example of the flaws within the counterreform theory: "Direct government hostility toward the zemstvos had little to do with the evolution of this law, although there was a general view in official circles that the zemstvos were not well equipped to handle famine relief. The immediate determination was the clash between the Ministries of Finance and Internal Affairs on the questions of budgetary unity, administrative costs and access to local resources. Beyond this lay broader differences in the philosophies and approaches of the two ministries. In this conflict the zemstvos were very much like the innocent bystander injured when two powerful vehicles collide." Ibid., p. 36.

107 Sipiagin gave his veto to the idea of zemstvo participation at the second session of the special conference, held on February 9, 1902. He reasoned that zemstvo liberals would only use the local committees as an excuse for discussing issues lying outside the sphere of the "needs of rural industry," such as national politics. TsGIA, f. 1233 (Osoboe Soveshchanie o nuzhdakh sel'skokhoziaistvennoi promyshlennosti) op. 1, ed. khr. 9, p. 52.

108 On September 8, 1902, Shipov praised Pleve in a letter to Chelnokov and denounced Osvobozhdenie as "foreign to the Russian spirit." TsGAOR, f. 810, op. 1, ed. khr. 492, pp. 17–22.

109 Letters to Chelnokov of September 18, October 3, and October 15, 1902. Ibid., pp. 28–37.

110 TsGAOR, f. 1233, op. 1, ed. 110, pp. 109–15. Pleve's remarks on the dominant influence within the zemstvo of the third element became a matter of public knowledge after they were reprinted in Osvobozhdenie on March 19, 1904, pp. 359–60. A paraphrased version of the above statement appeared around 1905 in a pamphlet on the third element written by an SD sympathizer. Achadov [F. A. Danilov], Tretii element (sluzhashchie po naimu v gorodskikh i zemskikh uchrezhdeniiakh). Ego znachenie i organizatsiia (Moscow, 1906), p. 15.

111 TsGAOR, f. 1233, op. 1, ed. 110, pp. 113–114.

112 Kuz'min-Karavaev, "Predely prava gubernatorov," p. 759.

113 Terence Emmons, "The Beseda Circle, 1899–1905," Slavic Review, September 1973, pp. 461–90. For the date of Beseda's first meeting, see Emmons's second article on the subject, "Additional Notes on the Beseda Circle, 1899–1905," Slavic Review, December 1974, pp. 741–3.

114 Korf, 1: 423–30.

115 Ibid., pp. 430–40.

116 Saratovskie gubernskie vedomosti, January 9, 1903, p. 2.

117 These words are from Pleve's letter to the tsar requesting that Governor Obolenskii be permitted to remain in the capital until the reform plans were completed. TsGAOR, f. 601, op. 1, ed. khr. 859, p. 8.

118 For more on this manifesto, see Judge, pp. 142–6

119 The members include P. N. Durnovo, B. V. Shtiurmer, N. A. Zinovev, A. N. Mosolov, S. A. Tol, and V. V. fon Val. V. S. Diakin, "Stolypin i dvorianstvo (Proval mestnoi reformy)," *Problemy krest'ianskogo zemlevladeniia i vnutrennei politiki Rossii. Dooktiabr'skii period* (Leningrad, 1972), p. 238. For the full text of the commission's hearings and a critique by the leading spokesman of the Union of Liberation, see P. B. Struve, *Usilenie gubernatorskoi vlasti: proekt fon Pleve* (Paris, 1904). Judge correctly argues that Pleve's reform, if implemented, would have probably ended the zemstvo's independent status. Judge, p. 213–17.

120 TsGAOR, f. 543, op. 1, ed. khr. 213, pp. 47–48.

121 Summarizing the minority opinion of seven governors, the text reads: "The right of state *vlast'* to issue direct executive orders at the expense of public organs runs contrary to the fundamental principles of self-government and will drive away from public affairs all the best elements of the public who have dedicated to it their efforts in various fields." Ibid., p. 25.

122 Ibid., p. 34. Emphasis added. Other Russians were also aware of the pressures exerted on local self-government by the conflicts among the ministries. Describing the controversy over state plans to reduce the role of the zemstvo in education, Boris Chicherin writes: "There was never any rivalry even between the zemstvo and the local clergy over schools; if they had been left alone, they would never have come into conflict. The rivalry exists not at the bottom but at the top, between two departments [*vedomstva*], each of which sought to expand its administration as much as possible and take as many matters into its own hands." (Chicherin is referring here to the rivalry between the Ministries of Education and Finance.) Chicherin, p. 74.

123 The best discussion of the zemstvo's clash with Pleve over the local committees can be found in Simonova, "Zemsko-liberal'naia fronda," pp. 150–216. In English, a good summary can be found in Shmuel Galai, *The Liberation Movement in Russia, 1900–1905* (Cambridge, 1973), pp. 153–6.

124 TsGAOR, f. 124, op. 11, ed. khr. 1333, 1902, p. 31. In June 1904, Zinovev and Shtiurmer were awarded for their efforts with a resolution of "Imperial gratitude." Judge, p. 556.

125 See the angry letter of Mikhail Chelnokov to a friend in Nizhnii Novgorod, dated October 22, 1903: "I find that these visits would be perfectly appropriate if they had occurred in the reign of Nikolai Pavlovich [Tsar Nicholas I] on one of Arakcheev's military colonies." Gosudarstvennyi arkhiv Gor'kovskoi oblasti, f. 1834 (E. V. Uvarova fond), op. 825, d. 1 (Pis'ma M. V. Chelnokova), pp. 2–3.

126 Gurko, pp. 184, 193, 239–41; Shipov, pp. 226–33; Urusov, p. 356.

127 TsGAOR, f. 124, (Ministry of Justice), op. 11, ed. khr. 1333 (Papers on N. F. Bunakov and S. V. Martynov), 1902, p. 31.

128 Urusov, pp. 359–64. The conference of 15 governors was held on January 25, 1904, under the chairmanship of A. S. Stishinskii. Macey, p. 281.

129 For more on this, see Terence Emmons, "Russia's Banquet Campaign," *California Slavic Studies*, 1977, no. 10, pp. 45–86.

130 "Chto zhe nam delat'?" *Osvobozhdenie*, December 19, 1902, p. 207.

7

The zemstvo and the education of the people

JEFFREY BROOKS

Primary schooling was the area of greatest zemstvo achievement, and on the eve of World War I education was the largest item in zemstvo budgets. Zemstvo educators in nineteenth-century Russia faced the task of spreading simple literacy in rural Russia, where the vast majority of the population lived and worked. Urbanization brought many country people to the cities in the late nineteenth and early twentieth centuries, but most migrants did not leave their villages until after they had passed school-entry age. If they were to be taught, the teaching had to take place in their villages. Schools had to be brought to the common people rather than the people drawn into the more literate urban life. Popular education was an endeavor that appealed to the hopes of zemstvo activists for a more Westernized society and to their fears of a volatile and ignorant peasantry. Zemstvo educators brought idealism, energy, and dedication to their task, and by the end of the old regime they could claim a great measure of success.

Although only 21 percent of the population of the Russian Empire (29 percent of the men and 13 percent of the women) were literate in 1897,[1] according to the census of that year, male literacy approached 40 percent in European Russia on the eve of the World War I and surpassed that level in 1920.[2] Literacy among recruits accepted into the army rose from approximately 10 percent at the end of the 1860s to almost 68 percent in 1913, and the literacy of the rural population of Russia rose from 5–6

The author wishes to thank the National Endowment for the Humanities, the International Research and Exchanges Board, and the Russian and East European Center of the University of Illinois for their support and assistance. I am also grateful to the following people for their helpful comments: Jean Hellie, Arcadius Kahan, C. Arnold Anderson, Richard Hellie, Karen Brooks, and Terence Emmons.

percent to 24–25 percent in roughly the same period, according to the Soviet demographer A. G. Rashin.[3] This half-century increase in literacy corresponds to changes that took two centuries or more in England and France, as determined by parish register signatures.[4] The most telling evidence that in the course of a half-century literacy had become commonplace throughout rural as well as urban Russia was the census of 1920.[5] According to this source, in the provinces of European Russia, literacy among children age 12 to 16, that is among the last children to pass through the prerevolutionary school system, was 71 percent for boys, 52 percent for girls, and 62 percent for both; literacy among 14-year-olds in the countryside of European Russia was at exactly the same level, compared with 91 percent in the cities. This was in part the achievement of zemstvo activists and other educators, who organized and administered a system of primary schools. How they accomplished the task is the subject of this chapter.

Peasants sought literacy for economic, administrative, and cultural reasons. The ability to read and cipher became increasingly important as the growing market economy brought opportunities for borrowing, lending, buying, and selling. The expanding market and industrial economy also increased the number of peasants involved in two distinct but related forms of activity that supplemented or replaced farm income: the *kustari*, home-based peasant craftsmen who produced everything from sheepskin coats and barrels to clay toys and agricultural tools; and the *otkhodniki*, off-farm workers who found seasonal and sometimes semipermanent work for wages outside their native villages in agriculture, industry, the railroads, and the job markets of the expanding cities. Literacy also smoothed the passage and facilitated location of a good plot of land for the literate among the millions of peasants who migrated to Siberia, Central Asia, and the Caucasus in the late nineteenth and early twentieth centuries in search of better living conditions. With the administrative restructuring of rural Russia that began with the reform of the economic and legal condition of the state peasants in the 1830s and continued through the emancipation and the establishment of local government, it became advantageous for peasant communes to have literate members to understand the official decisions that concerned them, to verify written contracts and tax decisions, and to defend their interests with the volost or district governments. When the army was reorganized in 1874 on the basis of universal military conscription, recruits with a primary school certificate served a four- instead of six-year term and the peasants soon learned that "among the soldiers the illiterate is a doomed man."[6] The cultural uses of literacy were more diffuse than the economic and administrative, but the expanding market and new consumption patterns brought religious works in Russian and Church Slavonic and many new secular books for individual and group readings. The literate could also participate more fully in the Orthodox Church service and in the movements of religious dissidence that gained force throughout Russia after the emancipation.

In education, as in other areas of zemstvo activity, the zemstvos were not the sole agents of change but acted in conjunction with other institutions and concerned groups. The development of popular education in prerevolutionary Russia was similar to that in other industrializing societies in that it depended on popular demand, the initiative of local educated activists and institutional leaders, and the intervention of the central government. The initiative of the common people, their decision to invest in education, was essential throughout the process of the development of a network of schools, but it was most crucial at the early stages. The educated activists, inside and outside the zemstvos, dominated the process at an intermediate stage, building a modern school system on the foundation of peasant demand and steadily raising the quality of instruction. Finally, the intervention of the state bureaucracy, most dramatic in the last years of the old regime, brought greatly increased financial resources to education and also greater central management and control, often at the expense of the zemstvos.

Education in prereform Russia

At the time of the zemstvo reform the three elements in education – consumer demand, initiative of local educated activists, and central government intervention – were apparent in three well-established types of primary schools: the peasant school of literacy (*shkola gramoty*), where those seeking instruction purchased it directly from "masters" willing and able to provide it; the clerical school, where a priest taught on a voluntary basis and offered instruction free of charge; and the bureaucratic school, where the state provided financial support and required school attendance, in order to train cadres for local administration. The schools of literacy were the best example of schools shaped by the initiative of the common people. Schools of this type existed in prereform Russia, but they flourished most dramatically in the first years following the emancipation, when peasant demand for literacy exceeded the efforts of other elements in society to supply schooling for them. In the simplest schools, the peasants hired a literate person to teach their children for a single winter in their own cottages. In turn they provided board and sent the tutor on his way when the job was done. It was also common for literate peasants to take on pupils from among their fellow villagers' children, as craftsmen took on apprentices. Occasionally peasants joined together as a commune to establish a more formal school, renting or borrowing a building, hiring a teacher, and either taxing themselves through communal government or paying the cost of schooling directly. Teachers in literacy schools were peasants, former soldiers, members of the clergy, spinsters, and uprooted wanderers of various sorts. Schools were frequently run by Old Believers or members of one or another of the Protestant-type rationalist sects, and instruction was often tinged with religious dissidence even in Orthodox villages. In such schools, the teachers were sometimes more mentors than hirelings.

The clerical school was the oldest type of school in Russia. Instruction took place in the church and was inseparable from church functions. The pupils learned to read religious books and were expected to participate in the service. The priest-teacher was first and foremost a religious figure to the children and their parents. He offered instruction as a representative of the church, and pupils were welcome to attend or not attend as they wished. Although by the middle of the nineteenth century few of these schools still existed, they served as an inspiration for clerical activists who tried to create a church-dominated school system in the latter part of the century. "In the parish school," wrote S. A. Rachinskii, the ideologue of the postemancipation church school system, "the priest does not appear as a hired teacher, but as the executor of his real duties toward his flock."[7]

The third type of school, the bureaucratic school, was integrated into the civilian administrative hierarchy. The state guaranteed financial support and required school attendance, and state authority insulated the school and teacher from the local population. Teachers held a rank in the state service, and they and selected pupils and school officials enjoyed rights and privileges denied the peasantry. Schooling of this type legitimized and reinforced legal class divisions by rewarding success with class privilege. The schools of the Ministry of Education, the Department of Crown Lands, and the Ministry of State Domains exhibited many characteristics of this pattern. The schools of the Ministry of Education were usually supported with state funds, whereas those of the Ministry of State Domains and Crown Lands were supported by compulsory levy on local peasant communes. Teachers in the Ministry of Education schools established in 1828 were in state service, with pension rights and privileges, including exemption from the head tax, conscription, and the risk of corporal punishment by volost authorities, as were teachers in the Ministry of Education district schools when these were reorganized into city schools in 1872. Teachers in the Ministry of State Domains and Crown Lands schools were usually priests paid 100 rubles a year by the ministry. Attendance at these schools was often compulsory in fact although not in law; pupils were recruited from communes by forced levy, and peasants often regarded schooling as a kind of corvée labor their children were forced to perform for the state.[8] The purpose of these schools was to prepare select state peasants to fill the lower ranks of the ministry and Crown Lands Department bureaucracies. In 1862, pupils who finished the course of the Ministry of Education district schools were granted immunity from corporal punishment by volost authorities.[9] Those named as school trustees for the Ministry of State Domains schools also received privileges.[10]

The numbers of schools of the three basic types on the eve of the zemstvo reform can be inferred from Table 7.1.

The Statute of 1864

The Zemstvo Statute of 1864 and other statutes dealing with education served as the framework in which zemstvo leaders, church and state authorities, and others interested in schooling acted to realize their objectives in supporting and founding primary schools. Fueled by both rivalry and cooperation among its supporters, primary education after the zemstvo reform developed in three phases. From 1864 to 1884 the Orthodox Church and the Ministry of Education reduced their educational activities in the zemstvo provinces, and a zemstvo school system was developed that incorporated some of the existing schools but drew most upon the example of the peasant schools of literacy and the schools supported by the communes. From 1884 to 1907, church authorities reasserted their claim to hegemony in schooling, and peasant literacy schools were placed under church authority, serving as the basis for a new system of parish schools that rivaled the zemstvo system. Finally, in the last decade of the old regime, the Ministry of Education reentered the field and began to establish central governmental authority over the primary schools at the expense of both the zemstvos and the church. The changing structure of rural primary schooling in Russia is shown in Table 7.2, which illustrates the development of different types of schools: those of the zemstvo, the church, and the Ministry of Education, as well as those financed

247

Table 7.1. *Type and composition of rural schools before the zemstvos*

Year	Type of school	Number of schools	Percent of all schools	Number of pupils	Percent of all pupils
	Bureaucratic schools				
1853	Department of Crownlands	204	1	7,477	1
1863	Ministry of Education	1,070	4	54,333	8
1865	Church schools	21,420	73	413,524	59
1866	Ministry of State Domains	2,754	9	137,582	20
1866	Schools of literacy	3,842	13	83,128	12

Sources: N. V. Chekhov, *Narodnoe obrazovanie v Rossii s 60-kh godov xix veka* (Moscow, 1912), pp. 27, 94; *Entsiklopedicheskii slovar'* (Brokgauz-Efron), vol. 20a (St. Petersburg, 1897), pp. 757–9.

Table 7.2. Number of rural primary schools, by type, 1879–1914

Year	Zemstvo	Commune	Church	Literacy	Ministry	Other	Total
1879–84[a]	9,108	—	4,213	—	—	—	22,770
1894	13,129	8,014	11,197	16,799	964	4,313	54,416
1911	27,944	11,051	31,202	4,291	5,752	9,478	89,718
1914	44,879	4,893	34,341	2,171	21,996		108,280

[a] Figures for 1879–84 are only for European Russia. All figures are for rural schools except in the case of the 1914 church schools. There the figure used is for one-class schools, which were almost all rural. A dash indicates that data are unavailable.

Sources: Statisticheskii vremennik rossiiskoi imperii, 3d series, no. 1 (St. Petersburg, 1884), pp. 290–5; G. A. Fal'bork and V. Charnoluskii, eds. Nachal'noe narodnoe obrazovanie v Rossii, vol. 2 (St. Petersburg, 1900), pp. x, 368; Odnodnevnaia perepis' nachal'nykh shkol Rossiiskoi imperii proizvedennaia 18 ianvaria 1911 goda, no. 16 pt. 2 (Petrograd, 1916), pp. 2–3, 19–20; Nachal'nye uchilishcha vedomstva ministerstva narodnogo prosveshcheniia v 1914 godu (Petrograd, 1916), pp. 76–77; Istoricheskii ocherk razvitiia tserkovnykh shkol za istekshee dvadtsatipiatiletie (1884–1909) (St. Petersburg, 1909), appendix, pp. 14–15; Tserkovnye shkoly Rossiiskoi imperii za 1914 god (Petrograd, 1916), p. 33.

primarily by peasant communes and volost administrations. Variations in the categorization of schools account for some inaccuracy, but the growth of the zemstvo schools, those of the ministry, and of the church, as well as the decline in the independent peasant schools (the literacy schools and the commune schools) is clear.

The legal mandate for zemstvo activity in schooling was outlined in the Zemstvo Statute of 1864 and the statute on primary education that followed it. Education was among the nonobligatory responsibilities assigned to the zemstvo institutions.[11] The July 14, 1864 statute on primary schools defined primary schools as those supported by the peasant communes and aided by various state departments.[12] The stated purpose of primary instruction was "to affirm religious and moral understanding in the people and to spread useful basic knowledge." The course of study was to include the Word of God (short catechism and sacred history), reading of Russian and Church Slavonic, writing, the four basic arithmetic operations, and church singing, where possible. The statute divided the economic and pedagogical supervision of schooling by granting authority over the finances of schools to the institutions that funded them and control over instruction to provincial and district school boards, composed of one representative each from the ministries of education and internal afffairs, other government departments that funded schools, the Synod, and two representatives from the zemstvo. In the zemstvo provinces the provincial school board was the chief school authority, whereas in the nonzemstvo provinces the main power was in the hands of the director of schools, an official of the Ministry of Education. Although the role of the Ministry of Education was diminished in the 1864 legislation, zemstvo authority did not entirely replace it and had to be exerted indirectly through the school board and through selective school financing. The school boards, not the zemstvos, were empowered to found new schools and supervise instruction.

Even before the 1864 legislation was complete some observers had noticed potential problems with the ambiguous position of the school trustees, the power of the peasant communes, and the paucity of staff to monitor the schools.[13] The last point troubled officials of the ministry, and within a year of the statute they began to formulate plans to control school boards in the zemstvo provinces.[14] D. A. Tolstoi, the conservative bureaucrat who became minister of education in 1866, when the flush of official liberalism faded, set out in 1869 to rectify this difficulty by appointing special school inspectors.[15] The inspectors were made permanent members of the school boards and were to bolster the never robust authority of those institutions. Their duties were elaborated in

250

1871 and 1873, and included responsibility for the quality of instruction, teachers' performance, and opening new schools and closing
unsatisfactory ones.[16] Zemstvo prerogatives in primary education were
again weakened with a plan to establish model schools under the
ministry and in late 1873, when Alexander II further diluted educational administrative authority by charging the marshals of the nobility
with the duty of monitoring schools.[17]

Primary school legislation of 1874

The 1864 statute was replaced by the May 25, 1874 statute on
primary schools, which served to define administrative relations in
primary education for the following 35 years.[18] The purpose of the new
law was to increase bureaucratic authority, but the changes were not
sufficient to reverse the direction of the earlier statute. Direct control
over schools still eluded the ministry, and teachers remained outside
the bureaucracy, answerable to many masters, including not only the
inspectors but also the zemstvos and the peasant communes that
funded the schools. The 1874 legislation established directors of
primary schools as supreme pedagogical authority in all zemstvo
provinces and placed two inspectors under them. The marshals of the
nobility were made chairmen of all school boards and also granted
power over school openings. The clergy remained responsible for
moral and religious instruction, and the governor for order. The
zemstvos retained their two representatives on the school board, which
now included, in addition to the marshal, two representatives from the
Ministry of Education, one from the Ministry of Internal Affairs, one
from the Synod, and representatives from the city governments that
aided schools. The zemstvos gained the right to choose school trustees,
and in 1875, the Ministry of Education recognized the right of those
who provided financial support for the schools to promote candidates
for teaching posts. Hiring was in the hands of the directors and
inspectors; the right to dismiss teachers remained with the boards.

Even under the new statute, neither the school boards nor the
inspectors were able to supervise and control the schools effectively.
The weakness of the boards was evident from the start. Many did not
meet, some never elected chairmen, and frequently district board
reports were not written. In the first three decades of zemstvo activity,
only 54 zemstvos put their expenditures in the hands of local school
boards, and by the 1890s, 21 had already reasserted financial authority.[19] As the minister of education stated in his report for 1868, the
district school boards for the most part lacked the means to monitor

251

schools except where the zemstvos provided funds or where members of the board took individual initiative.[20] The directors and inspectors were hardly more successful. The large number of schools under their responsibility, the short school year (150 days), and the poor roads and extreme weather conditions all discouraged frequent school visits.

The legislation mandating zemstvo involvement in schooling changed the status of the existing state and church schools, explicitly by redefining the peasants' obligations to these schools and implicitly by making provisions for funding educational alternatives. Peasant support for the Ministry of State Domains and Department of Crown Lands schools became voluntary with the inauguration of rural self-government institutions in 1868, despite some official efforts to continue compulsory levies on peasant communes.[21] At their communal meetings the peasants refused to vote funds for these schools and withdrew their children from them.[22] In some cases the schools were later converted into zemstvo or Ministry of Education model schools.[23]

The Orthodox Church was no more successful in maintaining its existing primary schools under the new legislation than the Ministry of State Domains and Department of Crown Lands had been. In March 1866, the chief procurator of the Synod appealed to the chairmen of the zemstvo boards to grant aid to church schools in their districts, and many zemstvos did initially allocate some funds for this purpose,[24] but zemstvo aid was most often token. The number of church schools declined rapidly in the late 1860s and early 1870s, falling from over 24,000 schools in 1866 to fewer than 8,000 in 1874, and to slightly more than 4,000 in 1880.[25] According to the 1880 school census of rural primary schools in the 60 provinces of European Russia, only 1,062 schools were funded entirely from church sources, less than 6 percent of the total. Although this figure excludes schools in which expenses were shared by the clergy, the zemstvos, and the peasant communes, it is still indicative of the decline of church schools.[26] The Ministry of Education had supported some church schools at the time of the emancipation, and the zemstvos rarely continued these payments. The refusal of the zemstvos to adopt the church parish schools did not always mean that the zemstvos set a higher standard than the church; some zemstvos were initially quite suspicious of peasant literacy.[27] The church schools proved unsuitable partly because of the priests and partly because the peasants themselves preferred alternative types of instruction.[28]

The ministry lacked control of the schools, but zemstvo authority was also precarious. The zemstvos lacked money and an executive arm. Their taxing authority was limited, as Veselovskii points out, by

252

self-interest as well as legal barriers.[29] The zemstvos had no officials to defend their interests at the village level so that the village schools were under the day-to-day suzerainty of those who owed no allegiance to the zemstvo and frequently were contemptuous of it, most notably the police.[30] Attempts by some zemstvos to establish administrative officers with special responsibility for primary education were unsuccessful, and the zemstvos' petitions for increased representation on the school boards were rejected.[31]

Under these conditions, zemstvo pedagogues favored schools voluntarily initiated and supported by the peasants, and these were, in most cases, schools of literacy. Zemstvo support transformed many of these into "zemstvo–commune schools," retaining their close dependence on peasant participation but gradually improving their quality. The zemstvos in effect used the peasant literacy schools as an indicator of latent demand for education and, by building on existing schools and working within established forms, minimized the need to spend limited resources on compelling or persuading pupils to attend the schools. "The zemstvo schools grew out of the peasant schools," wrote N. V. Chekhov, the pedagogue and journalist, in his history of prerevolutionary schools.[32] Many peasant schools received zemstvo aid, and some zemstvos opened their own literacy schools, many of which were subsequently converted into proper zemstvo schools in which the zemstvos paid the bulk of the expenses and determined the program. The peasant schools existed in a legal limbo from 1864 to 1874. In 1874 new regulations specified that only certified teachers (those approved by school boards or with a secondary credential) could teach. This made many peasant schools illegal, and they were often closed by the police until a ruling by the minister of education in 1882 exempted literacy school teachers from the 1874 regulation, in effect legalizing the schools.[33] In 1891 they were placed under church control, ending the zemstvos' connection with them.

Zemstvo–commune cooperation

The arrangements that zemstvos made to found schools as well as to aid the more viable literacy schools, to improve them, and ultimately to transform them into zemstvo schools, were generally based on agreements with communes. In the appendix to his pedagogical handbook, *The Russian Primary School* (1870), Baron Korf, the visionary educator who did so much to give the zemstvo school its particular cast, presents a sample communal agreement containing the particulars he found important for the proper development of a new zemstvo primary school.[34] The commune promised to provide: (1) 40 rubles for school supplies and materials; (2) a salary of 250 rubles for the teacher, plus three bushels of wheat, three of rye, and either a room with heating or 40 rubles to rent one, and board for bachelors; and (3) a caretaker and a hired cottage to serve as a schoolhouse for the first year, after which a proper building constructed by the commune would be ready. The commune was to choose a trustee to oversee the school and its finances, and the village elder was to pay the teacher's salary as the trustee directed. School funds were to come from a levy of one measure of grain per head of household, a communal plot to be farmed by the commune, and a money levy in which families with schoolchildren would pay more than others. Korf suggested that the question of a trustee be raised when the heads of households met to establish the school.[35] The trustee and school board were to recommend a teacher. The trustee was to protect the school and teacher in relations with the community and with village and volost authorities. Teachers would be further insulated against arbitrary decisions by the commune because the commune was not to remove a teacher without the approval of the board and was to guarantee three years of school support. School attendance was to be free for commune members and available at three rubles a year for outsiders if space permitted.

Actual conditions and the arrangements made by peasant communes differed significantly from this ideal commune agreement. Most of the efforts of zemstvo educators in the first two decades were attempts to bridge the gap between their expectations and the level of schooling the peasants were willing to support. Baron Korf assumed that the zemstvos could set the terms once they decided to encourage the founding of a school, but in fact many peasant communes reached agreements either independently or on the initiative of local elders or the clergy. The peasants presented the zemstvos and school boards with already functioning schools, or they agreed upon the kind of aid they were willing to give a school and then petitioned the zemstvo or the school board to assist them in establishing it. In both cases the peasant commune members had already agreed on the extent of their commitment to the school.

The value the peasants placed on literacy can be inferred from the wages they paid teachers in literacy schools, which were much lower than those Korf suggested. According to materials gathered by members of the Tver zemstvo, male teachers in literacy schools with a school-house, that is, the highest type of literacy school, received on average 32 rubles per winter; women, who may have been better educated or of a higher class, received 39 rubles.[36] Wages in other types of schools were lower; teachers of both sexes in the schools of the second type received 20 rubles, and itinerant male and female teachers received on average 14 and 20 rubles, respectively. The peasants in general did not see the need for a school building that differed substantially from their own dwellings, and they attached little importance to classroom aids. Communal arrangements for school support were less permanent than Korf had envisioned, with the result that communes maintained considerable control over the schools and the teachers. Communes refused to make long-term agreements and often would not sign a teacher's contract for more than a single winter; the saying was, "As long as the teacher works, he'll be paid."[37] The frequency with which peasants reneged on agreements to support schools and caused their closing led the Ministry of Education to complain to the Ministry of Internal Affairs, and that ministry suggested to provincial governors that they encourage local officials to compel continued communal support after a voluntary initial agreement.[38]

The zemstvo teacher

Zemstvo authorities and various representatives of official Russia could intervene to influence the material and administrative conditions of schooling, but it was the rural teacher who mediated the day-to-day meeting of peasant children and the written word. Zemstvo leaders sought to raise the quality of schooling through selecting and rewarding teachers. In the five decades of zemstvo school work, the profile of the primary school teaching profession underwent a gradual change in age, sex, and social origin. The rapid expansion of the educational system required continual addition of newly-trained young people. In the rural primary schools of European Russia in 1880, 76 percent of the women teachers and 44 percent of the men were 25 years old or younger.[39] By 1911 the percentage of women who were that young had fallen to 64 percent, and that of the men had risen to 49 percent.[40] The dominant group of teachers in the 1880s was men of clerical origins, but by 1911 women of several classes filled the majority of posts. In 1879 the 22,767 rural schools of all types in the 60 provinces of European Russia employed 24,389 teachers, and 80 percent of them were men.[41] In 1911 in the 43 zemstvo provinces alone there were 62,913 teachers in 38,272 rural schools under the authority of the Ministry of Education, and 62 percent of these teachers were women. In January 1915, 69 percent of the 90,597 teachers in rural schools of these provinces were women. The percentage of women in zemstvo schools was even higher, 71 percent in 1911.[42] The proportion

JEFFREY BROOKS

Table 7.3. *Percent of schoolteachers with various types of preparatory training, 34 zemstvo provinces, 1910*

Preparatory training	Women	Men	Both
Higher education	0.1	0.0	0.1
Secular secondary	35.3	1.5	25.5
Clerical secondary	24.6	7.3	19.6
Pedagogical secondary	4.9	38.1	14.5
Lower[a] and home-educated	35.2	53.1	40.3

[a]This includes city schools.
Source: *Odnodnevnaia perepis' nachal'nykh shkol Rossiiskoi imperii proizvedennaia 18 ianvaria 1911 goda*, no. 16, pt. 2 (Petrograd, 1916), p. 4.

of teachers of peasant origin in the 60 provinces of European Russia rose from 30 to 41 percent between 1880 and 1911, and the proportion from the clergy fell from 38 to 22 percent.[43] In 1911 a majority of the male teachers (57 percent) was from the peasantry, whereas most of the women were from clerical families and the middle strata (*meshchanstvo*) (29 and 22 percent, respectively.)[44]

Because teaching drew women primarily from the middle strata and the clergy, and men from the peasantry, their preparatory training necessarily differed (Table 7.3).

Men from the peasantry attended the special pedagogical institutions that were opened specifically for them, primarily by the ministry. Men who attended clerical institutions did not choose to teach in zemstvo schools. Women from the middle strata attended gymnasia, the secular secondary institution, and the progymnasia, all of which gave preparation superior to that offered in the special pedagogical institutions. Women of clerical origins went to clerical schools and chose teaching as a profession because the priesthood was closed to them. Women were of higher class origin and better educated on average than the men and chose teaching due to the limited array of opportunities. Men were able to use their education more to their advantage, and those with secondary education equivalent to that of the women teachers did not often choose to teach at zemstvo schools. The effect of alternative opportunities is particularly apparent in comparison of the proportions of male and female teachers in different economic regions; the percent-

256

Table 7.4. Percent of men and women teachers
in different economic regions

Region	Men	Women
Central industrial	26.0	74.0
Central agricultural	38.0	62.0
Little Russian Agricultural	38.0	62.0
Volga agricultural	39.0	61.0
Northern forest	43.5	56.5

Source: Vl. Akimov, "Narodnoe obrazovanie. Zemskaia rabota po podgotovke narodnykh uchitelei,"
Zhurnal Ministerstva narodnogo prosveshcheniia,
1915, no. 4, p. 170.

age of men was highest in the region of least opportunity, the northern
forest, and lowest in that of greatest opportunity, the central industrial
region (Table 7.4).

Zemstvo pedagogues had to recruit most of their teachers from
preparatory programs over which they had no influence. A few
zemstvos were able to found pedagogical institutions and organize
summer courses and conferences for teachers, but state authorities
severely restricted these activities. There were 5 zemstvo pedagogical
institutions in 1896, compared with 51 state institutions, and in 1910, 5
and 81, respectively.[45] Zemstvo summer courses for teachers were held
in a number of provinces in the late 1860s and early 1870s. Some
zemstvos considered the courses preferable to a teachers' school; others
saw them as supplementary. For still others they were a temporary
expedient until a school could be opened.[46] The courses were forbidden
by the authorities in the mid-1870s, and did not reconvene until the
early 1890s; between 1901 and 1911, 36 were held.[47] Many of the
barriers to the courses disappeared in 1906, and from that year teachers
from the provinces frequently journeyed to the capitals to attend
courses, their provincial zemstvos often providing stipends. The programs at the summer courses stressed teaching methods for basic
primary school subjects, but some courses included additional topics,
such as church singing, penmanship, drawing, and school hygiene.[48]

Teachers, hired by zemstvos or other school administrators, arrived
in their assigned villages to face a difficult job rendered more difficult
by inadequate training and by administrative and social relations that
frequently reminded them of their subservience, dependence, and
isolation. Professional and often personal survival required that teach-

257

ers maintain good relations with three separate constituencies, the zemstvo, the state officials, and the peasant community, but the obligation was seldom reciprocal.

Teacher–zemstvo relations

The administrative and legal position of the teachers was unambiguous; "Who is not the boss of the rural schoolteacher?" one observer queried rhetorically in the early twentieth century.[49] School boards were legally responsible for appointing and dismissing them after 1864; in 1869 the inspectors gained much of this power, and, in 1874, the marshals of the nobility. Local school trustees, priests, policemen, peace mediators, land captains, and volost and village elders could all interfere in the affairs of the school and treat the teacher as an inferior. Zemstvo board members could intervene if they suspected wrongdoing or immorality, whether they sat on the school board or not. Teachers could be dismissed without hearings, and the sessions of the school board that decided their fate were closed to them.[50] The ease with which teachers were removed and the slight pretexts that served as justification were noted in contemporary accounts.[51]

The zemstvo, the most likely source of moral support for rural teachers, appeared instead as an organization that paid salaries, provided books and supplies, and sometimes sent unannounced emissaries to promulgate policies decided upon far from the village and the schoolhouse. At the year-end pupil examinations, zemstvo school board members judged the teacher's effectiveness. Even this contact was generally infrequent and often arbitrary. The teachers complained that the zemstvos were concerned with numbers, pupil attendance, and course completion instead of quality and the reality behind the numbers. The zemstvos paid teachers' salaries and bonuses, and, in the process, often earned the resentment of their employees. After the late 1870s, the zemstvos assumed full responsibility for the salaries of teachers in zemstvo schools. In the earlier period, when the zemstvos had fewer funds, they rewarded selected teachers and only paid full salaries in the more solid schools. The reward system gradually gave way to more stable zemstvo salary payments in the early 1870s. The bonuses bred resentment, and teachers complained that such discretionary remuneration went only to the obsequious and subservient.[52]

Zemstvos made other contributions to the quality of schooling in existing schools. The most important additional item was school materials the communes were unable or unwilling to obtain, including school furniture, blackboards, individual slate boards, pens, paper, and school and library books. The communes continued to provide the heat, light, building maintenance, custodian, teachers' quarters, and usually the school building, although a few provincial zemstvos began to subsidize school construction with grants and loans in the 1870s and 1880s. The schoolhouse, whether rented or specially built, most commonly resembled a peasant cottage and had all of its disadvantages. It was damp, chilly, dark, and airless, and these problems were multiplied when the building was crowded with 20 or 30 pupils. The peasant cottages were, however, the cheapest quarters available. "No one can build cottages as cheaply as the peasants," commented one observer in *Vestnik Evropy* in 1869.[53] Some zemstvos provided nearly complete school support; in one district in Vologda Province the zemstvo in 1870 supplied nine schools with 170 rubles each for teachers' salaries, 40 for religious instructors, 15 for school supplies, 20 for heat and light, 15 for the pay of a custodian, and 40 for rent if the school did not have a permanent building.[54]

In some zemstvos, educators and school teachers shared common interests and objectives, and in these areas groups of teachers appealed for more effective zemstvo control of schools. More frequently teachers demanded participation of their own representatives in school management.[55] The differences in class and rank between zemstvo assemblies and school teachers were large at the beginning of the zemstvo era and increased as the number of male teachers of peasant origin rose. After 1890, the zemstvo became more clearly a gentry organization.[56] The political conservatism of the "lordly" zemstvo, as one commentator called it in the pedagogical magazine *Russkaia shkola*, was manifest most clearly in the period following the Revolution of 1905.[57]

Teachers had many complaints about the zemstvos – trustees who never visited the schools, board members ignorant of rural primary education, the lack of "moral force" within the zemstvo – but behind many of these accusations were the teachers' frustration and anger at zemstvo condescension. N. V. Chekhov wrote, "He [the teacher] was thought to be on the lowest rung of the social ladder."[58] "In the zemstvo office," a former teacher wrote to a pedagogical magazine, "he is greeted with suspicious looks, by an unbearably cold and haughty attitude toward him, and by indifference to the interests of the primary school."[59]

The teachers, the government, and the school board

Government officials and members of the school board legally responsible for conduct in the school, including representatives of the

259

zemstvo, constituted the teachers' second constituency. They exercised their authority through occasional unannounced inspections, and through year-end pupil examinations. Difficult as it was for inspectors to visit schools regularly, they did manage infrequent visits, and the nature and surprise of their calls inspired many teachers with trepidation. A more regular evaluation of the teachers' success was the spring examination of pupils by the school board. The pupils who passed received a certificate which in the late nineteenth century entitled them to a shorter term of military service Up to 1885 many of the exams involved the whole school; after 1885 the exams concerned only the pupils in the graduating section.[60] For a few outstanding pupils the exam was a step toward the teachers' institute and a secondary education, but in the majority of cases the results of the exam were of more importance to the teacher than the pupil because the teachers' performance was evaluated on this basis. After 1885, teachers sat on the examination committee, but the examiners were usually the more active members of the school board, and, as in the case of the inspection, questioning and grading were totally at their discretion. "Examiners of all types usually make completely arbitrary demands," wrote one commentator in Russkii narodnyi uchitel', who observed, "The teacher involuntarily submits and makes an effort to satisfy the demands." Twenty years later an article in the same magazine overstated a recognized problem: "What is demanded by the examiners becomes the main subject of school instruction."[61]

Although an officially approved program existed, it was vague, and no standard state examination forced compliance with it. From 1864 to 1897 the Ministry of Education program, to which the zemstvo schools were bound to conform, specified only the basic subjects to be taught. An expanded program, approved by the ministry on February 7, 1897, specified what was to be covered under each subject heading each year and also listed the number of hours to be spent on each subject per week: the Word of God, 6 hours; Church Slavonic, 3; Russian language, 8; writing, 2; and arithmetic, 5.[62] The teachers could, within the limits posed by local needs and preferences, stress what they wished in determining the overall character of their school.

Despite the efforts of the zemstvos and state officials, teachers were most susceptible to the influence of the peasant communities in which they lived and worked. Peasant contributions shrank relatively over the late nineteenth and early twentieth centuries as the zemstvos assumed a greater share of the expenses,[63] but Veselovskii calculated that zemstvo school expenditures did not equal the total communal contribution in money and kind until 1889.[64] The total monetary contribution to primary education by the communes in 1881 was 600,000 rubles in 34 zemstvo provinces, compared with approximately 3 million rubles spent on primary education by the zemstvos.[65] Communes retained the initiative in funding schools, partly as a result of limited zemstvo funds. Many zemstvos would support schools only where the peasants were willing to contribute substantially. Even when the zemstvo paid a large portion of school expenses, the agreement of the commune was necessary for a successful school. Most important to the successful school was a steady supply of pupils. A drop in regular attendance or a poor showing at the exam might mean the end of a teacher's job. Attendance fluctuated with the rhythm of the peasant economy, and it was difficult for teachers who did not have the confidence of the commune to get pupils back who had been withdrawn for seasonal tasks. In agricultural districts even young children worked in the fields throughout spring and fall. In areas of animal husbandry the routine differed, and work in cottage-industry districts followed still a third schedule. Teachers had no means to keep children in school when parents wanted to withdraw them. In one district teachers offered fathers two or three rubles for each child who stayed in school during the two weeks before the spring exam, but the fathers refused.[66]

The teacher's dependence on the commune was not obscured by any misunderstanding on the peasants' part. Teachers in the literacy schools, on which the zemstvo schools were modeled, were clearly subservient to the commune, unless they happened to be members. Peasants frequently considered the teachers hirelings without communal rights, and even teachers who wished to join in village life found it difficult to do so. Many did not want to or found themselves psychologically unable to close the distance between the peasants and themselves. Peasants who had left their villages for the three-year pedagogical training course could not go home again as peasants, or, in many cases, even as teachers. S. A Rachinskii, the theoretician of the church schools, observed that the teacher of peasant origins "is completely estranged from the peasant milieu, and, taking up his position far from his village, he is immediately attracted to the middle level of rural society – the clergy, the poor gentry, the barkeepers, and the village kulaks."[67] The directors of the Tver zemstvo teachers' school, the School of Maksimov, found that far from all the peasant girls who completed the course wished to return to their villages to teach; they felt it would be more difficult to inspire respect there and to win authority.[68] Teachers from the middle strata or clergy who went to the village were separated from family, friends, and colleagues. "You sit by yourself in one of the 'Godforsaken corners' of our fatherland, snowed in by drifts, separated by whole dozens of versts from cultural centers," wrote a teacher correspondent. "You sit and your soul is seized by melancholy, the tormenting melancholy of solitude."[69]

The teacher's isolation was compounded by the fact that most of them, both men and women, were unmarried. In 1911, in schools throughout the empire, only 47 percent of the male and 17 percent of the female teachers were married.[70] Due to both the lonely and difficult working conditions and the relatively low pay, teachers tended not to remain in the profession for long. In 1911, the average teaching experience throughout the empire was about nine years for men teachers and seven for women.[71] The short period of service was related to the high proportion of unmarried teachers; men postponed marriage until they moved on to more lucrative work, and women quit teaching when they married.[72]

Isolation and lack of effective outside support left teachers vulnerable to peasant demands and, correspondingly, gave the peasants a measure of influence over school curriculum. While the peasants withheld support from schools of which they did not approve, they showed a different attitude toward those in which instruction was effective and consistent with their wishes. They thought in general that education should be religious, that proper reading was done aloud, that instruction should be purely functional, and that the course should end when the child could read and cipher. The peasants stressed religious instruction, not necessarily because they did not value secular literacy but because they feared teachers might slight the sacred. Judging from their letters to pedagogical magazines, the teachers found that the inclusion of re-ligious instruction was a way to win peasant support for the school. Peasants hoped that education would make their sons into volost clerks, shopkeepers, and even gentry, but teachers found it easier to introduce reading of the Gospels than to assure occupational and class mobility. In 1889 a zemstvo teacher in Perm wrote to N. A. Rubakin, "In the beginning I recommended books on agronomy, but the peasants did not read them.... It is necessary to reconcile the facts of science with those of the Bible."[73] The peasants divided reading matter into useful religious writing and frivolous fairy tales, and teachers found that secular primers containing folk tales, such as K. D. Ushinskii's *Mother Tongue*, some-times provoked complaints.[74] The peasants' emphasis on reading aloud in Church Slavonic and Russian led teachers to complain that parents were interested only in mechanical reading, that "they teach their children only for the sake of reading, and not for enlightenment," as one teacher put it in 1882.[75] The demand for religious material led teachers to request such works from the zemstvos.[76]

Church singing instruction was another simple way to ensure community enthusiasm for the school. "The peasant values it more if his son sings in church and reads the Psalter over the deceased than if he is able to figure and can write a letter," wrote a teacher in 1894.[77] A teacher who had organized a church choir stressed singing "as a means of increasing the number of pupils in the school; the peasants one after the next tried to send their children to the school in the hope that their children would end up in the choir."[78] Some zemstvos, assuming that this was a way to advance schooling, made the teaching of singing compulsory, excluding teachers who proved incapable of doing it.[79]

Increased zemstvo participation

Commune control and initiative in zemstvo schools gradually declined as the zemstvos assumed a larger share of school expenses. Education became the largest item in zemstvo budgets in 1912, surpassing medicine. In 1893, the district zemstvos, the main dispensers of funds in education, spent over 70 percent of their education budgets on zemstvo schools and another 10 percent on aiding other primary schools.[80] The provincial zemstvos, on the contrary, which did not take such an active role in education, spent the bulk of their smaller educational budgets on elementary vocational education (over 30 percent) and pedagogical, secondary, and higher education (40 percent), and only a small proportion, less than 10 percent, on primary schools. Despite much discussion of adult education and extracurricular programs in the press, neither the district zemstvos nor the provincial zemstvos spent much money on them in 1893. The steady and rapid growth of zemstvo expenditures on education is shown in Table 7.5.

Much of the increased zemstvo activity in primary schooling in the two decades after the 1864 laws came at the expense of church influence in education. The decline in church authority was reversed in the early 1880s and 1890s, with new regulations on peasant literacy schools and the statute on church parish schools, which strengthened the position of the church and weakened that of the zemstvos. The 1884 rules on church parish schools gave the clergy a mandate to establish schools under their authority even where zemstvo schools already existed, and new rulings on literacy schools separated these schools from the zemstvo system. The new rules on literacy schools were particularly detrimental to the growth of the zemstvo system. The 1882 decision on literary schools legalized them and placed them under the surveillance of local authorities, including the parish priest,

Table 7.5. *Zemstvo expenditures on education, 1868–1913*

Year	Amount spent on all education (millions of rubles)	Ratio of school to all zemstvo expenditures (%)	Amount spent on rural primary schools (millions of rubles)
1868	0.7[a]	n.a.	0.6[b]
1871	1.5	n.a.	n.a.
1879			2.5[c]
1883	6.0	n.a.	n.a.
1893	9.0	n.a.	6.6
1900	15.6	17.7	n.a.
1906	25.3	20.4	n.a.
1910	42.6	25.4	n.a.
1912	71.4[d]	29.2	n.a.
1913	87.7[d]	30.7	n.a.

[a]Includes expenditures of 22 provincial and 215 district zemstvos.
[b]Includes expenditures of 13 provincial and 215 district zemstvos.
[c]Expenditures by uezd zemstvos.
[d]Includes the expenditures of zemstvos in 40 provinces.
Sources: I. Kornilov, "Summy na narodnoe obrazovanie," *Zhurnal Ministerstva narodnogo prosveshcheniia*, 1873, no. 1, p. 9, for 1868; G. S. Fal'bork, *Vseobshchee obrazovanie v Rossii* (Moscow, 1908) p. 207, for 1871; *Statisticheskii vremennik*, 3d series, no. 1 (St. Petersburg, 1884), p. 286, for 1879; *Statisticheskii vremennik Rossiiskoi imperii*, 3d series, no. 16 (St. Petersburg, 1886), pp. 57–61, for 1883; G. A. Fal'bork, ed., *Nachal'noe narodnoe obrazovanie*, vol. 3 (St. Petersburg, 1905), pp. vii–ix, for 1893; *Dokhody i raskhody zemstv 40 gubernii po smetam na 1913 g.* (St. Petersburg, 1915), p. xlix, for 1900–13.

thus beginning the expansion of church control over them.[81] Ten years later, the May 4, 1891 rules granted the church complete jurisdiction over these schools.[82] The literacy schools became part of the rapidly developing system of church schools, and neither the zemstvos nor the school boards on which zemstvo representatives sat had any further authority over them. The schools were placed under diocesan boards and local priests. Zemstvo petitions for permission to open their own literacy schools were denied.[83] Under the new rules the literacy schools became the foundation for the new church schools and served, as they had for the zemstvos, as the lowest level of a growing school system. The February 26, 1896 statute on parish and literacy schools confirmed the future conversion of literacy schools into proper church schools.[84] The 1891 law immediately established church educational authority in

Table 7.6. Number of church schools and literacy schools, 1899–1911

Year	Church parish schools	Literacy schools
1899	41,402	21,501
1904	43,841	18,118
1907	40,195	13,650
1911	33,942	4,397

Sources: Istoricheskii ocherk razvitiia tserkovnykh shkol za istekshee dvadtsa-tipiatiletie (1884–1909) (St. Petersburg, 1909), appendix, pp. 5, 14–18; Tserko-vnye shkoly Rossiiskoi imperii za 1914 god (Petrograd, 1916), p. 33; Odnod-nevnaia perepis' nachal'nykh shkol Rossiiskoi imperii proizvedennaia 18 ianvaria 1911 goda, no. 16, pt. 2 (Petrograd, 1916), pp. 2–3.

many villages where zemstvo educators had been active, and the nature of the zemstvo system changed. Before 1891 most zemstvo schools had grown out of functioning peasant schools, but after that year zemstvo schools were opened primarily in villages without schools, where demand for education had not yet been demonstrated.[85]

The decline of the church school

The expansion in the church system of education came to a halt in the first years of the twentieth century. The numbers of peasant literacy schools began to decline as these schools were converted into church parish schools, and then the number of church parish schools also declined (Table 7.6).

The church schools were funded largely by the church, local taxes, village and volost communes, and private donations until the second half of the 1890s, when the state became heavily involved in providing for these schools. Zemstvo contribtions to the church schools remained insignificant until the mid-1880s, when some zemstvos responded favorably to the new church system. Zemstvo funding of church schools in the 34 zemstvo provinces rose steadily in absolute figures until the early twentieth century, but as a percentage of the total funding of these schools, only until the mid-1890s (Table 7.7).

The total zemstvo support of church schools increased after 1903, however, as a result of the contributions of the zemstvos in the new zemstvo provinces. The contributions of these zemstvos in 1907 reached over 500,000 rubles.[86]

Table 7.7. *Zemstvo contribution to church schools, 1889–1907*

Years	Zemstvo contribution (thousands of rubles)	Zemstvo contribution as percent of total support of church schools
1889	117	6
1894	294	8
1899	419	4
1904	388	2
1907	347	2

Source: *Istoricheskii ocherk razvitiia tserkovnykh shkol za istekshee dvadtsa-tipiatiletiia (1884–1909)* (St. Petersburg, 1909), p. 118.

Universal primary education

During the last decade of the prerevolutionary period, bureaucrats of the Ministry of Education were able to supplant zemstvo authority in many areas, and the cause of the zemstvo's diminished control was, paradoxically, one of the goals most cherished by zemstvo pedagogues – universal primary education. The issue of universal primary education was raised in the 1890s in over 70 percent of the provincial zemstvos.[87] The issue in the 1890s differed considerably from attempts to institute compulsory school attendance in the 1860s and 1870s. No longer was it a question of penalizing illiterates and compelling peasants to attend the few schools that existed. Instead, the debate concerned the feasibility of placing schools within walking distance of children who wished to attend them. Almost all such plans required enormous amounts of money, and because the taxing power of the zemstvos remained limited, the logical source of new funds was the state treasury. When the ministry began seriously to consider plans for universal primary education at the turn of the century, many zemstvos petitioned for state subsidies to allow them to put the idea into effect.[88] The ministry adopted a plan to concentrate on the central zemstvo provinces where the school network was best developed and to establish ministry schools in those areas in every village without a school.[89] This plan, which would have supplanted zemstvo influence where it was potentially strongest, was abandoned in the confusion of the Russo-Japanese War and the Revolution of 1905. A new ministry project was presented to the Second State Duma on February 20, 1907, in which zemstvo authority over primary schools was affirmed and guidelines were established to the effect that there should be one teacher per 50 children, one school within three versts (1.6 miles) of

Table 7.8. *Ministry of Education expenditures on lowest type of primary schools, 1907–12*

Year	Expenditure (thousands of rubles)	Year	Expenditure (thousands of rubles)
1907	9,681	1910	29,364
1908	15,920	1911	39,650
1909	22,231	1912	47,083

Source: *Obzor deiatel'nosti gosudarstvennoi dumy tret'iago sozyva, 1907–12, chast'tret'ia, rassmotrenie gosudarstvennykh rospisei* (St. Petersburg, 1912), pp. 282–3.

every village, a general four-year course of instruction for all school-age children, and, in addition, a contribution by the state of from 360 to 390 rubles to each satisfactory school, primarily to support the teacher's and religious instructor's salaries. Although the law was not passed, the ministry began to dispense funds according to this program. As a result, most district and provincial zemstvos as well as city governments soon submitted plans to the ministry for adding additional schools and upgrading existing ones. There was an effort on the part of the zemstvos and also the church to make sure that existing schools qualified for state aid, and some marginal schools lost their support and closed.

The ministry's role in financing the expansion of the school systems in zemstvo provinces was affirmed in the law of May 3, 1908, and the ministry began to dispense 390 rubles from the treasury for each teacher with 50 pupils in a properly functioning school. The ministry also began to allocate other monies for primary education, and ministry expenditures for primary education rose rapidly (Table 7.8).

The increase in central state financing of primary education and the decline in relative importance of both the zemstvos and the local peasant communes are shown in Table 7.9.

Some ministry funds were granted to the zemstvo boards to allocate, but other funds were put in the hands of the curators of the school districts to use as they saw fit. In addition to salary payments and funds for school construction, the ministry began, in accordance with the law of June 1, 1910, to assume support and management of the pension funds for zemstvo schoolteachers.[90] Until 1900, individual zemstvos had made separate arrangements; in 1900, provision was made for uniform management, but the decision was left to individual zemstvos. In 1910 there were 1 district pension and 25 provincial funds.[91] The

Table 7.9. Sources of funding of rural schools in 34 zemstvo provinces, 1879 and 1910

Funding source	Percent of total received from each source		Ratio: 1910 to 1879 funds
	1879	1910	
Treasury and local taxes	9	45	48
Zemstvo	54	39	7
Peasant communes	27	7	3
Payment for instruction	2	1	5
Other	8	8	10

Source: Odnodnevnaia perepis' nachal'nykh shkol Rossiiskoi imperii proizvedennaia 18 ianvaria 1911 goda, no. 16, pt. 2 (Petrograd, 1916), p. 124.

1910 regulations made it possible for all teachers to participate in a single state plan; it was compulsory only for teachers in the schools of the Ministry of Education.

The increase in ministry funding of zemstvo schools led to greater ministry control. P. N. Miliukov, the liberal Kadet party leader, raised the issue in the State Duma in 1910, when he remarked that, to succeed in its attempt to control the zemstvo schools, the ministry needed only "an inspectorate and money." The Duma, he pointed out, was granting both in the name of universal primary education.[92] Through a series of administrative decisions in 1913, zemstvo schools were insulated from zemstvo authority and placed under the supervision of the ministry. Zemstvo schools became state property by a Senate decision in 1913, and in 1914 zemstvo leaders were forbidden to give direction to teachers in zemstvo schools.[93] In the same year, inspectors gained the power to appoint and dismiss zemstvo schoolteachers without notifying the zemstvo board and to reverse school board decisions.

Armed with new authority, ministry officials openly challenged the zemstvos for control of the zemstvo schools. A speaker for the ministry made this clear at the State Duma budget hearings in 1914. A few schools were still funded entirely from local sources, but most were supported jointly by the Treasury and the zemstvos. The spokesman observed, "The zemstvos consider them to be zemstvo schools because they receive zemstvo allocations, but the ministry considers them to be state schools because they also receive money from the state."[94] When the state began to pay the bills for schooling, it gradually assumed the means to control the schools, thus reducing the role of the zemstvos in primary schooling in the final period before the revolution. Zemstvo pedagogues were hampered in school management and policy making by the lack of effective administrative mechanisms, and although they developed standing commissions, special boards, and bureaus[95] for education in the late nineteenth and early twentieth centuries in an effort to circumvent legal restrictions, the pattern of zemstvo school management remained uneven. The zemstvos had provided an administrative umbrella for those who wished to advance primary education in the zemstvo provinces, but the zemstvos' restricted powers and ties to local and class interests were obstacles to their effecive management of a nationwide system with unified standards and funding. In nonzemstvo regions, there was little alternative to state management of the planning of universal primary education. The expansion of state financing in all areas of primary education signalled the gradual emergence of an increasingly centralized and uniform educational system. The reentry of the state authorities into the field of primary education was in many respects a logical consequence of the decision to provide universal primary education on a systematic scale in the absence of a more authoritative and perhaps more representative local administration to carry it out.

Zemstvo achievements

The measure of success of those who worked to develop a network of primary schools, the zemstvo educators, local communes, and state, church, and other school administrators, was ultimately the number of children educated and the quality of the schooling they received. Zemstvo educators and ministry officials were not optimistic about their accomplishments when they sought to calculate the additional needs of the educational system for the establishment of universal primary education on the eve of World War I. In arguing for more funds, they often pointed to a shortage of teachers and to the fact that the number of school-aged children (8–11, or 7–14) greatly exceeded the number of children actually attending school. In fact, the shortcomings of the educational system were often exaggerated in such computations, encouraging a negative evaluation of the effectiveness of the prerevolutionary educational system, and, later on, by implication, an overly positive view of early Soviet efforts. In appraising the requirements for universal primary education in 1915, Ministry of Education officials used as a model a 50-place school with one teacher and a

269

Table 7.10. *Data used by Ministry of Education to calculate needs of educational system in European Russia (51 provinces) and in all Russian Empire, January 1, 1915*

Data	European Russia	Empire
Number of 8- to 11-year olds in population	11,171,283	15,253,758
Number of children in school	6,490,174	7,788,453
Percent of all 8- to 11-year-olds in school	58	51
Number of teachers then employed	156,632	186,859
Number of teachers considered necessary[a]	223,425	305,075

[a]Assuming 1 teacher per 50 children.
Source: *Nachal'nye uchilishcha vedomstva ministerstva narodnogo prosveshcheniia v 1914 godu* (Petrograd, 1916), appendix, pp. vi–ix.

four-year course. Assuming that all children ages 8 to 11 should be in school, they derived a figure of 223,425 teachers as the number necessary for the school-aged population of European Russia, compared with the 156,632 teachers employed in 1915, and 305,075 compared with 186,859 employed in the empire. The figures used by the ministry are given in Table 7.10.

On the basis of a full four-year attendance pattern, one teacher in a 50-place school could serve a village that produced 12.5 children of school-entrance age every year. If, however, the children stayed in school for less than the full four-year course, the same school could serve more children. If the withdrawal pattern conformed to the 1911 average for all city and country primary schools throughout the empire, then the same teacher in the same 50-place school could serve 20.7 entrants per year. The patterns of attendance revealed by the 1911 school census are shown in Table 7.11.

Assuming that children attended according to the above pattern, the number of teachers required for a school-age population that produced 3.8 million school entrants (one-quarter of all 8–11-year-olds in the Russian Empire in 1911) was 183,575 and not the 305,975 calculated by the ministry. Since the actual pupil–teacher ratio was 41 rather than 50, a one-teacher school with 41 places would suffice for a village that produced 17.0 pupils annually. In this case, 223,529 teachers would be

Table 7.11. *Distribution of schoolchildren by grade, 1911*

	Rural schools			Rural and urban schools		
School year	Boys	Girls	Both	Boys	Girls	Both
1	38.2	48.6	41.3	38.6	47.4	41.4
2	31.3	38.0	33.3	31.6	37.7	33.6
3	18.1	6.7	14.7	17.5	7.6	14.3
4	8.7	4.7	7.6	8.6	5.2	7.5
5	3.7	2.0	3.2	3.7	2.2	3.2

Source: *Odnodnevnaia perepis' nachal'nykh shkol Rossiiskoi imperii proizve-*
dennaia 18 ianvaria 1911 goda, no. 16, pt. 2 (Petrograd, 1916), pp. 22–3, 103.
Given in the census are rates for years 1, 2–3, 4–5. Drop-out rates for the first
year were used to separate years 2 and 3. The census does not contain
information to divide fourth- and fifth- year pupils. I assume, somewhat
arbitrarily, that 70 percent are in the fourth and 30 percent in the fifth year.

required in order for all children to start school and remain there
according to the pattern observed in 1911, a 20 percent increase over
the 186,859 teachers employed in 1915, rather than the 63 percent
increase necessary if all the schools served 50 pupils for a full four
years. In European Russia, the number of teachers required to serve the
same pupil attendance pattern was 164,705, a modest 5 percent
increase over the 156,632 teachers employed in 1915. Variations in the
sizes of schools and in the concentrations of schools and teachers
probably necessitated a somewhat greater number of teachers, but the
ministry figures overstated the needs if the observed enrollment
patterns were to be allowed to continue rather than a four-year course
enforced on all pupils.

The proportion of children who attended school at some time in their
childhood can be inferred from the 1911 school census and the
attendance pattern presented in Table 7.11. In the matrix in Table 7.12,
the far right column gives the proportion of children of a given age in
school, according to the 1911 census. The attendance pattern presented
above shows that, of the children who began school, 81 percent
remained in school for all or part of two years, 35 percent for three, 18
percent for four, and 8 percent for five. These percentages allowed the
children of a given age in school to be separated according to the
number of years they had attended, by the following method. All
7-year-olds are assumed to be in first year. Of those, 81 percent
continue on to second year, so the remaining 8-year-olds observed in

Table 7.12. *Percent of children in Russian Empire attending each year of school, by age of children, 1911*

Age of child	Percent of children attending school year:					Percent of children in school
	1	2	3	4	5	
7	3.2					3.2
8	13.5	2.6				16.1
9	20.0	10.9	1.1			32.1
10	14.9	16.2	4.7	0.6		36.4
11	16.2	12.1	7.0	2.4	0.3	37.9
12	0.0	13.1	5.2	3.6	1.1	21.4
13	2.2	0.0	5.6	2.7	1.6	12.1
14	0.0	1.8	0.0	2.9	1.2	5.2
Estimated likelihood that child 7–14 will attend each school year	70.0	56.7	23.6	12.2	4.2	

The horizontal sums may not be exact, due to rounding, and due to the approximation of small negative numbers by 0.0, as in row 6.
Source: Derived from *Odnodnevnaia perepis' nachal'nykh shkol Rossiiskoi imperii proizvedennaia 18 iarvaria 1911 goda*, no. 16, pt 2 (Petrograd, 1916), pp. 103–4.

school must be in first year. After the 8-year-olds have been separated according to years attended, the result can be used to allocate the 9-year-olds, continuing until all the 7–14-year-olds in school have been divided according to the number of years in school. The result is displayed in Table 7.12.

The rows sum to the proportion of children of a given age in school, given by the 1911 census. The columns sum to the proportion of children aged 7 to 14 who attended school for a given number of years, assuming that there are approximately equal numbers of children of each age group in the total population of Russia and the empire. For example, 70 percent of all girls and boys ages 7 to 14 in the empire attended at least one year of school. In other words, there was a probability of about 70 percent that a child growing up in the empire in the decade before World War I would attend school for at least a year. Using attendance figures specific for sex and rural location, the school attendance probabilities for girls and boys and rural children can be calculated in the same way (Table 7.13).

Table 7.13. *Estimated likelihood that a child 7–14 will attend each school year, in Russian Empire, 1911*

School year	Rural and urban children			Rural children		
	Boys	Girls	Both	Boys	Girls	Both
1	87.8	52.4	70.0	83.6	46.9	66.1
2	72.0	41.4	56.7	68.6	36.6	53.5
3	38.5	8.0	23.6	38.7	6.4	22.8
4	18.6	5.4	12.2	18.9	4.5	11.65
5	6.1	1.8	4.0	6.0	1.5	3.8

Source: Derived from *Odnodnevnaia perepis' nachal'nykh shkol Rossiiskoi imperii proizvedennaia 18 iarvaria 1911 goda*, no. 16, pt. 2 (Petrograd, 1916), pp. 103–4.

A number of conclusions can be drawn from these figures. Most generally, the implied availability of schooling is greater than that suggested by the simpler figure, the proportion of school-aged children in school, used both by contemporary observers and subseqent analysts of schooling in late Imperial Russia.[96] The numerical preponderance of rural children makes the rural pattern very close to the pattern for all children. The numbers of boys observed in school at any time was greater than that of girls, both because boys were more likely to enter school and because they were more likely than girls to stay for more than one year; 84 percent of all rural boys started school, 69 percent went for two years, and 39 percent entered the third year.

Conclusion

The same figures that show the success of the school system also show its failures. Educators at the time considered that four years of schooling would convey a functional education for rural children in their society; most rural schools did not offer four years, and only 12 percent of the children went beyond the third year. The decision to withdraw a child from school was made by peasant parents. Keeping children in school for four years would have necessitated either compulsory measures with punishment for drop-outs or a reduction in the very real costs parents paid to keep a child in school. Such a lowering of costs could have been achieved through increased provision of school lunches and dormitories and bringing schools closer to the peasants. Unequal geographic distribution of schools made distances prohibitively great for some peasants, particularly in regions outside European Russia. Of the 30 percent of the children who never attended school, some actively sought schooling and were turned away for a number of reasons including overcrowding in some schools, which can be attributed to inadequacy either in the total number or distribution of schools. Despite the failures of the prerevolutionary school system, which fell so short of the ideals of zemstvo and other educators, schooling became available in the half-century following the zemstvo reform to the majority of peasant children, and they took advantage of it, acquiring the level of schooling they or their parents considered optimal under the circumstances of their lives. Their decision and the efforts of the educators contributed to the relatively high (61 percent; 71 percent for boys, 52 percent for girls) literacy rate among 14-year-olds in the countryside of European Russia in 1920.

Notes

1 I. M. Bogdanov, *Gramotnost' i obrazovanie v dorevoliutsionnoi Rossii i v SSSR* (Moscow, 1964), pp. 358–9.

2 A. G. Rashin, "Gramotnost' i narodnoe obrazovanie v Rossii v xix i nachale xx v.," *Istoricheskie zapiski* 1951, no. 37, pp. 49–50; Tsentral'noe statisticheskie upravlenie, *Gramotnost' v Rossii* (Moscow, 1922), pp. 10–11.

3 Rashin, pp. 38, 44–5.

4 Lawrence Stone, "Literacy and Education in England 1640–1900," *Past and Present*, February 1969, p. 120; for Russian parish registers, see *Pervyi obshchezemskii s"ezd po statistike narodnogo obrazovaniia 1913 goda. Doklady* (Kharkov, 1913), pp. 671–82.

5 *Gramotnost' v Rossii*, p. 29; D. Erde, *Negramotnost' i bor'ba s nei* (Sevastopol, 1926), p. 193.

6 V. V. Petrov, "Ob otnoshenii naroda k gramotnosti," *Vestnik vospitaniia (VV)*, 1900, no. 4, p. 129.

7 S. Rachinskii, *Zametki o sel'skikh shkolakh* (St. Petersburg, 1882), p. 44.

8 N. A. Korf, "Uchilishcha aleksandrovskogo uezda i mariupol'skogo okruga" *Zhurnal Ministerstva narodnogo prosveshcheniia (ZhMNP)*, 1867, no. 8, pp. 158–9.

9 *Entsiklopedicheskii slovar'* (Brokgauz - Efron), vol. 20a (St. Petersburg, 1897), p. 759.

10 N. A. Korf, "Itogi obshchestvennoi deiatel'nosti," *Vestnik Evropy (VE)*, 1876, no. 6, pp. 910–11.

11 L. Demis, *Zemskie uchrezdeniia. Polozhenie o gubernskikh i uezdnykh uchrezhdeniiakh* (St. Petersburg, 1866), pp. 119–25, reprints the text of the July 14, 1864 law.

The zemstvo and education

12 N. Nazar'evskii, "Istoricheskii ocherk zakonodatel'stva po nachal'nomu obrazovaniiu v Rossii," *ZhMNP* 1905, no. 2, pp. 167–8.

13 *Zamechaniia na proekt ustava obshcheobrazovatel'nykh uchebnykh zavedenii i na proekt obshchego plana ustroistva narodnykh uchilishch*, pt. 5 (St. Petersburg, 1862), pp. 189, 305, 521.

14 S. V. Rozhdestvenskii, *Istoricheskii obzor deiatel'nosti Ministerstva narodnogo prosveshcheniia 1802–1902* (St. Petersburg, 1902), p. 456.

15 *Sbornik postanovlenii po Ministerstvu narodnogo prosveshcheniia*, no. 4 (St. Petersburg, 1871), pp. 1221–4.

16 Rozhdestvenskii, p. 544; Allen Sinel, *The Classroom and the Chancellery: State Educational Reform in Russia under Count Dmitry Tolstoy* (Cambridge, Mass., 1973), pp. 230–1.

17 *ZhMNP*, 1874, no. 1, pp. 3–5.

18 A. S. Prugavin, *Zakony i spravochnye svedeniia po nachal'nomu narodnomu obrazovaniiu* (St. Petersburg, 1898), pp. 25–31.

19 Boris Veselovskii, *Istoriia zemstva za sorok let*, 4 vols. (St. Petersburg, 1909–11), 3: 178.

20 "Otchet Ministerstva narodnogo prosveshcheniia za 1868," *ZhMNP*, 1870, no. 1, pp. 39–40.

21 Demis, pp. 125–6.

22 "Sovremennaia letopis'," *ZhMNP*, 1872, no. 3, pp. 392–401.

23 M. Smirnov, "Nachal'nye uchilishcha Riazanskoi gubernii," *ZhMNP*, 1871, no. 8, p. 236.

24 "Sovremennaia letopis'," *ZhMNP*, 1867, no. 2, pp. 182–3; 1867, no. 6, pp. 108–9.

25 M. Kupletskii, "K voprosu o tserkovno-prikhodskikh shkolakh," *Pravoslavnoe obozrenie*, 1882, no. 12, pp. 710–11.

26 *Statisticheskii vremennik Rossiiskoi imperii*, 3d series, no. 1 (St. Petersburg, 1884), pp. 294–5.

27 "Sovremennaia letopis'," *ZhMNP*, 1867, no. 11, pp. 181–3.

28 *Tserkovnyi vestnik* 1883, no. 51, pp. 4–5.

29 Veselovskii, 1:77–81.

30 S. Frederick Starr, *Decentralization and Self-Government in Russia, 1830–70* (Princeton, 1972), pp. 312–13.

31 Veselovskii, 3:172; Prugavin, pp. 53–4; Rozhdestvenskii, p. 552.

32 N. V. Chekhov, *Narodnoe obrazovanie v Rossii s 60-kh godov xix veka* (Moscow, 1912), p. 70.

33 A. S. Prugavin, *Zaprosy naroda i obiazannosti intelligentsii v oblasti prosveshcheniia i vospitaniia* (St. Petersburg, 1895), pp. 513–14.

34 N. A. Korf, *Russkaia nachal'naia shkola. Rukovodstvo dlia zemskikh glasnykh i uchitelei sel'skikh shkol* (St. Petersburg, 1870), appendix, pp. 1–8.

35 Korf, *Russkaia nachal'naia shkola*, pp. 15–16.

36 V. Debel', "Krest'ianskie vol'nye shkoly gramotnosti v Tverskoi gubernii," *Russkaia shkola (RSh)*, 1890, no. 6, pp. 135–8.
37 S. Miropol'skii, "Inspektsiia narodnykh shkol i ee zadachi," *ZhMNP*, 1872, no. 6, p. 68.
38 Prugavin, *Zakony*, pp 52–3.
39 N. Kibardin, "Odnodnevnaia perepis' nachal'nykh shkol Rossiiskoi imperii," *ZhMNP*, 1917, no. 5, p. 36.
40 Kibardin, p. 36.
41 *Statisticheskii vremennik*, 3d series, no. 1, p. xlvii.
42 *Nachal'nye uchilishcha vedomstva Ministerstva narodnogo prosveshcheniia v 1914 godu* (Petrograd, 1916), pp. ix–xi; Kibardin, p. 35.
43 Kibardin, p. 36.
44 Ibid.
45 V. Charnoluskii, "Zemstvo i narodnoe obrazovanie," *RSh*, 1910, no. 3, pp. 30–8, 46; Prugavin, *Zakony*, pp. 433–45; see also V. R. Leikina-Svirskaia, *Intelligentsiia v Rossii vo vtoroi polovine xix veka* (Moscow, 1971), p. 162.
46 Charnoluskii, pp. 46–7.
47 Ibid., p. 48; Vl. Akimov, "Narodnoe obrazovanie," *ZhMNP*, 1915, no. 5, p. 15.
48 Akimov, pp. 15–16.
49 P. Salomatin, *Kak zhivet i rabotaet narodnyi uchitel'* (St. Petersburg, 191?), p. 98.
50 E. A. Zviagintsev et al., eds., *Shkola, zemstvo, i uchitel'* (Moscow, 1911), pp. 117–25.
51 Salomatin, pp. 141–50; "Khronika," *VV*, 1904, no. 7, p. 117; "Khronika," *VV*, 1897, no. 7, pp. 115–22.
52 "Golos iz Viatskoi gubernii," *Russkii narodnyi uchitel'* (*RNU*), 1881, no. 5, p. 356; "O nagradakh dlia uchashchikhsia," *RNU*, 1903, no. 2, p. 28.
53 E. Gordenko, "Zemstvo i narodnye shkoly," *VE*, 1870, no. 1, p. 231.
54 "Sovremennaia letopis'," *ZhMNP*, 1870, no. 12, pp. 170.
55 "O s"ezde uchashchikhsia," *RNU*, 1909, no. 11, pp. 4–8; "Rezoliutsii l-go vserossiiskogo s"ezda po voprosam narodnogo obrazovaniia," appendix *VV*, 1914, no. 8, pp. 45–6.
56 Charnoluskii, "Zemstvo i narodnoe obrazovanie," *RSh*, 1910, no. 12, p. 55.
57 "Pedagogicheskaia khronika," *RSh*, 1909, no. 10, p. 54.
58 Chekhov, p. 114.
59 "K voprosu o deputatakh," *RNU*, 1884, no. 2, p. 70.
60 Zviagintsev et al., p. 24.
61 *RNU*, 1882, nos. 6–7, p. 296; *RNU*, 1901, no. 5, p. 192.
62 Prugavin, *Zakony*, pp. 771–84.
63 *Statisticheskii vremennik*, 3d series, no. 1, pp. 248–87.
64 Veselovskii, 1:472.

65 *Statisticheskii vremennik Rossiiskoi imperii*, 3d series, no. 13 (St. Petersburg, 1886), p. 28–9.
66 *RNU*, 1892, no. 3, p. 31.
67 Rachinskii, p. 27.
68 O. Kaidanova, *Ocherki po istorii narodnogo obrazovaniia v Rossii i SSSR*, vol. 1 (Brussels, 1938), p. 173.
69 Kir'iakov, "Vystavochnye vpechatleniia narodnogo uchitelia," *RNU*, 1897, no. 6–7, p. 59.
70 Kibardin, p. 35.
71 Ibid.
72 *VV*, 1903, no. 5, p. 85.
73 Archive of N. A. Rubakin, Manuscript Section, Lenin Library, f. 358, k.5, ed. kh. 14.
74 *RNU*, 1882, no. 3, p. 191. I discuss these attitudes in "Readers and Reading at the End of the Tsarist Era," in William Mills Todd, ed., *Literature and Society in Imperial Russia: 1800–1914* (Stanford, 1978).
75 Ibid., p. 188.
76 *RNU*, 1890, no. 4, p. 62.
77 Nik. Nik-skii, "Chetyre lista iz pamiatnoi knizhki sel'skogo uchitelia," *RNU*, 1894, no. 10, p. 93.
78 *RNU*, 1886, no. 12, p. 607.
79 *RNU*, 1888, no. 2, p. 90.
80 G. A. Fal'bork and V. Charnoluskii, eds., *Nachal'noe narodnoe obrazovanie v Rossii*, vol. 3 (St. Petersburg, 1905), pp. vii–ix.
81 Prugavin, *Zaprosy*, pp. 513–14.
82 Prugavin, *Zakony*, pp. 374–8.
83 M. I. Mysh', *Polozhenie o zemskikh uchrezhdeniiakh 12 iiunia 1890 goda*, 4th ed., vol. 1 (St. Petersburg, 1904), p. 272.
84 Prugavin, *Zakony*, p. 392.
85 Chekhov, pp. 70-71.
86 *Istoricheskii ocherk razvitiia tserkovnykh shkol za istekshee dvadtsatipiatiletie (1884–1909)* (St. Petersburg, 1909), p. 118.
87 I. P. Belokonskii, *Novyi fazis v deiatel'nosti zemstva po narodnomu obrazovaniiu* (Moscow, 1898), pp. 3–4.
88 N. P. Malinovskii, "Ocherki po istorii nachal'noi shkoly," *RSh*, 1912, no. 12, pp. 70–1.
89 Chekhov, pp. 188–94, summarizes these plans.
90 N. P. Malinovskii, "Pedagogicheskaia khronika," *RSh*, 1912, no. 10, p. 64.
91 V. Charnoluskii, "Zemstvo i narodnoe obrazovanie," *RSh*, 1910, no. 11, pp. 115–19.
92 *Gos. Duma. Stenograficheskie otchety, 1910 g. Sessiia chetvertaia, zasedanie 2*, October 18, 1910, p. 19.
93 Paul N. Ignatiev, Dmitry M. Odinetz, and P. J. Novgorodtsev, *Russian Schools and Universities in the World War* (New Haven, 1929), p. 19.
94 *Doklady biudzhetnoi komissii*, no. 18 (St. Petersburg, 1914), p. 65.

95 V. Charnoluskii, "Zemstvo i narodnoe obrazovanie," *RSh*, 1910, no. 10, pp. 59–60.
96 See, for example, Rashin, "Gramotnost'," and A. Piskunov, ed., *Ocherki istorii shkoly i pedagogicheskoi mysli narodov SSSR. Vtoraia polovina xix v.* (Moscow, 1976); for a contemporary discussion of this question, see "Doklad Ia. Ia. Gurevicha i N. P. Malinovskogo," in *Pervyi obshchezemskii s"ezd po statistike*, pp. 533–8.

8

The zemstvo and public health

SAMUEL C. RAMER

Long before the zemstvo celebrated its fiftieth anniversary in 1914, its efforts in the field of public health had elicited broad acclaim. When judged by the standards most physicians shared, however, neither the quality nor the accessibility of health care in rural Russia was remotely satisfactory. Given contemporaries' awareness that, for all the zemstvo's efforts, the peasantry continued to live in a squalid environment which fostered high rates of chronic and epidemic disease, one may well ask why it was that zemstvo medicine enjoyed such strong support.[1] Here it is important to recognize that zemstvo medicine was an ideal as well as a series of functioning programs. For its architects and leading practitioners, its value as a model for the development of rural health transcended its inadequacies, however measured.

The Zemstvo Statute of 1864 did not create this or any other model, leaving the organization and financing of most public health measures to the discretion of each district (uezd) zemstvo assembly.[2] This splintering of authority into the hands of 350 different assemblies would make it impossible to speak of a single "zemstvo medicine" at all were it not for a few common principles to which most zemstvos adhered either as a result of their legislative mandate or at the behest of the physicians they hired. These principles, which both defined zemstvo medicine and enhanced its popular authority, were:

1. A primary commitment not only to make modern medical care available to the Russian peasantry but to convince the peasantry that such care was desirable
2. The administration of public health by representative institutions of local government rather than the tsarist bureaucracy

I would like to thank the Tulane University Committee on Research, the National Endowment for the Humanities, the International Research and Exchanges Board, the Fulbright–Hays Fellowship Program and the University of Illinois for their generous support of the research for this chapter.

279

3. The abolition of direct fees paid to the physician in return for medical care
4. An emphasis upon public hygiene and preventive medicine as equally as important as if not more important than therapeutic treatment in solving the problems of rural health

For the most committed zemstvo physicians these principles assumed the character of an ideology and for that reason deserve some elaboration here.

The zemstvo was not the first Russian institution to concern itself with the health of the peasantry, but it was the first to acquire responsibility for all elements of the rural population in the areas it administered. The Ministry of State Domains, for example, which had developed the most elaborate system of rural medicine prior to the zemstvo, had only provided for the state peasants. For privately owned serfs as well as most other rural dwellers there had been virtually no organized system of medical care. Such dedication to the welfare of the impoverished rural majority, however compromised in practice, was a major source of zemstvo medicine's appeal to liberal and populist intellectuals.

Contemporaries attest to the symbolic as well as practical importance of the transfer of medical administration from the central bureaucracy to the zemstvo. In the pre-zemstvo era what few district physicians there were presided over a medical administration that existed for the most part only on paper. They themselves were primarily urban practitioners in charge of hospitals that were infamous among the peasantry – with good reason – as houses of death (morilki).[3] These physicians ventured into the countryside for the most part only to engage in tasks that could be expected to alienate the peasantry, such as performing autopsies for forensic purposes or examining recruits for the draft.[4]

Zemstvo programs could not change this negative image overnight, and the stark contrast usually drawn between the socially committed zemstvo physician and his time-serving "bureaucratic" predecessor is both exaggerated and unfair.[5] Nevertheless, the new zemstvo framework did make two fundamental changes possible. First, it created ever greater numbers of salaried positions outside the state bureaucracy in which the enthusiastic members of a populist intelligentsia could serve the people. By transforming the physician's identity from state servant to servant of society, it also enhanced the potential authority of modern medicine among the peasantry.

Aside from its overall mission to reduce the suffering and horrendous mortality rate of the Russian peasantry, zemstvo medicine's most distinctive trait was its abolition of the commercial relationship between physician and patient that was the norm in Western Europe and urban Russia. Medical care, in short, became a public service which the community bore collectively through its taxes. This principle was not implemented everywhere immediately, but most districts retained direct payment only for medicines and hospital care. There were practical reasons why physicians and local zemtsy (elected zemstvo members) were able to agree on the need to provide "free," or tax-subsidized, health care. The most obvious was that individual peasants could not afford to pay physicians directly, or at least not enough to make survival in the countryside on fees alone an attractive or even viable prospect. Since many peasants were both fearful and suspicious of physicians, no medical system that added direct payment to these apprehensions could have made rapid headway among the rural population. Physicians anxious to win popular confidence saw the elimination of direct fees as imperative in their struggle against the authority and widespread practice of cheaper, more traditional village practitioners.

For many zemstvo physicians, the provision of medical care without direct fees was a moral as well as practical question. Imbued with the generally populist sympathies that dominated public life in Russia during the latter part of the century, physicians such as D. N. Zhbankov, M. Ia. Kapustin, and E. A. Osipov would see this aspect of zemstvo medicine as one which even more advanced countries would do well to emulate. Although the zemstvo was neither the first nor the only institution in Russia to provide medical care without direct fees,[6] its leading spokesmen's cultivation of this practice as a central feature of an articulate medical ideology would make zemstvo medicine an important precedent for socialized systems of medical care in the twentieth century, most obviously that of the Soviet Union.

Preventive medicine and public hygiene assumed a prominent position in zemstvo health programs at the persistent behest of physicians, who saw them as the only hope for any real improvement in rural health. No one denied the importance of therapeutic or curative medicine. On the contrary, much of the zemstvo's activity was directed toward increasing its availability through the hiring of more and better medical personnel and the construction of hospitals and clinics. But most physicians argued that any system of medical care which placed exclusive emphasis on treating the sick was doomed to remain an unsatisfactory palliative in Russia.

Influenced by the sanitary movement in the West, zemstvo "sanitary" physicians in particular sought to eliminate the very sources of disease. As I. I. Molleson, the first specialized "sanitary" physician to serve in the zemstvo, indicated in 1871, these sources were deeply rooted in peasant life. "Examine the peasant's yard, his barns and his cellars," Molleson wrote. "Sit down and eat with him. Lie down and sleep beside him. Walk side by side with him in the fields, to work, and so on. Everywere you will see one and the same thing: disease, disease, and disease."[7] In order to change this, he continued, the physician interested in preventive medicine would have to study "the whole ensemble of Russian life: mores, customs, habits, holidays, games, the raising of children, clothing, housing, baths, the preparation of food, and so on."[8] To be effective he should also understand peasants' "superstitions and overall vision of life (their hopes, beliefs, aims, and expectations), their mutual relationships, and popular medicine – all those things which kill and maim so many."[9]

This sweeping definition of tasks, which the most influential architects of zemstvo medicine accepted, necessarily involved physicians in all aspects of the peasants' individual and community life. The mandate of zemstvo medicine thus transcended medical care itself to include an attempt to transform the peasantry's entire worldview,[10] and physicians joined with teachers to form the "third element's" cutting edge in the zemstvo's effort to bring the Russian village into the modern world.

This chapter will explore how the zemstvo's overall medical system emerged, convey some notion of its operation in practice, and evaluate the results it achieved during the period 1864–1914. For the social and cultural historian, the most interesting question is that of how the medical culture of the modern era affected, and was affected by, the traditional medical culture of the village. Since cultures can only be defined and borne by real people, we will examine the kinds of people who worked as zemstvo medical practitioners, the popular attitudes and traditional healers they encountered in the countryside, and the ways in which both were affected by that encounter.

Emergence of the zemstvo medical system

Prior to the zemstvo's creation, the responsibility for public health in each province had been shared by four institutions with overlapping jurisdictions. The oldest and best endowed of these was the Office of Public Welfare (Prikaz obshchestvennogo prizreniia), headed by the provincial governor and consisting of two elected representatives apiece from the nobility, the townsmen of the provincial capital, and the free peasantry. This office, established by Catherine the Great, was essentially an urban institution, although its services existed in theory for the whole population. In the field of health care, the office maintained the provincial hospital and other welfare institutions such as foundling homes, institutions for the infirm, and insane asylums. These were usually located in the provincial capital, and the physicians hired to staff them rarely went beyond the city's immediate environs in their practice. Most of the patients in provincial hospitals were either urban dwellers or retired soldiers: the peasant population was for all practical purposes beyond their reach.

The so-called Committees of Public Health (*Komitety obshchestvennogo zdraviia*), created in 1845 and expanded in 1852, existed at both a provincial and a district level. Consisting of the local administrative and medical personnel, these committees were appointed by the provincial governor to deal primarily with epidemics and other emergencies. Their day-to-day role in providing health care for the peasantry was also minimal.

Only two institutions had a specific responsibility for rural health. They were the Ministry of State Domains (*Vedomstvo gosudarstvennykh imushchestv*), which administered the state peasants, and the Ministry of Appanages (*Vedomstvo udelov*), which had jurisdiction over all peasants living on lands belonging to the imperial family. Of these, the Ministry of State Domains made the most notable effort to organize an effective system of rural health care, and the programs it developed during the 1850s anticipate those of the zemstvo in several ways.

The ministry was first concerned to provide all state peasants with realistic access to some sort of trained medical personnel, a leveling impulse prominent in later zemstvo calculations. Unable to do this with physicians alone, the ministry emphasized the role of feldshers, or paramedics, as the primary means of serving the peasant population directly. These feldshers were stationed at various points throughout a district, where they opened outpatient clinics and functioned as independent practitioners. Their duties were much the same as those of the future zemstvo physician: receiving patients, traveling by horseback or cart to visit emergency cases, and supervising the vaccination which peasant "vaccinators" – generally teenage boys with virtually no medical training – had previously managed so poorly. The ministry's program provided that these feldshers would be periodically visited by one of the ministry's physicians, who would inspect and, to that extent at least, supervise the work. The effectiveness of this control can be judged from the fact that there was often only one physician for a whole province, leaving most feldshers entirely on their own.[11]

The ministry itself was under no illusions about these feldshers' abilities. The best – and largest single contingent – were graduates of feldsher schools run by the Moscow and Saint Petersburg foundling homes.[12] Others came from a variety of sources, the most important being the army. Whatever their background, their training had been for the most part quite superficial. In many cases they had received no formal instruction at all, serving instead as hospital orderlies or company medics during what amounted to an apprenticeship not for independent work but for continued employment in an auxiliary capacity.

The overall cultural development of these early feldshers was little higher than that of the population they served. (The popular literature of the time unfailingly portrayed them as drunks.) Whatever their actual abilities may have been, their reputation as medical practitioners was notorious among physicians. The chief physician of the Ministry of State Domains nevertheless reasoned that these feldshers were at least a beginning and preferable to nothing at all.[13] Early zemstvo medical systems continued to rely on feldshers scattered at independent feldsher receiving stations, while simultaneously endeavoring to improve the quality of their training through the establishment of zemstvo feldsher schools.

If unsatisfactory in practice, the ministry's system was at least an expression of concern for the state peasants' welfare. Lacking state-administered health programs of any kind, privately owned serfs had recourse to a variety of other medical practitioners. Like peasants of all categories, they frequently called upon the parish priest for medical assistance, and from the eighteenth century onward the state encouraged this by requiring seminarians to study medicine. In 1802 medicine became an obligatory subject in all seminaries.[14] Writing in 1853, the chief physician of the Ministry of State Domains confirmed the utility of the parish priests' medical role and sought to expand it.[15] Zemstvo physicians would also turn to local priests for assistance in outlying areas.

Some landlords maintained feldshers for their serfs, and on occasion whole peasant communities either hired their own feldsher or paid for one of their number to be trained as one (usually an orphan). In many cases the woman of the manor also served as a consultant for the serfs' ailments, however exaggerated the benevolent stereotype may be. For the most part, however, the peasantry in all areas turned to its own traditional healers and deliverers, the znakhar' (or znakharka) and the povitukha. The znakhar' was a faith healer specializing in magical chants (zagovory) and folk remedies. His regard for disease as a manifestation of divine mystery closely corresponded to the peasants' own vision, and the special powers he purportedly possessed combined with the occasional efficacy of his herbal remedies (or simply

284

with the peasant's natural recovery) to give him great popular authority in the village.[16]

The *povitukha*, an experienced village midwife without formal training, brought the same veneration for ritual and fear of divine retribution to her work. Popular confidence in her abilities was enhanced by her record of successful deliveries, her usefulness in taking over domestic chores for the mother still confined to bed, and the fact that she was one of the peasantry's "own" people, known to the local population. The latter was particularly important because of the reluctance peasant women had to allow anyone at all to assist in childbirth.[17] Zemstvo physicians would view their efforts to win popular confidence away from these traditional practitioners as their first task in the countryside. As I. K. Savitskii wrote in 1869, "The most important goal of zemstvo medical service in the beginning must be simply *to awaken* the people's consciousness of their need for modern medical care."[18]

The transfer of responsibility for rural health from these various state institutions to the zemstvo was neither immediate nor smooth. As a result, even those meager steps the government had taken were frequently allowed to lapse during the first years of zemstvo administration. In addition to the general difficulties with funding and personnel, which adversely affected all areas of the early zemstvo's activity and caused many early supporters of the zemstvo to lose their enthusiasm,[19] there were more specific reasons for the early zemstvo's failure to develop its health programs more rapidly. The first was the imprecise nature of the zemstvo statute itself, which accorded zemstvo institutions the right to care for public health without specifying the exact extent of their responsibility. As of 1865, at least, there were still other institutions, such as the Ministry of State Domains, that also had a concern for rural health. Zemstvo deputies, whose budget was paltry given the array of tasks before them, were understandably reluctant to devote a large share of their funds to public health until they found out exactly what their mandate was.

Budgetary considerations alone, however, do not account for the zemstvo's lackadaisical performance during the later 1860s. Many critics have emphasized the gentry's domination of zemstvo assemblies as the primary reason for their initial indifference to problems of public health.[20] B. B. Veselovskii cites 159 instances between 1865 and 1904 when the numbers of physicians to be funded by a zemstvo were actually cut, most of them occurring in the 1860s and 1870s.[21] He as well as other commentators have viewed the early zemstvo's preference for feldshers over physicians as an outgrowth of this same gentry indifference. Feldshers were cheaper than physicians, and the cost of supporting them could be transferred more easily to the village communities themselves. Zemstvo deputies argued variously that feldshers would ultimately be more effective in treating what were supposedly the peasant's "simpler" diseases, and peasant as well as gentry deputies could predictably be found who would insist that "the physician was the gentry's doctor, whereas the feldsher was the muzhik's doctor."[22]

Actually, one of the major reasons for the faltering nature of the zemstvo's first steps was that the corps of physicians who would lobby for a more active, populist conception of zemstvo medicine was still small and had not yet developed a sense of common identity. As their numbers grew during the 1870s, the debate over what Kapustin would call "the basic questions of zemstvo medicine" emerged from bureaucratic offices and even zemstvo assemblies to acquire an impassioned and intensely public character. One of the results of this debate, which included an insistence on the part of zemstvo physicians that the system of medicine they had developed was a pioneering effort different from earlier government initiatives, was a tendency to romanticize the zemstvo's early commitment and forget the disarray that reigned in rural medicine until the late 1870s. Without dwelling any longer on the difficult transition from several rural medical systems to the unified administration of the local zemstvo, let us proceed to examine the zemstvo's earliest programs.

First tasks of the zemstvo medical system

The zemstvo inherited the personnel and system of health-care delivery that the Ministry of State Domains had elaborated for the countryside, but its primary legacy in property was the buildings and capital of the Offices of Public Welfare. Overall, it inherited 335 hospitals and clinics from these offices,[23] which it was obliged to maintain. More than half of the beds (around 6,200) were in the 32 provincial hospitals, which were large urban institutions located in the provincial capitals. The rest were scattered among the more than 300 district clinics, most of which were in district capitals.

The earliest zemstvo physicians' reports on the condition of the large provincial hospitals, which were doubtless the best of the lot, indicate that insufficient numbers do not begin to describe their inadequacy. Out of the 28 provinces reporting, 24 stressed the generally poor physical condition of these hospitals, citing such factors as leaky roofs,

286

rotten floors, cracked walls, and a general state of disrepair so severe that in some case a total renovation was needed. Other factors almost universally mentioned were an overcrowding of beds and primitive toilet facilities. When these conditions were combined with an almost total lack of ventilation the result was, variously, "a horrible stench," "unimaginably foul air," or "a smothering odor."[24] There seems little reason to doubt the general impression that these early zemstvo reports convey; zemstvo hospitals would share the same defects for a long time.

Faced with the almost total absence of any effective hospital care for the rural population and lacking in medical personnel as well, the zemstvo's first steps were to hire physicians and feldshers, to repair and improve the hospitals they had inherited, and to expand the network of rural clinics (lechebnitsy), which might afford the peasantry at least the possibility of hospital treatment. In the first year of the zemstvo's existence 18 provinces hired 50 physicians. A year later, in 1866, 29 provinces had hired a total of 283 physicians.[25] By 1870, there were 756 physicians serving in 33 provinces.[26] Thenceforth the total number of physicians employed by the zemstvo would steadily increase. Their importance was less in their numbers than in the direction which they as a group succeeded in imparting to zemstvo medical programs. In a very real sense it was these physicians, the ultimate prototype of the "third element," who created zemstvo medicine, and the means by which they did so are worth exploring.

The most effective weapons zemstvo physicians had in their struggle to develop a unified zemstvo medicine were periodic physicians' congresses along with a medical press that reported the activities of these congresses as part of its own active concern for public health. These congresses were organized on a provincial, district, and later – through the Pirogov Society of Russian Physicians – even on a national level. The first provincial congress, summoned by zemtsy and physicians together, met in Tver in 1871. Tver's example was immediately followed by other provinces, so that the number of provincial congresses tended to grow. By 1899 all provinces had had at least one such congress; Moscow and Kherson provinces had held 13 apiece. Such congresses did not meet on a regular schedule, however. One reason for their infrequency, especially during the 1870s and 1880s, was the unapologetic suspicion with which many zemtsy viewed any organized efforts on the part of the "third element." In a number of cases physicians' congresses were temporarily abolished, with the zemtsy citing variously their uselessness, excessive cost, or the fact that "physicians discuss quite different questions than the zemstvo had in mind."[27]

Actually, provincial congresses only embodied the tension and potential conflict that existed between zemstvo physicians and the deputies and zemstvo boards that had hired them. The increased funds and more ambitious public health programs that physicians sought were not the only source of this conflict. Equally if not more important were more general questions of competence and jurisdiction. Zemstvo physicians committed to particular strategies of health care tended to claim an exclusive competence in health matters based on their medical expertise. In a more general way they were leaders in the Russian medical profession's attempt to establish itself as a free profession whose members should have the decisive voice in all matters of public health.[28] The zemtsy who controlled the purse strings were on the whole unwilling to recognize this exclusive competence and had their own ideas about health care as well. As one deputy from Chernigov province stated in 1881, arguing against the usefulness of physicians' congresses: "Questions related to the organization of zemstvo medicine...are questions not of medicine, but of administration, and their resolution is the business of the zemstvo assemblies. They can be discussed by every educated man, and there are physicians within the assemblies."[29]

Physicians' ability to affect the formulation of public health policies through their congresses depended on a whole series of chance factors, some of them personal. Where an assembly and the physicians it employed enjoyed a close relationship, for example, the organization of health-care delivery and public hygiene tended to move much more rapidly. The first provincial congresses, however, found their recommendations almost entirely ignored by the district assemblies, which alone had the power to implement them. The virtually autonomous power of the district assembly and district board in the actual administration of rural medicine made it imperative to form some sort of physicians' councils at the district as well as provincial level. Zemstvo physicians also sought to involve interested zemtsy, and particularly the heads of zemstvo boards, in their deliberations at all levels. Their hope was that such participation would promote understanding and sympathy for their ideas within the zemstvo assemblies themselves. Such cooperation gradually became the pattern even in those provinces which had originally rejected the need for physicians' congresses.

However useful in illuminating local problems, provincial and district congresses did not answer the need most physicians experienced for some sort of national organization that could coordinate their

288

efforts and allow physicians from many provinces to compare their experiences. Such an organization appeared only with the founding of the Pirogov Society of Russian Physicians, which held its first national congress in Saint Petersburg in December 1885. The Pirogov Society, and particularly the section on social medicine established at the second congress in 1887, quickly became the guiding organ of zemstvo medicine. Its congresses, which met every two or three years between 1885 and 1919, were major events in Russia's medical history, attracting anywhere from 1,000 to 2,500 participants. Sanitary physicians such as F. F. Erisman, I. I. Molleson, E. A. Osipov, D. N. Zhbankov, V. I. Dolzhenkov, A. I. Shingarev, and N. I. Teziakov were particularly influential in the society's congresses as well as its governing board, and as a result community medicine as opposed to individual therapy provided the main focus for the society's attention.[30]

The most important general function of all these congresses was to provide a forum where physicians could discuss common problems. The proceedings of provincial congresses were printed, albeit in small numbers, and shared unsystematically with other provinces. Together with the proceedings of the later Pirogov Society congresses they formed the ingredients of an ongoing discussion of the problems of public health. Moreover, such congresses were crucial in boosting the morale and commitment of physicians who had been separated too long not only from their professional peers but from educated society in general. The importance of this latter function cannot be overstressed given the acute loneliness and spiritual isolation experienced by most physicians who actually lived in the countryside and engaged in a rural practice. In this regard one woman serving in a rural area wrote: "You live here in what is truly a foreign land, where you and the inhabitants speak entirely different languages and neither understands the other. There is nobody with whom to exchange a few words, with whom to share impressions, to ask for advice or instructions."[31] As a result, she lamented, the physician in such areas was "completely isolated, with nowhere to turn for support or sympathy."[32] Certainly the notion of "two Russias," culturally distinct and only occasionally overlapping geographically, is nowhere more prominent than in the perceptions of dedicated but essentially urban physicians working among a people who were in many respects foreigners to them.

The circuit system versus the stationary system

The central question of how to deploy the zemstvo's limited personnel and funds in order to achieve the best care for the whole population generated a debate which was both passionate and repetitious. The first aspect of this debate, which was waged in zemstvo assemblies as well as physicians' congresses, involved the physician's most appropriate use of his own time. Originally most zemstvo districts had only one or two physicians, whose responsibility to care for the entire district exceeded all human capacity. Generally they lived in the district capital, maintaining whatever hospital existed there. In order to expand their services beyond this capital and make up for their small numbers, the earliest zemstvo physicians served their districts by means of what was called a "circuit" (*raz"ezdnaia*) system. This system, which was directly inherited from the Ministry of State Domains, emphasized the use of feldshers at various receiving stations throughout the zemstvo district. The district physician's role in this arrangement, aside from tending the district hospital for a day or two each week, was to "ride the circuit" of both feldsher stations and unmanned receiving points according to a fixed schedule, spending a day or less at each station. During these brief and frenetically busy visits he (or she) would treat outpatients, prescribe medicines, visit emergency cases in the surrounding area, leave instructions for followup care in such cases with the feldsher or with relatives, and be off.

Physicians opposed the circuit system from the very beginning. By forcing them to spend so much time traveling from one village to another, it drastically reduced the amount of time they had to engage in actual medical practice. Within the circuit system, they argued, they became little more than periodic, and thereby ineffective, supervisors of feldsher practice. The system also compromised the quality of what medical care they were able to give. Constantly on the move, they could not provide the followup care that was as important in serious cases as the original diagnosis and treatment. Physically exhausted by long hours on horseback or primitive peasant wagons, they frequently lacked any convenient place to treat the patients who had assembled. During the wintertime patients of all ages seeking to escape the cold jammed the small, dark room of the *izba*, or hut, that usually served as a clinic. In such cramped quarters privacy was unthinkable, and it was difficult to isolate patients even for examination. Finally, of course, there were no facilities where the physician could hospitalize those with serious diseases or injuries and keep them under observation.

In place of this circuit system, physicians suggested what they called a "stationary" system, in which they would spend most of their time at a centrally located clinic or hospital. One of the circuit system's great defects was that the population never knew where to find the physician at any given moment. His ideally punctual visitation schedule was not

290

well known to the population at large, who knew only when he was expected in their village, and circumstances frequently forced him to alter that schedule anyway. This unpredictability discouraged peasants from seeking the physician's help in all but the most serious cases, particularly since most of them were reluctant to sacrifice a working day for medical treatment. By establishing a regular routine of receiving outpatients at the hospital every day, usually in the morning, the physician could let it be known when and where he could be found. With less obligation to visit the distant corners of his district, he could more easily make himself available on holidays and market days, when peasants were likely to appear in the greatest numbers. In the afternoons, in addition to making rounds in his hospital, the physician could travel to visit those emergency cases which arose; so the stationary system left latitude for him to provide care outside the hospital. Overall, physicians argued, that system would allow them to make the maximum use of their medical expertise, and ultimately to treat the largest number of patients.[33]

Most zemtsy opposed this sort of stationary system during the 1860s and 1870s, arguing among other things that it denied peasants in remote areas the equal access to a physician's care for which they paid through taxes. Only by traveling his district regularly, they insisted, could the physician remain sensitive to the specific needs of the different areas within that district. This concern that the physician actually travel his district seems particularly understandable when we recall that a considerable proportion of the physicians employed by the district zemstvos (60 percent in 1870, and 32 percent as late as 1910) resided not in the countryside but in the district capital.[34] In many cases the zemtsy attributed physicians' preference for the stationary system to laziness or their desire to lead a more comfortable life.[35]

As long as the numbers of physicians working in rural areas were so few as to be virtually insignificant, the practical difference between these systems of health-care delivery was small; most peasants remained beyond a physician's care in either case. As the number of zemstvo physicians grew, however, the stationary system became increasingly practical: the zemstvo district was gradually subdivided into greater numbers of physician's *uchastki*, or bailiwicks, thereby reducing the area and population for which each physician was responsible. These reductions made it possible for physicians who devoted most of their time to a central clinic to supervise nearby feldsher stations and visit emergency cases. Beginning in the 1880s, therefore, the stationary system was increasingly favored by district zemstvos, and the stationary bailiwick became the central organizational unit of zemstvo medicine.[36]

Table 8.1. *Status of zemstvo medicine, 1870–1910*

	1870	1880	1890	1900	1910
Physicians employed by district zemstvos	613	1,069	1,558	2,398	3,082
Number of physician bailiwicks (*uchastki*)	530	925	1,440	2,010	2,686
Average population of physician bailiwick	95,000	58,000	42,000	33,000	28,000
Average radius of physician bailiwick (km)	42	31	25	21	18
Average area of physician bailiwick (km^2)	5,539	3,018	1,963	1,385	1,017
Number of independent feldsher receiving points	1,350	n.a.	2,800	n.a.	2,620

Note: Number of independent feldsher receiving points for 1880 and 1900 missing in original table.
Source: Z. G. Frenkel', *Ocherki zemskogo vrachebno-sanitarnogo dela* (St. Petersburg, 1913), pp. 121, 125.

Ideally, the physician's bailiwick would have a population of less than 10,000 and a radius of five to eight kilometers. (Experience had shown that peasants living further away were much less likely to consult the relatively remote physician.) This ideal was rarely achieved in the zemstvo period – only eight zemstvo districts reported a physician–patient ratio of less than 1:10,000 in 1910[37] – but steady progress was made toward its realization, as Table 8.1 indicates.

"Feldsherism"

If the circuit system gradually "withered away" with the increase in zemstvo physicians, the related issue of "feldsherism," or independent feldsher care, would remain a source of heated debate throughout the zemstvo's existence. The nature of this debate is important to understand not only because of the issue's contemporary prominence but because of what it reveals about the more fundamental cultural problems that zemstvo physicians encountered in trying to bring modern medicine to the countryside.

The reason for the widespread practice of feldsherism was simple enough: there were not enough physicians in the whole country to make a physician's care accessible to all of the widely scattered rural population, nor would there be in the foreseeable future. Because of that shortage, and even more because of the maldistribution of what physicians there were,[38] the feldsher – trained only to serve as a physician's assistant – was often forced to practice on his own.

In everyday practice physicians accepted the inevitability of this arrangement and sought to ameliorate its effects by improving feldsher training and reducing the size of the physician's bailiwick so that the feldsher would have a realistic opportunity to seek the physician's guidance in emergency cases. But to recognize such independent practice as legitimate, even as an interim measure, was another question entirely, and physicians as a group consistently refused to do so. Zemstvo physicians were particularly opposed to such recognition, since feldsherism represented an inadmissible compromise in the medical standards they sought to establish. Rather than sanction that compromise, which they feared would be interpreted as an acceptance of the feldsher as an adequate independent rural practitioner, they rationalized its de facto existence by emphasizing and seeking to strengthen the formal but largely illusory control they had over the isolated feldsher's everyday practice.

The independent feldsher was thus placed in the awkward position of being forced by the population's needs – and demands – to perform operations and prescribe drugs that were beyond his legal competence and thus to violate the law in his everyday work. Such "illegal" practice was a well-known phenomenon in rural life, and physicians tolerated it in the breach, however vociferously they may have denounced it in principle. (Witness the growth in independent feldsher receiving points between 1870 and 1910 in Table 8.1.) It should come as no wonder that one of the first professional demands which the feldshers made when they began to organize themselves at the end of the century was that the independent practice which was forced upon them by circumstances should be sanctioned by law.[39]

Feldsherism was also a question whose resolution could have real consequences in the zemstvo's hiring policies. We should recall that the debate over feldsherism began while the basic outlines of zemstvo medicine were still being drawn up. There was no European model for a rural health system on such a scale, and the only tradition of rural medicine the zemstvo inherited was the use of feldshers by the Ministry of State Domains. As of 1870, the number of physician bailiwicks in the countryside was less than half the number of independent feldsher receiving points, and they would outnumber those points only in the twentieth century (see Table 8.1). Physicians feared – with reason – that cost-conscious zemstvo assemblies, dominated by members of the gentry, might continue to opt for the cheaper feldsher as the fundamental rural practitioner. We have already seen that zemtsy on occasion advanced arguments in support of this policy, such as the notion that the peasantry somehow suffered from "simpler" diseases.

A more serious defense of the feldsher's independent role, which even some physicians would support, emphasized the distinctive characteristics of peasant culture and the need to consider this cultural context in developing public health policies. On the whole this line of argument stressed the feldsher's identity as one of the peasantry's "own" people.[40] He spoke their language, understood their problems, and in many cases had their confidence.[41] As such, it seemed, he could serve as a cultural link between modern science and the village. As Alexander Novikov put it, based upon his experience as a zemskii nachal'nik, better the feldsher who works "if not according to science, then at least in the name of science, than the znakhar', who undermines and seeks to undermine faith in science in every way."[42]

Most physicians refused to accept any variant of this argument, and many insisted that feldsher care was worse than none at all.[43] Reasoning in a fashion precisely opposite that of Novikov, they stressed that independent feldsher care tended to undermine whatever chances modern medicine had of winning popular confidence.[44] In their public statements physicians systematically ignored the feldsher's useful services, lest any praise be construed as sanction of independent feldsher care, and went on to attack not only the educational but the moral qualifications of feldshers as a group. In doing so they ignored the considerable differentiation in training and ability that had come to characterize the feldsher community by the late nineteenth century.

Beginning in the late 1860s and 1870s, zemstvos established increasing numbers of feldsher schools in order to replace the "company" (rotnye) feldshers and graduates of the Foundling Homes' feldsher schools with better-educated, competent physicians' assistants. Whereas the company feldshers had for the most part received only on-the-job training as corpsmen, students in zemstvo schools completed three- to four-year courses in medical training, usually at the provincial hospital. The ideal recruit for these schools during the 1860s and 1870s was "a simple peasant lad, of local origin, who is able and a nondrinker."[45] With time, the emphasis on peasant origin as a factor in admissions would be overshadowed by the factors of prior education and overall cultural development. Only one-third of those studying to be feldshers in 1910 were of peasant origin.[46]

This decline in peasant enrollment was caused in part by the increasing applications to feldsher schools made by urban students whose prior education was on the whole superior to that which peasant children had received. Particularly important here was the growing number of women from various social backgrounds who sought careers as feldshers after the opening of feldsher practice to women in 1871. Their education was so far superior to that of their male counterparts – many of them had completed a full course in gymnasium – that by the turn of the century the zemstvo was systematically trying to replace feldshers with feldsher-midwives. In 1910, for example, 71 percent of those studying in feldsher and feldsher-midwife courses throughout the empire were women, a dramatic shift from the exclusively male profession of the 1860s and an important harbinger of the prominent role of women in medicine during the Soviet period.[47]

By 1915, there were 80 civilian schools throughout the empire training feldshers and feldsher-midwives, 36 of them supported by the zemstvo. These zemstvo schools taught slightly over half of the 6,500 students enrolled in all schools.[48] The graduates of these increasingly sophisticated feldsher schools were on the whole quite respectable medical practitioners: most had completed at least 8 years of primary education plus 4 and sometimes 5 years of training in a feldsher school. A third, mostly women, had 10 to 12 years of primary and secondary education followed by the same feldsher training. As medical practitioners, these better-educated feldshers compare favorably with the American country doctor of the same period.[49]

The passion with which most physicians opposed independent feldsher practice – even though they knew it was an inevitable reality of everyday life – involved issues beyond that of the most rational way to employ medical personnel. In order to understand the implacable nature of their opposition, we must recall the primary mission zemstvo physicians had of transforming peasant culture. In the strictly medical sphere, this meant introducing modern, scientific, "rational" medicine into the countryside, sweeping away the web of "superstitious" practices associated with folk medicine. What was this "modern" medicine of which physicians spoke with such certainty? How did it differ from earlier practices, and why was it difficult to persuade the population of its efficacy?

Rational medicine, as zemstvo physicians understood it, was medicine whose contours are defined by the secular assumptions of the Enlightenment. It is a method rather than a set of specific cures. It is essentially empirical, involving attempts to draw informed conclusions from as large a body of data as possible. Unlike more traditional forms of healing, modern medicine focuses not only on the individual in collecting that data but on the community as it develops over time. The accumulation of statistics becomes a central step in the interpretation of factors that remained either unnoticed or incomprehensible when they appeared only as individual attributes.

Obviously modern medicine is not indifferent to the individual patient, but its practitioners, unlike traditional folk healers, claim no magic powers and are sustained in their frequently impotent everyday confrontation with death by the belief that in the long run the consistent application of the empirical approach to disease can reduce both its incidence and destructive power. The diagnosis or treatment in any given case may, and in fact often will be erroneous, but the secular faith underlying modern medicine argues that this empirical approach will achieve the best possible results for the community.

These abstract considerations were not easily appreciated by a largely preliterate Russian peasantry, whose traditions emphasized the divine origin of disease and the importance of the healer's charismatic gifts. The problem zemstvo physicians faced of acquiring the popular authority that peasants readily accorded traditional practitioners was thus a cultural task of no small magnitude. On the whole they were correct in their belief that this goal could never fully be achieved until the population was able to differentiate clearly between the two modes of medical care. This, in turn, required that modern medicine's therapeutic superiority be demonstrable through results the layman could appreciate. Since even the most advanced nineteenth-century medicine was still powerless to deal with most serious diseases once they had developed, physicians were not able to sustain their claims to exclusive medical competence on the basis of results alone. The fact that peasants often consulted physicians, feldshers, and znakhari concurrently,[50] even if for different purposes, suggests that they continued to evaluate competence in largely personal terms. They unquestionably perceived differences in the overall approach and specific talents of these practitioners, but they appear to have viewed them as variously gifted healers, each of use in his own way, rather than representatives of competing or mutually exclusive systems of medical care.

The feldsher's role as an independent practitioner was thus intolerable for physicians not only because of his limited abilities and the threat he represented to the hiring of physicians for the countryside but also because his very practice tended to blur popular distinctions between traditional and modern medicine. The zemstvo physician's university education and overall cultural achievements had imbued him with a deep faith in the long-range efficacy of modern medicine as a method. Many independently practicing feldshers, on the other hand, understood that method superficially at best. When isolated from whatever guidance and example the physician might provide, all but the very best-educated feldshers found it easy – and to some extent necessary – to adapt their methods of treatment to the expectations of their peasant clientele. This was not difficult because even with their castor oil and carbolic acid, "those 'alphas' and 'omegas' of all medical endeavors,"[51] their idea of medical practice often differed little from that of the peasantry, from which many of them had come. The feldsher's cultural proximity to the rural population could be advantageous in theory, allowing him to serve as a conduit of modern medicine into the countryside. The result in practice, however, was usually an interesting interpenetration of feldsher and *znakhar'* techniques, the former to various extents taking up folk medicine both to supplement his income and to augment his clientele, and the latter borrowing from the feldsher's "scientific" techniques to enhance his own storehouse of cures.[52] Physicians had just this blending in mind when they described feldsherism as nothing more than "enlightened *znakharstvo*." (Such a description would be less justified at the beginning of the twentieth century, with the increase in trained feldshers who consciously shared the cultural mission of their physician colleagues and had some real understanding of the principles of modern medicine. Throughout much of the zemstvo period, however, feldshers in independent practice tended to be either "company" feldshers or the worst graduates of the zemstvo schools, the best qualified usually seeking some sort of urban practice.[53])

The refraction of modern medical principles through the distorting medium of the independently practicing feldsher did not simply blunt zemstvo physicians' efforts to transform peasant culture; rather, it altered the nature of the changes zemstvo medicine produced and in some ways complicated the original task. This was particularly true in the case of the physician's authority. One of the major corollaries of modern medicine has been that the right to medical practice should be conferred only upon licensed physicians. Secular priests of a sort, these physicians ideally acquire as a group the exclusive competence to interpret medical truth, "rational" medicine at any given moment being what the community of licensed physicians says it is.[54] Since the immediate results of their everyday practice were not sufficiently impressive in themselves to win quick popular authority for modern medicine *as a system*, physicians considered their monopoly on independent practice as important as their empirical method in assuring the eventual triumph of a medical science whose superiority to folk medicine was not yet clear to the layman. The independent feldsher, of course, was an embodied denial of the physician's exclusive competence. Feldshers who acquired a popular following, even on the basis of their proven skill as practitioners, inevitably tended to postpone the

297

day when the physician's license itself might serve as an adequate claim for popular confidence. Affecting as it did the whole complex of medical and cultural tasks that zemstvo physicians had set for themselves, feldsherism generated a controversy that was both passionate and unabating.

Community medicine

In the eyes of most zemstvo physicians, the techniques of public hygiene and preventive medicine first developed in England and Germany were absolutely essential in Russia. Peasant living conditions and customs fostered disease and its spread. The number of trained physicians in rural areas was insignificant, and their therapeutic skills were limited, even in the best instances, by the narrow frontiers of contemporary medical knowledge. Their therapeutic inadequacy was nowhere more obvious, both to themselves and the frightened, potentially hostile population they were endeavoring to help, than in the case of epidemic disease. Frequent outbreaks of such epidemic diseases as smallpox, cholera, diphtheria, and typhoid fever made the urgency of a community approach to medicine apparent.[55]

It was one thing during the 1860s to speak of "sanitation" or of rooting out "harmful" popular customs, but where did one begin? What tasks were most important, and what kinds of institutions and personnel were needed to carry them out? Although no final answers to these questions were possible, early proponents of community medicine agreed that sanitary statistics were the most significant aspect of its practice.

Three early forums were particularly influential in urging the importance of such statistical studies. The first was a quarterly journal of the Medical Department entitled, *The Archive of Forensic Medicine and Public Hygiene* (*Arkhiv sudebnoi meditsiny i obshchestvennoi gigieny*), first issued in 1865. Under its editor S. P. Lovtsov, the *Archive* expanded the popular conception of community medicine beyond the traditional functions of a medical police to include the study of all aspects of community life.[56]

Among the more than 20 urban physicians' societies functioning during the late 1860s, the society formed in Kazan in 1868 played a particularly influential role in clarifying the early tasks of community medicine. Following the election of Professor A. V. Petrov as its chairman in 1870, the Kazan society actively pressed the Kazan zemstvo to undertake sanitary initiatives, prepared to publish its own journal,[57] and gained a national audience when it sponsored a section on community medicine at the Fourth Congress of Russian Natural Scientists, which met in Kazan in 1873. (This was the only national conference to give serious consideration to community medicine prior to the creation of the Pirogov Society in the 1880s.[58])

Early advocates of community medicine shared Lovtsov's view that the sanitary physician's most important general task was to establish a medical topography of the area he served, recording every possibly useful bit of information about the population, physical environment, economy, and climate.[59] In order to form a useful basis for comparative study, such information would have to be collected in as complete and systematic a fashion as possible. The Kazan society accordingly sought to develop uniform medical records and a single accepted nomenclature of disease to be used in the city of Kazan itself.[60] During the 1870s, it proved impossible to establish these prerequisites for any accurate statistical studies throughout all zemstvo provinces, in part because of the autonomy each zemstvo preserved in its own medical practice. The introduction of such uniform medical records throughout the country would be one of the Pirogov Society's major goals.[61]

The Kazan society ceased to exist in 1875, after a series of practical failures: the government refused to allow its journal, and the provincial zemstvo rejected most of its proposals for the development of community medicine in Kazan. Most of the 11 specialized sanitary commissions that provincial zemstvos had formed during the 1870s and 1880s also failed, usually as a result of the same general conflict with zemstvo deputies.[62] Many of the latter honestly doubted the practical worth of the sanitary studies physicians proposed and found the budgetary requests physicians' congresses made for such studies virtually fantastic given the zemstvo's limited funds. Their skepticism had a legitimate basis, at least during the 1870s, when no systematic collection of statistics on disease was possible in most areas because of the small number of physicians, their lack of training in statistics and hygiene, and their more than full-time work as therapeutic practitioners. Even those deputies who had originally supported such sanitary studies were reluctant to do so once they saw the inevitably long-range nature of their practical results.[63]

Sanitary physicians, for their part, made little effort to understand the zemstvo deputies' real budgetary dilemma, and their insistence on autonomy in running community medical programs inspired suspicion and hostility among zemtsy anxious to guard the administrative prerogatives they had so recently acquired themselves.[64] As a final explanation of the conflict that community medicine would continue to generate between physicians and zemstvo deputies, it should be kept in mind that the studies of social and economic conditions which physicians undertook in their role as hygienists were by their very nature subversive of Russia's existing social order, suggesting as they often did that no real improvement in public health was possible without drastically enhancing the economic well-being of the peasantry and embryonic working class.

Until the establishment of sanitary bureaus headed by physician-hygienists with responsibility for the ongoing collection and interpretation of medical statistics, which did not happen in most provinces until the 1890s and after, community medical programs were supervised by a variety of administrative and advisory bodies. The most important, at first, were the periodic congresses of zemstvo physicians and zemstvo deputies, which met with varying frequency in most provinces beginning in the 1870s. These congresses became particularly active in drafting sanitary proposals after 1879, when the zemstvo first acquired the authority to issue binding sanitary legislation within the province.[65]

As advisory bodies, these physicians' congresses suffered from a number of deficiencies. They were inconvenient to assemble and too unwieldy to be effective in giving advice on a day-to-day basis. They met irregularly and infrequently, with as much as 5 to 10 years intervening between many of their sessions. In an effort to supplement these larger congresses, zemstvos first resorted to ad hoc conferences of physicians and zemstvo boards. With time, however, most zemstvos would share physicians' perception of the need for a more regularly constituted, smaller body. The first such sanitary council (*sovet*) was established by the Moscow provincial zemstvo in 1885 as the permanent continuation of the Moscow sanitary commission, of which E. A. Osipov had been the secretary and guiding force since 1875. Under Osipov's leadership, to quote one contemporary, the Moscow sanitary commission had become "a sort of laboratory for all-Russian as well as Moscow zemstvo medicine, since all of zemstvo Russia tried to match the zemstvo medical organization of Moscow province."[66]

By 1910, all but 13 provincial zemstvos had sanitary councils, and they existed in many districts as well. Such councils brought physicians together with zemstvo boards and selected deputies on a regular basis, and they quickly became the most important administrative organs of zemstvo medicine. Although their decisions had no binding legal authority without the zemstvo assembly's approval, the councils themselves enjoyed considerable moral authority within the assembly because of the prominent role played by the zemstvo boards and deputies.[67]

For the development of community medical programs, sanitary councils depended upon full-time sanitary bureaus staffed by physicians trained in statistics and hygiene. Moscow again led in establishing such a bureau (1886), which had the function of not only assembling and

300

analyzing statistics but coordinating all of the zemstvo's medical activities by setting the agenda for physicians' congresses and meetings of sanitary councils. The sanitary bureau supervised the implementation of all sanitary measures, especially the precautions taken against epidemics.[68] By 1910, 31 provinces had experimented with these sanitary bureaus, and they were still functioning in twenty provinces.[69] Their proceedings, which were published under various titles, are one of the best sources historians have on the operation of zemstvo medicine at the local level. Leaving "high principles" for national congresses, physicians in these bureau meetings frankly discussed their needs and the deficiencies of the administration they headed.[70]

The usefulness of these sanitary bureaus remained a matter of dispute among physicians as well as zemstvo deputies, and their activities were periodically restricted, suspended, and even terminated. The reasons offered were familiar. In closing such a bureau in Bessarabia, for example, delegates noted that "a lot has been studied, a lot published," but that the practical results amounted to nothing.[71] Excessive cost was another prominent complaint. The efforts various provincial bureaus made to conduct statistical registrations (*kartochnye registratsii*) of the population elicited particular opposition. Many physicians thought such registration not only burdensome but worthless: "What we lie about in the registration," opponents of the Perm bureau grumbled, "you [sanitary physicians] treat as statistics."[72] District boards saw such registration – and the generally centralizing activity of the provincial bureaus – as an encroachment on the autonomy of their administration. Many district physicians shared this parochial resentment of the sanitary physician, whom one Riazan physician described as "the zemstvo general of medicine."[73] Finally, the sanitary bureaus proved to be the focus for the suspicion with which many zemstvo delegates viewed the activities of the "third element." Six bureaus were closed in 1906, for the most part as a result of the more general restriction on zemstvo activity that followed the revolutionary turmoil of the previous year. In at least one case (Tula), the sanitary bureau's abolition resulted from charges that it was engaged in party-oriented (*partiinyi*) political activity.[74]

The close monitoring of sanitary conditions was the most important single activity in which sanitary physicians engaged. In addition to making statistical studies possible, which could suggest other community medicine initiatives, it also facilitated zemstvo physicians' ability to detect the outbreak of epidemic diseases as early as possible. Because of the devastating character of such diseases once they reached national proportions, as in the cholera epidemics of 1892–93 and

1905,[75] it is often forgotten that smaller epidemics, at the provincial and district level, were virtually a constant factor in rural Russia throughout the zemstvo period. As one physician remarked on the basis of her experience in the 1880s, "There was not a single summer or winter without some kind of epidemic, each of which carried off no small number of victims."[76]

Two other problems that concerned sanitary physicians were vaccination and midwifery, both of which offered the possibility of cutting the mortality rate drastically. Better vaccine and an increased participation by physicians and better-trained feldshers brought about a gradual improvement in the vaccination programs that the zemstvo had inherited from the Ministry of State Domains. Unfortunately, the same cannot be said for midwifery. Proper obstetric care was particularly significant because of the high rate of infant mortality that existed in rural Russia: almost one out of two peasant children died before the age of five.[77] Unable to improve diet or living conditions overnight, physicians hoped that, by providing trained midwives to replace the village *povitukhi*, they might be able to prevent at least those deaths that were the result of incompetent assistance at birth. The zemstvos made considerable efforts to train qualified midwives who could accomplish this task, establishing 14 schools for that purpose as early as the 1870s. By 1905 there were over 10,000 trained midwives in practice throughout the empire, some 2,200 employed by the zemstvo.[78] If these numbers represented a vast improvement over the situation of the 1860s, they nevertheless were insignificant given the overall population of more than 125 million. At the very end of the zemstvo period, these trained midwives attended only 2 percent of all peasant births.

The almost total failure of modern midwifery to take hold in the countryside had two basic causes. The first was the reluctance of peasant women to seek any assistance at all during parturition, least of all that of a stranger. When they did recognize the need for help, they preferred that of the *povitukha*, who was one of their "own" people. Her willingness to assume household chores during the mother's confinement, coupled with her traditional, ritualistic attitude toward childbirth and her jealous defense of her practice against trained but inexperienced newcomers, gave her a popular authority that her frequently younger rivals found it difficult to challenge. Unable to maintain themselves in the countryside for lack of an extensive practice, many of these early trained midwives migrated to the city, which promised an income either in private practice or in nonmedical work. The city's attraction was also cultural, and even the peasant girls who dominated the earliest midwifery courses responded to its lure

302

when faced with the isolation and loneliness that rural practice afforded. By the turn of the century, over 90 percent of the midwives trained for rural practice rapidly qualified themselves for urban practice and moved to the city.[79] This trend was reinforced by the increasing precedence that prior education had over peasant origin as the most important factor in admitting students (a change in emphasis mirrored in feldsher recruitment as well). The best-qualified applicants were increasingly of urban origin, and less than a quarter of the midwives in training in Russia were peasants as of 1910.[80]

Another reason for these early trained midwives' failure to win popular acceptance was their inability to demonstrate their purely medical superiority over the *povitukhi*. Despite the horror physicians expressed at the *povitukhi's* methods, it appears that many were quite effective in assisting at births that required no active intervention. It was their primitive, often fatal techniques in cases of complicated births that contributed most to their notoriety outside the peasant community. Faced with similarly complicated circumstances, however, trained midwives were for the most part equally helpless, as were many physicians, and their refusal to act without a physician's assistance was a confession of incompetence more damaging to their prestige in the peasant community than the *povitukha's* efforts, however misguided.

Physicians offered a variety of proposals to increase the effectiveness of modern midwifery in the countryside. One suggestion was to offer crash courses in modern midwifery to the *povitukhi*, who already had popular confidence.[81] Such an approach was tried briefly in Saratov province in 1888, but discontinued for lack of any promising results. The most controversial proposal concerning rural midwifery was made in 1899 by Professor Dmitrii Ott, the director of the Imperial Clinical Obstetric Institute in Saint Petersburg.[82] He urged a renewed emphasis on peasant origin as the first criterion in trained midwives, arguing that such a temporary sacrifice of expertise in the face of existing reality was essential if any sort of trained midwives were to establish themselves in the countryside. Returning to arguments that had been prominent in the 1860s, he stressed both the cultural proximity of the peasant girls to the rural population, which could facilitate their practice, and the greater likelihood that girls of rural origin would remain in the countryside.

The Seventh Congress of the Pirogov Society, to which Ott made this recommendation, rejected it as "one which contradicts the basic tasks of zemstvo medical organization."[83] Most thought it impossible to transform peasant girls into competent midwives in only eight months, as Ott had proposed, and insisted that licensing poorly trained midwives who happened to be peasants would only complicate the original task of improving rural obstetric care. Here, as in the case of feldsherism, a minority of physicians – like Ott – remained convinced that Russia's relatively undeveloped situation made some compromise of ideal standards necessary. The practical solution most zemstvos adopted in the early twentieth century was to hire increasing numbers of female feldsher-midwives to replace both feldshers and midwives. The rationale behind this was that such feldsher-midwives, working as feldshers, would be able to establish a reputation as trustworthy practitioners in situations less intimate than that of childbirth. On the whole this proved to be the case, although the *povitukhi* would retain a significant rural practice until well into the Soviet period.[84]

The exact functions that sanitary physicians performed varied with local conditions. In Moscow province, for example, where industrial development affected most of the population, including the peasantry, factory medicine was an especially important concern. In provinces where a large annual influx of migrant agricultural laborers raised significant health problems, sanitary physicians sought to prepare for these workers by constructing shelters, making provisions for additional health personnel, and so on.[85]

Syphilis was an affliction that plagued the Russian peasantry in all provinces. In order to combat its spread, physicians who could do little to cure it tried to increase popular knowledge concerning its symptoms and transmission as well as to dispel the sense of shame that prevented many victims from seeking help. They also studied the ways in which seasonal labor migration and practices such as baby farming affected its incidence.[86] In a more general way, finally, physicians emphasized the importance, for health, of self-discipline and mutual respect in village and family life. Here their main target, which they fought in vain, was the frequent drunkenness of village males, which was the catalyst for so many fistfights, stabbings, and even more prevalent incidents of wife beating.

More than anything else, perhaps, zemstvo physicians saw themselves as enlighteners. The propagation of modern hygienic principles among the rural population was an aspect of community medicine in which they were all engaged, enlisting the aid of teachers and clergy wherever possible. Instruction could be oral, in the classroom or during the physician's visit, or could take the form of didactic pamphlets such as those sponsored by the Pirogov Society.[87] Improvements in housing (more space, better ventilation, the elimination of dirt floors, and the still widespread "black" or chimneyless cabins), adequate clothing, and proper diet were subjects that physicians stressed as well, although substantial changes were usually beyond the peasants' means. In an effort to improve the circumstances in which peasant children were raised, which frequently amounted to almost total neglect because of their parents' long working hours, zemstvo physicians advocated the establishment of summer nurseries and kindergartens. Because of their enormous cost and debatable sanitary impact, the zemstvos' willingness to sponsor such nurseries was limited to a comparatively few random experiments.[88] The same desire to protect the health of children involved sanitary physicians in detailed sanitary studies of early zemstvo schools and increasingly regular inspections of school conditions.[89]

Zemstvo medicine's shortcomings and achievements

The ambivalence with which contemporary observers regarded all aspects of zemstvo activity is particularly striking in the case of zemstvo medicine. Its deficiencies, on the one hand, were obvious to those who sought to expand the scope of its endeavors. The absence of a national zemstvo assembly and the limited powers of provincial assemblies, for example, left district zemstvos in possession of virtually autonomous authority except for their subjection to the relevant laws and regulations of the central government. Although this decentralization had the advantage of involving local people in administration, it also resulted in an enormous disparity in public health programs, even between districts in the same province. Such district autonomy, and the separatist spirit that accompanied it, frustrated collaboration between neighboring districts in the use of what few physicians and facilities there were.[90] The appearance of the Pirogov Society eliminated the intellectual vacuum surrounding zemstvo medicine at the national level, but it had no legislative or budgetary authority with which to implement its proposals.

At the provincial and district levels physicians waged a perpetual two-front war. On the one hand, they had to win the confidence of the people they served. On the other, they had to convince – and periodically reconvince – their zemstvo employers that their efforts were worthwhile and needed to be expanded. Such persuasion was complicated not only by disagreements over zemstvo medical policy but also by the conflicting perceptions physicians and deputies had of what their own mutual relationship should be. For many zemstvo deputies the physician (not to speak of the feldsher or midwife) was simply an employee who could be treated arbitrarily. He could advise on medical

305

matters, but only they could consent. Physicians understandably viewed their dependence upon the gentry-dominated zemstvo assemblies as a less than ideal basis for a medical system. They resented the social condescension of zemstvo deputies as well as the petty indignities they frequently suffered at the hands of capricious zemstvo board members. Conflicts over medical administration fueled the political radicalism of many physicians, particularly during the period leading up to the Revolution of 1905 (see Chapter 9). This radicalism, in turn, enhanced the suspicion with which many zemstvo deputies regarded the "third element" as a whole.

To a considerable degree, contemporaries tended to quantify zemstvo medicine's shortcomings and achievements. In the standard works by Osipov, Frenkel', Veselovskii, and others, for example, there is a persistent effort to measure such factors as the number of physicians and other health personnel working for the zemstvo, the resulting physician–patient ratios, square kilometers per physician bailiwick, numbers of hospitals and independent feldsher stations, patients treated, and, finally, the budgetary appropriations for medical care on which these activities depended. These statistics, although indicating a significant improvement in all categories between 1870 and 1910, nevertheless constitute a measure of zemstvo medicine's inadequacy when considered as absolute figures (see Table 8.1).

Given the zemstvo's responsibility for the health the peasantry, which made up over 80 percent of the population in most zemstvo provinces, its most glaring deficiency was its failure to hire more than 20 percent of the civilian physicians in Russia. The resulting maldistribution meant that physician bailiwicks remained for the most part enormous in size, with huge and scattered populations. By 1910, as we have noted, only 8 districts (out of 359) had achieved physician–patient ratios of less than 1 to 10,000 (Table 8.1). In quantitative terms, therefore, zemstvo medicine's success was quite limited.

These statistical shortcomings, however, must be seen as part of a larger social and scientific context. To understand zemstvo delegates' failure to appropriate more funds for medicine, for example, three factors should be kept in mind. First is the zemstvo's overall budgetary limitations. These limitations, as Professor Atkinson has shown in Chapter 4, rested on the peasants' unwillingness to pay higher taxes for any services as well as the government's refusal to allow the zemstvo more freedom in taxing itself. Second, it should be recalled that public health was the single largest item in the zemstvo budget throughout most of the zemstvo period, rivaled only by education. Such a prominent allocation, outlined in Table 8.2, hardly reflects an indifference to

306

Table 8.2. *Zemstvo allocations for health and education, 1868–1913*

Year	Percent of total for:		Total amount for health (thousands of rubles)
	Health	Education	
1868	8.6	4.9	1,298
1875	14.1	12.0	3,933
1885	21.7	15.7	9,388
1890	22.5	15.3	10,505
1900	27.6	17.6	24,322
1910	28.4	25.4	47,665
1912	26.3	30.2	57,704
1913	25.1	31.4	63,781

Source: V. F. Karavaev, "Zemskie smety i raskladki," in B. B. Veselovskii and Z. G. Frenkel, eds., *Iubileinyi zemskii sbornik: 1864–1914* (St. Petersburg, 1914), pp. 167, 170.

public health on the part of zemstvo deputies as a group. A final factor of some importance in explaining zemstvo deputies' refusal to appropriate all the funds that physicians wished was the limitation of medicine itself during the nineteenth century. A larger budget would indeed have made certain obvious improvements possible, at the very least in hiring and outfitting physicians, but the correlation between appropriating more money and saving lives was not nearly so direct as it later became when antibiotics were introduced.

The zemstvo's expenditures on public health were dramatic compared with those of nonzemstvo provincial governments, as were the resulting achievements. A survey made by D. N. Zhbankov in 1892 gives some idea of the disparity between the two systems (Table 8.3). The zemstvo's commitment to public health is even more impressive when one realizes that, measured in real rubles, the total budget for health care in the RSFSR as late as 1925–6 was at best 89 percent of what the zemstvo appropriated.[91]

In the last analysis, however, no figures can account for the appeal that zemstvo medicine exerted. This appeal was in large part a result of the ideals that physicians who served in the zemstvo articulated so forcefully in their professional gatherings and their everyday lives. Zemstvo medicine began the process of converting the mass of the Russian people to modern medicine and set forth the tasks that a medical administration should seek to accomplish in an overwhelmingly peasant country. In doing so it established the intellectual foundations and organizational framework for a viable system of public health in rural Russia.

Table 8.3. *Status of public health achievements in zemstvo and nonzemstvo provinces, 1892*

Average physician's bailiwick	Zemstvo provinces	Nonzemstvo provinces
Square kilometers	1,120	5,382
Population	42,060	101,800
Independent feldsher stations (per bailiwick)	1.6	5.6
For every 10,000 inhabitants:		
Beds in hospitals	8.0	4.2
Numbers seeking help (annually)	3,210	1,594
Numbers treated in hospitals	123	47
Kopeks spent per person	34.0	16.6

Source: E. A. Osipov, I. V. Popov, and P. I. Kurkin, *Russkaia zemskaia meditsina* (Moscow, 1899), p. 206.

Notes

1 The mortality rate in the zemstvo provinces did fall by a quarter over the half-century from the reform period to the eve of the First World War, but the role of medical care in producing this decline was marginal at best. In the western, nonzemstvo provinces, whose expenditures for public health were much lower, the mortality rate fell even faster. Nutrition and a variety of cultural factors related to national differences were the most important reasons for this differential mortality rate. For statistics see A. G. Rashin, *Naselenie Rossii za 100 let (1811–1913 gg.): statisticheskie ocherki* (Moscow, 1956), pp. 189–91, 193.

2 *Svod zakonov Rossiiskoi imperii* 3d ed., 16 vols. (St. Petersburg, 1857–1915), 2: 398–9, 409. Both the original statute and its amendment in 1890 were ambiguous about the respective jurisdictions of the provincial and district zemstvos in health care, providing only that the provincial zemstvo should have control over problems that affected the whole province or several of its districts. For a discussion see A. V. Korchak-Chepurkovskii, "Otnosheniia mezhdu gubernskim i uezdnymi zemstvami v dele organizatsii zemskoi meditsiny," *Vestnik obshchestvennoi gigieny, sudebnoi i prakticheskoi meditsiny,* January 1900, pp. 33–4.

3 S. I. Mitskevich, *Zapiski vracha-obshchestvennika (1888–1918),* 2d ed. (Moscow, 1969), p. 58.

4 I. K. Savitskii, "Ob ustroistve vrachebnykh posobii dlia sel'skogo naseleniia," *Arkhiv sudebnoi meditsiny i obshchestvennoi gigieny* May 1869, pp. 9–10.

5 I. D. Strashun, "Polveka zemskoi meditsiny (1864–1914)," in P. I. Kal'iu, ed., *Ocherki istorii russkoi obshchestvennoi meditsiny (k stoletiiu zemskoi meditsiny): sbornik statei* (Moscow, 1965), pp. 30–6.

6 Programs of government medicine in the nonzemstvo provinces also attempted to provide physicians' services without direct fees.

7 I. I. Molleson, *Zemskaia meditsina* (Kazan, 1871), p. 8. For a German translation of this work, see I. I. Molleson, *Der russische Landarzt im 19 Jahrhundert: Die Zemstvo-Medizin*, trans. and intro. Heinz Muller-Dietz (Stuttgart, 1970).

8 Ibid., p. 49.

9 Ibid. Molleson's emphasis.

10 The phrase is N. I. Pirogov's, quoted in E. A. Osipov, I. V. Popov, and P. I. Kurkin, *Russkaia zemskaia meditsina. Obzor razvitii zemskoi meditsiny v Rossii voobshche i otdel'no v Moskovskoi gubernii s kratkim statisticheskim ocherkom strany i ee sanitarnogo sostoianiia* (Moscow, 1899), p. 43. In outlining these fundamental traits of zemstvo medicine I have relied on the following standard monographs in addition to those of Osipov, Popov, and Kurkin, Kal'iu, and Molleson: Z. G. Frenkel', *Ocherki zemskogo vrachebnosanitarnogo dela* (St. Petersburg, 1913); V. Ia. Kanel', "Obshchestvennaia meditsina v sviazi s usloviiami zhizni naroda," *Istoriia Rossi v XIX veke*, 9 vols. (St. Petersburg, 1909–11), 8: 156–262; M. Ia. Kapustin, *Osnovnye voprosy zemskoi meditsiny* (St. Petersburg, 1889); L. N. Karpov, *Zemskaia sanitarnaia organizatsiia v Rossii* (Leningrad, 1964); M. M. Levit, *Stanovlenie obshchestvennoi meditsiny v Rossii* (Moscow, 1974); M. Slobozhanin, *Iz istorii i opyta zemskikh uchrezhdenii v Rossii* (St. Petersburg, 1913), p. 489–524; and P. E. Zabludovskii, *Meditsina v Rossii v period kapitalizma (razvitie gigieny; voprosy obshchestvennoi meditsiny)* (Moscow, 1956). As for all aspects of the zemstvo's activity, B. B. Veselovskii's *Istoriia zemstva za sorok let*, 4 vols. (St. Petersburg, 1909–11), is of critical importance. See particularly volume 1, pp. 267–434. The most extensive bibliographies for the period prior to 1905 are D. N. Zhbankov, *Bibliograficheskii ukazatel' po zemsko-meditsinskoi literature* (Moscow, 1890), and its continuation, *Bibliograficheskii ukazatel' po obshchestvennoi meditsinskoi literature za 1890–1905 gg.* (Moscow, 1907).

11 As of 1853, for example, the ministry employed only 124 physicians for the state peasants of the entire empire. TsGIA, f. 1297, op. 97, d. 69, p. 138. Strashun indicates that this number had not increased as of January 1, 1857. "Polveka zemskoi meditsiny," p. 33.

12 Not all feldshers were orphans, but the notion that orphans should receive preference in feldsher recruitment was embodied in law as well as practice. *Svod zakonov Rossiiskoi Imperii*, 13:228.

13 TsGIA, f. 1297, op. 97, d. 69, p. 1 ob. For the detailed attention that the ministry focused on feldsher training, see TsGIA, f. 1297, op. 98, d. 101, vol. 1, pp. 324–408 ob., and f. 1297, op. 98, d. 102, vol. II, pp. 42–89.

14 Gregory Freeze, *The Russian Levites: Parish Clergy in the Eighteenth Century* (Cambridge, Mass., 1977), p. 264.

15 TsGIA, f. 1297, op. 97, d. 69, pp. 49–49 ob.

16 *Znakharstvo* was not a phenomenon restricted to the countryside. As Alexander Novikov noted in 1904: "The culture of urban dwellers is not far removed from the culture of the villages, and now, still, you encounter barbaric examples of *znakharstvo* right and left in the capitals." *Zapiski o gorodskom samoupravlenii* (St. Petersburg, 1904), pp. 150–1. With less emphasis upon faith healing than herbal medicine, *znakharstvo* remains prominent even in the contemporary Soviet Union, to judge by the number of pamphlets issued to combat it. Solzhenitsyn's *Cancer Ward* conveys the atmosphere in which this is the case.

17 For a review of popular attitudes toward childbirth, see G. E. Rein, *O russkom narodnom akusherstve* (St. Petersburg, 1889), and V. F. Demich, "Pediatriia u russkogo naroda," *Vestnik obshchestvennoi gigieny, sudebnoi i prakticheskoi meditsiny*, August 1891, pp. 125–45; September 1891, pp. 187–212; October 1891, 66–76; November 1891, pp. 111–23; December 1891, pp. 169–86.

18 Savitskii, p. 27. Author's emphasis.

19 On this point, see S. Frederick Starr, *Decentralization and Self-Government in Russia, 1830–1870* (Princeton, 1972), pp. 304–6, 324–5.

20 Veselovskii, 1:335–6; Kanel', p. 169. These are only two examples of a prevailing analysis.

21 Veselovskii, 1:333–4.

22 Ibid.; Osipov, Popov, and Kurkin, eds., p. 76.

23 Osipov, p. 63. The number would be 350 if we were to add the reasonable estimate of one clinic apiece for each district not reporting.

24 Ibid., p. 64.

25 Strashun, p. 36.

26 Osipov, p. 90. Strashun records only 599 physicians in zemstvo service in 1870 (p. 36).

27 Quoted in Veselovskii, 1:303. For a breakdown of these congresses by province, see Veselovskii, 1:301–2; and D. N. Zhbankov, *O deiatel'nosti sanitarnykh biuro i obshchestvenno-sanitarnykh uchrezhdenii v zemskoi Rossii; kratkii istoricheskii obzor* (Moscow, 1910), pp. 8–14.

28 See Nancy M. Frieden, "Physicians in Pre-Revolutionary Russia: Professionals or Servants of the State?" *Bulletin of the History of Medicine* (1975) no. 1, pp. 20–9.

29 Quoted in V. Skalon, "Zemstvo i narodnoe zdravie," Russkaia mysl'
    1883, no. 5, pp. 72–3.
30 M. M. Gran, "Pirogovskie s"ezdy. Obzor i svod postanovlenii Pirog-
    ovskikh s"ezdov," in M. M. Gran, Z. G. Frenkel', and A. I Shingarev,
    eds., Nikolai Ivanovich Pirogov i ego nasledie: Pirogovskie s"ezdy
    (St. Petersburg, 1911), pp. 179–83; and Iu. Lisitsyn and Iu. Shilinis,
    "Meditsinskie s"ezdy," in A. N. Bakulev, ed., Bol'shaia meditsin-
    skaia entsiklopediia, 2d ed., 36 vols. (Moscow, 1956–64), 17:783. On
    the fate of the Pirogov Society after 1917, see Peter F. Krug, "Russian
    Public Physicians and Revolution: The Pirogov Society, 1917–1920"
    (Ph.D. dissertation, University of Wisconsin, 1979).
31 D. I – va, "Iz zapisok zemskogo vracha," Russkaia mysl', 1884, no. 12,
    p. 78.
32 Ibid.
33 For a summary of the arguments on this subject, see Kapustin, pp. 2–28;
    and Peter F. Krug, "The Debate Over the Delivery of Health Care in Rural
    Russia," Bulletin of the History of Medicine, Summer 1976, pp. 226–41.
34 Frenkel', p. 125.
35 Veselovskii, 1:351.
36 Frenkel', pp 110–24.
37 Ibid., p. 96.
38 The vast majority of physicians lived and worked in urban areas. In
    1907, for example, 72 percent of Russia's 18,215 civilian physicians
    lived in cities. Over 80 percent of the population, of course, lived in
    the countryside. Ministerstvo vnutrennykh del, Otchet o sostoianii
    narodnogo zdraviia i organizatsii vrachebnoi pomoshchi v Rossii za
    1907 god (St. Petersburg, 1909), p. 190.
39 On the ambiguity of the feldsher's legal position as a medical
    practitioner, see N. G. Freiberg, Vrachebno-sanitarnoe zakonodatel'
    stvo v Rossii, 2d ed. (St. Petersburg, 1908), pp. 148–51.
40 The Medical Soviet of the Ministry of Internal Affairs made it clear in
    an internal circular of 1897 that "feldsher schools maintained by
    zemstvos train for the most part children from the peasant popula-
    tion, and by the nature of things should train such children." L. F.
    Ragozin, ed., Svod uzakonenii r rasporiazhenii pravitel'stva po
    vrachebnoi i sanitarnoi chasti v imperii, 3 vols. (St. Petersburg,
    1895–8), 3:298.
41 National differences could also be important in this respect, although
    this was less of a problem in the predominantly Russian zemstvo
    provinces.
42 Novikov, Zapiski o gorodskom samoupravlenii, p. 150.
43 One of the earliest diatribes against independent feldsher practice
    was Molleson's Zemskaia meditsina, pp. 17–24. Insisting that feld-
    shers could be of no benefit at all to the people, Molleson noted (p.
    22) that "one after another they bury those who had the misfortune to
    turn to a feldsher for help."

44 For one of many arguments to this effect, see D. N. Zhbankov, "Qvazi prakticheskaia i poleznaia organizatsiia zemskoi meditsiny i feldsher-izm," *Zemstvo*, 1882, no. 1, p. 10.

45 TsGIA, f. 1297, op. 216, d. 262, p. 6.

46 TsGIA, f. 1298, op. 1 d. 1754, pp. 8 ob., 9.

47 Ibid.

48 P. Kalinin, *Profdvizhenie srednego meditsinskogo personala v Rossii: istoricheskii ocherk* (Moscow, 1927), p. 7. Enrollment figures here are based on school reports from 1914–15 in TsGIA, f. 1288, op. 13, d. 9. passim.

49 Richard Shryock points out that during the mid- to late nineteenth century "many 'doctors' in the United States were second-grade men in a professional sense. As will be noted, it was assumed by some observers that such men were needed to look after the poor. But most Americans, in the absence of open distinctions, probably thought that they were cared for by real physicians. It might have been safer, or at least more candid, to have given many of these 'docs' some lesser title." The situation had changed little at the turn of the century. "In 1898," Shryock reports, "Dr. L. Connor told the American Academy of Medicine that the profession still contained a 'vast number of incompetents, large numbers of moral degenerates, crowds of pure tradesmen' and so on" (epithets Russian physicians usually reserved for "company" feldshers). Richard Harrison Shryock, *Medical Licensing in America, 1650–1965* (Baltimore, 1967), pp. 33, 60. The exact proportion of these better-trained, non-"company" feldshers in practice at the turn of the century is not known. With 774 graduates in 1907 alone, from feldsher schools which in many cases had been operating for over a decade, it would appear that the number formally trained was approaching a majority. *Otchet o sostoianii...za 1907 god*, appendix, pp. 204–6. An extremely approximate survey of medical personnel made in 1920 reported that 45 percent of a total of 29,088 feldshers were graduates of feldsher schools; 38 percent described themselves as "company" feldshers, and 17 percent did not indicate their training. *Statisticheskie materialy po sostoianiiu narodnogo zdraviia i organizatsii meditsinskoi pomoshchi v SSSR za 1913–1923 gg.* (Moscow, 1926), p. xxii. On the general problem of feldsher qualification, see my article, "Who Was the Russian Feld-sher?" *Bulletin of the History of Medicine*, Summer 1976, pp. 213–25.

50 "To put it in a word, there's hardly a single sick person in the village who won't make use of his *znakhar'* sooner or later." N. D. Rudinskii, *Zapiski zemskogo vracha* (St. Petersburg, 1906), p. 140.

51 Ibid., p. 75.

52 Ibid., pp. 145–6.

53 TsGIA, f. 1297, op. 216, d. 262, p. 4.

54 On the social dimension of scienific inquiry, see Thomas Kuhn, *The Structure of Scientific Revolutions*, 2d ed., enlarged (Chicago, 1970).

55 The term *community medicine* will be used here to denote what contemporaries referred to variously as "sanitary medicine," "preventive medicine," and public hygiene.

56 Osipov, Popov, and Kurkin, eds., pp. 119–22. For an analysis of the *Archive*'s role in the development of factory medicine, see Reginald E. Zelnik, *Labor and Society in Tsarist Russia: The Factory Workers of St. Petersburg* (Stanford, 1971), pp. 268–82.

57 For the proposed contents of this journal, see Strashun, pp. 46–7.

58 Osipov, Popov, and Kurkin, eds. p. 135.

59 Ibid., pp. 119–22.

60 Ibid., p. 135.

61 See Gran, "Pirogovskie s"ezdy," pp. 207–14, for evidence of the Pirogov Society's continuing interest in this problem.

62 Zhbankov, *O deiatel'nosti sanitarnykh biuro*, pp. 5–7; Osipov, Popov, and Kurkin, eds., pp. 137–8.

63 Osipov, Popov, and Kurkin, eds., pp. 150–1.

64 Zhbankov, *O deiatel'nosti sanitarnykh biuro*, pp. 5–7.

65 Osipov, Popov, and Kurkin, eds., p. 146.

66 Mitskevich, p. 67. Quoted in E. Ia. Belitskaia, "Razvitie zemskoi meditsiny v Moskovskoi gubernii," in Kal'iu, p. 70. For the fullest discussion of Moscow's medical organization, see Osipov, Popov, and Kurkin, eds., pp. 211–340.

67 Zhbankov, *O deiatel'nosti sanitarnykh biuro*, pp. 14–15.

68 Ibid., p. 21. Indeed, it was often the threat of an epidemic that called such bureaus into being.

69 Ibid., p. 20.

70 For a list of these proceedings under their various titles, see Veselovskii, 1:313–14; and Zhbankov, *O deiatel'nosti sanitarnykh biuro*, pp. 59–63.

71 Zhbankov, *O deiatel'nosti sanitarnykh biuro*, p. 25.

72 Ibid.

73 Ibid., p. 26.

74 Ibid., p. 27.

75 For a recent discussion of the epidemic of 1892–93, see Nancy M. Frieden, "The Russian Cholera Epidemic, 1892–93, and Medical Professionalization," *Journal of Social History*, June 1977, pp. 538–9.

76 D. I – va, p. 74.

77 D. A. Sokolov and V. I. Grebenshchikov, *Smertnost' v Rossii i bor'ba s nei* (St. Petersburg, 1901), pp. 20–4.

78 *Otchet o sostoianii narodnogo zdraviia i organizatsii vrachebnoi pomoshchi v Rossii za 1905 god* (St. Petersburg, 1907), p. 180.

79 Dmitrii Ott, *Proekt organizatsii akusherskoi pomoshchi sredi sel'skogo naseleniia (Doklad sektsii akusherstva i zhenskikh boleznei VII s"ezda russkikh vrachei v pamiati N. I. Pirogova)* (St. Petersburg, 1899), p. 15.

80 TsGIA, f. 1298, op. 1, d. 1754, pp. 3–9.

81 P. A. Kalinin and N. I. Teziakov, eds., *Gubernskie s"ezdy i soveshcha-niia zemskikh vrachei i predstavitelei zemskikh uprav Saratovskoi gubernii s 1876 po 1894 god (Svod postanovlenii)* (Saratov, 1894), p. 53.
82 Ott.
83 A. P. Artem'ev, "Kak trudno byt' sostavitelem proekta organizatsii akusherskoi pomoshchi v Rossii," *Zhurnal akusherstva i zhenskikh boleznei*, February 1900, p. 1.
84 For a fuller discussion of the problems rural midwifery presented, see my article "Childbirth and Culture: Midwifery in the Nineteenth-Century Russian Countryside," in David L. Ransel, ed., *The Family in Imperial Russia* (Urbana, Ill., 1978), pp. 218–35.
85 Osipov, Popov, and Kurkin, eds., pp. 161–2.
86 David L. Ransel, "Abandonment and Fosterage of Unwanted Children: The Women of the Foundling System," in Ransel, pp. 189–217.
87 For a study of this hygienic literature, see Nancy M. Frieden, "Child Care: Medical Reform in a Traditionalist Culture," in Ransel, pp. 236–59.
88 Veselovskii, 1:320–2.
89 For examples, see D. P. Nikol'skii, "Obzor deiatel'nosti gubernskikh s"ezdov zemskikh vrachei (okonchanie)," *Vestnik obshchestvennoi gigieny, sudebnoi i prakticheskoi meditsiny*, June 1892, pp. 62–4.
90 Veselovskii, 1:377–9.
91 Christopher Davis, "Economic Problems of the RSFSR Health System: 1921–1930," Soviet Industrialisation Project Series, no. 19 (University of Birmingham Centre for Russian and East European Studies, 1978), pp. 26–7. I am grateful to Professor Davis for permission to quote from this informal discussion paper.

9

The politics of zemstvo medicine

NANCY M. FRIEDEN

Zemstvo medicine, a pioneering system of rural health protection, became a vital interest of the Russian medical profession. Physicians employed in the zemstvos and their colleagues in other medical work valued zemstvo medicine as a model health program, an outstanding example of their service goals and ability to translate scientific expertise into practical programs.[1] Although the medical program gained the physicians' firm and continuing support, the zemstvo deputies who administered it frequently provoked their animosity. Discord dominated the politics of zemstvo medicine. Deep and persistent conflicts between physicians and the deputies characterized the first three decades of the program; an uneasy alliance between these two groups formed an atypical interlude in the decade before the Revolution of 1905; and after 1905 that alliance disintegrated and the earlier tensions reappeared. The period of alliance, although of brief duration and a deviation from the broader pattern of conflict, is of interest as part of the process of radicalization on the eve of 1905. As a case study of the politics of zemstvo medicine, the uneasy alliance demonstrates the obstacles to political cooperation within the zemstvo milieu.

The early decades of zemstvo medicine

Tensions between zemstvo deputies and their medical employees seriously hampered progress in zemstvo medicine. Many deputies refused to cooperate with the medical personnel, meddled in their professional activities, and often treated them with disdain. The

For research and travel support the author wishes to thank the National Library of Medicine (NIH Grant RO1 LM 02590), the International Research and Exchanges Board, and the Ministry of Higher and Specialized Education of the USSR, the staffs of the Central State Historical Archives of the USSR in Leningrad and the Central State Medical-Scientific Library of the USSR in Moscow, and the American Council of Learned Societies.

315

report of the first zemstvo medical meeting in Kazan province, according to one participant, might have been entitled "The Tears of the Zemstvo Physicians" because "from beginning to end it was filled with the complaints about the unfortunate position of zemstvo physicians, whom the zemstvo board and deputies treated as masters had treated their former serfs."[2] Disagreements flared up over specific issues – the type and amount of medications to be purchased, the quality of hospital food, the hiring and firing of paramedical personnel. More basic were differences on the interpretation of the zemstvos' proper role in public health. Both leaders and the rank and file of the medical profession endorsed current theories that emphasized the prevention of disease, the only logical approach, in fact, where a low doctor–patient ratio made it impossible to provide medical treatment to the entire population. The zemstvo authorities often misunderstood and resisted some medical efforts. Surveillance of local sanitary conditions sometimes threatened the interests of owners of industrial or agricultural enterprises, who then blocked this form of preventive medicine. In the early years, when most physicians became convinced of the drawbacks of the "traveling system," the zemstvos resisted change, sometimes accusing the physicians of laziness or avarice in their quest for stationary posts.[3]

Social tensions underlay the political wrangling. The physicians, almost without exception, had more humble origins than the deputies, who rarely let them forget that social gulf. When physicians offered recommendations on issues of policy, they might be castigated for their "pretensions" in trying to participate in the legislative process; but constitutional issues concerned the deputies less than their resentment of such assertiveness on the part of their social "inferiors." A sensitive point in this relationship was educational disparity, for frequently the physicians had the more advanced general education, as well as special expertise. It is remarkable that in this fractious, often highly disagreeable environment, an outstanding program evolved and acquired an enthusiastic following. Traditional interpretations have credited that success to a few deputies and dedicated physicians, but actually the central government initiated and encouraged zemstvo medicine in its early stages. Regardless of the origins and stimuli, as the program improved many deputies took pride in it and cited it as proof of their political competence. They even argued that zemstvo medicine demonstrated the benefits of representative government and proved that Russia was ready to be "crowned with a roof" – a national assembly.

For very different reasons physicians supported zemstvo medicine. The zemstvos had little appeal to them as models of constitutional progress for few of them owned the property needed to qualify as

316

deputies or even to vote for them. Ideology may have influenced some, who wished to serve the common folk according to the "ideals of the 1860s" or the "movement to the people" of the 1870s. More important were professional imperatives and personal experiences. Zemstvo medicine had been conceived as the most cogent means to serve the nation's needs with Russia's limited capabilities: it utilized statistical health and organizational methods tested in the 1850s and regarded as scientifically sound, and it adapted current medical thinking on preventive medicine to rural needs. By the 1880s the splendid system of Moscow zemstvo medicine had attracted wide attention as the model for community medicine in all zemstvos and also in other public institutions throughout Russia.[4]

Personal contact convinced many physicians of the practical attributes of zemstvo medicine. The program employed from 15 to 20 percent of the profession at a given time, and because of a rapid turnover in zemstvo service about one-half of all physicians had some zemstvo experience. Medical students often worked in the zemstvos during summer vacations and then for a few years after graduation until they found a different, usually urban position. N. F. Filatov (1847–1902), who became a professor of medicine and pediatrics, had a characteristic attitude: beginning his career as a zemstvo physician in a remote district of Penza province, he left as soon as he had earned enough to finance postgraduate training. Others had only brief contact with the program. During epidemics all physicians had the legal obligation to serve if called, and many enlisted, including professors, writers such as Chekhov, and urban physicians; the experience often overwhelmed them and stimulated their moral and financial support of zemstvo colleagues. Vital assistance came from professors of medicine who taught postgraduate courses for rural physicians and gave generously of their time and advice.[5] By the end of the 1880s, with an upsurge of approval from the medical press and the national medical association, the Pirogov Society, zemstvo medicine became a major focus of professional consciousness.[6]

In addition to its practical advantages, zemstvo medicine provided a tangible means for physicians to reconstruct their public image. Before the reform era they had worked as *chinovniki* with very little prestige. With improvements in medical training and rapid advances in medical science their self-perception changed, but social acceptance and recognition lagged. The success of zemstvo medicine encouraged them to wage a subtle but effective propaganda campaign to project an improved image. Espousing the "ideals of the 1860s" they claimed to have effectively implemented those ideals, in contrast to the record of

317

many of the intelligentsia who failed to translate programs into practice. The average physician recognized that his professional status had become inextricably bound to zemstvo medicine and willingly fostered an idealized view of the program. There gradually emerged a "mystique of the zemstvo physician," who embodied the profession's best qualities.[7]

Despite the practical and professional attractions, very few physicians devoted entire careers to zemstvo service. The program had a number of negative aspects. Zemstvo physicians had the highest mortality rate of all physicians, probably because of frequent exposure to the virulent epidemics that invaded the countryside. Cultural and political reasons also caused a rapid turnover. Many physicians worked in what they termed the "distant corners" and "silent depths" until their children reached school age but then moved to areas with better educational facilities. Frequently physicians left in defiance and disgust because their position as "hirelings" was unpleasant and even degrading.[8] Unsatisfactory employment conditions turned many away, but this did not detract from their high regard for the contributions of the actual zemstvo medical programs. On balance, then, the medical profession approved the zemstvos' efforts in the field of public health, but deplored the demoralizing conflicts that obstructed medical progress.

In the history of zemstvo medicine, the positive role played by the central government has been largely overlooked. The legislation of the 1860s set up a dual public health structure in the provinces: the gubernatorial authorities retained control of major health responsibilities; and the zemstvos supervised only secondary problems, primarily the welfare of the poor and feeble. In the 1870s, however, a series of epidemics demonstrated the superiority of the zemstvos' medical organization and caused the central government to shift more medical powers to the zemstvos.[9] The dual structure remained on paper, but the zemstvos gained a substantial area of jurisdiction. The Zemstvo Statute of 1890, although one of three measures that eventually received the pejorative label of "counter reforms," actually strengthened some aspects of zemstvo medicine. The statute raised hopes among zemstvo physicians that they would have more authority in the area of their expertise.

The new zemstvo statute attempted to resolve some of the problems that persisted in Russia's "undergoverned provinces." In the zemstvo institutions many factors militated against their effectiveness: reluctant participation of some deputies, limited funds and disagreement on their use, tensions within the zemstvo milieu, and so forth. More serious, the original zemstvo legislation inadequately defined the distribution of functions among the local, provincial, and central administrations and thereby invited confusion and conflict.[10] In a few areas of competence the zemstvos acquired wide powers and some independence, but as a whole the system lacked rational organization. Greatly disparate programs of zemstvo medicine attested to the absence of order in a system that varied according to the personal whims, prejudice, or special interests and expertise of the deputies and administrators.[11] Throughout the 1880s, government circles debated fundamental administrative changes, and the statutes that resulted drew the zemstvos more tightly into the central bureaucracy. Provincial governors and the Ministry of Internal Affairs gained greater control over the zemstvo and city governments; some provincial officials became members of the zemstvo assemblies; members of the zemstvo boards received ranks (from 7 to 5) as state officials; and a new executive organ composed of a minority of deputies and a majority of nonzemstvo bureaucrats became the essential link in a newly minted chain of command between the center and the local institutions.[12]

For a variety of reasons, zemstvo partisans and the liberal press did not detect, at least at first, the implications of the new law. For many who had feared that the zemstvos might be abolished altogether, the 1890 statute produced a feeling of relief because it fell far short of their pessimistic predictions. *Russkie vedomosti* criticized the augmented powers of the governors and the Ministry of Internal Affairs and objected to new voting regulations but also declared that "the foundations of self-government have remained inviolable."[13] The governors' veto power, although an incursion on the zemtsvos' former rights, seemed limited by the zemstvos' right of petition to the Senate or the Committee of Ministers.[14] In addition, criticism may have been muted because the famine and cholera crises (1891–3) delayed the measure's implementation and prevented an assessment of its practical effects.

The mild opposition to the Zemstvo Statute of 1890 also stemmed from its imprecision, which reflected the contending groups that fashioned it. One faction would have fully incorporated the local governments into the bureaucratic hierarchy; another argued that these institutions should retain their limited independence. As a consequence, the new statute strengthened the web of governmental control, but certain safeguards indicated that the zemstvos did not face the danger of extinction.[15] A rough-hewn compromise, the 1890 zemstvo statute could be interpreted as either support for the local governments or a threatening wedge into their jurisdiction. A contemporary professor of law noted that this dualism complicated interpretation of the statute; and in 1899 Minister of Finance S. Iu. Witte observed that some of its articles did indeed amplify the zemstvos' powers.[16] The tendency of the liberal press and zemstvo circles to interpret the statute in a positive manner rested on a plausible construction of the document.

The medical profession evaluated the new statute's impact on zemstvo medicine, noting that it shifted many health responsibilities from the district to the province zemstvos, thereby facilitating health planning, coordination, and control. Broad regional and national organization had been under discussion for many years, and health reformers had repeatedly recommended greater uniformity.[17] Enthusiasm for central control had faded, however, as the regime revealed its limited capacity to handle epidemics, deal with agricultural and industrial health problems, and address the nation's general health needs; the glaring failure of the Botkin Commission, appointed in 1886 to find measures to reduce Russia's high mortality rate, reduced most hopes for effective central leadership.[18] Consequently most physicans worked independently or under the guidance of interested professors, medical societies, the newsletter *The Physician* and other publications, and, in some zemstvo provinces, zemstvo medical councils. Health reform had progressed surprisingly well considering the obstacles and lack of coordination, but the restrictions on meetings, publications, and other cooperative work were keenly felt.[19]

The new statute promised useful changes. Medical personnel in province zemstvos gained an expanded realm of activity, including jurisdiction over factory conditions and workers' health. The zemstvos could impose obligatory regulations on local sanitary conditions and establish surveillance to prevent diseases related to industrial growth.[20] Provision for additional machinery and staff enhanced the position of physicians, and the zemstvo boards were enjoined to appoint personnel to "fulfil zemstvo obligations that demand special knowledge and preparation."[21] Whereas previously physicians had relied on interested deputies to present their reports and recommendations to the assemblies, now they could participate when those meetings considered medical matters. It is ironic that, according to one official statement, the statute had been devised to limit the influence of "the intelligentsia, eager to experiment with political theories"[22] and that an official guide asserted that after 1890 the zemstvos had become more representative of "the most intelligent class, the nobility."[23] Actually, some of the nonnoble hired experts who carried out the zemstvos' daily functions had acquired tangible gains.

Focusing on the letter of the law, the physicians had interpreted the zemstvo statute of 1890 as a means to strengthen their position with respect to the zemstvo authorities. They soon discarded this optimistic view, when

320

the government announced a hospital statute to go into effect July 1, 1895.[24] This measure threatened to drive a sizable wedge into zemstvo competence and to draw the local medical programs into a highly centralized framework. The regime's policies, instead of fortifying zemstvo physicians against their traditional adversaries, forged a bond between the two groups.

The campaign against the hospital statute

The reversal in the politics of zemstvo medicine reflected the sharp break in Russian history in the mid-1890s. The crisis of famine and cholera after 1890 exposed the gravity of Russia's backwardness, the trauma caused by rapid industrialization, and the urgent need for change.[25] The radical intelligentsia became more strongly committed to revolutionary programs, stepped up propaganda work in industrial centers, and embarked on a vital stage of the revolutionary process.[26] At the same time, the liberal movement began to coalesce, attracting local activists, the liberal press, the professions, and the "third element." The first cooperative action by the liberals, their campaign of 1894 against the proposed hospital statute, reveals the inner dynamics of the zemstvo opposition in its early stage.

The origins and leadership of the liberal opposition have not been fully explored, and some interpretations remain untested. A few participants of the Revolution of 1905 who later analyzed its course argued that the third element, especially zemstvo physicians, played a dominant role. These revolutionaries manqué were hardly free from prejudice. Writing shortly after 1905 and disappointed by deputies who had defected from their cause, they minimized the contributions of gentry activists to the opposition movement. Perceiving the third element as a substitute for the middle class – in Russia weak and disconcertingly oblivious of its historic task – they assigned the zemstvo employees a function similar to that of the Third Estate in France.[27] Interesting though this interpretation may be, it is contradicted by the facts. In the mid-1890s the deputies, not zemstvo employees, controlled the political mechanism and determined the course of the zemstvos' activities. Many physicians may have cooperated in a series of zemstvo campaigns, but theirs was a secondary and subordinate position. The campaign against the hospital statute inaugurated a decade of "uneasy alliance" between two groups of unequal powers.

The hospital statute attempted to standardize hospital care throughout Russia. Hospitals would be classified into five groups according to their size, to be determined by the number of patients; the composition of the medical staff would in turn depend upon the hospital classifica-

321

tion. This rigid structure bordered on the absurd, with the physicians' rank (8 to 5) decided not by qualifications or service but by the number of patients they supervised. Hospital management and personnel would be transferred to the Ministry of Internal Affairs, which would control hospital architecture, food supply, admissions policy, registration forms, and the employment of physicians. Applied to the zemstvo and the city hospitals, the statute deprived the local governments of administrative control but required their continued financial obligations.[28] It also mandated costly improvements for the large provincial hospitals within the zemstvos' jurisdiction, obligations which would necessarily reduce the local governments' expenditures for other aspects of their health programs.

During deliberations on the statute, legal advisors to the State Council warned that the law had serious defects and would provoke opposition:

> One should bear in mind that when the zemstvo and city governments were asked to participate in...the protection of public health, the lawmakers did not deem it useful to regulate their operations in this field... It was assumed that zemstvo and city activists, with their knowledge of local conditions...would best be able to find ways and means for the appropriate management of the hospitals. Subsequent experience entirely justified these expectations.[29]

Citing the superiority of zemstvo hospitals over others, the advisers predicted that the change would "weaken the energy of the self-governing bodies in public health work"; if relegated to being mere rubber stamps, the deputies would "undoubtedly refrain from further participation." These critics also argued that the zemstvo and city statutes of 1890 and 1892, respectively, gave the Ministry of Internal Affairs sufficient means to control hospitals within the self-governments' purview.[30]

However cogent these arguments may have been, they did not prevail because they controverted the expressed wishes of I. N. Durnovo, the minister of internal affairs from 1889 to 1895. His personal intervention had dictated that the hospital statute be extended to zemstvo hospitals,[31] and Durnovo succeeded in imposing his will. The published statute received special sanction from the tsar, whose imperial rescript rebuked the critics:

> Against the recommendations of the Combined Departments that it would be neither desirable nor necessary to subordinate the zemstvo and city hospitals to the projected supervision of the ministry of internal affairs, His Majesty declared that: "It was entirely desirable," and in regard to the changes proposed by the Department empowering the Minister with the above-mentioned supervision: "with these changes I am not in agreement, but approve that which was introduced by the Minister of Internal Affairs."[32]

Durnovo had won the first round.

The prediction that the zemstvos would object to the hospital statute proved correct. Zemstvo activists analyzed the measure with care, coordinated a campaign against it, and achieved an unusual victory that surprised and invigorated zemstvo partisans. For the medical profession that campaign had broad ramifications. Confronted with a threatening innovation, the profession recognized its inability to resist the change by isolated efforts such as personal contacts with medical professors and administrators or pressure exerted by medical societies and the medical press. In the course of the campaign, and especially with its successful outcome, the profession discovered many sympathetic and effective allies in the zemstvo institutions.

The first evidence of local resistance (subterfuge may be a more accurate term) occurred in March 1894, when several zemstvos altered architectural plans for some hospitals in order to reduce their accommodations to under 60 beds. They calculated that thus reclassified these hospitals would be beyond the purview of the reorganized hospital administration,[33] but this maneuver failed. In July, Durnovo directed the governors to "begin without delay" to implement the changes specified in the hospital statute.[34] Zemstvo activists perceived this as a direct and blatant attempt by the government to control zemstvo medicine and, more important, an indirect challenge to the principles of local self-government.

In marked contrast to the rather tepid initial reaction to the 1890 zemstvo statute, stiff resistance arose quickly. *Vestnik Evropy* considered the hospital statute a much greater threat to the zemstvos:

> The Zemstvo Statute of 1890 materially changed the composition of the zemstvo assembly, limited its independence, and incorporated the zemstvo boards into the local administrative offices, but left inviolable – at least in broad outlines – *the zemstvos' sphere of activity*. One ventured to think that the zemstvos retained the ability to continue as before, meeting obstacles and difficulties more often but not parting from the tasks entrusted to them in 1864.

The hospital statute, on the other hand, had changed what "one ventured to think" about the future role of the zemstvos; one of "an entire series of measures recently instituted or projected that significantly narrow zemstvo competence...[it] bureaucratizes zemstvo and city hospitals and subordinates them to the province administration under the supervision of the Ministry of the Interior."[35] When *Moskovskie vedomosti*, the conservative supporter of the imperial government, welcomed the statute as the "subordination of zemstvo medicine to the government,"[36] it proclaimed official intentions of a direct assault on the zemstvos.

323

The question of the zemstvos' competence to administer medical programs became a sensitive issue and important rallying point. Zemstvo medicine received more funds than any other zemstvo function (32.8 to 42 percent of provincial zemstvo budgets). It was extolled as "the pride and glory of the zemstvos, Russia's unique contribution to public health, developed without previous example in the West and adapted especially to Russian needs," whereas the hospital statute would replace this dynamic program with discredited, ineffectual, and "rigid bureaucratic controls."[37]

Physicians had their specific objections. Despite the numerous drawbacks of zemstvo medicine, it was their model program of health care and a focus of medical professionalization. The new statute threatened to destroy that program and reinstate undesirable methods of centralized medical work. The medical press focused on the projected renovation of the large province hospitals; their fate could determine that of zemstvo medicine. Inherited by the zemstvos from the prereform system and vestiges of a period when the peasantry looked upon hospitals as jails and death traps to be avoided at all costs, the province hospitals symbolized the inferior medical care considered characteristic of the central administration. To overcome the fear engendered by these institutions, the zemstvos had instituted separate, decentralized programs, and zemstvo physicans served the populace through small outpatient clinics and infirmaries with only a few beds. Sixty percent of zemstvo physicians lived in rural areas and only 12 percent in the province capitals, the usual site of province hospitals.[38] Their willingness to carry medical care to the "remote corners" of Russia became a major attribute of the program and a source of pride for the profession. The recent cholera epidemics had demonostrated conclusively that rural Russia needed these small local clinics with permanent medical personnel whom the peasantry would trust, as opposed to large, forbidding, and inaccessible hospitals.

Currently the province hospitals impeded zemstvo medicine by draining funds that the zemstvos preferred to spend on rural services. In the province of Nizhnii Novgorod, 20 percent of zemstvo expenditures financed the province hospital, which served a predominantly urban population. The zemstvos regarded the rural areas as their legitimate concern and argued that their support of province hospitals permitted city governments to evade medical responsibilities. Province hospitals were "only a burden for the zemstvos" and should have "no role in the future of zemstvo medicine,"[39] but the hospital statute strengthened these hospitals and would absorb most zemstvo funds earmarked for rural health care.

Physicians had limited means to oppose the statute. One physician urged his colleagues to encourage the local zemstvos to take a stand, as he had, at a meeting of zemstvo physicians and the zemstvo board, where he convinced the deputies to introduce a petition against the statute to the zemstvo assembly. Because the issue was "basic to zemstvo medicine" and "significant to all zemstvo physicians," he "hoped to hear other voices" join in an effort to rescind the law.[40] Zemstvo physicians, lacking real influence over zemstov activites, could give advice and exert some pressure. But the deputies, among whom physicians were rarely numbered, held the reins of power and coordinated the campaign.

Following the prescribed form of political action, district zemstvo assemblies sent petitions to province assemblies, which in turn petitioned the Ministry of Internal Affairs to delay, change or rescind the hospital statute. The widely read medical newsletter *The Physician* gave prominent space to the campaign and, in late December 1894, published two lengthy articles urging all physicians to support the zemstvos' agitation. The author, D. N. Zhbankov, a prominent member of the Pirogov Society and head of the medical-statistical bureau of the Smolensk province zemstvo, reviewed the debate. He tersely brushed aside as legal hairsplitting current arguments that the statute could be interpreted as inapplicable to zemstvo medicine:

> The juridical side of this affair, the interpretation, is of limited importance. It is not necessary for zemstvo physicans to become lawyers and get lost in interpretation. What is important is the essence... The essence of the misunderstanding is that the new statute introduces difficulties for the successful development of zemstvo medicine. Rather than consider the theoretical difficulties, I will explain...the simple practical considerations.[41]

The most serious defect, according to the Smolensk petition, was that the anticipated changes would alter the character of zemstvo medical work:

> The problem is that each zemstvo physican who administers a hospital has many other important obligations in addition to treating inpatients: epidemic controls, vaccination, home visits to the seriously ill, inspection of schools and examination of school children; in a word, the hospital physician of a given district is responsible for the public health of the entire district. The new statute pertains only to the hospital, chains the physician to it, and does not mention his other activities... It will squeeze zemstvo medicine into narrow confines and hinder its further development.[42]

By the end of 1894 zemstvos throughout Russia had voted unanimously to petition against the hospital statute[43] because "its introduction would destroy the entire zemstvo medical structure. Zemstvo medicine is new and dynamic work, developed on the basis of decentralization; placing it in a narrow framework and introducing formalism would undoubtedly retard the correct development of medical care for the populace." And, Zhbankov added, "If all these petitions are rejected and the new statute is introduced...there will be great difficulty for the zemstvos and the administration."[44]

After years of dissension between zemstvo physicians and their employers, the medical profession could be deeply gratified by the tenor of these petitions. The Kostroma zemstvo acknowledged the physicians' vital role: "Popular medicine, created entirely by the zemstvo, established hospitals and clinics in the remote districts... zemstvo medical personnel have sacrificed their work, time and knowledge – and zemstvo medicine has gained the trust of the *narod*." The current organization had distinct advantages over the projected change:

> The zemstvo physician is head of the entire medical district with the hospital at the center and the *feldsher* stations at various points. The new statute recognizes only the hospitals, as if isolated from the area where they are located and for which they exist. A hospital with more than 16 beds would bind the physician to it, and the zemstvo would not have his services as a district physician...The statute concentrates all attention on the hospitals and leaves to arbitrary fate the medical care of the entire peasant population of the district.

The statute would debase the role of the physician who "would have to present reports on the hospital's medical...and financial administration. In this manner the physican would be converted into an accountant and bureaucratic official with no time to devote to medicine."[45] A deputy in Samara province drew the same conclusion: the statute would convert zemstvo physicans into *chinovniki* and "the serious work of public health, which should be in the hands of society itself...would revert to outdated methods of the Bureau of Public Welfare."[46] These petitions expressed a good measure of confidence in zemstvo physicians and their medical goals.

The hospital statute clarified the government's position on the question of autonomy – that of the zemstvos and the medical profession. The optimistic interpretation of the Zemstvo Statute of 1890 as a means for physicians to improve their role turned out to be faulty. Several articles of that statute did indeed grant medical experts a wider range of functions, but the medical profession and liberal commentators had not detected that the statute's overall thrust was to draw the zemstvos and their employees into the bureaucratic orbit. The further development of zemstvo medicine and perhaps the viability of the local self-governments depended upon the outcome of the campaign.

The opposition mobilized during a sensitive period. Alexander III (1881–94) died in October 1894, and on January 17, 1895, Nicholas II (1894–1917) antagonized zemstvo liberals with his declaration that any hopes for the introduction of constitutional rights were but "senseless dreams." The outcome of the campaign against the hospital statute is all the more unusual in the light of these better-known developments. At the end of 1894 the minister of internal affairs received a flood of petitions from the zemstvo and city governments and also several delegations of deputies who argued against the statute.[47] The Moscow province zemstvo, by virtue of its position of leadership in zemstvo medicine, spearheaded the campaign. F. F. Erisman, professor of public health at Moscow University and for many years a leader of Moscow zemstvo medicine, convinced the province medical council that the statute could be interpreted as inapplicable to zemstvo hospitals. On the council's advice, the Moscow zemstvo requested an administrative review of its contention that the statute violated past laws and practices and should be rescinded. The press carefully followed the legalistic sparring, for the outcome could decide the issue for all zemstvo provinces. On January 15, 1895, *Russkie vedomosti* reported that the administration had indeed concurred with Erisman's construction of the statute,[48] and within a few months the provincial governors received notice that the implementation of the hospital statute had been "postponed for an indefinite time."[49]

The liberal press hailed the "postponement" as the validation of zemstvo prerogatives. Journalists argued that the effective use of the "right of petition regarding local needs and welfare" to defeat the statute had demonstrated that the local self-governments possessed basic, incontrovertible powers.[50] They greatly inflated the zemstvos' power of petition and underestimated the strength of the minister of internal affairs. Forced to delay the introduction of the hospital statute, the minister also appeared to have limited control over its revision:

> He could not determine how the highest government institutions would respond to zemstvo petitions for changes of specific articles or for the review of the entire statute, or for the remote date to be fixed for its implementation. All petitions, though presented by the governors to the minister of internal affairs, may not be declined except by the command of the Committee of Ministers.[51]

Perhaps the initial elation reflected zemstvo partisans' belief that they had effectively reversed a new general policy. They now realized that changes embodied in the counterreforms and typified by the hospital statute profoundly altered the local governments; but the postponement of the statute raised hopes that these changes might be delayed,

327

mitigated, or even reversed.[52] Actually the victory was but a temporary triumph, a solitary achievement to be followed by a steady stream of defeats. The episode became memorable precisely because it was unique, one instance of concerted action among the zemstvos that had produced positive results.

The uneasy alliance

The significance of the campaign against the hospital statute does not lie in any long-range constitutional advance but in its immediate impact. Occurring when the zemstvo movement first gained momentum, the positive results certainly encouraged zemstvo partisans. "In its time this victory created a strong impression," wrote one zemstvo activist. "It was remarkable that all the province zemstvos passed similar petitions on this question. Within six months the hospital statute had been postponed for an indefinite time. This was the sole occasion that the minister [of internal affairs] was forced to yield and to give up his position in his actions against the zemstvos."[53] The campaign may have influenced the central administration; according to Witte it had a chastening effect and convinced the Ministry of Internal Affairs to be more cautious in controverting "established practice and habit."[54] At the same time, the achievement of compelling the imperial government to make a hasty retreat emboldened zemstvo activists and encouraged them to use similar tactics in the future.

As a case study of the emerging zemstvo opposition, the campaign illuminates that political process. The zemstvo physicians and their employers, although joined in pursuit of shared immediate goals, had different long-range objectives. The deputies interpreted the hospital statute as a direct challenge to their political rights. In this and later confrontations with the central government, they argued for the preservation of the original zemstvo statute and for further constitutional development. Their focus on overarching political goals may have blurred the area of disagreement that separated them from the physicians. The deputies' primary purpose was to maintain their jurisdiction over local functions, including public health, whereas the physicians continued to seek greater authority in the medical programs. The two groups might join forces against the central government, but they would clash eventually on the issue that had long divided them – zemstvo medicine.

The physicians had made an unusual political choice, considering the history of their acrimonious relations with the zemstvo authorities. With a critical need for allies, they forged the coalition in the hopes

328

that the local governments could provide a shelter for their model health programs. The alliance seemed to be a viable political strategy and was renewed whenever rumors spread that the hospital statute – which had merely been "postponed" – might be resurrected.[55] Still, it could not be an equal partnership. Contrary to the interpretation that the third element acted as prime movers of the zemstvo opposition, in this and subsequent campaigns the deputies controlled the political process and pulled the physicians into the fray; followers, not leaders, the physicians lent assistance to attain immediate political goals.

The Sixth Congress of the Pirogov Society in Kiev, April 1896, sealed the alliance. Some participants recalled the recent battle over the hospital statute and mustered arguments to convince their colleagues that they must defend zemstvo medicine and the local governments. One resolution emphasized the positive role of deputies as well as of physicians: "The correct and progressive advancement of rural medicine is possible only with the direct participation of the physicians and the local population. The absence of local community power is the primary reason for the weak development and defects of rural medicine in the nonzemstvo provinces."[56] The support for the local institutions fostered a negative attitude toward central controls. When the congress reconsidered an old proposal for a Ministry of Health, Professor Erisman expressed the growing antipathy toward the regime:

> Yesterday we reached the unanimous conclusion that the weak side of rural medicine in nonzemstvo provinces consists for the most part in the lack of community participation, and the fact that the administration...does not possess the necessary familiarity with local conditions. But this proposal consists in establishing new administrative echelons without incorporating the local community. Of course, public health in Russia is not brilliant. All the same, it is undoubtedly advancing, and it would be quite unfortunate to remove it from the self-governments and to transfer it to the administration.

A Ministry of Health, Erisman concluded, would be as counterproductive as the hospital statute, "inconvenient and not in accord with the normal development of public health work in Russia."[57]

After the Sixth Pirogov Congress, many physicians actively supported the zemstvo opposition in a series of campaigns. The pattern of cooperation set during the campaign against the hospital statute continued to the eve of 1905. In each political undertaking the physicians addressed the issues in a distinctive manner; and, in the political action that centered in the zemstvos, the deputies continued as the natural leaders, with the physicians cast in a subsidiary role.

A group of zemstvo constitutionalists resolved that the next major cooperative effort would be a campaign to abolish corporal punishment.[58] Many liberals deplored the persistence of this legal penalty for some segments of the population and on both legal and cultural grounds sought to change the law. As experts on the physical and psychological impact of corporal punishment, individual physicians, medical societies, professors of medicine, and zemstvo medical councils all contributed to the spate of literature on the subject. The sharp emotional tone of the medical arguments reveals how professional and personal concerns shaped the physicians' point of view. They spoke with the tone of the expert on the damages of corporal punishment. The deputies might argue fine legal points such as the allocation of powers (which became germane to this dispute), but the legalities were open to dispute and the central authorities could claim the final word. The realm of science had different imperatives. Regarding their evidence as incontrovertible, physicians believed that their advice should influence relevant areas of public policy. They should be heeded as well as heard.

Sometimes the physicans capitalized on their humble origins to claim a special understanding of the common folk. In a related campaign to end the use of the familiar form of address for patients, one physician argued:

> Many of us have come from the narod: there are among us even those whose fathers perished under the yoke of serfdom. How can we encroach upon the honor and good name of simple people in general and the peasants in particular..."tykan'e" [addressing as thou], like corporal punishment, is a remnant of serfdom... Let it be understood that to the sick the doctor should not be nor seem to be a baron or a bureaucrat.[59]

Their legal arguments differed also. Physicians serving in the military, prisons, and other governmental posts could be required to "officiate" at corporal punishments. The physician might be asked to decide the safe number of lashes, to observe the proceedings in order to stop them when the victim's life became endangered, and then to treat the victim afterwards.[60] Such participation, making them accomplices to cruel and unjust treatment, conflicted with their medical oath. Throughout the campaign against corporal punishment the tenor of physicians' arguments indicated their personal involvement and distinguished them from other activists.

In other zemstvo campaigns to oppose limitations on famine relief and on taxation, the physicians and deputies again shared political goals but had distinct positions. On the question of famine relief the deputies asserted jurisdictional rights; physicians contended that their specialized knowledge of the peasantry and the relationship of famine to disease entitled them to an authoritative role. When in 1900 the Ministry of Internal Affairs barred the Pirogov Society from an active role in famine relief, some members responded with great anger: the policy challenged their ability as experts and also insulted their honor as citizens.[61] Both groups opposed limitations on taxation imposed in 1900, but physicians focused on the consequences for public health, and one even predicted that it spelled the "end of the growth of zemstvo medicine."[62] More than matters of degree, these examples suggest fundamental differences.

The cooperation forged to achieve mutual political goals could not mask the underlying tensions born of a long history of strife. Fissures in the alliance widened after 1902, when some deputies began to withdraw support for medical goals, while the zemstvo physicians became more strident in their opposition. The central government contributed to the split. The Ministry of Internal Affairs announced an impending reorganization of the medical-sanitary structure of the empire and set in motion activities toward that end.[63] N. A. Zinovev, the assistant minister, made a series of investigations of zemstvo governance and found much to fault in the area of public health. He insisted that zemstvo physicians had usurped functions and undermined the powers of elected officials, that through the provincial medical councils they had expanded their competence and now controlled most medical policy and programs. Disregarding the fact that these councils developed under provisions of the 1890 zemstvo statute, he castigated the provincial zemstvos for fostering the imbalance between district and provincial institutions.[64] His critique expressed dissatisfactions of several groups: district deputies who objected to their loss of power; the conservatives in the zemstvo movement who wished to preserve their own rights but opposed the extension of those rights to the third element; and some who were receptive to Zinovev's patronizing comments about the medical employees who must be kept in their proper place. Now alerted to these new "pretensions" and jealous of their own political power, some deputies became less inclined to support physicians' claims for expanded rights and functions.

The liberal wing of the opposition movement continued to work with medical activists and especially the Pirogov Society, although the area of agreement shrank. The Ninth Pirogov Congress of January 1904 passed resolutions that resembled those of other liberal groups and also some that reflected professional needs. Employment insecurity, an ever present problem for physicians, had become acute with a wave of political reprisals against a few activists and stern restrictions on all medical hiring. The Congress passed a resolution aimed at job security that by implication censured those zemstvos that cooperated with the regime's repressive policies. On the issue of future electoral policy, the physicians generally preferred universal suffrage, but a deputy who addressed one of the Pirogov sessions, although he expatiated on the noble deeds of zemstvo physicans, proposed voting restrictions that would have disqualified many of his listeners. Other sessions devoted to the nation's socioeconomic problems showed that the physicians' welfare goals far outstripped those of the average zemstvo activist.[65]

The alliance began to disintegrate during 1904. A vituperative attack on zemstvo physicians ended the moratorium on the rancorous politics of zemstvo medicine. Writing in a medical journal and signing himself merely as a "zemstvo deputy" (zemets), the author upbraided the current generation of zemstvo physicans for failing to continue the humanitarian tradition of their predecessors.[66] He rekindled old resentments and triggered a furious counterattack. Physicians interpreted the criticism as characteristic of the deputies' disdain for them and as a threat to force them back into a subordinate position. Moreover, the charge assaulted the keystone of the profession's public image – the idealized zemstvo physican whose medical abilities, humanitarian qualities, and personal sacrifices were now claimed to be representative of all Russian physicians. During the campaign against the hospital statute in the 1890s, the deputies had graciously acknowledged these fine qualities, but now some supported the charges levelled against their medical employees. What had changed? The cooperation undertaken to oppose the central government was weakened by a countervailing force: the reappearance of the power struggle over zemstvo medicine.

The end of the alliance and its legacy

As the nation moved toward revolution the alliance faltered. Physicians and their zemstvo allies disagreed on the correct policy to adopt toward new "cholera regulations" issued by the central government. The Pirogov Society called a special "cholera congress" in March 1905, which declared the innovations administratively unsound, contrary to precedent, and potentially dangerous for medical personnel. The dominant objection was that the proposed mechanism of control might inflame popular discontent and provoke disorders as serious as those of 1892. At first some zemstvos supported the physicians, but gradually they turned against them, accusing them of improper interference in local politics and dereliction of duty in a time of crisis. The physicians urged the zemstvos to support their cause, arguing that the new administrative controls undercut the authority of the zemstvos in addition to placing medical personnel in a vulnerable position. When a cholera epidemic did not materialize in the summer of 1905, the physicians lost a very potent ally; at the same time the zemstvo opposition began to splinter as some liberals retreated to less advanced positions. Many zemstvos rejected the demands of the physicians, who countered with a series of boycotts and mass resignations.[67]

The split in the uneasy alliance became irreparable at the end of 1905. Some community physicians, increasingly alienated from the deputies with whom they had tried to cooperate, sought instead a political base among the workers and peasants. Utilizing the professional positions that placed them in close contact with these groups, they lectured and distributed pamphlets to encourage political action.[68] No matter that only several hundred or at most a thousand activist physicians became enmeshed in this agitation; their record cast suspicion over most of the profession. Especially when social revolution erupted in the countryside, accusations of fostering popular discontent were leveled at physicians. To the central authorities and also to many deputies, these activities smacked of treason and were treated accordingly: 1,324 physicans experienced some form of repression and were listed in the "martyrology" of the Pirogov Society.[69]

The period of attempted cooperation in zemstvo politics thus ended tragically for some physicians and posed a warning to the rest. Many who supported the zemstvos as administrators of an exceptional medical program had joined the opposition movement to defend these institutions and – they assumed – zemstvo medicine. With what in restrospect may be judged as political naiveté, they expected their zemstvo allies to place general political goals over personal imperatives. But many deputies, for all their seeming commitment to constitutional principles, shifted political gears; property holders with vested interests in the zemstvos as institutions to serve their own class needs, they lent their weight to the political reaction that swept through rural Russia after 1905. In a fierce backlash against their erstwhile colleagues in the opposition movement, the deputies singled out the medical programs for major cutbacks, dismissed many physicians, and disbanded the medical councils that directed the most progressive programs. In some provinces the tensions reached proportions that precluded future cooperation of the sort that had existed before 1905.[70]

333

The politics of zemstvo medicine reverted to the traditional, antagonistic pattern. Once more physicians supported zemstvo medicine but harbored deep distrust of the deputies and endeavored to increase their own political leverage. They made some progress. The repression of zemstvo medicine could not be permanent because of the nation's pressing health needs; cholera, that prime catalyst of public health activity, compelled the zemstvos to reinstate medical programs and personnel, and by 1910 the system had been rejuvenated.[71] Still, the deputies retained political control, and the physicians continued to demand more influence in their area of expertise. These conflicts persisted in the period of war and revolution, as William Gleason and William Rosenberg have shown in Chapters 11 and 12.

When the zemstvo institutions disintegrated in 1917, their medical employees continued to function and eventually adjusted to a changed medical administration. Some accommodations had to be made. The new government gave assurances that in the future medical experts, not bureaucrats, would be in charge of public health; and Bolshevik leaders who had been zemstvo physicians convinced many of their medical colleagues that their traditional objectives would be realized.[72] The readjustment of past accomplishments to the new needs included some linguistic gymnastics. Z. P. Solovev, a veteran of zemstvo medicine and evidently learned in the language of its politics, gave a new twist to an old phrase. "The building of zemstvo medicine," he wrote in 1914, "reflects the energy of its founders – the zemstvo medical workers – but stands unfinished and awaits a proper host, who will cover it in the appropriate fashion."[73] As an organizer of Soviet health care, Solovev believed he had constructed an appropriate "roof" for the unfinished edifice.

Notes

1   See Nancy M. Frieden, *Russian Physicians in an Era of Reform and Revolution, 1856–1905* (Princeton, 1981), ch. 4, "Zemstvo Medicine: The Formative Years," for a full treatment of this attitude.

2   A. P. Zhuk, *Razvitie obshchestvenno-meditsinskoi mysli v Rossii v 60–70-kh godakh XIX veka* (Moscow, 1963), pp. 142–3.

3   Peter F. Krug, "The Debate over the Delivery of Health Care in Rural Russia: The Moscow Zemstvo, 1864–1878," *Bulletin of the History of Medicine*, Summer 1976, pp. 226–41, and "Doctors and the Administration of Russian Zemstvo Medicine: The Province of Moscow, 1864–1885" (M.A. thesis, University of Wisconsin, 1974); V. V. Khizhniakov, *Polozhenie rabochikh v sel'sko khoziaistve v sanitarnom otnoshenii* (Kherson, 1899).

4 For the origins and early development of zemstvo medicine, see Nancy M. Frieden, "The Roots of Zemstvo Medicine," *Actes du Congrès*, I: *Colloque* (Proceedings of the 25th International Congress of the History of Medicine, Quebec, 1976), and *Russian Physicians*, ch. 3, "The Great Reforms and New Roles for Physicians," and passim.

5 D. N. Zhbankov, "Itogi zemskoi meditsiny," *Vrach*, 1894, no. 19, pp. 546–51, gives the pattern of zemstvo medical employment; *Russkaia mysl'* 1890, no. 9, p. 435, cites the example of Kherson province, 1865–90, where out of 37 zemstvo physicians only 1 served over 12 years and over half worked there less than 4. For Filatov's career, see *Liudi russkoi nauki*, vol. 3: *Biologiia, meditsina, sel'skokhoziaistvennye nauki*, ed. I. V. Kuznetsov (Moscow, 1963), pp. 565–8; and *Russkii vrach*, 1902, no. 11, p. 444. Emergency medical service is covered in Nancy M. Frieden, "The Russian Cholera Epidemic, 1892–93, and Medical Professionalization," *Journal of Social History*, Summer 1977, pp. 538–59; and E. B. Meve, *Meditsina v. tvorchestve i zhizni A. P. Chekhova* (Kiev, 1961), pp. 185–207. On the postgraduate training, see I. I. Orlov, "O vzaimnykh otnosheniiakh mezhdu universitetskimi klinikami i zemskimi lechebnitsami," *Vos'moi pirogovskoi s"ezd (Moskva, 3–10 ianvaria, 1902)*, 2 vols. (Moscow, 1903), 2:92–6.

6 Frieden, *Russian Physicians*, ch. 5, "Medical Professionalization in Russia."

7 Ibid.

8 The mortality figures are in V. I. Grebenshchikov, "Material'naia obezpechennost' i smertnost' sredi russkikh vrachei za gody s 1890 po 1902," *Trudy deviatogo s"ezda obshchestva russkikh vrachei v pamiat' N. I. Pirogova*, 6 vols. (St. Petersburg, 1904), 5:238–54. Regarding the conflicts, see, for example, S. N. Korzhenevskii, *Zemskaia meditsina v Tverskoi gubernii* (Tver, 1903), pp. 73–4; *Vrach*, 1895, no. 5, pp. 130–3; and a zemstvo physician's letter describing his unbearable conditions: TsGIA, 1297 (Meditsinskii departament MVD), op. 243, d. 7.

9 *Polnoe sobranie zakonov Rossiiskoi imperii (PSZRI)*, 2nd series, vol. 54, no. 59399 (March 9, 1879), and no. 60109 (October 24, 1879). For official correspondence leading to the expansion of the zemstvos' responsibility during epidemics, see TsGIA, f. 1297, op. 87, d. 173 "Ob uiasnenii obiazannostei zemstva...v otnoshenii predotvrashcheniia...zarazitel'nykh boleznei," July 30, 1871–7 April 1878. According to the *Journal of the Committee of Ministers*, improvements by eight zemstvos in mental institutions convinced the committee to shift more responsibility to the zemstvos in this field: TsGIA, f. 1263 (Komitet ministrov), op. 1, 1879 g., d. 4048, pp. 191–214 ob. For welfare policy and changes in welfare programs after the great reforms, see Adele Lindenmeyr, "Public Poor Relief and Private Charity in Late Imperial Russia" (Ph.D. dissertation, Princeton University, 1980), chs. 1–2.

10 S. Frederick Starr, *Decentralization and Self-Government in Russia, 1830–1870* (Princeton, 1972), pp. x–xi, 289–90, 299–336. The three "counterreforms" are *PSZRI*, 3d series, vol. 9, no. 6196 (July 12, 1889); vol. 10, no. 6927 (June 12, 1890), the zemstvo statute; and vol. 12, no. 8708 (June 11, 1892), the city statute. These measures are discussed in P. A. Zaionchkovskii, *Rossiiskoe samoderzhavie v kontse XIX stoletiia* (Moscow, 1970), pp. 355–428; and L. G. Zakharova, *Zemskaia kontrreforma, 1890 g.* (Moscow, 1968).

11 *Obshchestvo russkikh vrachei v pamiat' N. I. Pirogova, Zemskomeditsinskii sbornik* (Moscow, 1890–6), a seven-volume compendium of the first 25 years of zemstvo medicine, displays this disparity.

12 Zaionchkovskii, pp. 366–401; N. P. Eroshkin, *Istoriia gosudarstvennykh uchrezhdenii dorevoliutsionnoi Rossii* (Moscow, 1960), pp. 237–9; *PSZRI*, 3d series, vol. 10, section 2, 1890, supplement, p. 399, gives the following ranks on province zemstvo boards – chairman, 5; member, 6; on district zemstvo boards – chairman, 6, member, 7. N. M. Korkunov, *Russkoe gosudarstvennoe pravo*, 2d ed. 2 vols. (St. Petersburg, 1897), 2:392–6. The new executive organ was the Gubernskoe po zemskim delam prisutstvie.

13 *Russkie vedomosti*, 1890, no. 181, quoted in Zakharova, p. 160; L. G. Mamulova, "Zemskii vopros v russkoi periodicheskoi pechati epokhi kontrreform," *Vestnik Moskovskogo universiteta, Seriia IX: Istoriia*, 1966, no. 2, pp. 57–68. B. B.Veselovskii, *Istoriia zemstva za sorok let*, 4 vols. (St. Petersburg, 1909–11), 2: 140, states that the "zemstvos hardly noticed the new law" of 1890.

14 *PSZRI*, 3d series, vol. 10, no. 6927 (June 12, 1890), art. 87–94.

15 Zaionchkovskii, pp. 401–11.

16 Korkunov, 2: 395, 438–9; S. Iu. Witte, *Samoderzhavie i zemstvo: Konfidentsial'naia zapiska Ministra Finansov Stats-Sekretaria S. Iu. Witte (1899g.)*, 2d ed. (Stuttgart, 1903), p. 143.

17 *PSZRI*, 3d series, vol. 10, no. 6927 (June 12, 1890), article 80–94, 108. *Obshchestvo russkikh vrachei v pamiat' N. I. Pirogova, Trudy vtorogo s"ezda* (Moscow, 1887), pp. 6–13, discusses the previous lack of province-level direction in zemstvo medicine. For the impact of the Zemstvo Statute of 1890 on zemstvo medicine, see N. G. Freiberg, *Vrachebno-sanitarnoe zakonodatel'stvo v Rossii* (St. Petersburg, 1910), pp. 61–3.

18 The Ministry of Internal Affairs appointed the Botkin Commission in response to a report on Russia's high mortality rates, delivered by N. V. Ekk to an International Sanitary Conference in Rome, 1885; Ekk later published his findings: *Opyt' obrabotki statisticheskikh dannykh o smertnosti v Rossii* (St. Petersburg, 1888). For the dismal record and criticism of the commission, see E. A. Osipov et al., *Russkaia zemskaia meditsina* (Moscow, 1899), p. 35; V. Portugalov, "Sanitarnaia polemika," *Zemskii vrach*, 1888, no. 6, pp. 92–4; no. 7, pp. 101–9.

19 The Pirogov Society communicated its resolutions on community medicine to local medical societies and zemstvo and city governments. *The Physician (Vrach)*, a forum for cooperative efforts, published reports of meetings, proposals for change, and analyses of public health advances. For the restrictions, see Osipov et al., p. 167; and V. Ia. Skalon, "Zemstvo i narodnoe zdravie," *Russkaia mysl'*, 1883, no. 5 pp. 58–92.

20 *PSZRI*, 3d series, vol. 10, no. 6927 (June 12, 1890), article 108, paras. 6, 12. Osipov et al., p. 292, n. 1, describes how the Moscow province zemstvo instituted sanitary regulations under this article.

21 *PSZRI*, 3d series, vol. 10, no. 6927 (June 12, 1890), articles 73, 105. Some commentators on the 1890 zemstvo statute, because they assumed it to be an impediment to local action, have puzzled over the fact that "despite the various governmental restrictions, the 1890s witnessed a sharp rise in the economic and welfare activities of the zemstvos" (Shmuel Galai, *The Liberation Movement in Russia, 1900– 1905* [Cambridge, 1973], p. 31). Actually the rapid growth arose logically out of the considerable powers granted to the province zemstvos.

22 A. D. Pazukhin, *Sovremennoe sostoianie Rossii i soslovnyi vopros* (Moscow, 1886), p. 59.

23 Chancery of the Committee of Ministers, ed., *The Statesman's Handbook for Russia* (Paris, 1896), p. 328.

24 "Ustav lechebnykh zavedenii vedomstva Ministerstva vnutrennykh del," *Sobranie uzakonenii i rasporiazhenii pravitel'stva 1893 goda*, no. 99 (St. Petersburg, 1894), pp. 2206–22. Brief notice of the statute appeared in *PSZRI*, 3d series, vol. 13, no. 9787 (June 10, 1893). Extensive discussions by nonmedical officials in the State Council preceding the promulgation of the statute indicate the limited influence of medical doctors on the policy: TsGIA, f. 1149 (Department zakonov gosudarstvennogo soveta), op. 11, 1893 g., d. 43, pp. 798–861, 930–70. For the opinion of the director of the medical department of the MVD, see ibid., pp. 1–59, 861–7, 934 ob.–45.

25 Richard G. Robbins, Jr., *Famine in Russia, 1891–92* (New York, 1975); Frieden, "The Russian Cholera Epidemic." For contemporary medical views on the relationship between modernization and disease, see D. N. Nikol'skii, "O tife v niazepetrovskom zavode v 1882–83 gg.," *Meditsinskii vestnik*, 1884, no. 40, pp. 652–3; D. N. Zhbankov, "Neskol'ko zametok o kholere," *Vrach*, 1893, no. 50, pp. 1377–82 (on improved communications as a major cause of the rapid spread of cholera); and A. V. Smirnov, "Kholera v Vladimirskoi gubernii v 1892 g.," *Zemskii vrach*, 1893, no. 13, pp. 313–16.

26 Alan K. Wildman, *The Making of a Workers' Revolution: Russian Social Democracy, 1891–1902* (Chicago, 1967); Leopold H. Haimson, *The Russian Marxists and the Origins of Bolshevism* (Boston, 1955).

27 Cherevanin [F. A. Lipkin], "Dvizhenie intelligentsia," in L. Martov, et al., eds., *Obshchestvennoe dvizhenie v Rossii v nachale XX-ogo veka*, 4 vols. (St. Petersburg, 1909–14), 1:259–90; 2 (pt. 2):146–202; L. D.

Briukhatov, "Znachenie 'tret'ego elementa' v zhizni zemstva," in B. B. Veselovskii and Z. G. Frenkel', eds., *Iubileinyi zemskii sbornik (1864–1914)* (St. Petersburg, 1914), pp. 186–205. This interpretation is repeated in George Fischer, *Russian Liberalism, from Gentry to Intelligentsia* (Cambridge, Mass., 1958), pp. 49, 121; and Galai, pp. 31–2.

28 "Ustav lechebnykh zavedenii," p. 2222, defined the system:

Classification	Number of beds	Physicians' ranks
1	Over 300	8–5
2	101–300	8–6
3	61–100	8–7
4	16–60	8
5	5–15	8

The statute mandated the qualifications of head physicians (art. 18) and the number of hospital employees (art. 26), and required the chief physician to be hired and dismissed by the MVD and the other physicians to be approved by the governor or city prefect (arts. 63,65). Articles 57 to 70 applied the statute to hospitals within the purview of the zemstvo and city governments, whose competence in this area had been defined by article 85 of the Zemstvo Statute of 1890 and article 81 of the City Statute of 1892 *PSZRI*, 3d series, vol. 10, nos. 6927 (June 12, 1890), 8708 (June 11, 1982).

29 "Po proektu novogo ustava o lechebnykh zavedeniiakh grazhdanskogo vedomstva," *Otchet po deloproizvodstvu Gosudarstvennogo soveta (za vremia s 1 ianvaria 1892 g. po 31 maia 1893 g.)* (St. Petersburg, 1893), 1: 557; the partial transcript is ibid., pp. 542–88. "Legal advisors" refers to the *Soedinennye departamenty zakonov, ekonomikh i grazhdanskikh;* their discussions, February 13, April 3, 10, 14, 1893, and the debate in the State Council, May 24, 1893, are in TsGIA, f. 1149, op. II, 1893 g., d. 43, pp. 930–90, 1077–83.

30 "Po proektu novogo ustava," pp. 558–9; the critics also predicted that the statute would impose financial strain on the local institutions (ibid., pp. 563–5). One critic asserted that the statute did not accomplish its aim of unifying hospital administration nor adequately differentiate between public and private hospitals and claimed that the statute had been designed before publication of the zemstvo and city statutes of 1890 and 1892, and therefore was not adapted to current practice in the local self-governments: TsGIA, f. 1149, op. 11, 1893 g., d. 43, pp. 961 ob.–5, 970.

31 "Po proektu novogo ustava," p. 555. TsGIA, f. 1149, op. 11, 1893 g., d. 43, pp. 863–7 ob., 944–6. I. N. Durnovo served as chairman of the Committee of Ministers from 1895 to 1903.

32 TsGIA, f. 1149, op. 11, 1893 g., d. 43, pp. 1083 and ob.; "Po proektu novogo ustava," p. 588.

33 *Vrach*, 1894, no. 14, p. 426, carried the following items on the reduction of the number of beds in zemstvo hospitals: in Kherson, from 100 to 55; in Vologda, from 90 to 60; in Voronezh, the zemstvo board asked the assembly to decide the correct number of beds that would permit the hospitals to remain under zemstvo control. Art. 14 of the hospital statute seemed to provide the loophole.

34 *Vrach*, 1894, no. 28, p. 808.

35 "Vnutrennee obozrenie," *Vestnik Evropy*, 1894, no. 6, pp. 390–1 (emphasis in original).

36 Ibid., p. 393, citing *Moskovskie vedomosti*, 1894, no. 279.

37 *Vestnik Evropy*, 1894, no. 6, pp. 391–2, quoting *Entsiklopedicheskii slovar'* (Brokgauz-Efron), s.v. "Zemskaia meditsina," vol. 12A (1894), pp. 482–91; Veselovskii, 1:260–2, analyzes the allocation of funds. For a summary of the arguments by a zemets, see D. V. Drutskoi-Sokol'nitskii (kn.), "Zemstvo po polozheniiu o zemskikh uchrezhdeniiakh 12 iiunia 1890," *Vestnik Evropy*, 1895, no. 3, pp. 391–409. *Nedelia*, September 18, 1894; and *Vrach*, 1894, no. 38, p. 1060, argued the advantages of the zemstvo health program. Even the MVD agreed: when it introduced medical services into nonzemstvo provinces, it reproduced the zemstvo system. *PSZRI*, 3d series, vol. 7, no. 4377 (April 14, 1887).

38 *Vrach*, 1894, no. 18, p. 514.

39 Ibid., no. 44, p. 1230.

40 P. P. Efreimov, "K voprosu o vliianii novogo ustava lechebnykh zavedenii na khod zemskoi meditsiny," ibid., no. 43, p. 1195. The general medical press assumed the same position as did *Vrach*; see especially *Zemskii vrach*, 1894, pp. 81–6, 109–11, 144–8, 179–85, 206–9.

41 D. N. Zhbankov, "O zatrudneniiakh vvedeniia s 1 iiulia 1895 g. novogo ustava lechebnykh zavedenii," *Vrach*, 1894, no. 51, pp. 1393–5.

42 Ibid.

43 TsGIA, f. 1287 (Khoziaistvennyi departament MVD), op. 15, 1895 g., d. 1415, p. 9.

44 *Vrach*, 1894, no. 51, p. 1395; "Eshche po povody novogo bol'nichnogo ustava," ibid., no. 52, pp. 1421–2.

45 Ibid., no. 52, p. 1433.

46 Ibid., and no. 49, p. 1366. The Bureau of Public Charity had a justly deserved bad reputation for its inadequate services in the prereform era.

47 TsGIA, f. 1287, op. 15, 1895 g., d. 1415, pp. 2 ob., 9–9 ob.

48 *Russkie vedomosti*, October 14, November 12, 1894; January 15, 1895; *Vrach*, 1895, no. 3, p. 81. The Moscow zemstvo immediately secured its victory by passing new regulations that clearly defined the zemstvo's control of district and province hospitals. Osipov et al., pp. 273–5.

49 *Vestnik Evropy*, 1895, no. 3, pp. 847–51. TsGIA, f. 1287, op. 15, 1895 g., d. 1415, pp. 1–11, a memorandum by the director of the Department of Economy of the MVD, listed the petitioning campaign as one of the insurmountable obstacles to implementing the statute.

50 "Poriadok napravleniia zemskikh khodataistv," *Russkie vedomosti*, March 14, 22, 1895, reviews the law and the history of zemstvo petitioning since 1864, and concludes that the governors must forward zemstvo petitions and that the Committee of Ministers had final authority.

51 *Vestnik Evropy*, 1895, no. 3, pp. 850–1. Ironically, I. N. Durnovo became chairman of the Committee of Ministers in October 1895.

52 TsGIA, f. 1287, op. 15, d. 1568, shows that in 1897–8 the MVD concluded that the local self-governments should retain most supervisory functions over their medical programs.

53 V. M. Khizhniakov, *Vospominaniia zemskogo deiatelia* (St. Petersburg, 1916), pp. 208–9. See also D. N. Shipov, *Vospominanii i dumy* (Moscow, 1918), p. 198; E. D. Maksimov, *Iz istorii i opyta zemskikh uchrezhdenii v Rossii* (St. Petersburg, 1913), p. 524; I. P. Belokonskii, *Zemstvo i konstitutsiia* (Moscow, 1910), p. 36; *Entsiklopedicheskii slovar'* (Brokgauz-Efron), s.v. "Lechebnye zavedeniia," vol. 18 (1896), p. 198.

54 Witte, p. 147.

55 See, for example, the petition of the Seventh Pirogov Congress (1899) to the MVD to include medical faculties, medical societies, and representatives of the local self-governments in the deliberations on a new hospital law, rumored to be in preparation. K. I. Shidlovskii, ed., *Svodka khodataistva Pirogovskogo obshchestva* (Moscow, 1904), p. 40.

56 *Dnevnik shestogo s"ezda Obshchestva russkikh vrachei v pamiat' N. I. Pirogova*, ed. Prof. A. V. Khodin (Kiev, 1896), supplement no. 7, pp. 3–4. A paper advocating local control, read at the congress, appeared in the general press: M. Levitskii, "Sel'skaia meditsina v ne-zemskikh guberniiakh," *Vestnik Evropy*, 1895, no. 4, pp. 789–807.

57 *Dnevnik shestogo s"ezda*, supplement no. 6, p. 25.

58 N. M. Pirumova, *Zemskoe liberal'noe dvizhenie. Sotsial'nye korni i evoliutsiia do nachala XX veka* (Moscow, 1977). For an analysis of the "legal wasteland" and the "unofficial patrimonial organs" for peasant "justice," see Peter Czap, Jr., "Peasant Class Courts and Peasant Customary Justice in Russia, 1861–1912," *Journal of Social History*, Winter 1967, pp. 149–78. A publication of the Pirogov Society presents the medical evidence: D. N. Zhbankov and Vl. L. Iakovenko, *Telesnye nakazaniia v Rossii v nastoiashchee vremia* (Moscow, 1899).

59 V. F. Bushuev, "Obrashchenie s bol'nymi na 'ty' " (Paper delivered at the Eighth Pirogov Congress, 1902), reprinted in *Russkii vrach*, 1903, no. 5, pp. 173–5; "Po povodu telesnykh nakazanii v voiskakh," *Vrach*, 1897, no. 41, pp. 1171–5.

60 D. Mamin-Sibiriak, "Na pokoe," Russkie vedomosti, 1897, nos. 139, 144, 150, 159; V. Kokovsov, "Ispolnenie sudebnogo prigovora," in V. I. Dmitrieva, Vrachi-Nizhegorodtsy (Gorky, 1960), p. 77; A. P. Chekhov, Ostrov Sakhalin Polnoe sobranie sochinenii i pisem A. P. Chekhov, ed. S. D. Balakhatii, 20 vols. (Moscow, 1944–51), 10: 296–302.

61 D. N. Zhbankov, "O pomoshchi golodaiushchim," Vrach, 1901, no. 50, p. 1539; "O pomoshchi golodainshchim ot Pirogovskogo obshchestva russkikh vrachei," Russkii vrach, 1902, no. 17, pp. 655–6; and I. A. Rozhdestvenskii, addressing the Eighth Pirogov Congress, Vos'moi Pivogovskii s"ezd, 7:371.

62 D. N. Zhbankov, "Konets rostu zemskoi meditsiny," Vrach, 1900, no. 39, pp. 1168–71; "Eshche o vliianii zakrepleniia zemskikh smet na razvitie zemskoi meditsiny," Vrach, 1900, no. 49, pp. 1481–5; and S. N. Korzhenevskii, "Zemskaia meditsina pri fiksatsii zemskikh smet," Vos'moi Pirogovskoi s"ezd, 6:312–24, 7:394–5.

63 The circular of April 6, 1902, and the responses of governors and zemstvos to it are in TsGIA, f. 1287, op. 15, d. 1970 "Po voprosu ob organizatsii vrachebnogo i sanitarnogo dela v imperii." A typical, irate reaction of a physician is K. I. Efimov, "Po povodu ministerskogo tsirkuliara o preobrazovanii vrachebno-sanitarnogo dela v Rossii," Russkii vrach, 1903, no. 45, p. 1610.

64 Kurskoe zemstvo, Otchet po revizii proizvedennoi v 1904 gody Senatorom N. A. Zinov'evym, 2 vols. (St. Petersburg, 1906), 2: 10–36. Pravitel'stvennyi vestnik, June 29, 1904. For a similar investigation by another official, see TsGIA, f. 1282 (Kantseliariia MVD), op. 2, d. 1842, "Sekretno. Obozrenie uchrezhdenii Tverskoi gubernii, 1903."

65 Frieden, Russian Physicians, ch. 10, "The Pirogov Society and the Liberation Movement, 1902–1904."

66 "Zemets," "Zemstvo i vrachi," Russkii meditsinskii vestnik, April 16, 1904, pp. 277–85, and May 1, 1904, pp. 307–14. Among the many physicians' responses, see N. Zolotavin, "Zemskie vrachi i g. 'zemets'," Russkii vrach, 1904, no. 46, pp. 155–7; Zhurnal Obshchestva russkikh vrachei v pamiat' N. I. Pirogova, May 1904, p. 180.

67 The details of the physicians' radical activities in 1905 are treated in I. A. Slonimskaia, Meditsinskie rabotniki v revoliutsii 1905–07 gg. (Moscow, 1955); E. I. Rodionova, Ocherki istorii professional'nogo dvizheniia meditsinskikh rabotnikov (Moskow, 1962); and Jonathan Sanders, "The Union of Unions: Political, Economic, Professional and Human Rights Organizations of the 1905 Revolution" (Ph.D. dissertation, Columbia University, 1980).

68 On November 8, 1905, the editorial group of the Pirogov Society's Commission for Popular Hygiene Education approved Listok no. 13, "Chto neobkhodimo dlia uspeshnoi bor'by s zaraznymi bolezniami," which asserted that adequate health protection could not be organized under the present regime. Over 100,000 copies were distributed:

Zhurnal Obshchestva russkikh vrachei v pamiat' N. I. Pirogova, April 1906, p. 273.

69 *Zhurnal Obshchestva russkikh vrachei*, February 1906, pp. 65–8; March 1906, pp. 169–73; April 1906, pp. 289–92; Report of the Pirogov Board, "Ob usloviiakh deiatel'nosti Pravleniia za 1904–1906 gg.," *Doklady pravlenii Obshchestva russkikh vrachei X-omu vserossiiskomu s"ezdu vrachei* (April 25–May 2, 1907) (Moscow, 1907), pp. 7–9, p. 9, n.l.

70 Roberta Thompson Manning, "Zemstvo and Revolution: The Onset of the Gentry Reaction, 1905–1907," in Leopold H. Haimson, ed., *The Politics of Rural Russia, 1905–1914* (Bloomington, 1979), pp. 48–49 and passim; and "The Russian Provincial Gentry in Revolution and Counter-revolution, 1905–1907" (Ph.D. dissertation, Columbia University, 1975), pp. 337–47.

71 D. N. Zhbankov, *O deiatel'nosti sanitarnykh biuro i obshchestvenno-sanitarnykh uchrezhdenii v zemskoi Rossii: kratkii istoricheskii obzor* (Moscow, 1910), pp. 337–47.

72 Peter F. Krug, "Russian Public Physicians and Revolution: The Pirogov Society, 1917–1920" (Ph.D. dissertation, University of Wisconsin, 1979).

73 B. D. Petrov and B. M. Potulov, *Z. P. Solov'ev* (Moscow, 1976), p. 32 and passim.

10

Liberal professionals and professional liberals: the zemstvo statisticians and their work

ROBERT E. JOHNSON

In December 1905, as the advisors of Nicholas II were debating election proposals for the newly created Duma, P. N. Durnovo spoke out strongly against admitting "medical aides, zemstvo statisticians and so forth, individuals who had recently been marshals of predatory gangs, raiding [the landowners'] estates."[1] The stereotype of the statisticians as a politically unreliable, potentially subversive force in the country-side was widely held among Russian conservatives, who in calmer moments were inclined to describe the researchers as outsiders who lacked a proper appreciation of local conditions, "young people, unknown to any of [the local landowners], sauntering through the districts on zemstvo money."[2]

At the opposite end of the political spectrum, Russian Social Demo-crats sometimes supported the statisticians in disputes with local authorities, but did not regard them as reliable allies. Lenin, although he drew upon many statisticians' work in his *Development of Capital-ism in Russia*, was quite harsh in his criticism of these publications, describing their authors as naive, prejudiced, and even grossly negli-gent in their computations.[3]

Were any of these complaints or accusations warranted? Unfortu-nately an answer to this question is not readily at hand. Despite the enormous volume of their publications, the zemstvo statisticians are barely mentioned in most histories of the zemstvo "movement." Veselovskii, who devoted 11 chapters of his mammoth study to zemstvo medicine and 13 to education, did not assign even a single chapter to the statisticians, and later writers have generally followed his lead. The would-be historian of zemstvo statistics is thus faced with a dual problem of abundance and scarcity. On the level of primary sources, there is almost an embarrassment of riches, yet at the same

343

time many crucial questions remain unanswered and unanswerable. Within these limits, the present chapter cannot pretend to offer a comprehensive assessment, or even a comprehensive summary, of the statisticians' work. Instead, it will attempt to isolate a few central themes and problems: the institutional and political constraints within which they operated, the career patterns of their most prominent members, and the overall significance of their labors.

The political-administrative context

Although the first statistical investigations were begun as early as 1870–1, the great bulk of zemstvo statistical work was carried out in two relatively brief periods, the mid-1880s and the period 1906–14. Prior to 1880, there were only 4 zemstvo statistical bureaus operating, but the following decade saw the creation of 17 more. By 1893, household inventories had been carried out in 23 different provinces, and, of these, 5 had been studied in entirety. From the early 1890s to 1905, however, the number of published studies fell off sharply, while the relations between the statisticians and local officials deteriorated. After 1906 there was a new surge of activity, during which some new methods were applied (for example, to the study of household budgets) and a large volume of publications was produced.

Essentially these long-term trends were a result of the changing opportunities and restrictions that the statisticians encountered in their work. Their activities were supervised by the local zemstvo, the provincial governor, and ultimately the central administration in Saint Petersburg. Any of these could veto projects, withhold funds, and dismiss (or reject the appointment of) staff members, yet their control over the statisticians was not total; in cases of conflict, as in their everyday work, the statisticians were able to provide a certain amount of assistance to one another and to appeal to a broader public for support. Thus, the environment in which the researchers operated was determined not just by the decisions of a particular governor or zemstvo board but by many external factors: the range of opinion in different ministries and different levels of government as well as in the press, the universities, and public associations.

Even before the first zemstvo statistical bureaus were established, there had been a virtual "explosion" of statistical research in Russia, stimulated in part by the Great Reforms, in part by the needs of expanding commerce, industry, and transport. In the 1850s, and even more in the 1860s under the vigorous leadership of P. P. Semenov, both the Imperial Geographic Society and the Central Statistical Commis-

sion undertook a whole range of demographic and economic investigations that were far more ambitious than any previous studies.[4] At the
same time, Russians began to take an active interest in the international
development of statistical science, symbolized by the holding of the
Eighth International Congress of Statisticians in Saint Petersburg in
1872.

In such a climate it was natural that the zemstvos should embark
upon a program of statistical research. The Law of January 1, 1864,
which created zemstvo institutions did not assign them any specific
responsibilities in the gathering or publishing of statistics. Such
responsibilities could be inferred, however, from two provisions of the
law: first, the famous "elastic clause," which empowered the zemstvo
to care for local economic needs and wants; and, second, the provisions
for taxation, which would require some manner of economic survey in
order to make a fair assessment of taxable property. Needless to say,
these two clauses were pointing in very different directions, the first
toward extensive investigation of social and economic conditions, the
second toward a down-to-earth, rubles-and-kopeks approach. In later
years, as zemstvo statistics developed and changed, the tension between these two approaches was to manifest itself on numerous
occasions.

The first zemstvo statistical studies began in 1870, but only toward
the end of the 1870s were large-scale systematic investigations
launched. Four provinces created statistical bureaus and began investigations of local economic conditions. In contrast to the practice of older
governmental agencies, which had usually collected statistics by
circulating questionnaires to local officials, the bureaus recruited their
own staffs to conduct firsthand studies. Almost immediately these
investigators came under attack from local conservatives, and two of
the bureaus were forced to cease operations. The statisticians were
accused of trying to prepare an uprising among the peasantry. In
addition, said the critics, these young people were unqualified for the
task of land appraisal and were gathering information carelessly from
unreliable sources.[5] Defenders of the statisticians retorted that these
objections were but a smokescreen for more selfish motives; the
conservatives, in this view, were trying to keep down their own taxes –
first by reducing or eliminating the statisticians' budget, and second by
preventing the statisticians from gathering information which might
result in higher tax assessments against powerful landowners.[6]

In Chernigov and Kherson, the conservatives succeeded in obstruct-
ing the statistical investigations for a time, but within a few years both
bureaus were revived. In the course of the following decade, most of

the other zemstvo provinces created bureaus of their own, and economic surveys were carried out in a total of 171 separate districts.[7] (For the most part, these studies were organized and carried out under the auspices of the provincial zemstvo, although in certain instances the district assemblies also sponsored statistical surveys.[8]) Echoes of the Chernigov conservatives' objections were heard more than once in these years but were not often heeded.

The fact that statistical studies flourished in the mid-1880s, at a time when other zemstvo activities were being cut back, is remarkable.[9] It can be explained in part by the presence of influential supporters in the zemstvo assemblies and boards, individuals such as M. A. Sablin in Moscow province, A. S. Gatssisskii in Nizhnii Novgorod, or A. S. Posnikov in Smolensk. Such individuals were usually landowners of liberal persuasion, and some of them (such as the three just named) had had extensive experience in statistical studies. Within the borders of their native provinces, and sometimes in other provinces as well, they were often able to exert a positive influence on behalf of the statisticians and their studies. In other cases the prestige of individual statisticians was so great that they themselves could exert such an influence.[10]

On the other hand, such support was not always decisive. When I. I. Petrunkevich, for example, tried to defend the Chernigov statistical bureau, he ended up being exiled to another province. By the same token, the prestige of statistical science also had its limits. When N. F. Annenskii was arrested in 1879, the police eagerly seized upon his photographs of the recent International Statistical Congress; in the course of the investigation it became apparent that, seeing the word "International" printed in the Roman alphabet, they were sure they had apprehended a member of the dreaded International Workingmen's Association.[11]

If the statisticians' prestige and local support were not powerful enough to explain the successes of the 1880s, perhaps other factors were at work. It seems likely that the tsarist administration saw some utility in the provincial studies. Despite the reactionary tone of the 1880s – the reversal of many of the previous era's reforms, the rebuffs to independent zemstvo initiatives – the government of Alexander III initiated a series of major economic changes in the countryside in the early 1880s. These included the institution of compulsory land redemption, the lowering of redemption payments, the abolition of the poll tax, the creation of the Peasant Land Bank, and the establishment of a program to facilitate peasant migration. Such measures stood a greater chance of success if they were based on an accurate appraisal of

346

the rural economy, yet the statistics that were available outside the zemstvo were often unreliable.[12] Instead of relying upon local police officials who had no statistical training, the zemstvo bureaus were sending specially trained researchers out to gather information directly from peasants and landowners.[13] Administrative officials may thus have had good reason to look kindly upon the bureaus, or at least to tolerate their work.[14]

One more factor that helped to promote the development of zemstvo statistics in the 1880s was the creation of a permanent statistical section within the Moscow Juridical Society. Up to this time the provincial zemstvo organizations had been forbidden to consult among themselves,[15] but in 1882 the minister of internal affairs relaxed this rule in response to a proposal from the society. By 1883 the statistical section had a membership of 59, 22 of them from provinces other than Moscow. The section's founders (M. A. Sablin, A. I. Chuprov, and V. I. Orlov) had hopes of establishing a uniform program of statistical study for all provinces, and many specific proposals were debated, but in the final analysis the section served mainly as a clearinghouse for information. In 1887 its members approved a set of general guidelines for future economic research, calling for universal household inventories as the basic unit of investigation. The members soon realized, however, that local conditions – both the phenomena being studied and the funds available for research – varied widely from province to province, making it impossible to implement any standardized format for asking questions or processing information.[16]

Even in the years of greatest activity, the statisticians did not have a free hand in setting their own agenda. They did generally succeed, however, in avoiding a narrowly functional definition of their work. Instead of simply assessing the value of landholdings, the statisticians of the 1870s and 1880s carried out household inventories, which compiled detailed information on the economic well-being of every peasant family. Their aim was to illuminate the causes of poverty and indebtedness and to provide factual data that could lead to reforms. In certain specific instances, such as the famine of 1891–2, statisticians were directly involved in providing assistance to the peasantry, even though this brought them into conflict with local conservatives.[17]

By the late 1880s, however, the favorable climate for statistical studies seemed to be disappearing, and with it the independence of the statisticians. In 1888 the Ministry of Internal Affairs disbanded the Samara statistical bureau and issued a circular requiring that all local studies be submitted to the Central Statistical Commission for approval; the bureaus, moreover, were now forbidden to touch upon questions of a fiscal character. Meanwhile, local zemstvo boards and assemblies began to put more obstacles in the way of statistical studies, and the total number of statistical bureaus was reduced from 19 to 10.[18] Not just the pace but the very spirit of zemstvo statistics was affected. The number of publications fell off, and the number of new studies dropped even more sharply. The statistical section of the Moscow Juridical Society met less and less frequently, until finally in 1898 the society itself was closed by administrative order.

Of all the laws and instructions passed in the early 1890s to transform the zemstvo, the one of greatest importance for statisticians was that of June 8, 1893, which assigned zemstvos the task of carrying out property assessment. A precise formula was spelled out for computing the value and profitability of land, and the statisticians' work was to be placed under much closer supervision. The burden of gathering statistics, moreover, was to switch from the provincial to the district level, where conservative influences were generally stronger.[19]

Leading statisticians expressed strong opposition to these changes, especially to the provisions that imposed a narrowly fiscal definition on their research. In a series of articles and public statements, they insisted that the population's tax-paying capacities could only be determined through a comprehensive (*sploshnoi*) survey of each household's condition by means of household inventories. The issue was debated at length in the statistical section of the Ninth Congress of Naturalists and Physicians in 1894. Of the 100 statisticians who took part, the vast majority indicated support for the continuation of comprehensive inventories.[20] Four years later, R. I. Baskin and A. V. Peshekhonov made the same argument before the final statistical conference of the Moscow Juridical Society and once again received overwhelming support. Meanwhile, however, broadly conceived studies were cut short for lack of funds or vetoed by the zemstvo assemblies.

The conditions of zemstvo work were further altered in 1899, when the tsarist government, in restoring assessment responsibilities to the provincial level, created an entirely new system for financing local surveys. Instead of the zemstvos paying the whole cost themselves, the government would subsidize the statisticians' work, to a total of one million rubles annually, a most impressive sum.[21] This removed one source of difficulty for the statisticians but by no means ended their conflicts with local or central authorities, for the money was provided for specific purposes and the activities of the recipients were closely supervised.

By 1900, then, the statisticians found themselves facing a configuration of forces different from those they had dealt with in earlier decades. They now had larger budgets and could hire a larger staff than ever before, yet they had less opportunity to set their own agenda for research. The net effect of these forces was described by A. V. Peshekhonov in 1901 as a crisis of zemstvo statistics.[22] Large numbers of new people, he argued, were being brought into the statistical bureaus, but they lacked the broad vision and commitment of their predecessors. In contrast to earlier years, the bureaus were instituting a strictly hierarchical division of labor and restricting individual initiative. Statisticians found themselves under increasing pressure to conform to externally imposed regulations, and the ablest among them were abandoning their posts in favor of more congenial ones in the cities, the central government, and the universities.

Another symptom of this crisis atmosphere, according to Peshekhonov, was a series of clashes between statisticians and government or zemstvo officials. In 1896 S. M. Bleklov and his entire staff resigned from the statistical bureau of Orel province after a disagreement with the provincial zemstvo board. In 1899, the director of the Ufa bureau quit, and in the following 3 years there were at least 11 other cases of conflict. Some statisticians were dismissed, or even exiled to other provinces, but others managed to reconcile their differences with the local chairmen or zemstvo boards.

Peshekhonov's view of this "crisis" may be simplistic. The statisticians, it seems, were not merely succumbing to bureaucratic intereference but were also showing a greater sense of themselves as a group with common interests. As early as 1898, a subcommittee of the Moscow Juridical Society tried to outline the professional needs and concerns of statisticians. Although this committee gave considerable attention to a demand for administrative independence, it also raised the question of standardized training for statisticians. It proposed the creation of a central library, mutual aid society, and nationwide organization of statisticians, as well as a clearinghouse for job seekers and potential employers.[23] These proposals were not implemented, but they do suggest that a spirit of professionalism was developing. In some cases this spirit manifested itself in political protests, but in others it may have been a source of specialization and hierarchy in the local statistical bureaus. Professionalism brought some statisticians into conflict with local governors or zemstvo leaders, but it did not make them all into oppositionists. On the contrary, as will be seen below, some of the most prominent leaders of the statistical movement published their works under the auspices of the central government, or even entered its service.

The "awakening" of the zemstvo in the years 1900 to 1905 produced few positive results for the statisticians. Difficulties with the central government were compounded after 1902 when the minister of internal affairs, responding to peasant uprisings in Kharkov and Poltava provinces, categorically prohibited any further contact between statisticians and the peasantry.[24] Another result of the disputes and turmoil of this period was that ongoing projects were disrupted or abandoned, leaving previously collected materials unpublished.[25] Meanwhile some of the most outspoken statisticians were drawn into broader oppositionist campaigns. The majority, however, do not seem to have played a very active role in the zemstvo movement of these years. This pattern may seem anomalous, since other "third-element" groups such as physicians were quite vocal in this period. The statisticians, however, had less reason to make common cause with the zemstvo activists. Their responsibilities in tax assessment put them into potential conflict with any and all property owners, and their emerging professionalism may have led some to take a hands-off attitude toward oppositionist struggles.

The conditions of zemstvo statistical work did not change drastically after 1905. Statistical bureaus continued to be funded at a level substantially higher than in the pre-1900 period, and close administrative supervision continued. Great numbers of clerks and junior statisticians were hired, and the volume of publications soared once again. The political clashes of earlier years receded, in part because a few of the most outspoken statisticians had been drawn off into other fields of endeavor.

In these years statisticians continued to seek a national forum for exchanging information and pursuing common interests. The Twelfth Congress of Russian Naturalists and Physicians in 1910 was a step in this direction; it heard a total of 49 statistical reports, of which 19 dealt with zemstvo topics.[26] Moscow University was another focus of attention when, at the instigation of N. A. Kablukov, it created a statistical section with its own library and meeting room. In 1912 this section became the nucleus of the newly formed Chuprov Society, which played a role similar to that of the Juridical Society in the 1880s, bringing together statisticians from different provinces and holding conferences on matters of general interest.[27] In contrast to the earlier society, however, questions of statistical theory received more attention and the practical tasks of zemstvo studies less.

To the extent that the post-1905 period saw significant innovation in the field of applied statistics, it was carried out mainly by individuals who were not zemstvo statisticians. The most notable example is the detailed peasant budget studies developed by A. V. Chaianov and other members of the so-called organization and production school. This group consisted of agricultural economists and agronomists and carried out its earliest studies with the aid of the Moscow Committee of Credit and Savings Cooperatives. Its members were quite critical of the zemstvo statisticians' habit of amassing "sterile" data or failing to analyze it. The methods that Chaianov developed ignored the precedent of zemstvo statistics. Instead of sending professional statisticians into the field, his studies used simplified questionnaires which were filled out by agricultural officers, and budget records which the peasants themselves could keep.[28]

All local statistical work was disrupted by the outbreak of World War I. During the war years, many zemstvo statisticians played a role in surveying national economic resources, and in 1917 some of them took part in the work of land commissions. In later years, many took up statistical posts in the Soviet government, but there was little continuity between their new posts and their prerevolutionary efforts.

Career patterns

Despite the restrictions and obstacles they encountered, many statisticians still managed to secure a certain degree of independence in their work. The course of their research was defined, not just by bureaucratic directives but by the statisticians themselves, who argued strenuously in favor of some lines of research and against others. Their background and training, political sympathies, and relations with one another all helped to determine what subjects would be studied and what methods used to gather information. The composition of the statistical staff was therefore an important variable, affecting the very nature of the statisticians' research as well as their relations with bureaucracy and society.

Unfortunately the materials for a full-scale collective biography are not at hand. Only a small – and presumably unrepresentative – minority of statisticians became prominent enough to be listed in biographical dictionaries, encyclopedias, or other similar sources.[29] Despite this limitation, a fair amount of indirect evidence does exist; so without knowing the histories of many specific individuals one can still trace the experiences of the group as a whole.

One of the first questions to arise is whether the statisticians were a homogeneous group. Durnovo and other conservatives tended to lump them all together as subversives, but was there any justification for such a view? Even a superficial examination of the statistical bureaus discloses a great diversity in the skills, responsibilities, and career patterns of the statistical employees. At the very top were a few dozen individuals, chief statisticians and directors of provincial bureaus, who played the greatest role in organizing zemstvo research throughout the country. Below them were a hundred or so senior investigators, who supervised local studies and sometimes had special training in specific fields (for example, public health). These were assisted by a group of statistical clerks, numbering in the low hundreds, and a mass of several hundred part-time interviewers who were hired for the duration of particular studies. Members of the latter group were recruited from the universities and from the lower ranks of zemstvo service (for example, feldshers, schoolteachers), but their employment rarely lasted for more than a few months. In addition to all these categories of paid employees, thousands of volunteer correspondents, mainly priests and literate peasants, contributed to statistical publications on an irregular basis by providing reports on crops, weather, and other details of life in their own villages.[30]

Although provincial statistical bureaus studied a wide range of topics, including fertility, mortality, factory industry, public health, and education, their main concern was the agricultural economy. Here zemstvo statistics made its most distinctive contribution and deployed its greatest resources; predictably, this was also the field with the fullest and most hierarchical division of labor among statisticians. In the early days of the 1870s and 1880s, occupational stratification was incomplete. Some researchers performed even the most mundane tasks themselves,[31] and a few individuals rose from humble beginnings to prominent posts without formal training or higher education.[32] By the end of the century, however, clearer lines were drawn between junior and senior statisticians. A much higher proportion of the latter group had attended universities or other postsecondary institutions, and their salaries were more than double those of their subordinates.[33] The senior group took on more of the attributes of a profession, whereas the junior clerks became more of a bureaucracy.

Statisticians were often described – by friends as well as foes – as changing employment at regular intervals, but in fact the individuals who did so were few and far between. It is true that this mobile minority included some of the leading lights of zemstvo statistics: V. I. Orlov, who in his short lifetime studied five provinces and helped to organize statistical bureaus in several others; A. A. Rusov, who worked in three different provinces and directed municipal censuses in four cities; A. V. Peshekhonov, who worked in four provinces before being barred from zemstvo employment by the Ministry of Internal Affairs; and V. N. Grigor'ev, who moved from Moscow to Riazan to Bessarabia to Voronezh and back to Moscow in the space of five years. Nonetheless the more typical career pattern was to spend one's entire career in a single locality. In 1893 V. P. Blagoveshchenskii compiled a list of 219 researchers who had published statistical reports under zemstvo auspices, and of these only 25 had published in more than 1 province.[34]

Mobility was closely correlated with education (graduates of Moscow University and the Petrovskaia Agricultural Academy tended to be especially mobile), and political activism. Statisticians' perambulations, however, were less a result of professional attributes than political ones. A certain number had participated in oppositionist circles in their student days, and an even greater number came into conflict with local officials while working in the statistical bureaus. Such individuals ran the risk of being labeled as politically unreliable, a charge which could result in dismissal from zemstvo employment and even involuntary departure from a province.

The members of this mobile, conspicuous minority exerted a disproportionately great influence on the course of zemstvo statistics. They tended to occupy higher posts, from which they could provide advice or even set the agenda for other statisticians' research. Being more visible, they also helped to create an image of all statisticians in the minds of officialdom and "society." Here the conservatives' stereotypes were sometimes echoed by liberals:

> For a long time the zemstvo statisticians were the most energetic and oppositionist element of the zemstvo intelligentsia. Practially speaking, the first statisticians were narodnik-propagandists...[The opportunity] to have direct ties with the people, legally to study their needs and, as far as possible, independently assist in the satisfaction of those needs through the zemstvo...attracted to statistics a large percentage of the most thoughtful intelligentsia.[35]

To what extent, though, can the political experiences or ideological convictions of "activist" statisticians illuminate the lives of the majority? This question can best be answered by reviewing the course of statisticians' oppositionist activity.

The first and best-known confrontation between statisticians and conservatives was the Chernigov incident of 1877, which was briefly described in the first section of this chapter. Statisticians were accused of fomenting unrest among the peasantry, and in the ensuing controversy the statistical bureau was closed. In addition, I. I. Petrunkevich, the statisticians' most outspoken defender in the zemstvo assembly, was exiled from the province for his efforts. Although no direct evidence of agitational activities was produced, biographical sources make it clear that several Chernigov statisticians had been involved in illegal activity. V. E. Varzar, a recent graduate of the Saint Petersburg Technical Institute and a co-founder of the Chernigov statistical bureau, was the author of one of the most widely circulated agitational pamphlets of the 1870s, "The Clever Trick." His colleague A. A. Rusov, although not personally involved in agitation, operated a model farm at which a number of young students tried to become familiar with agricultural life; one of these was I. P. Belokonskii, who was shortly arrested and exiled to Siberia for his connection with the Land and Liberty organization.[36] Rusov also took part in the publishing and distribution of Ukrainian literature after 1876, defying the government's ban on use of the Ukrainian language.[37] A third co-founder, P. P. Chervinskii, had been banished from Saint Petersburg in 1871 for participating in a student demonstration.

Although the Chernigov case involved a certain amount of questionable behavior, none of the principal statisticians was arrested or punished at this time. All three resumed their posts when the statistical bureau reopened in 1880, and both Varzar and Chervinskii eventually moved on to occupy prominent statistical positions in the tsarist bureaucracy. Their experience suggests that higher tsarist officials gave little credence to the accusations that were circulated in Chernigov and that these statisticians were not seriously involved in revolutionary activity.

I have been able to identify six other future statisticians who were expelled from university, arrested, or exiled in the 1870s, and it seems likely that the actual number was much higher. I find no evidence, however, to suggest that these individuals were working in zemstvo statistics prior to their arrest or expulsion or that they were using zemstvo work as a cover for illegal activity. Instead, their zemstvo service seems to have been a consequence of youthful radicalism. Barred from residence in certain cities and provinces and regarded with suspicion by local officials, individuals such as I. P. Belokonskii and N. F. Annenskii found themselves unemployable and penniless after a period of detention or exile.[38] In such cases, as Belokonskii put it, "Just as for the Russian muzhik there was nowhere to go except 'one beaten path–to the tavern,' so too for every type of 'unreliable,' 'former,' or 'person under surveillance' there was only one beaten path – to zemstvo statistics."[39] In some zemstvo circles the returning exiles were welcomed, in others barely tolerated, but the obstacles they encountered were fewer than in other occupations. This is not to suggest that the newly hired statisticians of the 1880s had no interest in the zemstvo or its statistical investigations but only to point out that their choice of employment was often dictated by circumstances.

This pattern continued after the revival of student activism in the 1890s. By this time some of the "unreliables" of the 1870s had become senior statisticians and were able to hire a second generation of like-minded subordinates.[40] These appointments were sometimes blocked by provincial governors, and in several instances senior statisticians were criticized or even dismissed for choosing "subversive" staff members. Belokonskii's memoirs suggest that there was some basis for these complaints in that political considerations did influence the selection of junior staff members. As the head of the Orel statistical bureau, Belokonskii consulted with colleagues in other provinces about the qualifications of job applicants and knowingly chose several who had been involved in oppositionist activity.[41] Although this hiring pattern might seem conducive to political unrest, the controversies that these appointments aroused were an effective obstacle to illegal actions by the statisticians, for they resulted in close police surveillance and obstruction of the researchers' work.[42]

Despite numerous allegations of radicalism, there is little reliable evidence of agitational or subversive activities on the part of statisticians. When conflicts and controversies erupted in the 1880s and 1890s, they were almost always centered on the details of statistical research: whom to hire, how to gather information, which results to publish. Often disputes arose between the statisticians and the zemstvo itself, as in Kursk province, where the work of I. A. Verner was publicly burned after complaints from conservative delegates.[43] The only case of clearly illegal activity, however, was the participation of a small circle of statisticians in the People's Right party during its brief existence in 1894, and even then there was no effort to agitate among the peasants.[44]

When unrest did flare up among the peasants of Kharkov and Poltava in 1902, Minister of Internal Affairs V. K. Pleve became convinced that zemstvo statisticians were to blame. He responded by exiling the director of the Poltava statistical bureau, A. A. Rusov, and forbidding any further contact between statisticians and peasants in 10 other provinces until their work could be redefined to his satisfaction. The minister's reaction, however, is not proof that statisticians had actually engaged in subversive acts. As far as can be determined, no specific statistician was ever named or accused by police, nor were any specific charges brought against the director of the bureau. Pleve's own statements, in fact, described a system of agitation that seems incompatible with the pattern of the statisticians' work. He alleged that malcontents had traveled secretly through the countryside, scattering seditious literature from trains and carriages; other agitators, he added, had established propagandist circles to instruct the peasants in revolutionary ideas.[45] Statisticians would have found it difficult to act in either of these ways. Their work required them to identify themselves to peasants and local officials wherever they traveled, with the result that their movements through the countryside could easily be traced. Their

355

contact with any one peasant village, moreover, was of such short duration that systematic propaganda would have been impossible.

It seems more reasonable to suppose, as many contemporaries did, that Pleve's charges were unfounded. This supposition is reinforced by the recollections of Rusov's widow who, writing long afterward with no reason to conceal the truth, suggested that the unrest of 1902 had taken her husband and his associates completely by surprise.[46]

Evidence of legal or moderate oppositionist activity is more abundant. Some of the best-known zemstvo statisticians were outspoken critics of Russian autocracy, contributing numerous articles to liberal and populist publications and playing a prominent part in public demonstrations and campaigns. In later years several former statisticians were active in the leadership of the Cadet and Popular Socialist parties, and three were elected to the State Duma. Although such individuals were a small minority among statisticians, the views they espoused – sympathy for the peasantry and its traditions, criticism of bureaucratic abuses, concern over economic hardship and suffering – were shared by the great majority of their subordinates. These concerns lay behind many of the "procedural" battles that were fought in provincial statistical bureaus, such as the demand for a comprehensive survey of peasant well-being or the efforts of many statisticians to publicize famine conditions in 1891–2.[47]

This review of oppositionist activity suggests several conclusions. In the first place, an activist minority of statiticians does seem to have exercised a disproportionately large influence over the course of zemstvo research. Through their own publications, professional standing, and contacts with oppositionist circles, they helped to decide how local studies should be conducted. When their senior colleagues became embroiled in disputes, the leading statisticians provided moral and material support, sometimes by attempting to intervene through central bureaucratic channels, sometimes by offering alternate employment. By consulting among themselves, the senior statisticians also served as an informal job referral network for junior staff, thereby reinforcing their own influence over the course of local research.

Although many senior statisticians seem to have shared a sense of purpose in their work, their goals were broadly educational rather than revolutionary. Statistical research was not treated as a pretext for illegal activity but as a means of serving the *narod* by illuminating its life and problems. Agreement about goals and purposes, moreover, did not prevent statisticians from disagreeing among themselves about many aspects of their work. The oppositionist sympathies that have been outlined in the preceding pages did not prevent several prominent

356

zemstvo statisticans from accepting employment in the tsarist bureaucracy or discourage others from participating in government-sponsored publications. A notable example was the controversial 1897 study of harvests and grain prices; edited by A. I. Chuprov and A. S. Posnikov and issued under the auspices of the Ministry of Finance, it included essays by 11 prominent statisticians challenging the widely held view that the peasant standard of living was falling from year to year.[48]

One more point worth noting is that, mobile as some of the activist statisticians were, only a few of them ever abandoned statistical work. Whether they moved from province to province, taught in universities, or accepted bureaucratic posts, the majority remained statisticians throughout their careers. The prevalence of this pattern seems to reinforce the conclusion that a spirit of professionalism was growing among the statisticians. At the same time that they were discussing standardized training and nationwide organization and seeing their own research bureaus become more hierarchical and bureaucratic, many researchers were coming to regard statistics as their life's work. Although they might agree among themselves about ethical or political principles, they tended more and more to make their research an end in itself. For this reason their participation in broader currents of oppositionist or revolutionary activity – inside or outside the zemstvo – was not great.

Achievements and shortcomings

If success could be measured in the volume of their publications, the zemstvo statisticians' place in history would be secure. The list of their works includes at least 3,500 items, some of them more than a thousand pages in length.[49] In household inventories alone (the largest single category of investigation) the statisticians interviewed an estimated total of 4.5 million peasant families in 34 provinces, using questionnaires that sometimes took hours to complete. The work is all the more impressive when one realizes that the statisticians had no precedent to follow but had to devise all their procedures themselves.

Having amassed such a volume of data, however, the statisticians were much less successful at pulling it together and explaining what it meant. Some critics have accused them of naive populism, suggesting that unconscious bias colored their reports and discredited their conclusions. Others have faulted them for making a fetish of numbers, accumulating information without purpose or direction.[50] Whether one blames the statisticians themselves or the conditions in which they worked, such criticism casts a long shadow over their efforts and helps to explain why they have generally been ignored by posterity. How well founded, though, are these objections?

In the first place, the picture of the statisticians as "obsessive-compulsives," treating their data as an end in itself, is incorrect. No matter how great the shortcomings of their publications, the zemstvo statisticians were consistently aware of the policy implications of their work. They raised important questions about social and economic life – the viability of the commune, the causes of poverty and indebtedness, the possibility of strengthening the peasant economy through cooperation and handcrafts – and fought long and hard to keep them on the agenda, despite the objections of officials and zemstvo conservatives.

The evidence that was collected in the zemstvo surveys, moreover, was not published in a haphazard or undigested form. On the contrary, a great deal of energy was invested in seeking appropriate ways of combining and analyzing data. Discussions of statistical methodology were held at the Moscow Juridical Society, the Conferences of Naturalists and Physicians, the Free Economic Society, and the Chuprov Society. In the 1880s and early 1890s, a few prominent individuals developed formulas for combining economic variables for purposes of categorizing peasant households; instead of using a single variable such as the size of landholdings, the number of head of livestock, or the extent of indebtedness, this method grouped a number of variables into a system of combined tables.[51] In later years, when budgetary and administrative constraints prevented statisticians from continuing broadly based socioeconomic surveys, much attention was given to the methodology of case studies and systematic sampling, through which a larger population could be studied by investigating a smaller one. Still later members of the Chuprov Society, using zemstvo statistics as their data, began to examine the mathematical relationships among socioeconomic variables.[52] None of these experiments was entirely successful, but the issues and methods that were discussed were new to statistical science, not just in Russia but worldwide. The fact that they received attention from the zemstvo researchers seems a sign of vitality and breadth of vision.

Even though the statisticians did not consciously subordinate their research to preconceived goals or conclusions, unspoken assumptions can often be discerned in their work. The categories and terminology they used sometimes led them to overlook or discount certain aspects of their data. The clearest example is their treatment of social differentiation among the peasantry. Zemstvo reports of the 1880s and 1890s tended to describe peasant life on the basis of simple averages, thereby disregarding any inequality that might have existed between households. It seems that many statisticians were predisposed to think of the peasantry as a more or less undifferentiated mass, and they either overlooked economic polarization or assumed that it was not a serious problem.[53] Similarly, a sympathy for traditional crafts and the village commune caused many statisticians to underestimate the influence of capitalism in the countryside. Even so, their methods of collecting and summarizing data were objective enough that other investigators, proceeding from different premises and asking different questions, were able to use the zemstvo data abundantly in their work. Here, too, the critics' objections to zemstvo statistics seem overstated.

In the disputes and controversies outlined earlier in this chapter, the statisticians consistently asserted the primacy of research over administrative politics, and this struggle for independence must be counted as part of their achievement and legacy. Here, as in their efforts to develop a standard methodology and training for statisticians, they were trying to lay the groundwork for statistics as an autonomous social science. If that goal was not achieved, the fault lay not with the statisticians but with the restrictive, sometimes stifling conditions in which they worked.

Notes

1 Quoted in Ann Erickson Healy, The Russian Autocracy in Crisis (Hamden, Conn., 1976), p. 96. Three years earlier, an unnamed "highly esteemed" correspondent had written to Moskovskie vedomosti to complain that at least two-thirds of all statisticians were anarchist revolutionaries. Moskovskie vedomosti, 1902, no. 96.

2 V. Korolenko, "Tretii element (Pamiati N. F. Annenskogo)," Russkoe bogatstvo, 1913, no. 7, p. 266, recounting a debate in the Nizhnii Novgorod zemstvo assembly in 1891.

3 V. I. Lenin, Sochineniia, 4th ed., 45 vols. (Moscow, 1941–67), 1; 7, 2; 333–4, 3; 176–9, 20; 65–71.

4 For an account of the statistical "awakening" of the 1860s, see S. Frederick Starr, Decentralization and Self-Government in Russia, 1830–1870 (Princeton, 1972), pp. 97–8; Z. M. Svavitskaia, "Moskovskii universitet i zemskaia statistika," in Ocherki po istorii statistiki SSSR, sbornik 2 (Moscow, 1957), pp. 61–77; and N. A. Svavitskii, Zemskie podvornye perepisi (Moscow, 1961), ch. 1.

5 The most celebrated controversy involving statisticians in the 1870s was the Chernigov incident of 1877, described in V. E. Khizhniakov, Vospominaniia zemskogo deiatelia (Petrograd, 1916), pp. 150–1; and B. B. Veselovskii, Istoriia zemstva za 40 let, 4 vols. (St. Petersburg, 1909–11), 1:81–3.

6 The Chernigov statisticians had concluded that roughly one-eighth of the privately owned land in the province had been left off previous

assessment rolls and that the landowners' holdings had been under-valued by as much as 50 percent. Veselovskii, 1:81.

7   The surveys included almost 70,000 villages, with a population of 25 million. D. Rikhter, "Zemskaia statistika," in *Entsiklopedicheskii slovar'* (Brokgauz–Efron), vol. 24 (St. Petersburg, 1894), p. 494.

8   K. Ermolinskii, *Sbornik statisticheskikh svedenii po Khotinskomu uezdu Bessarabskoi gubernii* (Moscow, 1886), pp. iii–iv.

9   Of a total of 140 studies of land rental, carried out between 1870 and 1892, 92 percent were done in the years 1882–7. N. Karavaev, "Krest'ianskie vnenadel'nye arendy," *Itogi ekonomicheskogo izsledo-vaniia Rossii po dannym zemskoi statistiki*, vol. 2 Derpt, 1892, p. xvii.

10 V. I. Orlov, for example, was known to have been offered the director-ship of the Central Statistical Committee in 1882. He declined, but his prestige was so great that he could influence the course of statistical work in many other provinces. In 1884 he interceded with the governor of Samara province on behalf of K. E. Paprits, a statistician who had been accused of stirring up the peasants. R. A. Eidelman, "Russkii zemskii statistik V. I. Orlov," in *Ocherki po istorii statistiki SSSR, sbornik 4* (Moscow, 1961), p. 22.

11 A. Annenskaia, "Iz proshlykh let (Vospominaniia o N. F. Annen-skom)," *Russkoe bogatstvo*, 1913, no. 1, p. 80.

12 The same could be said of factory statistics. Here, too, major legislation was being prepared, yet the government's own factory inspectors began work only in 1884; meanwhile certain zemstvos (notably Moscow) had embarked upon large-scale investigations of factory life that could have a direct bearing on the legislative proposals.

13 On the shortcomings of statistics that were collected by nonspecialists, see Svavitskii, p. 38; S. N. Veletskii, *Zemskaia statistika* (Moscow, 1899), pp. 2, 348–51.

14 The fact that N. Kh. Bunge, an economist, statistician, and former university teacher, was serving as minister of finance between 1881 and 1887 also helps to explain the government's relatively tolerant policy toward the statisticians in these years.

15 V. V. Garmiza, *Potgotovka zemskoi reformy 1864 g.* (Moscow, 1957), p. 251.

16 Svavitskaia, pp. 81–4.

17 Korolenko, pp. 260–75, provides an account of N. F. Annenskii's efforts in Nizhnii Novgorod in 1891.

18 Veselovskii, 3:302. The curious reference to fiscal questions was not intended to restrict tax assessment but to prevent discussion of the national budget and its effects on the peasantry.

19 This latter arrangement proved unworkable, apparently because local landowners, strongly entrenched in the district assemblies, were able to obstruct assessment of their property. In 1899 new legislation restored responsibility for assessment to the provincial zemstvo. Ibid., 1:84.

20 A few prominent economists and statisticians dissented from this position: I. I. Ianzhul, A. P. Shlikevich, and N. N. Chernenkov, the latter two on the basis of long experience in zemstvo statistics. So too did A. A. Kaufman, but for opposite reasons. He argued that fiscal concerns were incompatible with broader scientific objectives and proposed to make a sharp distinction between the two. Svavit-skaia, pp. 99, 101.

21 By way of comparison, Moscow province had spent an average of 10,000 rubles annually in the years 1879–89, during which time its statistical bureau was the most active and prolific in Russia. Velet-skii, pp. 95–7.

22 A. V. Peshekhonov, *Na ocherednye temy* (St. Petersburg, 1904), pp. 307–31.

23 S. N. Veletskii, "O nekotorykh voprosakh, vozbuzhdennykh v zase-daniiakh statisticheskogo otdeleniia moskovskogo iuridicheskogo obshchestva s 9-go po 18-e fevralia 1896 g.," *Trudy Vol'nogo eko-nomicheskogo obshchestva*, 1900, no. 6, pp. 202–10.

24 I. P. Belokonskii, *Zemskoe dvizhenie*, 2nd ed. (Moscow, 1914), pp. 131–6; Veselovskii, 3:545–6.

25 Svavitskii, pp. 295–8.

26 Svavitskaia, pp. 121–2.

27 Ibid., pp. 123–7, 131–2.

28 Basile Kerblay, "A. V. Chaianov, Life, Career, Works," in A. V. Chaianov, *The Theory of the Peasant Economy* (Homewood, Ill., 1966), pp. xxx–xxxv.

29 In preparing this chapter I have been able to locate biographical information for a total of 61 zemstvo statisticians.

30 Information gathered through correspondents was described as cur-rent (*tekushchaia*) to distinguish it from "fundamental" (*osnovnaia*) statistics, which were gathered by full-time staff members. The turnover among correspondents was extremely high, and their train-ing was minimal; as a result, I have excluded them from considera-tion in the remainder of this chapter.

31 An extreme example was N. A. Tereshkevich, director of zemstvo statistics in Poltava province in the early 1880s, who contracted a fatal illness while traveling through the countryside in bad weather to conduct interviews. S. M. Bleklov, "Pamiati N. A. Tereshkev-icha," *Iuridicheskii vestnik*, 1891, no. 10, p. 265.

32 Peshekhonov, pp. 308–12. This author himself exemplified the pat-tern, having risen to the rank of director of a provincial bureau despite a lack of formal training.

33 In a survey taken in 1898, 65 percent of bureau directors had attended university, as compared with 40 percent of their subordi-nates. The former group received an average salary of 2,260 rubles, whereas statisticians were paid an average of 962 and statistical clerks 403.

34 N. A. Blagoveshchenskii, *Svodnyi statisticheskii sbornik khoziaist-vennykh svedenii po zemskim podvornym perepisiam*, vol. 1 (Moscow, 1893), pp. 262–4.

35 Belokonskii, p. 36.

36 I. P. Belokonskii, *Dan' vremeni* (Moscow, 1918), pp. 79–80.

37 Jurij Lawrynenko, "Ševčenko and His Kobzar in the Intellectual and Political History of a Century," in V. Myakovskyj and G. Shevelov, eds., *Taras Shevchenko, 1814–1861, A Symposium* (The Hague, 1962), p. 194. I am grateful to Yury Boshyk for this and subsequent references to Rusov's career.

38 Annenskaia, "Iz proshlykh let," *Russkoe Bogatstvo*, 1913, no. 2, pp. 56–65.

39 I. P. Belokonskii, *V gody bespraviia* (Moscow, 1930), p. 43.

40 Like-mindedness was a matter of degree. Though their careers followed similar patterns, the students who were expelled or exiled in the 1890s tended to be more sympathetic to Marxism than their seniors. In my biographical file I have identified three who were active Social Democrats, including two members of the Union of Struggle for the Emancipation of the Working Class.

41 Belokonskii, *V gody*, pp. 122–5, 141–4.

42 Statistical researchers were sometimes refused permission to travel in the countryside. When permission was granted, they might discover that police officers had visited the villages before them or warned the peasants against cooperating too closely with them. Peshekhonov, p. 326. Belokonskii reports that in Orel province statisticians were not only forbidden to discuss sensitive topics when interviewing peasants but were enjoined from expressing opinions through "negative movements of the body" such as shrugs, winks, or facial expressions. Belokonskii, *V gody*, p. 51.

43 Belokonskii, p. 116.

44 Belokonskii, *Zemskoe dvizhenie*, pp. 46 ff.; idem. *V gody*, pp. 85–90; V. V. Shirokova, *Partiia "Narodnogo prava"* (Saratov, 1972), appendix.

45 The text of the minister's order, as well as his correspondence with provincial governors, is reproduced in Belokonskii, *Zemskoe dvizhenie*, pp. 132–5.

46 S. Rusova, *Pamiati Oleksandra Rusova*, pt. 2 (Lvov, 1938), p. 184.

47 On the 1891 famine in particular, see Korolenko, "Tretii element." For the statisticians' sense of commitment, see Belokonskii, *V gody*, p. 52.

48 Theodore Von Laue, *Sergius Witte and the Industrialization of Russia* (New York; 1963), pp. 115–16.

49 The fullest available survey of this evidence is V. N. Grigor'ev, *Predmetnyi ukazatel' materialov v zemsko-statisticheskikh trudakh s 1860-kh po 1917 g.*, 2 vols. (Moscow, 1926–7). Grigor'ev exhaustively catalogs 3,432 separate publications. For a bibliography of secondary sources, see Svavitskii, pp. 349–53.

50 V. I. Smirnskii, "Iz istorii zemskoi statistiki," in *Ocherki po istorii statistiki SSSR*, sbornik 3 (Moscow, 1960), pp. 130–44; Eidelman, "V. I. Orlov."

51 Svavitskii, ch. 3.

52 Svavitskaia, pp. 108, 126.

53 For criticism of this tendency, see Lenin, 3; 138–40; Eidelman, "V. I. Orlov." Lenin tried to correct some of the zemstvo statisticians in his *Development of Capitalism*; in response, several leading statisticians, including N. A. Kablukov and P. A. Vikhliaev, tried to answer him in kind, marshalling masses of statistics in support of their conclusions. Lenin's response was to accuse them of making a fetish of numbers.

11

The All-Russian Union of Zemstvos and World War I

WILLIAM GLEASON

World War I, it has often been noted, was an unmitigated nightmare for Romanov Russia. The ravages of disease in town and countryside alike, the discontent of millions of permanently uprooted refugees, and above all, the dissolution of the homefront into savage class struggle – these were but a few of the seemingly endless disasters to batter against the fragile foundation of the state, eroding its social base by wearing down public confidence.

At the same time there were crosscurrents. Writing of the war's impact upon the industrial economy, Norman Stone, a British historian, has seen the conflict "not as a vast run-down of most accounts, but as a crisis of growth, a modernization crisis in thin disguise."[1] Reduced to its essentials, Stone's view is that the war accelerated the consolidation of Russian industry, leading in the end to a significant spurt in output and productivity. The point is well taken: the Great War, at first imperceptibly but soon with relentless force, thrust the nation into situations that required public planning, organizations, and – especially – technical competence. Indeed, if we apply the concept of modernization to local government a somewhat similar picture emerges. There the war sharply increased the need for specialists and expert workers of all skills to assist the overburdened and understaffed municipal and zemstvo councils.[2] The story of the All-Russian Union of Zemstvos (*Vserossiiskii zemskii soiuz*) illustrates the ascendancy of the technical and professional intelligentsia within local government on the eve of its demise.[3] It also highlights the ultimate consequence of the division within the rural assemblies between the enfranchised

The author gratefully acknowledges the assistance of the staffs of the Lenin Library and the Central State Archive of the October Revolution in Moscow. Special appreciation goes also to E. D. Chermenskii, Professor of History at Moscow State University, for his advice and encouragement during my stay several years ago in the Soviet Union.

zemtsy, coming in most cases from the landed gentry, and the zemstvo employees, better known as the third element.

The union: origins and organization

The union of zemstvos came into existence scarcely hours after the German declaration of war.[4] On August 7, 1914, the Moscow provincial zemstvo convened in emergency session to pledge its energies to the war effort. Simultaneously a more far-reaching proposal was broached: formation of an empire-wide association of zemstvos to better manage the nation's meager medical resources. As suggested, the union's objectives were to facilitate the evacuation of soldiers and civilians from the front, to staff hospitals for the sick and wounded, and to provide medical supplies for the army.[5] Less than one week later, again in Moscow, delegates from 35 provinces gathered in anticipation; never before, not even in 1905 at the height of the Liberation Movement, had so many prominent zemtsy joined hands in common cause. Following a brief discussion they resolved to "create an all-Russian union of zemstvos for aid to the wounded; to organize provincial and smaller local organs of the union...[and] to leave the method of organization of these bodies to the discretion of the zemstvos."[6] Prince G. E. Lvov, whose credentials included direction of the General Organization of Zemstvos, a similar but smaller volunteer relief agency during the Russo-Japanese War, easily won election as the union high commissioner.[7]

The central government quickly extended its blessings. On August 28 an imperial decree announced that the union was to exist for "the duration of the war...under the flag of the Red Cross."[8] As initially constituted, then, the union stemmed from a twofold and potentially contradictory process: the consolidation of the zemstvos coupled with the act of official consent. Not until 1916 was legislation introduced to clarify the union's status, but the State Duma, caught up at that point in a political donneybrook with the Council of Ministers, failed to act on the bill before the 1917 February revolution.

The union's task and jurisdiction were strictly defined: to receive the sick and wounded at railway centers earmarked by the Ministry of War and thence to convey them to rural hospitals. In August the head of the Red Cross drew a straight line on a map to demarcate the intended zone of union operations from the zone reserved for the army medical staff. It was a division of jurisdiction based entirely on geography; east of the line, running from Moscow through Orel to Kharkov, the union was to go about its business; west of the line, to the army's rear and in the immediate vicinity of the front, the Red Cross was entrusted with "exclusive responsibility for private care."[9] In this way the union was confined to the homefront area, completely disregarding the fact that 15 provincial zemstvos west of the line already had joined the union and had undertaken preparations for the treatment of casualties. For the moment their efforts were ignored.

Structurally the union was a loosely textured, somewhat open-ended association. There was no written constitution or fixed set of rules. Membership was available to any zemstvo on the basis of a voluntary commitment, usually in the form of a council resolution. There were no requirements for membership dues because the union officers believed that all of the committees would contribute regularly to the general account – and most of them did.

The union situated its headquarters in Moscow, partly in order to symbolize the action taken there by the zemstvo assembly and partly to maintain continuous contact with its municipal counterpart, the All-Russian Union of Towns. At the national level the policy-making unit was the congress, which formulated resolutions and selected the central committee. Elected by the provincial zemstvos, congress delegates convened on a regular basis, at six-month intervals. The primary concern of the central committee was to direct the trains filled with wounded from clearing stations, which were located just outside the war zone, to the interior provinces, where the zemstvos supervised the medical care. At the outset the central committee was quite small, consisting of Lvov, several assistants, and a few specially chosen representatives from the most important local areas. All of these individuals were members of the gentry class, with long-standing records of public service. Within several months, however, when the union broadened its area of activity and entered the fighting zone, the central committee expanded, and professional consultants were placed in positions of authority. Still later the committee itself became too unwieldy to function smoothly, and a smaller executive bureau, staffed with doctors, sanitation engineers, and statisticians, was established to handle day-to-day affairs.

Since the union represented the zemstvos one would expect that their work in the provinces would have been carried out by the established institutions of local government. As it turned out this was not the case; the union simply could not function on the basis of the prewar zemstvo franchise, however great the enthusiasm of the civic-minded nobility. Prince Lvov, among others, was fully aware of conditions as they existed locally, aware of the fact that the zemstvos were narrowly constituted and not empowered by law to act as they

367

saw fit. Before 1914 these county assemblies had been dominated, by and large, by the nobility. Even the sizable third element – thousands of professionals hired by the zemstvos to develop better schools, hospitals, and farming methods – was left without a voice.[10] Nevertheless, in order to discharge the responsibilities of public welfare, zemstvo leaders depended upon the advice of the third element because they themselves were not always – indeed, not usually – sufficiently well versed in the complexities of such matters as scientific farming or public hygiene.

That tendency was reinforced by the war as union spokesmen ranged far beyond the limits of the zemstvo class franchise and drew in outsiders belonging to the professions who were debarred by law from voting in the assemblies. The actual process of reorganization varied from area to area. Some provincial councils did not find it necessary to appoint parallel committees. These bodies either entrusted the work to their regular board (uprava), authorizing it to co-opt the services of specialists, which most of them did, or selected representatives from among their own number to take part in the local organizations. This was the case in the provinces of Bessarabia, Olonets, Tula, Pskov, and Tauride.

But these zemstvos were the exception. Most affiliates formed ad hoc committees. Many followed the so-called Moscow Plan, emulating the parent organization under its chairman, F. V. Shlippe. Here the provincial committee was composed of 10 men chosen by the assembly, the entire staff of the provincial board, 1 representative from each district committee, 1 from the provincial sanitation bureau, and 1 from the provincial sanitation board.[11] This arrangement was followed in the Viatka, Kaluga, Yaroslavl, Vitebsk, and Petrograd provinces. In a few provinces we find committees of an exceedingly mixed composition. For instance, the Nizhnii Novgorod zemstvo added a good number of community leaders to its roll, whereas in Kiev the provincial zemstvo ballooned to 74 delegates, with representatives from all the district hospitals sitting on the board. In the districts, committee duties were performed entirely by the district boards, who enrolled anybody – usually doctors and sanitation engineers – who might prove useful.[12]

The de facto but significant transformation of the social composition of local government was underscored by two additional developments: first, by the willingness of the regime, usually at the insistence of the army high command, to permit the union to engage in activities that properly were the duty of the state; second, by the domestic reverberations of the war, which magnified the union's place in society. We shall consider these points in turn.

The zemstvos' wartime role

Everyone in Russia, like many people in other combatant countries, had assumed in August 1914 that a heavy struggle under terrible conditions would be settled in some fashion by Christmas. Neither the high command, the dynasty, nor the general public was prepared for a protracted engagement. Thus it soon became evident that official plans for the evacuation of wounded and medical supply beyond points immediately adjacent to the battlefield were virtually nonexistent and that the army medical staff was unable to operate with the facilities at its disposal.[13] Consequently, in September 1914 the Council of Ministers turned unabashedly to the union of zemstvos and the union of towns for the purpose of organizing victory in the rear. For the first six months that task entailed provisioning hospitals, including staff, for the homefront. Some of the figures are staggering. By November 1914, for instance, some 90 days after the mobilization order, 1,667 hospitals units of varying size and description stood ready under union aegis.[14] The job was made easier by the fact that zemstvo doctors and junior medical officers automatically obtained exemption from the draft, a sorely needed privilege in view of the overall shortage of medically trained personnel.

As one of the most important medical centers in Russia, the union of zemstvos compiled information concerning every conceivable dimension of hospital administration. Over 2,000 centers regularly filed reports pertaining to treatment facilities, numbers of patients, and medical staff. Although laden with statistics the reports provide a brief glimpse of the war's impact on Russia's institutional resources. For example, we find that, although the towns and larger cities had better physical facilities, they suffered from a shortage of doctors, even by comparison with the villages.[15] This situation can be explained along several lines. First, the smaller community centers received far fewer patients than the towns. Second, before the war the cities were impoverished in the area of health care, whereas the network of rural hospitals, built largely by the zemstvos, was relatively impressive. Finally, in many cities the available reserve of doctors was depleted by the military call-up. In Moscow alone over half the doctors were taken by the army in the first month. It is no accident therefore that the union of zemstvos employed over six times as many doctors as the union of towns and that it was called upon and did play a larger part in the administration of hospital services.

In the meantime the army had thrown itself on the mercy of the union in yet another capacity: the operation of evacuation carriers, including those trains running inside the war zone. On September 30 the General Staff (*Stavka*) asked Prince Lvov to outfit five trains and dispatch them to Belostok, right at the line dividing the interior from the battlefront. This was just the beginning: weeks later zemstvo trains dotted the countryside in Poland, East Prussia, and Galicia; by February 1915 the union had readied 45 carriers, of which 31 moved to the west of Moscow in the zone once earmarked for the army.[16] Ultimately the union maintained 50 trains which carried as many as 16,000 sick and wounded at one time. They were spread across European Russia, as far west as Brest-Litovsk and Belostok; as far east as Saratov and Riazan.[17]

All of this was terribly expensive; a great deal of money was needed and in a hurry. As far as the trains were concerned, the union and the army, in effect, split the cost: the War Ministry provided the trains, with unequipped cars, and defrayed all railroad charges; in return the union provisioned the trains, including staff, inventories, laundry material, and so forth. The total order from the War Ministry involved an initial outlay for the union of 560,000 rubles, with an additional 280,000 rubles for operations every month thereafter. The Council of Ministers approved the credit and subsequently channeled all allocations through a single agency, a special body with the General Staff.[18]

As the union entered the area of battle, the army encouraged it to extend its operations as fully as possible, whatever the cost. By mid-1916 the network of services ranged from the Zemgor, a joint committee of the unions to increase the flow of munitions, to schemes to improve the cleanliness of the troops, to the procurement and delivery of meat for army consumption. Some of the programs, in particular the Zemgor, were poorly conceived and never amounted to much.[19] In other instances, such as the transportation of wounded from the front, the union acquitted itself well, and it was only through its efforts that anything like adequacy was achieved in ambulance work. Similarly, the zemstvos successfully completed the assignment of provisioning the army with meat, thus reversing a desperate supply shortage from the previous year.[20] Finally, when it came to the care and treatment of refugees in the war zone the unions, acting together, provided an element of civil administration that had not been fashioned at all. In 1915 tens of thousands of people along the western front as well as in Caucasus were fed, clothed, and registered by the unions, which took on the additional burden of telling Petrograd what was going on. The union of zemstvos also provided housing for boys and girls who had lost their parents; by mid-1916 the operation embraced some 300 orphanages where 50,000 children had found a place to live.[21]

Domestic reverberations

These examples illuminate the degree to which the General Staff looked to the union of zemstvos for assistance. They do not, however, constitute the only vantage point from which to view the union's place in history. For many people, and certainly for the men of both unions, the problems of public health care, economic dislocation, and handling refugees from the western provinces lost to the Germans during the Galician campaign of 1915 symbolized the legacy of the war. Attention, correspondingly, centered increasingly on these concerns, sometimes almost to the extent of overlooking the demands of the army. In each instance the unions acted in advance of the authorities and urged the regime to broaden its commitment to and care for the civilian population. In each instance the unions, in varying degrees and with varying intensity, instituted welfare programs exceeding in scope and plenitude the traditional systems of private charity and government-sponsored philanthropy that had predated the war. The services of the union of zemstvos included job rehabilitation for disabled veterans and job training and employment for refugees.[22]

When the government failed to respond to the prodding of the unions, often coupling that failure with a refusal to endorse initiatives beyond the range of bureaucratic controls, it marked the isolation of the regime and its inability to cope with the challenge of modern, total war. By contrast the response of the unions to the problems engendered by the struggle – in the form of professional programs and services – revealed the dynamic of educated society and its potential for development. Certainly the government needed no convincing; from its perspective the unions clearly served as agents for change in the structure and functioning of the old order of society. At a governor's conference in 1916, B. V. Shtiurmer, chairman of the Council of Ministers, put it this way: "The union of zemstvos was culled from persons of a definite coloration...each free unit was saturated with the third element ... moreover, it was impossible to liquidate this problem because the administration could not manage without them." He was no less emphatic about the union of towns:

> If a permanently active...Municipal Union were formed, Russia would have two governments, of which the public one would be independent not only of governmental authority, but also in general of the state ...furthermore...town life – in its economic and administrative entirety – would be completely in the hands of lawyers, technicians, and others from the best segments of the urban population.[23]

During the first 18 months of the fighting the government watched the proliferation of practical public initiative with growing alarm. However, as it was impossible to win the war without accepting a degree of popular assistance, the ministers displayed an ambivalent attitude toward the unions, alternating between heartfelt effusions for the help received and dark suggestions that Lvov and others secretly were maneuvering to destroy the regime's credibility. An example of this ambivalency came when the tsar, while touring the front in 1915 and praising the unions for their "patriotic endeavors," corresponded with Nicholas Maklakov, his minister of internal affairs, who wrote that "all the public figures were... attempting to darken the brilliance of your glory and to weaken the holy immemorial and eternally saving idea of the autocracy."[24] Despite Maklakov's warning the other ministers moved cautiously, confining themselves to periodic reminders that the unions were financially dependent upon the state, not vice-versa.

When at last it became apparent that the unions were going to press forward on such key issues as refugee and public health care, thereby indirectly calling into question the regime's authority, the latter stepped up its attack. An effort was made to curtail the number of union meetings, and in April 1916 a total ban was placed on public congresses and conferences. The ban brought loud protests from the State Duma and from Lvov; in a letter to the war minister, the union high commissioner complained that the "inability to convene... places us in jeopardy and directly paralyzes our work."[25] In September, in response to these protests, the ministers momentarily back-pedalled: the April ban was lifted with the ministers "reserving the right to police any future session, private or public."[26] However, it was too late for lasting compromise: in December, when union representatives gathered in Moscow to consider remedies for the spreading food shortages in the major northern cities, the government resorted to strong-arm police tactics. In a stormy confrontation the congresses were shut down and the delegates forcibly dispersed.[27]

At this point a question arises: Did the union of zemstvos in fact constitute a concrete threat to the authority of the state? Put another way, was the ministers' expressed fear of the union – more precisely of both unions – justified? It is absolutely correct to say that the towns and zemstvos lacked certain crucial powers, power to legislate for their localities or to expand their revenues in time of need. In the first instance they were thoroughly dependent on the Duma; in the second, on the governors and ministers who retained final authority to confirm (or deny) supplemental fund requests.

372

On the other hand the unions undoubtedly were potential sources of subversion: they had under their jurisdiction tens of thousands of civilians; they conducted their business at all levels of society and in all parts of the empire; and, unlike the Duma, they operated yearround and could not be disbanded without an inexcusable increase in human suffering and distress. Even more meaningfully, in some instances, as with hospitals and medical supply, they developed considerable auton- omy, and in the war zone, thanks to the army's control there and its pronounced bias for union-sponsored programs, the public organizations were quite independent. This was especially true for the union of zemstvos, because of the magnitude of its medically related endeavors. Finally, both the army and the ministers – the latter notwithstanding their obsessive status fears – believed that the unions played a vital part in the wartime drama. The government declined to disband them even when they were suspected and accused of disloyalty. Therefore, if so inclined, union leaders could have demanded such reforms as drastic local reorganization, most fundamentally updated municipal and zemstvo statutes, as the price for continued support of the tsar. They could have backed these demands with a threatened work stoppage in the field, in the capital, or everywhere. They could even have appealed to the high command for assistance, insisting that this was an act of patriotism.

Extreme possibilities perhaps, but not altogether beyond the realm of speculation. It will not do to argue that the notion of a military-backed coup defied tradition because the argument from precedent is irrelevant in this case: there was no precedent for the upsurge of voluntary activity during World War I, let alone for the intimate, one might even say cozy, relationship between civilian and military elites. From first to last Lvov extolled the unity of the army and the people, with thinly veiled scorn for the ministers, "whose actions are motivated by mistrust."[28] And, as hopes turned to despair and despair to bitterness, oblique references turned to open threats. Thus in a publicly circulated letter in June 1916, the union high commissioner notified the minister of war that, "as conditions stand now, it would be better for the union to turn aside from additional work as long as the government continues to behave irresponsibly."[29] Lvov soon backed down, however, and the political muscle of the union remained unexploited for reasons that had much less to do with the war than customarily has been claimed.[30]

Zemtsy and the third element

Histories of the union, most notably that by Tikhon Polner, describe it as an organization for the "direct participation of the masses in work for the army."[31] According to this view the union was a national service agency, and its members, in hundreds of local committees, labored mightily at the tasks to which they were set. The conclusion suggests that their patience was tried *only* by the ineptness of the regime and that they, along with all the other elites of the old society, finally deserted the monarchy in February 1917.[32]

There can be no doubt that the founders of the union were to a man driven by a sincere desire to extend a helping hand to the tsar's military machine. Evidence abounds, furthermore, that the disdain for political partisanship on Lvov's part was indeed traceable to the war: time and again he used the public platform to spur his fellow zemstvoists on to greater efforts. However, in my opinion, Polner's portrayal of the union is much too one-sided. An examination of the archival record reveals that the union's fate can in large measure be understood against the backdrop of the patterns of social interaction that characterized the zemstvos at critical junctures throughout the reign of the last tsar. In 1905, to take the most telling illustration from the prewar decade, the organizational momentum of the third element sparked a widespread reaction by conservative *zemtsy* who, having gained the upper hand in the provinces in the aftermath of that turbulent year, moved to mutilate essential features of zemstvo life. For well-nigh two years the local nobility, and not agents for the imperial police, stampeded the zem-stvos into an era of self-liquidation.[33]

During World War I a similar process occurred and with similar results. In basic terms the union's political quiescence – its loyalty to the regime – transcended the war. Simply put, it was grounded in the opposition of the elected nobility in the provinces to the concerted drive by the rank-and-file third element for a more significant place in the local polity.

Ostensibly it might seem that, by virtue of working together for the benefit of the army, the zemtsy and their assistants would have been governed by comparable interests. In reality the gentry representatives and the third element all too often held differing views not only on how best to fulfill their tasks but also with regard to just what the tasks were. Doctors and statisticians, for example, some of them right under Lvov's nose in Moscow, banded together at the very outset "to exploit the union for the purpose of democratizing the zemstvos." By their own admission the war provided a unique opportunity to secure legislative passage of a new zemstvo statute. The employees of the Moscow provincial zemstvo formed a clandestine body within the council "to meet once a month to coordinate the activities of the third element." Alexander Lositskii and Vladimir Dmitriev, both statisticians, were the organizors of the movement.[34] Their group, numbering some 60 individuals when first formed, called itself the "Assembly of Delegates," and combined forces with white collar workers from the union of towns. The assembly was an expressly political group, directing its energies at the "mobilization and unification of the third element of the All-Russian Union of Zemstvos."[35]

Perhaps a period of national emergency, in particular a war, is an inappropriate moment for special interest groups to mount a political assault, however limited in scope. But was it senseless for the third element to think about the future? To deliberate, for example, on its role during postwar reconstruction? I think not. From 1914 onwards, as we have seen, the union employed vast cadres of specialists in its headquarters and provincial and district branches. For two and one-half years hundreds of doctors, nurses, statisticians, and agronomists not only streamlined resources for the war effort but also tried to give more substance to the local administrative units. In this endeavor they were the prime witnesses to the tragic results of a top-heavy, archaic bureaucratic system.

Moreover, the third element was not alone in its concern. Resolutions were passed in the State Duma throughout 1915 calling for changes in the local government laws. Expectations were strongly reinforced by the formation of the Progressive Bloc in August of that year and by the bloc's program, which included planks on most of the serious wartime problems of the empire.[36] Finally, in their campaign for a political voice the professional intelligentsia of the zemstvos found support in the Pirogov Society, the arm of Russia's medical community. In April 1916, at its annual meeting, attended by 1,500 delegates and numerous union-affiliated doctors, the Pirogov Society appealed for the "politicization of the third element and a movement of doctors to the people." The three-day convention concluded with an endorsement of the "reconstruction of our rural and urban institutions on the basis of universal suffrage."[37]

None of this, however, took into account the tenacity of the old-line zemstvo leadership. To the very end of the imperial regime, the nobility – or, to be more exact that portion of the nobility active in zemstvo affairs – maintained a resourceful and determined resistance to initiatives that threatened their position. They did this by various means. They used their numerical preponderance in the provinces to monopolize the selection of delegates to the union congresses and, on rare occasion, when "politics" appeared to intrude on the agenda, to suppress the debate.[38] They controlled the contents of the union journal. Whole articles, sometimes running to 30 and 40 pages, elaborated on the latest sanitation device, therapeutic cure, or hospital design. All these grand subjects were discussed in a vacuum as if nothing else mattered, as if fundamental issues connected with improving the war effort could be divorced from politics and society.

Nor was the union high commissioner, Prince Lvov, much help. It is a truism among Western writers that the Revolution of 1917 descended decisively from the first of the twentieth century's catastrophic horrors. Yet, as previously noted, when it came to Lvov, the war served as an anti-revolutionary force. For, although aware of the dynamite inherent in an awakened though retarded society governed by a stagnant dynasty, Lvov always insisted that the defeat of Germany took precedence over everything else:

> Gentlemen, we are faced with tasks...that would burden the citizen of the most perfect state system...Russia awaits a word from us. Speak it calmly, conscious of your duty...and don't undermine the belief of the Russian people in their own resources, and don't for a moment doubt the final outcome. No world is impossible for us. There is no yoke that the Russian people cannot take upon themselves.[39]

Spoken to a union conference in 1915, in the midst of the headlong summer retreat in Galicia and Poland, these words convey the single-mindedness with which the high commissioner pursued the goal of victory.

Lvov's refusal to use his organization for partisan ends, together with the political conservatism of the zemtsy, produced bitter recriminations within the union. The trouble began in September 1915, at the height of the public clamor over the government's prorogation of the Fourth State Duma. A principal reason for the prorogation was the demand by Duma leaders for the enfranchisement of professional and middle-class elements in the towns and zemstvos. At a union congress in Moscow, groups of doctors and statisticians circulated a petition among the delegates condemning the government's cavalier disregard of the Duma and urging the union to curtail operations in the war zone pending final enactment of the legislative reforms. Lvov's only suggestion and the only response of the congress delegates was to organize a three-man delegation to the throne to put "Nicholas in touch with society." Nothing came of the action, of course, because the tsar declined to receive the delegation. Lvov, in turn, urged his colleagues "to bow before the decision," politics being, in his words, "a waste of time."[40]

Frustrated in their appeals to Lvov, zemstvo employees took matters into their own hands. In 1916, in Minsk, where the union was heavily committed to refugee relief work, doctors and hospital orderlies stopped operations "to protest the class-dominated unions."[41] The tsarist high command, with headquarters at nearby Mogilev, warned against a continuation of the boycott, and Lvov ordered his own investigation. When word came back that the protest was being engineered from Moscow by Lositskii and Dmitriev, Lvov offered to fire his staff assistants. The threat boomeranged: the protests spread to adjoining areas along the front, including Mogilev. In desperation Lvov dispatched Polner to Minsk to intercede with the workers. An on-the-spot police communiqué observes that, once in Minsk, Polner found himself "surrounded by people of leftist tendencies." In Mogilev the situation had further deteriorated: there, Polner discovered that zem-stvo employees were affiliated with the Bolshevik underground which was engaged in the spreading of antiwar propaganda. Apparently Polner recommended that no action be taken against the strikers, but when the police ignored his advice and moved in to arrest over two dozen employees of the Mogilev provincial zemstvo neither he nor Lvov resisted.[42] Small wonder that three months later, at a conference of consumer cooperatives in Moscow, with spokesmen for the union third element in attendance, a resolution was passed condemning the union for "its estrangement from the democratic intelligentsia."[43]

Ironically the unfolding panorama of conflict and dissension within the union hierarchy coincided with a change of heart on the part of the union high commissioner. In the fall of 1916, Lvov announced his support for full-scale political reform. In consultation with his staff, he called for the introduction into every rural district of an all-class volost zemstvo to aid the peasant economy. He recommended the abolition of franchise distinctions based on property and the granting of the vote as well as membership in the volost assemblies to the third element.[44] Although Lvov did not editorialize on the motivation behind the belated interest in reform, a probable impetus lay with the escalating cry for change by the union intelligentsia. Also pertinent, no doubt, was the assumption of authority by groups of specialists who, it will be remembered, by the summer of 1916 had taken charge of the provision-ing of meat for military units in the war zone. One can infer some anxiety on Lvov's part over this turn of events because it was here, along the western front, that audible rumblings of discontent had surfaced among the third element.

In any event Lvov coupled his suggestions with an invitation to the local assemblies to come forth with their recommendations. To his great disappointment and chagrin no response came. In my opinion the silence should not have been surprising; the old-line zemstvos still were very much the political preserve of the militantly intransigent nobility. As a result Lvov, along with the third element, stood alone, suspended in midair, so to speak, between the zemstvos below and the ministry above, a ministry secure in its waning weeks that the nobility constituted the flower of the land.[45]

Conclusion

The union of zemstvos survived the February Revolution, continued to function under the Provisional Government, and finally was dissolved in January 1918 by decree of the Bolsheviks. Nevertheless, from a practical standpoint the union had ceased to exist before the collapse of tsarism: by the end of 1916 many workers had left the committees, and field operations had fallen off dramatically. Furthermore, in 1917 the union was radically restructured in line with the democratic goals of the Provisional Government, thus assuming a new and, from the pre-1917 perspective, unrecognizable social profile.

In the conclusion to his book Polner would have us believe that the disintegration of local government which followed the introduction of the wide-ranging changes was the result of the cumulative shocks of war and revolution. Only in 1917, we are told, did "extremist elements" within the zemstvos demand reorganization from top to bottom.[46]

It cannot be denied that the war interrupted the application of the new administration and that the very revolution which had made the reforms possible speedily rendered them obsolete. At the same time, as we have tried to show, the divisions within the zemstvos, manifest in the union, were visible and consequential before 1917. The play of forces was organic in nature, reflecting the inferior standing of the third element and its aspiration for recognition commensurate with its civic responsibility. The contribution of the third element to the wartime mobilization of human and material resources served only to whet its appetite for power. In the union the reality of class in time overshadowed that of dedication to a patriotic cause. From 1914 to 1917 the myth of the zemstvo as an aggregate of high-minded individuals stood revealed; likewise the shape of things to come once the empire gave way.

Notes

1   Norman Stone, The Eastern Front 1914–1917 (New York, 1975), p. 14.
2   For an analysis of the war's impact on the cities, see William Gleason, "The All-Russian Union of Towns and the Politics of Urban Reform in Tsarist Russia," Russian Review, 1976, no. 3, pp. 290–303.

378

3 Many zemstvo specialists who launched their professional careers during the Stolypin ministry provided a link with early Soviet society when they survived the Bolshevik insurrection of 1917 and were again at work in the 1920s, this time under the auspices of the People's Agricultural Commissariat. See George Yaney, "Agricultural Administration in Russia," in James Millar, ed., *The Soviet Rural Community* (Urbana–Champaign, Ill., 1971), pp. 3–36.

4 Soviet and Western historical literature takes little note of the union. The principal published source is Tikhon J. Polner, *Russian Local Government During the War and the Union of Zemstvos* (New Haven, 1930). Polner was a high-ranking member of the union central committee, and his account, written nearly a half-century ago, constitutes a good starting point for an investigation of the union. For a recently published study of the union's handling of the wartime food crisis, see Thomas Fallows, "Politics and the War Effort in Russia: The Union of Zemstvos and the Organization of the Food Supply, 1914–1916," *Slavic Review*, 1978, no. 1, pp. 70–90. For an unpublished history of the union, see William Gleason, "The All-Russian Union of Towns and the All-Russian Union of Zemstvos in World War I: 1914–1917" (Ph.D. dissertation, Indiana University, 1972). For the only published Soviet assessment, see A. P. Pogrebinskii, "K istorii soiuzov zemstv i gorodov," *Istoricheskie zapiski*, 1941, no. 12, pp. 39–60.

5 Vserossiiskii zemskii soiuz (VZS), *Obzor deiatel'nosti glavnogo komiteta 1 avgusta 1914–1 fevralia 1915* (Moscow, 1915), pp. 21–5.

6 Ibid., p. 18. Seven of the eight unrepresented zemstvos sent telegrams of support for the union. Eventually only the Kursk provincial council refused to join, being dominated by ultraconservative zemtsy.

7 A detailed description of the general organization of zemstvos as well as Lvov's role throughout this period can be found in Tikhon J. Polner, *Zhiznennyi put' Kniazia Georgiia Evgen'evicha L'vova* (Paris, 1932).

8 TsGAOR, f. 102, op. 17, ed. khr. 343, August 16, 1914, p. 151. This archival source, a police report, contains the recommendation of Nicholas Maklakov concerning the legal status of the union. Maklakov was the minister of internal affairs at the start of the war.

9 By a decree of July 12, 1913. This decree, issued before the war, was intended to specify the exact jurisdiction of the Red Cross and the army medical staff. Now it was used to limit the union's activities to the interior of the country.

10 Altogether in 1910 the zemstvo third element "comprised no less than 65,000 or 70,000 employees." See B. B. Veselovskii, *Istoriia zemstva za sorok let*, 4 vols. (St. Petersburg, 1909–11), 2:494. Another source notes that in 1906, in the two capitals alone, 27,000 individuals worked for the zemstvo and municipal councils. See *Samoupravlenie*, 1906, no. 2.

11 For more details on the Moscow provincial zemstvo during the war along with the activities of its chairman, see "Shlippe Memoirs," Russian and East European Archive, Columbia University, New York.

12 VZS, pp. 24–5.

13 General Danilov, chief supply officer for the northwest front, later recalled that "our health department had given little thought in peacetime to guaranteeing the troops a sufficient number of doctors during the war." See Iu. N. Danilov, *Rossiia v mirovoi voine 1914–1915 gg.* (Berlin, 1924), p. 116–17.

14 *Izvestiia VZS*, 1915, no. 26, p. 19.

15 Village hospitals had one doctor for every 16.4 patients as compared with ratios of 20.8 and 43.5, respectively, for the district and provincial towns. Ibid., 1915, no. 29, p. 19.

16 VZS, pp. 299–301.

17 *Izvestiia VZS*, 1915, no. 15, pp. 11–13.

18 Ibid., 1916, no. 32, pp. 65–6. For the first 18 months the union received over 150 million rubles in state subsidies. By 1916, as relations between the union and the regime began to deteriorate, the ministers charged that union leaders deliberately "misspent millions." The charge is difficult to accept since the state comptroller had on several occasions audited the union books, concluding each time that they were in good order. On the other hand, there is some evidence that the government's criticism was, to a degree, politically motivated. In testimony before the Provisional Government in 1917, Alexander Protopopov, minister of internal affairs in late 1916, admitted that the ministers reacted to the union's influence during the war by reminding its leaders of their "financial subserviency." See *Padenie tsarskogo rezhima*, 7 vols. (Leningrad, 1926–7), 4:72.

19 The Zemgor worked with small factories and cottage industry (*kustari*), whose technical backwardness was too great to permit the manufacture of sophisticated weaponry. Heavy industry, which possessed the requisite technology, dealt directly with government contractors who paid handsomely for their services. Union leaders were well aware of these shortcomings, and it is inaccurate to say, as Norman Stone does in his history of the war, that Lvov and others inflated the Zemgor's contribution to the war economy. See Stone, pp. 201 ff. Stone's sources do not include the union's published reports and summaries.

20 The memoirs of Alexander Naumov, minister of agriculture in 1916, are quite clear on this point. Naumov notes that when he came into office in November 1915, there was no overall meat provisioning plan for the army and that "only in the spring of 1916, due to the statistical and organizational endeavors of the zemstvos," were improvements made. In 1916, Army Chief of Staff General Alekseev informed Naumov that the army was stocked with a three months'

supply of meat. See A. Naumov, *Iz utselevshikh vospominanii,
1868–1917 gg.*, 2 vols. (New York, 1955), 2:471, 476.

21 *Izvestiia VZS*, 1916, nos. 41–42, pp. 123–7.

22 The last effort was especially interesting. Jobs for refugees came
through the Labor Exchange, a central employment bureau established by the two unions in 1915. By 1916 the exchange operated
through 100 local outlets, and in Petrograd the Ministry of Trade and
Industry empowered the union bureau to act as the principal employment agency for the northern capital area. Ultimately the enterprise
proved too difficult because the unions had little if any leverage when
it came to negotiating contracts, wages, and salaries. Consequently
they gradually phased out the exchange and in September 1916
closed its doors forever.

23 *Krasnyi arkhiv*, 1929, no. 2, pp. 150–1.

24 V. P. Semennikov, ed., *Monarkhiia pered krusheniem* (Moscow,
1927), p. 95.

25 *Izvestiia Vserossiiskogo soiuza gorodov*, 1916, no. 37, 26–7.

26 B. B. Grave, ed., *Burzhuaziia nakanune fevral'skoi revoliutsii* (Moscow, 1927), pp. 152–3. This documentary collection contains the
ministerial instruction to the local authorities to relax their vigilance
in light of the union's importance to the war effort.

27 TsGAOR, f. 102, op. 17, ed. khr. 343[3c], tom 5, pp. 31–4.

28 VZS, *Sobranie upolnomochennykh gubernskikh zemstv v Moskve, 5
iiuniia 1915* (Moscow, 1915), pp. 5–9.

29 Tsentral'nyi Gosudarstvennyi Voenno-Istoricheskii Arkhiv (TsGVIA),
f. 12564, op. 1, d. 80, p. 80.

30 In my dissertation I maintained that the war was indeed the primary
restraint on the union's oppositional profile to the autocracy. Subsequent investigation in the Soviet archives revealed a more persuasive
perspective, set forth in this article.

31 Polner, *Russian Local Government*, p. 9.

32 On the other hand, Thomas Fallows, in his study of the union
leadership, argues that politics was uppermost in the minds of the
zemtsy in their response to the food crisis. Politics, in this case, is
taken to mean a desire on the part of zemstvo officials for autonomy
from the government in the organization of food supply. Against this
position two points are in order, in my opinion. First of all, as Fallows
himself admits, there is ample evidence to suggest that much of the
movement for the establishment of a food supply apparatus derived
from practical necessity – the union acted in large measure to
coordinate the variety of zemstvo programs to procure food for the
army. Secondly, I quite agree with Fallows that Lvov was unhappy
with the government. That much is evident from the published
sources. The question is, Why, given the degree of disillusionment,
didn't Lvov and the union respond in some fashion to intimidation by
the ministers throughout 1916? The answer, as suggested in this

chapter, will not be found in the published record. See Fallows, pp. 70–90.

33 Veselovskii, 4: 64 ff. Paradoxically the zemstvo *likvidatorstvo* occurred exactly when the authorities in Saint Petersburg were more than willing to admit that Russia's professional elite had a part to play in transforming the countryside and schooling the peasantry. Because of this the rural public service sector expanded, and the cadre of technical intelligentsia showed a sharp increase. The most notable proliferation of personnel and program under zemstvo aegis came with the implementation of the land reform acts of Stolypin. In 1912, to take one example, over 1,000 agronomists drew their pay from the zemstvos, a figure which takes on meaning when it is noted that 12 years earlier only 200 specialists had performed a similar task. See V. E. Brunst, "Zemskaia agronomiia," in Z. G. Frenkel' and B. B. Veselovskii, eds., *Iubileinyi zemskii sbornik* (St. Petersburg, 1914), pp. 327–8.

34 TsGAOR, f. 102, op. 17, ed. khr. 343, tom 3, pp. 69–70. The source material for this section of the paper comes for the most part from a series of reports by the union third element. The reports are located in the Moscow section of the tsarist police file.

35 Ibid., tom 4, p. 305.

36 Michael F. Hann, "The Progressive Bloc and Russia's Fourth State Duma" (Ph.D. dissertation, Indiana University, 1971), chs. 1–2.

37 TsGAOR, f. 102, op. 17, ed. khr. 338, pp. 83–4.

38 Newspaper reports regularly stressed the reluctance of the union delegates to "weigh issues of a general state character." See, for example, *Utro Rossii*, February 18, 1915 or *Rech'*, February 15, 1916.

39 *Izvestiia VZS*, 1915, nos. 22–23, p. 17. Emphasis added.

40 According to a Soviet scholar, Nicholas II initially was prepared to meet the delegation but, "under great pressure from Alexandra and the court," finally refused to do so. The rejection decision was relayed to Lvov by word of mouth "in order to keep matters out of the press." See V. S. Diakin, *Russkaia burzhuaziia v gody pervoi mirovoi voiny, 1914–1917* (Leningrad, 1967), pp. 125–6.

41 TsGAOR, f. 102, op. 17, ed. khr. 343, tom 4, p. 99.

42 Ibid., pp. 43–4.

43 Ibid., p. 94. Quite possibly these incidents proved so embarassing to Polner that he chose to ignore the political history of the third element in his account of the union. That would explain the discrepancy between the published and unpublished records on the political background of the zemstvos in the period before the February Revolution.

44 *Izvestiia VZS*, 1916, no. 49, pp. 156–7.

45 In November 1916, Lvov criticized the zemstvos for their lax attitude toward reform, an unusual gesture; generally he denied any suggestion of intraorganizational friction. See *Izvestiia VZS*, 1916, no. 50, p. 100.

46 Polner, *Russian Local Government*, pp. 306–7.

12

The zemstvo in 1917 and its fate under Bolshevik rule

WILLIAM G. ROSENBERG

Like those which preceded it, the final chapter in the history of the zemstvo is rife with irony and contradiction. For liberals like Prince Lvov and others in the zemstvo union, the tsar's abdication seemed finally to remove the impediments that had blocked zemstvo development for more than 50 years and that many saw as a root cause of Russian political backwardness. The revolution promised civil liberties and a rule of law, and the full development of legitimate organs of self-government at a local level. For those who felt ideologically committed to these objectives or who had struggled for years within the zemstvo apparatus to broaden liberal prerogatives and improve social welfare, February was a time of genuine rejoicing.

But it soon became apparent, as the revolution began to unfold, that this one "traditional" organ of government often considered potentially progressive and democratic was becoming almost everywhere a barrier to social reform, and in most places a symbol of reaction. By the summer of 1917, the zemstvo had also become an arena of conflict rather than an instrument of social harmony; by the fall, many zemstvo activists actually felt themselves "subverted" by democratic processes, as efforts at improving local welfare were rejected by peasants as unwarranted interference in their affairs.[1]

The problem, of course, was partly one of timing and the difference between orderly, liberal change and radical social transformation; but even more so it reflected the contradiction between the realities of past zemstvo politics and social relations, and the objectives to which liberal zemstvo figures hoped to press these institutions in a new era of democracy and freedom. In this as in so many other areas of Russian life, 1917 represented the violent interface of historical legacy and revolutionary aspiration, a time when traditional institutions and values lay open to scrutiny and assault and when only that which was deeply rooted in popular need, habit, or consciousness stood much chance to survive. For many, what made the final chapter of zemstvo history so agonizing was not only that the zemstvos collapsed just when their full development as liberal, democratic institutions seemed finally within reach but that a free Russian peasantry regarded them with hostility and, perhaps even worse, indifference. More than five decades of effort to improve rural life and establish effective local government seemed to lead precisely nowhere.

Approaching this final chapter of zemstvo history in terms of the contradictory processes of tradition and change reveals much about the zemstvo itself, but is also highly suggestive in terms of the revolution generally. The decline in zemstvo authority reflects a process of peasant emancipation from traditional government institutions and raises questions about the nature of political democratization in 1917. Through the zemstvo one can observe the developing contrast between democratization as a means for legitimizing state authority, as supported by the vast majority of moderate socialist and liberal political figures, and democratization as an effort to broaden the unilateral powers of ad hoc class-bound bodies like the peasant *skhod*, which involved peasant fears about outsiders gaining control of local affairs. One gets a sense as well of the growing problem of urban–rural relations generally and of the interesting process of introversion in the countryside in 1917, which involved a closing off of the villages and the development of a virulent hostility on the peasants' part toward representatives of any central administrative bodies. Similarly, the manner in which an ostensibly progressive institution became a barrier to change reflects the myriad problems of securing "orderly" reform and allows one to observe in some detail the ways in which liberal democrats rapidly shed their principles and their commitments, a complex process of psychological, social, and economic displacement as well as political transformation. The issues here involve method as well as purpose and raise important general questions of means and ends in a period of revolutionary upheaval.

I must confess that in approaching the zemstvo in 1917, these larger issues have concerned me at least as much as zemstvo activities themselves. This chapter reflects a strong bias against institutional history detached from broad political concerns. In one sense, however, the bias is appropriate to my task: one simply could not present a full institutional history of the zemstvo in 1917 in 40 pages, much less an analysis of its fate under Bolshevik rule. Zemstvos operated at all administrative levels during these months – province, district (uezd), and volost – as well as through such organizations as the All-Russian Union of Zemstvos. Activities varied widely from region to region, from town to village, and from month to month. Divisions developed among zemstvo leaders themselves, and zemstvos in different areas assumed quite different aspects under the Bolsheviks and during the Civil War.

The situation is similar with larger patterns of zemstvo institutional history. The preceding chapters in this volume have suggested rather strongly that the zemstvos' fate had largely been determined even before the February revolt, set by such factors as gentry reaction in the country-side (particularly after 1905), tsarist repressive violence, third-element conflict with zemstvo boards and assemblies, zemstvo tax policies, and the limited conception on the part of many zemstvos of peasant welfare and need. Since the ways in which such legacies affected zemstvo performance in 1917 also varied widely from province to province, they, too, are not really susceptible to detailed scrutiny. But, at the same time, one might possibly get at some general issues of principle. The opportuni-ties presented by the revolution had been eagerly awaited by a number of zemstvo activists for years, and the liberal government's hopes for effective rural self-government rested on zemstvo reform. In a sense, therefore, 1917 was a test of long-time liberal zemstvo assumptions and might be analyzed at least in part in these terms.

In the discussion that follows, my effort will be to highlight the most important features of zemstvo history in 1917, particularly at the volost level, and try to suggest ways in which this history reflects broader problems. I have distinguished five separate phases of zemstvo develop-ment and trust that my periodization, albeit somewhat loose, does not do violence to historical continuities. The first phase is roughly between March and May and is a period of political democratization, both from "above" and "below." Then, between May and August, comes a period of maximum government investment in zemstvo functions and a time when the zemstvos themselves began to mirror Russia's growing social polariza-tion, revealing different meanings of the terms *revolution* and *democracy* to different social groups. Then follows a period of battle, when zemstvo elections generally became the focal point of rural dissidence; followed in turn by the period after October, when for many zemstvo employees, particularly in the zemstvo union, the issue was not political democracy but social welfare. Finally, and briefly, I will survey the final phase of zemstvo activity in anti-Bolshevik Russia and abroad.

The zemstvo and liberal democracy

The February Revolution meant "democracy" for Russia, and all but the most confirmed supporters of Nicholas and his entourage seemed genuinely excited by its prospects. There were doubts, of course, and also a good deal of fear. Liberals like V. D. Nabokov thought it "dangerous to venture out" and spent several days in their apartments "in a kind of stupor and anxious waiting." But Nabokov himself emerged on March 2 with a deep sense of "spiritual elation," and others must have felt the same.[2] Duma leaders like Rodzianko and Maklakov worried about Russia's "readiness" for democracy but moved quickly to ensure an orderly transition, "securing" the Ministry of Justice and taking control of various state institutions in the new government's name.[3] In the zemstvos, there was little doubt things would change for the better. Many provincial bodies "keenly resented" tsarist economic policies and had loudly demanded greater administrative authority.[4] Work in relief of sick and wounded soldiers, aid to refugees, and other important functions of supply and welfare had all been hampered by tsarist administrators, and few zemstvo figures doubted the new government would move quickly to give them more power.

They were not disappointed. As early as March 4, at one of its very first meetings, the new Provisional Government indicated how great an investment it was prepared to make in the zemstvos by dismissing all tsarist governors and vice governors and entrusting their offices to the chairmen of provincial zemstvo boards. At the same time, chairmen of district zemstvo boards were appointed "district commissars" of the new regime and officially charged with all duties of district government administration in the interest of "establishing order" and "guaranteeing the uninterrupted functioning of all governmental and public institutions."[5] In a single stroke, zemstvo leaders throughout Russia thus became guardians of public welfare and official representatives of Russia's "new democratic order."

Shortly afterward, zemstvo groups serving the army were also given more authority, and on March 20, the government initiated plans to extend zemstvo organization into Russia's more than 9,000 volosts, smaller rural divisions of the districts (uezdy).[6] Broadening zemstvo operations in this way had been a goal of democratic zemstvo figures for years, beginning, in fact, as early as the reform period itself, when many zemstvo liberals were distressed at the tsar's decision to limit the new institutions to district and province levels. Some of these units were enormous. One or two districts approached the size of Holland or Denmark and contained upwards of 100,000 inhabitants; Okhansk and Glazovsk in the Urals had almost 3,000 villages and some half-million inhabitants. Even on the average there were some 30 to 40 villages in each volost, with some 20 volosts per district.[7] Hopes were high after

1905 that the tsar would extend zemstvo functions to the volost level, and there were repeated appeals for such a reform at various party and professional meetings. The State Council consistently blocked Duma legislation to this end, however, even plans drafted by Fourth Duma representatives with conservative support.[8]

The March 20 announcement was thus the culmination of many years of struggle. Calling volost zemstvo organization an "urgent task," the new regime formed a special zemstvo section of the Ministry of Interior to supervise volost zemstvo organization and indicated that legislation "formalizing" volost bodies would soon be forthcoming. In the meantime, Lvov and his colleagues empowered provincial and district zemstvo board chairmen (now government "commissars") to organize "temporary volost committees." Pending the election of volost zemstvo assemblies, these committees were to assume the tasks of rural government, particularly those of "supplying the army, maintaining order, and preserving intact the buildings and files of the [tsarist] volost administration."[9]

The process of political democratization had thus begun, reflecting in the zemstvo structure the broader pattern of Russian society as a whole. With hindsight, some flaws in these developments seem obvious. Provincial zemstvo figures in many places were identified with the staunchest gentry reaction, and, as Chapter 5 in this volume has shown, had even opposed aspects of Stolypin's Third of June system as insufficiently safeguarding their interests. If one can appreciate why the new regime appointed zemstvo chairmen as commissars in early March, given fears of counterrevolution and the desire to draw as much gentry support as possible for the new government, the authority of the chairmen was still bound to lead to conflict. The government's misconception in this regard was that peasant support for a revolutionary regime would be far more secure than that of the gentry, whose resources and alliances might lead to a dangerous fronde; but, in retrospect, what is surprising is not the liberal government's intentions but its failure to recognize the degree of past peasant alienation from the zemstvo and the likelihood that extending "democratic" authority through zemstvo officials was bound to raise peasant suspicions about the new order's orientation as a whole.

Also, the liberal regime was democratizing the zemstvo by fiat, something of a contradiction in terms. The new government even used the word *ukaz* in announcing zemstvo reforms, certainly a gratuitous identification with the old order, even to many who recognized the necessity of proceeding at this stage by decree. As those familiar with this period realize, contradictions of this sort were also emerging in other areas of Russian life in March and April, notably in connection with the war; they lay at the heart of the growing problem of dual power. But the liberal ministers' actions themselves hardly augured well for the success of democratic zemstvo self-government.

These first zemstvo reforms also suggest other problems with the process of political democratization, at once more subtle and more revealing. For one thing, Russia's new regime was attempting to give official sanction to what was, in effect, an ad hoc political reconstruction, reflecting at a state level the same tendency of various special interest groups to take local matters into their own hands. Unilateral government decrees were, of course, an inevitable and necessary consequence of overthrowing the autocracy, but the new regime's power depended on popular support and its ability to justify what it was doing. In this regard the obvious is worth remembering: Lvov and his colleagues were deliberately using institutions and procedures consonant with liberal traditions but which for many had come to represent the essence of Russia's estate system with its special prerogatives for those with wealth and education. For those who rejected liberal premises, whether peasants or social democrats, or who saw the zemstvos as institutions protecting gentry interests, there was no obvious justification to building a new system of local government based on the zemstvo, as opposed, say, to allowing peasants themselves to organize new volost councils or perhaps delegating democratic State Duma representatives to perform temporarily the functions of provincial commissars.

Also, some provincial zemstvo boards were already beginning to move directly into areas of production and commerce. A special Iaroslavl province conference, for example, resolved in April to assign up to 15,000 rubles toward plans for a zemstvo agricultural machinery plant "in the interests of raising the productive forces of the country," and similar plans were underway elsewhere.[10] In some places, like Kostroma, zemstvo groups had already used their new freedom to buy into manufacturing enterprises.[11] Such steps may actually have been motivated by altruistic as well as entrepreneurial concerns, but they tended further to identify the zemstvos as "bourgeois" institutions, weakening their prospects for popular support.

Lvov and his colleagues felt pressed for time and acted as they did out of concern for gentry reaction and peasant violence. The zemstvos were established, gentry-controlled welfare institutions, and their employees possessed valuable expertise. It was logical to assume they could be used to preserve rural order and carry on functions of local government. There was also what might be called historical expectation in this regard, and the absence of any other comparable "all-class" institution. But it was also logical for those hostile to gentry zemstvo figures to interpret government democratization procedures as a means of extending gentry power. In the process, moreover, even progressive "third-element" people could not help but be tainted with a social identity most of them probably did not have. Thus one cannot be fully surprised to find reports as early as the third week of March rejecting the authority of zemstvo personnel and even demanding the dismissal of zemstvo teachers, agronomists, and other third-element professionals.[12]

Also, the very size of prerevolutionary zemstvo districts meant that even district personnel were often strangers to thousands of local villagers. As these persons became Provisional Government officials, charged with such matters as directing local finances and mobilizing army supplies, they were bound to appear as outside authorities, little different in the peasants' view from those they had replaced. In addition, many zemstvo figures actually were former tsarist administrators themselves, identified with unpopular tax policies. Already by April the Ministry of Internal Affairs had begun to recognize the "general discontent" that province and district zemstvo board members were creating in their new roles. In a circular dated April 27, the ministry admitted that zemstvo board chairmen "have never enjoyed the confidence or good will of the people" and that "the idea of appointment has not fit in with the popular understanding."[13] What the circular failed to say, of course, is that the government itself in this way may have generated considerable confusion in the countryside about the meaning of liberal democracy and perhaps even helped arouse the very passions and conflict it hoped to avoid.

Conflict may also have stemmed from the fact that these first reforms failed to consider that peasants themselves were *not* disorganized in rural localities, despite the absence of volost zemstvo bodies. Throughout Russia peasant councils (*skhody*) often unofficially performed the functions of local government, and, as tsarist officials disappeared from the countryside, these rudimentary governing bodies began to expand their activities. In Vologda province, councils were organized at a volost level in some 90 districts in the first half of March, some 25 percent of the total. Another 175 volosts organized by the first of April. According to a report in *Severnyi khoziain*, these were organized almost entirely by peasants themselves, without outside help; peasants constituted 76 percent of their members.[14] In addition, in Samara, Nizhnii Novgorod, and Iaroslavl, representatives from volost peasant councils convened their own provincewide congresses. The sources do not reveal how successful these gatherings were or what they discussed, but what is clear is that in addition to other more familiar peasant groups organizing at this time, like the SR (Socialist Revolutionary) "Peasants Union," and local peasant soviets, Russia's peasants were also developing governing institutions on their own. The evidence is fragmentary, but the council may also have been the one institutional form that the peasants themselves most trusted.[15]

The implications of this in terms of expanding the zemstvos are evident. As "temporary volost committees" came "down" from district and province zemstvos, peasant delegates themselves came "up" from the villages. Conflict of some sort was inevitable unless institutional ambitions could be reconciled. In Tver, a number of volost peasant councils sent delegates to district zemstvo boards with demands for full control over all aspects of rural life; in Samara, a number of the councils announced that they would not respect the authority of prerevolutionary zemstvo officials.[16] Elsewhere, peasants simply delegated representatives to sit on existing zemstvo bodies, supplementing rather than replacing authorized deputies.[17] The local SR paper in Saratov editorialized strongly against this "spontaneous democratization," calling instead for orderly reconstruction "from top to bottom"[18] but in Kazan a group of provincial zemstvo members complained themselves that new peasant delegates had no "legitimate authority" and hence the "democratized" zemstvo was itself without legal foundation.[19] Thus the conflict was not only one of institutional competence but of the manner and form of peasant control over peasant affairs. In Kazan, democratization was rejected "from above" precisely because it involved surrendering power to "illegitimate" peasant delegates; in Tver, it was rejected "from below" because it involved the surrender of council powers to the zemstvos.

Many observers, of course, identified growing peasant power with anarchy, violence, and social disintegration in the spring of 1917, and sharply questioned peasant competence in government matters. Violence was indeed increasing in April and May, but one must remember that it was largely purposeful, in support of the peasants' quest for land, and hence bespeaks an impatience with Western legal procedures rather than random chaos or administrative incompetence. Whether the peasants' own newly elected leaders actually did lack competence in managing their affairs is an interesting question that cannot be investigated here. An "unofficially democratized" peasant zemstvo board in Ustiug thoroughly reorganized the local court structure and managed to secure a bank loan of some 400,000 rubles, which suggests that it was something more than a group of dullards.[20] In Kremenchug, another exclusively peasant zemstvo board resolved as its first measures to broaden the program of zemstvo schools, prepare teachers in Ukrainian, and organize a lecture series on current events.[21] But here as elsewhere in 1917, the mere conception many Russians had of peasant activism as a blind, anarchic force may have been as compelling in structuring the course of revolution as actual peasant activities; and in any event, the increasingly complex and spontaneous process of zemstvo reorganization pushed the government to move as rapidly as possible toward official, regularizing legislation.

This legislation was finally ready in May in the form of three decrees, one introducing "the most pressing changes" in the statute on province and district zemstvos, pending the promulgation of an entirely new statute by the Constituent Assembly; one setting out rules on the election of province and district zemstvo members; and a comprehensive statute on volost zemstvo administration, including rules for elections, and new provisions concerning the volost zemstvos duties in collecting taxes. Together, the three constituted a radical restructuring of Russian provincial self-government. According to *Russkie vedomosti*, they were "of utmost importance" for Russia's democratic future.[22]

The new zemstvos and their contradictions

Publication of these decrees signalled the start of a second phase in zemstvo history during 1917, a phase in which the new government made an extraordinary investment in the zemstvo as the primary instrument of local government for democratic Russia. The new legislation involved both a broadening of zemstvo functions and a formal substitution of an expanded zemstvo hierarchy for the old tsarist administrative structure in the countryside. Zemstvo institutions were now charged with virtually all matters of local government and economy as well as "other matters assigned to them by specific legislation." These included:

> Elimination of shortages and high prices of foodstuffs and articles of prime necessity; promoting consumers societies and the organization of food shops, bakeries and the like; maintenance of roads, piers, and local means of communication; administration of zemstvo medical institutions; care of the poor, the incurably ill, the insane, and orphans and cripples; organization and maintenance of elementary schools and other educational institutions; book publishing; organization and maintenance of public libraries; veterinary and veterinary police measures; protection of labor; organization of public works, public

> workshops, overnight lodging houses, labor exchanges, and interme-
> diary employment offices; and public security...[and] meeting the
> requirements of the military and civil administrations.

This last was a catch-all provision which virtually subordinated the
zemstvo to military command. In addition, the new volost zemstvos
were made responsible for the administration of zemstvo taxes, in
money and kind, to the extent determined by the district zemstvo
assembly. Volost zemstvo jurisdiction extended to continuous districts
formed from all types of holdings located outside municipalities, and
to all persons residing within these limits regardless of status; and
central government authorities were permitted to interfere in local
zemstvo decisions only if they were "clearly illegal."[23]

This was, indeed, a remarkable range of responsibilities for new
organs of local government. In ordinary times, it would have presented
serious challenges even to experienced administrators; in the midst of a
war and a "deepening" revolution, the new legislation shifted responsibility for a series of urgent tasks onto a political matrix that few rural
Russians really thought of as their own. The decrees created some
9,500 new volost zemstvo cells, each consisting of an elected assembly
and a zemstvo board. Assemblies were required to convene at least
once a year and had to assemble within a period of two weeks upon
application of one-fifth of the assembly members or on the request of
the zemstvo board, an executive body of at least three persons elected
by the assembly. Thus virtually all issues of volost government were
susceptible almost immediately to democratic review. With an average
of some 30 members per assembly, the Provisional Government was
also creating almost 300,000 new local officials, each of whom was to
be elected on the basis of secret and direct elections. An additional
40,000 persons were likely to be drawn into the administrative work of
local zemstvo boards.[24] Reforms on the district and province level were
somewhat less comprehensive, but here, too, assembly members were
to be democratically elected and charged with direct review of zemstvo
affairs.[25]

It is possible to see in these provisions some hesitation on the part of
government liberals to purge the zemstvo apparatus entirely of its
traditional estate orientation. When temporary volost committees were
established in March, Prince Lvov and his colleagues called specifically for the participation of local landowners and especially for the
involvement of village "intellectual forces," who "inspired the greatest
confidence of the population."[26] These attitudes were also reflected in
review powers now officially granted to provincial zemstvo boards, in
the indirect form of provincial assembly elections, and in the various

requirements at the district and province level for ministerial review. But more significant in terms of the developing problems of revolutionary government is the way in which the new legislation still reflected genuine liberal aspirations. The new government *wanted* effective, orderly popular rule in the countryside guided by liberal zemstvo professionals, even as disillusionment with democratic authority grew; and for those whose hopes had been placed for many years on the full realization of zemstvo potential, the statutes themselves, even more than the new institutions they created, seemed a worthy culmination of struggle.

Thus liberal and populist papers alike greeted the legislation in euphoric terms. According to *Zemlia i volia*, the new volost zemstvo was the "foundation of a new government order," the means for "realizing the will of the whole rural population"; Soviets and other committees had only "temporary significance" and were not institutions for substantial growth and development.[27] *Russkoe slovo* saw the volost zemstvo as a vehicle for "the great, creative national work of the peasantry," and *Russkie vedomosti* and *Rech'* expressed high hopes for institutions based "on truly democratic principles."[28]

Even as the statutes were being published, however, few could really doubt that the gap between vision and reality in the case of the zemstvos was likely to be very large indeed. Zemstvos represented "revolution" in terms of political democracy, not social reform; and while many would argue that one simply had to precede the other if reform was to have legal foundation, the connection was not so obvious in the countryside, where many peasants must have already felt they had control over their own affairs, and where "revolution" and "democracy" both meant, above all, a change in social relations and the end of gentry dominance. The new zemstvo legislation, in fact, reflected the remarkable shift which even three months of revolution had wrought on the meaning of constitutionalism in Russia. Almost to the moment of Nicholas II's abdication, insistence on a legislative foundation for both local and national government was a progressive, if fundamentally conservative political outlook, aimed at containing the arbitrariness of tsarist officials. Now such legislation had almost instantaneously become a means of both asserting the prerogatives of Russia's new central authority and containing local radicals. As such, it could not help but draw significant opposition, despite its liberal content. Thus it presented to the provisional regime an extraordinary need to muster the support and cooperation of village elders or other local leaders in whom the peasants themselves had confidence.

393

In several ways, however, the zemstvo statutes could only alienate local peasant leaders and intensify rather than reduce political conflict. For one, the new volost zemstvos were specifically authorized to *replace* existing peasant councils (*skhody*), and the positions of volost elders (*starshiny*), board members, clerks, and other local officials were to be eliminated.[29] One can appreciate the logic of this provision if the new zemstvos were to become "legitimate" local government bodies in the sense of having a strictly defined electoral base. But it set up the new zemstvos as a challenge to the peasants' own substantial mechanism of self-government and could not help but breed enormous local dissatisfaction in many places, even if one could assume that displaced peasant leaders might take on comparable functions in the zemstvos.[30]

Further, the government was not consistent in displacing local institutions and vesting the zemstvo with full power. At the very moment when Petrograd officials were announcing the elimination of volost peasant councils, new legislation was being drafted to establish a network of rural land committees, headed by a "main committee" in Petrograd, and an entirely separate network of food supply committees was already in operation. The function of the land committees was to gather information for the Constituent Assembly in preparation for land reform, but the enabling legislation of April 21 gave the committees broad powers and stressed the need for "popular representation" in their membership, thus giving them the appearance of local government bodies.[31] The food supply organs were the collecting points for all grain not specifically exempted for the peasants' own needs, and hence an administrative network of considerable importance and complexity.[32] There were ample reasons why both these bodies would alienate Russian peasants, but in terms of the future place of local zemstvo organs the greatest difficulty lay in the government's effort to impose yet additional agencies on rural life from above, while displacing the peasant councils and the peasants' own ways of conducting affairs. Here, in essence, was the town in conflict with the countryside in 1917, the peasantry promised democracy but forced to accept new administrative controls imposed from without, the government fixed on the primacy of political legitimacy over social reform.

Three further dimensions to this problem in May and June 1917 deserve brief mention. First, the proliferation of new rural authorities weakened the power of each; and, as John Keep has pointed out, the principle of hierarchical representation on which the new institutions were organized, with deputies from lower organs being sent on to those above, added to the confusion by making consistent and thoughtful policy difficult to formulate.[33] Second, new conflict was bound to develop between formal government agencies like the zemstvos and land committees and ad hoc groups like local soviets and new cooperative institutions. The soviet problem is well known and bears mention only insofar as rural soviets in many places were already assuming precisely the functions the regime was assigning to the zemstvos; it added the familiar difficulties of dual power to the problem of functional redundancy within the government's own institutions. It is interesting to speculate what might have happened had the government invested local soviets with official power rather than establishing new zemstvos. Such a step was virtually impossible, of course, given the political view of Lvov and his colleagues and even the ideological biases of many soviet leaders themselves; but one can at least imagine the regime building a somewhat stronger base in the countryside. As it was, the soviets were bound to become magnets for antigovernment dissidence, accelerating both political and social polarization. The cooperatives, meanwhile, were also rapidly proliferating. In most places they restricted themselves to matters of consumption or production, but in some localities they had extensive credit operations and were much more familiar and trustworthy groups for the peasants than the zemstvos.[34] As we shall see, the Bolsheviks moved quickly against the zemstvos after October but retained and strengthened the cooperatives, which suggests that they, like the soviets, had a relatively greater degree of popular support.

The final problem to emerge during the late spring of 1917 was more subtle and touched the question of the so-called rural intelligentsia. As the councils and other peasant bodies were officially being displaced by new zemstvos and as the government attempted to circumscribe the authority of local peasant leaders, there is some evidence that zemstvo figures also attempted to reestablish directive roles for teachers, agronomists, and other third-element personnel whom the peasants themselves had discharged in many places. In Tambov and Samara, zemstvo board members urged that rural *intelligenty* be hired for "cultural-educational" work and offer special courses on "the present political moment." Elsewhere, rural professionals were hired to set up the temporary volost zemstvos.[35] Whether this effort had any specific political bent, particularly in terms of extending SR influence, is difficult to tell. What is clear is that considerable sums were spent from zemstvo accounts for this purpose and that many in the movement hoped a cultural blitz of this sort might counter the growing dangers of peasant violence. The result, however, was often just the opposite. One finds increasing reference in the newspapers in May and June to clashes between third-element lecturers and organizers and various unspecified "dark forces," who challenged arguments and disrupted meetings.[36] The role of the third element itself in extending the zemstvos thus seems to have accelerated, rather than reduced social polarization, at least in some places; and by giving employment to persons towards whom the peasants themselves had shown hostility, particularly as prices rose and peasant economic security grew more tenuous, the zemstvos themselves may have further complicated their own task of becoming authoritative, popular local organs.

The electoral battleground

Many in Moscow and Petrograd recognized these problems, of course, and grew increasingly nervous. The solution seemed to be to set the zemstvos on the foundation of electoral democracy as quickly as possible and turn them into popular and genuinely representative organs of government through the ballot box. "The zemstvos are the means by which Russia can be saved from social chaos," the liberal *Russkie vedomosti* editorialized, "the foundation on which community life can be firmly built, and by which citizens can be guided in constructive work."[37] Like other moderate socialist organs, *Izvestiia* in Moscow shared this view, urging all parties "to bend every effort so that the new zemstvo becomes the active representative of the people."[38] Elections on the volost level were set for August and early September in most places, and it was hoped new zemstvos could be functioning smoothly at all levels by sometime in October. Thus began the third phase of zemstvo revolutionary development in 1917, a period in which many liberals desperately hoped that zemstvo elections might finally bring orderly government to the countryside.

Such expectations were hopelessly unrealistic, of course, and not only because the proliferation of authorities and the peasants' press for agrarian reform made rural conditions so unstable. There were also basic administrative difficulties and a problem of peasant political understanding. Before elections could be held, volost committees had to divide their districts into electoral wards, organize lists of electors, print ballots, and explain the complex system of proportional representation to the voters. The electoral statute even required that local groups determine the actual size of zemstvo assemblies, stating only that they had to be between 20 and 50 members.[39]

When third-element people tried to cope with these problems, peasant suspicion and hostility increased. Long arguments ensued over various provisions of the law, and many peasants apparently thought the zemstvo officials themselves were responsible for the law's complexity. In Moscow province, a number of villages went so far as to reject the proportional system outright as a "violation of basic rights" because fixed candidates' lists prevented them from voting directly for an individual candidate. Many places within a district also insisted they have their "own" local candidate list, and when this was refused, they demanded that "their" people be added to lists set up for the volost as a whole. Sometimes, in open violation of the electoral law, villagers actually succeeded in forcing temporary zemstvo committees to accept a direct majority system.[40]

There was also a great deal of suspicion about secret ballots, which seemed manipulative and arcane in comparison to the way the peasant council ran its affairs, and fears that the new volost bodies would be nothing more than tax collectors. Even where the zemstvo's purpose was clear, its premises were not. "Why do we need to be literate?" was one common response, according to newspaper reports. "We have lived without literacy in the past, and things were better!"[41] "We need food, not elections," was another. "First give us bread, and then we will think about voting."[42] When instructors tried to respond they were often attacked: "Each time there is an attempt to explain the essence of volost zemstvo legislation," one discouraged instructor wrote from Kutozov volost near Zhitomir, "the villagers grab pikes and chase us away."[43]

In some places, like Volynia province and the Don region, resistance went even further. Whole areas simply refused to organize volost zemstvo elections. In the Don, resistance had to do with fears that the zemstvos would weaken Cossack influence vis-à-vis non-Cossacks (*inogorodtsy*).[44] In Volynia, peasants had "had such a lack of trust in the old, estate-based (*tsenzovoe*) zemstvo, that the new one was discredited by analogy."[45] Provincial authorities tried in response to convene representatives "of all rural peasant councils and demand categorically that no obstacles be placed in the way of electoral organization," but in some areas not a single district had organized electoral lists by mid-August. In Ostrog, Novogradvolynsk, Ovruch, and Zhitomir districts, entire volosts simply refused to participate in the elections at all.[46] "The new zemstvo will take our money, and that is all," peasants in Tver were quoted as saying; in Ufa, a volost peasant assembly declared "zemstvo" a "harmful word" and voted to form their own self-government rather than recognize zemstvo authority.[47] In some places, the electoral mechanism itself gave new power to rural soviets, exactly what government leaders had hoped to avoid. Popular electoral lists were easy to prepare in these relatively well-organized institutions, and party activists could carry them throughout the volost.

They therefore gained acceptance much more readily than those drawn up by volost electoral committees, and often because they appeared as *antizemstvo* lists.[48]

This, of course, was not the situation everywhere in Russia, and one must appreciate the difficulties of generalizing from limited sources. But accounts throughout the country indicate that zemstvo election meetings everywhere were becoming battlegrounds between peasants and zemstvo officials, and the elections themselves a vehicle for further social and political fragmentation, part of the complex process of introversion in the summer of 1917, whereby peasant communities turned away from outside authorities and settled affairs on their own. It would be impossible, of course, to survey this process in detail and, in fact, scarcely necessary in terms of the broad social and political picture, even if the evidence were available. The important point is that peasants almost everywhere regarded the elections at best with indifference and at worst with deep hostility. "Down with Commissars, Teachers, and Jews!" peasants shouted in the village of Groianovo as ballot boxes were burned. "Outsiders, foreigners, stay away from our villages!"[49] There is scarcely a shred of evidence in any source to suggest that peasants were concerned whether local government, as liberal zemstvo leaders perceived it, was established at all.

Several aspects of the elections are, however, worth noting, before turning briefly to a review of the results. First, the magnitude of peasant indifference was startling even to the most pessimistic. In Samara province, only one-fourth of the eligible electors participated, despite the fact that electoral preparations here had been relatively smooth.[50] In Krasnoiarsk, many volosts had no elections at all; in Kovrov, scarcely one elector in six cast a ballot.[51] *Vlast' naroda* reported a "representative" village in which only 172 out of 1,500 persons voted, a figure so small that a second day was set aside for additional balloting. Even so, only 87 new votes were cast, and these, reportedly, were "mostly from the intelligentsia."[52] The situation was somewhat better in Moscow, Kostroma, and Tver provinces and also, apparently, in Saratov. But even in Moscow a number of districts had not finished their preparations by the date set for voting.[53]

One should also note the resistance of many peasant women to voting, and, inferentially, the way volost elections challenged broader peasant social traditions. The SR paper in Petrograd, *Zemlia i volia,* gave considerable space to this question, and frequently exhorted peasant women to assume their new democratic responsibilities.[54] Women in some places apparently thought it would be "sinful" to vote and regarded the elections as a whole as "devil's work." *Izvestiia* of the

Moscow Soviet regarded this as an indication of the special backwardness of women in the countryside and worried about its political implications; *Vlast' naroda* pointed out that villagers were being asked to cast ballots for one institution or another almost every two weeks, for food committees, land committees, soviets, councils, and all sorts of conference and congress delegations, and women in particular found it difficult to sort out the importance of one election as opposed to another.[55] By the end of the summer, it was simply much easier to leave such questions up to village elders and go about one's business.[56]

Further, there is the obvious but noteworthy point that the zemstvo elections, like those to local soviets, dumas, and other organs of popular representation, gave considerable advantage to political groups that had managed to form rudimentary local organizations, and in many places this meant that the Bolsheviks did much better in the zemstvo voting than almost anyone had thought possible. As with the local duma campaigns, the Bolsheviks were assiduous in calling revolutionary socialists to vote. In Moscow, they devoted considerable space in *Sotsial demokrat* to both the volost and district zemstvo balloting. Conditions in many places were far from easy for Lenin's supporters. In Pavlovsk volost near Zvenigorod, for example, where elections were held on August 15, Bolsheviks were not allowed to speak at election meetings and in several villages were driven off with pitchforks.[57] Elsewhere Bolshevik election lists (*spiski*) were systematically destroyed, and party agitators "cruelly slandered," according to the party press.[58] Still, the Bolsheviks sent teams of agitators deep into the countryside and persisted doggedly in their effort to win village support. In Moscow, the party drafted a special zemstvo election platform, calling for the immediate transfer of land directly to the peasants and describing the role "revolutionary zemstvo organizations" might have in facilitating the transfer of goods from town to countryside.[59] In fact, the Bolsheviks seem to have been practically alone among the parties in taking the difficult task of campaigning seriously. No other party newspaper in Moscow or Petrograd gave such attention to organizing for the zemstvo elections, and none published comprehensive "platforms." The Kadets in most places did not even bother to organize their own list of candidates, preferring instead to join local "nonpartisan" or "professional" lists; and the SRs, whether from complacency or a greater concern for the Constituent Assembly campaign, seemed content in the main to let matters simply take their course.

In many places, consequently, the results of Bolshevik efforts showed in the balloting. In Pavlovsk volost mentioned above, for example, Lenin's supporters received 1,269 out of 6,283 votes cast, to the Mensheviks' 309, and the SRs' 2,607, with the remainder scattered among various lists of "nonpartisans."[60] Party leaders rightly considered these results quite respectable. In elections to the district zemstvos, which took place in Moscow province shortly after the volost balloting in August, Bolsheviks in some places received as much as 40 percent of the vote.[61] There is, to repeat, no available systematic collation of zemstvo balloting, but at the time of the Second All-Russian Congress of Soviets in October, the Bolsheviks queried their delegates on a variety of issues, one of which concerned the party's influence in city and zemstvo voting. Among 139 responses, local committees reported Bolshevik zemstvo representation in some places to be as high as 60 percent.[62]

This is not to suggest, of course, that Lenin's supporters emerged as a dominant force in the new volost zemstvos during the early fall of 1917. According to the fragmentary material I have been able to examine, the overwhelming majority of new volost deputies were local peasants, or members of local peasant soviets, with Left SR, SR, or nonpartisan sympathies. But the degree of Bolshevik success, coupled with the violent nature of the volost election process itself, does serve to indicate how widely misplaced the hopes of liberal zemstvo leaders turned out to be. Far from setting local government on a firm, "legitimate" foundation, the elections served in many places actually to discredit the zemstvos and to demonstrate their lack of popular support. New volost assemblies were increasingly in the hands of persons either hostile to the Provisional Government and its goals or "hopelessly unable" in the view of some observers to carry out the zemstvos' extensive new responsibilities.[63] Most jarring of all to liberal zemstvo figures was the degree of peasant antagonism to third-element personnel. By the fall of 1917, *village intellectual* was a term of derision in many places; even in Moscow province, more industrialists and landowners were apparently elected to volost zemstvo assemblies than those designated as members of "free professions."[64]

All of this, obviously, put national zemstvo figures in a hopeless bind. By the summer of 1917, few believed seriously that zemstvos could remain effective as traditional, estate-based institutions; even conservative zemstvo union officials supported some form of democratization. But in this, as in virtually every other aspect of Russian life in 1917, the impossible practical question was to define democracy's limits; and the difficult task intellectually was to recognize that "of" and "by" the people were inextricably linked in popular consciousness, and that broadening popular responsibility might very well involve a weakening of institutional competence. The difficult line for

400

many to draw was the one that ran between reform in the interest of democratic political ideals and preservation of an existing apparatus in the interest of administrative effectiveness. Many believed deeply that a genuine commitment to popular welfare actually mandated resist-ance to further reform, a position which was hard to separate from one that simply defended established interests; others recognized that institutions like the zemstvos either had to broaden greatly popular participation as a means of gaining popular confidence or become adversary institutions to the very people they hoped to serve. In these dilemmas, and indeed in this very split among national zemstvo figures, the whole process of zemstvo reform in 1917 mirrors the problematic character of Russian democracy as a whole.

As late as August, the broader tendency among national zemstvo leaders continued to be in favor of new reforms. At the Moscow State Conference in mid-August, S. S. Salazkin spoke as a representative of this tendency and urged Russia to accept the Soviet-sponsored "Declar-ation of the United Democratic Organization," read by Chkheidze, as a program for national development.[65] Full support for Salazkin's speech came from some 18 provincial zemstvo groups, including ones in Riazan, Vitebsk, Saratov, Kostroma, Simbirsk, Tver, and the Tauride, traditional centers of the liberal gentry. Partial support came from Penza, Petrograd, Chernigov, Kiev, Tambov, and some seven other regions.[66]

Opposed to this position was A. E. Gruzinov, who spoke for "tsen-zovye zemstvo interests" at the Moscow conference, and represented 13 of the 31 zemstvo groups that had sent delegates to Moscow.[67] Gruzinov stressed the problems of local disunity, paralyzed law enforcement, disrupted finances, and the like and urged his country-men to resist platitudinous solutions to difficult, complex problems. "In both old and new zemstvos and in the committees, a new strange kind of attitude has appeared – that money is bourgeois and therefore can be spent freely. Never has money been spent as recklessly as now."[68] But like others who condemned an ill-defined "left" at the Moscow sessions, Gruzinov chastised the "recklessness" of those claiming to speak without offering much in the way of constructive suggestions. The fact was that there was little he or other conservative liberals could propose within a democratic framework.

In the aftermath of the Moscow conference, and especially after the Kornilov uprising two weeks later, the dilemmas of national zemstvo officials only intensified. At a meeting of zemstvo delegates to the Democratic Conference in September, representatives from the Tauride region, Kharkov, Mogilev, and Saratov introduced a resolution of protest against "the participation of Zinovev and Lenin, [who were] fugitives from justice," but the proposal evoked such a storm of feeling on both sides that it was not even discussed.[69] Two days later the delegates agreed simply to warn their countrymen about the grave danger of impending civil war and to appeal urgently for resistance to calls for class struggle, from whatever quarter they might come:

> Let our soldiers throw their energy into defending their country from the foreign enemy; let the workers increase the productivity of their labor; let the rich give up their millions of profits, the intelligentsia carry its knowledge to the dark masses, the peasants and landowners open their storehouses and give bread to the people...Russia's very future existence is possible only through the unification of all her vital forces, excluding only those interested in reestablishing the old regime.[70]

But even this was rejected by some left-wing delegates, and subsequent discussion was restricted to minor issues. Questions of zemstvo democratization and future zemstvo policies were simply too contentious for orderly debate.

In September and early October a number of additional zemstvo election results became known, including those for the district assemblies of Moscow province. Some of these showed a dramatic increase in Bolshevik strength, as for example in Podolsk district (Moscow province), where Lenin's supporters secured almost 5,000 of the 14,600 votes cast, and 15 of 42 delegates.[71] Reports from Perm and Chernigov showed comparable results, and even more worrisome for many were additional accounts of violence against zemstvo officials and the general breakdown of local zemstvo activities.[72] In a number of places newly elected zemstvos refused to collect badly needed taxes, seeking funds instead from province zemstvo organs or the government. Moscow province zemstvos alone showed a deficit of some 3 million rubles for the month of October.[73]

But above all it was the violence in the countryside that most agitated national zemstvo figures and made them most pessimistic. "In our penchant for making 'verbs of battle' to describe ordinary occurences," N. Valentinov wrote gloomily in *Vlast' naroda*, "we must now create something along the order of 'to volost' [*vzvolostnut'*, *vzvolostit'*], as in 'I will volostize you' [*Ia tebia vzvolostnu'*], to depict the especially brutal force being used against zemstvo electoral commissions, their *razgon* (mighty Russian word!), and the senseless destruction of ballot boxes, ballots, and electoral lists."[74] The reconstruction of Russian local government by formal democratic procedures was being rejected in the countryside out of ignorance, animosity, radicalism, and a tradition of peasant self-government at odds with the Western liberal premises on which the zemstvo reforms were structured. Liberal democracy was dead in the villages, perhaps even stillborn, well before the Bolsheviks came to power; for many who had worked long years to liberalize the zemstvos and broaden them into viable institutions of local government, the realization of failure came as a crushing blow.

Conflict after October and the zemstvos' dissolution

When the Bolsheviks came to power in October, there began what the liberal editors of *Russkie vedomosti* called "the most difficult moment in the entire history of zemstvo existence."[75] *Russkie vedomosti* focused on Lenin's "usurpation" and, like much of the later literature, saw the drama of this period in terms of the zemstvos' struggle for survival against spreading Bolshevik power. At heart, of course, the struggle *was* political, but politics was hardly its only dimension, and bolshevism was not at the root of zemstvo political difficulties. Rather, the drama for many centered on the conflict between continuing social welfare work, which necessarily involved some accommodation with "illegitimate" authorities, and struggling themselves against the Bolsheviks, which meant leaving one's post and disrupting desperately needed social services. The root of zemstvo political troubles after October, however, remained peasant hostility. Zemstvos collapsed everywhere in the countryside during the first months of Bolshevik rule because peasants refused to support them.

This is not to suggest that the Bolsheviks did not play up to peasant sentiment and in many places simply order local zemstvos closed. Often, as in Nizhnii Novgorod province, in Smolensk, and throughout Moscow province, Bolsheviks seized zemstvo offices and threw out or even arrested local zemstvo officials. The latter often tried to retaliate and in some places attempted to consolidate an anti-Bolshevik front with local soviets. As far as one can determine, this typically occurred in areas of substantial SR strength, such as Vladimir province, where in early November a meeting of Melenkov district peasant representatives voted to dissolve volost soviets and transfer their functions entirely to the zemstvos.[76] Similarly in Tver and Nizhnii Novgorod, provincial zemstvo boards convened congresses in November to organize anti-Bolshevik forces; and in Novgorod, on December 23, a congress of provincial zemstvo officials declared itself the "sole authority" in the province.[77] In Perm province, several zemstvo boards organized armed militia bands (*druzhiny*) to protect "legitimate" authority; and in Saratov, apparently, zemstvo officials enlisted military cadets to "pacify" the peasants and prevent the confiscation of estates.[78] Where this happened, of course, local Bolsheviks mobilized whomever they could, and battle lines were clearly drawn.

But Lenin's supporters were not uniformly anxious at first to move forcefully against all zemstvo institutions; they seemed particularly concerned in some places not to disrupt the service and welfare functions that a number of zemstvos continued to provide. For the moment, the countryside was a secondary front. The agrarian revolution was fully under peasant control, and if zemstvos continued to function they did so with a modicum of popular support which was easier to accommodate then to challenge. Where possible, the Bolsheviks tried to use the zemstvo apparatus, or at least to subordinate essential zemstvo services to local soviet or party control. In places where Bolshevik cadres themselves had been elected to zemstvos, as in Kursk province, zemstvo meetings became new battlegrounds over political orientation, with the result in some cases being the alignment of zemstvo assemblies and boards with the new Bolshevik power. Such was the case, for example, in Sestroretsk and Tsarskoe Selo in Petrograd province, in several volosts in Orel and Chernigov provinces, and in Abdulinsk volost in Samara province, where the Bolsheviks had elected 29 of 47 members to the zemstvo assembly.[79] The ephemeral nature of Bolshevik "success" in these cases, however, was hinted at by *Russkie vedomosti* in early January, when the rapid disintegration of Bolshevik zemstvos in Kozlov was described with ill-concealed satisfaction: "When the Bolsheviks took over the zemstvos a month ago," the paper reported, "they thought they could work wonders. Now the treasury is empty, taxes are not being paid, and nothing is happening."[80]

Elsewhere, local zemstvos came under the control of various local soviets after October, sometimes as a result of Bolshevik influence, sometimes not. Again, the evidence is fragmentary, and again this process had begun in some places well before October. In Tsivilsk district (Kazan province), pressures on zemstvo figures were such that a conference of volost representatives simply declared themselves to be a soviet of peasant deputies, perhaps hoping to preserve their authority through political mimicry.[81] In other places, soviets sent various commissars and officials to supervise and control zemstvo operations. Again, there was no uniformity either to local Bolshevik policy in this regard or to that of the local zemstvos. Some local soviets, even with substantial Bolshevik representation, continued to support the forthcoming Constituent Assembly and apparently moved to supervise zemstvo operations as a matter of efficiency; elsewhere, particularly in areas where the zemstvos themselves were strongly anti-Bolshevik, the assault of local soviets had much more deliberate political objectives. In any event, the amalgamation of local zemstvo and soviet functions was itself only a stage in the transformation of Russian local government, since the latter soon underwent its own process of "bolshevization."

Through all this, one can in retrospect detect two broad and interrelated patterns, both of which signified the end of effective local zemstvo operations. One was the final rejection by Russia's peasants after October of local zemstvos as organs of authority or even social welfare. In the main, "democratic" zemstvos were not even looked upon as focal points for resisting further encroachment by central (Bolshevik) government authority. The revolt of the countryside in 1917 was surely as much an explosion against outside interference in peasant affairs as it was a striving for agrarian reform; and, in the course of this upheaval, as we have seen, local zemstvos were identified as instruments of both the gentry and the towns, vehicles for outside control. Thus, despite desperate welfare needs, the Provisional Government's fall led not to a consolidation of zemstvo functions but to the creation of hundreds of new local peasant councils, now often misidentified as soviets, which replaced and terminated zemstvo activities. In Perm province alone in the first three months of 1918, some 500 such bodies were organized, and the pattern elsewhere was similar.[82] It is likely that most local Bolsheviks supported this process but highly unlikely that it occurred under their impetus or direction. In the winter of 1917–18, Russia's peasants ruled their own affairs.

The second pattern, which is really only the converse of the first, is that the local zemstvos for the most part continued to function only very briefly into 1918, before being "liquidated" in one way or another. In December 1917, according to one report, zemstvo boards were dissolved in some 8 percent of all volost units, but this figure grew to 45 percent in January and to some 85 percent by February.[83] If these figures are correct, then the formal decision of the Bolsheviks themselves to dissolve the zemstvos, which came in a Commissariat of Internal Affairs directive at the end of February 1918, was largely after the fact. In the main, it was the force of social rather than political revolution that had led to the zemstvos' demise.[84]

Meanwhile in Moscow, at the highest levels of zemstvo structure, a similar drama was unfolding in the headquarters of the zemstvo union. Here, however, the central issue was not popular support, but Soviet control over union operations; and the essential issue was whether third-element union employees could and should continue serving Russia under the Bolsheviks. Because of the prominent personalities involved and the attention of the still-functioning liberal press, the issues here were also set in bold relief. *Russkie vedomosti* presented the story like a nineteenth-century novel, with liberal forces of Westernization and Progress arrayed against a Coarse and Ruthless Nativism. At the heart of the drama was the continued commitment of third-element personnel to the social welfare of a populace that rejected their efforts, anxious now to appear "nonpolitical" while recognizing that political forces controlled their fate. The episode is worth following briefly, if only to complete the final chapter of zemstvo existence in Bolshevik Russia and to glimpse the last struggle of third-element personnel as zemstvo workers.

As earlier chapters in this volume indicate, this struggle had taken various forms in the long history of the zemstvo and had reached a peak of sorts in the wholesale purge of "liberal" and "radical" employees during the reactionary period after 1905. Antagonism between rightist boards and progressive professionals continued through the war period, however, and cleavages over appropriate zemstvo policies became particularly sharp in the zemstvo union, as William Gleason has suggested in Chapter 11. After February, there was significant pressure within the union not only to realign its policies, as indicated above, but also to democratize its membership; however, the issue was not resolved before the Bolsheviks came to power. Third-element personnel in various places (particularly Moscow province) pressed the union's board to rid itself and the zemstvos as a whole of their *tsenzovoe* image, and one of the great ironies of zemstvo history during 1917 is surely the way in which these very people were assaulted by peasants for reflecting values they themselves rejected. Pressure also came from outside, particularly from the Moscow Soviet, which in early October formed its own delegation to participate in the activities of the union's Main Committee (*Glavnyi komitet*), while at the same time pledging "full power" to the committee pending the convocation of an all-Russian congress of democratic zemstvos.[85] The Main Committee resisted the soviet's effort, but by November the pressure was overwhelming. At a conference of representatives from various provincial zemstvo boards called by the Main Committee in early December, a number of local zemstvo workers stated directly that the Main Committee no longer enjoyed the trust of its own employees.[86]

In response, the Main Committee formed a special commission, headed by D. M. Shchepkin, a former assistant minister of internal affairs under the Provisional Government and a well-known Moscow liberal, to broaden its membership. The Main Committee as a whole apparently hoped to democratize itself by adding regular union employees to its membership along with selected representatives from the "democratic organs," presumably the soviets. Shchepkin's commission was unwilling to go this far, however. According to *Russkie vedomosti*, it feared such a move would weaken the "stability" of union functions.[87] Instead, it brought back to the conference a plan to establish a special "control" organ to "supervise" a democratized Main Committee and, presumably, to retain control of some 2 million rubles in union funds.[88] After considerable debate, the conference accepted this scheme; but the Bolsheviks, apparently watching rather closely, took the conference decision as a signal to march against the union. The following day Red Guards seized the union's treasury and froze its accounts. Shortly afterward, Lenin's supporters went one step further and declared the Main Committee a counterrevolutionary organization.[89]

All of this has a familiar ring in terms of the broad pattern of Bolshevik activity in the winter of 1917–18, of course, but two aspects of the story make it particularly interesting. One is the extraordinary tentativeness of the Bolsheviks' approach, rather than the decisiveness one might have expected. There was by this time no secret about the antipathy with which zemstvo leaders viewed Lenin's party and the October coup. There was also reason to suspect that zemstvo figures were in close contact with anti-Bolshevik groups like the Committee to Save the Fatherland and Revolution and good reason to expect that zemstvo funds might be used to subvert Bolshevik power. But, rather than dissolve the union straightaway, Lenin's supporters announced instead that a special commission was being formed to supervise its reorganization and that the seizure of union funds was only to assure their proper disbursement.[90]

Thus the Bolsheviks were apparently still undecided about whether the zemstvos should be preserved. Perhaps they also overestimated zemstvo popularity among the peasants; perhaps they were simply cautious about disrupting zemstvo services and unnecessarily strengthening their opposition, especially while the forthcoming Constituent Assembly was still a potential rallying point. In any event, the Bolsheviks tried to use the zemstvo institution and persuade union employees to stay at their posts.

Second, this in turn put enormous pressure on those among the union's third-element personnel who continued to consider themselves "progressive." Many zemstvo employees were no doubt ready to reach some form of accommodation with Lenin's supporters if this would assure the continuation of union welfare activities. Seizing the union's funds, however, had the effect of drawing battle lines. In response, a special meeting of "socialist zemstvo workers" announced the "definite possibility" of a zemstvo workers' strike if an agreement with the soviet could not be reached on the basis of "preserving the autonomy of the All-Russian Union of Zemstvos and the...noninterference in the internal affairs of the zemstvo union by outside forces."[91] Undeterred, the soviet proceeded to organize its new commission. When the union's Main Committee refused to cooperate the soviet went one step further. On December 23, it ordered the entire committee to dissolve.[92] For their part, Shchepkin and his colleagues now publicly rejected the December 23 decree, stating that only representatives of provincial zemstvo boards could dissolve the Main Committee and indicating that they would continue to conduct union affairs despite the soviet's actions. The stage was thus set for a dramatic encounter on December 30, when Shchepkin and his colleagues arrived for a regular, scheduled meeting, only to find soviet counterparts seated in their place.[93]

There followed a tortuous month in the history of both the zemstvo union and its third-element employees, one in which the principles of service clashed head on with the problems of politics, and zemstvo workers of various persuasions groped for solutions to what were essentially insoluble problems. In response to the Soviet's "occupation" of zemstvo union offices and its dissolution of the "legitimate" Main Committee, union workers in Moscow went on strike and asked their zemstvo colleagues elsewhere to join them. Similar strikes had been called in the late fall of 1917,[94] but the union strike was the most extensive and effective work stoppage of this sort. In both practical and symbolic terms it culminated the long and heroic struggle of the third-element employees to serve Russian welfare needs effectively. In fact, as a number of zemstvo workers themselves recognized, it was not so much the Bolsheviks or the zemstvo right that now lay at the heart of the problem as the country's own lack of commitment to the zemstvo as an institution. In this sense, the union employees' last struggle was simply one more chapter in a history of comparable struggles stretching back some five decades.[95]

At first the strike was widely supported by zemstvo union employees. Almost 2,400 workers voted on the question early in January just after the Bolsheviks closed the Constituent Assembly, and 1,858 voted to strike.[96] Workers in health and food services were exempted. But just as in the case of other civil service strikes in this period, the resistance of union employees soon began to weaken. Some simply felt the strike was not effective as a weapon of resistance and were doubly discouraged by the fact that the dissolution of the Constituent Assembly had not precipitated any additional organized resistance. For others, perhaps, the question was one of personal survival; employees were not being paid, and the Bolshevik seizure of union accounts effectively shut off a strike fund. But for most the question turned on the issue of politics versus social service and the morality of "deserting the people" at a time of overwhelming social need.[97] Soviet spokesmen themselves played heavily on this tension, repeatedly appealing for zemstvo people to go back to their jobs. By the third week of January, sentiment had turned in favor of negotiating a *modus vivendi*. On January 21, a special meeting of union employee delegates voted 73 to 17 (with 2 abstentions) to begin discussions with soviet representatives.[98]

In the meantime, a national congress of zemstvo and city organizations (Zemgor) had opened in Petrograd, and Shchepkin and his colleagues on the deposed zemstvo union's Main Committee had managed to convene an "all-Russian" congress of the zemstvo union, which met in Moscow on January 13. Both gatherings were relentless in their attack on Lenin and his supporters despite a substantial delegation of radicals at the Zemgor sessions.[99] In Moscow, a new Main Committee was elected,[100] and passionate appeals were issued to workers and peasants over various party signatures calling for further resistance and condemning, as Menshevik delegates put it, "the torrent of violence threatening the most precious and valuable gains of the revolution."[101]

By this time, however, volost and district zemstvos had virtually been destroyed throughout Moscow province, as various representatives reported, and the situation elsewhere was similar. In fact, had the Bolsheviks themselves decided at this juncture to breathe new life into the zemstvos, it is most unlikely they could have done so. Instead, as a special delegation of zemstvo union workers finally sat down to negotiate with Russia's new authorities, the latter moved officially against the zemstvo network as a whole. On January 27, a Moscow province congress of soviet representatives decreed all volost, district, and provincial zemstvos "liquidated" and ordered the transfer of zemstvo assets and functions to local soviets. Zemstvo workers not discharged by soviet authorities were ordered to remain at work "under pain of judgment by revolutionary tribunals."[102] On February 21, zemstvo union spokesmen announced that zemstvo workers would stay at their posts and presented a new set of conditions under which zemstvo employees would work in the future for the Bolsheviks.[103] But by now the Bolsheviks had made their own decision, and late in February, as noted above, the Commissariat of Internal Affairs officially dissolved all zemstvo institutions organized prior to October 1917.

The zemstvo outside Soviet Russia

Before offering some general comments about the fate of the zemstvos in the 1917 revolution, let me sketch out very briefly, for the sake of completeness, the subsequent final chapter in zemstvo history. Much, of course, could be written about zemstvo activities in Siberia and southern Russia during the Civil War as well as zemstvo functions in emigration. The story in some ways reflects the best in zemstvo tradition: the commitment to service and personal sacrifice in the face of serious material deprivation, the struggle to liberalize reactionary governments, the effort to mitigate harsh and trying circumstances of dislocation and resettlement. My charge here, however, has been to look at the zemstvo movement in 1917, and a bare-bones outline will have to suffice.

As the Bolsheviks closed in on the zemstvo union and absorbed the functions of volost and district zemstvos in regions under their control, the zemstvo network as a whole in Russia rapidly dissolved. The new Main Committee elected at the January 1918 congress of provincial zemstvos was not permitted to function; and after ordering zemstvo officials throughout Russia to protect zemstvo property and continue their work, if possible, they left the capitals for southern Russia, along with members of the Union of Cities.[104] In the late summer of 1918 a unified zemstvo-city organization was reestablished in Ekaterinodar, and in January 1919, as the Bolsheviks were driven from the Don and northern Caucasus areas, local committees of the zemstvo union again began to function. On February 22, 1919, a "Constituent Assembly" of the All-Russian Union of Zemstvos convened in Ekaterinodar, elected a new executive organ, and declared its intention to serve General Denikin's volunteer army in "an entirely practical capacity." Shortly afterward, in April 1919, Denikin and his Special Council affirmed the "legitimacy" of zemstvo union activities in southern Russia; and, in May 1919, the zemstvos were given broad authority to "serve the material needs of the local populace."[105]

In fact, however, volunteer army officers had little use for zemstvo figures, and much of the population itself remained hostile. In August 1918, Ataman Kaledin and the Don Cossack administration had attempted to block the extension of zemstvo activities into Cossack areas; democratic zemstvo figures in army support units on the southwestern front had pulled out of the zemstvo union and requested its liquidation.[106] As the volunteer army expanded, local commanders rode roughshod over local zemstvo committees and in many places effectively prevented their operations. The situation was perhaps worst of all in the Crimea, where liberal zemstvo activists had helped establish an autonomous regional government and where Denikin's troops eventually arrested a number of prominent zemstvo figures as "radicals" and "separatists."[107] In the fall of 1919, left-wing Kadets in Rostov pressed angrily for greater zemstvo control as the only means to prop up faltering local support for the anti-Bolshevik movement. In a long report to Denikin, Nicholas Astrov called the army's weakness in this area a prime reason for the army's impending collapse.[108] But if left Kadets continued to overestimate the zemstvo's popularity as an institution and failed even now to appreciate its image as an outpost of gentry privilege, the Kadet Central Committee in southern Russia believed that "radicals" in local zemstvo and town duma organs were more interested in "political struggles" than "meeting the primary needs of the population and reestablishing economic and cultural life" and asked that their functions be curtailed, a view reflecting that of Denikin's administration as a whole.[109] In any event, the issue by this time was irrelevant. Most zemstvo union officials evacuated southern Russia with the remnants of Denikin's army in 1920, and, after working briefly with General Wrangel's regime, set up relief operations abroad.

In Siberia, meanwhile, the chronicle was much the same. Zemstvo figures there were grouped around the regional autonomy movement rather than the All-Russian Union of Zemstvos and played an active role in the formation of P. I. Derber's Siberian Regional Government in January 1918, which angered those who wanted to establish an authoritative national government in the region.[110] As early as the summer of 1918, Kadets supporting General Khorvat in eastern Siberia attacked zemstvo personnel as "undoubtedly pro-Bolshevik"[111] and were bent on bringing local zemstvo bodies under "centralized control." Kolchak's minister of internal affairs (later premier) and leading advisor, the right Kadet V. N. Pepeliaev, was particularly hostile. Throughout the winter and spring of 1918–19, he consistently opposed autonomy for the zemstvos, generally equating zemstvo activities with organized opposition to Kolchak.[112] Pepeliaev was not entirely wrong in this view, but he failed to see that "organized opposition" was not a movement in support of Lenin but an effort to reorganize Kolchak's administration on the basis of liberal democratic principles and a necessary step to secure even a modicum of popular local support. In the summer of 1919, zemstvo figures led by I. A. Iakushev, the former president of the Siberian regional Duma, proposed the convocation of an elected regional congress (*zemskii sobor*). Iakushev's plan was to draw together representatives from a range of Siberian regional groups and construct a government based "on broad social trust and responsible to popular representatives."[113] Not surprisingly, Kolchak and Pepeliaev, along with members of the Kadet party's "Eastern Central Committee," stoutly resisted this effort, and it was only in the weeks immediately before the total collapse of Kolchak's regime that Pepeliaev finally recognized the merits of the plan.[114] By that time, of course, it was much too late. With the Bolshevik advance, most zemstvo figures tried to maintain their efforts in the areas of food supply and social welfare, and a number of local zemstvos may well have continued to function into the 1920s. But "accommodationist" sentiment was obviously not enough to assure their survival, and the movement here, as elsewhere, quickly faded.[115]

The only area under White control where the zemstvos played a "legitimate" role in the Civil War was northern Russia. Here the Provisional Government under N. V. Chaikovskii officially entrusted the zemstvos with all matters relating to cultural and economic life, including legal administration, food supply, land and forest administration, and social welfare facilities. In the Archangelsk region, zemstvo authorities apparently succeeded in reopening a number of schools and aiding local agricultural production, even opening a small factory for the manufacture of agricultural implements. Working closely with local cooperative societies, they also took charge of food distribution.[116]

The most dramatic work of the zemstvos in the north, however, related to land reform. In September 1918, the northern Russian government abolished the old land committees of 1917 and transferred their tasks and duties to the zemstvos, including the administration of lands seized or redistributed during the revolution. On January 13, 1919, as a result of joint efforts by the government and zemstvo leaders, a law was passed transferring all cleared land to zemstvo control with the object of subsequent redistribution "to those who till it."[117] This was regarded as the first step in a comprehensive land reform, although little additional progress was made apparently before the area was again under Bolshevik control. In anticipation of the reform, new local elections were also held in the region in which, according to one report, between 40 and 70 percent of the population voted. "By an overwhelming majority," new board members belonged to socialist parties.[118] (Here one can perhaps briefly glimpse an orientation that might possibly have brought the volost zemstvo some degree of popular support in the spring of 1917, although such speculation admittedly jars the reasonable limits of historical probability.) In any event, just as in the Crimea, where local zemstvo figures also struggled valiantly to preserve democratic rule, the course of events in northern Russia was

412

well beyond control. Recognizing this, a northern Russian zemstvo delegation established itself in London in 1919 to pressure the British government for support, but these efforts, of course, were also destined to fail.[119] As things turned out, the London Committee and others like it became instead the nucleus of Russian émigré relief operations.

In fact, zemstvo operations abroad had begun sometime earlier, even before Russia had pulled out of the European war, when the Main Committee in Moscow sent delegations abroad to secure additional supplies for the Russian army. After the Bolshevik revolution and Brest-Litovsk, these groups turned instead to the problem of supplying the Whites, while at the same time ministering to the needs of an increasing number of refugees. By the end of 1921 zemstvo committees were functioning in Serbia, Bosnia, Bulgaria (Sofia), France (Paris), Egypt, Cyprus, and Constantinople as well as London, with the center of operations near the remnants of Denikin's and Wrangel's army around Gallipoli. Unified under the Emigré Committee of the All-Russian Union of Zemstvos in Constantinople, these agencies became a crucial means of support for thousands of White Russian refugees. A number continued to function well into the 1930s.

In 1920 and 1921, zemstvo efforts centered on charitable relief: night shelters, canteens, orphanages, and various forms of health care. With the passage of time, this changed in the direction of what was called "relief through work." In various places, particularly the Balkans and France, labor bureaus were set up along with job training facilities and retail craft outlets.[120] A number of loans were also made to various individuals and groups to enable them to open workshops, set up farming colonies, or otherwise get themselves reestablished. Legal aid was also provided.[121] Funds for this came from old Russian state accounts, which the union had managed to retain, as well as from several foreign governments and humanitarian organizations and contributions from émigrés themselves. By 1923, however, Russian state funds had been exhausted, and international assistance generally diminished. As a consequence, zemstvo activities began to wind down.[122] By the late 1920s, the zemstvo committee continued to support 6 labor bureaus, 4 legal assistance offices, and a number of libraries, but most attention and the major portion of zemstvo funds were devoted to education: the committee subsidized some 80 different institutions in some 13 different European states, either directly or through the offices of local zemstvo groups.[123]

In this way, and with considerable success in humanitarian terms, the zemstvos played out their historical role.

Conclusion

As the preceding chapters in this volume have suggested, the zemstvo was an institution of contradiction and paradox. Conceived initially as a means of preserving harmonious social relations in the countryside and designed to link state and society closely together, the zemstvo in most places soon became a bastion of gentry prerogative. As Dorothy Atkinson has shown in Chapter 4, it imposed heavy taxes on peasants alone for what were perceived as common local interests and increasingly reflected the tensions between Russia's two antagonistic rural estates rather than facilitating their harmonious resolution. The zemstvos' role in Russian constitutional development was also, at best, ambiguous, as Roberta Manning argues convincingly in Chapter 5: while contributing to the establishment of central representative institutions, after 1905 zemstvos became openly hostile to government plans for local reform, hindered programs deemed incompatible with gentry interests, and significantly undermined Stolypin's efforts at building a conservative constitutional order. The zemstvos did, of course, spawn and support the remarkably progressive third element, dedicated populist professionals whose commitment as a social group to improving popular welfare is perhaps unmatched in modern European history. But we learn from Samuel Ramer, Jeffrey Brooks, and Nancy Frieden in Chapters 8, 7, and 9, respectively, that zemstvo relations with these rural professionals was one of continuing tension and discord – an "uneasy alliance" often reflecting master–serf attitudes and one which largely fell apart after the first Russian revolution. If the work of zemstvo employees in the field of education and public health won well-deserved acclaim, it is, as Professor Ramer suggests, very hard to credit the zemstvos themselves with these achievements.

The importance of these conclusions is not only that they help revise common Western assumptions about the zemstvos as essentially liberal institutions but also that they form a background against which the demise of the zemstvo in 1917 becomes fully comprehensible. The collapse of the old regime left Russia in the control of liberals whose assumptions and values bore increasingly little relation to social realities and popular aspirations. Zemstvos became agencies of Provisional Government authority in the countryside in part because they were well-established institutions and could help maintain the political loyalty of the gentry but also because the new regime misperceived their past political function and mistakenly assumed their history as welfare institutions would secure peasant support. However, for many in the countryside, the zemstvos symbolized reaction, not progress,

414

and appeared as institutional barriers to social reform. Thus their identification as bodies of Provisional Government authority not only worked to discredit the new regime but also helped identify liberal democracy with the preservation of gentry interests.

There was perhaps no escape from this dilemma, and certainly the new government's fault was not one of intention. The necessities of political liberalism irreconcilably contradicted the need to build mass support, which could only be done by accepting a radical solution to the land problem, cultivating the allegiance of respected village authorities, and risking gentry anger and displacement. This was done during the Civil War in northwestern Russia, where the evidence suggests that the zemstvos were finally supported as local government institutions. But the paradox of success here lay in the wreckage of democratic politics; it is hard to imagine any liberal regime moving in this direction before October 1917 without precipitating civil war.

One is left with a distressing sense of the zemstvo almost as an institutional screen behind which the antagonistic base of Russian social relations in the countryside was artfully concealed – from everyone, that is, but the peasants. What is disturbing about this image is the way it suggests the misapprehensions of even Russia's most progressive liberals, who remained unable even after February 1917 to perceive the depths of peasant estrangement. Ironically, moreover, it was not only the gentry which bore the brutal consequence of this misapprehension and became the focus of peasant antizemstvo feeling but also the third element, which was used throughout Russia in 1917 to explain electoral laws, organize balloting, and oversee the formation of new volost assemblies. Having fought for years against reactionary zemstvo assemblies and boards, the village "intelligentsia" found itself derided as an agent of its own antagonist. One can hardly be surprised by the relative ease with which many from this group eventually made their peace with the Bolsheviks and continued in many cases to work in the area of social welfare well into the 1920s.

Finally, it is also worth noting that the long history of third-element brutalization was only finally completed during the period of high Stalinism and that the process of peasant introversion, which played such a significant role in the zemstvos' fate in 1917, was similarly only resolved a full decade later, and perhaps not even then. The history of the zemstvo is at heart a study of antagonistic social and political relations in the countryside and largely takes its broader meaning in these terms. If the fate of the zemstvo as an institution outlines the failures of both tsarist society and liberal democracy to come to grips with the dual problem of peasant politics and agrarian economics, it also suggests the dimensions of Bolshevik tasks in this regard. Thus the history of the zemstvo in 1917 perhaps also sets the background for a fuller understanding of the Bolsheviks' own ultimate disasters in this area.

Notes

1 See the speech by D. M. Shchepkin to the Congress of Provincial Zemstvo Representatives, January 18, 1918, in *Russkie vedomosti*, 1918, no. 11.
2 V. D. Nabokov, "Vremennoe pravitel'stvo," *Arkhiv russkoi revoliutsii*, 1922, no. 1, pp. 14–16.
3 *Kak sovershilas' velikaia russkaia revoliutsia* (Petrograd, 1917), pp. 1–6; M. M. Ichas, "27 i 28 fevralia 1917 g.," *Poslednie novosti*, March 12, 1927.
4 T. J. Polner, *Russian Local Government during the War and the Union of Zemstvos* (New Haven, 1930), p. 87.
5 *Sbornik tsirkuliarov Ministerstva vnutrennykh del za period mart–iiun' 1917 goda*, 1917, no. 891–932. See the discussion on this decree in William G. Rosenberg, *Liberals in the Russian Revolution* (Princeton, 1974), p. 59, n. 24.
6 *Sbornik tsirkuliarov MVD*, 1917, no. 91.
7 E. A. Zviagintsev, *Chto takoe melkaia zemskaia edinitsa ili volostnoe zemstvo?* (Moscow, 1917), p. 10.
8 Polner, pp. 287–9.
9 *Sbornik tsirkuliarov MVD*, 1917, no. 91.
10 *Proizvoditel'nye sily Rossii*, 1917, no. 6, p. 41.
11 Ibid.
12 *Zemlia i volia*, 1917, no. 3.
13 "Mart–mai 1917 goda," *Krasnyi arkhiv*, 1926, no. 16, pp. 40–1.
14 As cited in *Vlast' naroda*, 1917, no. 113. See also *Zemlia i volia*, 1917, no. 9. According to the survey in *Severnyi khoziain*, the average *skhod* was around 400 persons, with the largest having 715 members, the smallest 172. Almost all members were between the ages of 30 and 50; 56 percent had finished primary school, and only 2 percent were illiterate.
15 See, for example, the interesting discussion of peasant communes and gatherings in D. J. Male, *Russian Peasant Organization Before Collectivization* (Cambridge, 1971), passim.
16 *Zemlia i volia*, 1917, nos. 3, 39.
17 *Russkie vedomosti*, 1917, nos. 110, 121.
18 *Zemlia i volia*, 1917, no. 14.
19 *Russkie vedomosti*, 1917, no. 112. This paper also has a number of reports, however, of old and new zemstvo representatives participating in sessions together in a "harmonious" and "orderly" way. See,

for example, 1917, nos. 110, 126, which contain accounts of assemblies in Kovrov and Novgorod.

20 Ibid., 1917, no. 121.
21 *Zemlia i volia*, 1917, no. 34.
22 *Russkie vedomosti*, 1917, no. 124.
23 *Polozhenie o volostnom zemstve* (Petrograd, 1917), pp. 11–41.
24 M. D. Zagriatskov, *Zemstvo i demokratiia* (Moscow, 1917), pp. 45–6.
25 District and province zemstvo boards had more independent authority than their volost counterparts and were given more responsibility for the conduct of current business in accordance with zemstvo assembly decisions. The latter apparently could not convene at their own initiative but had to be called at least once a year by the board. Still, district assembly members were to be elected directly from both municipalities and new rural election districts and were themselves responsible for both the election of the district zemstvo board and the selection of members to the provincial organization. Thus the principle of democratic review operated here as well, although specific provisions were also established for the review of decisions by central government authorities.
26 *Sbornik tsirkuliarov MVD*, 1917, no. 91.
27 *Zemlia i volia*, 1917, no. 48.
28 *Russkie vedomosti*, 1917, no. 124, *Russkoe slovo*, 1917, no. 192.
29 *Polozhenie*, p. 6. (This is Article 6 of the "Postanovlenie Vremennogo pravitel'stva o volostnom zemskom upravlenii," dated May 21, 1917.)
30 See the discussion in Zviagintsev, pp. 13–14; and *Zemlia i volia*, 1917, no. 13, which details the activities and concerns of the peasant delegates to a general peasant congress in Iaroslavl province in March.
31 The legislation is reprinted in R. Browder and A. Kerensky, eds., *The Russian Provincial Government 1917. Documents*, 3 vols. (Stanford, 1961), 2:528–32. See the discussion in P. N. Pershin, *Agrarnaia revoliutsiia v Rossii*, 2 vols. (Moscow, 1966), 1:301–2, 364–6; and the useful, if somewhat tendentious essay by N. K. Figurovskaia, "Bankrotstvo 'agrarnoi reformy' burzhuaznogo Vremennogo pravitel'stva," *Istoricheskie zapiski*, 1968, no. 81, pp. 23–67. See also the discussion in V. I. Kostrikin, *Zemel'nye komitety v 1917 godu* (Moscow, 1975), esp. pp. 144 ff.
32 See Browder and Kerensky, 2:615, 625–6; and the interesting discussion in John Keep, *The Russian Revolution: A Study in Mass Mobilization* (New York, 1976), pp. 173–5.
33 Ibid.
34 See the discussions in *Russkie vedomosti*, 1917, nos. 110, 143; and V. V. Kabanov, *Oktiabr'skaia revoliutsiia i kooperatsiia* (Moscow, 1973), esp. pp. 109–20.
35 *Zemlia i volia*, 1917, nos. 63, 78.

36   See, for example, the reports in *Russkie vedomosti*, 1917, no. 131; and *Zemlia i volia*, 1917, no. 102.

37   *Russkie vedomosti*, 1917, no. 200.

38   *Izvestiia Moskovskogo soveta rabochikh deputatov*, June 9, 1917.

39   *Polozhenie*, pp. 15–16.

40   *Russkie vedomosti*, 1917, nos. 193, 200.

41   *Vlast' naroda*, 1917, no. 122.

42   *Russkie vedomosti*, 1917, nos. 194, 217.

43   *Bor'ba trudiashchikhsia Volyni za vlast' sovetov (mart 1917–dek. 1920 g.)* (Zhitomir, 1957), p. 55.

44   *Den'*, 1917, no. 141. See also ibid., 1917, no. 194, which contains a summary of events.

45   *Delo naroda*, 1917, no. 148.

46   *Volynskaia rech'*, 1917, no. 62, as cited in *Bor'ba trudiashchikhsia Volyni*, pp. 46–8; *Delo naroda*, 1917, no. 160.

47   *Delo naroda*, 1917, no. 148.

48   *Russkie vedomosti*, 1917, no. 193.

49   Ibid., 1917, nos. 193, 194, 227.

50   Ibid., 1917, no. 227.

51   Ibid., 1917, nos. 206, 227.

52   *Vlast' naroda*, 1917, no. 133.

53   *Russkie vedomosti*, 1917, nos. 193, 217; *Vlast' naroda*, 1917, no. 105; *Izvestiia Moskovskogo soveta*, 1917, no. 177.

54   See, for example, 1917, no. 123.

55   *Vlast' naroda*, 1917, no. 122.

56   Ibid., 1917, no. 114; *Izvestiia Moskovskogo soveta*, 1917, no. 155.

57   *Sotsial demokrat*, 1917, no. 136.

58   Ibid., 1917, nos. 135, 136.

59   Ibid., 1917, no. 138.

60   Ibid., 1917, no. 136.

61   For example, in Podolsk district, where the Bolsheviks received 4,735 out of 14,579 votes and returned 12 of 38 delegates. See *Izvestiia Moskovskogo soveta rabochikh deputatov*, 1917, no. 173.

62   *Vtoroi Vserossiiskii s"ezd sovetov rabochikh i soldatskikh deputatov. Sbornik dokumentov* (Moscow, 1957), pp. 227–386. Scattered election returns appear in most major Moscow and Petrograd newspapers in late August and September. See esp. *Russkie vedomosti*, 1917, no. 200, et seq.; *Sotsial demokrat*, esp. 1917, no. 162, et seq.; *Delo naroda*, 1917, no. 160; and *Izvestiia* (Moscow), 1917, no. 171. Newspaper accounts show Bolsheviks doing extremely well in Perm, Moscow, and Riazan provinces. In Semenovka volost (Chernigov province), 7,167 out of 8,265 votes cast ballots for a bloc of Bolshevik and SD (Menshevik) Internationalist candidates, according to several newspaper reports; in Verkhnii Ufalei volost in Perm province, Bolsheviks won 35 of 39 volost zemstvo seats. Scattered returns of this sort are meaningless as indicators of peasant sentiment, of

418

course, but undoubtedly they had some impact on public opinion generally as they were prominently reported in Moscow and Petrograd papers.

63 *Russkie vedomosti*, 1917, no. 217.
64 Ibid., 1917, no. 194.
65 *Gosudarstvennoe soveshchanie* (Moscow, 1930), pp. 165–6.
66 Ibid.
67 Ibid., pp. 160–3.
68 Ibid., pp. 162–3.
69 *Den'*, 1917, no. 164.
70 Ibid., 1917, no. 166.
71 *Izvestiia* (Moscow), 1917, no. 173.
72 *Vlast' naroda*, 1917, no. 137; *Sotsial demokrat*, 1917, no. 167.
73 *Russkie vedomosti*, 1918, no. 17; see also 1918, no. 10.
74 *Vlast' naroda*, 1917, no. 134. *Razgon* might be translated "dispersal," but it is much more powerful than its English counterpart.
75 *Russkie vedomosti*, 1918, no. 15.
76 Pershin, 1:469, citing TsGAOR, f. 393, op. 5, d. 33, p. 227.
77 Pershin, 1:469–70, *Delo naroda*, 1917, nos. 212, 242.
78 *Informatsionnyi listok otdela mestnogo upravleniia NKVD*, 1918, no. 6.
79 *Velikaia oktiabr'skaia sotsialisticheskaia revoliutsiia. Khronika sobytii*, 4 vols. (Moscow, 1957), 3:449, 486, 517, 520; 4:170, 197, 228, 264.
80 *Russkie vedomosti*, 1918, no. 6.
81 E. N. Gorodetskii, "Bor'ba narodnykh mass za sozdanie sovetskikh gosudarstvennykh organov (1917–1918 gg.)," *Voprosy istorii*, 1955, no. 8.
82 *Russkie vedomosti*, 1917, no. 271; *Ustanovlenie sovetskoi vlasti na mestakh v 1917–1918 godakh* (Moscow, 1953), p. 295. In Perm there were also widespread complaints about paying zemstvo salaries and adamant refusal to pay zemstvo taxes, which undoubtedly helped encourage the formation of new local *skhody* as well.
83 Gorodetskii, p. 31.
84 *Vestnik otdela mestnogo upravleniia NKVD*, 1918, no. 14.
85 *Russkie vedomosti*, 1917, no. 234.
86 Ibid., 1917, no. 271.
87 Ibid.
88 Ibid., 1917, no. 272.
89 Ibid., 1917, nos. 271, 272.
90 Ibid., 1917, no. 272.
91 Ibid.
92 Ibid., 1917, no. 278. The board members appointed by the Sovnarkom were identified in the press as Serebriakov, Vasilev, Kobelev, Rogov, Margolin, Kameron, and Gortinskii.
93 Ibid., 1917, no. 279.

94 Large-scale strikes apparently occurred at Kolomna and Saratov, among other places, as well as in Minsk and Simferopol.

95 *Russkie vedomosti*, 1918, no. 1.

96 Ibid., 1918, no. 4.

97 Zemstvo workers resolved "to take all possible measures to preserve zemstvo cultural and welfare institutions, and with this aim, not to prolong the strike but to support as much as possible the independence and autonomy of service collectives not supporting the Bolshevik government." See ibid., 1918, no. 10. This was short, however, of a decision to end the strike.

98 Ibid., 1918, no. 4.

99 The composition of the Zemgor conference, according to ibid., 1917, no. 7, was as follows:

	City delegates	Zemstvo delegates
Right SR	48	83
Left SR	4	32
Nonparty	28	88
Mensheviks	27	10
Bolsheviks	1	16
Kadet	10	1
NS (Popular Socialists)	6	2
Edinstvo	1	2

100 The new committee is listed in ibid., 1918, no. 12.

101 Ibid., 1918, no. 18.

102 Ibid., 1918, no. 21.

103 The conditions included a provision for "collegial management" of zemstvo affairs through a committee elected by zemstvo employees; return of confiscated zemstvo property; and the participation in the new collegial executive organ of one representative from the Soviet government "for purposes of practicality and contact." See ibid., 1918, no. 28.

104 Vr. Glav. Kt. Vserossiiskago zemskago soiuza, *Ocherk deiatel'nosti Vserossiiskago zemskago soiuza za granitsei (aprel' 1920–1 ianvaria 1922 g.)* (Sofia, 1922), pp. 3–4.

105 Ibid., pp. 6–10. The new Main Committee included S. P. Shlikevich, Baron A. K. Vrangel, V. G. Kolokovtsov, S. A. Balavinskii, and Count S. L. Kopnist.

106 *Delo naroda*, 1917, no. 134; *Russkie vedomosti*, 1917, no. 131.

107 See the discussion in Rosenberg, esp. pp. 368–9, 375.

108 *Donskaia rech'* (Rostov), 1919, no. 24, et seq.; N. I. Astrov, "Neskol'ko spravok o 'novom politicheskom kurse' " (Ms. in Panina Archive, Columbia University, n.d.), pack. 3, fold. 40.

109 Appeal of the Kadet Central Committee to Local Party Organizations, October 14, 1919, in the Panina Archive, pack. 3, fold. 33. See also N. M. Melnikov, "Grazhdanskaia voina na iuge Rossii" (Ms. in Archive of Russian and East European Culture, Columbia University, n.d.), esp. pp. 18–24; B. A. Shteifon, *Krizis dobrovol'chestva* (Belgrade, 1928).

110 See Rosenberg, pp. 386–7.

111 Konstitutsionno-demokraticheskaia partiia, *Vremennyi pravitel' Khorvat i ego delovoi kabinet* (n.p., 1919) (Broadside of the Siberian Regional Kadet Committee).

112 Telegram of E. L. Harris (U.S. consul in Omsk) to Washington, D.C., no. 65, May 16, 1919, in E. L. Harris Archives, Hoover Institution, Stanford, Calif.

113 I. A. Iakushev, "Komitet sodeistviia sozyvu zemskogo sobora," *Sibirskii arkhiv*, 1929, no. 2, p. 76.

114 See Rosenberg, pp. 415–16.

115 N. V. Ustrialov, "Belyi Omsk " (Ms. in N. V. Ustrialov Personal Archive, Hoover Institution); Iakushev, pp. 77 ff.

116 Union of Russian Zemstvos and Towns, London Committee, *North-Russian Zemstvos and Municipalities* (London, 1919), pp. 15–17.

117 Ibid., p. 19.

118 Ibid., p. 22.

119 The membership of this group included P. Mamontov, P. Koptiakov, S. Matskevich, and A. Petrov.

120 *Ocherk deiatel'nosti*, pp. 12–15.

121 Vserossiiskii zemskii soiuz, *The Educational Work of the Russian Zemstvos and Towns Relief Committee Abroad* (Paris, n.d.), passim.

122 Ibid., p. 8.

123 Ibid., pp. 17–19.

13

The zemstvo in historical perspective

TERENCE EMMONS

Rather than give the customary résumé of the individual contributions to this volume, I would like to offer here a few observations about the main points made in them, according to my reading, and then I should like in the light of these observations to reconsider the problem of political alternatives existing in Russia during the crisis period of the old regime. In doing so, I hope to demonstrate some of the implications of these chapters for major questions in modern Russian history – from one observer's perspective. I would not expect all the contributors to be in agreement with me about all that I have to say here.

It is well known that the emancipation of 1861 left the peasants an order apart, economically, legally, and in matters of general administration and justice, with a system of communal land tenure, their own village and volost administrations, and separate class courts. The zemstvo was the one institution to emerge from the reforms of the 1860s in which all three principal estates of provincial Russia – nobility, peasantry, and merchantry (or large private landowners, communal peasantry, and owners of substantial nonagricultural property) – were to come together on a regular basis, through their elected representatives, for the administration of a variety of common local affairs (see Chapter 4). Together with the other reforms of the 1860s, however, the zemstvo reform brought a cautious and partial dismantling of the old estate order with the lord–peasant relation at its center. Ensured by the suffrage system and enhanced by peasant indifference and the costs and inconveniences of participation, dominance in the new zemstvo institutions was for the representatives of the landed gentry.

Gentry domination of the zemstvos was such an obvious fact of life in these "all-class" institutions of local self-government that it drew attention, and criticism, from the very beginning, long before the "counterreform" of 1890 institutionalized specifically *noble* dominance (as opposed to that of private landholding in general) and deprived the peasants of the right to elect their "representatives" directly to the district assemblies (see Chapter 3). What the present studies do, accordingly, is not so much shed new light on the overall level of gentry domination of the zemstvos,[1] but rather to point up the extent to which the zemstvos tended, by and large, to defend the perceived interests of a broader constituency of gentry proprietors and to explore the implications of that situation for the zemstvos' relations with the peasantry, the third element, and the government.

The zemstvo gentry were themselves not a homogeneous lot, although they were almost all drawn from a relatively small pool of 25–30,000 middle-to-large landowners. Although the zemtsy very widely shared a number of goals – increased independence of the zemstvos from the government, expansion of education and medical care, even the ideas of "crowning the edifice" with some kind of national zemstvo assembly and giving it a "foundation" by creating a volost-level zemstvo – it would be wrong, as Roberta Manning forcefully argues in her essay, to equate the views of the zemstvo gentry at large with those of the liberal activist minority whose concepts of the "zemstvo idea" fairly dominated prerevolutionary writing about the zemstvos and whose activities have attracted the attention of historians. Present in the zemstvos from their inception, this rather small minority[2] took advantage of their gentry status and property qualifications to pursue in the zemstvos the progressive political and social goals they had acquired in the Europeanized culture of educated, urban Russia. Among them, again from the beginning, there were those who looked on the zemstvos primarily as the first step toward establishment of a constitutional order.[3] Although the latter were able to capitalize on growing gentry discontent with government policies and performance to bring the bulk of the zemstvo establishment by the early days of the Revolution of 1905 into the active political opposition that was pushing for constitutional reform, by the autumn of that year, fear of a peasant jacquerie (*pugachevshchina*) had engendered a reaction in the zemstvos which in the course of the ensuing 20 months effectively withdrew them from the political opposition and removed the constitutionalist leadership of 1905 from zemstvo governing boards almost without exception.

Following the Revolution of 1905, the government returned to the job of dismantling the old estate order it had begun in the 1860s to 1880s, and specifically to removing the various legal and fiscal disabilities of the peasantry and encouraging dissolution of communal tenure. On the eve of World War I, it was, ironically, above all in the original "all-class" institution of the zemstvo that the old estate categories and distinctions not only remained in force but were reinforced by comparison with the situation established at the time of the reforms half a century before. The suffrage system for zemstvo elections remained the estate-based one that had been formally eschewed (except for the communal peasants) in the system introduced in 1905 for elections to the national parliament, the Duma, and the numerically and economically diminished gentry more exclusively dominated the zemstvo assembly halls and governing boards than ever before, and in a manifestly more self-interested manner (Chapter 4).

The precariousness of the situation of the zemstvo under these conditions did not by any means escape contemporary notice. The editors of the fiftieth-anniversary volume on the zemstvo, most of whose contributors were second- and third-element veterans of the constitutional reform movement, made a point of it in their introduction:

> There can no longer be any argument about the urgent need to reform the 1890 statute, which gave the zemstvo into the hands of a nobility that is progressively losing its significance in local cultural life...
>
> The work of the zemstvo has grown enormously and continues to grow irrepressibly; it is becoming ever more involved with the variegated interests of the population. To leave representation in the zemstvo in its present form, in the hegemony of a small group of nobility – ever poorer in land, paying almost no taxes into zemstvo coffers, rotting on the vine – is quite impossible. The existing situation represents a threat to the foundations of zemstvo self-government, and to the cultural future of the country.[4]

The prophetic implications of this last remark were borne out in 1917–18 in a spectacle whose proportions its authors, one imagines, could hardly have anticipated. The events of the 1917 revolution in the countryside, described here in the essay of William Rosenberg, revealed plainly the gulf that, after half a century of "all-class" local administration, still separated peasant Russia from the Russia of the gentry and the bureaucracy. As village Russia, taking the gentry's lands with it, turned in upon itself with the breakdown of political authority and of the economic ties linking town and country, it turned its back on all the institutions that had been imposed upon it from "outside" (with the exception of the exclusively peasant institutions, now freed of bureaucratic supervision).

The indifference, often mixed with hostility, that the peasants by and large demonstrated toward the zemstvo institutions in the revolution was clearly perceived by contemporaries. It was by implication the main element in the "existing situation" deplored by the authors of the

425

passage just quoted, and it was explicitly discussed by many prerevolutionary writers. V. D. Kuzmin-Karavaev, a man with long experience in both zemstvo and government, wrote, for example, in another anniversary collection, as late as 1911:

> Neither the character of zemstvo activity nor the desire of the zemstvo to serve the interests of the peasantry have been capable of merging the zemstvo and the peasantry into a single whole. In the eyes of the peasants the zemstvo was and remains an organization that is foreign to them: a collective name for some kind of undefined administration [nachal'stvo], whether identical with the district office [of administration], the marshal [of nobility], the policeman [ispravnik], the land captain [zemskii nachal'nik], or distinct from them – it is not clear.[5]

The essential accuracy of Kuzmin-Karavaev's characterization of the prevailing peasant attitude toward the zemstvo is confirmed in the essays in this volume, especially in the chapters by Dorothy Atkinson and Rosenberg, but also in the studies dealing with the third element (see below). It is particularly important to remark the apparent identification of the zemstvo by the peasantry with a single gentry–bureaucratic "establishment." If, as the historians of the nobility and the bureaucracy tell us, the nobility by the end of the nineteenth century had been effectively bifurcated into a landless service nobility on the one side and a provincial landed gentry, increasingly aware of itself as a separate interest, on the other,[6] the peasants appear to have been quite oblivious to this distinction. And well they might have been, since the gentry-run zemstvo was also the government's main collector of direct taxes after the abolition of the poll tax in the 1880s, and, especially after creation of the office of zemskii nachal'nik in 1889, most of the main representatives of government authority in the district with whom the peasants had contact were also local noble landowners: the barin and the chinovnik were often one and the same person, the pillar of the order that taxed them and prevented them from taking possession of the gentry's lands, which they believed to be their right as a matter of elementary justice.

There does not seem to be need for recourse to abstract notions about "lack of political culture" or "prepolitical mentality" in order to understand peasant indifference toward the zemstvos; it was grounded in a sober, if in some respects not very farsighted, sizing up of the real character of the zemstvo institutions and what they were capable of doing for the peasants. Widespread nonparticipation by peasants in zemstvo elections is a case in point: peasant indifference to the elections was clearly linked to simple recognition that the peasant vote did not amount to much in the zemstvos, especially after the 1890 legislation reduced the proportion of peasant deputies in the district assemblies and deprived the peasantry of the right of direct election of these deputies altogether.[7] By contrast, when the suffrage system elaborated for the first national elections (law of December 11, 1905) offered considerable weight to the peasant vote and it appeared that the Duma was going to take up agrarian reform as the major substantive item on its agenda, peasants took a lively interest in the elections to the first two Dumas convened under that system and sent to the provincial electoral assemblies, and thence to the Duma, a considerable number of alert representatives who were prepared to pursue peasant interests aggressively.[8] (This kind of activism was not carried on into the elections to the Third and Fourth Dumas, in which peasant weight in the elections had been drastically undercut by the revision of the electoral law on June 3, 1907; nor was it to the post-1905 "reactionary" zemstvos, despite restoration in 1906 of the peasantry's right to direct election of their deputies.)[9]

Ironically, the third-element intelligentsia, despite their idealism, real service to the people, and noninvolvement in land relations, were in the peasants' view just as much outsiders – representatives of the establishment – as was the gentry "second element."

The zemstvo intelligentsia's persistent sense of isolation from the peasantry is a frequent refrain in these chapters, one which reminds us of the distance that, right up to the revolution, still separated the two cultures of Russia: the traditional culture of peasant Russia, and the European culture that emanated from its towns. It is remarkable that a profound sense of estrangement seems to have been felt not only by the more highly educated third-element specialists who were city people by origin but even by representatives of the "peasant intelligentsia" who may have been away from the village for only a few years in attendance at a teachers' seminary or technical school. How deep and widespread the estrangement was in the case of the "peasant intelligentsia" is impossible to judge. It is known that in the first national elections in 1906, peasant gatherings (*volostnye skhody*) frequently elected just such peasant *intelligenty*, and a fair number of them made it all the way to the Duma. They were selected precisely because of that which made them different from their electors: their literacy and assumed familiarity with the ways of the other Russia, where the peasants' interests would need defending. Of course, these particular representatives of the "peasant intelligentsia" were also (by statutory requirement) householders in the volosts from which they had been elected.[10]

In any event, to the extent that they involved themselves in 1917 in the attempt to reconstruct local government on the basis of a reformed zemstvo, peasant *intelligenty* had visited upon them the same animosity

427

and even violence the peasants displayed toward everyone else involved in that work; indeed, as William Rosenberg suggests in Chapter
12, they often seem to have borne the brunt of peasant antagonism, for
they were widely used in the reconstruction effort as "shock troops" by
zemstvo leaders, in the mistaken belief that the peasants would heed
them.

Despite its size (50,000 by the turn of the century and perhaps as
many as 70,000 by the eve of the war) and great importance in modern
Russian history, we still have only the most impressionistic knowledge
of the third element as a social and professional group, or congeries of
groups, and it has begun to receive serious scholarly attention only in
the last few years.[11] Some of the most illuminating pages of this book
deal with third-element groups. Although they deal with professional
groups of diverse educational, income, and status levels, the essays
dealing with the third element are linked by common themes, one of
which, generalized estrangement from the peasantry, has already been
mentioned.

The predominant theme running through the essays, however, is that
of tension and conflict between the third element and its second-
element, mostly gentry, employers: the deputies and members of the
governing boards of the district and provincial zemstvos.

Low pay and difficult working conditions – which seem to have been
the lot of most of the third element – naturally aroused resentment and
tended to underline the third element's subordinate, employee status.
The subordinate status of the third element was reinforced by differences in social backgrounds: most of the third element were of
nonnoble origin, *raznochintsy*. An air of condescension appears to
have frequently attended the dealings of the zemtsy with their third-
element employees, including not only the lowly schoolteachers and
clerical personnel, many of them not far removed from the peasant
village, but even such groups as the zemstvo physicians, who were
better educated than most of their employers.[12]

Closely linked to these status differences as a source of friction
between the second and third elements were differences in the values
and goals they respectively brought to their zemstvo work. As the
studies of Ramer, Frieden, and Johnson show, tensions arising from
this source were particularly acute between the *zemtsy* on the one side
and physicians and statisticians on the other. Although the physicians'
general goal of developing modern community medicine outside the
framework of the central government bureaucracy found widespread
and enduring support in the provincial zemstvos,[13] serious differences
arose between the physicians and the *zemtsy* over the specific forms

428

that zemstvo medical care should take, differences grounded, on the one side, in concern for establishing professional autonomy and standards and, on the other, in a desire to retain administrative control, budgetary considerations, and so on. On the whole, the physicians seem to have had their way in shaping the character of zemstvo medical service, but only through persistent struggle and, for the time and place, remarkable feats of organization and publicity.

Things were different with the statisticians, and the issue of goals accordingly became a greater source of friction between the two elements than in the case of the physicians. In the early days of zemstvo statistics, the populist ethos was particularly marked among the statisticians, who brought to their work the desire "to illuminate the causes of [peasant] poverty and indebtedness, and to provide factual data that could lead to reforms" (Chapter 10). This approach required broad and diverse inquiries, especially detailed peasant household surveys. The zemstvos themselves (and the central government, whose agents they were in this activity) tended to set a much more narrowly conceived task for their statisticians: to provide statistical data needed for tax assessments. The scope of the inquiries they were willing to support was correspondingly more restricted. These conflicting goals led to repeated clashes between zemstvo statisticians and their employers and, on occasion, to resignations by entire statistical bureaus attached to provincial zemstvos, especially toward 1900, by which time the progressive growth in the size of the zemstvos' statistical apparatus and the progressive restriction in the scope of its activities had combined to produce a sense of crisis in zemstvo statistical circles.

The present studies do not appear to contest the generally held opinion that the third element (or at least its better-educated members) was largely populist-oriented and generally held more radical social and political views than most of the second element; however, they do call into question received views on the level of political activism obtaining within the third element in general and on their role in the zemstvo opposition movement leading into 1905 in particular. It is argued here that the zemstvo physicians were largely preoccupied with professional advancement and autonomy and were generally followers rather than leaders of the second element in the organization of the zemstvo opposition (Chapter 9). The work of the zemstvo statisticians, the classical "subversive" third-element group in the eyes of government officials, was broadly reform-oriented, but it appears that only a small "elite" used their professional positions as a cover for political activity. (It seems, moreover, that this highly politicized minority generally got involved in zemstvo statistical work out of necessity – as a source of livelihood in provincial exile – rather than by design.) The majority of zemstvo statisticians apparently stayed out of politics in the years of the Liberation Movement and the Revolution of 1905 – partly, it seems, because of estrangement from the gentry second element and partly as a result of the considerable degree of professionalization and specialization in statistical work that had been reached by that time: instead of remaining a fairly homogeneous group, statisticians were increasingly dividing into a more or less highly trained professional elite, whose goals were broadly educational rather than specifically political, and an army of scantily educated clerks. Most of the politicized generalists of the first generation of zemstvo statistics had been drawn off into other endeavors well before the political crisis of the early years of this century, in large measure due to the increasing circumscription of zemstvo statistical work.

With all due concession to the influence that some of the third element might have had on the views of those members of the second element with whom they had sustained contact (principally members of governing boards), it would appear that the growth of political opposition in the zemstvos before 1905 was mainly a development internal to the predominantly gentry second element.[14]

Greatly strained by the zemstvo reaction that followed the Revolution of 1905, when many zemstvos cut back drastically on their programs and some carried out wholesale purges of their third-element personnel, relations between the third and second elements seemed to be stabilizing by 1908, and the size of third-element staffs began to rise once again. The coming of World War I showed, however, that all the old sources of conflict between the two elements were still present; indeed, it greatly aggravated them.

The social tensions and conflicting goals that were endemic to the relations between the two elements naturally entailed a contestation by the third element of the formally undivided administrative authority of the gentry-dominated zemstvo boards; this in turn focused attention on the issue of reforming the suffrage system for elections to the institutions of local self-government. The sharpness of that issue, that is, the third element's demand for participation, had grown apace with the size and importance of the third element itself. Instead of producing a moratorium on the demand for democratization of the zemstvo suffrage which was coming from third-element quarters, the enlistment of the zemstvos in the war effort through the zemstvo union only exacerbated it. As William Gleason points out in Chapter 11, the second element became increasingly dependent on the third element during the war

430

because of the technical nature of the demands it made on the
zemstvos; the third element was drawn into the governing units of the
zemstvos – whether the established boards or special committees for
the war effort – on an ad hoc basis. This "de facto transformation of the
social composition of local government" (Chapter 11) went unaccom-
panied, however, by any signs that the gentry *zemtsy*, by and large,
were willing to recognize it de jure.

Using the leverage their role in the war effort gave them, some
third-element circles began early on to mobilize support for democratization of the zemstvo suffrage system. Conflict on this issue, together
with the unwillingness of the established second-element leadership of
the zemstvo union to make political demands on the increasingly
incompetent yet increasingly interfering government, brought the
tension between the second and third elements to an unprecedented
level of acuity on the eve of the February Revolution.

The reformers who came to the fore during the early years of the war
finally got their way under the Provisional Government in 1917: a
series of reforms ended the domination of the zemstvos by the gentry,
but by the time these reforms began to be put into effect in mid-1917
the possibility that the zemstvos, however constituted, could assume
the primary role in local administration assigned them by the Provisional Government had vanished in the great wave of anarchy that
swept away the social and institutional foundations of the old regime.

Most nonacademic observers of relations between state and zemstvo,
from Witte to Lenin, have agreed that there was an inherent conflict
between the institutionalization of the principle of self-government in
the zemstvo and the centralizing bureaucratic traditions of the autocracy.[15] Both of the two contending theories about the nature of the
zemstvo administration that were elaborated in prerevolutionary Russia, the "societal" (*obshchestvennaia*) theory and the "statist" (*gosudarstvennaia*) theory, however, rejected the inevitability of conflict.[16] It
is noteworthy that the two theories were in vogue consecutively, in
differing circumstances, which suggests that in each instance the
theory was put in service by those who for one reason or another
wished to protect the zemstvo institutions from accusations of incom-
patibility with autocracy.

The societal theory, in vogue at the time of the reform's promulgation, held that elective self-government occupied itself with a special
complex of local affairs that lay outside the sphere of state administration. It appears that this theory was advanced by supporters of the
reform to reassure a bureaucracy, jealous of its prerogatives, of the
absence of a systemic threat in the introduction of an elective, public

431

element into the administrative structure at a time when the government was desperately seeking the means to improve governance, that is, especially fiscal control, over the provinces.[17]

The statist theory held that local self-government was a direct extension of the general system of state administration – there are no purely "local" affairs – whose only peculiarities were its element of public participation and a certain level of independence; both were considered purely functional attributes. This theory came into its own in the 1880s during the reaction under Alexander III, and appears to have been advanced by liberal academic and publicist circles as a means of reassuring the regime, which seemed bent on undoing the reforms of the 1860s, that the 1864 zemstvo reform had not constituted a violation of state tradition: the zemstvos were compatible with autocracy.

By the 1890s, however, the proposition that the zemstvos and the autocracy pursued incompatible goals had come to the fore and did not pass from the political scene until the demise of both the autocracy and the zemstvos. In the long perspective, it seems, only the 'state theory' held credence in the Russian tradition. From their several points of view bureaucrats, law professors, constitutionalist reformers, and the peasants all agreed about this.

The history of the relations between the autocracy and the zemstvo seemed to be repetitive in a fundamental way of a pattern that became established in Russian history no later than the mid-sixteenth century: the central government, casting about for the means to extract revenues from the provinces and keep them under control, would turn in periods of crisis to the practice of involving elected representatives of "society" in local administration; then, almost as soon as the reform was completed, there would begin the process of tightening central controls over the "self-administration," circumscribing its area of competence, and assimilating its officials into the state bureaucracy: "The elected institutions are progressively transformed into subordinate, second-level executors of various tasks assigned them by the bureaucracy, losing in the process their vital moral tie with the communities that had elected them and all traces of independent initiative in the conduct of their affairs."[18]

Manifestations of this pattern were in evidence almost immediately after the promulgation of the zemstvo reform, and it seemed to be in full sway with the promulgation of the 1890 "counterreform," which so dramatically increased the governors' control over the zemstvos and laid the groundwork for transforming the elected officials of the zemstvos into regular government functionaries. This time, however,

432

in contrast to all earlier experience, the bureaucracy encountered determined resistance from within the institutions it had created; the bureaucratic reflex was confronted by a persistent drive to expand the zemstvo's field of competence and by the system's tendency to "replicate itself upwards" (see Chapter 2), that is, to create a national zemstvo organization, which, in the view of quite a few of its proponents, would be the national parliament: the principle of self-government institutionalized at the central government level – a constitutional monarchy.

This confrontation, which was until the eve of the 1905 revolution the focal point of the broader confrontation between autocracy and civil society (*obshchestvo*, the Russian term used to render this classical concept of British political theory), occurred for the first time only in the late nineteenth century. Until that time the absence of an independent civil society of any significant proportions precluded challenges to the regime's undivided political authority. Only toward the end of the nineteenth century had administrative, educational, and economic development combined to produce a civil society of sufficient size and autonomy to challenge the regime's monopoly on political authority.[19] Whatever elements of civil society that had developed prior to the emancipation of the serfs, especially following the elevation of the nobility to the status of a semi-autonomous corporation under Catherine II, were held in check by the institution of serfdom, which compelled dependence of the nobility upon the state.

The zemstvos' crucial contribution to the mounting of the political challenge to the autocracy on the part of civil society is, together with the undeniable cultural services they performed, a major factor accounting for the ambivalence toward the zemstvos that is reflected in most of the literature about them. The confrontation between the zemstvo and the government was, however, far more complex than the struggle between a "progressive" public and a "reactionary" bureaucracy that it is sometimes made out to be. Not only were the zemstvos throughout most of their existence extremely timid in their confrontations with the government. Their motives in them cannot be considered uniformly progressive, just as the government's cannot be considered uniformly reactionary. In various conflicts the question of whether the zemstvos or the local representatives of the bureaucracy were best serving the public interest is moot. Moreover, as the famous rivalry between the Ministries of Finance and Internal Affairs illustrates, the government's attitude toward the zemstvos was far from monolithic. Overall, much of zemstvo–state relations could better be described as cooperative rather than competitive, and some zemstvo

433

programs that have generally been considered progressive were accomplished not despite state interference but because of support within the central government.[20]

Thomas Fallows argues persuasively in Chapter 6 that the exacerbation of relations between the zemstvos and the government over the decade preceding the Revolution of 1905 was due primarily to two factors: on the one hand, the competition between the Finance Ministry and the zemstvos over tax revenue sources, the former bent on channeling all available resources into industrial development, the latter seeking to expand their services and staffs; on the other, the actions of the Interior Ministry resulting from a growing fear of "revolution." It was Pleve's conviction that the zemstvos were becoming havens for "revolutionaries" (perpetrators of political violence) rather than any general notion of the zemstvos as the locus of a constitutional reform movement that provoked the aggressive actions against the zemstvos characteristic of Pleve's ministry (1902–4). There is an interesting parallel here with the ministry's treatment of the gentry opposition around the time of the serf emancipation: in both instances the government, when presented with a challenge to its undivided authority, lumped all its opponents into a single category and took action accordingly in a way that could only alienate its more moderate opponents and make its categorization take on the attributes of a self-fulfilling prophecy.[21]

It would be quite wrong to think that contemporary proponents of the "zemstvo cause" believed that the zemstvo as it existed was a democratic institution, that they were unaware that it was dominated, by and large, by gentry who were not neglectful of their own class interests while functioning as deputies or board members. What they did believe was that the zemstvo could contribute to the economic and cultural development of the country and that, by virtue of its inclusion, however disproportionately, of all the major social groups, it held the potential for democratization and the expansion of public participation in governance. This was the liberal myth about the zemstvo: a myth in the sense of "an idea embodying...cultural ideals" rather than in the more usual sense of a "received idea" or "half-truth."[22]

The zemstvo reform movement began, in effect, even before the institution came into existence, in the liberal critique of the administrative statutes of the emancipation legislation and of the preliminary plans for the zemstvo; the zemstvo–liberal reform program was already elaborated before the creation of the zemstvo and remained intact until the eve of the 1905 revolution, when the movement split into two distinct streams, the one (ascendant until the autumn of 1905) going on

434

from the traditional call for a "crowning of the edifice" (a national zemstvo organization) to the demand of the left opposition as a whole for a constituent assembly and, by implication, a regime of parliamentary sovereignty; and the other, retreating to the Slavophile ideal of consultation between tsar and people without formal constitutional adjustments.

The liberal reform program had two essential goals: social integration or democratization (*sliianie soslovii*), the breaking down of class and cultural barriers in provincial society; and the establishment of popular representation at the national level. From the beginning, as noted, there were those who saw the zemstvo reform as the first step toward a parliamentary order.

Proponents of social integration perceived that the order being arranged in the emancipation statutes presented serious obstacles to their goal by maintaining the commune and setting up an administrative–judicial order for the peasants that kept them isolated from the rest of local society and directly subordinate to government officials. This realization led to proposals for creating an all-class volost, or what was later to be called the "small zemstvo unit," an organ of local self-government for all the population below the district level that would have contact with the day-to-day existence of the people. Proposals along these lines were made as early as 1858 in several of the provincial committees of nobility convened to discuss the reform statutes. The leading advocates of this idea were the majority of the Tver committee, who declared their aim to be "to replace the former patriarchal ties...with new ones, with ties of social benefit and mutual interest, and in the name of this significant principle, to unite equally all inhabitants of the region."[23]

This and related desiderata of the gentry liberals were not realized in the statutes of emancipation, and they went on in the gentry assemblies of 1861–2 to reiterate them and, citing the demonstrated inability of the regime to carry out adequate reforms by purely bureaucratic means, to call for the establishment of a national consultative assembly elected on a democratic franchise.[24] The demand for "crowning the zemstvo edifice" did not pass from the zemstvo agenda from the moment the institutions were set up, although it was made the subject of zemstvo petitions to the throne for the first time (not counting an abortive attempt by the Petersburg provincial zemstvo assembly in 1865) only during the political crisis of 1878–81.

This idea was not without supporters in the government. As V. G. Chernukha has demonstrated, there was a nearly general assumption among the advisors of Alexander II (probably not shared by him) that, sooner or later, representative institutions would be introduced in Russia as part of the country's general advancement toward the status of a modern European polity.[25] (In his famous memorandum, Witte called this view – that Russia's political evolution was destined to follow the path taken by the Western constitutionalist states, particularly England and France – "the great myth of our generation.") And a long series of reform plans was generated within the government bureaucracy, stretching from Speranskii's well-known project of 1809 to Sviatopolk-Mirskii's scheme in 1904, which were based on the principle of public representation from permanent bodies of local self-administration rather than by means of special elections to a central assembly. The first bureaucratic plan to adapt that principle to the zemstvo institutions, P. A. Valuev's, was actually drawn up before they were put into operation, in a project submitted to the tsar in 1863. It provided for elected zemstvo representation in a sort of appendage to the State Council. Others followed.[26] It looked as if a modest step toward implementing this plan was about to be taken at the beginning of the 1880s, but Count Loris-Melikov's reform project was aborted by the assassination of Alexander II (March 1, 1881) and the reaction that set in under his successor, Alexander III (1881–94).[27] When the regime was finally brought back to serious consideration of political reform during the crisis of 1904–5, it soon became clear that this traditional scheme could no longer satisfy the level of demand for political participation existing in the country: it was rejected on these grounds in the earliest planning sessions within the Interior Ministry following the Bulygin manifesto (February 18, 1905) in favor of special elections to a separate assembly.[28] The zemstvo edifice received its "crown" in the form of the national zemstvo congresses, which became legal after October 1905 (although they met rarely thereafter, and not at all after 1907), and a remnant of Valuev's idea of attaching zemstvo representatives to the State Council was preserved under the law of February 20, 1906, which transformed the State Council into an upper house in parity with the new Duma: half of its membership was elected from various corporations, including the zemstvos.[29] The idea of building national representation on the institutions of local self-government came to naught, however, with the creation of the Duma. (It was briefly revived in the government as one of the alternative schemes for rewriting the suffrage law in connection with Stolypin's coup d'état of June 1907.)

Plans for giving the zemstvo a proper "foundation" fared no better under the old regime. The demands for an all-class volost put forward during the preparation of the emancipation legislation were echoed through the succeeding decades and taken up in a particularly intense way just after the turn of the century, when many provincial and district zemstvos passed resolutions in favor of creating the small zemstvo unit, as did a significant proportion of the local committees convened by the government in 1902–3 to discuss the agrarian situation (the Witte committees). The national congresses of zemstvo leaders that began to gather about the same time and were continued into the 1905 revolution all included the demand for a small zemstvo unit in their protocols.[30]

Plans for creating a local-level zemstvo were accompanied from the beginning by demands for democratization of the zemstvo suffrage system, although they were much less widely supported in zemstvo circles, especially in the radical form of universal direct suffrage. All the national congresses of zemstvo leaders that gathered after the turn of the century called for democratization of the zemstvo suffrage system in general terms, but it was not until the April 1905 congress that the zemstvo leaders went so far as to call for universal direct suffrage as the basis for local self-government elections. This demand was carried into the program of the Constitutional Democratic (Kadet) party, but most zemstvos in 1904–5 would go no further in their support for suffrage reform than a return to the 1864 law, which had been altered by the 1890 legislation.[31]

Following the Revolution of 1905, the Kadets introduced into the Second Duma a bill on the small zemstvo unit linked with total democratization of the suffrage, and the government introduced its own, much less radical, bill for a general volost-level administrative unit that would, nevertheless, have significantly increased representation of the peasantry and other nongentry groups.[32] But the volost zemstvo was never created, nor was the suffrage system significantly changed, before the fall of the old regime.

The mutual isolation of the peasantry and the gentry that was built into the emancipation legislation of the 1860s was intended by its architects to protect the peasants from the nobles during the transition period from serfdom to civil equality: the main purpose of the reform had been to dissolve the liens of personal dependency which were considered to be potentially productive of a peasant uprising, à la Pugachev. The planners of the reform were not opposed in principle to the idea of an 'all-class volost' and the general process of social integration to which it was linked; they saw this arrangement as temporary, to be revised, if necessary, with the passage of time, just as they considered the preservation of the peasant commune a temporary necessity.[33]

437

It is one of the great ironies of modern Russian history – although fully in conformity with the regularity with which the anticipations of reformers of all sorts are confounded by the simple fact that the new conditions they help create produce new circumstances they could not possibly have foreseen – that the anticipations of the reformers were so massively frustrated. The institutional arrangements that were considered to be only the first step toward the breakdown of the old society of orders and the evolution of the Russian polity and society along the path already followed by Western countries were turned to different purposes and given a prolonged existence in the 1880s during the reign of reaction under Alexander III. That reign yielded the elaboration, in the words of one early twentieth-century writer, of "the estate–police tendency," which reinforced the separate and unequal status of the rural orders while simultaneously subjecting them to increased bureaucratic tutelage.[34]

The reinforcement of the estate principle in general, and of peasant isolation in particular, was continued as official government policy until the Revolution of 1905.[35] Within the context of that policy, which was still being intoned as a matter of principle in imperial manifestos on the very eve of the 1905 revolution, the possibility of the government's taking on an overhaul of the zemstvo administration was made even more remote by the aforementioned rivalry between the Ministries of Finance and Internal Affairs, which continued unabated over most of this period. Following the government's abandonment of the policy, signified by its aggressive turn after 1905 toward encouraging the breakup of communal tenure among the peasants, the likelihood that Stolypin's agrarian reforms would be accompanied by reform of the zemstvos was made remote by the linkage of that issue to broader political issues, even though the Stolypin government and the Duma majority (even after June 3) both favored creation of an all-class volost and zemstvo suffrage reform.[36] Discussions of zemstvo reform, particularly of the zemstvo suffrage system, took place in an increasingly polarized atmosphere against a background of two contending tendencies within the enfranchised, largely gentry, public of the "Third of June system." These tendencies were starkly described in a minority opinion presented to the 1907 zemstvo congress:

> Two sociopolitical tendencies have taken shape in the zemstvo milieu: a majority which consistently defends the class character of the zemstvo, with predominance in it of large landowning; and the other, which believes in the impending triumph of the idea of a democratic and nonclass [bessoslovnogo i vneklassovogo] zemstvo in a constitutional Russia.[37]

438

A major factor causing the zemstvo reform plan to be stuck for several years in Duma committees and then buried altogether in the State Council was resistance among the provincial gentry, heavily represented in both institutions, out of concern that they might be overwhelmed by the peasants in a reformed zemstvo (with particular anticipated consequences, perhaps, in the area of tax assessment),[38] together with the fact that the government's reform plan for the volost was linked to a plan for replacing the gentry marshal as chief administrative official in the district with a government appointee, who would oversee the new volost administration with the help of *chinovniki* directly under his supervision.[39]

Was, then, the idea, held by generations of zemstvo liberals, that Russia's political development would follow that of the Atlantic countries, its old regime yielding to a parliamentary order, nothing but a pious hope, a "myth" in the more usual sense of the word?[40] The old regime survived longer in Russia than in any other European state, and when the end came the outcome was not only uncommonly violent; it was quite different in character from anything that had happened in the European countries where divine right monarchy had been challenged by civil society in the name of popular sovereignty: neither a full-fledged constitutional-parliamentary order as in England and France nor the *Scheinkonstitutionalismus* of post-1848 Germany and Austria, but a truly new departure, "the first socialist state." (Despite the conventions of Soviet historiography there never was a "bourgeois revolution" in Russia.)

If, as has been widely (though not universally) conceded, the chances for a "European" issue from the crisis of the old regime were remote by 1914 and by 1917, after three years of extreme dislocation of the political and economic order by the ravages of the first total war, perhaps altogether excluded, then there was a brief period at the opening phase of the general crisis of the old regime – essentially that embraced by the outbreak of the Russo-Japanese War in early 1904 at the outset and by the Stolypin coup d'état of June 1907 at the close – when the possibility for a moderate, "European" solution to the crisis of the old regime, most likely a proper constitutional monarchy with effective political authority shifted from crown to parliament, did, in my opinion, exist.

The confrontation between the autocracy and civil society that occurred at that time produced the concession by Emperor Nicholas II of the Manifesto of October 17, 1905, which promised in general terms to introduce civil and political liberties and to summon a legislative assembly elected on a broad franchise.[41] In retrospect it appears that the issuance of the October Manifesto broke up the opposition sufficiently to allow the monarchy to withstand the challenge to its authority. For many contemporaries, however, the revolution was not over, and the contest for political authority was carried over – following the failure of the urban movement of workers, students, and revolutionary partisans in late 1905 to rekindle the general strike that had extracted the promises of the manifesto from the regime so as to bring about its definitive capitulation and the summoning of a constituent assembly – into the first national assembly, the Duma. In the First Duma, convened at the end of April 1906, the opposition, led by the Kadets, the leading party there, attempted to shift the center of political authority from the monarch and his ministry to the Duma. The First Duma was dismissed after 72 days, but the issue continued to be contested by the Kadets, although more cautiously and with less support from groups to their left, in the Second Duma, which was convened in the spring of 1907. The end for the Second Duma came in its turn in a little less than three months, when the Stolypin government, having now pacified the rebellious countryside by the extensive application of physical force and summary justice, moved to rewrite the suffrage law so as to ensure convocation of a Duma that would be dominated by elements – chiefly landed gentry and other large property owners – who would pose no constitutional threat to the regime. Russia had entered its brief "post-constitutionalist period," as some contemporaries liked to call it. Up to that moment, or at least until shortly before it, the contest for political authority was still open, its issue by no means predetermined. The strategy of the Kadets was not favored by the odds, but neither was it entirely unrealistic; some of the best political minds of the generation played the game seriously.[42]

Throughout most of the years stretching from the mid-1860s to the denouement of 1907, the constitutionalist movement had been centered in the zemstvos. Although liberal activists had at no time over these years been more than a modest minority among zemstvo deputies, it was generally understood among Russian liberals that no concessions would be forthcoming from the autocracy without mobilization of the zemstvos for constitutional reform. When the Liberation Movement was gotten underway just after the turn of the century to reach beyond the zemstvo milieu in seeking support for constitutional reform, its leaders (many of them veterans of the zemstvo movement) nevertheless paid primary attention to the zemstvos. Thus the zemstvos played an indispensable role in the constitutional reform movement, both by the active demands forwarded by the zemstvos themselves through their national congresses, in petitions, resolutions, and so forth and through the organizational basis they provided for the most important constitutionalist-reform party of the first two Dumas, the Kadets. Approximately three-quarters of the zemstvo participants in the national congresses of 1905 went on to join that party, and many of the local branches of the party that sprang up in the winter of 1905–6 to contest successfully the first national elections were founded by veterans of the zemstvo movement. Most of the other congress participants joined the moderate constitutionalist Union of October 17, and zemstvo veterans also played an important part in the formation of its local network.[43]

If the zemstvos in the post-October period generally failed to support the Duma in its constitutional struggle with the regime, and after 1907 may have helped, through their representatives in the State Council and elsewhere in the central government, to thwart the conservative reformism of Stolypin's ministry, the fact remains that the zemstvo was a crucial factor in the prerevolutionary political reform movement that came close to extracting definitive political concessions from the crown.

What role the zemstvo might have played in the crisis of the old regime and what its outcome might have been had the zemstvo been reformed according to the demands of liberal and democratic critics some significant time before the onset of the general crisis is impossible to say. It seems reasonably clear, however, given the outbreak of the war in 1914, that introduction of these reforms only after the 1905 revolution would have been too late to prevent the great agrarian revolution that lay behind the political drama of 1917. A harbinger of the treatment liberal constitutionalist Russia was to receive at the hands of the peasants in 1917 had already been seen in 1906. Following the imperial order dissolving the First Duma on July 9, 1906, about a third of the First Duma deputies, led by the Kadets, crossed over the Finnish border to Vyborg, where they signed and published the next day a manifesto "To the Citizens of All Russia." The Vyborg manifesto described the dissolution of the Duma as a violation of the people's right of representation and explained the government's action as the result of its wish to stop the Duma from carrying out its reform program, particularly the radical agrarian reform sponsored by all Duma groups from the Kadets leftward, and warned that the government might act in the immediate future to prevent reconvention of the Duma altogether. In a second part, the manifesto called on the people to engage in civil disobedience by refusing to pay taxes or submit to military recruitment in order to force the government to summon a new Duma promptly.[44]

The liberals' attempt to appeal directly to the people to support the Duma in its struggle for political sovereignty was answered by what can only be called a deafening silence from "the people," that is, the population at large and the peasantry in particular. By September, the Kadet party leader Paul Miliukov, in his speech to his party's fourth congress, had relegated the manifesto to the status of "a historical document."[45] (This marked the end of the Kadets' uncharacteristic adventure into "illegal" action. [The signers of the manifesto were tried and sentenced to a few months in prison for their act.] In the post-June 1907 order the Kadets' once impressive provincial organization quickly atrophied, and the basis of the party's political power was restricted almost exclusively to publicism.)

One can imagine that the peasants' failure to respond to the Vyborg appeal was in large measure due to the simple fact that, given the state of literacy and communications prevailing in rural Russia, most of them never heard of it. But this only points up the isolation of peasant Russia from urban Russia and with it the political significance of the absence of a democratized, grass-roots zemstvo institution. This situation in turn underlines the immense historical consequences of a single event, the assassination of Alexander II. It does not seem unrealistic to suggest that had the projected reforms of Loris-Melikov been gotten underway in the 1880s instead of only after the 1905 revolution, and fitfully at that, the zemstvo might have been transformed before the cataclysm of 1914 into a solid foundation for a liberal-democratic political order, and the existence of the peasantry as an order apart might have been sufficiently overcome to have precluded the great rustication of 1917–18.

In conclusion, I should like to quote from the ruminations on this theme in the unpublished memoirs, written shortly after the Bolshevik revolution, of Alexander Kornilov, the historian of nineteenth-century Russia, long-time government functionary in the peasant administration, and liberal politician:

> It is obvious to me now that no matter how small may have seemed the concessions made by Alexander II to Russian society under the influence of Loris-Melikov, all the same these concessions, and in particular Loris-Melikov's projected plan for further measures in regard to the peasant problem and zemstvo self-administration, were sufficient to have turned Russia onto the path of reforms that had been abandoned by our government after Karakozov's attempted assassination [of Alexander II] in 1866. At the present time I see quite clearly that had there been no catastrophe on March 1 and the enduring

reaction that followed upon it, by which the revolutionaries of that time were in any case swept away without having achieved anything, we would have had a broad and solid development of democratic zemstvo self-administration, and moreover it would have been given the foundation it lacked, in the form of a *small zemstvo unit* of one kind or another. At the same time we would have seen the free development of *popular education*, so necessary for Russia.

Those democratic circles of Russian society capable of thought should have clearly perceived the necessity of both the one and the other, and the fatal consequences of their absence, on two occasions that I have witnessed: the first time was during the revolution of 1905–1906, especially in the fiasco that overtook the revolution following the dispersal of the First Duma as a result of the complete lack of consciousness of the popular masses, *who failed to give the conscious support to their own representatives which they needed at that moment.* The second occasion is the revolution we are now living through, which is accompanied by such terrible and destructive universal chaos.[46]

Notes

1   Roberta Manning, Chapter 5, nevertheless points out that the degree of gentry dominance has generally been underestimated for most provinces, especially at the district level.

2   See the work of N. M. Pirumova (cited in Chapter 5). She estimates the liberal or oppositionist minority to have amounted to a few hundred, or about 20 percent of deputies overall in the 1890s. The zemstvos of some provinces were much more opposition-minded than others.

3   I have discussed this group in my book, *The Russian Landed Gentry and the Peasant Emancipation of 1861* (Cambridge, 1968).

4   B. B. Veselovskii and Z. G. Frenkel', eds., *Iubileinyi zemskii sbornik, 1864–1914* (St. Petersburg, 1914), pp. x–xi.

5   V. D. Kuz'min-Karavaev, "Krest'ianstvo i zemstvo," in *Velikaia reforma. Russkoe obshchestvo i krest'ianskii vopros v proshlom i nastoiashchem,* 6 vols. (Moscow, 1911), 6:286.

6   With the exception of the highest reaches of the bureaucracy, where the landed connection remained predominant to the end. On the nobility, see the new authoritative work of A. P. Korelin, *Dvorianstvo v poreformennoi Rossii, 1864–1904 gg. Sostav, chislennost', korporativnaia organizatsiia* (Moscow, 1979). For a guide to Russian-historical bureaucratic studies, see Daniel Orlovsky, "Recent Studies on the Russian Bureaucracy," *Russian Review,* 1976, no. 4, pp. 448–67; and the new work, Walter Pintner and Don Rowney, eds., *Russian Officialdom. The Bureaucratization of Russian Society from the Seventeenth to the Twentieth Century* (Chapel Hill, 1980).

7 Between 1890 and 1906, the peasants did not elect their deputies to the district zemstvos but only presented lists of candidates from which deputies were selected by the governors.

8 Kuz'min-Karavaev, p. 287. Peasant behavior in the first national elections is analyzed in my work, *The Formation of Political Parties and the First National Elections in Russia* (forthcoming), chs. 6–7.

9 See the contributions of Robert Edelman and Eugene Vinogradoff to Leopold H. Haimson, ed., *The Politics of Rural Russia, 1905–1914* (Bloomington, 1979).

10 Emmons, *The Formation of Political Parties*, ch. 6.

11 In the work of Robert Johnson presented here, and in the researches of Natalia Pirumova, Thomas Fallows, and a few others, which remain for the most part unpublished.

12 Perhaps only physicians like Mikhail Petrunkevich, S. V. Martynov, or A. I. Shingarev, who were also noble members of the second element, were entirely exempt from condescension.

13 Between the 1890s and the war of 1914, medicine was the largest single item in the zemstvo budget, reaching 31 percent of total by 1913. (Education, only about one percentage point behind medicine over most of this period, enjoyed a large direct contribution from the central government, especially after 1907.)

14 Compare the standard work on the zemstvo constitutionalist movement, which assigns the decisive role in activating the zemstvo opposition to the "classless intelligentsia," the third element: I. P. Belokonskii, *Zemskoe dvizhenie*. 2d ed. (Moscow, 1914), pp. 35–7.

15 Witte's famous (ghostwritten) statement of this proposition was the 1899 memorandum, *Samoderzhavie i zemstvo. Konfidentsial'naia zapiska Ministra finansov Stats-Sekretaria S. Iu. Vitte (1899g.) s predisloviem i primechaniiami R. N. S.* (Stuttgart, 1901). For Lenin's views, see note 3 of Chapter 1.

16 See P. P. Gronskii, "Teoriia samoupravleniia v russkoi nauke," in Veselovskii and Frenkel', eds., pp. 76–85.

17 S. F. Starr, *Decentralization and Self-Government in Russia, 1830–1870* (Princeton, 1972).

18 A. A. Kizevetter, *Mestnoe samoupravlenie v Rossii. IX–XIX st. Istoricheskii ocherk*, 2d ed. (Petrograd, 1917), pp. 117–18.

19 An analysis of the ideological currents that came together in this challenge is provided by Leopold H. Haimson, "The Parties and the State: The Evolution of Political Attitudes," in C. E. Black, ed., *The Transformation of Russian Society: Aspects of Social Change since 1861* (Cambridge, Mass., 1967), pp. 110–44. An acute discussion of the character and political significance of Russian civil society in this period may be found in the essay by Martin Malia, which appeared after this article was prepared for press: *Comprendre la Révolution russe* (Paris, 1980).

20 The contributions to this volume, especially that of Thomas Fallows, appear to confirm the recent observations on this subject by George Yaney: *The Systematization of Russian Government: Social Evolution in the Domestic Administration of Imperial Russia, 1711–1905* (Urbana, Ill. 1973), pp. 346–60, esp. 349.

21 I discuss relations between the government and gentry in the reform period in *The Russian Landed Gentry and the Peasant Emancipation of 1861.*

22 *The American Heritage Dictionary of the English Language* (New York, 1970) p. 869.

23 Emmons, *The Russian Landed Gentry,* p. 136.

24 Ibid., ch. 8.

25 V. G. Chernukha, *Vnutrenniaia politika tsarizma s serediny 50-kh do nachala 80-kh gg. XIX v.* (Leningrad, 1978), ch. 1.

26 Excerpts from these plans are available in English in Marc Raeff, ed., *Plans for Political Reform in Imperial Russia, 1703–1905* (Englewood Cliffs, N.J., 1966).

27 P. A. Zaionchkovskii, *Krizis samoderzhaviia na rubezhe 1870–1880-kh godov* (Moscow, 1964).

28 S. E. Kryzhanovskii, *Vospominaniia* (Berlin, 1938), pp. 36–107.

29 The texts of the constitutional documents of 1905–7 may be conveniently consulted in N. I. Lazarevskii, ed., *Zakonodatel'nye akty perekhodnogo vremeni 1904–1906 gg.,* 2d ed. (St. Petersburg, 1907).

30 The intensification of interest in this reform is described and reflected in the collection *Melkaia zemskaia edinitsa,* published in Petersburg in 1902 and then followed by a second, expanded edition with supplementary volume in 1903. The background to this and related publications is described in my article, "The Beseda Circle, 1899–1905," *Slavic Review,* 1973, no. 3, pp. 461–90. See also B. B. Veselovskii, *Istoriia zemstva za sorok let,* 4 vols. (St. Petersburg, 1909–11), 3; supplement, chs. 4–5.

31 See Roberta Manning, "Zemstvo and Revolution: The Onset of the Gentry Reaction, 1905–1907," in Haimson, pp. 51–2.

32 Veselovskii, 4: ch. 19; V. S. Diakin, *Samoderzhavie, burzhuaziia i dvorianstvo v 1907–1911 gg.* (Leningrad, 1978).

33 See I. M. Strakhovskii, "Krest'ianskoe soslovnoe upravlenie," in *Melkaia zemskaia edinitsa,* 2d ed., vol. 1 (St. Petersburg, [1903]), pp. 275–303, esp. 284. See also Starr, ch. 4. On the aims of the planners of the reform in the Editing Commissions, see L. G. Zakharova, "Pravitel'stvennaia programma otmeny krepostnogo prava v Rossii," *Istoriia SSSR,* 1975, no. 2, pp. 22–47; and for the fate of these aims to the end of the reign of Alexander II, see the extremely informative works of V. G. Chernukha, *Krest'ianskii vopros v pravitel'stvennoi politike Rossii (60–70 gody XIX v.)* (Leningrad, 1972); and *Vnutreniaia politika tsarizma.* A plan to end the administrative isolation of the peasantry by creating an all-class volost was introduced as early as 1864 by

Minister of Internal Affairs Valuev. See Peter Czap, Jr. "P. A. Valuyev's Proposal for a *Vyt'* Administration, 1864," *Slavonic and East European Review*, July 1967, pp. 391–410.

34 G. A. Evreinov, quoted in G. Shreider, "Melkaia zemskaia edinitsa v usloviiakh russkoi zhizni," in *Melkaia zemskaia edinitsa v 1902– 1903 gg. Sbornik statei. Vypusk vtoroi* (St. Petersburg, 1903), p. 4.

35 As Alexander Gerschenkron has noted, even the abolition of the institution of joint responsibility among the communal peasantry, generally regarded as an essential element of the communal system, which constituted the first significant step in the government's about-face in its peasant policy (1903), was accompanied by solemn invocation of the inviolability of the commune (*obshchina*) and the necessity of maintaining the communal peasantry as a special estate. A. Gerschenkron, *Continuity in History and Other Essays* (Cambridge, Mass., 1968), pp. 231–2.

36 Veselovskii, 4:167–8. Even the "reactionary" zemstvo congress of 1907 went on record in favor of the small zemstvo unit and expansion of the suffrage system. It should be noted that the government project of these years differed from that of the Duma in that it did not directly treat the reformed volost as the "small zemstvo unit."

37 Veselovskii, 4:168.

38 On the whole, gentry lands were taxed at a lower rate than communal lands, on the grounds that they contained a higher proportion of nonarable land. See Chapter 4.

39 See Diakin. These matters are discussed at some length in Haimson, ed., *The Politics of Rural Russia*, and the book of G. A. Hosking, *The Russian Constitutional Experiment: Government and Duma, 1907– 1914* (Cambridge, 1973).

40 There can be no doubt that this assumption was very widespread and was held as something like an article of faith in prerevolutionary Russian liberal and Marxist circles.

41 The most detailed history in English of the 1905 revolution is Sidney Harcave, *The Russian Revolution of 1905* (London, 1970) (originally published as *First Blood* in 1964). See the analytical comments of Martin Malia in *Comprendre la Révolution russe*.

42 These issues are discussed in my work, *Formation of Political Parties*. See also V. I. Startsev, *Russkaia burzhuaziia i samoderzhavie v 1905–1917 gg.* (Leningrad, 1977).

43 Emmons, *Formation of Political Parties*, ch. 2–5.

44 *Vyborgskii protsess* (St. Petersburg, 1908), pp. 6–9; M. M. Vinaver, *Istoriia Vyborgskogo vozzvaniia (Vospominaniia)* (Petrograd, n.d.).

45 The words are taken from Professor Nathan Smith's translation of the text of Miliukov's speech, which was never published in full. A copy is preserved in the Columbia University Russian Archive.

46 *Arkhiv Akademii Nauk* (Moscow), f. 518 (V. I. Vernadskii), op. 5, no. 68, p. 22.

Index

congress, national zemstvo, 152–3, 154, 164, 195, 227, 437; government prohibition, 205, 347, 348, 436; zemstvo opposition movement, 146, 221, 437, 440–1
Congress of Naturalists and Physicians, 348, 350, 358
Congress of Russian Natural Scientists, Fourth, 298
conservatives, 373–8, 387; and statisticians, 343, 345, 347, 353, 355, 358; see also gentry
Constantinople, 413
Constituent Assembly, 391, 394, 399, 404; and Bolsheviks, 407–9
Constitutional Democratic Party, 152, 356, 399, 411, 412, 437; creation, 145, 147; and liberal history of zemstvo, 135, 138; and Octobrists, 148, 165; and opposition, 161, 162, 166, 356, 440–2
cooperatives, 395
corporal punishment, 110, 204, 330
corruption, 10–11, 19, 23–4, 202
cossacks, 85, 114, 143, 397, 410
Council of Ministers, 371; and zemstvo union, 366, 369, 370
Council on the Affairs of the Local Economy, 158–9, 166
courts, 12, 144
Crimea, 411–12
Crown Lands, Department of, 246–7, 252
Cyprus, 413

Decembrists, 26
Declaration of the United Democratic Opposition, 401
Democratic Conference, 401
democratization of the zemstvo, 387, 389, 400–2, 430; as liberal goal, 384–5, 393, 434, 437; see also small zemstvo unit
Denikin, A.I., General, 410–14
Derber, P.I., Siberian politician, 411
district commissars, 386, 387
Dmitriev, Vladimir, statistician, 374–5, 377
Dolgorukov, Princes, 145, 205, 226
Dolzhenkov, V.I., physician, 289
Don region, 33, 34, 397, 410
dual power, 388, 395
Dubasov, F.V., Admiral, 150
Duma, local, 63, 399
Duma, State, see State Duma
Durnovo, I.N., interior minister, 35, 183, 343; hospital statute, 190, 322–3; as marshal of the nobility, 238–9n

Eastern Central Committee, 412
education, 243–4, 424; universal primary, 155, 165, 166, 167, 266–9; and zemstvo expenditures, 119–20, 196, 263n; see also schools; teachers; Education, Ministry of
Education, Ministry of, 255, 266–9; jurisdiction, 197, 246–7, 251, 260; model schools, 252, 269–73
Egypt, 413
Ekaterinoslav, province and zemstvo, 33, 137n, 149–50n, 225
elections: 7–21 passim; electoral curiae, 38–41, 79–84, 87; peasants to commune, 8, 9; Provisional Government electoral statute, 396, 398; proxies, 201–3; urban, 19; to zemstvos, 31, 84–7, 206, 398–403, 425, 426
emancipation of serfs, 80, 135, 143, 433, 434; and social integration, 244, 423, 435, 436–7
Emigré Committee, 413
England, 95, 413, 436, 439
Erisman, F.F., physician, 289, 327, 329
Ermolov, Aleksei, agriculture minister, 237
Ershov, M.D., zemstvo activist, 154

estates: organizations, 32; prior to zemstvo, 7–19; under 1864 statute, 80, 81, 84; under 1890 statute, 41–2, 87–96, 438; see also gentry; peasants; towns
evacuation of soldiers, 366
Extraordinary Investigating Commission of the Provisional Government (1917), 155

Fallows, Thomas, 381–2n, 434
famine: government response, 217, 222, 319; statisticians, 347, 356; zemstvo opposition, 319–21, 330–1
Far East, Russian, 35
February revolution, 385–91
Feldshers, 56, 290, 326, 352; feldsherism, 292–8; training of, 283–6n, 294–5, 302–3; see also medicine; physicians
Filatov, N.F., physician, 317
Finance, Ministry of, 62, 216–18, 233, 357, 434; rivalry with Interior, 180, 433, 438; see also Witte; Vyshnegradskii; Sipiagin
fire insurance, 196
First World War, 148, 166, 441; voluntarism, 373, 430; zemstvo union, 48, 134, 351, 365–78
fon Val, V.V., bureaucrat, 239n
food supply committees, 394, 399
France, 413, 436, 439
Free Economic Society, 7, 205, 358
Freemasons, 23
Frenkel, Z.G., historian, 306
Frieden, Nancy, 414, 428

Gatssisskii, A.S., zemstvo activist, 346
Geiden, P.A., Count, 145–6
General Organization of Zemstvos, 366
gentry, 20–1, 80–1, 83–4, 85–7, 151, 163, 367, 430–1; family ties in zemstvo, 160–1; political schooling, 12–15; predominance in zemstvos, 142–3, 156, 375–8, 423–4; reaction, 167, 385, 387, 393, 415, 439; relations with communes, 10, 123; relations with towns, 18, 26
gentry marshal, see marshal of the nobility
Germany, 439
Gerschenkron, Alexander, historian, 446n
Gleason, William, 334, 406, 430–1
Goremykin, I.L., interior minister, 217, 238n
Gorky, Maxim, 181–2
Gorodilov, K.A., peasant deputy, 124
governing boards, zemstvo, 52–6, 85; compensation to board members, 95; district, 40–1, 49, 61–3; provincial, 31, 41, 52–6, 288, 392–3
government, central, 344, 366, 392; conflicts with zemstvos, 179, 183, 188, 214–28; zemstvo medicine, 316, 318; see also bureaucracy; and individual ministries
governor, 32, 50, 53–6, 159, 177–214 passim, 283, 386; inspection, 59; prior to zemstvo, 13, 14, 24, 96; and third element, 344, 355; under 1890 statute, 88, 319, 432
Grigorev, V.N., statistician, 352
Grimm, K.N., Octobrist, 162
Grodno, province, 34
Gruzinov, A.E., zemstvo activist, 401

Haxthausen, August von, Baron, 8, 15, 21
Health, Ministry of (proposed), 329
historiography: liberal, 1, 124, 177, 192, 214; Soviet, 1, 216, 439; Western, 1, 134, 142, 148
Hosking, Geoffrey, 64
hospital statute (1893), 190, 197, 320, 321–9, 332
hospitals, see medicine
household inventories, 344, 347, 348, 357, 429

Iakushev, I.A., zemstvo activist, 411–12
Ianzhul, I.I., statistician, 361n

448

449

Moscow, province and zemstvo, 33, 87, 95, 118, 199, 226, 369, 397, 398; and Bolsheviks, 400, 402, 403, 409; and third element, 287, 300, 304, 317, 327, 346, 406; zemstvo opposition, 137n, 149–50n; zemstvo union, 366, 367, 374–5, 376–8
Moscow Committee of Credit and Savings Cooperatives, 351
Moscow Juridical Society, 347, 348, 349, 350, 358
Moscow Plan, 368
Moscow Soviet, 406
Moscow State Conference, 401
Moscow University, 350, 353
Moskovskie vedomosti, 112, 195, 323, 359n
Mosolov, A.N., official, 239n
Muravev, M.N., General, 15
Muravev, Nikolai, justice minister, 188

Nabokov, V.D., Kadet, 386
Naryshkin, A.A., zemstvo activist, 153
Neigardt, D.S., governor, 231n
Nekliudov, P.V., governor, 231n
Netchiki (naysayers), 13
Nicholas I, Emperor, 12–13, 15
Nicholas II, Emperor, 225, 372, 378, 383, 439–40; antagonizes zemstvo liberals, 63, 136–7, 139–40, 327
Nizhnii Novgorod, province and zemstvo, 33, 195, 231, 324, 346, 368; and 1917 revolution, 389, 403; zemstvo opposition, 137n, 149–50n, 210
Novgorod, province and zemstvo, 33, 49, 115, 202, 205, 136–7n, 403
Novikov, Alexander, land captain, 294, 310n

Obolenskii, Ivan, zemstvo publicist, 213–14, 225, 239n
Obrok (duties in cash), 20–1
Octobrists, *see* Union of October 17
Old Believers, 246
Olonets, province and zemstvo, 33, 49, 95, 368; peasant zemstvo, 119–21, 143; zemstvo opposition, 137n, 149–50n
Olsufev, D.A., zemstvo activist, 154
Orel, province and zemstvo, 33, 153, 201, 231, 349, 404; zemstvo opposition, 136–7n, 149–50n, 154
Orenburg, province and zemstvo, 33, 34, 123
organization and production school, 350–1
Orlov, V.I., statistician, 347, 352, 360n
orphanages, 14, 18, 370
Osipov, E.A., physician, 281, 289, 300, 306
Ott, Dmitrii, physician, 303–4

Pares, Bernard, historian, 212
parliamentarism, 160–3
Paul I, Emperor, 19
Pazukhin, A.D., official, 35, 36
Peace mediators, 40, 62, 144
peasant *intelligenty*, 427–8
Peasant Land Bank (1883), 63, 91, 103, 346
peasant zemstvos, 119–21, 143
peasants, 20–1, 26, 181, 279; agrarian crisis, 11, 101–8, 141, 145; agrarian disorders, 138, 141, 147, 150, 216, 221, 345; attitudes toward zemstvo, 111–15, 383–5, 387, 388, 393, 402, 403, 405, 415, 425–6; delegates' behavior, 115–19; *otkhodniki* (off-farm workers) 244; participation in zemstvo boards, 89–90, 92–3; political schooling, 7–11; status, 44, 62, 358–9, 423; *see also* commune; estate
Peasants Union, 390
Pegeev, Pavel, statistician, 220
Penza, province and zemstvo, 10, 33, 94, 317, 401; zemstvo opposition, 137n, 149–50n
People's Right Party, 355

Pepeliaev, V.N., Kadet, 411–12
Perm, province and zemstvo, 33, 208, 402, 403, 405; peasant zemstvo, 119–21, 143; third element 262, 301; zemstvo opposition, 137n, 149–50n
Peshekhonov, A.N., statistician, 348, 349, 352
Peter I, Emperor, 17
petitions, 63, 139–40, 159, 204–5, 264, 325, 327
Petrograd, province and zemstvo, 368, 401, 404
Petrov, A.V., physician, 298
Petrovskaia Agricultural Academy, 353
Petrukenvich, Ivan, zemstvo activist, 145, 184, 205, 235n, 237n, 346, 353
Petrunkevich, Mikhail, physician, 145, 444n
physicians, 56, 280–6, 286–9, 291, 295–8, 317–8, 369, 376–8; and American country doctor, 295, 312n; conflict with zemstvo, 305–6, 315–34, 316, 428; feldsherism, 292–8; loneliness, 289, 318, 428; professional and political issues, 324, 330, 330–1, 331–2, 333; zemstvo union, 367, 374; *see also* feldshers; medicine; third element
physicians' congresses, 287–9, 290, 300–1
physicians' councils, 288, 320, 333
physicians' societies, 298, 320; *see also* Pirogov Society
Pirogov Society of Russian Physicians, 303–4, 305, 317; congresses, 287, 331–2, 329, 332–3; founded, 289, 299; political opposition, 325, 331, 333, 375
Pirumova, N.M., historian, 143, 443n
Pleve, V.K., interior minister, 138–9, 159, 183, 218, 221, 238n; and third element, 222–8, 355–6, 434
Podolia, province and zemstvo, 34
Podolinskii, S.S., zemstvo activist, 160
police, 13, 18, 36, 253, 258; department of, 220, 221, 222, 226; and economic administration, 96, 106–7; *ispravnik*, 13, 32, 425; and statisticians, 347, 355; *see also* Internal Affairs, Ministry of
political parties, 161, 165; *see also* individual *political parties*
Polner, Tikhon J., historian, 46, 48; in zemstvo union, 373–4, 377–8, 379n
Polovtsov, A.A., official, 236–7n
Poltava, province and zemstvo, 33, 49, 87, 143, 197, 199, 208, 361n; agrarian unrest, 221, 222, 350, 355; zemstvo opposition, 136–7n, 149–50n, 204
Popular Socialist Party, 356
population growth, 100
Populism, 216, 280, 286
Posnikov, A.S., statistician, 346, 357
Prikaz obshchestvennogo prizreniia (Bureau of Public welfare, Office of Public Welfare, Social Welfare Board), 13, 14, 15, 19, 282–3, 286, 326
professionalization, 208–9; of physicians, 317–18, 324; of statisticians, 349–50, 357, 430
Progressive Bloc, 148, 375
Proizvol (bureaucratic abuse), 188, 190, 208
Protopopov, A.D., Octobrist, 151
Provincial Bureau of Zemstvo Affairs, 43, 58–61, 134
Provincial Reform (1775), 11, 13, 18, 25–6
Provisional Government, 378, 386, 393, 405, 406; peasant hostility, 387, 414–15; proliferation of officials, 389, 392, 400; zemstvo made universal, 34, 431
Pskov, province and zemstvo, 17, 33, 159, 368; zemstvo opposition, 136–7n, 149–50n
Pugachev revolt, 12, 147, 424
Purishkevich, V.M., conservative deputy, 156
Pushkarev, S.G., historian, 8, 27n

450

quartering soldiers, 98

Rachinskii, S.A., official, 246, 261
Ramer, Samuel, 414, 428
Rashin, A.G., historian, 244
Rech' (Petrograd), 393
Red Cross, 366–7
Red Guards, 407
redemption payments, 83, 106, 108, 204, 346
reformatories, 14
refugee relief: émigrés, 413, 410; zemstvo union, 370–1, 372, 386
religious dissidence, 245, 246
Revolution of 1905, 90, 141, 159, 161, 424, 430; demarcation point in zemstvo history, 64, 148; peasants, 92, 108; zemstvo opposition, 138, 146–7, 161
Riazan, province and zemstvo, 33, 95, 118, 199, 401; third element, 301, 352; zemstvo opposition, 136–7n, 149–50n, 205, 210
road work, as zemstvo obligation, 98, 195
Rodichev, F.I., zemstvo activist, 156, 145, 235n
Rodzianko, M.V., State Duma president, 156, 386
Rosenberg, William, 334, 425–6, 428
Rubakin, N.A., educator, 262
Rusov, A.A., statistician, 352, 354, 355–6
Russkaia shkola, 259
Russkie vedomosti (Moscow), 195, 319, 327, 396; and Bolsheviks, 403, 404, 405, 407; and Provisional Government statute, 391, 393
Russkii narodnyi uchitel', 260
Russkoe slovo, 393
Russo-Japanese war, 227, 266, 439; zemstvo opposition, 138, 146; zemstvo union, 48, 366
Russo-turkish War, 137–8, 139

Sablin, M.A., zemstvo activist, 346, 347
Saint Petersburg, province and zemstvo, 19, 33, 225; zemstvo opposition, 136–7n, 139–40, 149–50n
Saint Petersburg Technical Institute, 353
Salazkin, S.S., zemstvo activist, 401
Saltykov-Shchedrin, M.E., writer, 233n
Samara, province and zemstvo, 33, 60, 118, 205, 389, 390, 398, 404; third element, 218–21, 226–7, 326, 347, 395; zemstvo opposition, 136–7n, 205
sanitary movement, 281–2, 299, 302–3; *see also* medicine
Saratov, province and zemstvo, 33, 162, 231n, 303, 390, 398; Bolsheviks, 401–2, 403–4; peasants, 197–8, 221; zemstvo opposition, 136–7n 149–50n, 210
Savitskii, I.K., physician, 285
schools, 14, 18, 193, 196, 197–8; attendance figures, 270–3; boards, 250, 258, 259, 259–63; bureaucratic, 245–7; church, 245–6, 252; course of study, 250; directors of, 251–3; examinations, 260; inspectors, 250–1, 252, 258, 260, 268; literacy schools, 245–6, 247, 253, 261, 263–5; parish, 165, 167, 247, 263; pedagogical institutions, 256–7, 261; primary, 243–74; primary school statute of 1874, 61, 251–3; pupil-teacher ratios, 270–3; state school council, 197; trustee, 254, 258, 259; *see also* education; Education, Ministry of; teachers
scribe (*pisar'*), 9
self-government, theory of: *gosudarstvennaia* (statist), 36–7, 178, 431–2; *obshchestvennaia* (societal), 36–7, 178, 431–2
Semenov, P.P., geographer, 344–5
Senate, 31, 105, 288, 319
Serbia, 413
serfdom, 26, 80

Severnyi khoziain, 389
Shakhovskoi, D.I., Prince, 145
Shamshin, I.I., Senator, 60, 234n
Shchapov, A.P., historian, 123
Shchepkin, D.M., zemstvo activist, 406–9
Shidlovskii, S.I., zemstvo activist, 156
Shingarev, A.I., physician, 289, 444n
Shipov, D.N., zemstvo activist, 146, 153, 195, 221, 237–8n; and Pleve, 222, 226
Shlikevich, A.P., statistician, 361n
Shlippe, F.V., zemstvo activist, 368
Shlippe, V.K., governor, 225
Shtiurmer, Boris V., official, 226, 235n, 239–40n, 371
Siberia, 410, 411
Siberian Regional Government, 411
Sievers, Jacob, official, 18
Simbirsk, province and zemstvo, 33, 137n, 149–50n, 151, 225, 401
Sipiagin, D.S., interior minister, 139, 217–18, 221–2, 238n; restricts zemstvo activity, 201, 223, 239n; Samara incident, 220, 226
Skhod (assembly), 9, 384, 389, 394, 427
slavophile ideology, 8, 9, 222, 435
Sleptsov, P.A., governor, 226
small zemstvo unit, 90, 111, 122, 435, 437, 443; *see also* volost zemstvo
Smolensk, province and zemstvo, 162, 198, 346, 403; zemstvo opposition, 136–7n, 149–50n, 205, 325
Social Democrats, 221, 343, 362n, 388
Socialist Revolutionary Party, 399–400, 403; third element, 221, 390, 395
Solovev, Z.P., physician, 334
Solzhenitsyn, Alexander, 310n
Sotsial-demokrat (Moscow), 399
Soviets, peasant, 390, 393, 395, 403, 404; elections, 397, 399, 400; zemstvo union, 407–9
Special Conference on the Needs of Agriculture (1902–5), 63, 112, 205, 221
Speranskii, Mikhail, Count, 11–12, 15, 436
Spiro, Herbert J., 25
Stakhovich, M.A., marshal of the nobility, 154, 226
Stalin, J.V., 8, 415
Starosta (village elder), 8, 23, 82, 258
Starshina (volost elder), 82, 118, 393, 394, 399
State Council, 19, 35, 50, 51, 56, 58, 81–2, 236n, 322, 436; introduction of zemstvos, 33–4, 123; predominance of gentry, 156–8, 166; representatives from zemstvos, 48, 64, 90, 138; thwarts reform proposals, 387, 441, 439
State Domains, Ministry of, 8, 21, 62; medicine, 280, 283–6, 293; schools, 246–7, 252
State Duma, 34, 123, 147, 154, 155, 159, 436, 440; gentry and parliamentarism, 151, 152, 153; reform of local government, 375, 438, 439; representatives from zemstvos, 64, 90; Second, 133, 165, 266–7, 437; Third and Fourth, 160, 162, 166, 376–8, 387, 427; zemstvo unions, 366, 372
state peasants, 244, 247, 280, 283–6
state properties and appanages, 49
state treasury, 108, 155–6, 266
statistical bureaus, 344–51, 352, 429
statisticians, 343–59, 376–8, 430; career pattern, 351–7; political-administrative context, 344–51, 428–9; zemstvo union, 367, 374–5; *see also* third element
Stavropol, province and zemstvo, 34, 108–10
Stolypin, P.A., prime minister, 34, 64, 90–1, 151, 441; agrarian reform, 109, 438; coup d'état of June 3, 1907, 134, 155–67, 387, 414, 436, 439–40; reforms of local government, 105, 152, 441
Stone, Norman, 365

452